APPLIED ECONOMICS
An introductory course

Fourth Edition

Alan Griffiths and Stuart Wall (editors)

Longman
London and New York

Longman Group UK Limited
Longman House, Burnt Mill, Harlow
Essex CM20 2JE, England
and Associated Companies throughout the world

Published in the United States of America
by Longman Inc., New York

© Longman Group Limited 1984, 1991

First published 1984
Second Edition 1986
Third Edition 1989
Fourth Edition 1991

British Library Cataloguing in Publication Data
Applied economics: an introductory course. – 4th ed.
  1. Applied economics
  I. Griffiths, Alan *1944–*   II. Wall, Stuart *1946–*
  330
ISBN 0–582–07235–2   *168369*

Library of Congress Cataloging in Publication Data
Applied economics: an introductory course / Alan Griffiths and Stuart
  Wall, editors. – 4th ed.
    p.   cm.
  Includes bibliographical references and index.
  ISBN 0–582–07235–2: $12.50
  1. Economics.   2. Great Britain – Economic conditions – 1945–
I. Griffiths, Alan, 1944–   . II. Wall, Stuart, 1946–   .
HB171.5.A65   1991
330 – dc20   90–22269
                                                      CIP

Set in 10/12 Linotron Times

Produced by Longman Singapore Publishers Pte Ltd
Printed in Singapore

APPLIED ECONOMICS
An introductory course

Contents

Preface

As any teacher or student of economics well knows, the vitality of the subject depends largely upon a continual synthesis of theory with observation, and observation with theory. Unfortunately this exercise is costly in terms of the time and the effort involved in finding sources, in assembling and interpreting data, and in searching journals and periodicals for informed comment on contemporary events. That the exercise is, however, ultimately worth while, is eloquently expressed by Professor James Meade in the following quotation taken, with his permission, from a letter to the authors:

The great tradition of Political Economy in this country is the application of basic economic analysis to the central economic problems of the time. For this purpose students must have a knowledge of institutions and quantitative relationships over a very wide range of sectors of the economy; and this instruction about the facts must be accompanied with guidance about methods of applying economic theory to the problems which arise over a very wide range of topics. Guidebooks to the UK economy which combine information and analysis in this way are all too rare; and the authors are to be highly commended for undertaking a comprehensive survey of this kind.

Our hope is that *Applied Economics* will take the reader some distance along this route, by combining information with analysis over twenty-seven separate topic areas. The book also examines in detail the major economic issues arising within each topic area. These are of interest in their own right and, more pragmatically, often form the substance of examination questions. Although the focus of *Applied Economics* is the UK, extensive reference is made throughout to the experience of the other advanced industrialized countries, helping the reader place any observations on the UK in a broader international context.

Each chapter concentrates on a particular topic area and begins with a synopsis, setting out the issues to be investigated, and ends with a conclusion, reviewing the major findings. The largely self-contained nature of each chapter gives the book a useful degree of flexibility. For instance chapters can be read selectively, in any order appropriate to the reader's interest or to the stage reached in a programme of study. This may be helpful to the reader as courses rarely follow the same sequence of topics. On the other hand the topics have been arranged with an element of progression, so that the reader may begin at Chapter 1 and read the chapters consecutively. The book then takes the form of a 'course' in applied economics.

Applied Economics is designed for undergraduate students in the first and second years of degree courses in economics, the social sciences and business studies, and for those taking professional courses with an economic content. The material will also be useful to many involved in Higher and National

Diplomas and Certificates of the BTEC, and to the serious A level student. Much of the content begins at an introductory level and is suitable to those with little or no previous exposure to economics, although the diverse nature of the various topic areas inevitably means some variation in the level of analysis, and indeed in the balance between information and analysis. Overall, the book is best read in conjunction with a good introductory text on economic theory.

We are indebted to many individuals for help during the course of this project. The major debt is, however, clearly owed to those who contributed the various chapters, and this is acknowledged more fully at the end of the book. Thanks are also due to Professor James Meade and Dr Paul Stoneman for help on particular aspects of the manuscript. We would also like to thank Olga Peppercorn, Librarian at the Department of Applied Economics, Cambridge University, for access to a wide range of empirical sources, and Fred Chambers, formerly Head Librarian at the Anglia Higher Education College (AHEC), for much helpful direction. For typing the various drafts of the manuscript, our thanks go to Jenny Connor, ably assisted by Margaret Nichols and Barbara Mornin. Finally, for patience and forbearance during many months of absence from normal family activities, our thanks go to Sylvia and Eleanor. Of course any errors and omissions are entirely our responsibility.

We were delighted that the first three editions of *Applied Economics* were so well received by teachers and students across a wide range of courses. Our intention is to keep the book at the forefront of economic debate and events. Accordingly, in this fourth edition we have thoroughly updated all the data and empirical material and added new economic analysis where appropriate, including a new chapter on Transport, a topic of increasing importance to the UK economy.

Alan Griffiths
Stuart Wall
Cambridge 1991

Acknowledgements

We are grateful to the following for permission to reproduce copyright material:

Bank of England for figs. 11.8, 16.3, 22.3, 22.5, and tables 15.2, 15.3, 15.4, 16.2, 16.3, 16.7, 17.3; Barclays Bank plc for tables 16.6, 22.4, 22.6; Basil Blackwell Ltd. for tables 3.2, 3.3; The Confederation of British Industry for table 28.6; Croom Helm for fig. 7.6; The Economist Intelligence Unit, Business Internation, for fig. 5.6; The Financial Times for figs. 2.12, 2.13 and tables 10.1, 22.7; Haymarket Marketing Publications for table 6.6 from *The Campaign Report* and table 3.4 from *Management Today*; the Controller of Her Majesty's Sationery Office for figs. 1.1, 7.1, 7.3, 7.5, 13.1, 13.2, 13.3, 13.4, 13.5, 14.4, 15.2, 15.3, 17.2, 18.2, 18.3, 18.5, 22.2, 28.2 and tables 1.1, 1.2, 1.4, 1.7, 1.8, 1.9, 4.1, 6.1, 6.2, 6.3, 7.3, 8.1, 8.2, 8.3, 8.4, 8.4a, 8.4b, 8.5, 9.4, 9.6, 12.1, 13.1, 14.1, 14.2, 14.3, 14.4, 14.5, 15.3, 15.5, 15.7, 15.8, 16.1, 16.4, 17.1, 17.4, 18.1, 18.4, 20.1, 20.5, 21.2, 21.3, 21.4, 21.5, 21.6, 22.1, 22.2, 22.3, 23.1, 25.1, 26.3, 26.4, 26.8, 28.1, 28.2, 28.3, 28.4; The International Monetary Fund for tables 27.3, 27.4, 27.6, 27.9; Lloyds Bank plc for figs. 7.2, 7.4 and table 7.4; Macmillan Press Ltd. for fig. 5.1; Midland Group for fig. 16.9; the Organization for Economic Co-operation and Development for tables 12.2, 12.3, 12.4, 12.5, 12.6, 13.3, 26.5, 26.7; Oxford University Press for fig. 18.7; Royal Bank of Scotland for fig. 16.6; Racal Communications Ltd. for fig. 2.14; Sears plc for figs. 2.1, 2.2, 2.3, 2.4, 2.5, 2.8; Shell U.K. Ltd. for table 4.3; Whitehall Press for fig. 9.2.

Though every effort has been made to trace the owners of copyright material, in a few cases this has proved impossible and we take this opportunity to apologise to any copyright holders whose rights may have been unwittingly infringed.

1   Changes in the UK economic structure

In this chapter we review the changing economic structure of the UK, particularly the declining significance of industrial output and employment as compared with the service sector. Some comparisons are made with international experience. Alternative explanations of industrial decline are examined, such as economic 'maturity', low-wage competition, the advent of North Sea oil, 'crowding out' by the non-market public sector and low UK productivity *vis-à-vis* its competitors. We consider whether the changes observed in the UK are a cause for concern, or merely a reflection of changes experienced in other advanced industrialized countries.

The popular view of the UK as an industrial economy, a manufacturing nation, is now inaccurate. Over the past thirty years the structure of the economy has been transformed. Manufacturing now contributes less than 23% of total output and employs some 3½ million fewer people than in 1964. Two of the most prominent of today's industries, North Sea oil and gas, did not even exist twenty-five years ago, and service activities have now outstripped the industrial and manufacturing sectors, both in terms of output and employment. There are even suggestions that the UK is becoming a 'post-industrial' economy, i.e. one in which information-handling activities are predominant. We shall consider the causes and consequences of these changes, and in so doing point out that structural change has implications for other important economic issues.

Structure defined

An economy may be analysed in terms of its component parts, often called 'sectors'. Sectors may be widely drawn to include groups of industries (e.g. the engineering industries) or narrowly drawn to identify parts of industries (e.g. fuel-injection equipment), depending on our purpose. Structural change is often discussed in terms of the even more widely drawn 'primary', 'secondary' and 'tertiary' (service) sectors. It will be useful at the outset to define these, and other conventional sector headings: (a) *the primary sector* – includes activities directly related to natural resources, e.g. farming, mining; (b) *the secondary sector* – covers all the other goods production in the economy, including the processing of materials produced by the primary sector. Manufacturing is the main element in this sector which also includes construction and the public utility industries of gas, water and electricity, which are classed as 'other energy and water supply' in the 1980 Standard Industrial Classification; (c) *the tertiary sector* – includes all the private sector services, e.g. distribution, insurance, banking and finance, and all the public sector services, such as health and defence; (d) *the goods sector* – the primary and secondary sectors combined; and (e) *the production industries* – includes the entire secondary sector except construction, together with the coal and coke industries and the extraction of mineral oil and natural gas. There is an index of industrial production on this basis, and the term 'industry' usually refers to this sector heading.

Structural change means change in the relative size of the sectors, however defined. We may judge size by output (contribution to Gross Domestic Product (GDP)),[1] or by inputs used, either capital or labour. Usually more attention is paid to labour because of the interest in employment and also because it is more easily measured than capital.

Through time we should *expect* the structure of an economy to change. The pattern of demand for a country's products will change with variations in income or taste, affecting in turn both output and employment. For instance, if economic growth occurs and real incomes rise, then the demand for goods and services with high and positive income elasticities[2] will tend to increase relative to those with low or even negative income elasticities. For example, between 1978 and 1988 total real consumer expenditure at 1985 prices rose by 38%, but expenditure on goods and services classified as 'recreation, entertainment and education' increased by 47.6%, whilst expenditure on 'food' increased by only 7.3%. Within the 'recreation, entertainment and education' category, consumer tastes favoured 'radio, TV and other durable goods', where real spending increased by 218%, at the expense of 'newspapers and magazines' where spending increased by a mere 1.6% in real terms. These changes have clear implications for the pattern of output and employment.

The pattern of demand is also responsive to changes in the age structure of the population. The UK, like other developed countries, is experiencing important demographic changes which mean that by 1995 there will be 1.2 million fewer people in the 16–24 year old age group. So, for example, the 'recreation, entertainment and education' sector may find this a constraint on its growth, unless it can adapt to the changing characteristics of the market. This smaller age cohort will form fewer new households than previous cohorts, so reducing demand for housing, furniture and consumer durables below what it would otherwise have been. In the longer term, a further demographic factor will be the continuing rise in the numbers of people aged over 75, who will place increasingly heavy demands on the medical and care services.

It is not only the demand side which initiates structural change. The reduced supply of young people in the labour market is already increasing their earnings relative to other workers, which has encouraged firms such as supermarkets to recruit older workers. Employers may also respond by substituting capital for labour and so changing employment patterns, or by raising product prices which would reduce the growth of output and in turn influence employment.

Also on the supply side, technical progress makes possible entirely new goods and services, as well as new processes for producing existing goods and services. In Chapter 10 we note that microelectronics not only gives us new products, such as word processors and video games, but also reduces costs of production, whether through the introduction of robotics in manufacturing, or computerized accounting methods in banking services. Where such 'process innovation' raises total factor productivity, unit costs fall. The supply side is therefore itself initiating new patterns of demand, output and employment, by creating new products or by reducing the prices of existing products and raising quality.

Changes in resource availability may also initiate structural change, as happened so dramatically with oil in 1973 and again in 1979. When the oil-producing and exporting countries (OPEC) restricted world output, oil-based products rose sharply in price, with *direct* consequences for substitutes (e.g. coal and gas) and complements (e.g. cars). In response to higher oil prices not only did the demand for substitutes rise, and for complements fall, but decisions had also to be taken throughout the economy, by both producers and consumers, to use less energy. As a result there was a decline in output and employment in energy-intensive industries, a prime example being steel.

Oil has had further *indirect* effects on the structure of the UK economy by means of the exchange rate. The development of North Sea oil production enabled the UK to be self-sufficient in oil by 1980, but also bestowed 'petro-currency' status on the pound. This meant that the sterling exchange rate was now responsive to changes in oil prices, which between 1979 and 1983 tended to keep the pound higher than would otherwise have been the case. The result was to make UK exports dearer and imports cheaper in the early 1980s, with adverse consequences for output and employment in sectors facing international competition, both abroad and at home. During 1986 this was partially reversed. The oil price halved and sterling fell 9.2% (on average), providing a stimulus to industrial output during 1987. Although by 1990 the UK was not much more than self-sufficient in oil, the pound still behaved as a petro-currency during the Gulf crisis. Following the invasion of Kuwait by Iraq, and the rise in the oil price, the pound appreciated by just over 6% during July and August 1990.

International competition is a potent force for change in the economic structure of the UK. Changing consumer tastes, the creation of new products and changing comparative costs result in the redistribution of economic activity around the world. The demise of the UK motorcycle industry in face of Japanese competition, for example, was the result of UK manufacturers failing to meet consumer demand for lighter, more reliable, motorcycles which Japan could produce more cheaply. As we see in Chapter 23, for most products the major impact on UK output and employment has come not from Japanese producers, but from those EC countries which, unlike Japan, have unrestricted access to the UK market. Membership of the EC inevitably meant accepting some restructuring of the UK economy, in accordance with European comparative advantages. This is certainly true for industrial production, with the EC a protected free trade area, though less true for agriculture (see Ch. 26).

Decisions on the location of industrial production are increasingly taken by *multinational enterprises*. In the UK motor industry, decisions taken by

Ford and General Motors during the 1970s and early 1980s to supply more of the European market from other EC plants, contributed to the fall in UK car output from 1.3 million in 1977 to 1.1 million in 1987, despite real consumer spending on cars and vehicles more than doubling in that period. On the other hand by 1995 the UK should increase its car output by half a million cars per year, if the plans of Nissan, Toyota, Honda and Peugeot-Citroen materialize.

Structural change in the UK

The data we shall use to trace changes in the UK economic structure are contained in Tables 1.1, 1.2 and 1.4. The choice of years in these tables is not arbitrary; 1964, 1969, 1973 and 1979 are the peaks of successive trade cycles. By using these years we shall be comparing like with like. Some activities, e.g. construction, show much more fluctuation in output and employment during the course of a trade cycle than do others, e.g. the public sector services. We must therefore compare years which have similar economic conditions if we are to avoid reaching wrong conclusions. It is, however, interesting to observe the way the recession affected the different sectors, so data are provided for 1981. The year 1988 appears to have been a turning point in the upswing which began in 1982. During 1989 and 1990, GDP continued to grow, but at a slower rate.

Changes in output

Table 1.1 presents index numbers of output at constant factor cost,[3] recording changes in the volume of output for the various sectors.

In the **primary sector**, agriculture, forestry and fishing grew at a rate of 1.8% per annum between 1964 and 1979, which increased to a remarkable 6.5% per annum between 1979 and 1984, stimulated by EC policies and unaffected by the recession. Since then agricultural output has declined by almost 5%. Coal and coke is the only UK industry where output has fallen throughout the period. The decline of the coal and coke industry's output was most rapid between 1964 and 1973, an annual average fall of 6.3% per annum compared with 2.4% per annum between 1979 and 1988. In sharp contrast, the output of mineral oil and natural gas rose dramatically between 1973 and 1979, and continued to grow at 6.4% per annum between 1979 and 1986, though falling sharply since then. The high real prices for energy after the oil price 'shocks' of 1973 and 1979, made possible both the reduced rate of contraction for the coal industry and the rapid exploitation of high-cost North Sea oil fields. However, after the halving of the oil price in 1986, UK oil production had fallen 10% by 1988.

In the **secondary sector**, 1973 is again a significant date. Output from both manufacturing and construction rose steadily between 1964 and 1973 (at annual rates of 2.9 and 1.8% respectively), but between 1973 and 1979 output from both these sub-sectors actually fell, and fell still more sharply between 1979 and 1981. Manufacturing output fell by as much as 15.5 points between 1979 and 1981, and construction output by slightly more. By 1981 output in these sectors had been cut back to levels last seen in the mid-1960s.

	1964	1969	1973	1979	1981	1986	1988
Primary							
Agriculture, forestry and fishing	69.3	73.5	87.4	90.1	102.6	118.8	117.8
Coal and coke	205	148.8	114	97.6	97.3	79.3	78.4
Extraction of mineral oil and natural gas	—	0.3	2.2	98.7	110.3	153.0	136.1
Secondary							
Mineral oil processing	75.3	99.9	126.9	113.7	93.0	99.0	107.4
Manufacturing	87.6	103.0	114.1	109.5	94.0	104.7	117.9
Construction	104.2	117.6	122.4	105.8	89.9	102.1	128.1
Other energy and water supply	56.7	68.9	87.1	102.2	99.6	112.2	120.3
Tertiary							
Distribution, hotels, catering, repairs	85.8	92.2	107	107.9	98.4	120.4	136
Transport	76.5	84.8	100.8	103.6	99.0	108.7	123.7
Communication	49.8	65.5	81.8	97.2	102.2	130.8	145.6
Banking, finance, insurance, business services and leasing	53	66	81	95	104	154	185.8
Ownership of dwellings	69	80	87	99	101	107	108.3
Public administration, national defence and compulsory social security	86	90	99	99	101	99	101
Education and health services	62	72	82	99	101	105	112.6
Other services	72	76	82	95	98	120	134
GDP	75.6	85.5	96.4	103	98.4	114	125
Production industries	76.6	89.7	99.5	107.1	96.6	110.2	118.1

Source: CSO (1983, Table 2.3; 1987b, Table 1.5 and Table 2.4; 1989, Table 2.4 (rebased from 1985 to 1980)).

Table 1.1 Index numbers of output at constant factor cost 1980 = 100

Since 1981 there has been a marked recovery of output in both manufacturing and construction, so that by 1988 both sectors were producing more than in the previous peak of 1973. Output continued to grow in 1989 and in 1990, but at a slower rate. Output from the gas, water and electricity industries ('other energy and water supply') grew at 4.9% per annum between 1964 and 1973, slowing to 2.8% per annum between 1973 and 1979 and showing a slight fall in output during the recession of the early 1980s. With the revival of growth in manufacturing, a major user of energy, there has been a steady growth of gas, water and electricity output at almost 3% per annum since 1981.

The index of output for the *production industries* (see above), is presented in the last row of Table 1.1. We see that industrial production grew between 1964 and 1973 by 22.9 points, an annual rate of 2.9%, but then grew more slowly between 1973 and 1979, and fell sharply between 1979 and 1981. This definition includes the contribution of North Sea oil and gas, which helped to compensate for the sharp decline of output in manufacturing since 1973. Exploitation of a non-renewable natural resource is, however, more akin to the consumption of capital than it is to the production of goods and services. The North Sea is providing the UK with a once-and-for-all 'windfall' gain in output over other less fortunate countries. To some extent this masked the full extent of the decline in *non-oil industrial output* which fell by 14.6% between 1973 and 1981, resulting in *non-oil GDP* being 2.5% lower in 1981 than in 1973.

After 1981, growth of UK industrial output resumed, led by the recovery of manufacturing output, and averaged 2.9% per year through to 1988. Industrial output in the 1980s was again growing at the rates of the 1960s, and changing oil output did not significantly affect the index.

International comparisons highlight the failure of British industry during the 1960s and 1970s. Industrial production in the industrial market economies grew at a weighted average of 6.2% per annum between 1960 and 1970, slowing to what in the UK would still be regarded as a healthy 2.3% per annum between 1970 and 1983 (World Bank 1985). However during the 1980s, the growth of UK industry relative to the rest of the OECD clearly improved. The OECD index of industrial production (excluding construction) shows growth in the UK of 16.5% between 1981 and April 1987, compared with 14% in the OECD as a whole. Unfortunately this improved UK industrial performance was not maintained into the late 1980s. Between 1985 and January 1990, UK industrial production increased by 10.3%, but the OECD average increased by half as much again, at 15.2%. Even the most optimistic interpretation of this data can only conclude that the UK's *relative industrial decline* merely slowed during the 1980s. It will be interesting to see whether this 'improvement' can be maintained, or whether the long run trend of accelerating decline will resume.

In the **tertiary or service sector**, Table 1.1 shows that output has grown in every sub-sector throughout the whole 1964–79 time period. Even during the recession of 1979–81 output fell in only two of the eight sub-sectors. The pace-setters have been communications, and banking, finance, insurance, business services and leasing. The contrast in growth experience between the service sector and the industrial sector has changed the share of total output attributable to each (see Table 1.2). However, even in the service sector, growth of output in the UK at 2.9% per annum between 1965 and 1980 lagged behind the average for the industrial market economies which was 3.9% (World Bank 1987). Between 1980 and 1988 UK service sector growth was, at 2.6% per annum, a relative improvement as the average for the industrial market economies had fallen to a similar figure. The poor UK industrial performance outlined above may also have contributed to this relatively poor service sector performance, since many services are marketed to industry or to people whose incomes are earned in industry. A growing industrial sector generates an induced demand for the output of the service sector.

The GDP can be obtained by aggregating the various sectors outlined above. It grew from 75.6 in 1964 to 103.0 in 1979, i.e. by around 38%. This represents an average annual growth rate of about 2.2% between 1964 and 1979, slowing to 1.1% between 1973 and 1979. The GDP actually declined between 1979 and 1981 by 4.4% whilst the OECD average GDP continued to rise slowly. By international standards the UK growth performance was poor between 1964 and 1981. For instance the weighted average annual growth rate for industrial market economies, our key trading partners, was 5.1% between 1960 and 1970 and 3.2% between 1970 and 1979. In the eight years following the recession of 1981, UK real GDP grew at an average of 3.3% per annum, well above the UK rates of the 1960s and above the OECD average of 3.1%. During the 1980s, therefore, the UK's relative economic decline was halted, but at these rates its reversal will be a very slow process.

Changes in shares of output

Table 1.2 uses percentage shares of total output (GDP at factor cost), to show changes in the relative importance of the sectors presented in Table 1.1.

Table 1.2 Percentage shares of GDP at factor cost*

	1964	1969	1973	1979	1986	1988
Primary	5.8	4.3	4.2	6.7	5.3	3.8
Agriculture, forestry and fishing	1.9	1.8	2.9	2.2	1.7	1.3
Coal and coke	3.9	2.5	1.1	1.3	1.0	0.7
Extraction of mineral oil and natural gas	—	—	—	3.2	2.6	1.8
Secondary	40.8	42.0	40.9	36.7	32.2	31.3
Mineral oil processing	0.5	0.5	0.4	0.6	0.7	0.3
Manufacturing	29.5	30.7	30.0	27.3	23.0	22.4
Construction	8.4	8.4	7.3	6.2	5.8	6.2
Other energy and water supply	2.4	2.4	2.8	2.6	2.7	2.4
Tertiary	53.8	53.0	54.9	56.5	62.3	64.8
Distribution, hotels, catering, repairs	14.0	13.3	13.1	12.7	13.3	13.2
Transport	4.4	4.4	4.7	4.8	4.3	} 6.9
Communication	1.6	1.9	2.3	2.5	2.6	
Banking, finance, insurance, business services and leasing	8.3	8.6	10.7	11.0	15.0	18.4
Ownership of dwellings	5.4	5.5	5.1	5.8	5.5	5.1
Public administration, national defence and compulsory social security	7.6	7.0	6.1	6.1	6.9	6.5
Education and health services	6.9	7.1	7.7	8.1	8.6	8.5
Other services	5.6	5.2	5.1	5.7	6.1	6.2

Calculated from GDP at factor cost, at current prices and unadjusted for financial services and residual error.
* Totals may not sum to 100 due to rounding.
Source: CSO (1983, 1985, 1987b, 1989).

The **primary sector** was in relative decline between 1964 and 1973 because of the contraction of output in coal-mining. From a low point of 4.2% of GDP in 1973, the primary sector sharply increased its share to 6.7% in 1979 and 9.5% in 1984 (not shown), an unusual trend in a developed economy and almost entirely attributable to the growth of North Sea oil and gas production. By 1988 the primary sector's share slumped to 3.8%, and that of oil and gas from 7% in 1984 to 1.8% in 1988. This dramatic change was caused by the collapse of oil prices during 1986. Self-sufficiency in oil has meant that the UK's national interest in energy prices is no longer necessarily the same as that of the other (non-oil-producing) industrial nations.

The **secondary sector**'s share of output fell from a peak of 42.0% in 1969 to 36.7% in 1979, and to only 31.3% in 1988. This decline is due largely to the loss of output share by manufacturing, made inevitable by the decline in volume of output after 1973. By 1988 manufacturing produced only 22.4% of UK GDP. Despite the strong recovery in UK output since 1981, there has been no reversal in the long run decline of the secondary sector's share of GDP.

The **tertiary sector**'s share of output has grown throughout the period since 1969 so that by 1988 almost two-thirds of UK output was from the service sector. Within this sector, banking, finance, insurance, business services and leasing have raised their output volume more rapidly than GDP, and so have significantly increased their share of total output.

With the exception of the growth of the North Sea sector, these changes in economic structure have occurred throughout the advanced industrial countries (see Table 1.3). The fall in the share of manufacturing in GDP in

Table 1.3 Industrial market economies distribution of GDP; weighted averages

	1960 (%)	1985 (%)
Agriculture, forestry and fishing	6	3
Industrial production	40	36
Manufacturing	(30)	(23)
Services	54	61

Source: World Bank (1985, 1987).

the UK is typical of the other industrial market economies, and the growth in the share of the service sector has been similar to the average for such economies. This has led some to interpret the changes in UK economic structure as inevitable, giving more recently industrialized countries a glimpse of the future. However, to be complacent because the *relative* position of the sectors in the UK has changed in line with that in other advanced industrialized countries, is to ignore the UK's dramatic and unrivalled fall in the volume of non-oil industrial production between 1973 and 1981, outlined above in the section on changes in output (p. 4). Even the recovery since 1981 had by 1988 only raised UK non-oil industrial output by about 11% above its 1973 level.

Changes in employment

Employment has obviously been influenced by the changes in output already described. It has also been influenced by changes in technology, which have affected the labour required per unit of output. Table 1.4 gives numbers employed in each sector, together with percentage shares of total employment. The table shows that in the **goods sector** (primary and secondary) there were fewer jobs in 1979 than in 1964, with a still more rapid decline in jobs between 1979 and 1988.

In the **primary sector**, employment was reduced by 60% between 1964 and 1988. Employment in coal and coke fell as output contracted. More surprisingly, agricultural employment continued to fall despite the rapid rise in output after 1979, indicating strong growth in output per worker. The rise of the North Sea sector had directly created only 33,000 jobs by 1984, which had fallen to 26,000 by 1988 as the industry responded to lower oil prices. The outcome was that between 1964 and 1988 the primary sector's share of total employment fell from 5.1 to 2.1%.

In the **secondary sector**, employment fell by over 2.05 million between 1964 and 1979, and again by almost 2.32 million between 1979 and 1988. Manufacturing, as the largest part of this sector, suffered most of these job losses, with manufacturing employment falling by 3.67 million in the period

	1964 ('000s)	1964 (% of total employment)	1969 ('000s)	1969 (% of total employment)	1973 ('000s)	1973 (% of total employment)	1979 ('000s)	1979 (% of total employment)	1981 ('000s)	1981 (% of total employment)	1988 ('000s)	1988 (% of total employment)
Agriculture, forestry and fishing	540	2.3	399	1.7	432	1.9	368	1.6	363	1.6	313	1.4
Coal and coke					336	1.5	304	1.3	285	1.3	135	0.6
Extraction of mineral oil and natural gas					5*	—	20	0.1	24	0.1	26	0.1
Total primary	1,201	5.1	845	3.6	773	3.4	692	3.0	672	3.0	474	2.1
Mineral oil processing					28*	0.1	33	0.1	31	0.1	12	0.1
Manufacturing	8,909	38.1	8,923	38.6	7,861	34.7	7,259	31.3	6,221	28.4	5,239	23.2
Construction	1,659	7.1	1,493	6.5	1,320	5.8	1,253	5.4	1,130	5.2	1,045	4.6
Other energy and water supply					364*	1.6	366	1.6	366	1.7	298	1.3
Total secondary	10,978	46.9	10,821	46.8	9,573	42.4	8,911	38.5	7,748	35.4	6,594	29.2
Distribution, hotels and catering, repairs					3,950	17.4	4,252	18.4	4,172	19.1	4,627	20.5
Transport	1,665	7.1	1,577	6.8	1,062	4.7	1,051	4.5	987	4.5	939	4.1
Communication					445	2.0	422	1.8	438	2.0	471	2.1
Banking, finance, insurance, business services and leasing					1,442	6.4	1,663	7.2	1,738	7.9	2,528	11.2
Public administration, national defence and compulsory social security	9,513	40.7	10,737	42.5	1,664	7.3	1,721	7.4	1,623	7.4	1,690	7.5
Education and health services					2,781	12.3	2,876	12.4	2,908	13.3	3,106	13.8
Other services					976	4.3	1,571	6.8	1,600	7.3	2,139	9.5
Total tertiary	11,178	47.8	12,314	49.3	12,320	54.4	13,556	58.5	13,465	61.4	15,500	68.7
Total employment†	23,357		23,086		22,664		23,158		21,891		22,586	

* 1974 data.
Figures for 1973, 1979 and 1984 are on the basis of the 1980 SIC (Standard Industrial Classification). Figures for 1964 are on the basis of the 1958 SIC and 1969 on the basis of the 1968 SIC. Blanks for 1964 and 1969 indicate incompatibility with the 1980 SIC.
† Totals may not add up to total employment because of rounding, and numbers not classified in the annual Census of Employment.
Source: CSO, *National Income and Expenditure*. 1964–74, 1984, 1989.

Table 1.4 Employees in employment, UK at mid June

1964–88. The *share* of manufacturing in total employment fell from 38.1% in 1964 to as little as 23.2% in 1988.

As employment fell in the goods sector between 1964 and 1979, employment in the **tertiary sector** expanded by 2,378,000, enabling total employment to be held at around 23 million. This expansion was concentrated in the financial sector, and in various professional and scientific services.

The rough balance between employment losses in the goods sector and gains in the service sector broke down after 1979. Between 1979 and 1981 service sector employment actually fell slightly. Not until 1984 did the growth of service sector employment again compensate for the loss of goods sector employment. Over the whole period 1979–88 service sector employment grew by around 2 million whilst employment in the goods sector fell by 2.53

million. As a result total employment fell by 590,000, at a time when the number of people in the labour force was steadily increasing (see Ch. 18).

Similar changes in the pattern of employment have, however, taken place throughout the industrial world (see Table 1.5). By comparison with other advanced economies the UK has relatively small agricultural and (now) industrial sectors, leaving services with a larger than average share of total employment.

Table 1.5 Industrial market economies distribution of the labour force (weighted averages)

	1960 (%)	1985 (%)
Agriculture, forestry and fishing	16	7
Industrial production	39	35
Services	45	58

Source: World Bank, World Development Report (1981 and 1987).

Causes of structural change

As the world's oldest industrial nation the UK might reasonably lay claim to being its most developed or 'mature' economy. Several variants of the maturity argument provide explanations of industrial decline which appear rather reassuring.

Stage of maturity

A first variant suggests that the changing pattern of UK employment since 1964 may be seen as analogous to the transfer of workers from agriculture to industry during the nineteenth century; a transfer necessary to create the new industrial workforce. In a similar way, the argument here is that those previously employed in industrial activities were required for the expansion of the service sector in the 1960s and 1970s. However, this line of argument looks rather weak from the mid- to late 1970s onwards, with rising unemployment surely providing the opportunity for service sector expansion without any marked decline in industrial sector employment.

The hypothesis that economic maturity is associated with falling industrial employment may be crudely tested by reference to Table 1.6. In the period

Table 1.6 Changes in industrial employment (%)*

	1964–79	1979–83
UK	−14.8	−18.9
Canada	+35.7	− 8.7
USA	+27.2	− 6.4
Japan	+28.3	+ 4.1
Austria	− 3.2	− 8.3
Belgium	−18.6	−15.2
France	+ 2.3	− 7.4
West Germany	−10.3	− 8.5
Italy	+ 2.2	− 3.8
The Netherlands	−14.0	−12.4
Norway	+ 9.1	− 2.7
Sweden	−10.9	− 7.1
Switzerland	−21.1	− 3.3

* Calculated from data in OECD (1985a).

1964–79 the experience of the UK, Austria, Belgium, West Germany, the Netherlands, Sweden and Switzerland lends support to the hypothesis, whilst the experience of Canada, the USA, France and Norway contradicts it. Italy and Japan also experienced rising industrial employment, but it might be contentious to call these economies 'mature' in this period. Between 1964 and 1979, the evidence does therefore suggest that decline in industrial employment in the UK was by no means an inevitable result of economic development. The data since 1979 are more difficult to interpret as they cover a period of recession, but only Japan experienced a rise in industrial employment.

A second variant of the 'maturity' argument is that our changing economic structure simply reflects the changing pattern of demand that follows from economic development. It has been argued that consumer demand in a mature economy shifts away from goods and towards services (higher income elasticities) and that this, together with increased government provision of public sector services, adds impetus to the growth of the tertiary sector. This may be a sound explanation for some of the UK's structural change, but not all. The pattern of UK demand simply does not fit such a stylized picture; for instance, UK trade data clearly show UK demand for manufactured imports growing faster than UK manufactured exports (see Ch. 23). This growth in manufactured imports is hardly consistent with a major switch of UK demand away from industries producing goods.

In a third variant of the 'maturity' argument, Rowthorn and Wells (1987) have pointed out that the demand for manufactured goods is at least as income elastic as the demand for services, when valued at constant prices, that is, in terms of volume. A successful industrial sector would therefore achieve increases in the volume of output at least matching the growth of GDP. Faster growth of productivity in the industrial sector could then cause prices to fall relative to those in the service sector, thereby reducing the industrial sector's *share* of both output at current prices and employment. The 'maturity' argument should, in the view of Rowthorn and Wells, be based on *productivity* changes and not on demand changes. In the case of the UK, the relative stagnation of the *volume* of industrial output hardly supports this variant of the 'maturity' argument.

A fourth variant of the argument is that the UK has always been a reluctant manufacturing nation, and that we are now specializing in services, a sector in which we enjoy a comparative advantage and a protected domestic market. However since the mid-1970s, any need to exploit comparative advantages in services could again have been met from unused resources rather than by reducing industrial output and employment.

Low-wage competition

Foreigners, especially from the Third World, make a convenient scapegoat for UK problems and are particularly blamed for providing 'unfair', low-wage competition. Wages in the Third World are extremely low but are usually accompanied by low productivity, a lack of key categories of skilled labour, and a shortage of supporting industrial services and infrastructure. The UK is not unique in facing this competition and is itself a low-wage economy by developed country standards. In some sectors (e.g. textiles and cheap electrical goods) Third World competition has been important but, as yet, the scale of Third World involvement in the export of world manufactures is too small (14.5% of OECD manufactured imports in 1984) to be regarded as a major cause of UK structural change. As we see in Chapter 23, the main competition comes from other industrial market economies.

The North Sea

Free market economists often argue that the contribution of North Sea oil to the UK balance of payments has meant inevitable decline for some sectors of the economy. The mechanism of decline is usually attributed to the exchange rate, with the improvement in the UK visible balance (via removal of the oil deficit) bringing upward pressure on sterling. In terms of the foreign exchange market, higher exports of oil increase the demand for sterling, and lower imports of oil decrease the supply of sterling. The net effect is, allegedly, a higher sterling exchange rate than would otherwise have been the case, particularly in the late 1970s and early 1980s. The new status of sterling as a petro-currency may also attract an increased capital inflow, further raising the demand for sterling, and with it the sterling exchange rate. The higher price of sterling then makes UK exports more expensive abroad, and imports cheaper in the UK. United Kingdom producers of industrial exports, and import substitutes, are the most seriously disadvantaged by a high pound, since the major part of UK trade is in industrial products (around two-thirds of both exports and imports). In this way a higher pound produces a decline in industrial output and employment.

The argument that North Sea oil, through its effect on the exchange rate, inevitably resulted in the decline in UK manufacturing output and employment observed in the late 1970s and early 1980s, is rather simplistic. The Government could have directed surplus foreign exchange created by oil revenues towards imported capital equipment. This increase in imports of capital equipment would have eased the upward pressure on the pound,[4] whilst providing a basis for increased future competitiveness and economic recovery. Equally, the upward pressure on sterling could have been alleviated by macroeconomic policies aimed at raising aggregate demand, and with it spending on imports, or by lower interest rates aimed at reducing capital inflow.

North Sea oil cannot be wholly to blame for the observed decline in UK industrial output and employment. These structural changes began in the mid-1960s, yet North Sea oil only became a significant factor in the UK balance of payments in 1978. The periods of high exchange rate between 1978 and 1981, whilst certainly contributing to industrial decline, were by no means an inevitable consequence of North Sea oil. Different macroeconomic policies could, as we have seen, have produced a lower exchange rate, as indeed has been the case since the early 1980s.

Crowding out

Bacon and Eltis (1976) argued that the decline of British industry was due to its being displaced ('crowded out') by the growth of the non-market public sector. Some of the (then) public sector, such as steel, is itself industrial and markets its output in the same way as any private sector company. However, some of the public sector, such as health and education, provides services which are not marketed, being free at the point of use. This non-market public sector uses resources and generates income, but does not supply any output to the market. It requires investment goods for input, and consumes goods and services, all of which must be provided by the market sector.

We might usefully illustrate the 'crowding out' argument by first taking a closed economy with no government sector. Here the income generated in the market would equal the value of output. The income-receivers could enjoy all the goods and services they produced. However they could no longer do so if a non-market (government) sector is now added, since the non-market sector will also require a proportion of the goods and services produced by the market sector. The market sector must therefore forgo some of its claims on its own output. It is one of the functions of taxes to channel resources from the market sector to support non-market (government) activity. The rapid growth of the public sector after 1945, it is argued, led to too rapid an increase in the tax burden (see Ch. 14), which adversely affected investment and attitudes to work, to the detriment of economic growth. Also, in the face of rising tax demands, workers in both market and non-market sectors sought to maintain or improve their real disposable income, thereby creating inflationary pressures.

If the market sector does not accommodate the demands of a growing non-market sector by forgoing claims on its own output, then in an open economy adjustment must be made externally. The higher overall demand *of both sectors combined* can then only be met either by reducing the exports of the market sector, or by increasing imports. A rising non-market public sector in this way contributes to balance of payments problems.

Bacon and Eltis see the rapid growth of the non-market public sector as being the cause of higher taxes, higher interest rates (to finance public spending), low investment, inflationary pressures and balance of payments problems. The growth of the non-market public sector has in these ways allegedly 'crowded out' the market sector, creating an economic environment which has been conducive to UK decline.

These ideas have provided intellectual backing to the Conservative Party's approach to public spending and tax policies since 1979. The irony is that attempts to cut public spending and taxation after 1979 simply accelerated industrial decline, eroded the tax base and prevented the desired reduction of the tax burden (see Ch. 14). Bacon and Eltis's ideas provide a coherent theory of industrial decline helping us to appreciate some of the complex linkages in the process. However, experience since 1979 calls into question the basic propositions. High unemployment during the 1980s made it impossible to argue that industry was denied labour, although it did lack capital investment. It may be that low investment had more to do with low expected returns than with the high interest rates said to be necessary to finance the growth of public expenditure. There are, of course, several other determinants of UK interest rates in addition to public expenditure. The 'crowding out' argument also neglects the importance of public sector services as *inputs* to the private sector. Of the non-marketed services, education is especially important in increasing the skills of the work force.

Productivity

The total output of any economy is determined partly by the quantity of factor input (labour, capital, etc.), and partly by the use to which factors are put. Different economies may achieve different volumes of total output using similar quantities of factor input, because of variations in productivity. Productivity is the concept relating output to a given input, or inputs. If we include all inputs then we have total factor productivity (TFP):

TFP = total output/input of all factors

In National Income accounting terms this ratio is always equal to 1, since the total output of any industry is equal to the total incomes (including profit) paid to its factors of production, i.e. the value of its inputs. The ratio may, however, be made meaningful by revaluing both output and inputs in the prices of a base year. We then have both numerator and denominator reflecting changes in 'real' output or real factor input. The resulting ratio then shows changes in physical as opposed to value productivity, the latter being in part the result of price changes.

Total factor productivity may be broken down into labour productivity and capital productivity, both of which are partial factor productivity (PFP) concepts. In practice capital goods and the services flowing from them, are difficult to value so that both TFP and capital productivity are less frequently used measures than labour productivity. This neglect does not imply any judgement on the relative importance of capital and labour to the growth of output.

Labour inputs may be measured in terms of persons employed or person hours worked. So, for example, labour productivity may be defined as:

Output per person employed = total output/total persons employed

or

Output per person hour = total output/total hours worked

Table 1.7 United Kingdom productivity and manufacturing output: (1985 = 100)

	UK output per person employed	
	Whole economy	Manufacturing industries
1964	65.7	54.7
1969	74.8	65.0
1973	83.5	76.6
1979	89.1	79.9
1988	107.4	115.8
1989	107.1	120.1

Source: CSO (1990a), *Economic Trends Annual Supplement and Economic Trends* (1990b).

Table 1.7 presents productivity data for the UK since 1964. Between 1964 and 1973, output per person in UK manufacturing increased by 21.9 points, or an annual average of 3.8%, but in the period between 1973 and 1979 the increase was only 3.3 points, or an annual average well below 1%. Most other advanced economies experienced slower productivity growth after 1973, but throughout the period 1964–79 UK productivity growth lagged behind that in other countries.

What matters of course is not only the *growth* in labour productivity but the *base level* from which that growth takes place. Also we must consider UK productivity in manufacturing *and non-manufacturing* activities if we are to get a rounded picture of UK competitiveness. Such data are difficult to derive, but Table 1.8 will help in both respects. It shows that the UK's poor labour productivity compared to other industrialized nations was most marked in manufacturing. In 1980 UK workers in manufacturing averaged $6,800 of output per year at constant 1973 prices, whilst workers in manufacturing in other countries averaged between $10,400 and $16,800 per year.

	Output per employed worker – year 1980 by sectors* ($US'000) (1973)					GDP (at market prices)
	Agriculture	Fuel and power	Manufacturing	Construction	Services	
USA	16.7	30.8	16.8	11.0	14.7	15.3
The Netherlands	11.8	64.7	16.0	11.0	12.1	14.3
France	8.1	27.8	12.8	13.2	12.8	14.2
Belgium	10.5	29.1	12.2	12.6	12.6	14.0
West Germany	4.7	24.3	13.8	17.3	12.6	13.5
Italy	4.4	32.3	10.4	10.3	10.9	10.3
Japan	2.7	16.6	14.5	7.1	10.2	10.3
UK	10.7	17.4	6.8	9.5	8.7	9.2

* Or nearest available year.
Source: NIESR (1982).

Table 1.8 International labour productivity

The UK service sector also displays lower labour productivity than the service sector of other countries, although the comparison is not quite so unfavourable. It is only in agriculture that UK labour productivity is on a par with other countries, comparing favourably with all but the Netherlands in Europe, and with the USA outside Europe.

Returning to Table 1.7 we see that between 1979 and 1988 there was an increase in the rate of growth of labour productivity, led by manufacturing with a 40.2 point increase (4.1% per annum) against an 18 point increase (1.9% per annum) in the whole economy. UK labour productivity in manufacturing grew faster than that of our major competitors over the period 1980 to 1986. Table 1.9 shows index numbers of manufacturing output per hour worked in the same seven countries as Table 1.8. In each year the base, equal to 100, is the UK. The table shows that in US manufacturing in 1980, output per hour worked was 273% of the UK output per hour. By 1986 UK manufacturing had improved its labour productivity relative to the US, but the US figure was still 267% of the UK's. Over the six years, the UK has made progress in catching up all the countries in the table, especially West Germany, Belgium and the Netherlands, but a huge productivity gap still remains.

Changes in the UK economic structure

Table 1.9 Labour
productivity (output per
hour worked) in
manufacturing. UK = 100

	1980	1984	1986
USA	273	262	267
Japan	196	177	176
France	193	179	184
West Germany	225	205	178
Italy	173	156	153
Belgium	207	215	154
The Netherlands	269	267	205

Source: NIESR (1987).

The causes of low labour productivity in the UK economy, and especially in its manufacturing sector, have received much attention. The problem is complex and involves many of our national institutions, social relationships and attitudes, so that any attempt at a complete appraisal must go beyond the usual boundaries of economics. Here, for simplicity, we approach the problem in terms of one important factor input, namely capital investment.

Productivity and
capital investment

The capital stock employed in UK manufacturing grew more slowly than that of France and West Germany throughout the 1960–85 period (National Economic Development Office (NEDO) 1980, 1987). Between 1960 and 1975 the gross capital stock in UK manufacturing grew at 3.4% per annum, that of West Germany grew at 6.1% per annum, and that of France at 6.9%. In the 1975–85 period these growth rates fell to less than 2% per annum in the UK and between 3 and 4% in France and West Germany. The USA also experienced low investment in manufacturing, but unlike the UK was already a high-productivity economy. Anecdotal evidence of ageing UK industrial equipment supports the general picture given by the above data. Nevertheless, as Chapter 12 shows, UK overall investment (excluding housing) is not unduly low, perhaps suggesting that we should question the allocation of investment funds.

Even where investment has been made in manufacturing, productivity is often lower than in other countries. The Ford Motor Company provides the media with many examples which are interesting when they offer direct comparisons of the same products and productive plant. Ford Escorts are produced at both Halewood (England) and Saarlouis (West Germany). Between 1973 and 1980 labour productivity did not rise at Halewood despite extensive investment, whereas it rose 30% at Saarlouis (Taylor 1981). Ford achieved substantial productivity gains in the UK during the 1980s but nevertheless by 1988 productivity at both Halewood and Dagenham was still trailing behind the norms elsewhere in Europe. For example, Dagenham needed 67 hours on average to build a Sierra and 57 hours for a Fiesta, whereas Genk (Belgium) required only 40 hours for a Sierra and Valencia (Spain) only 33 hours for a Fiesta. At Halewood it took an average of 59 hours to produce an Escort (Done 1990). National Economic Development Office data support the general conclusion that returns to manufacturing investment are low in the UK (NEDO 1980), e.g. in the period 1961–77, the average increase in net manufacturing output per unit of investment was 130% greater in France than in the UK; with the excess being 81% in West

Germany and 32% in the USA. More recent data (OECD 1985b) confirm these trends, with output per unit of net capital stock in manufacturing 95% higher in West Germany than the UK, and 110% higher in the USA. The relatively low levels of manufacturing investment in the UK may be seen as a rational response to low returns in the UK, so that whilst low investment may contribute to low productivity so also low productivity discourages more investment.

Differences in average returns may be explained either by poor selection of projects, and/or by poor utilization of capital equipment, as at Halewood. In both cases we might seek explanations in terms of the contribution of management. In the latter case we might examine the skills and work practices of the labour force. Management is responsible for selecting projects, organizing the flow of work and the utilization of resources, so that effective management is a 'necessary' condition for good productivity performance. It is not, however, 'sufficient', since a labour force which possesses inappropriate skills, or which refuses to adapt its work practices and manning levels to new technology will prevent advances in productivity, whatever the merits of management. A major issue in many industries is workers' lack of flexibility between tasks, resulting in overmanning and also a disincentive to innovation which may lead to disputes about manning. Lack of flexibility can result from union restrictive practices, but is also caused by badly trained workers and managers who are unable to cope with change. There is increasing evidence of low standards in UK education which mean that many school leavers are ill-equipped for the growing complexity of work. S. J. Prais has found that the *average* Japanese *15$\frac{1}{2}$* year old has about the same attainment in mathematics as the *top 30th percentile* British *16$\frac{1}{2}$* year old (Prais, 1987).

Throughout British industry there is less emphasis on training than in other countries. Davies and Caves (1987) point out that British managers are only marginally better qualified than the population at large, for example very few production managers are graduate engineers. Amongst production workers only a quarter in Britain have completed an apprenticeship compared with about half in West Germany (NIESR 1985). Very few British foremen have formal qualifications for their job but in West Germany foremen are trained as craftsmen and then take the further qualification of *Meister*. Higher levels of skill enable West German firms to make better use of their capital equipment and to adapt to change of all kinds, so investment in human capital raises productivity of both physical capital and labour, whilst also achieving consistently higher quality of output. To return to the example of Ford, the decision was taken in 1990 to switch Sierra production to Genk, leaving Dagenham producing only the Fiesta and so greatly simplifying the operation of the plant. The aim of this rationalization is to raise productivity and also to raise the quality of the Fiestas produced to match those in Valencia by 1992.

We turn now to the *consequences* of low productivity growth. It might be argued that faster productivity growth would destroy yet more manufacturing jobs. It is certainly true that UK manufacturing could produce its present output with little more than half its present labour force if labour productivity were raised to the levels prevailing in the other EC countries shown in Table

1.9. Presented in this way it may appear that productivity growth threatens jobs. However, the flaw in the argument is that it assumes constant output, yet, as we note in Chapter 10, a higher UK productivity rate may well mean that the UK would produce more output. Higher productivity may reduce costs, lower prices and stimulate both domestic consumption and overseas consumption (i.e. exports). Whether output would increase sufficiently to raise aggregate employment after productivity increase is an empirical question, considered more fully in Chapter 10.

It would still be possible to remain price-competitive with overseas producers even with low labour productivity, if real wages were also low. Labour costs per unit of output (unit labour costs) are determined by the wages of the workers as well as the output per worker. International competitiveness, in terms of unit labour costs, is also influenced by exchange rates. Depreciation of the currency can even compensate for poor productivity and high money wages, though it also has the effect of raising import prices.

Figure 1.1 reveals the sources of the changes in UK cost competitiveness in manufacturing since 1976, relative to its major competitors. The UK's *relative productivity* is shown by Schedule 'C', which indicates the changes in UK manufacturing productivity *relative* to its major competitors since 1976. We see that in 1986 UK manufacturing productivity was at about 95% of its 1976 level relative to those competitors. The *relative cost of UK labour* had risen by as much as 54% over this period. The impact of these changes on UK competitiveness was, however, moderated by a fall in the *effective exchange rate* to 84% of its 1976 level. As a result, *relative unit labour costs* (RULC) were only 30% above their 1976 level. The calculation of RULC is as follows:

$$\frac{\text{Relative labour costs}}{\text{Relative productivity}} \times \frac{\text{sterling effective}}{\text{exchange rate}} = \text{RULC}$$

Fig. 1.1 Cost contributions: sources of changes in UK cost competitiveness in manufacturing
Source: National Economic Development Office (1987)

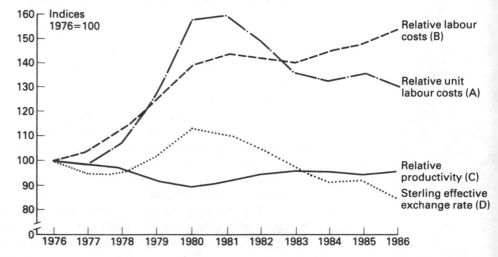

We should not of course conclude from this that the 1976 position was 'just right'. Nevertheless, we have already shown that manufacturing output and employment had fallen dramatically by 1984. A restoration of UK competitiveness, even to 1976 levels, would in all probability generate more output and more employment than currently experienced.

The above formula emphasizes that lower *relative unit labour costs* could be achieved either by reducing relative labour costs, *or* by raising relative productivity, *or* by lowering the effective exchange rate, or indeed by a combination of all three. If the *exchange rate alone* were to be used, a *depreciation* of 23% would have been required in 1986 in order to restore RULC in the UK to its 1976 level. Figure 1.1 draws attention to the fact that the sterling effective exchange rate *appreciated* between 1978 and 1981 (see also Ch. 22). This happened at the very time that relative labour costs were rising rapidly and relative productivity was falling. Hardly surprising, therefore, that the UK's competitive position deteriorated by about 50% during this period, as indicated by the sharp rise in RULC. This was a major factor in the marked decline in manufacturing output and employment in the UK between 1979 and 1981.

After 1980/81 the competitive position improved (RULC is on a downward trend) as the decline of the sterling effective exchange rate more than compensated for the resumed rise in relative labour costs. Notice that improvements in relative productivity contributed little to the falling RULC after 1983. By 1990 there was again concern about the comparative position as the pound rose to around 3.0 DM.

The 'logic' of low productivity, namely lower real wages and pensions and inferior social services, has not readily been accepted in the UK. It is in any case doubtful whether the option of a low-wage, low-productivity industrial economy is viable, given the role of technology. Technical change is frequently embodied in the latest capital equipment, and has the effect of changing not just the volume of output per worker, but also the quality of products. For instance, robot welders and paint-sprayers on car production lines offer a dependable quality which previously more labour-intensive methods did not. If, as a consequence of lower real wages, older and more labour-intensive methods are retained in the face of competition from new technology, markets will often still be lost on the basis of quality, *even if* prices can be held at apparently low levels. In these circumstances, the UK would be producing goods under similar conditions to many newly industrializing Third World countries.

Low productivity, not fully compensated by low wages or by a lower exchange rate, leaves UK companies in a weak market position. They are faced with the choice of raising prices and risking lost orders, or continuing to sell on lower profit margins. Markets differ in their sensitivity to rising prices, but in all markets rising prices tend to reduce sales *volume*, which usually means less employment. Multinational companies located in the UK may, to avoid raising price, supply an increasing proportion of their market from overseas plants, again reducing UK output and employment.

Firms which absorb rising unit costs by taking lower profit margins may be able to maintain their levels of output and employment, at least in the short run. But in the long run profits are vital to industrial investment, both in providing investment finance and in influencing expectations of future rates of return, and hence investment plans. Investment is also required in many industries to raise productivity, and thereby profits, and so we come full circle. Profits depend on productivity, which is affected by investment, which depends on profits! The process is self-reinforcing; low productivity gives low profits, low investment and therefore little productivity improvement. In contrast, once productivity is raised, profits and investment increase, which further raises productivity. This cumulative upward spiral is still further reinforced in that market share and factor incomes rise, so that demand is created for still higher output. New technology is also more easily accepted in situations of rising output, perhaps leading to still higher profits, stimulating further investment, and so driving the process on. The UK's problem is to break out of a low-productivity trap.

The consequences of low productivity and poor competitiveness are felt mainly in the industrial sector of the economy, largely because its exposure to international competition is greater than that of the service sector. Structural change, in the form of a *reduced share* of output and employment for the industrial sector, is then almost inevitable. In the UK this has also become a decline in *absolute level* of employment and, from 1973 to 1981, in output of the industrial sector.

Consequences of structural change

Deindustrialization

There is little agreement as to what 'deindustrialization' actually means. For some time politicians on the left have used the term to mean loss of industrial employment. Thirlwall (1982) also favours this view. Others extend the term to include situations of declining industrial output, and still others to include declining *shares* of employment or output.

We have shown that the UK has undergone deindustrialization on each and every one of these criteria. Declining industrial employment is not unusual in other advanced economies (see Table 1.6), and neither is a decline in the industrial sector's share of employment (Table 1.5) or of GDP (Table 1.3). Where the UK *is* unusual is in its declining volume of non-oil industrial output after 1973.

Declining industrial employment need not be a problem; there is every indication that many British people would not freely choose industrial employment. There will, however, be the problem of rising unemployment if declining industrial employment is not compensated by increasing non-industrial employment. Until 1979 this problem did not arise; as we saw in Table 1.4, employment levels were broadly maintained until 1979, but since then the growth of service sector employment has *not* compensated for falling industrial employment. The costs of deindustrialization have been particularly felt in those regions where declining industries were concentrated. The Midlands, the North, Yorkshire and Humberside, the North West, Wales and Scotland all experienced a prolonged period with unemployment rates well above 10% during the 1980s, as the industrial base contracted. By May 1990, the recorded rates of unemployment in the North and Scotland (at 8.5% and 8%) were still above the 5.4% average rate for Great Britain.

Some writers view these changes as part of a move towards a post-industrial society, where the main activities involve the creation and handling of information. However, a decline in the share of industrial activity within the economy would be less worrying if *absolute* industrial output had grown since 1973 at the same rate as in other advanced economies.

Growth prospects

As we saw in Table 1.7, in the recovery since 1981 it is manufacturing which has led the way in productivity growth. Manufacturing lends itself to rapid growth of labour productivity because of the scope for capital investment and technical progress. Growth of manufacturing output, of GDP, and of productivity, are closely related, and manufacturing has in the past been the engine for growth. As workers found new jobs in manufacturing during the nineteenth century they left agriculture and other relatively low-productivity sectors. Those in the new jobs raised their productivity, and the average productivity of those remaining in agriculture was raised by the removal of marginal workers. At the same time rising incomes in manufacturing generated new demand for goods and services, the multiplier process encouraging still further growth of output, and with it productivity.

In parts of the service sector there is little scope for improved productivity; even the concept itself is often inappropriate. First, because there is often no clear output – how do you measure the output of doctors, or nurses? Second, even where a crude output measure is devised, it often fails to take into account the quality of service – are larger class sizes an increase or decrease in educational productivity? The national accounts often resort to measuring output by input (e.g. the wages of health workers), so that productivity is by definition equal to 1. There are, however, some services where productivity can be meaningfully measured and in these there is scope for productivity growth, especially where the new information technologies can be applied. But many workers who lose manufacturing jobs move into service sector jobs, where their productivity may be lower, into unemployment or out of the labour market altogether. There is no mechanism for growth in this process, quite the reverse.

Balance of payments

An alternative definition of deindustrialization is offered by Singh, based on the traditional role of manufacturing in UK trade flows. Historically the UK was a net exporter of manufactures, so that surplus foreign exchange was earned which enabled the country to run a deficit on its trade in food and raw materials. Singh (1977) defines an 'efficient' manufacturing sector as one which 'not only satisfies the demands of consumers at home but is also able to sell enough of its products abroad to pay for the nation's import requirements'. Singh also states that this is subject to the restriction that 'an efficient manufacturing sector must be able to achieve these objectives at socially acceptable levels of output, employment and exchange rate'. A country such as the UK would then be 'deindustrialized' if its manufacturing sector did not meet these criteria, leaving an economic structure inappropriate to the needs of the country. It can now be argued that this is indeed the position in the UK. The current account can only be kept in balance by surpluses in the oil and service sectors and by earnings from overseas assets. Any reflation of aggregate demand stimulates an even faster growth in imports of manufactured goods which pushes the current account towards deficit. The UK current account deficit re-emerged during the second half of 1987 and quickly grew to what many regard as unsustainable levels. The decline of UK manufacturing has recreated the balance of payments constraint on macroeconomic policy which many had hoped North Sea oil would remove. This, allied to the fact that UK output and employment are hardly at *socially acceptable* levels, suggests that the UK could be regarded as 'deindustrialized' on Singh's definition.

It might be argued that the service sector can take over the traditional role of manufacturing in the balance of payments accounts. A difficulty here is that unlike manufactures many services cannot, by their nature, be traded internationally (e.g. public sector services), with the result that trade in manufactures is on a vastly bigger scale than trade in services (see Ch. 23). The House of Lords Committee (1985) points out that a 3% rise in service exports is required merely to offset a 1% fall in manufacturing exports. In some services which can be traded, the UK is already highly successful (e.g. financial services), and if even bigger surpluses are to be earned then the UK would have to move towards a monopoly position in those services. In fact, international competition is increasing in traded services and the UK may find it difficult to hold its current share of the market. This is borne out by data from the *Financial Times* in 1985 which showed the UK world market share of invisibles to have fallen from 12% in 1978 to 8.5% in 1983.

Thirlwall (1982) points out that Singh's definition would leave most of the non-oil-producing industrial countries categorized as 'deindustrialized' because, despite growing industrial output, their macroeconomic policies have been constrained by their balance of payments positions since the 1973 and 1979 oil price rises. Although Singh's definition is not entirely satisfactory, his work does highlight the serious balance of payments consequences of deindustrialization in the UK.

Inflation

If deindustrialization in the UK is so advanced that the economy is not capable of producing goods to match the pattern of market demand, then there may be implications not only for imports but also for prices. Any increase in overall demand will meet a shortage of domestic suppliers in many industrial sectors. This will both encourage import substitution and provide opportunities for domestic suppliers to raise prices. As a result, despite unemployment of over 1.6 million, there may be little effective spare capacity in the UK in sectors where deindustrialization has been excessive. Structural change may then have increased the likelihood of the UK experiencing demand-led inflation in the event of a sustained increase in aggregate demand, such as that of the late 1980s.

Conclusion

There have been profound structural changes in the UK economy since 1964, resulting in relative stagnation of industrial output and declining industrial employment, and these have transformed the sectoral balance of the economy. The causes of these changes are not agreed. We reviewed various suggestions, such as economic 'maturity', low-wage competition, the advent of North Sea oil, 'crowding out', and low productivity. Our view has been that low productivity, resulting in a substantial loss of competitiveness, has been central to the structural changes observed. Certainly no other major industrial country has experienced the fall in volume of non-oil industrial output recorded in the UK after 1973. The consequences of industrial decline are widespread, contributing to unemployment and balance of payments problems, increasing inflationary pressures and hampering growth. Judged by the growth of output and productivity there was an improvement in the performance of the UK economy during the 1980s, sufficient to reverse the earlier decline in industrial output, but not sufficient to restore the 1979 levels of employment. The decline in UK productivity relative to our competitors has been halted, but an enormous 'catching up' task remains.

Notes

1. The GDP is the total value of output produced by factors of production located in a given country.
2. Income elasticity of demand is given by:

$$\frac{\%\ \text{change in quantity demanded}}{\%\ \text{change in income}}$$

3. 'Factor cost' means that 'market price' valuations of output have been adjusted to take account of the distortions caused by taxes and subsidies. Taxes raise market prices above the true cost of factor input and so are subtracted. Subsidies reduce market prices below factor cost and so are added.

   'Constant factor cost' means that the valuations have been made in the prices of a given base year (in this case 1980). This eliminates the effects of inflation, so that the time series shows 'real' output.
4. Buying the foreign currency to pay for the extra imports would increase the supply of sterling on the foreign exchange market, reducing the price of sterling.

References

Bacon, R. and **Eltis, W.** (1976) *Britain's Economic Problem – too few producers*. Macmillan.
Bell, D. (1973) *The Coming of Post Industrial Society*. Basic Books, New York.
CSO (1964–74, 1984, 1989)*National Income and Expenditure*.
CSO (1983, 1987b, 1989) *National Accounts*.
CSO (1985) *Annual Abstract of Statistics*.
CSO (1990a) *Economic Trends, Annual Supplement*.
CSO (1990b) *Economic Trends*, June.
Davies, S. and **Caves, R. E.** (1987) *Britain's Productivity Gap*. CUP, Cambridge.
Done, K. (1990) Time to do or die at Dagenham, *Financial Times*, 26 June.

House of Lords (1985) *Report from the Select Committee on Overseas Trade*. HMSO.

National Economic Development Office (1980, 1985, 1987) *British Industrial Performance*.

National Institute of Economic and Social Research (NIESR) (1982) *National Institute Economic Review*, 101, Aug. p. 29.

National Institute of Economic and Social Research (1985) *National Institute Economic Review*, Feb.

National Institute of Economic and Social Research (1987) *National Institute Economic Review*, May.

OECD (1985a) *Labour Force Statistics 1963–1983*. Paris.

OECD (1985b) *UK Country Report*.

Prais, S. J. (1987) Educating For Productivity: Comparisons of Japanese and English schooling and vocational preparation. *National Institute Economic Review*, Feb. 1987.

Rowthorn, R. E. and **Wells, J. R.** (1987) *Deindustrialization and Foreign Trade*. CUP, Cambridge.

Singh, A. (1977) UK industry and the world economy: a case of deindustrialization? *Cambridge Journal of Economics*, **1**, 2, June.

Taylor, R. (1981) *Observer Business*, Nov.

Thirlwall, A. P. (1982) Deindustrialization in the United Kingdom, *Lloyds Bank Review*, 144, April.

World Bank (1985, 1987) *World Development Report*. OUP, New York.

2 Company accounts as a source of financial information

The price paid by public and private companies for the privilege of limited liability is the preparation and publication of annual accounts. The required level of reporting is specified by the Companies Acts and for most companies the actual disclosures made are the legal minimum. Company accounts are complex documents which are as likely to mislead and misinform the shareholders and potential investors as they are to provide them with the data to make rational economic decisions. This chapter examines the content and presentation of conventional accounts, and identifies a number of useful accounting ratios which can be extracted from the balance sheet, with Sears p.l.c. (1990), whose activities include the Miss Selfridge and Saxone stores, used for illustration. It goes on to consider attempts to derive a *single* index of company performance, testing whether it would have predicted company liquidations. The chapter concludes with a detailed analysis of a further source of information to company investors, the Financial Times Share Information Service, and the indices and ratios it contains.

Company accounts and the assessment of company performance

The separation of control and ownership in the majority of public companies[1] creates an atmosphere in which management might wish to present to shareholders as favourable a picture as possible of the company's activities. Fear of the effects of competition and of adverse investor reaction may also mean that companies seek to give away as little as possible – usually by disclosing the legal minimum of information. Many p.l.c.s, however, regard the presentation of their annual accounts as a matter of corporate pride, and pay great attention to the quality and relevance of the documents.

Published financial statements should provide sufficient information to enable shareholders and potential shareholders to make economic decisions about whether to buy, hold or sell shares in a company. If shareholders are unable to assess the company's performance from the accounts, or to estimate the likely risk of their future involvement, then much of the blame for this must rest with those who prepare the accounts, or with governments for failing to introduce legislation requiring companies to provide such information. This problem is often less acute where numerical accounting data are supported by narrative description.

An examination of the typical elements that make up a company report reveals a mixture of statutory items, requirements of the accounting profession, additional Stock Exchange requirements and voluntary disclosures. The most important items in the general picture that emerges are the following:

(a) Chairman's review;
(b) Directors' report;
(c) Balance sheet;
(d) Profit and loss account;
(e) Notes to the accounts;
(f) Funds flow statement;
(g) Auditors' report;
(h) Historical summary.

It is worth while investigating each of these elements to identify those features which may be helpful in assessing a company's overall performance.

Chairman's review

There is no statutory requirement for a chairman to report separately from his directors, so any statement usually contains voluntary information. The chairman's review of operations often seeks to explain why the company has performed as it has over the past year, indicating strategy for the immediate future. Plans for expansion, diversification, overseas growth and the development of new products would usually be included.

However, the chairman's position as the figurehead of the company demands that he maintain confidence in the company's activities, so he is likely to concentrate on the encouraging aspects of performance and ignore the weak points. Thus Geoffrey Maitland Smith, chairman of Sears, was able to state:

Sears financial strength has served us well in this challenging year and emphasises the wisdom of past prudent management. Over many years we have worked to build the Group's financial strength which enables us to maintain growth programmes at a time when some competitors are finding it difficult to finance ongoing operations. Plans for the coming year include a continuing programme of capital investment totalling over £110 million.

Directors' report

This includes a statement of the principal activities of the company and of any significant changes that have taken place in the holding of fixed assets (e.g. property sales or the acquisition of subsidiaries). Details of the directors and their financial interest in the company are also mentioned as any significant change in their holdings may reflect their view of the company's future prospects.

Balance sheet

This shows the position of the company at the particular time of its financial year end, usually 31 December, but for retailers like Sears, the relatively 'quiet' date of 31 January is used. It details the assets of the business and balances them against its liabilities; in other words, what the company *owns* (assets) is exactly matched by what it *owes* (liabilities) in terms of funds required to finance those assets.

The balance sheet is essentially a 'snapshot' of the state of the company on one day, though the actual position could appear very different a few days before or after. A number of criticisms can be made of the way balance sheets are normally presented. They do not show how the final position was arrived at; for instance, the company may attempt to 'clean up' its balance sheet by repaying loans just before the year end only to incur the debt again early in the new financial year. This is known as 'window dressing'. They also ignore those items which cannot be measured objectively in monetary terms, such as expertise or harmonious labour relations.

Accounting ratios

Despite these difficulties, the construction of several simple ratios from the information contained within the balance sheet can give a clear assessment of the company's performance in specific areas.

Differences in size between companies mean that absolute values cannot easily be compared. The most common method of removing the size factor is to deflate absolute values, dividing through by one of several alternative measures of size: (a) sales turnover; (b) total assets; (c) shareholders' funds; (d) net capital employed; and (e) net worth. Not only are there a number of possible deflators, but each one can be defined in a number of alternative ways. For instance, sales turnover might appear a straightforward concept but it is shown in the accounts net of VAT (a figure which may be 13% less than the cash through the tills) or, for a group, net of intra-company trading. The result of all this is a large number of possible ratio values.

Even when we have dealt with the size factor by selecting a *particular* ratio, we must adopt some standard for comparison. This usually means one or more of the following:

1. Comparison of a company's performance with its *own* performance in previous time periods.
2. Comparison of its performance with that of *other companies* in the same sector, and/or
3. Comparison of its performance with *accepted standards* of performance, i.e. with particular values ('norms') for each ratio.

Figure 2.1 shows the 1990 balance sheet for Sears p.l.c., a retailing group. Several accounting ratios have been calculated by extracting the 1990 figures from the table and *comparing them* with the corresponding annual sales turnover (£2,091m. for Group sales to outside customers – see the profit and loss account of Fig. 2.2). For comparative purposes the same ratios have been calculated for Tesco p.l.c., also in the retailing sector, and for Blue Circle Industries in the manufacturing sector.

Leverage ratios   These reflect the financial risk to which the company is subject, by measuring the capital structure of the company and the degree to which it relies on external borrowings.

Gearing ratio.   One of the most important leverage ratios is the gearing ratio. This can be calculated in various ways, including:

$$\text{Gearing ratio} = \frac{\text{external borrowing}}{\text{total capital employed}}$$

$$= \frac{\text{loan capital} + \text{bank overdraft}}{\text{loan capital} + \text{bank overdraft} + \text{ordinary shares and reserves}}$$

Company accounts as a source of financial information

CONSOLIDATED BALANCE SHEET

31 JANUARY 1990	Notes	1990 £m	£m	1989 £m	£m
Fixed assets					
Tangible assets	10	1,183.2		1,138.5	
Investments	11	27.5		20.1	
			1,210.7		1,158.6
Current assets					
Stocks	12	463.1		443.6	
Debtors	13	387.8		362.9	
Investments	11	—		2.1	
Cash at bank and in hand	14	174.1		508.5	
		1,025.0		1,317.1	
Creditors (due within one year)	15	637.5		583.4	
Net current assets			387.5		733.7
Assets less current liabilities			1,598.2		1,892.3
Creditors (due after one year)	15	196.1		559.7	
Provisions for liabilities and charges	17	42.3		35.0	
Minority interests in subsidiaries		13.5		13.5	
			251.9		608.2
			1,346.3		1,284.1
Capital and reserves					
Called up share capital	18		378.9		378.1
Share premium account	18		5.4		4.5
Revaluation reserve	19		202.9		242.4
Profit and loss account	19		759.1		659.1
			1,346.3		1,284.1

NOTES ON THE ACCOUNTS
DEBTORS

	Group 1989/90 £m	1988/89 £m
Due within one year:		
Trade debtors	261.9	255.9
Group companies	—	—
Taxation recoverable	—	1.1
Other debtors	45.8	29.6
Prepayments and accrued income	52.1	43.1
	359.8	329.7
Due after one year:		
Trade debtors	5.4	5.3
Other debtors	0.4	6.7
Prepayments and accrued income	3.0	2.9
Advance corporation tax	19.2	18.3
Deferred taxation recoverable	—	—
	387.8	362.9

CREDITORS

	Group	
	1989/90 £m	1988/89 £m
Due within one year:		
Debentures, loans and overdrafts	167.3	100.0
Trade creditors	137.3	120.1
Other creditors	67.7	42.6
Group companies	—	—
Taxation on profits	71.6	121.7
Other taxes and social security	37.3	31.1
Accruals and deferred income	98.6	113.0
Dividends accrued and proposed	57.7	54.9
	637.5	583.4
Due after one year:		
Debentures and loans	188.8	543.3
Taxation on profits	7.3	15.8
Accruals and deferred income	—	0.6
	196.1	559.7

The total capital employed is made up of external borrowings (debentures,[2] other loans and bank borrowing) and internally generated funds (ordinary shares and reserves). The *cost* of external borrowing is loan interest payments, whilst that for internal funds is the dividend that must be paid to shareholders.

The gearing ratio shows the proportion of total capital that is provided externally and gives an indication of the burden of interest payments to which the company is committed irrespective of its profitability. A gearing ratio around 33.3% is usually regarded as acceptable for a company, suggesting that it is not over-reliant on external borrowing. A figure in excess of this indicates a relatively highly geared company. High gearing ratios are most suitable to those companies with steady and reliable profits, whose earnings are sufficient to cover interest payments and where total dividends are low. Wide fluctuations in profitability make the highly geared company extremely vulnerable to a downturn in market conditions – profits may be so low that interest payments cannot be covered, leading to receivership. The 1990 accounts reveal a relatively low gearing ratio of 21% for Sears, $(167.3 + 188.8)/(167.3 + 188.8 + 1,346.3)$, a value lower than the 32% of Blue Circle and the 25% of Tesco. Furthermore, Sears had £174.1m cash at bank and in hand at the end of 1990, which when offset against loans and overdrafts, effectively reduces its gearing level to 10.7%.

Debt/equity ratio. The most common alternative leverage measure is the debt/equity ratio, which compares external borrowings directly with internally generated funds.

$$\text{Debt/equity ratio} = \frac{\text{loan capital} + \text{bank overdraft}}{\text{ordinary shareholders' funds}}$$

$$= \frac{\text{loan capital} + \text{bank overdraft}}{\text{ordinary shares} + \text{reserves}}$$

The smaller denominator makes this ratio a more sensitive measure of the overall borrowing position than the gearing ratio, with a 50% figure regarded as typical. Sears has a fairly low ratio of 26.5% (167.3 + 188.8)/(1,346.3) from Fig. 2.1, although this shows a decrease from 50% in 1989. Blue Circle with 49%, and Tesco with 34%, again exhibit higher figures. Note that Sears' figure falls to 13.5% if the cash balances are offset against the loans and overdrafts.

However, both of these ratios are concerned only with borrowings on which interest charges are incurred. They ignore completely liabilities which constitute interest-free loans. One such major item is that of 'trade creditors' – money which is owed by the company to its suppliers. Both the gearing and debt/equity ratios tend to understate the dependence of companies on external borrowings and it is useful to extend the 'loan' item to 'liabilities'. The numerator would then become: 'short and long-term liabilities' and produce a ratio which is a more realistic basis for comparison when linked with 'shareholders' funds'. The ratios for the three companies are: Sears 62%; Blue Circle 54%; Tesco 66%.

Operating ratios   These can be used to gauge the efficiency with which various aspects of the company's trading are managed.

Stock turnover ratio.   The holding of stock, in the form of unsold finished, and partly finished, goods, is an expensive activity for companies, so that considerable attention is paid to the stock turnover ratio:

$$\text{Stock turnover ratio} = \frac{\text{stocks}}{\text{sales turnover}}$$

This ratio reflects the level of stockholding used to support sales. We would expect companies to carry the minimum level of stock (inventories) consistent with the efficient running of the business. The appropriate figure will vary widely according to the industrial sector involved. Sears' ratio is 22.1% (463.1)/(2,091.9). Tesco had a ratio of only 4%, reflecting the extremely fast throughput of their stock. Blue Circle had a ratio of 12.5%.

Debtors' turnover ratio.   This ratio can be used to monitor a company's credit control procedures, by comparing the amount it is owed by consumers, to whom credit facilities have been extended, with its total sales.

$$\text{Debtors' turnover ratio} = \frac{\text{debtors}}{\text{sales turnover}}$$

$$= \frac{\text{average amount owed to the group by customers}}{\text{sales turnover}}$$

Businesses like retail supermarkets are run almost exclusively on a cash-and-carry basis so have almost zero debtors (the Tesco Group debtors' turnover figure of 0.7% reflects this). However, the tendency for retail supermarkets to introduce their own charge card for credit trading (e.g. Marks and Spencer, 1985) increases the debtors' figure. Even so, it may generate sufficient additional sales actually to reduce the debtors' turnover ratio. For other businesses an average credit period might be six weeks, equivalent to a debtors' turnover figure of around 12%, which was the figure for Sears (261.9 + 5.4)/2,091.9.

Creditors' turnover ratio.   This ratio indicates the size and period of credit a company receives from its suppliers, by comparing the total amount the company owes to its creditors with its sales.

$$\text{Creditors' turnover ratio} = \frac{\text{creditors}}{\text{sales turnover}}$$

$$= \frac{\text{average amount owed by the group to its suppliers}}{\text{sales turnover}}$$

It may (after evaluating the possibility of pre-payment discounts) be very much in the company's interests to exploit its suppliers by extending the credit period. However, Sears shows a figure of 6.6% (137.3/2,091.9), reflecting its close links with its suppliers.

It is important to avoid confusion between the term 'creditors' when meaning 'trade creditors' (i.e. money owed to suppliers) as against meaning 'total creditors' (i.e. liabilities of all varieties). All further references in this chapter will equate 'creditors' with 'trade creditors'.

Working capital/sales ratio.   'Working capital' represents the funds available internally to finance the future operations of the company.

$$\text{Working capital/sales ratio} = \frac{\text{stocks} + \text{debtors} - \text{creditors}}{\text{sales turnover}}$$

In its simplest form working capital is calculated as current assets − current liabilities, i.e. the short-term funds still available after meeting those liabilities which must be repaid in the following year. In practice 'cash' and 'overdraft' are easily manipulated in the accounts, and companies adopt differing practices for dealing with them – so for purposes of comparison they are often excluded from the working capital definition. This leaves stocks (inventories) + debtors − creditors as the main elements in working capital. The value of the working capital ratio will vary widely according to the complexity of the business. In the heavy engineering sectors, where high stock levels are necessary to operate an effective after-sales service, the ratio is sometimes as high as 50%.

An efficient retailer, without credit-card facilities, will have a very low, perhaps even negative, ratio. This will follow from having low stocks, few debtors and extensive credit from suppliers.

Liquidity ratios   These give an indication of the company's short-term financial position. In other words, the availability of cash or marketable assets with which to meet current liabilities.

Current ratio.   The current ratio measures the extent to which currently available assets cover current liabilities, i.e. those requiring repayment within one year.

$$\text{Current ratio} = \frac{\text{current assets}}{\text{current liabilities}}$$

$$= \frac{\text{stocks} + \text{debtors} + \text{cash}}{\text{overdraft} + \text{creditors} + \text{taxation} + \text{dividends}}$$

A figure of 1.5 may be taken as prudent, showing that current liabilities are more than covered by current assets. A ratio value of more than 1.5 is not necessarily helpful, since it may mean excessive stocks, or debtors, or an uneconomic use of liquid funds. Sears has a ratio of 1.6 (1,025)/(637.5).

Food retailers are unusual in that their rapid turnovers, together with the cash-and-carry nature of their business, will give low 'stock' and 'debtor' items respectively. In this way 'current assets' will be small, and so a low current ratio is to be expected. Tesco's 1989 figure of 0.5 must be viewed in this context.

Quick assets ratio (acid test).   This ratio provides a better indication of short-term liquidity by ignoring stockholdings and concentrating on those assets which are more easily convertible into cash.

$$\text{Quick assets ratio} = \frac{\text{current assets} - \text{stocks}}{\text{current liabilities}}$$

A yardstick of 1.0 is usually sought, indicating that sufficient liquid assets are available to cover current liabilities. Sears' figure is about right at 0.9 (561.9)/(637.5) though Blue Circle is above the manufacturing sector average with a ratio of 1.7.

Traders with a rapid turnover of cash sales will have a lower level of current assets, and often a very low ratio. This is the case with Tesco's quick assets ratio of 0.14 for 1989.

The current and quick assets ratios are probably the best-known and most widely used financial ratios, so it is no surprise that some companies might resort to 'window-dressing' of the accounts in order to create an impression that these ratios are a little better than they actually are.

The calculation of the above eight ratios from balance sheet information, i.e. (a) *leverage* ratios: gearing; debt/equity; (b) *operating* ratios: stock turnover; debtors' turnover; creditors' turnover; working capital; and (c) *liquidity* ratios: current; quick assets; permits an assessment of a company's performance with regard to accepted standards across a given sector. This assessment is further improved by considering the information provided by the profit and loss account.

Profit and loss account

This is a summary of transactions for a stated period, usually a year, and sets revenues against costs in order to show the profit, or loss, made. The statement discloses summarized figures for the expenses of the business (e.g.

the cost of goods sold), but makes no evaluation of the risks incurred in order to earn the given profit levels. Neither is there any indication of the degree to which the given profit level conforms with the company's objectives.

Fig. 2.2 Profit and loss account for Sears p.l.c. *Source:* Sears Accounts

CONSOLIDATED PROFIT AND LOSS ACCOUNT

FOR THE YEAR ENDED 31 JANUARY 1990

	Notes	1989/90 £m	1988/89 £m
Turnover	1		
Continuing businesses		2,091.9	2,038.7
Discontinued operations		—	667.2
		2,091.9	2,705.9
Cost of sales		(1,310.3)	(1,881.0)
Gross profit		781.6	824.9
Distribution costs		(490.0)	(452.4)
Administration expenses		(91.2)	(94.0)
Trading profits	1	200.4	278.5
Share of related company profits		5.7	5.1
Other income	3	43.5	25.4
Exceptional items	4	(7.6)	—
Interest	5	(10.6)	(36.2)
Profits on ordinary activities before taxation		231.4	272.8
Taxation	6	(63.8)	(87.1)
Profits after taxation and before extraordinary items		167.6	185.7
Minority interests – dividends paid		(0.6)	(0.6)
Extraordinary items	7	—	312.3
Attributable to Sears plc		167.0	497.4
Dividends on preference shares		(0.2)	(0.2)
Attributable to ordinary shareholders		166.8	497.2
Dividends on ordinary shares:	8		
Interim paid – 11 December 1989		(23.0)	(21.7)
Proposed final – payable 6 July 1990		(57.6)	(54.8)
Added to reserves	19	86.2	420.7

Figure 2.2. shows the profit and loss account of Sears for 1990 and indicates the various deductions that take place from sales revenue to derive profit or loss. Profit is either distributed to shareholders in the form of dividends or retained by the company to boost reserves. Dividends may still be paid to shareholders even when losses have been incurred, but only by running down reserves.

The profit figure remains the single most important figure in the company accounts and various profitability measures can be employed to assess relative performance.

Profit margin

$$\text{Profit margin} = \frac{\text{profit before interest and tax}}{\text{sales turnover}}$$

The profit margin is a ratio of profit, after the deduction of trading expenses but before the payment of interest on borrowings (financing charges) and corporation tax, to sales turnover. A normal figure of 8–10% would be typical for manufacturing industry. Activities such as food retailing, with high volumes and competitive prices, might expect a ratio around 3%, which might still yield high absolute levels of profit. In fact, Tesco exhibits an encouraging result with a ratio of 5.2% for its profit margin. Sears shows 9.5% (200.4)/(2,091.9), whilst Blue Circle produces a healthy 16%.

Return on assets

$$\text{Return on assets} = \frac{\text{profit before interest and tax}}{\text{total assets}}$$

Measurement of the rate of return on total assets offers a popular alternative assessment of profitability, despite the fact that it compares a 'dynamic' item (profits) with a 'static' item (total assets). On this basis the Sears figure is 10.4% (231.4)/(2,235.7), whereas Blue Circle yields 9.7%, and Tesco 12.8%.

For comparative purposes it is essential that profits are calculated on a consistent basis. Ratios based on the profits generated from normal operations should therefore exclude income from other sources, particularly from the sale of fixed assets. For example, the profit on the sale of subsidiary companies by Sears in 1989 (£312.3m) was treated as an 'extraordinary item', and would have been excluded from profit calculations in that year.

Calculations of the return on assets will clearly vary, sometimes substantially, with the basis used for measurement. This is a strong argument for using a standard approach and accountants are now expected, under their *Accounting Standard No. 12*, to revalue assets at regular intervals to avoid outdated valuations being used.

A consideration of these profitability ratios, together with earlier information on leverage, operating and liquidity ratios, can give an overall impression of Sears' financial position in 1990. The company appears to be one which is fairly low geared, with good profitability. It conforms in most respects to the average company 'profile'.

Notes to the accounts

There is far more information contained in notes to the accounts than is within the balance sheet and profit and loss account. The regulatory framework of accounting has broadened since the early 1970s to include not only the Companies Acts but also *Accounting Standards*, which are issued by the accountancy profession to standardize procedures and suggest 'best practice'.

The notes always commence with a statement of the accounting policies adopted by the company (Fig. 2.3), and there will follow many pages of detailed information required either to comply with the Acts or the relevant standards. It is unusual for companies to give more than the minimum requirements, but the auditors' report will confirm whether or not such requirements have been met.

Funds flow statement

This attempts to analyse the sources from which funds have been raised and the ways in which they have been employed during the period between the last two balance sheets. Figure 2.4 shows the funds flow statement (referred

Fig. 2.3 Accounting policies
Source: Sears p.l.c., 1990

ACCOUNTING POLICIES

BASIS OF ACCOUNTS

The accounts are prepared under the historical cost convention, as modified by the revaluation of certain properties. The accounts of all principal subsidiaries are included for either 52 or 53 week periods ending within one week of 31st January. The accounts of one subsidiary, whose activities and net assets are immaterial to the group, are made up to 31st December.

The trading results of subsidiaries acquired or sold are included in the consolidated profit and loss account from or until the effective date of acquisition or disposal respectively.

FIXED ASSETS AND DEPRECIATION

(a) Tangible assets

The majority of the group's properties are valued at regular intervals and are stated in the balance sheet at valuation, less depreciation if appropriate. Additions since valuation dates and all other fixed tangible assets are stated at cost, less depreciation if appropriate. Interest on borrowings to finance major building construction work undertaken by the group is capitalized, net of taxation, as part of the cost of those assets.

Fixed tangible assets are depreciated as follows: –

Retail and office properties –
> It is the group's policy continually to maintain its properties in a state of good repair. In the case of freeholds and long leaseholds it is considered that the residual values and lives of these properties are such that their amortisation would not be significant. Therefore, no amortisation is provided on freehold or long leasehold properties. The book amounts of short leasehold properties are amortised by equal instalments over the remaining length of the leases.

Industrial premises and warehouses –
> Freeholds and long leaseholds are amortised at 2% per annum; short leaseholds by equal instalments over the remaining length of the leases.

Plant, machinery, fixtures and fittings –
> At various rates, generally between 5% and 20%, calculated to write off these assets over their remaining useful lives.

An amount equivalent to that part of the charge for annual depreciation of revalued assets which relates to the surplus over cost is transferred from revaluation reserve to profit and loss account.

Property disposals –
> The difference between the depreciated original cost and the net proceeds is dealt with through the profit and loss account and any realized revaluation surplus or deficit is eliminated from revaluation reserve. Surpluses or deficits on disposals, other than those relating to the relocation of retailing sites or to the property development activity, are included in other income.

(b) Investments

(i) Shares in subsidiaries are included in the Company's balance sheet at the Company's share of the net assets of those subsidiaries.

(ii) The consolidated profit and loss account includes the group's share of the results of related companies. In the balance sheets, investments in related companies are stated at the aggregate of cost and the group's share of undistributed reserves of those companies since acquisition.

(iii) Other investments are included at the lower of cost and directors' valuation.

GOODWILL

Fair values are ascribed to tangible assets and liabilities of subsidiaries at dates of acquisition and any surplus or deficiency between such values and the purchase consideration is dealt with through reserves. Subsequent adjustments are also dealt with through reserves.

STOCKS AND WORK IN PROGRESS

Stocks and work in progress are stated at the lower of cost and net realizable value.

DEFERRED TAXATION

Deferred taxation in respect of capital allowances and other timing differences is provided under the liability method to the extent that a liability or an asset is expected to crystallize in the foreseeable future.

TURNOVER

Turnover represents sales, excluding value added tax, to external customers, and the aggregate amount of rental income from operating leases.

OPERATING LEASES

Rentals receivable and payable under operating leases are dealt with on a straight line basis over the lease term.

FOREIGN CURRENCIES

Trading results are expressed in sterling at the average of the rates ruling during the year and include exchange differences realized in the normal course of trade. Assets and liabilities denominated in foreign currencies are expressed in sterling at rates of exchange ruling at balance sheet dates. Unrealized exchange differences arising on the translation of net assets of overseas subsidiaries and on related foreign currency borrowings are dealt with through reserves.

PENSION COSTS

The amount charged to profit and loss account reflects the cost, based on actuarial estimates, of providing for pension benefits arising in the year. Any excess or deficit of contributions paid into pension schemes compared to the cumulative pension cost is included in prepayments or accruals. This represents a change of accounting policy following publication of SSAP 24. In previous years, the charge to profit and loss account comprised contributions made by the group to the schemes.

Fig. 2.4 Funds flow statement
Source: Sears p.l.c., 1990

SOURCE AND APPLICATION OF FUNDS

FOR THE YEAR ENDED 31 JANUARY 1990

	1989/90		1988/89	
	£m	£m	£m	£m
Source of Funds				
Trading profits less interest		189.8		242.3
Adjustment for items not involving the movement of funds:				
Depreciation		49.1		46.7
Other	(23.0)		(15.5)	
Total generated from operations		215.9		273.5
Proceeds of disposals:				
Fixed tangible assets	90.1		69.7	
Investments	5.4		1.5	
Subsidiaries	—		331.6	
New loans	13.6		507.0	
New share capital	1.7		1.1	
		110.8		910.9
		326.7		1,184.4
Application of funds				
Tax paid	106.6		74.9	
Dividends paid	78.6		71.3	
Additions to:				
Fixed tangible assets	144.9		160.4	
Investments	4.4		—	
Goodwill	—		0.4	
Subsidiaries	—		11.2	
Purchase of minority interests	—		1.2	
Loan repayments	286.7		138.8	
Exceptional items	7.6		—	
Extraordinary items	—		5.1	
		628.8		463.3
		(302.1)		721.1
Increase/(decrease) in working capital:				
Stocks	19.5		32.1	
Debtors	25.1		(32.2)	
Trade and sundry creditors and provisions	(27.0)		318.5	
Net exchange movements	0.6		1.9	
Movement in net liquid funds:				
Increase/(decrease) in net cash and short term deposits	(320.3)		400.8	
		(302.1)		721.1

Effect of acquisitions and disposals of subsidiaries in 1988/89

	Acquisitions	Disposals
Increase/(decrease) in net assets:		
Fixed tangible assets	1.0	(31.8)
Stocks	2.7	(1.4)
Debtors	0.4	(19.9)
Net cash	0.5	(11.8)
Creditors and provisions	(5.4)	12.9
Taxation	—	22.5
Bank loans	—	14.2
Goodwill on acquisition	12.0	—
Extraordinary items	—	(316.3)
Cost/(net proceeds)	11.2	(331.6)

to as the Source and Application of Funds statement) for the Sears plc for 1990 and 1989. In each case, the statement shows the way in which funds (mainly from trading profits) have been employed, largely in the purchase of fixed assets, the payment of taxation and dividends and the repayment of loans. The emphasis on fixed asset purchase reflects the company's active store development policy, with the relocation of existing stores and extensions and improvements to stores.

In general terms a match is sought between the time periods of funds and assets, so that if borrowing is necessary to finance the purchase of fixed assets (long term) we would expect the funding to be similarly long term (i.e. share issues or long-term loans). Short-term funds, on the other hand, e.g. creditors and bank overdrafts, should be financing short-term assets and working capital.

Auditors' report

The auditors are required to report to shareholders on whether the company accounts have been properly prepared, in accordance with the Companies Act, and whether they give a true and fair view of the activities of the company. Where the preparation and presentation of accounts are satisfactory this report is usually very short. Figure 2.5 provides a typical

Fig. 2.5 Auditors' Report
Source: Sears p.l.c., 1990

REPORT OF THE AUDITORS

To the members of Sears plc

We have audited the accounts on pages 30 to 34 in accordance with Auditing Standards.

In our opinion the accounts give a true and fair view of the state of affairs of the company and of the group at 31 January 1990 and of the profit and source and application of funds of the group for the year then ended and have been properly prepared in accordance with the Companies Act 1985.

Price Waterhouse
Chartered Accountants
Southwark Towers
32 London Bridge Street
London SE1 9SY

9th May 1990

example. But the auditors may qualify their approval of the accounts if they feel that the records have not been well kept or if all the information they require is not available. Such qualifications usually fall into two categories: (1) those relating to accounting policy, and (2) those relating to unsatisfactory levels of information. Whilst very few plc's receive a *qualified* audit report, an example of such a report, given in circumstances where the auditors *fundamentally disagree* with the directors, is shown in figure 2.6 on the next page. Also shown (Fig. 2.7) is an example of a qualified auditor

Fig. 2.6 Auditors' Report
(Qualified)

================================ *Auditor's Report* ================================

To the Members of No-Hope PLC

We have audited the financial statements on pages 11 to 20 in accordance with approved Auditing Standards.

As more fully explained in note 15 no provision has been made for losses expected to arise on certain long-term contracts currently in progress because the directors consider that such losses should be offset against expected but unearned future profits on other long-term contracts. In our opinion provision should be made for foreseeable losses on individual contracts as required by Statement of Standard Accounting Practice No. 9. If losses had been so recognized the effect would have been to reduce the profit before and after tax for the year and the contract work in progress at 31st December 1990 by £4.5m

In view of the significant effect of the failure to provide for the losses referred to above, in our opinion the financial statements do not give a true and fair view of the state of the company's affairs at 31st December 1988, and of its profit and source of application of funds for the year then ended.

In other respects the financial statements in our opinion comply with the Companies Acts 1985 and 1989.

---

report where the company's status as a going concern is subject to the issue of additional share capital.

Historical summary

Over 90% of the companies subject to the requirements of the Stock Exchange Listing Agreement provide some sort of historical summary, usually over a five- or ten-year period, but with no uniform approach to content (Fig. 2.8). A simple overall picture of the company's progress is usually provided, along with difficulties encountered, such as problems of coping with inflation over the period or with changing accountancy practice.

Towards a single index of company performance

The recession of the early 1980s saw many business failures. The retail, and building and constructing sectors were particularly hard hit. Amongst the companies to fail were household names like Laker Airways, Lesney Products (makers of Matchbox toys), Airfix (makers of Meccano), and Norvic (shoes). Whilst these failures may have shocked the ordinary shareholder, they should have come as no surprise to the skilled financial analyst, since statistical methods exist to give advance warning. These methods often seek to establish a single measure of performance, bringing together elements from the diverse accounting ratios outlined above.

One important statistical method is known as Z-score analysis (Taffler and Tisshaw 1977; Earl and Marais 1982). The Z-score combines the most important aspects of a company's performance, as measured by a group of financial ratios, into a *single* score, in an attempt to overcome the misleading

Fig. 2.7 Auditors' Report
where doubt exists
concerning *going concern*
status of company

HOPELESS plc

Report of the Auditors
for the period ended 31 March 1989
To the Members of Hopeless plc

We have audited the accounts in accordance with approved Auditing Standards.

As stated in Note 1 to the Accounts the Company has arranged for the issue of additional shares which will provide working capital. This arrangement together with other proposals require the approval of both shareholders and stockholders and are conditional upon the Council of The Stock Exchange agreeing to grant permission to deal in the new Ordinary Shares and Convertible Loan Stock in the USM and the conditions in the placing agreement being fulfilled or waived by the broker. The accounts have been drawn up on a going concern basis on the assumption that the necessary approvals will be obtained and the other conditions stated above will be satisfied.

Subject to all the proposals contained in the Prospectus being implemented, in our opinion the accounts give a true and fair view of the state of affairs of the Company and the Group as at 31st March 1989 and of the loss and source and application of funds of the Group for the fourteen months then ended and comply with the Companies Act 1985.

Chartered Accountants
London

---

impression that can be created by the consideration of numerous individual accounting numbers in isolation. The actual ratios employed to calculate the Z-score differ between models, but might be expected to include measures of profitability, gearing, liquidity and working capital.

The model developed in Fig. 2.9 (Smith 1983) distinguishes bankrupt from solvent companies on the basis of only three familiar financial ratios. The model can therefore be illustrated in terms of a three-dimensional 'decision cube'.

The cube has 'gearing' – measuring financial risk – on the vertical axis, with 'liquidity' and 'profitability' on the horizontal axes. Failed companies were found to be associated with high values of gearing, low values of liquidity and low, perhaps negative, values of profitability. The failed group thus occupies a high position within the cube, clustered close to the near corner. The solvent group, on the other hand, combines low gearing with relatively high liquidity and profitability values, and produces a cluster around the lower far side of the cube. The cube helps isolate potential company failures in the manufacturing and construction sectors, using only three variables. It is less helpful in assessing the prospects for retail companies, as the nature of their business often means relatively low liquidity values even for efficiently run operations.

The cube implies an index of performance derived from the following equation:

Index $= a + b$ (profitability) $+ c$ (gearing) $+ d$ (liquidity)

Fig. 2.8 Five year record
Source: Sears p.l.c., 1990

THE PAST FIVE YEARS

	1985/86 £m	1986/87 £m	1987/88 £m	1988/89 £m	1989/90 £m
Turnover – adjusted to exclude discontinued operations	1,132.2	1,290.5	1,453.6	2,038.7	2,091.9
Trading profits					
Retailing and home shopping	125.4	145.5	167.6	185.0	143.6
Property	21.0	33.5	48.0	72.7	56.8
	146.4	179.0	215.6	257.7	200.4
Discontinued operations	36.9	39.7	16.5	20.8	—
	183.3	218.7	232.1	278.5	200.4
Share of related company profits	4.8	4.1	4.6	5.1	5.7
Other income	7.3	14.6	39.6	25.4	43.5
Exceptional items	—	(7.6)	(28.9)	—	(7.6)
Interest	(8.6)	(11.1)	(1.7)	(36.2)	(10.6)
Profits on ordinary activities before taxation	186.8	218.7	245.7	272.8	231.4
Taxation	(64.0)	(77.5)	(81.6)	(87.1)	(63.8)
Profits after taxation and before extraordinary items	122.8	141.2	164.1	185.7	167.6
Minority interests and preference dividends	(0.8)	(0.8)	(0.8)	(0.8)	(0.8)
Extraordinary items	(3.7)	1.0	(47.1)	312.3	—
Ordinary dividends	(50.4)	(59.7)	(69.0)	(76.5)	(80.6)
Added to reserves	67.9	81.7	47.2	420.7	86.2
Earnings per share	8.3p	9.4p	10.9p	12.3p	11.1p
Dividends per share	3.4p	4.0p	4.6p	5.1p	5.355p

Fig. 2.9 Decision cube

☐ Bankrupt set of companies

▦ Solvent set of companies

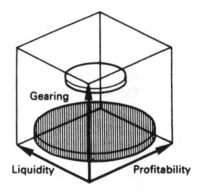

where *a* is a constant, and *b*, *c*, *d* are coefficients reflecting the relative importance of each ratio. The signs of *b* and *d* will be positive, and that of *c* negative, so that the more positive the index, the 'better' the performance; the more negative the index, the 'worse' the performance. Values for the coefficients were then established by discriminant (similar to regression) analysis, using the ratio profile of fifty bankrupt companies, and fifty solvent ones – subject to the constraint that zero be the index score that separates the two groups. The following model is generated:

$$Z = -2.53 + 6.87\left(\frac{PBT}{TA}\right) - 1.78\left(\ln\left(\frac{TL}{TA}\right)\right) + 2.01\left(\frac{QA}{CL}\right)$$

where PBT = profit before tax;
$\quad\quad TA$ = total assets = current assets + fixed assets;
$\quad\quad TL$ = total liabilities = current liabilities + long-term liabilities;
$\quad\quad QA$ = quick assets = current assets − stocks;
$\quad\quad CL$ = current liabilities;
$\quad\quad \ln$ = a log natural (to base e) transformation of the financial risk
$\quad\quad\quad\quad$ ratio.

Figure 2.10 outlines the index scores for a selection of companies. A clear

Fig. 2.10 Solvency indicator

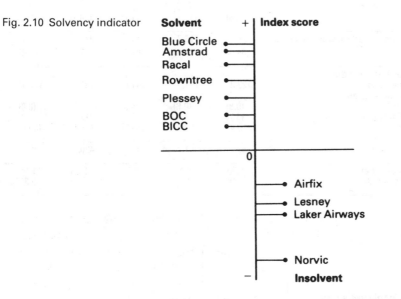

contrast is visible between the solvent group of Blue Circle, Racal, Amstrad, Plessey (electronics), Rowntree (confectionery), BOC (industrial gases) and BICC (cables), all with positive index scores, and the failed group of Laker, Lesney, Airfix and Norvic, all with negative scores.

Figure 2.11 plots the index scores of four companies over a period of seven years from 1979 to 1986 in order to produce a performance trend. It suggests, for instance, that the apparent astonishment in the media over the demise of Laker Airways was misplaced, since the time trend shows persistent negative scores. The time trend also illustrates Dunlop's slide into the negative region during 1981 and the poor financial position of the Lotus Group – the latter prompting a rescue operation in August 1983 from the British Car Auction Group and Toyota, prior to its being acquired by General Motors. In contrast Racal Electronics remain clearly in the solvent region throughout the period, though hit by the troubles of the electronics sector in 1985.

As a predictive tool, the main problem with the model appears to be that of overstating the likelihood of failure. A negative index score is not an explicit prediction of impending liquidation but rather an indication that the company closely resembles previous failures. Whilst a negative score is a necessary condition for failure it is not a sufficient one, as evidenced by the

Fig. 2.11 Performance trend

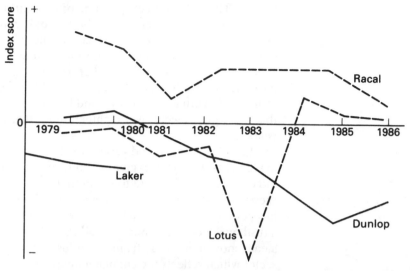

large number of companies who continue to trade despite scores suggesting impending liquidation. Although no company with a solvent profile is likely to fail, only about one-third of those with an insolvent profile will fail; the remainder will recover, remain at risk, or be taken over.

External sources of financial information

Of the various elements in the company accounts, the chairman's review is the most widely read. None of the other elements, despite the importance of the information contained, receives more than the passing attention of the average reader. Comparability between company reports has been increased considerably due to two factors. Firstly, the Companies Act requirement that all balance sheets and profit and loss accounts should be presented according to standard *formats*. Secondly, the accounting profession has, since 1971, issued a wide range of *Accounting Standards* which set out 'best practice' to be followed by *all* accountants when faced with certain complex areas including the treatment of foreign currency translation and accounting for research and development costs. However, users of financial information still often prefer to use secondary sources of information, including those provided by the Central Statistical Office, the financial press and other external agencies. Smith (1990) emphasizes the importance of non-financial indicators (NFI) as important alternatives to financial indicators. These may allow potential problems to be spotted prior to the publication of sterling outcomes. Here we consider in detail the Financial Times Share Information Service, which is perhaps the most inexpensive, comprehensive and readily available source of data on company and sector performance.

Financial Times Share Information Service

FT Industrial Ordinary 30-Share Index   The *Financial Times* (FT) prints over eighty UK indices of market activity, but this particular one is usually referred to as *the* FT Index. The index is recalculated every time one of the share prices of its constituents changes and the updating is published every minute. The index reflects the tone of the market by including movements in thirty shares, considered representative of the market as a whole and not unduly influenced by overseas factors. The selection of thirty shares (equities),[3] gives a group which, though small enough to be sensitive to changes in the mood of the market, is still large enough to absorb abnormal movements in individual shares. The 30-Share Index commenced operation in July 1935 with a base of 100, and by July 1990 it stood at 1,838, suggesting that share prices were over eighteen times higher than they were fifty or so years ago.

The index is calculated geometrically,[4] to make it less sensitive to extreme movements, though this gives it a downward bias compared to arithmetic indices. Despite the need to maintain consistency for comparison purposes, there have been over thirty changes in the constituent companies since the inception of the index, such as the replacement of Dunlop Holdings by Trusthouse Forte in January 1984. A feature of such revision has been a steady movement away from the industrial sector and towards the service sector which reflects the changing involvement across the ordinary share market. Despite its popularity the 30-Share Index is most useful as a short-term market indicator, with the FT Stock Exchange 100 Index and the All-Share Index providing better standards against which to judge the performance of share portfolios over the long term.

FT Stock Exchange 100 Index   The FT Stock Exchange 100 Index (FTSE 100), pronounced 'footsie', was launched on 13 February 1984 after an initial test period. It is composed of the shares of the 100 largest companies in terms of *market capitalization* and has a base of 1,000, as of 30 December 1983. The FTSE 100 is calculated on a 'real time' basis, and is more broadly based than the 30-Share Index, representing 70% of the value of all shares quoted on the Stock Exchange. As a result it is sensitive to movements in the service-orientated industries as well as in the manufacturing industries. It includes companies such as Reuters 'B', Tesco, Royal Insurance and the 'big four' clearing banks, as well as the majority of manufacturing companies also included in the 30-Share Index. In contrast to the geometric calculation of the 30-Share Index, the FTSE 100 (like the All-Share Index – see below) is an arithmetic index.

The FTSE 100 is useful in that, being broadly based, it gives a better 'instant' picture of the state of the market than that given by the 30-Share Index. The constituent shares of the FTSE 100 are changed from time to time by a joint committee comprising both the Stock Exchange and market users. In its first year of operation, nearly one-sixth of the constituent shares were replaced by other shares.

By 31 July 1990, the FTSE 100 Index stood at 2,316.5, a rise of almost 150% in share prices since the end of 1983.

FT Actuaries All-Share Index: sector share movements   The All-Share Index[5] integrates the movements of some 679 constituent shares, covering 7 sector groups, and 35 sectors, based on April 1962 = 100. Figure 2.12 shows the nature of the information provided, with the various indices (see below) and trends published separately for each sector group, as well as for selected sectors within those groups.

FT-ACTUARIES SHARE INDICES

Equity groups and sub-sections Figures in parentheses show number of stocks per section	Index No.	Day's Change %	Est. Earnings Yield % (Max.)	Gross Div. Yield % (Act at 25%)	Est. P/E Ratio (Net)	Year ago (approx.) Index No.
1 **CAPITAL GOODS (194)**	865.89	−0.6	13.36	5.36	9.15	990.24
2 Building Materials (26)	1115.07	−0.1	13.70	5.41	9.01	1215.05
3 Contracting, Construction (36)	1438.61	−0.3	16.52	5.72	7.87	1624.16
4 Electricals (10)	2424.34	−0.5	11.83	5.49	10.40	2941.47
5 Electronics (26)	1763.25	−1.3	10.74	4.55	12.19	2262.74

Monday July 30 1990

Trend in value of index −22%

Sector price/earnings ratio = 12.19

Sector gross dividend yield = 4.55%

Sector earnings yield = 10.74%

Decrease on day = 1.3%

Sector index = 1763.25

No. of shares used to construct sector index = 26

	Index No.	Day's Change %	Est. Earnings Yield % (Max.)	Gross Div. Yield % (Act at 25%)	Est. P/E Ratio (Net)	Year ago (approx.) Index No.
6 Engineering-Aerospace (8)	458.96	−0.4	14.15	5.13	8.42	0.00
7 Engineering-General (46)	490.18	−0.5	12.12	5.22	10.00	0.00
8 Metals and Metal Forming (6)	481.35	−0.5	23.99	6.98	5.07	531.29
9 Motors (13)	349.64	+0.2	16.14	6.69	7.20	359.51
10 Other Industrial Materials (23)	1536.67	−1.0	11.33	5.19	10.19	1689.03
21 **CONSUMER GROUP (179)**	1301.93	−0.3	9.32	3.88	13.26	1325.09
22 Brewers and Distillers (22)	1643.02	+0.7	9.27	3.55	12.96	1451.71
25 Food Manufacturing (20)	1088.71	−0.3	10.44	4.35	11.86	1197.52
26 Food Retailing (16)	2607.75	−0.4	8.68	3.16	14.74	2535.21
27 Health and Household (15)	2532.40	−0.8	6.83	2.74	17.40	2370.46
29 Leisure (33)	1442.44	−0.2	10.05	4.29	12.12	1757.13
31 Packaging & Paper (12)	602.97	−0.9	10.99	5.72	11.19	601.25
32 Publishing & Printing (16)	3335.86	−1.8	10.79	5.54	11.58	3797.26
34 Stores (34)	810.83	−0.3	10.91	4.65	11.87	889.01
35 Textiles (11)	488.28	−0.3	12.61	7.37	10.01	558.21

	Index No.	Day's Change	Day's High (a)	Day's Low (b)	Jul 27	Year ago
40 OTHER GROUPS (107)	1144.46	−0.2	11.28	5.19	10.70	1185.34
41 Agencies (16)	1492.24	+0.1	6.87	2.61	17.61	1479.51
42 Chemicals (24)	1216.00	+0.2	10.92	5.45	10.82	1311.14
43 Conglomerates (15)	1603.86	−0.4	10.63	6.23	11.30	1706.05
44 Transport (13)	2321.45	−0.2	10.60	4.46	11.98	2475.65
46 Telephone Networks (2)	1173.93	−0.1	11.42	4.80	11.39	1078.34
47 Water (10)	2002.80	+0.2	16.02	6.76	6.98	0.00
48 Miscellaneous (27)	1727.69	−0.6	12.77	5.20	8.92	2019.88
49 INDUSTRIAL GROUP (480)	1155.20	−0.3	10.89	4.64	11.23	1217.84
51 Oil & Gas (20)	2351.11	−0.9	12.49	5.25	10.50	2158.79
59 500 SHARE INDEX (500)	1254.97	−0.4	11.11	4.72	11.12	1297.94
61 FINANCIAL GROUP (108)	787.59	−1.2	—	5.83	—	788.54
62 Banks (9)	836.91	−1.7	19.54	6.49	6.70	783.25
65 Insurance (Life) (7)	1452.44	−1.6	—	5.07	—	1177.11
66 Insurance (Composite) (6)	659.19	−1.0	—	6.27	—	627.40
67 Insurance (Brokers) (8)	961.63	−0.3	8.95	6.69	14.72	979.90
68 Merchant Banks (7)	436.13	−0.4	—	4.65	—	371.13
69 Property (47)	1086.43	−0.6	8.07	4.35	15.91	1374.90
70 Other Financial (24)	288.29	....	10.58	6.79	12.25	379.78
71 Investment Trusts (66)	1202.56	−0.4	—	3.22	—	1223.87
91 Overseas Traders (5)	1431.76	−0.5	9.83	6.38	12.15	1414.11
99 ALL-SHARE INDEX (679)	1142.87	−0.5	—	4.85	—	1173.25
FT-SE 100 SHARE INDEX	2316.5	−13.6	2322.4	2311.5	2330.1	2297.0

Fig. 2.12 FT actuaries share indices
Source: Financial Times 31/7/90

A comparison of *sector* index numbers with that for the All-Share Index allows the buoyant and depressed sectors to be quickly and clearly identified. For instance, publishing and printing (3,335.86) and food retailing (2,607.75) represent the high-fliers when compared to the All-Share figure of 1,142.87 whilst Engineering-Aerospace (458.96), motors (349.64), merchant banks (436.13) and other financial institutions (288.29) represent the opposite end of the spectrum.

The *individual company* Share Information Service – of which Fig. 2.13 is an abstract – can usefully be viewed in conjunction with the All-Share Index. The performance of an individual company can then be assessed in the context of the performance of the industrial sector in which it operates.

FT data on individual share movements   Share (equity) price movements are published daily, with shares ordered alphabetically within particular industrial sectors. The price quoted is the middle price, i.e. midway between the buy and sell prices on the stock market. Figure 2.13 shows an abstract of the information provided for a number of companies in the electricals sector. Data can be extracted from Figs 2.12 and 2.13 to permit a detailed assessment of the current position of each company, especially when combined with published accounting data from its profit and loss statement.

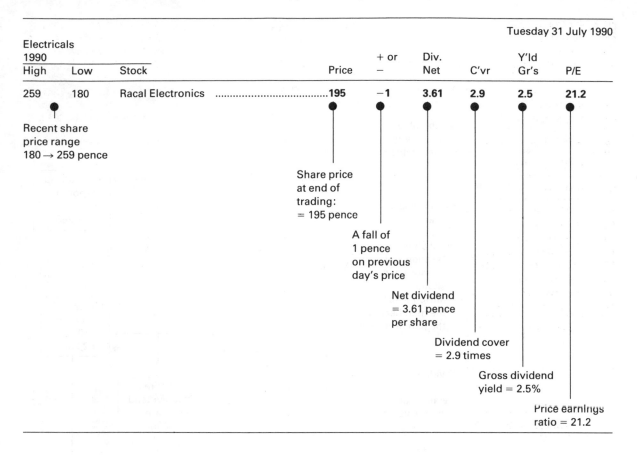

Tuesday 31 July 1990

Electricals 1990				+ or	Div.		Y'ld	
High	Low	Stock	Price	–	Net	C'vr	Gr's	P/E
259	180	Racal Electronics 195		–1	3.61	2.9	2.5	21.2

Recent share
price range
180 → 259 pence

Share price
at end of
trading:
= 195 pence

A fall of
1 pence
on previous
day's price

Net dividend
= 3.61 pence
per share

Dividend cover
= 2.9 times

Gross dividend
yield = 2.5%

Price earnings
ratio = 21.2

Fig. 2.13 FT Share
Information Service

Figure 2.14 outlines these possibilities, using Racal Electronics and the electricals sector for illustration.

The FT of Tuesday 31 July 1990 (see Fig. 2.13) revealed that at the close of the day's trading the Racal share price stood at 195p, a fall of 1p on the previous day's closing price, much lower than the highest price recorded since January 1990. We can make a more thorough assessment of Racal's current position if we examine the technical headings of Fig. 2.13, in conjunction with Racal's own profit and loss statement.

Price/earnings ratio = 21.2.   The price/earnings (P/E) ratio is the most important single measure of how the market views the company, and is the most common means of comparing the market values of different shares. The P/E ratio tells us the number of years' earnings that will be necessary to accumulate the current share price. Usually the more highly regarded is the company, the higher will be its P/E ratio, with the market anticipating a sustained earnings performance over a lengthy period. The P/E ratio will depend in part upon the company's past record, but also upon that of the industrial sector of which it is a part, and upon the overall level of the stock market. A P/E ratio of 10–12 might be regarded as typical.

$$\text{P/E ratio} = \frac{\text{share price}}{\text{earnings per share}}$$

Fig 2.14 FT ratios: Racal
Electronics (1990)

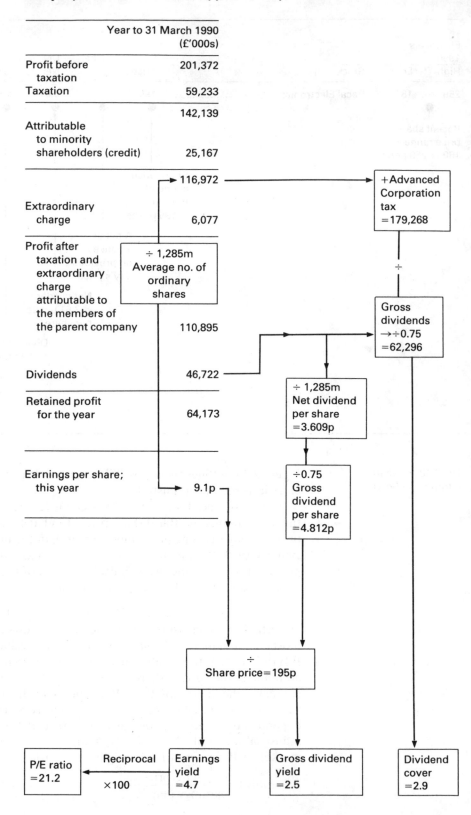

	Year to 31 March 1990 (£'000s)
Profit before taxation	201,372
Taxation	59,233
	142,139
Attributable to minority shareholders (credit)	25,167
	116,972
Extraordinary charge	6,077
Profit after taxation and extraordinary charge attributable to the members of the parent company	110,895
Dividends	46,722
Retained profit for the year	64,173
Earnings per share; this year	9.1p

÷ 1,285m
Average no. of
ordinary
shares

+Advanced
Corporation
tax
=179,268

÷

Gross
dividends
→÷0.75
=62,296

÷ 1,285m
Net dividend
per share
=3.609p

÷0.75
Gross
dividend
per share
=4.812p

÷
Share price=195p

P/E ratio =21.2	Reciprocal ×100	Earnings yield =4.7	Gross dividend yield =2.5	Dividend cover =2.9

where earnings per share is profit after tax divided by the number of ordinary shares.

The group figure of 12.19 for electronics is itself higher than average, whilst Racal's own P/E ratio of 21.2 is much greater and indicates its position as a market leader within that sector. With 21.2 years of earnings required to accumulate Racal's current share price, the market is clearly expressing confidence in Racal's long-term prospects. Changes in future expectations will affect both share price and the P/E ratio, of which the share price is the numerator.

Earnings yield = 4.7%.   Earnings yield is simply the reciprocal of the P/E ratio, expressed as a percentage. It helps to identify quickly those shares whose earnings are high compared to their price.

$$\text{Earnings yield} = 1/\text{P/E} \times 100 = \frac{\text{earnings per share}}{\text{share price}} \times 100$$

Racal's earnings yield of 4.7% (100/21.2) is low compared to the 10.74% in Fig. 2.12 for the electronics sector as a whole. Of course, this merely reflects the fact that Racal has a higher P/E ratio, due to market confidence in its potential for sustained growth.

Dividend cover = 2.9.   The dividend cover is the number of times by which profits available for distribution as dividends (i.e. after the deduction of corporation tax) cover the actual dividends paid to shareholders.

$$\text{Dividend cover} = \frac{\text{profit after tax} + \text{advance corporation tax}^6}{\text{gross dividends}}$$

The higher this figure, the higher the proportion of profits retained for future investment, and perhaps the more secure the prospects for future dividends. The maximum distribution of profits will correspond with a dividend cover approaching 1.0. A value less than this must mean that dividends are being paid out of capital reserves, and not out of current earnings.

With profits available for distribution almost three times the actual dividends paid, Racal has a high rate of investment, which suggests a secure future dividend.

Gross dividend yield = 2.5%.   This shows the return on the investment before the deduction of income tax at the basic rate, as a percentage of the share price.

$$\text{Gross dividend yield} = \frac{\text{gross dividend per share}}{\text{share price}} \times 100$$

Racal's gross dividend yield is below the sector figure of 4.55%. However, a relatively low gross dividend yield is typical for a secure company with high growth potential. Such companies will have a high current share price (the denominator), and the potential for increased future dividends. A high gross dividend yield, with low dividend cover, usually indicates a risky venture paying levels of dividend it may not be able to sustain. Companies in declining industries often exhibit a high gross dividend yield, since current dividends may be raised by the absence of investment.

These technical figures, particularly the P/E ratio and the gross dividend yield, provide an excellent indication of current company performance and prospects. If this FT information is used alongside balance sheet information, narrative company reports, particularly that of the auditors, and narrative Press statements about recent company activities, then the shareholder will be better able to assess the management of his investment.

Conclusion

Clive Jenkins, a leading trade unionist, is reputed to have complained that 'published accounts are utterly and absolutely useless' (Holmes and Sugden 1986). Clearly there remain opportunities to revise the content and improve the presentation of company accounts so that they provide the shareholder with a better service. Nevertheless our earlier analysis makes it difficult to agree with Mr Jenkins. Various accounting ratios, properly understood, give useful insights into specific aspects of company performance. Taken together they can also provide a more general guide to overall company prospects. Indeed, recent models have sought to incorporate separate accounting ratios into a single index of performance through Z-score analysis. The content of the published accounts, together with external sources, notably the FT Share Information Service, provide an excellent basis for the assessment of company performance and the evaluation of investments.

Notes

1. Evidence suggests that in as many as 58% of public companies, the controlling management has little or no stake in the ownership of the company. The directors of Sears plc, for example, had beneficial ownership of only 0.04% of the company's issued equity capital.
2. Fixed interest stocks issued by companies, usually redeemable at a set date, and backed by an agreement similar to a mortgage.
3. Of the thirty companies making up the original index of July 1935 only seven now remain:

Blue Circle Industries	Hawker Siddeley Group
Courtaulds	Imperial Chemical Industries (ICI)
General Electric (GEC)	Tate and Lyle
Guest Keen and Nettlefolds (GKN)	Vickers

4. FT Industrial 30-Share Index $= 30 \sqrt{\dfrac{P_1}{S_1} \times \dfrac{P_2}{S_2} \times \ldots \dfrac{P_{30}}{S_{30}}}$

   where $P_{1-30} =$ the current share price for companies 1 to 30;
   $\qquad\quad S_{1-30} =$ the base year share price for each company at 1 July 1935, adjusted so that capital changes such as share issues do not affect continuity.
5. The All-Share Index is an arithmetic average of price relatives weighted to reflect the market valuation of the shares included.

   $$\text{All-Share Index} = \frac{w_1 \, (P_1/S_1) + w_2 \, (P_2/S_2) + \ldots + w_{750} \, (P_{750}/S_{750})}{w_1 + w_2 + \ldots + w_{750}}$$

where w_{1-750} = market valuations (i.e. current share price × number of ordinary shares) for each share included;

P_{1-750} = current share price of each share;

S_{1-750} = base year share prices for April 1962.

6. Advance corporation tax was introduced in April 1973 as a means of preventing distributed profits being taxed twice. Whenever a company pays dividends to shareholders, it pays to the Inland Revenue a sum equivalent to the basic rate income tax that would be payable on the dividends. This sum represents part of the company's corporation tax liability for the period in which the dividend is paid – the remaining part is 'mainstream' corporation tax.

References

Earl, M. J. and **Marais, D. A. J.** (1982) *The prediction of corporate bankruptcy in the UK using discriminant analysis*, Oxford Centre for Management Studies, **5**.

Holmes, G. and **Sugden, A.** (1986) *Interpreting Company Reports and Accounts*. Woodhead-Faulkner, Cambridge.

Smith, M. (1983) 3-D charting signals possible problems, *Accountancy Age*, 3 Feb.

Smith, M. (1990) The rise and rise of the NFI, *Management Accounting*, May.

Taffler, R. and **Tisshaw, H.** (1977) Going, going, gone: four factors which predict, *Accountancy*, **88**, 1003, March.

3   Firm objectives and firm behaviour

Economists have put forward various theories as to how firms behave in order to predict their reaction to events. At the heart of such theories is an assumption about firm objectives, the most usual being that the firm seeks to maximize profits. The first part of the chapter examines a number of alternative objectives open to the firm. It begins with those of a maximizing type, namely profit, sales revenue, and growth maximization, predicting firm price and output in each case. A number of non-maximizing or behavioural objectives are then considered. The second part of the chapter reviews recent research into actual firm performance, and attempts to establish which objectives are most consistent with how firms actually operate. We see that although profit is important, careful consideration must be given to a number of other objectives if we are accurately to predict firm performance. The need for a perspective broader than profit is reinforced when we consider current management practice in devising the corporate plan.

Firm objectives

The objectives of a firm can be grouped under two main headings: maximizing goals and non-maximizing goals. We shall see that marginal analysis is particularly important for maximizing goals. This is often confusing to the student who, rightly, assumes that few firms can have any detailed knowledge of marginal revenue or marginal cost. However, it should be remembered that marginal analysis does not pretend to describe *how* firms maximize profits or revenue. It simply tells us *what* the output and price must be if they do succeed in maximizing these items, whether by luck or by judgement.

Maximizing goals

Profit maximization   The profit-maximizing assumption is based on two premises: first, that owners are in control of the day-to-day management of the firm; second, that the main desire of owners is for higher profit. The case for profit maximization as 'self-evident' is, as we shall see, undermined if either of these premises fails to hold.

Profit is actually maximized where marginal revenue (MR) equals marginal cost (MC), i.e. where the revenue raised from selling an extra unit is equal to the cost of producing that extra unit. In Fig. 3.1 total profit (TP) is a maximum at output Q_p, where the vertical distance between total revenue (TR) and total cost (TC) is the greatest ($TP = TR - TC$). Had the marginal revenue and marginal cost curves been presented in Fig. 3.1, they would have intersected at output Q_p.

Fig. 3.1 Variation of output
with firm objective

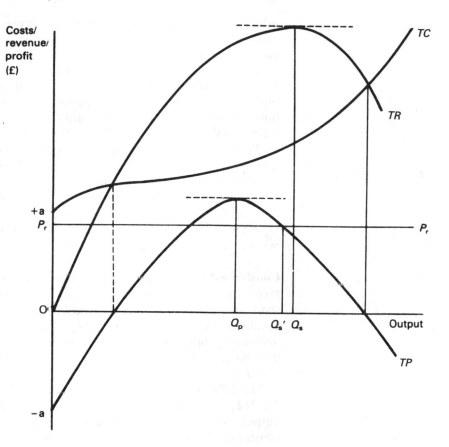

Sales revenue maximization   Where ownership and control are in the hands
of the same person or small group of people (as in a small firm), then the goal
of owners, usually assumed to be profit, can be pursued without conflict.
However, with the rise of the public limited liability company, ownership and
control may have become separated, with ownership in the hands oi voting
shareholders and day-to-day control in the hands of management. If
management should have different goals from shareholders then the
possibility of conflict arises.

The extent to which a firm's top management can override the owners'
goals will depend on the structure of the firm. It is typical of some larger
organizations that managers have virtually complete discretion over their
actions, i.e. ownership and control are sharply separated. Where managers
do have control it will be *their* goals which predominate.

W. J. Baumol (1959) suggests that the manager-controlled firm is likely to
have sales revenue maximization as its main goal. His argument is that the
salaries of top managers, and other perks, are more closely correlated with
sales revenue than profits.

Williamson's (1963) managerial theory of the firm is similar to Baumol's in
stressing the growth of sales revenue as a major firm objective. However, it is
broader based, with the manager seeking to increase satisfaction not only, as
Baumol suggests, in terms of salary and perks (car, expense account, luxury

offices, etc.), but also through the greater expenditure on both staff levels and projects made possible by higher sales revenue. Increased staff levels give the manager greater status and seniority, whilst expenditure on 'discretionary' projects – those which are beyond the normal operation of the firm – give management the satisfaction of following their own personal preferences. Funds for greater expenditure can come from profits, external finance and sales revenue. In Williamson's view, however, increased *sales revenue* is the easiest means of providing additional funds, since higher profits have in part to be distributed to shareholders, and new finance requires greater accountability. Baumol and Williamson are describing the same phenomenon, though in rather different terms.

If management seeks to maximize sales revenue without any thought to profit at all (pure sales revenue maximization) then this would lead to output Q_s in Fig. 3.1. This last (Q_s^{th}) unit is neither raising nor lowering total revenue, i.e. its marginal revenue is zero.

Constrained sales revenue maximization   Both Baumol and Williamson recognize that some constraint on managers can be exercised by shareholders, as at the annual general meeting. Maximum sales revenue is usually considered to occur well above the level of output which generates maximum profits. The shareholders may demand at least a certain level of distributed profit, so that sales revenue can only be maximized subject to this constraint.

The difference a profit constraint makes to firm output is shown in Fig. 3.1. If P_r is the minimum profit required by shareholders, then Q_s' is the output which permits the highest total revenue whilst still meeting the profit constraint. Any output beyond Q_s' up to Q_s, would raise total revenue TR – the major objective – but reduce total profit TP below the minimum required (P_r). Q_s' therefore represents the constrained sales revenue maximizing output.

Although there may be some constraints, managerial goals are assumed to be dominant for firms in which ownership and control are separated. So far we have assumed that the goals of owners (profits) have been in conflict with the goals of management (sales revenue). Marris (1964), however, believes that owners and managers have a *common* goal, namely maximum growth of the firm.

Growth maximization   Marris (1964) argues that the overriding goal which *both* managers and owners have is growth. Managers seek a growth in demand for the firm's products or services, to raise power or status. Owners seek a growth in the capital value of the firm to increase personal wealth.

It was also true in Baumol's theory that growth in the firm's demand, and therefore sales revenue, raised managerial power and status. However Baumol's theory was essentially static, whereas that of Marris is dynamic. To Marris, managers are motivated not so much by the achievement of absolute size, such as a given value of sales revenue, but rather by *changes* in size. For instance, he contends that managers would prefer to *expand* the firm to a particular size rather than to move job to a company which has already achieved such size.

Growth of the firm's capital (fixed assets, stocks, short-term assets and cash reserves) is assumed by Marris to be the major goal of the shareholder-owner. The basis of this assumption that the owner wants capital growth rather than distributed profits, is not entirely clear. It presumably implies that shareholder-owners wish to maximize their *wealth* rather than their current income.

It is important to note, therefore, that it is through the *growth* of the firm that the goals of both managers and owners can be achieved. Also central to the analysis of Marris is the ratio of retained to distributed profits, i.e. the 'retention ratio'. If managers distribute most of the profits (low retention ratio), shareholders will be content and the share price will be sufficiently high to deter takeover. However, if managers distribute less profit (high retention ratio), then the retained profit can be used for investment, stimulating the growth of the firm. In this case shareholders may be less content, and the share price lower, thereby increasing the risk of a takeover bid.

The major objective of the firm, with which both managers and shareholders are in accord, is then seen by Marris as maximizing the rate of growth of the firm's demand *and* the firm's capital ('balanced growth'), subject to an acceptable retention ratio. Figure 3.2 shows the trade-off between higher balanced growth and the average profit rate.[1]

Fig. 3.2 Trade-off between average profit and balanced growth

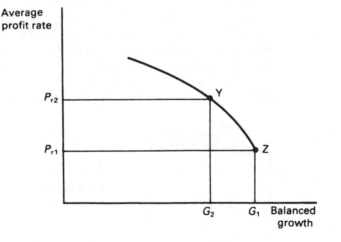

For 'balanced growth' to increase, more and more investment in capital projects must be undertaken. Since the most profitable projects are undertaken first, any extra investment must be reducing the average profit rate. Point Z is where the balanced growth rate is at a maximum (G_1), with an implied retention ratio so high that all profitable investment projects have been pursued, giving an average profit rate P_{r1}. Risk avoidance by managers may, however, enforce a lower retention ratio with more profits distributed. Point Y is such a constrained growth-maximizing position (G_2), with a lower retention ratio, lower investment and higher average profit (P_{r2}) than at point Z. How close the firm gets to its major objective, Z, will depend on how constrained management feels by the risk of disgruntled shareholders, or a takeover bid, should the retention ratio be kept at the high rates consistent with points near to Z.

Non-maximizing goals

The traditional (owner control) and managerial (non-owner control) theories of the firm assume that a single goal will be pursued. The firm then attempts to achieve the highest value for that goal, whether profits, sales revenue or growth. The *behaviouralist* viewpoint is rather different, and sees the firm as an organization with various groups, workers, managers, shareholders, customers, etc., each of which has its own goal, or set of goals. The group which achieves prominence at any point of time may be able to guide the firm into promoting its goal set over time. This dominant group may then be replaced by another giving greater emphasis to a totally different goal set. The traditional and managerial theories which propose the maximization of a single goal, are seen by behaviouralists as being remote from the organizational complexity of modern firms.

Satisficing   One of the earliest behavioural theories was that of H. A. Simon (1959) who suggested that in practice managers are unable to ascertain when a marginal point has been reached, such as maximum profit with marginal cost equal to marginal revenue. Consequently, managers set themselves *minimum* acceptable levels of achievement. Firms which are satisfied in achieving such limited objectives are said to 'satisfice' rather than 'maximize'. This is not to say that satisficing leads to some long-term performance which is less than would otherwise be achieved. The achievement of objectives has long been recognized as an incentive to improving management performance and is the basis of the management technique known as management by objectives (MBO). Figure 3.3 illustrates how the attainment of initially limited objectives might lead to an improved long-term performance.

Fig 3.3 Development of aspiration levels through goal achievement

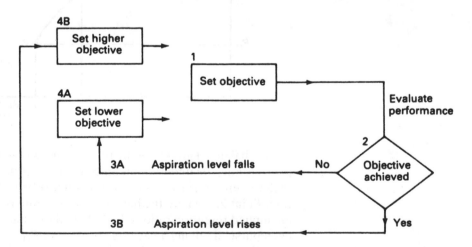

At the starting point 1, the manager sets the objective and attempts to achieve it. If, after evaluation, it is found that the objective has been achieved, then this will lead to an increase in aspirational level (3B). A new and higher objective (4B) will then emerge. Thus, by setting achievable

objectives, what might be an initial minimum target turns out to be a prelude to a series of higher targets, perhaps culminating in the achievement of some maximum target, or objective. If, on the other hand, the initial objective is not achieved, then aspirational levels are lowered (3A) until achievable objectives are set. Simon's theory is one in which no single objective can be presumed to be the inevitable outcome of this organizational process. In fact, the final objective may, as we have seen, be far removed from the initial one.

Coalitions and goal formation   If a firm is 'satisficing', then who is being satisficed – and how? R. M. Cyert and J. G. March (1963) were rather more specific than Simon in identifying various groups or coalitions within an organization. A coalition is any group which, at a given moment, shares a consensus on the goals to be pursued.

Workers may form one coalition wanting good wages and work conditions and some job security; managers want power and prestige as well as high salaries; shareholders want high profits. These differing goals may well result in group conflict, e.g. higher wages for workers may mean lower profits for shareholders. The behavioural theory of Cyert and March, along with Simon, does not then view the firm as having one outstanding objective (e.g. profit maximization), but rather many, often conflicting, objectives.

Top managers have, ultimately, to set the firm's goals in the key areas for decision-making of production, inventory, sales, profit and market share. Cyert and March suggest that their aim is to set goals which resolve the conflict between opposing groups. This will inevitably involve compromise, with management setting minimum targets in the key areas, i.e. the objective is to satisfice rather than maximize. To encourage compromise, a number of techniques may be used:

Time constraints. Restricting bargaining time creates pressure for compromise between the groups.
'Agreed' limits. Some budgets are set at the outset, limiting the area of conflict to how the given 'cake' is to be distributed. This is never more apparent than when strongly enforced cash limits are imposed.
Structure. Conflict can be reduced by structuring the firm in such a way that group discretion is limited. This may involve clearly demarcated areas of responsibility for each department.
Money payment. Payment, in lieu of other demands, is often used to reduce conflict. Part of this may well be what Cyert and March call 'organizational slack', i.e payments in excess of what is necessary to keep the group stable.
Sequential problem-solving. Top management will seize on the process of achieving one goal as a way of limiting the demands of other groups at any given moment. For example, they could use an increase in wages to explain why more equipment could not be purchased.

Contingency theory   The contingency theory of company behaviour suggests that the optimal solutions to organizational problems are derived from matching the internal structure and processes of the firm with its external environment. However the external environment is constantly changing as industrial markets become more complex, so that the optimum strategy for a firm will change as the prevailing environmental influences change. The result of this is that firms may not have a single goal such as the maximization of profits or sales, but will have to vary their goals and strategies as the environment changes around them. It has been argued by some economists that there may be as many as two thousand different strategic behaviour patterns, depending on the nature of the firm and its environment (Ansoff 1984). In today's rapidly changing world market it is not easy for a company to maintain one overall goal and the contingency theory helps us to understand why firms will not always be able to follow a single optimizing course through time.

To summarize, the various behavioural theories look at the *process* of decision-making. They recognize that the 'organization' is not synonymous with the owner – nor with any other single influence, but rather that the firm has many objectives which relate to the many different groups acting within the organization. These objectives may be in conflict and so management will use a number of techniques in order to reduce that conflict. The behavioural approach has been criticized for its inability to yield precise predictions of firm activity in particular settings. However, where management processes are recognized, such as in strategic planning (see p. 62), then specific short-term predictions can be made.

Does firm objective matter?

The economist is continually seeking to predict the output and price behaviour of the firm. Figure 3.1 indicates that firm *output* does indeed depend upon firm objective, with the profit-maximizing firm having a lower output than the sales-maximizing firm (pure and constrained). If we remember that price is average revenue (i.e. total revenue/total output) we can see from Fig. 3.4 that firm *price* will also vary with objective.

Fig. 3.4 Variation of price with firm objective

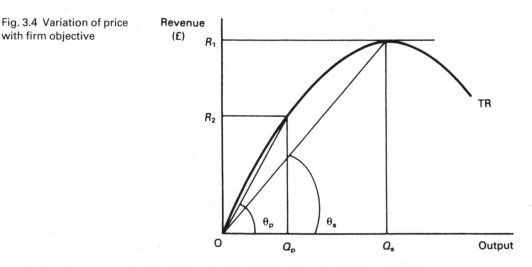

Price in the *pure sales-maximizing* firm $= \tan \theta_s = R_1/Q_s$
Price in the *profit-maximizing* firm $\quad = \tan \theta_p = R_2/Q_p$
$$\tan \theta_s < \tan \theta_p$$

i.e. the price of the pure sales-maximizing firm is below that of the profit-maximizing firm.

It is clear that it really *does* matter what objective we assume for the firm, since both output and price depend on that objective. We turn now to firm performance to assess which of the objectives, if any, can be supported by how firms actually behave.

Firm behaviour

Ownership and control in practice

Profit maximization is usually based on the assumption that firms are owner-controlled, whereas sales and growth maximization usually assume that there is a separation between ownership and control. The acceptance of these alternative theories was helped by early research into the ownership of firms. Studies in the USA by A. Berle and G. Means in the 1930s, and by R. Larner in the 1960s, suggested that a substantial proportion of large firms (44% by Berle and Means and 85% by Larner) were manager-controlled. Later research has, however, challenged the definition of 'owner-control' used in these early studies. Whereas Berle and Means assumed that owner-control is only present with a shareholding of more than 20% in a public limited company, Nyman and Silberston (1978) used a much lower figure of 5% after research had indicated that effective control could be exercised by owners with this level of shareholding. This would suggest that owner-control is far more extensive than previously thought. In fact Burch (1972) suggests that up to 60% of US companies may be family-controlled, and in the UK Nyman and Silberston estimate that over 56% of the largest 224 firms are owner-controlled.

A further aspect of owner-control is the role of financial institutions and pension funds. Between them they now own over 40% of the shares of public companies in the UK, compared to only 17.9% in 1957. Financial institutions are more likely than individuals to bring influence to bear on chief executives, being experienced in the channels of communication and sensitive to indices of firm performance. Their influence can either be direct, as a shareholder, or indirect through interlocking directorships of commercial and merchant banks.[2] The effect of this influence is seen by Nyman and Silberston as moving the firm towards the profit-maximizing (owner-controlled) type of objective.

Profit

Profit maximization In a major study, Shipley (1981) concluded that only 15.9% of his sample of 728 UK firms could be regarded as 'true' profit-maximizers. This conclusion was reached by cross-tabulating replies to two questions shown in Table 3.1.

Because answers to questionnaires can often be given loosely, Shipley considered as 'true' maximizers only those who claimed both to maximize profit (answered (a) to Question 1) and to regard profit as being of overriding importance (answered (d) to Question 2). Only 15.9% of all the firms replied with both 1(a) and 2(d), and were considered by Shipley as true profit-maximizers. Given the significance of the profit-maximizing assumption in

Firm objectives and firm behaviour

Table 3.1 Sample of 728
firms

	All respondents (%)
(1) Does your firm try to achieve:	
(a) Maximum profits,	47.7
(b) 'Satisfactory' profits?	52.3
(2) Compared to your firm's other leading objectives, is the achievement of a target profit . . . regarded as being:	
(a) Of little importance	2.1
(b) Fairly important	12.9
(c) Very important	58.9
(d) Of overriding importance?	26.1
Those responding with both 1(a) and 2(d)	15.9

Source: Adapted from Shipley (1981).

economic analysis, this result is surprising. However, some consideration of the decision-making process may serve to explain this low figure.

Traditional theory assumes that firms invest in the most profitable projects first, and then choose projects of descending profitability, until the return on the last project just covers the cost of funding that project, i.e. marginal revenue = marginal cost, and profit is maximized. In fact, the process of choosing projects is much more complicated and subject to many influences. First, many companies do not have access to sufficient funds to reach the marginal position. Second, project appraisal is based on perception and educated guesses about how markets will react. Instead of assessing a *single* revenue and cost outcome for the project, to which marginal analysis could be applied, outcome is often evaluated in terms of 'scenarios'. In this way, firms are in practice forced away from marginal analysis. In addition, they often rely on pre-set 'hurdle' rates of return for projects, with managers given some minimum rate of return as a criterion for project appraisal. As a result they may not consciously see themselves as profit-maximizers, since this phrase suggests marginal analysis. Yet in setting the hurdle rates, top management will be keenly aware of the marginal cost of funding, so that this approach may in some cases relate closely to profit maximization. In other words, the response of management to questionnaires may understate the true significance of the pursuit of profit.

Profit as part of a 'goal set'   Although few firms appear to set out specifically to maximize profit, profit is still seen (even in response to questionnaires) as an important factor in decision-making. In the Shipley study the firms were asked to list their principal goal in setting price. Table 3.2 shows that target profit was easily the most frequently cited, with 73% of all firms regarding it as their principal goal. Even more firms (88%) included profit as at least part of their 'goal set'.[3]

If responses to questionnaires are to be believed, profit *is* important to firms. Haspeslaugh (1982) also found that in the USA profit was the most highly ranked issue of importance amongst 345 companies carrying out strategic business planning. Hilton (1978), in reviewing a series of reports by chairmen and employees in published UK annual accounts, concludes that

Table 3.2 728 firms in UK. Principal pricing objectives

	Principal goal*	Part of goal set
Target profit or ROCE†	486	639
Prices fair to firm and customers	94	353
Price similarity with competitors	56	350
Target sales revenue	54	342
Stable volume of sales	37	182
Target market share of sales	16	129
Stable prices	11	120
Other	10	38

* Thirty-four respondents cited two or more principal objectives.
† Return on capital employed.
Source: Shipley (1981).

profit is clearly regarded as a major objective by employer and employee alike.

Profit – long term vs short term   Long-term profit may be even more important than short-term profit in firm objectives. Shipley found that 59.7% of his sample gave priority to long-term profits, compared to only 20.6% giving priority to short-term profits (see Table 3.3).

Table 3.3 Relative importance of profits in alternative time horizons

486 firms declaring profits as the principal pricing objective	
(%)	Profit priority given to
20.6	Short term
59.7	Long term
19.7	No priority

Source: Shipley (1981).

Shipley found long-term profit to be a significant influence in all sizes of company, though particularly in those of medium/large size. Haspeslaugh also found in the USA that long-term profit was the major objective for larger firms, with short-term profit in sixth position.

However, in practice 'long-term' profitability is an elusive concept to manage, firms having different philosophies. When Hanson Trust took over Berec, later British Ever Ready, it made major changes in order to increase the profitability of the firm in the short term. It sold off overseas subsidiaries with strong market shares and cut back heavily on what Berec, and long-term participants in the industry, believed to be essential investment in production and research and development (R & D) for the future. Subsequently the firm returned substantial profits. In 1987 the Hanson Annual Report mentioned further R & D to improve Silver Seal batteries but, according to one private stockbrokers' report, it is not Hanson's policy to invest in fundamental technological research in this area. The higher recorded profits might, in this case, be deemed short-term rather than long-term.

A more obvious example of pursuing long-term profits would seem to be that of Rank Xerox which, throughout the 1980s, faced heavy international competition. The chairman, Derek Hornby, commented that 'we have, in all the years I have been chairman, had profit as our number one objective'. However, a change in corporate philosophy, critical to its long term survival, took five years to implement, the first three years of which saw no improvements in what were relatively poor profits. The move paid off only in the fourth and fifth years after the radical change was initiated.

To summarize therefore, although there may be no open admission to profit maximization, the strong influence of owners on managed firms, and the use of pre-set hurdle rates, may in the end lead to an objective, or set of objectives, closely akin to profit maximization.

Sales revenue

Sales revenue maximization   Baumol's suggestion that management-controlled firms will wish to maximize sales revenue was based on the belief that the earnings of executives are more closely related to firm revenue than to firm profit. A number of studies have sought to test this belief, though the results are inconclusive. Although Smyth, Boyes and Peseau (1975) and Ciscel (1974) found that sales revenue did closely affect executive incomes in the USA, Masson (1971) and Llewellen and Huntsman (1970) came to exactly the opposite conclusion.

However, even if economists cannot decide whether sales revenue has more effect on executive income than does profit, there is general support for the contention that *firm size* is directly related to executive income. In a study of over 1,000 large UK companies, Meeks and Whittington (1975) found that the larger the asset value of the company, the larger the executive salary. Yarrow (1972) in a study of eighty-five US corporations came to a similar conclusion. Sawyer (1981), summarizing various studies along these lines, pointed to the importance of size in general rather than sales in particular as an influence on executive income. However, a recent analysis of published accounts (Management Today, 1990) found *profitability* to be much more important than size or sales revenue in determining director salaries in the top 250 UK companies. Profit-related pay was an important element in the salaries of a substantial number of chief executives.

Sales revenue as part of a 'goal set'   The results of Shipley's analysis tell us little about sales revenue *maximization*. Nevertheless, Table 3.2 showed that target sales revenue was the fourth-ranked principal pricing objective, and that nearly half the firms included sales revenue as at least part of their set of objectives. Larger companies cited sales revenue as an objective most frequently; one-seventh of companies with over 3,000 employees gave sales revenue as a principal goal compared to only one-fourteenth of all the firms. Since larger companies have greater separation between ownership and management control this does lend some support to Baumol's assertion. However, we see below that the nature of planning in large organizations must also be considered, and that this may temper our support for sales revenue being itself the major objective, at least in the long term.

Strategic planning and sales revenue   Current thinking on strategic planning would support the idea of short-term sales maximization, but only as a means to other ends (e.g. profitability or growth). Research in the mid-1970s by the US Strategic Planning Institute (Schoeffler, Buzzel and Heany 1974) links market share – seen here as a proxy for sales revenue – to profitability. These studies found that high market share had a significant and beneficial effect on both return on investment and cash flow, at least in the long term. However, in the short term the high investment and marketing expenditure needed to attain high market share, reduce profitability and drain cash flow. Profit has to be sacrificed in the short term if high market share, and hence future high profits, are to be achieved.

Any observation that firms seek to maximize sales revenue (market share) may then merely reflect tactical short- to medium-term strategy, rather than long-term objective, i.e. a means to an end (higher profits) rather than an end in itself. This does not reduce the value of the theory of sales maximization for predictive purposes, as long as the time-scales involved are recognized. In the short to medium term, sales maximization may be the most useful assumption for predictive purposes. In the longer term, profit maximization would appear to be still supreme (see Table 3.3 above).

Constrained sales revenue maximization The fact that 88% of all companies in Shipley's study included profit in their goal set indicates the relevance of the profit constraint to other objectives, including sales revenue.

Growth

There are a number of reasons why firms should wish to grow. Marris (1964) suggests that managers seek to increase their status by increasing the 'empire' in which they work. This means not only expansion within the firm, i.e. at the expense of fellow managers, but also growth in the size of the firm. Others would argue that although growth is an important company objective it is a means to an end, e.g. higher profit, rather than an end in itself as Marris would suggest.

When we examine the facts however, there is little to indicate that faster growth really does mean higher profits. We can see from table 3.4(a) that none of the top 10 most profitable firms in the UK are also in the top 10 growth firms. From table 3.4(b) we can see that none of the top 10 highest growth firms are in the top 20 of profitable ones. Table 3.4 is in line with the results of a study by Whittington (1980) who found that profit levels did not increase as the firm grew in size. Both of these lend some support to those, like Marris, who see growth as a separate objective from profit.

In fast-moving markets, such as high-technology electronics and pharmaceuticals, companies need flexibility to move rapidly to fill market niches. To achieve this, some firms are moving in quite the opposite direction to growth, i.e. they are de-merging. 'De-merging' occurs when the firm splits into smaller units, each separately quoted on the Stock Exchange. For example, in 1987 ICI announced the de-merging of its fast growth businesses from its more traditional areas, so that adequate funding could be obtained from the markets. This is a clear sign that professional investors do not merely equate larger size to greater profit.

In a similar vein, Tom Peters, co-author of *In Search Of Excellence*, says

Firm objectives and firm behaviour

Table 3.4
(a) The ten most profitable UK corporations in 1990 and their position in the 'growth' league of the largest 250 UK companies.

Rank in profits**	Firm	Rank in growth* of 250 top UK firms 1980–89
1	Manpower	126
2	Reuters	144
3	Rentokil	102
4	Thomas Robinson	96
5	Wilson Bowden	225
6	Argyll	53
7	Nu-Swift	17
8	Smith and Nephew	65
9	Hestair	29
10	BTR	36

(b) The ten fastest growing UK corporations 1990 and their position in the profitability league of the largest 250 UK companies.

Rank in growth*	Firm	Rank in profitability** of 250 top UK firms
1	Pentland	81
2	Albert Fisher	35
3	Polly Peck International	42
4	Parkfield	49
5	Williams	26
6	Amstrad	122
7	BM	40
8	Dunhill	46
9	Glaxo	33
10	Macallan-Glenlivet	206

* Growth in shareholders' ordinary capital over 10 years 1980–89.
** Net profit before tax as a percentage of total capital invested for financial year ended 1989.
Source: Management Today, June 1990.

that 'quality and flexibility will be the hallmarks of the successful economy for the foreseeable future' (Peters 1988). This premise leads to a view that size, with its inherent inflexibility and distance from the end-customer, is a *disadvantage*. Indeed, recent analysis by The Strategic Planning Institute (Buzzel and Gale 1987) shows an *inverse* relationship between market size and the rate of return on investment in the USA. In market segments of less than $100m (£55m), the return on investment averaged 27% in their study; however, where firms operated in market segments of over $1bn (£550m), the return averaged only 11%. They found that organizations sought to reduce the disadvantages of size by restructuring, either by creating decentralized strategic business units (SBU's) or by demerging.

Non-maximizing behaviour

We have seen that the non-maximizing or behavioural theories concentrate on how firms actually operate within the constraints imposed by organizational structure and firm environment. Such theories usually predict that firms will 'satisfice', i.e. seek non-maximizing solutions. Minimum targets may, for instance, be set over a whole range of variables: profit, sales revenue, growth, inventory-holding, etc. Recent evidence on management practice broadly supports the behavioural contention, namely that it is unhelpful to seek a single firm objective as a guide to actual firm behaviour. This support, however, comes from a rather different type of analysis, that of portfolio planning.

Work in the USA by the Boston Consulting Group on the relationship between market share and industry growth (Henderson 1970) gave rise to an approach to corporate planning known as 'portfolio planning'. Firms, especially the larger ones, can be viewed as having a collection or 'portfolio' of different products at different stages in the product life cycle. If a product is at an early stage in its life cycle, it will require a large investment in marketing and product development in order to achieve future levels of high profitability. At the same time another product may have 'matured' and, already possessing a good share of the market, be providing high profits and substantial cash flow.

The usual strategy in portfolio planning is to attempt to balance the portfolio so that existing profitable products are providing the funds necessary to raise new products to maturity. Haspeslaugh (1982) found that in his survey 45% of the top 500 companies in the USA used portfolio planning to some extent. Companies saw the method as a way of making the best use of resources. Sizer (1982) indicates that UK companies such as Reckitt and Colman, Rowntree Mackintosh and Cadbury Schweppes have a similar approach to corporate planning. This approach has become a classic part of strategic decision making. However, the decision criteria have changed. In the late 1970s the focus was on market growth; in the 1980s it was on coherency in the overall business (concentrating on core business or 'sticking to the knitting'). The uncertainties and speed of technological change in the 1990s have moved the emphasis to shorter payback periods, hence the importance of rapid innovation, niche markets and higher added value (Peters 1988, Ohmae 1982, Porter 1985).

If a firm is using the portfolio approach in its planning then it may be impossible to predict the firm's behaviour for individual products or market sections on the basis of a single firm objective. This is because the goals of the firm will change for a given product or market sector *depending on the relative position of that product or market sector within the overall portfolio*. Portfolio planning, along with other behavioural theories, suggests that no single objective is likely to be useful in explaining actual firm behaviour, at least in specific cases.

Conclusion

The traditional theory of the firm assumes that its sole objective is to maximize profit. The managerial theories assume that where ownership and control of the organization are separated, the objective which guides the firm will be that which the management sets. This is usually thought to be maximization either of sales revenue or growth. It is important to know which, if any, of the maximizing objectives are being pursued, since firm output and price will be different for each objective. Behavioural theory tends to oppose the idea of the firm seeking to maximize any objective. For instance, top management may seek to hold the various groups within the organization in balance by adopting a set of minimum targets. Even where a single group with a clear objective does become dominant within the firm, others with alternative objectives may soon replace it.

In practice, profit maximization *in the long term* still appears to be paramount. Sales revenue seems quite important as a short-term goal, though even here a profit target is still part of the goal set. The prominence of the profit target may be an indication that ownership is not as divorced from the control of large firms as may once have been thought. One reason why sales revenue may be pursued in the short term is found in an analysis of current strategic planning techniques, which link short-term sales revenue to long-term profit. Sales revenue may therefore be useful for explaining short-term firm behaviour, but with profit crucial for long-term behaviour. Those who, like Marris, argue that growth is a separate objective from profit, find some support in the lack of any clear relationship between growth and profitability. Growth may also be a means of securing greater stability for the firm. It may reduce internal conflict, by being an objective around which both owner-shareholders and managers can agree, and possibly reduces the risk of takeover. Also large firms experience, if not higher profits, then less variable profits (see Whittington 1980 and Schmalensee 1989). Beyond these points, there is little empirical evidence to support growth as a major objective. In fact, a recent and widely used technique in the management of larger firms, portfolio planning, would seem to support the behaviouralist view, that no single objective will usefully help predict firm behaviour in a given market.

Notes

1. Average profit rate is total profit divided by total capital employed.
2. Some examples of these interlocking or linked directorships are identified by Nyman and Silberston (1978).
3. See Table 3.2. Shipley even assumes that 'fair' prices might be considered to have a profit element, in which case 97% of all firms included profit in their goal set.

References and further reading

Ansoff, I. (1984) *Implementing Strategic Management*. Prentice Hall.
Baumol, W. J. (1959) *Business Behaviour, Value and Growth*. Macmillan.
Berle, A. A. and **Means, G. C.** (1934) *The Modern Corporation and Private Property*. Macmillan, New York.
Burch, B. C. (1972) *The Managerial Revolution Reassessed*. Lexington Books, Lexington, Mass.
Buzzel, R. and **Gale, B.** (1987) *The PIMS Principles*, Strategic Planning Institute.
Ciscel, D. H. (1974) Determinants of executive compensation, *Southern Economic Journal*, **40**.
Cyert, R. M. and **March, J. G.** (1963) *A Behavioural Theory of the Firm*, Prentice-Hall, New York.
Haspeslaugh, P. (1982) Portfolio planning, uses and limits, *Harvard Business Review*, **60**, 1, Jan./Feb., 58–73.
Henderson, B. (1970) Intuitive strategy, *Perspectives*, **96**, The Boston Consulting Group, Boston.

Hilton, A. (1978) *Employee Reports: how to communicate financial information to employees.* Woodhead-Faulkner, Cambridge.

Larner, R. J. (1970) *Management Control and the Large Corporation.* Dunellan, Cambridge, Mass.

Llewellen, W. G. and **Huntsman, B.** (1970) Managerial pay and corporate performance, *American Economic Review*, **60**, June/Dec.

Management Today (1987) British Business Growth League, June.

Marris, R. (1964) *The Economic Theory of Managerial Italism.* Macmillan.

Masson, R. T. (1971) Executive motivation, earnings and consequent equity performance, *Journal of Political Economy*, **79**, 6, Nov./Dec.

Meeks, G. and **Whittington, G.** (1975) Directors' pay, growth and profitability, *Journal of Industrial Economics*, **24**, 1, Sept.

Nyman, S. and **Silberston, A.** (1978) The ownership and control of industry, *Oxford Economic Papers*, **30**, 1, March.

Ohmae, K. (1982) *The Mind of the Strategist.* McGraw Hill.

Peters, T. (1988) *Thriving On Chaos.* Macmillan.

Porter, M. (1985) *Competitive Strategy.* McGraw Hill.

Sawyer, M. C. (1981) *The Economics of Industries and Firms.* Croom Helm, p. 175.

Schmalensee, R. (1989) Intra-Industry profitability in the US. *Journal of Industrial Economics*, **36**, 4.

Schoeffler, S., **Buzzel, R. D.** and **Heany, D. F.** (1974) Impact of strategic planning on profit performance, *Harvard Business Review*, **52**, March/April.

Shipley, D. D. (1981) Primary objectives in British manufacturing industry, *Journal of Industrial Economics*, **29**, 4, June.

Simon, H. A. (1959) Theories of decision making in economics, *American Economic Review*, **69**, 3, June.

Singh, A. and **Whittington, G.** (1968) *Growth, Profitability and Valuation.* CUP, Cambridge.

Sizer, J. (1982) Pricing and product profitability analysis, *Management Accounting (UK)*, **60**, 2, Feb.

Smyth, D., **Boyes, W. J.** and **Peseau, J. E.** (1975) *Size, Growth, Profits and Executive Compensation in Large Corporations.* Macmillan.

Whittington, G. (1980) The profitability and size of United Kingdom companies, *Journal of Industrial Economics*, **28**, 4.

Williamson, O. E. (1963) Managerial discretion and business behaviour, *American Economic Review*, **53**, Dec.

Yarrow, G. K. (1972) Executive compensation and the objectives of the firm, in: Cowling K. (ed.) *Market Structure and Corporate Behaviour.* Gray-Mills.

4   The small firm

The small firm is the subject matter of this chapter. It begins by outlining the difficulties of finding an adequate definition, along with problems of measurement. Fragmentary statistical evidence is reviewed, to see whether the small firm really is becoming more important in UK employment and net output, and to compare the small firm in the UK with its position in other countries. We consider the historical reasons for the neglect of the small firm, and why, in more recent times, there has been a resurgence of interest in them. Measures to help the small firm are outlined, from both government and private sources. The chapter concludes with a cautionary note against placing too heavy a reliance on the small firm for economic regeneration.

Definition of the small firm

The difficulties of deriving a single, simple definition of a small firm were amply illustrated in the Bolton Committee Report (1971). The committee's terms of reference had defined small firms as broadly those with not more than 200 employees, but in practice it found this definition to be totally inadequate. Instead, it suggested that a definition was needed which emphasized those characteristics of small firms which might be expected to make their performance and their problems significantly different from those of large firms. They concluded that three main characteristics had to be taken into account:

1. A small firm is one that has a relatively small share of its market.

2. It is managed by its owners or part-owners in a personalized way, and not through the medium of a formalized management structure.

3. It is independent, in the sense that it does not form part of a large enterprise, so that its owner-managers are free from outside control when taking their principal decisions.

These characteristics formed the 'economic' definition of the small firm. However, to make this operational, the committee needed a statistical definition, although it recognized that no single quantifiable definition could be entirely satisfactory. In attempting to reflect the three characteristics above, the committee found that for statistical purposes the criteria of a small firm would have to vary from sector to sector. For manufacturing it retained the usual '200 employees or less' definition, though in construction and mining the upper limit for small firms was reduced to '25 employees or less'. In the motor trades, retailing and miscellaneous services, the statistical definition was based not on the number of employees, but on a specified upper limit for annual turnover, e.g. £200,000 for the motor trades, and £50,000 for retailing and miscellaneous services. For road transport the definition adopted was based on the number of vehicles operated (less than five), whereas in catering all enterprises were to be included except multiples and brewery-managed public houses.

Problems of defining the small firm are not confined to the UK. Bannock (1980) points out that the definition often used for small firms varies widely, from less than 50 employees in the Netherlands, to less than 1,000 employees in the USA! Whether within a single country, or between countries, there will inevitably be a strong element of arbitrariness in the statistical definition used for the small firm.

Importance of the small firm

The problem of finding an appropriate statistical definition for small firms makes it difficult to assess their contribution to economic activity, and the dearth of government statistics in the small business field compounds the difficulty. For instance, in a survey of the Paisley area in 1982, Dr Alan Leyston found that 70% of the small firms contacted had never filled in any government census or leaflet relating to their business. For instance, establishments employing fewer than twenty persons are not required to complete returns for the Census of Production. It is hardly surprising, therefore, that even when the statistical definition of the small firm has been agreed, the lack of data may still cause estimates of the number of small firms to vary widely. In the UK such estimates have varied from 1.3 million to 2.5 million. Despite these difficulties we now consider whether there is any indication that small firms are becoming more important in the UK economy.

Table 4.1 Analysis of private sector enterprises by size of employment (all manufacturing)

Size of firm	1958 Total employment (%)	1958 Total net output (%)	1968 Total employment (%)	1968 Total net output (%)	1987 Total employment (%)	1987 Total net output (%)
1–24	5.8	5.2	5.9	5.2	} 24.4	} 19.0
25–99	9.9	8.4	7.6	6.3		
100–199	8.0	6.9	5.6	4.7	6.8	5.5

Sources: Business Monitor, Report on the Census of Production, PA 1002, Summary Table, 1990 and earlier dates.

Table 4.1 shows the size distribution of private sector firms in UK manufacturing. The contribution of small firms (with less than 200 employees) fell between 1958 and 1968 in terms of both employment and net output, but rose between 1968 and 1987. Since 1968 the sharpest rise has been for firms with less than 100 employees; from 13.5% of total employment in 1968 to 24.4% in 1987, and from 11.5% of total net output in 1968 to 19.0% in 1987.

The data in Table 4.1 provide information about the presence of small firms in manufacturing but do not provide an adequate picture of the economy as a whole. An important study of the size distribution of *all* UK firms published in 1990 has helped to remedy this deficiency (Bannock and

The small firm

Daly 1990). The study included statistics of all companies registered for VAT. To these were added the number of businesses which were not registered for VAT, which includes a large number of sole proprietors and partnerships. It is also worth noting that all self employed persons working on their own are treated as separate firms in this study and that the study includes both the goods and service sectors. From Table 4.2 it can be seen

Table 4.2 Number of businesses, employment and turnover share by size band

Employment size band	Number of businesses (Thousands)	Share of total (per cent)		
		Number of businesses	Total employment	Total turnover
1–2	1,579	63.9	9.7	5.0
3–5	473	19.1	8.9	4.0
6–10	190	7.7	7.2	4.4
11–19	140	5.7	10.0	7.4
20–49	44	1.8	6.7	7.3
50–99	20	0.8	6.9	10.5
100–199	14	0.6	9.9	18.1
200–499	8	0.3	11.9	13.8
500–999	3	0.1	10.5	12.2
1,000+	1	0.0	18.2	17.2
	2,472			

Source: Bannock and Daly (1990).

that there were 2,472,000 businesses in the UK in 1986. Businesses employing less than 20 people accounted for 96.4% of the total number of businesses, 35.8% of total employment and 20.8% of total turnover. The study shows quite clearly the contribution of small businesses to the UK economy as a whole. Although not shown on this table, the share of *total employment* accounted for by small companies employing less than 20 people increased, from 27% in 1979 to almost 36% by 1986. The study also defined small businesses in relation to annual turnover. It showed that no less than 78% of businesses had a turnover of less than £100,000 in 1986, and that these firms accounted for 18.3% of total employment and 5.3% of total turnover.

It is interesting to compare the contribution of small firms in the UK with their contribution elsewhere. We have already noted that each country has a different definition for the small firm. Nevertheless, the contribution of small firms does seem to be less in the UK than in other advanced industrialized countries. Table 4.3 suggests that in comparison with the UK, the USA has 1.57 times as many small firms per head of population, whilst France and Japan have more than twice as many, and the Netherlands nearly four times as many.

A similar pattern emerges when an international comparison is made of small firms in the manufacturing sector alone. Table 4.4 shows that some 94% of the number of manufacturing establishments (plants) in the UK may be defined as small, having less than 200 employees. Although this proportion is similar to that of West Germany, the USA and Canada, it is much less than in Japan or Italy. As regards the numbers employed in each

Table 4.3 Number of small firms* relative to population – selected countries

Rank		Small-firm population (million)	No. of small firms per 1,000 of population (UK = 100)
1	The Netherlands	1.2	370
2	France	3.1	250
3	Japan	5.4	202
4	USA	8.0	157
5	West Germany	1.9	133
6	Canada	0.6	109
7	UK	1.3	100

* The definition of small firms for each country was decided upon after consultation with the relevant government departments of those countries.
Source: Bannock (1980).

Table 4.4 Small firms* in manufacturing

	Manufacturing Establishments		Manufacturing Employment		
	Total ('000s)	Small-firm share (%)	Total (million)	No. of estab. per 100,000 employed	Average no. of employees per establishment
Italy	628.5	99	5.30	11,850	8
Japan	744.3	99	10.89	6,830	15
Canada	32.0	95	1.70	1,880	53
USA	350.8	94	18.52	1,890	53
UK	108.0	94	7.11	1,520	66
West Germany	93.1	93	7.48	1,240	80

* Small firms are defined as those having less than 200 employees.
Source: Adapted from *Financial Times*, 3 May 1983.

manufacturing establishment, the UK is, with sixty-six employees, second highest to West Germany. In manufacturing, as in the economy as a whole, there is clearly scope for growth in small-firm activity before parity is reached with our major competitors.

The neglect of small firms

Early economic theory was broadly favourable to the small firm. The theory of perfect competition had shown that in markets where many small firms produced identical products, the eventual equilibrium would be at the 'technical optimum', i.e. the level of output with lowest average cost. Monopoly, on the other hand, was regarded with suspicion, the exploitation of market power giving the opportunity for restricting output and raising prices (see Fig. 9.1).

The rise of limited liability and the development of the capital market had, by the end of the nineteenth century, made it easier for firms to raise finance for growth. There was also a greater awareness that increased size could secure substantial economies of scale. These developments shifted the focus of attention away from small firms and towards large firms. During the inter-war period, economic theory gave further grounds for viewing large-scale production in a more favourable light. The theory of imperfect competition developed during the 1930s showed that many small firms producing differentiated products could, as with monopoly, produce output below the technical optimum, with prices above the competitive level.

Bannock (1981) argues that after the Second World War attitudes towards large firms became still more positive, with attention being focused on the innovatory role of large firms. Particularly influential was the American economist Schumpeter, who wrote in 1943 that 'the large-scale establishment . . . has come to be the most powerful engine in [economic] progress and in particular of the long-run expansion of total output' (Bannock 1981). Price competition in traditional competitive theory was, to Schumpeter, less important than the 'gales of creative destruction' which replaced old products, processes and organizations, with new ones. Technical progress to bring about these innovative changes would, in Schumpeter's view, require substantial monopoly profits to fund research and development (R & D). The large sums needed to research and develop products in the aerospace, nuclear and computer industries lent weight to this argument. The fact that in the two decades after the Second World War, increasing industrial concentration coincided with the most rapid and sustained period of economic growth in the twentieth century was seen by many as supporting Schumpeter's view.

British Government policy reflected this growing preoccupation with larger size as a means of reaping economies of scale and reducing unit costs of production, so that UK products would become more competitive on world markets. For example, in 1966 the Government announced the formation of the Industrial Reorganization Corporation (IRC). The White Paper inaugurating the IRC (HMSO 1966) had emphasized the need for increased concentration in British industry, so that firms could benefit from economies of scale in production and increase expenditure on R & D. The IRC was set up to encourage the reorganization of UK industry, which in practice led to it promoting mergers through financial and other assistance. Although the IRC was wound up in 1971, the Industry Acts of 1972 and 1975 continued financial help to industry on a selective basis in order to encourage modernization, efficiency and expansion, in particular through the activities of the National Enterprise Board (NEB).[1] However, emphasis on increasing size as a means of achieving greater efficiency began to wane by the early 1970s, with a reawakening of interest in small firms.

The renewed interest in small firms

Empirical and other evidence began to accumulate in the late 1960s which challenged the views of Schumpeter that large firms must be the engine of economic progress.

First, it began to be felt that large firms may not always be the most innovative. Instead of large firms growing still larger by capturing new markets as a result of product and process innovation, they often grew by taking over existing firms with established products and processes. A study by Hannah and Kay (1977) has shown that virtually all the increase in concentration that occurred in the UK between 1957 and 1973 resulted from mergers between existing companies and not from internal growth.

Second, evidence began to be published which indicated that small firms were themselves beginning to play an important role in innovation. The Bolton Committee had found in its survey of important innovations between 1945 and 1970, that small firms only accounted for some 10% of these innovations, but that this was twice as high as their share of total R & D. It has been argued, therefore, that small firms use skilled manpower and research equipment more efficiently than larger firms. Similarly in a nationwide study of 800 firms, covering 1,200 innovations, Oakey, Thwaites and Nash (1980) had found that 23% of these innovations came from single-site independent companies. In the fast-growing instrument engineering and electronic sectors, the small firms' share of innovations was even higher. The fact that small firms are prominent in the most dynamic, high-technology sectors, may mean that they still have an important role to play as innovators.

Third, Prais (1976) produced evidence that the growth in size of firms (business units) was not, in the main, due to the growth in size of plants (production units). According to his calculations the share of the 100 largest manufacturing *plants* remained at about 11% between 1930 and 1968, whilst the share of the 100 largest *firms* rose from about 22 to 41% in the same period. Concentration had increased because firms had built or acquired more plants, not because they had built larger ones. Put another way, Prais showed that increasing concentration was not explained by increased technical economies of scale at plant level. The small firm may therefore be able to compete with the large firm even though it produces in relatively small plants.

Fourth, evidence began to accumulate that acquisitions do not always have particularly beneficial effects on financial performance. A number of studies (Singh 1971; Meeks 1977) showed that the profitability of the combined enterprise usually fell after merger. In fact Newbold (1970) found that only 18% of all the mergers investigated could be linked in any way to technical or financial economies of scale. Again, such evidence gave grounds for optimism that the small firm may be at less of a disadvantage in terms of profitability than had earlier been thought.

Fifth, there is evidence that small firms have contributed a major part of the gains in employment whilst larger firms have been shedding labour. Birch (1979) in his study of changes in employment in the USA, concluded that small firms (those with twenty or fewer employees) generated 66% of all new jobs in the USA in the period 1969–76. In the UK, Gudgin (Gudgin, Brunskill and Fothergill 1979) showed that the main source of employment growth in the regions has been through the setting-up of new, small, indigenous firms, rather than through the inward migration of large firms. Gudgin's studies indicate that small firms originate in a localized fashion, with people who work in small firms more likely to set up in business themselves than are employees of large firms. The existence of a greater number of small firms might therefore increase prospects for gains in employment through new 'start-ups'. Also, in the UK, the 'shake-out' of jobs in recession has appeared to come mainly from large firms (see Ch. 7) which has again added to government interest in small firms. The Conservative

Central Office pamphlet *Small Business, Big Future* noted that: '. . . more than one job in three outside the public sector is in small businesses. If they were encouraged to do so they would become the main source of new jobs' (Conservative Central Office 1982). More recent evidence of the role of small firms in employment creation suggests that between 1985 and 1987, small firms employing less than 20 staff accounted for 295,000 out of a total of 307,000 net jobs created (Gallagher, Daly and Thomason 1990).

Sixth, the role of small firms in foreign trade has been shown to be more significant than was first thought. Hannah and Kay (1977) quote unpublished figures from a survey undertaken in 1973 by the Department of Trade. These show that firms with a turnover of less than £10m. exported 14.5% of turnover, whilst firms with a turnover of over £250m. exported only 10%. As recently as 1990, the yearly 'Queens Awards for Exports and Technology' gave 46% of its awards for export excellence to firms employing less than 100 employees.

For all these reasons there has been a renewed interest in the small firm, which has been reflected in recent government policy.

Measures to help small firms

The Conservative Government has aimed 'to establish the conditions for a sustainable growth in output and employment' (Treasury 1981). As part of its policy, the Government has sought to stimulate the supply side of the economy, with special attention being paid to the small-firms sector. Specifically, action has been taken in three directions.

Small firms and Government

Equity and loan capital   The flow of equity and loan capital has been augmented to enable an individual who wishes to exploit an idea or to expand his business to do so. The following schemes have been introduced.

The Business Expansion Scheme.   This scheme was introduced in the 1983 Budget. It was the successor to the Business Start-Up Scheme of 1981, which sought to encourage individuals to take up equity (shares) in new unquoted companies. Under the Business Expansion Scheme, individuals can invest up to £40,000 a year in both established and new unquoted companies and can claim income tax relief (against taxable income) on this sum. Also, if investors hold on to their shares for five years or more, they can sell them free of capital gains. Over £365m was invested under the BES scheme in 1989. By 1990 many of the new issues were in a variety of sectors, such as residential properties (companies such as Airways Homes and BESRES Lakeland), cargo transport (Short, Sea Europe) and chemist shops (Broadoak Pharmacy). Under the Business Expansion Scheme, companies can normally raise £750,000 of finance per year, although firms in the shipping, timber and residential property business who let their property to secured tenants may raise up to £5m over the same period.

Loan Guarantee Scheme.   This was introduced in 1981 as a pilot scheme for three years. It was intended to cover situations where potential borrowers were unable to provide sufficient collateral, or where the banks considered the risk went beyond their normal criteria for lending. The Government now encourages 'approved' financial institutions to lend to small firms by guaranteeing 70% of each loan (the original figure had been 80%) up to a maximum of £100,000. The borrower usually pays interest at 2½% above base rate and a premium of 2½% extra interest on the *guaranteed* part of the loan. A report by the accountants Robson Rhodes in 1983 found, however, that one in five companies receiving loans through this scheme had failed, and by April 1985 this figure had risen to one in three. Nevertheless, a study in June 1985 calculated that the Loan Guarantee Scheme had created some 44,500 jobs nationally at an average cost of only £2,200 per job, even after allowing for the estimated future costs of failures (Woodcock 1985). The scheme was re-launched in April 1989 after an evaluation exercise and more recent statistics show that between 1981 and 1990, the scheme guaranteed 24,797 loans to more than 21,000 small firms. The total value of this lending was £812m and the average amount of each loan was £32,700. The net exchequer cost of the scheme per person leaving the unemployment count was estimated to be only about £450.

The Unlisted Securities Market. The Unlisted Securities Market (USM) was introduced in November 1980 and was intended to enable small- and medium-sized firms more easily to acquire venture capital on the London Stock Exchange. Previously, smaller firms have been discouraged by the prohibitive cost of a full listing on the Stock Exchange (upwards of £200,000) and the fact that a minimum of 25% of shares had to be in the hands of the public. The cost of joining the USM is considerably below that of a full listing on the Stock Exchange, perhaps as little as £10,000, and there is greater flexibility since companies need only place a minimum of 10% of shares in public hands. The advantages of the USM for the small- or medium-sized firm include access to equity capital, which is one of the cheapest forms of company funding, the opportunity to engage in rights issues and placings, and the ability to offer shares as well as cash when seeking to grow through acquisition. Although there is no rigid limit to the size of firms joining the USM, they have ranged from £1m. to £5m. in terms of market capitalization. This is smaller than is normal for companies which seek a full listing. Companies such as Reliant Motors, Acorn Computers and Intersun Leisure were amongst the 283 companies which had used the USM by mid-1985. These companies had raised over £803m. from their flotations. In 1987 companies raised a total of £935m. *in that year alone* in the USM.

Share Buy-back. Changes in the law have made it possible for small business owners to sell shares to outside investors and make an agreement with them that the company will buy back the shares after a certain time period. This benefits small firms who want to raise capital but who do not want to part with their equity permanently.

Tax allowances and grants In order to help small businesses, tax allowances have been modified, and grants offered.

Corporation tax. This has been made more generous for small firms – small companies in 1990 pay a reduced rate of 25% (up to a limit of £200,000) compared to a standard rate of 35%.

The Enterprise Allowance Scheme.   This scheme is designed to help unemployed people who wish to set up their own business and have £1,000 available to invest. A weekly allowance of £40 is paid for the first year in order to compensate them for the loss of unemployment benefit they would have received if they had not embarked on the scheme. By 1990, over 425,000 had participated in the scheme and 57% of those who started on the scheme and 65% of those who completed a full year on it were still trading three years later. Some £132m is planned to be spent on the scheme in 1990/1, at a cost of £2,100 per person.

The Enterprise Initiative.   As part of this initiative, grants are provided for companies employing fewer than 25 people in the Development Areas under the Regional Enterprise Grant Scheme. For *investment* projects the Department of Trade and Industry pays 15% of the expenditure on fixed assets up to a maximum grant of £15,000 and for *innovation projects* the DTI pays 50% of eligible costs up to £25,000 (see Ch. 19).

Less government interference   A number of measures have been taken to reduce the amount of government administrative interference. For example:

1.   Certain small firms are now exempted from some requirements relating to industrial tribunals, maternity reinstatement, and unfair dismissal procedures.

2.   Small firms have the right to pay business rates by instalments.

3.   New schemes to assist smaller firms in accounting for VAT have been introduced.

The concern of Government to simplify administrative requirements for small firms has even led to a White Paper *Lifting the Burden* (HMSO 1985) in late 1985. This proposed a *single* requirement to replace the current *variety* of requirements concerning the filing of company returns. It also suggested simplifying building regulations and planning procedures for small firms, and eliminating the statutory auditing requirement.

Other sources of advice and training for small firms.   By the early 1990s many schemes were in place to help and advise small firms. For example, there are some 400 independent, privately run *Local Enterprise Agencies* (enterprise trusts in Scotland) in the UK which offer business advice and counselling (usually free) to small firms. Under the Government's *Enterprise Initiative*, launched in 1988, a series of subsidized consultancy packages are available to small firms. Consultancies cover areas such as marketing, design, business planning, information technology and financial planning. Between 1988 and 1990, nearly 36,000 applications for assistance had been approved under the scheme. Also, the Government, through the *Training Agency*, has attempted to provide relevant and practical training courses for small companies, in subjects such as bookkeeping, computers and marketing. In

1989, the *Business Growth Training Programme* was launched to help 100,000 small and medium sized firms. This was a catch-all title for a number of training programmes which were already in existence and some new ones. More recently, the *Training and Enterprise Councils* (Tecs) have been set up on a local basis to take over the running of the training initiatives which were previously under the auspices of the Training Agency.

All these training initiatives are absolutely essential since surveys have shown that between 80% and 90% of small companies have no business training and have received no formal preparation for company board responsibility (Batchelor 1990).

These examples do not represent the full range of government policy measures relating to the small firm, with over 100 introduced since 1979, but they do indicate the general thrust.

Small firms and the banks

The main retail banks have set up small business centres at their main branches, offering advice and arranging loans in suitable cases. Generally speaking, small business loans of between £2,000 and £15,000 secured on a mortgage basis are offered, although longer period loans above £15,000 are obtainable from some banks. The maximum repayment period in many cases is five years and the rate of interest is fixed at between 2.5% and 3% above base rate. Some banks have targeted certain types of small companies, such as those involved in developing technology. For example, in May 1989 the National Westminster bank launched its Technology Unit which provides venture capital of between £5,000 and £50,000 for firms in the developing technology-based business. This bank has also secured about 33% of all small businesses bank lending and has more than one million small business accounts, which generate 200m transactions a year!

In addition to UK banks, there are funds available from overseas banks, such as the European Investment Bank (EIB) of the EEC, which provides increasing amounts of long-term finance for small firms. The UK has received the second largest amount of money from the EIB of any country in Europe.

Despite all these schemes, both government and private, small businessmen often feel that they are treated less than sympathetically. For example, funds obtained under the Loan Guarantee Scheme are by no means cheap; borrowers pay a full commercial rate for the loan, part as interest to the lending institution and part as a guarantee premium (2½%) to the Government. The schemes are numerous, making it difficult for firms or even lending institutions to be aware of all the possibilities. Small firms often fail to obtain money which is available from the EIB, both because of lack of information, and the complex processes involved in obtaining finance.

Conclusion

Renewed interest in small firms derives from changes in economic thought and has been given impetus by the particular policies pursued by the Government, partly for ideological reasons, partly as a means of producing new jobs, and partly as a corollary of 'supply side' monetarist policies.

However, there is a danger in placing too heavy an emphasis on the role of small firms in rebuilding the UK's industrial base. Storey (1982) stresses that most small firms stay static or die. In his study of all the new manufacturing firms started in Cleveland, County Durham, and Tyne and Wear from 1965 to 1978, he found that only 774 survived out of 1,200. Of the survivors, more than half still had less than ten employees in 1982, and nearly three-quarters had less than twenty-five. In fact, the probability of a new business employing more than 100 people after a decade was less than three-quarters of 1%. For every new job created by a small firm in these three counties over the thirteen-year period, four jobs were lost from large companies employing over 1,000 persons. Storey *et al.* (1987) found that in their survey of single-plant independent manufacturing companies in northern England, one-third of the new jobs were found in less than 4% of the new starters. Although the Conservative Government has claimed to have introduced over 100 measures to help small firms since 1979, it is clearly possible to overestimate the role they can play in generating new employment.

Small-firms policy may also have a regional impact. The start-up rate is related to entrepreneurial characteristics which are unevenly spread across the regions. Storey draws up a table ranking the regions as regards factors such as further education, dominance of large manufacturing plant, and owner occupation – the start-up rate being seen as directly related to these entrepreneurial characteristics. The South-east scores highest, and Wales and the North-east lowest. It is not, therefore, surprising that the South-east has most innovations per head of population, and Wales the least (Oakey, Thwaites and Nash 1980). Also, a study of 242 small firms located all over the UK showed that northern firms tended to be less profitable, invested less in management resources and were more likely to be supported by grants than southern firms. Small firms in the south tended to be older and less likely to be involved in manufacture, thus reflecting the long term buoyancy of the south and the greater success of the service firms over manufacturing (Batchelor 1989). Likewise, in a study of the distribution of venture capital, it was found that 60% of venture capital was invested in the South East, where only 47% of the recipient firms were located. These various figures indicate once more the regional inequalities which continue to persist (Mason 1987).

At least two implications follow. First, that the regional problem may even be aggravated by too heavy an emphasis on small-firm creation. Second, that if the Government wishes to maximize the rate of new start-ups, then selective help must be given to small firms in the disadvantaged regions. In other words, the Government may need to introduce a regional dimension to its small-firm policy. Gudgin, Brunskill and Fothergill (1979) have, however, questioned the desirability of encouraging small firms in the regions on welfare grounds, because they tend to pay lower than average wages and offer fewer fringe benefits than large firms.

For all these reasons, the net advantages of small firms may be less than is commonly supposed. Nevertheless small firms are able to find market niches, especially where economies of scale are not easily obtained, as in providing specialized items for small markets, and in developing products used as components by large firms. A US survey (Woo and Cooper 1982) has shown that as regards manufacturing, it is in low-growth markets, producing industrial components with high value added, that small firms with low market share are most likely to be profitable and successful. The 'small firm', like the poor, will always be with us, but whether it can be used as a vehicle for economic regeneration is quite another matter.

Note

1. For an account of the policies pursued by the IRC and the NEB see Howe (1978).

References and further reading

Bannock, G. (1980) *The Promotion of Small Business: a seven-country study*, vols 1 and 2. Prepared by the Economists Advisory Group for Shell UK.
Bannock, G. (1981) *The Economics of Small Firms*. Blackwell, Oxford, Ch. 6.
Bannock, G. and **Daly, M.** (1990) Size Distribution of UK firms. *Employment Gazette* **98**, 5.
Batchelor, C. (1989) Research into Small Business. *Financial Times*, 5 Dec.
Batchelor, C. (1990) Growing Business. *Financial Times*, 23 July.
Birch, D. L. (1979) *The Job Generation Process*. Massachusetts Institute of Technology, mimeo.
Bolton Committee (1971) *Small Firms: report of the Committee of Inquiry on Small Firms*. Cmnd 4811, HMSO.
Conservative Central Office (1982) *Small Business, Big Future.*
Employment Gazette (1978) How big is British business? **86**, 1.
Employment Gazette (1990) 1989 Labour Force Survey – preliminary results, **98**, 4.
Gallagher, C., Daly, M. and **Thomason, J.** (1990) The Growth of UK Companies 1985–87 and their contribution to job generation. *Employment Gazette* **98**, 2.
Ganguly, P. (1983) Lifespan analysis of business in the UK (1973–82), *British Business*, 12 Aug.
Gudgin, E., Brunskill, I. and **Fothergill, S.** (1979) *New Manufacturing Firms in Regional Employment Growth*. Centre for Environmental Research.
Hannah, L. and **Kay, J. A.** (1977) *Concentration in Modern Industry*. Macmillan.
HMSO (1966) *Industrial Reorganization Corporation*, Cmnd 2889.
HMSO (1985) *Lifting the Burden*, Cmnd 9571.
Howe, W. S. (1978) *Industrial Economics*. Macmillan, Ch. 9.
Mason, C. (1987) Venture Capital in the United Kingdom: a Geographical Perspective. *National Westminster Bank Quarterly Review*, May.
Meeks, G. (1977) *Disappointing Marriage: a study of the gains from merger*. University of Cambridge, Department of Applied Economics, Occasional Paper 51, CUP, Cambridge.
Newbold, A. (1970) *Management and Merger Activity*. Guthstead, Liverpool.
Oakey, R. P., Thwaites, A. T. and **Nash, P. A.** (1980) The regional distribution of innovative manufacturing establishments in Britain, *Regional Studies*, **14**, 3.

Prais, S. J. (1976) *The Evolution of Giant Firms in Britain*. CUP, Cambridge.
Singh, A. (1971) *Takeovers*. CUP, Cambridge.
Storey, D. (1982) *Entrepreneurship and the New Firm*. Croom Helm.
Storey, D., **Keasey, K.**, **Watson, R.** and **Wynarczyk, P.** (1987) *The Performance of Small Firms*. Croom Helm.
Treasury (1981) *Economic Progress Report*. HMSO, 132, April.
Woo, C. T. and **Cooper, A. C.** (1982) The surprising case for low market share, *Harvard Business Review*, Nov.–Dec.
Woodcock, C. (1985) Loan scheme moribund, *Guardian*, 9 Dec.

5 Mergers and acquisitions in the growth of the firm

A well-established maxim suggests that a company must grow if it is to survive. Mergers and acquisitions have become two of the more widely used methods of achieving growth in recent years, accounting for about 50% of the increase in assets and 60% of the increase in industrial concentration. The years 1984–89 provided a sustained merger boom greater than that experienced in either 1968 or 1972, in that the *expenditure* on mergers was extremely high compared to the number of mergers involved. This chapter examines the types of merger activity, such as horizontal, vertical, conglomerate and lateral mergers, and the motives for such activity. These include financial motives which may be related to valuations placed on a firm's assets, the desire to increase 'market power' or to secure economies of scale, and managerial motives related more to firm growth than profitability. Legislation affecting merger activity is considered both in the UK and the EEC. The UK approach to mergers is then contrasted with that of the USA. The chapter concludes with a brief review of recent tendencies to de-merge.

Definitions

One of the most significant changes in the UK's industrial structure during this century has been the growth of the large-scale firm. For example, the share of the 100 largest private enterprises in manufacturing net output has risen from 22% in 1949 to a maximum of 42% in 1975, before falling back to 39% by the late 1980s. Most of the growth in size was achieved by acquisition or merger rather than by internal growth.

A merger takes place with the mutual agreement of the management of both companies, usually through an exchange of shares of the merging firms with shares of the new legal entity. Additional funds are not usually required for the act of merging, and the new venture often reflects the name of both the companies concerned.

A takeover (or acquisition) occurs when the management of Firm A makes a direct offer to the shareholders of Firm B and acquires a controlling interest. Usually the price offered to Firm B shareholders is substantially higher than the current share price on the stock market. In other words, a takeover involves a direct transaction between the management of the acquiring firm and the stockholders of the acquired firm. Takeovers usually require additional funds to be raised by the acquiring firm (Firm A) for the acquisition of the other firm (Firm B), and the identity of the acquired company is often subsumed within that of the purchaser.

Sometimes the distinction between merger and takeover is clear, as when an acquired company has put up a fight to prevent acquisition. This was the case when, in 1982, British Sugar sought to prevent their takeover by S. & W. Berisford and when Spillers sought to prevent their takeover by Dalgety. However, in the majority of cases the distinction between merger and takeover is difficult to make. Occasionally the situation is complicated by the use of the words 'takeover' and 'merger'. For example, in 1989 the press announced that SmithKline Beckman, the US pharmaceutical company, had 'taken over' the UK company Beecham for £4,509m. However, technically speaking it was a 'merger' because a new company SmithKline Beecham was created which acquired the shares of the two constituent companies to form a new entity.

Types of merger

Four major forms of merger activity can be identified: horizontal integration, vertical integration, the formation of conglomerate mergers, and lateral integration.

Horizontal integration

This occurs when firms combine at the same stage of production, involving similar products or services. During the 1960s over 80% of the total number of mergers were of the horizontal type, but by the late 1980s this figure had fallen to 62% as other forms of mergers increased in importance. The British Airways takeover of British Caledonian in 1988, and the Ford takeover of Jaguar in 1989, were examples of horizontal mergers. Horizontal integration may provide a number of economies at the level both of the plant (productive unit) and the firm (business unit). *Plant economies* may follow from the rationalization made possible by horizontal integration. For instance, production may be concentrated at a smaller number of enlarged plants, permitting the familiar technical economies of greater specialization, the dovetailing of separate processes at higher output,[1] and the application of the 'engineers' rule' whereby material costs increase as the square but capacity as the cube. All these lead to a reduction in cost per unit as the size of plant output increases. *Firm economies* result from the growth in size of the whole enterprise, permitting economies via bulk purchase, the spread of similar administrative costs over greater output, and the cheaper cost of finance, etc.

Vertical integration

This occurs when the firms combine at different stages of production of a common good or service. Only about 5% of mergers are of this type. Firms might benefit by being able to exert closer control over quality and delivery of supplies if the vertical integration is 'backward', i.e. towards the source of supply. Factor inputs might also be cheaper, obtained at cost instead of cost + profit. The acquisition of Hall Ham River Ltd, the sand and gravel quarry company, by Ready Mix Concrete Ltd, was an example of backward vertical integration. The takeover of Texas Eastern, an oil exploration company, by Enterprise Oil in 1989 for £419m, serves as another example of backward vertical integration. Of course, vertical integration could be 'forward' – towards the retail outlet. This may give the firm merging 'forward' more control of wholesale or retail pricing policy, and more direct customer contact. The British Oxygen Company's (industrial gases) acquisition in 1982 of Mountain Medical, a US company manufacturing mobile oxygen concentrators for home care, was an example of forward vertical integration.

Vertical integration can often lead to increased control of the market, infringing monopoly legislation. This is undoubtedly one reason why they are so infrequent. Another is the fact that, as Marks and Spencer have shown, it is not necessary to have a controlling interest in suppliers in order to exert effective control over them. Textile suppliers of Marks and Spencer send over 75% of their total output to Marks and Spencer. Marks and Spencer have been able to use this reliance to their own advantage. In return for placing long production runs with these suppliers, Marks and Spencer have been able to restrict supplier profit margins whilst maintaining their viability. Apart from low costs of purchase, Marks and Spencer are also able to insist on frequent batch delivery, cutting stockholding costs to a minimum.

Conglomerate merger

This refers to the adding of different products to each firm's operations. Diversification into products and areas with which the acquiring firm was not directly involved before, accounted for only 13% of all mergers in the 1960s. However, by the late 1980s the figure had risen to 34%. The major benefit is the spreading of risk for the firms and shareholders involved. Giant conglomerates like Unilever (with interests in food, detergents, toilet preparations, chemicals, paper, plastics, packaging, animal feeds, transport and tropical plantations – in seventy-five separate countries), are largely cushioned against any damaging movements which are restricted to particular product groups or particular countries. The various *firm economies* outlined above may also result from a conglomerate merger. The ability to buy companies relatively cheaply on the stock exchange and to sell parts of them off at a profit later, became an important reason for conglomerate mergers in the 1980s. The takeovers of the Imperial Group and of Consolidated Goldfields by Hanson Trust in 1986 and 1989 respectively, provide good examples of the growth of a large conglomerate organization.

Lateral integration

This is sometimes given separate treatment, though in practice it is difficult to distinguish from a conglomerate merger. The term 'lateral integration' is often used when the firms which combine are involved in different products, but *have some element of commonality*. This might be in terms of factor input, such as requiring similar labour skills, capital equipment, or raw materials; or it might be in terms of product outlet. The merging of J. Hepworth (menswear retailer) with Kendalls (womenswear) in 1980, which it then transformed into Next (ladies' fashions) in spring 1982, allowed the successful Next venture to use a further 190 retail outlets under Hepworth's control.

Economic theory and merger activity

A number of theories have been proposed in an attempt to explain merger activity.

The value discrepancy hypothesis

This theory is based on a belief that two of the most common characteristics of the industrial world are imperfect information and uncertainty. Together, these help explain why different investors have different expectations of the prospects for a given firm.

The value discrepancy hypothesis suggests that one firm will only bid for another if it places a greater value on the firm than that placed by its current owners. If Firm B is valued at V_A by Firm A and V_B by Firm B then a takeover of Firm B will only take place if $V_A > V_B$ + costs of acquisition. The difference in valuation arises through Firm A's higher expectations of future profitability, often because A takes account of the improved efficiency with which it believes the future operations of B can be run.

It has been argued that it is in periods when technology, market conditions and share prices are changing most rapidly that past information and experience are of least assistance in estimating future earnings. As a result differences in valuation are likely to occur more often, leading to increased merger activity. The value discrepancy hypothesis would therefore predict high merger activity when technological change is most rapid, and when market and share price conditions are most volatile.

Evidence Gort's (1969) test of the value discrepancy hypothesis in the USA gives some support, finding a statistically significant relationship between merger rate and the parameters noted above. In the UK the merger booms of the late nineteenth century, of the 1920s, the 1960s and the mid-1980s, seem also to have occurred during periods of accelerating technological change and volatile share prices. However, although this theory points to the general economical conditions surrounding merger activity, it rarely provides an insight into the particular reasons behind merger activity.

The valuation ratio

One factor which may affect the likelihood of takeover is the valuation ratio, as defined below:

$$\text{Valuation ratio} = \frac{\text{market value}}{\text{asset value}} = \frac{\text{no. of shares} \times \text{share price}}{\text{book value of assets}}$$

If a company is 'undervalued' because its share price is low compared to the value of its assets, then it becomes a prime target for the 'asset stripper'. If a company attempts to grow rapidly it will tend to retain a high proportion of profits for reinvestment, with less profit therefore available for distribution to shareholders. The consequence may be a low share price, reducing the market value of the firm in relation to the book value of its assets, i.e. reducing the valuation ratio. It has been argued that a high valuation ratio will deter takeovers, whilst a low valuation ratio will increase the vulnerability of the firm to takeover. For example, the property company British Land purchased Dorothy Perkins, the womenswear chain, because its market value was seen as being low in relation to the value of its assets (prime high street sites). After stripping out all the freehold properties for resale, the remainder of the chain was sold in 1982 to the Burton Group.

In recent years the asset value of some companies has been seriously underestimated for other reasons. For example, many companies have taken years to build up brand names which are therefore worth a great amount of money; but it is often the case that these are *not* given a money value and are thus not included in the asset value of the company. As a result, if the market value of a company is already low in relation to the book value of its assets, then the acquirer gets a double bonus. One reason why Nestlé was prepared to bid £2.5m (regarded as a 'high' bid, in relation to its book value) for Rowntree Mackintosh in 1988 was to acquire the 'value' of its consumer brands cheaply, because they were not shown on the asset sheet. Finally, it is interesting to note that when the valuation ratio is low and a company would appear to be a 'bargain', a takeover may originate from *within* the company; in this case it is referred to as a Management Buy Out (MBO).

Evidence   Kuehn (1975) in his study of over 3,500 companies in the UK (88% of companies quoted on the Stock Exchange) between 1957 and 1969, found that those firms which maintained a high valuation ratio were much less susceptible to takeover. Figure 5.1 indicates this inverse relation between

Fig. 5.1 Valuation ratio and probability of takeover
Source: Kuehn (1975)

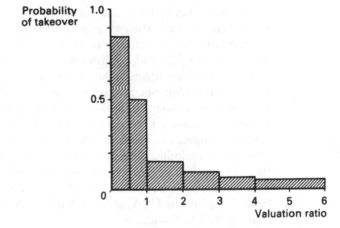

valuation ratio and the probability of acquisition. The suggestion is that potential raiders are deterred by the high price to be paid, reflecting a more realistic market valuation of the potential victims' assets. However, the valuation ratio may not be as important as Kuehn's study implies. For example Singh (1971), in a study of takeovers in five UK industries (which included food, drink and electrical engineering industries) between 1955 and 1960, found that a relatively high valuation ratio may not always guarantee protection against takeover. An even stronger conclusion against the valuation ratio hypothesis was drawn by Newbold (1970), when he compared the valuation ratios of 'victim' firms with those of the 'bidding' firms during the merger period of 1967 and 1968. His conclusion was that the valuation ratio of actual 'victim' firms exceeded the average for the industry in thirty-eight cases but was below the average in only twenty-six cases. In other words, a high valuation ratio did not seem to deter takeover activity.

**The market power
theory**

The main motive behind merger activity may often be to increase monopoly
control of the environment in which the firm operates. Increased market
power may help the firm to withstand adverse economic conditions, and
increase long-term profitability.

Three situations are particularly likely to induce merger activity aimed at
increasing market power:

1. Where a fall in demand results in excess capacity and the danger of price-
    cutting competition. In this situation firms may merge in order to secure
    a better vantage point from which to rationalize the industry. In 1982
    Montague Meyer, Britain's largest timber firm, merged with
    International Timber Corporation, its largest independent rival. The
    motive was largely defensive, in response to the recession in housing
    construction and the movement in tastes from hardwood to softwoods.
    Meyer saw the merger as necessary to their survival, allowing a more
    rational treatment of overcapacity, and even reducing that overcapacity
    through the prospect of forcing many small timber importers out of
    business.

2. Where international competition threatens increased penetration of the
    domestic market by foreign firms. Mergers in electronics, computers and
    engineering, have in the past produced combines large enough to fight
    off such foreign competition. British examples range from the formation
    of GEC (from AEI and English Electric) in the 1960s, to the formation
    of Northern Engineering Industry (from a merger between Reyrolle
    Parsons, the turbine generator makers, and Clarke Chapman, the
    boilermaking firm) in the 1980s. On the European scene, the acquisition
    in 1990 of the ailing German computer firm Nixdorf by Siemens, the
    country's largest electrical and electronics group, was partly to
    rationalize the industry and partly to increase Siemens market share in
    the very competitive European computer market. This move would
    make Siemens/Nixdorf the second largest computer business in Europe,
    behind IBM of the USA, and much larger than Olivetti of Italy or
    Groupe Bull of France.

3. Where a tightening of legislation makes many types of linkages between
    companies illegal. Firms have in the past adopted many practices which
    involved collusion in order to control markets. Since restrictive practices
    legislation has made many of these practices illegal between companies,
    merger, by 'internalizing' the practices, has allowed them to continue.

For these reasons merger activity may take place to increase a firm's market
power. However, the very act of merging usually increases company size,
both in absolute terms and in relation to other firms. It is clear, therefore,
that increased size will be both a by-product of the quest for increased market
power, and itself a cause of increased market power.

Evidence Newbold (1970) in his study of thirty-eight mergers between 1967
and 1968 found that the most frequent reason cited by managers for merger
activity was risk reduction (48% of all mergers), as firms sought to control
markets along the lines of market power theory. These conclusions were

substantiated in a study by Cowling, Cubbin and Hall (1980) of nine major mergers including such names as Thorn–Radio Rental (1968), Courtaulds–British Celanese (1969), and Rowntree Mackintosh (1969). The study concluded that the mergers did generate elements of market power, often to the detriment of consumers.

There is also fragmentary evidence that the termination of restrictive agreements encouraged some firms to combine formally. Elliot and Gribbin (1977) found that the five-firm concentration ratio increased faster in industries in which restrictive practices had been terminated than in those in which no such practices existed.

Empirical work does suggest that an increase in the size of a firm raises its market power. For example, Whittington (1980) found that large firms often experience less variability in their profits than small firms, indicating that large firms may be less susceptible to changing economic circumstances as a result of their greater market power. Studies by Aaronovitch and Sawyer (1975) also show that large firms are less likely to be taken over than small- or medium-sized ones, and that a given percentage increase in size for an already large firm reduces the probability of takeover much more than the same percentage increase for a small to medium-size firm. It would appear that size, stability and market power are closely interrelated.

Economies of scale

It is often argued that the achievement of lower average costs (and thereby higher profits) through an increase in the scale of operation is the main motive for merger activity. As we noted in the earlier part of this chapter such economies can be at two levels. First, at the level of the plant, the production unit, including the familiar technical economies of specialization, dovetailing of processes, engineers' rule, etc. Second, at the level of the firm, the business unit, including research, marketing, administrative, managerial and financial economies. To these plant- and firm-level economies we might add the 'synergy' effect of merger, the so-called '2 + 2 > 4' effect, whereby merger increases the efficiency of the combined firm by more than the sum of its parts. Synergy could result from combining complementary activities as, for example, when one firm has a strong R & D team whilst another firm has more effective production control personnel.

Evidence   Economies of scale seem less important in merger activity than is traditionally supposed. Prais (1976) points out that technical economies, through increased plant size, have played only a small part in the growth of large firms. For instance, the growth of the 100 largest plants (production units) in net output has been much slower than the growth of the 100 largest firms (business units) in net output. Firms seem to grow not so much by expanding plant size to reap technical economies, but by acquiring more plants. Of course, evidence that firms seek to grow as an enterprise or business unit, through adding extra plants, could still be linked to securing 'firm level' economies of scale.

Newbold (1970), however, found that only 18% of firms surveyed admitted to any motive that could be linked to plant- or firm-level economies of scale. Cowling, Cubbin and Hall (1980) conclude in similar vein that the 'efficiency gains' (economies of scale) from mergers were difficult to identify in the firms examined. Finally, Whittington (1980) found profitability to be independent of firm size. This might also seem to argue against any significant economies of scale, otherwise larger firms, with much lower costs, might be expected to secure higher profits.

Although we cannot test the synergy effect directly, there is case evidence that it plays a part in encouraging merger activity. Nevertheless, the hopes of substantial benefits through this effect are not always realized. Unsuccessful attempts at pursuing synergy are widespread, notably by companies who mistakenly believe that they have the management expertise to turn around loss-making companies into efficient, profitable ventures. Thus PMA doubled the size of their furniture industry holdings in 1979 through the purchase of Gower and Harris Lebus, only to be so stretched by liquidity problems resulting from an increased borrowing commitment, that even the resale of Gower could not save it from bankruptcy.

Managerial theories

In all the theories considered so far, the underlying principle in merger activity is, in one way or another, the pursuit of profit. For example, market power theory suggests that through control of the firm's environment, the prospects of profit, at least in the long run, are improved. Economies of scale theory concentrates on raising profit through the reduction of cost. Managerial theories on the other hand (see also Ch. 3) lay greater stress on non-profit motives.

With the rise of the public limited company there has been a progressive divorce between ownership by shareholders, and control by management. This has given managers greater discretion in control of the company, and therefore in merger policy. The suggestion by Marris, Williamson, and others, is that a prime objective of managers is growth of the firm, rather than absolute size. In these theories the growth of the firm raises managerial utility by bringing higher salaries, power, status, and job security to managers. Managers may therefore be more interested in the rate of growth of the firm than in its profit performance as suggested by the work of Jensen and Meckling (1976).

Managerial theories would suggest that fast-growing firms, having already adopted a growth-maximization approach, are the ones most likely to be involved in merger activity. These theories would also suggest that fast-growing firms will give higher remuneration to managers, and will raise job security by being less prone to takeover.

Evidence It does appear that it is the fast-growing firms that are mainly involved in merger activity. For example, Singh (1971, 1975) noted that the acquiring firms had a significantly higher growth rate than the acquired firms, and possessed many of the other attributes of a growth maximizer, such as a higher retention ratio (see Ch. 3), higher gearing and less liquidity (Ch. 2). Similarly Aaronovitch and Sawyer (1975) report that in the period before an acquisition, the acquiring firm generally grew much faster than the acquired firm.

As regards higher managerial remuneration through growth, Firth (1980) found a significant increase in the salaries of directors of the acquiring company after merger. The chairman's salary increased by an average of 33% in the two years following merger, compared to only 20% for the control group of companies not engaged in merger activity. Meeks and Whittington (1975) also found that company size was the main factor affecting executive income.

Managerial theories place less stress on profit performance, and more on growth of the firm. The fact that, at least in the short run, the profit level often deteriorates for the acquiring firms is taken by some as further evidence in support of the managerial approach. For example, Utton (1974) showed that firms involved in mergers tended to have lower profitability levels than non-merging firms; again in the studies of Meeks (1977), Kumar (1985), and Cosh, Hughes and Singh (1985), mergers were found to have negative effects on profitability.

We have already noted that large firms, whilst not necessarily the most profitable (Meeks and Whittington 1975), were less likely to be taken over than small to medium-sized firms. In fact, any given percentage increase in size was much more significant in reducing the probability of takeover for the large firm, than it was for the small to medium-sized firm (Aaronovitch and Sawyer 1975; Singh 1975). The small to medium-sized firm has therefore an incentive to become large, and the large firm still larger, if takeovers are to be resisted. Further evidence in support of the suggestion that small to medium-sized firms *are* active in acquisitions comes from a more recent survey of some 2,000 firms in UK manufacturing industry between 1960 and 1976 (Kumar 1985). The study concluded that there was indeed a tendency for firm growth through acquisitions to be *negatively* related to firm size. Once firms become large they appear to be more 'stable' and less prone to takeover. Such evidence is consistent with managerial theories which stress the importance of growth as a means of enhancing job security for managers. However it should be noted that the merger boom of the late 1980s showed that even large firms were no longer safe from takeovers; this was in part due to firms now having easier access to the finance required for takeover activity.

The evidence clearly points away from traditional economies of scale, whether at the level of 'plant' or 'firm', as the motive for merger. Survival of the firm, and control of its environment, seems to be at the heart of most merger activity. This often implies the sacrifice of profit, at least in the short run. Such an observation is consistent with market power and managerial theories, both of which concentrate on objectives other than short-run profit (see also, Ch. 3).

Trends in UK merger activity 1949–1989

Having looked at both theory and evidence relating to merger activity, it may be helpful to trace briefly the trends in merger activity since 1949, in order to obtain a more practical view of the merger process in the UK. Figure 5.2 shows the intensity of takeover activity by using two series of statistics and expressing the values of takeovers and mergers as a percentage of capital stock.[2]

Fig. 5.2 Merger and takeover activity in the UK 1949–1989
Source: M. King 'Takeover Activity in the United Kingdom' in *Fairburn and Kay* (1989) (updated).

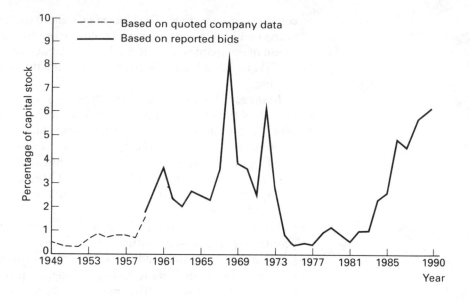

Merger activity was particularly active during the 1958–62, 1966–69, 1971–73 and 1982–89 periods, with merger peaks around 1961, 1968, 1972 and 1989. After a quiet period during the 1940s and early 1950s, there was intense activity in the 1958–73 period. The first wave of mergers involved many types of industries, including the merger of three main airframe manufacturing companies to form British Aircraft Corporation in 1959. In the same year, mergers took place in publishing (Odhams Press takeover of George Newnes) and in food (Schweppes takeover of Hartleys). A year later, in 1960, there was a rapid reorganization of the electrical industry, with EMI taking over Morphy Richards and Pye merging with E K Cole. The second wave of mergers occurred between 1966 and 1968 and involved much structural change. In the electrical industry, the giant GEC made a hostile takeover of AEI in 1967 and then merged with English Electric in 1968. Meanwhile, in the vehicle industry, the Leyland bus and truck group took over British Motor Corporation (BMC) to form the British Leyland Corporation in 1968. The third wave of merger activity was largely concentrated in the 1972/3 fiscal year, when Grand Metropolitan Hotels acquired Watney Mann (brewing) and the Imperial Group (tobacco, food and drink) acquired Courage (brewing). Other major acquisitions included the Bowater (paper, international trading) takeover of Ralli International (commodity brokers and dealers) and the British and American Tobacco (BAT) takeover of International Stores (food retailers).

The most notable features which tended to galvanize such merger and takeover activity were the following.

● First, the growth of national and international markets created circumstances favourable to economies of scale, while at the same time world tariff barriers were being reduced under the guidance of GATT. The result was fierce competition between nations which often led to a rationalization of production since larger firms were seen to have important cost advantages. For example, in the electrical industry the number of UK firms producing televisions declined from 60 in 1964 to 7 by 1969 (Hannah 1976).

● Second, improved communication methods, such as telephones and computers, made it easier for large companies to grow, while the adoption by many companies of a multi-divisional structure encouraged horizontal mergers.

● Third, there had been a rapid growth of financial intermediaries, such as insurance companies and investment trusts. They had begun investing heavily in company equity, thereby providing a ready source of finance for companies who wanted to issue more shares and then to use the money received to support a takeover bid. At the same time, there was a dilution of managerial control; for instance, by 1972 the median holding of equity by the board of directors of the largest manufacturing companies was half a percent, as compared to 20% in the inter-war period (Prais 1976). This 'divorce of ownership from control' made takeover activity easier because directors now had a less-close relationship with the company, and were therefore less committed to its continuing in an unchanged form.

● Fourth, the period 1957 to 1972 saw an increase in the 'gearing ratio' of companies, i.e. an increase in the ratio of debt (debenture and bank borrowing) to shares (equity). Loan finance was attractive because the interest paid on debentures and loans was deducted from company profits *before* it was taxed. Therefore companies had a tax incentive to issue loan stock, the money from which they could then use to mount a takeover bid.

After a quiet period for merger activity between 1973 and the early 1980s, there was renewed activity after 1984. One of the interesting points about the recent merger activity has been its dominance by large acquisitions involving an expenditure of over £10m. These accounted for only 18% of the *number* of mergers, but 90% of the *total expenditure* on mergers. Takeover activity was particularly high in the food, drink and tobacco industries. Also, this merger period witnessed a significant rise in the number of Management Buyouts (MBO), where managers have bought their company from the existing shareholders (in many cases the parent company). The general takeover movement in the period 1984 to 1989 included the acquisition of Arthur Bell by Guinness, followed by the celebrated Guinness takeover of Distillers in 1986 (see below). Other major takeovers included that of the House of Fraser by the Fayed brothers in 1985 and the acquisition of Debenhams by the Burton Group in the same year. The Imperial Group and Consolidated Goldfields were acquired by Hanson Trust in 1986 and 1989 respectively. In the confectionery industry, Rowntree Mackintosh was acquired by Nestlé, the Swiss firm in 1988, and in the same year British Petroleum acquired Britoil. On an international note, 1989 also saw the sale of the UK pharmaceutical firm Beecham to SmithKline of the US for £4,509m, and the sale of Jaguar to the Ford Motor Company for £1,560m.

The motives for such intense takeover activity have been varied. For example, many of the 1985–87 mergers were of the *horizontal* type suggesting that one important motive for such activity was production economies arising from rationalization. This motive may have been strengthened by the desire to integrate technology and to improve marketing expertise in order to increase market power. There is also some evidence that target companies tended to be less dependent on debt finance, which suggests that some acquisitions may have been due to the desire of the acquirer to increase cash flow and to reduce its dependency on debt finance. However, on a general point, it is important to note that the period up to 1987 was one in which company liquidity rose rapidly, equity markets were buoyant, and interest rates relatively low. Such conditions created a substantial pool of liquidity to finance takeovers. However, despite the decrease in stock market prices and the interest rate rises in 1988 and 1989, large takeovers continued, with takeover bids now tending to involve cash rather than the exchange of shares. At the beginning of the 1990s, the difficult state of the stock market, the high interest rates, the rapid fall in company liquidity, and the publicity relating to the Guinness and House of Fraser 'affairs', together with the collapse of the 'junk bond' market in the US, resulted in a relatively quieter period of merger activity.

Control of mergers and acquisitions

We have seen that mergers may be a means of extending market power. We now consider how the UK, the EEC and the USA, have sought to exercise control over merger activity in order to prevent the abuse of such power.

The UK experience

United Kingdom legislation has been tentative in its approach to merger activity, recognizing the desirable qualities of some monopoly situations created through merger; it therefore seeks to examine each case on its individual merits. The first UK legislation, the Monopolies and Restrictive Practices (Inquiry and Control) Act, dates from 1948 and set up the Monopolies Commission. This Act empowered the Board of Trade (now the Department of Trade and Industry) to instruct the commission to report on situations in which any one firm (unitary monopoly), or group of firms acting together, could restrict competition through the control of at least one-third of the market. Although the commission was successful in revealing the extent of monopoly power in the UK, its position as an advisory body left it powerless to effect change. The commission took on average more than two years to complete a report, and the majority of its recommendations were virtually ignored.

Restrictive practices legislation   The Restrictive Trades Practices Act of 1956 separated unitary monopoly investigations from restrictive practices operated by groups of firms. A restrictive practice operated by groups of firms had now to be registered with a Registrar of Restrictive Practices. It was his responsibility to bring cases to the Restrictive Practices Court, consisting of five judges and ten lay members with the status of a High Court. Such restrictive practices were deemed against the public interest unless they could satisfy at least one of seven 'gateways':

1.   That it protects the public against injury.

2. That it confers specific benefits on consumers.
3. That it prevents local unemployment.
4. That it counters existing restrictions on competition.
5. That it maintains exports.
6. That it supports other acceptable restrictions.
7. That it assists the negotiation of fair trading terms for suppliers and buyers.

Even having satisfied one or more of the 'gateway' conditions, the firms had still to show that the overall benefits from the restrictive practice were clearly greater than the costs incurred. This 'tail-piece' was largely responsible for the prohibition of many restrictive practices. Since the passing of the 1956 Act, over 3,000 restrictive practices have been registered. Although less than fifty practices have been brought before the court, the majority of such practices have been 'voluntarily' ended by the parties themselves in anticipation of an unfavourable decision by the court.

In 1968, 'information agreements' (i.e. agreements whereby information concerning prices, conditions, etc. are formally exchanged) were for the first time considered a restrictive practice. Also in 1968 an eighth 'gateway' was added, namely 'that the agreement neither restricts nor deters competition'. The Fair Trading Act of 1973 gave permission for restrictive practices legislation to be extended to cover services as well as the production of goods, though this was only implemented three years later. The 1976 Restrictive Practices Act consolidated previous legislation, with the Director-General of Fair Trading now responsible for bringing restrictive practices before the court.

Despite the apparently comprehensive nature of current restrictive practices legislation, loopholes still exist. For instance the action of the Secretary of State for Industry in July 1983 in abandoning the investigation of Stock Exchange practices, contrary to the wishes of the Office of Fair Trading, vividly highlighted the power of the minister in such cases. This action has set a legal precedent in the field of restrictive practices which may also have implications for merger procedures (see below).

Monopolies and mergers legislation   The 1965 Monopolies and Mergers Act provided for the investigation of mergers or acquisitions which might produce or strengthen a monopoly, if they involved the takeover of assets in excess of £5m. The Board of Trade could prohibit those cases found by the commission to be 'contrary to the public interest', and could set conditions under which certain mergers might be allowed to proceed. The effect of the 1965 Act was to slow down the trend towards greater industrial concentration rather than seriously to inhibit the growth of larger firms. Indeed, the Labour Government of the late 1960s actively promoted mergers in engineering and computers, with the assistance of the Industrial Reorganization Corporation (IRC),[3] in order to make better use of scarce entrepreneurial talent and to provide units of sufficient size to compete effectively on an international basis. The political climate has remained a major factor in the implementation of mergers policy, so that the vast majority of mergers and acquisitions proceed unopposed. Since 1965, less than 3% of mergers eligible for consideration by the Monopolies Commission have, in fact, been referred to it, with fewer than 1% ruled against the public interest.

The 1973 Fair Trading Act together with the 1980 Competition Act represent the current state of monopoly and merger legislation, and have introduced a number of changes.

1. The unitary monopoly definition is extended to situations where at least 25% (rather than 33%) of the market is controlled by a single buyer or seller. This market share test may be applied to sales at local, as well as at national level. In addition, monopoly situations stemming from nationalization can now be investigated.

2. Under the Acts, two interconnected companies (e.g. a parent + subsidiary) which control a 25% share of the market can now be investigated, as can two quite distinct companies operating in such a way as to restrict competition without any formal agreement, e.g. the case of price leadership or tacit collusion (see Ch. 6).

3. As regards mergers, investigation can take place when the merging firms together control at least 25% of the market, or when the merger involves gross assets of over £30m.

4. The 1973 Fair Trading Act created the Office of Fair Trading (OFT) and new post of Director-General of Fair Trading (DGFT). The director-general can refer cases of monopoly situations to the renamed Monopolies and Mergers Commission (MMC), and chairs a mergers panel which can collect information on mergers which fall within current legislation. He may then advise the secretary of state on whether the mergers investigated (by the panel) should be referred to the commission for a decision on whether or not they are against the 'public interest'.

After the preparation of the commission's report (a delay of around three months), the director-general recommends action to the secretary of state based on the commission's conclusions. However, as is apparent from the flow chart (Fig. 5.3), various alternative outcomes are possible. We might usefully follow through Fig. 5.3, using recent data and cases for illustration.

About 28% of takeover bids are contested by the boards of 'raided' companies or by third parties (a), and in over 40% of cases the boards are able to defend themselves successfully, so that the proposals are abandoned (b). For example, Pilkington, the glass maker, successfully fought a long and bitter battle in 1986/7 to prevent being taken over by BTR. Of the cases that remain (voluntary mergers and unsuccessful defences by boards), only a small proportion, less than 3%, are recommended for referral by the Director-General of Fair Trading to the MMC (c). In 1989, for example, the DGFT scrutinized 427 mergers and recommended to the Secretary of State for Trade and Industry that 14 should be referred to the MMC. Of the mergers referred, two were abandoned after the reference, eight were cleared, and two rejected.

The director-general may refer mergers to the MMC if he feels that they will infringe the public interest through adverse effects on competition. Where such considerations are unclear, as with conglomerate mergers, strong additional circumstances are usually necessary to bring about referral.

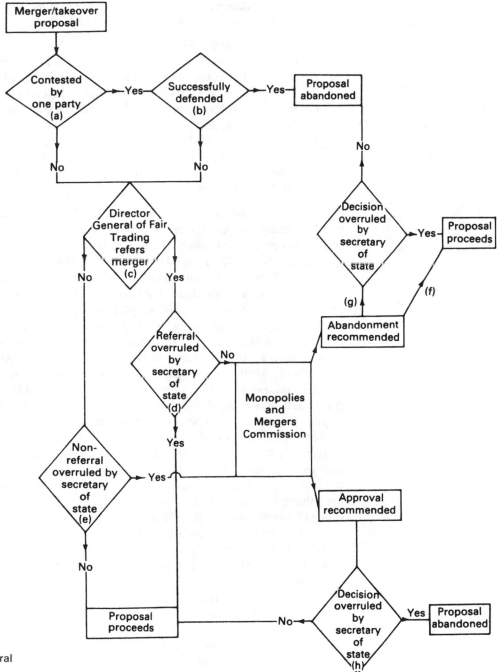

Fig. 5.3 The referral procedure

However, the director-general has no power to implement his decisions, as shown by two instances in 1982 and 1990 when his recommendations were overruled:

1.   His advice to refer the takeover by Woolworth of the Dodge City do-it-yourself chain in 1982 was rejected by the Secretary of State (d), who

allowed the deal to go through without investigation on the grounds that jobs would otherwise be lost in areas of high unemployment.

2. In February 1990 the Secretary of State, Mr Nicolas Ridley, overruled the recommendation of the DGFT. He decided to refer the bid by Ransomes (the maker of grass cutting machinery) for Westwood (a garden tractor maker) to the MMC despite the fact that the DGFT did not feel that a referral was needed (e). He felt that the merged company would have an unacceptably high UK market share in 'ride-on' domestic lawnmowers. The MMC's report recommended that the takeover was *not* against the public interest and it was allowed to continue. This was only the third time in a decade that the Secretary of State had overruled the DGFT in this way.

The MMC was strengthened by the 1973 Fair Trading Act, being given a free hand to define the 'public interest', so that it could more easily maintain and promote competitive trading conditions. However, the decision-making process involved in the referral of mergers has remained somewhat arbitrary and unsatisfactory to the companies concerned. The very action of referral has itself led to the immediate abandonment of about one-third of proposed mergers – as with the referral of Argyll Foods' bid for Linfood. Argyll had borrowed £20m. to build up a 30% stake in Linfood but decided not to incur the estimated £1.75m. in interest charges necessitated by the usual six months' wait for the conclusion of the commission investigation.

When the MMC has reported, it is by no means certain that its recommendations will be implemented. For instance, if the MMC rules a proposal against the public interest, *but by less than a two-thirds majority*, the secretary of state has no powers to implement the MMC recommendation (f) preventing the merger taking place. The acquisition of Herbert Morris, the engineering firm, by Babcock and Wilcox was one bid which went ahead in such circumstances. Even if the ruling is achieved with a two-thirds majority the secretary of state *need not* implement the recommendation of the MMC even though he now has the power to do so (g). This happened for the first time in December 1982 with the decision to allow Charter Consolidated, the South African mining company, to bid for Anderson Strathclyde, the Glasgow-based mining engineers,[4] despite the greater than two-thirds majority by the MMC against the bid. If, on the other hand, the MMC recommends approval of the merger, it is still not clear that it can proceed as the secretary of state may overrule the decision and propose the abandonment of the merger (h). As well as the problems noted above, both referrals by the director-general and approvals of the secretary of state often give the impression of extensive behind-the-scenes political activity, rather than a detailed assessment of economic arguments. The vast majority of merger bids do not infringe issues of competition, making referral decisions marginal and questionable. In borderline cases the absence of a ministerial statement explaining the costs and benefits of proposed mergers is particularly unsatisfactory.

The UK approach to mergers is based on the principle that they can be forbidden if they operate, or can be expected to operate, against the public interest. A Labour Government Green Paper in 1978 argued that it was wrong to place the onus on the MMC to find that a merger was against the public interest because it tended to encourage the MMC to look for problems. As a result, it recommended that the MMC should not only recognize the possibility that a loss of competition might result from mergers but also that benefits might accrue. However, when the new Conservative Government came to power in 1979, its new Competition Act of 1980 cast a more sceptical attitude towards the supposed benefits from mergers, especially conglomerate ones. In a practical sense, most of the references to the MMC since July 1984 have followed the guidelines proposed by the then Secretary of State, Norman Tebbitt. These guidelines suggest that, apart from the statutory 'market share' criterion, references should be made to the MMC on the more practical grounds of possible loss of competition as a result of the merger. For example in 1990, the MMC rejected the Kingfisher/ Dixons merger in the UK retail market for electrical appliances, because it would 'clearly remove competition between the two market leaders; in our view it would also significantly weaken competition in the retailing of electrical appliances' (*Financial Times* 1990a).

The Companies Act of 1989 has attempted to modify and improve merger operations in two main ways. First, the Act provides for a formal pre-notification procedure to help reduce the uncertainties involved in merger policy. Under this procedure, the companies involved must submit a merger notice to the OFT, together with a completed questionnaire containing basic details of the proposed merger, and a fee to cover the cost of merger reference. In uncomplicated cases the details given in the questionnaire will be the basis of the DGFT's recommendation to the Secretary of State. Generally, companies will have automatic clearance if no merger reference is made to the MMC within twenty days of the receipt of the notice. Second, even if the DGFT has recommended that the Secretary of State should make a reference to the MMC, the Secretary of State need not in fact make the reference. Instead he might ask the companies involved in the proposed merger to sell off some of their assets in order to decrease any excess-power they may acquire as a result of the merger. If they agree to this, the Secretary of State may still allow the merger without reference to the MMC. Basically, these new aspects are merely modifications to the main aspects of merger legislation, which otherwise remain intact.

Self-regulatory controls   As well as the legal controls noted above, there are also *self-regulatory* controls on UK merger activity which are imposed by the Stock Exchange and the Panel on Takeovers and Mergers, both of which are responsible to the *Council for the Securities Industry*. The London Stock Exchange imposes self-regulatory controls on all companies which are listed on the Stock Exchange or on the Unlisted Securities Market (USM). These rules were mainly developed in order to keep all shareholders adequately informed of certain important changes in share ownership. For example, the quotations department of the Stock Exchange must be given certain information about companies which acquire more than 5% of the assets of another company or which divest more than 5% of their own assets. If the figure is between 5% and 15%, only the Stock Exchange and the press need be notified; but if the figure rises to 15% or more, the Department of Trade and Industry, the shareholders, and the press should be notified. The *Council for the Securities Industry* also issues a 'City Code on Takeovers and Mergers'. This is administered by the Panel on Takeovers and Mergers and relates to both listed and unlisted companies but not to private companies. One function of the Code is to make sure that each shareholder is treated equally during takeover bids. For example, an offer given to some shareholders early in a bid, and which they have accepted, must also be left open to all other shareholders. Another function of the Code is to set out 'rules' for the conduct of companies during a takeover, covering items such as 'insider dealing' and other complicated aspects of such bids. If companies fail to follow these rules, the Council can refuse them the facilities of the securities market.

Difficulties which can emerge during takeover bids have been clearly shown in the UK in two recent cases. The first case relates to the Egyptian Al Fayed brothers' takeover of the House of Fraser (which owns Harrods, the London store), in 1985. An investigation into the takeover by the Department of Trade and Industry in 1990, found that the brothers gave incomplete information about their finances to the Monopolies Commission and to the OFT, which were investigating the takeover in 1985. During this period, the Takeover Panel, under its self regulatory role, did not ask for detailed financial information from the Al Fayed brothers but only asked (as was normal) for a general statement of their personal wealth. The Panel relied instead on the accuracy of the information presented by the financial advisors employed by the brothers (in this case the merchant bank Kleinwort Benson) about the financial standing of the bidders. This information turned out to be incomplete and the reputation of the merchant bank was weakened. However, in addition to this unofficial control, it was possible under UK law to disqualify the Fayeds as co-directors of any UK company (under section 8 of the Company Directors Disqualification Act of 1986) for such incomplete disclosure. They were also liable to two years imprisonment for false and misleading information to the Secretary of State, the OFT and the MMC, under section 151 of the Companies Act 1989. The Secretary of State did *not* take action against the brothers, because he did not believe it to be in the long run in 'public interest'.

The second case involves the so called 'Guinness Scandal' which related to the problems of corporate fraud in the UK drinks industry during the Guinness takeover of Distillers in 1986. The takeover by Guinness involved the swapping of Guinness shares for Distillers shares, so that the higher the value placed by the market on Guinness shares, the higher would be the value of the Guinness takeover offer. To achieve this, Guinness, through its chairman and the director of financial strategy, set up a 'share support scheme' whereby other companies such as Heron International, Compagnie Internationale de Finance Commerce (linked to S&W Berisford) and Zentralsparkasseund Kommerzial Bank Wien of Austria, were asked to buy shares in Guinness in order to support the share price. If such a share support operation involved the companies in any losses, then it was agreed that these would be covered by Guinness. Also Guinness would pay a 'success' fee to these companies if the takeover itself was completed successfully. However, in the UK it is an offence in law, except in a few limited cases, for a company to provide financial assistance for the purchase of its own shares. There were other fraud and conspiracy charges involved in the case and the verdict given in August 1990 involved jail sentences for four leading businessmen. Since the Guinness bid for Distillers in 1986, the power of the Takeover Panel has been reinforced by the 1986 Financial Services Act. This requires self-regulatory organizations and professional bodies to comply with the Code, and penalizes those which fail to do so. Also disclosure requirements during takeovers have been tightened and the Stock Exchange computer now provides more detailed information on daily dealings in takeover stocks which the panel monitors and investigates if necessary.

On a wider issue, the whole question of 'insider dealing' came to the fore during this period. This type of dealing occurs when company shares are bought by those who have special privileged information about the future of the company, e.g. the possibility of an imminent takeover. By buying shares *before* a takeover announcement, for example, they can make huge gains as share prices rise when the excitement of the takeover begins. Basically, the UK has one of the most advanced insider-dealing regulations in the world. The main act is the Companies Securities (Insider Dealing) Act 1985, although it should be noted that insider dealing was made a criminal offence under the Companies Act of 1980. The 1985 Act prohibits individuals connected with a company from dealing on a recognized Stock Exchange in the securities of that company while in possession of unpublished price sensitive information. This covers not only 'insiders' but also Crown servants, lawyers and consultants, etc. who may have been supplied with information in the course of their work (*Financial Times* 1990b).

The EEC experience

Many European countries have long histories of state intervention in markets so it is hardly surprising that the European Commission accepts the case for intervention by member governments. Apart from agriculture, competition is the only area in which the EEC has been able to implement effectively a common policy across member countries. The commission can intervene to control the behaviour of monopolists, and to increase the degree of competition, through authority derived directly from the Treaty of Rome:

1. Article 85 prohibits agreements between enterprises which result in the restriction of competition (notably relating to price-fixing, market-sharing, production limitations and other restrictive practices). This article refers to any agreement affecting trade between member states and therefore applies to a large number of British industries.

2. Article 86 prohibits a dominant firm, or group of firms, from using their market power to exploit consumers.

3. Articles 92–94 prohibit government subsidies to industries or individual firms which will distort, or threaten to distort, competition.

European Economic Community competition policy has been criticized for its lack of comprehensiveness but in December 1989, the Council of Ministers agreed for the first time on specific cross border merger regulations. The criteria for judging whether a merger should be referred to the European

Commission covers three aspects. First, the companies concerned must have a combined world turnover of more than 5bn ECU. In the case of banks and insurance companies the figure is based on total assets rather than turnover. Second, at least two of the companies concerned in the merger must have a Community wide turnover of at least 250m ECU each. Third, if both parties to the merger have two thirds of their business in one and the same member state, the merger will be subject to national and not Community controls.

The Commission must be notified of merger proposals which meet the criteria noted above within one week of the announcement of the bid and it will vet each proposed merger against a concept of 'a dominant position'. Any creation or strengthening of a dominant position will be seen as incompatible with the aims of the Community if it significantly impedes 'effective competition'. The Commission has one month after notification to decide whether to start proceedings and then four months to make a final decision. If a case is being investigated by the Commission it will not also be investigated by national bodies such as the British Monopolies and Mergers Commission for example. Member states may prevent a merger which has already been permitted by the Community only if it involves public security, involves some aspects of the media or if competition in the local markets is threatened. The new policy took effect in September 1990 and it is thought that it will result in only 40 to 50 cases per year because the thresholds for investigations are so high.

There have been some reservations about the legislation. First, a main aim of the legislation was to introduce the 'one stop shop' which means that merging companies would either be liable to European *or* national merger control and not both. However, as can be seen above, there are situations where national merger control can override EC control in certain instances so that there may be a 'two stop shop'! Second, it is not clear how the rules will apply to non EC companies. For example, it is quite possible that two US or Japanese companies each with the required amount of *sales* in the Community, but with no actual Community *presence*, could merge. While such a case would certainly fall within the EC merger rules, it is not yet clear how seriously the Commission would pursue its powers in such cases. Third, guidelines are also needed on joint ventures. The new regulations make a distinction between 'concentrative' joint ventures and 'cooperative' joint ventures which needs further clarification. The new Commission rules apply to the first type which is seen to concentrate power, but not to the second (which is merely seen as a method to coordinate competitive behaviour). The second type will be covered by articles 85 and 86 of the Treaty of Rome as before. As can be seen, there are still problems to be resolved, but the first major breakthrough has been achieved.

The EC merger vetting process described above has been developed alongside another set of proposals which cover the behaviour of companies during a takeover, i.e. takeover rules. The aim of the so called 13th company law directive is to govern the way in which European takeovers are conducted. Once adopted, the directive will have statutory power in the member states and thus bring to an end the informal non statutory UK approach to the regulation of bids and deals through such bodies as the UK Takeover Panel. The amendments to the directive on January 1990 involved four alterations. First, it limited the field of application of the rules to companies quoted on a Stock Exchange. Second, predators now have to explain how they intend to finance the bid and what the financial effect of the bid will be on the target company. Third, companies can call an extraordinary general meeting during the offer period in which case the 'takeover bid shall be suspended from the day on which this meeting is called to the day after it is held'. Finally, the amendment sets down a number of guiding principles for the supervisory authorities of each member state.

The US experience

American legislation reflects a much more vigilant attitude towards mergers, dating from the Sherman Anti-Trust Act of 1890. Monopolies were considered illegal from the outset, resulting in a much less flexible approach to the control of monopoly power.

Since 1968, US merger guidelines have directed attention to the market power exerted by the four largest companies in any market. The rigidity of using merely the four largest companies (see the discussion on Fig. 5.4 below) for evaluating merger proposals has been extensively criticized, and in June 1982 the US Justice Department issued new proposals. These included establishing a new 'screening' index to alert the Justice Department as to which merger proposals were worthy of closer scrutiny and which should be immediately prohibited or 'nodded through'. That index was to reflect the whole market and not just the four largest firms.

The so-called 'Herfindahl–Hirschman Index' of market concentration was devised for this screening purpose, together with a number of guidelines for policy action. This index is constructed simply as:

$$\sum_{i=1}^{n} (\% \text{ market share})^2$$

for all n companies in the market. Using a squaring procedure places greater emphasis on the large firms in the market. We can illustrate this by first considering an index which adopts an additive procedure. If a simple additive procedure had been used[5] over all n companies:

Fig. 5.4 Hypothetical markets in the construction of market concentration indices

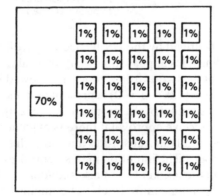

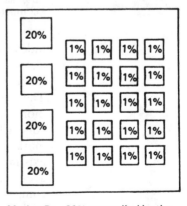

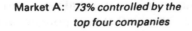

Market A: *73% controlled by the top four companies*

Market B: *80% controlled by the top four companies*

Market A : Index = 1(70) + 30(1) = 100
Market B : Index = 4(20) + 20(1) = 100

Here the markets would be evaluated as equally competitive, yet a strong
case could be made for Market B being the more competitive. Using the
Herfindahl–Hirschman Index we have:

Market A : Index = $1(70)^2 + 30(1)^2 = 4,930$
Market B : Index = $4(20)^2 + 20(1)^2 = 1,620$

The lower the index, the more competitive the market, so that Market B is
deemed more competitive. The index could, in fact, vary in value from
10,000 (i.e. 100^2) for a pure monopoly, to almost zero for a perfectly
competitive industry. For example, an industry consisting of 1,000 companies
each with a tiny 0.1% share of the market would produce an index value of
only 10 (i.e. $1,000(0.1)^2$).

Once constructed, the interpretation of the index is still, however,
subjective. Figure 5.5 illustrates the range of the index and the three zones of

Fig. 5.5 The Herfindahl
Index as an instrument of
merger policy

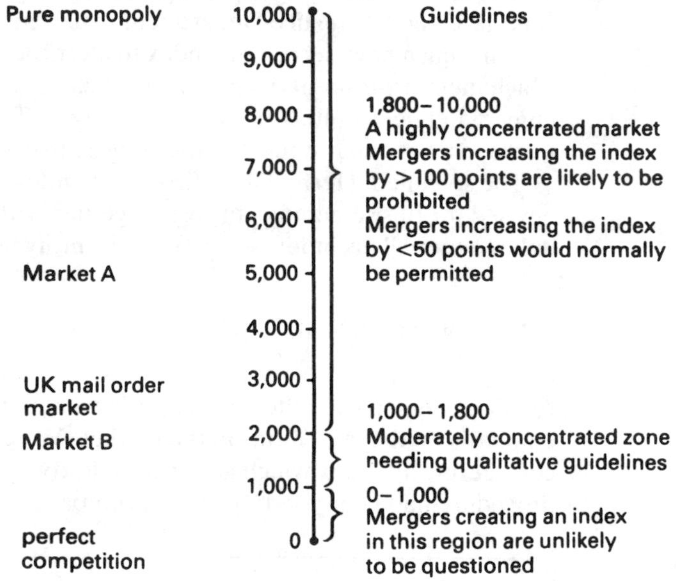

Pure monopoly	10,000	Guidelines
	9,000	
	8,000	**1,800–10,000** A highly concentrated market Mergers increasing the index
	7,000	by >100 points are likely to be prohibited
	6,000	Mergers increasing the index by <50 points would normally
Market A	5,000	be permitted
	4,000	
UK mail order market	3,000	**1,000–1,800**
Market B	2,000	Moderately concentrated zone needing qualitative guidelines
	1,000	**0–1,000**
perfect competition	0	Mergers creating an index in this region are unlikely to be questioned

index value identified by the US Justice Department for policy purposes. The
chosen dividing lines appear somewhat arbitrary, though it is clear from the
guidelines that the two extreme zones are viewed in radically different lights.
The central zone (1,000–1,800) represents a policy 'grey' area, requiring
more detailed scrutiny of the proposed merger. In practice, mergers in this
zone will only receive approval if there is evidence of easy entry into the
market, freely available substitutes and no collusive arrangements between
existing members. The intention in this central zone is to prevent further
acquisitions in the market by a market leader, whilst allowing smaller
companies to combine more freely. The 'highly concentrated' zone (> 1,800)
of the index would, for instance, include any market in which two companies
have shares of over 30%, so that their potential for growth of market share

by further acquisition is slim – even the addition to one of these firms of a further 2% of acquisition would trigger the 100-point condition. Yet in the same market, two smaller companies with market shares of less than 5% each could combine without infringing anti-trust policies. The purchase of just one of the competing companies in hypothetical Market A of Fig. 5.4 by the dominant firm would increase the index to 5,070 (i.e. $1(71)^2 + 29(1)^2$), triggering the 100-point condition in the process and attracting the attentions of the Justice Department.

It is both interesting and instructive to note how such guidelines might operate within a UK context if they were used to produce a more systematic approach to mergers. Figure 5.6 shows the 1982 market shares of the

Fig. 5.6 Market share of UK catalogue mail order business (1982)
Source: EIU Retail Business, Aug. 1982

£2,370m. UK catalogue mail-order business. The individual market shares would produce an overall market index of at least 2,872 (i.e. $1(40)^2 + 1(32)^2 + 1(12)^2 + 1(6)^2 + 1(8)^2 + 1(2)^2$). In 1982 Great Universal Stores (with Marshall Ward, Trafford and John England catalogues) attempted to merge with Empire Stores. The bid was referred to the MMC, ultimately rejected, and the proposal abandoned. Great Universal Stores was ordered to reduce its shareholding in Empire Stores from 29.9 to 10%.

Had the market index been in operation such a combine would have increased its value to 3,352 (i.e. $1(46)^2 + 1(32)^2 + 1(12)^2 + 1(8)^2 + 1(2)^2$), an increase of 480 points, clearly in contravention of the US guidelines. With such a system it would have been apparent to Great Universal Stores from the outset that such a merger was bound to fail, and they would have been saved the considerable cost of building up a substantial shareholding in Empire. Interestingly, the same guidelines would allow an Empire–Grattan combine, but prevent an Empire–Grattan–Freemans combine being created as a substantial third force in mail-order, since the index would rise by 96 and 332 points respectively, the latter triggering the 100-point condition.

Such an index could not, however, cope with vertical or conglomerate mergers since they cannot be viewed merely in terms of increasing market concentration. As a result, even with this index, non-horizontal mergers between companies in different industries or market sectors remain an area of uncertainty in terms of Justice Department reaction. This is particularly serious as the large majority of mergers in the USA are of the conglomerate type (Smith 1983).

Corporate restructuring

Two of the most important developments during the 1980s and early 1990s have been the acceleration in the trend towards corporate restructuring, and the financing of takeovers by 'leveraged debt'.

While larger mergers have been continuing, other forms of restructuring seem to have gone against this trend (Gressle 1990). Restructuring has taken two directions; the taking apart of diversified conglomerates, and the putting together of focused global companies. There are obvious advantages in creating diversified conglomerates, such as less risk of financial distress and a decreased threat of being taken over. However, in recent years many larger conglomerates have found that they need to concentrate on operating a more limited range of companies, especially those which can generate cash. For example, companies involved in major disinvestment and restructuring in 1989 included the Gateway Corporation's sale of sixty-one of its stores to Asda, and the sale by Grand Metropolitan of its William Hill (betting shops) interest to Brent Walker (UK). Disinvestment by UK companies of their foreign subsidiaries in 1989 included the sale by Sir James Goldsmith of the US supermarket chain, Grand Union, and the sale by Hanson of American Aggregates (US). Similarly, ICI sold its ICI (non-prescription drugs) (US) arm and Grand Metropolitan sold its S&A Restaurants (US) in the same year.

The restructuring of companies into a relatively more focused area of operation has been made more possible by the emergence in the UK and abroad of the 'leveraged buyout'. This means that companies obtain a high percentage of the finance they need in order to takeover another company by issuing high interest unsecured bonds (Junk Bonds) or by borrowing through high interest unsecured loans (mezzanine finance). The former was a method favoured in the US while the latter form of borrowing is the favoured UK method. This development has had two important repercussions for corporate strategy. First, it has meant that even managers of very large companies can be subject to a takeover bid from a smaller company which has managed to borrow large amounts of debt finance. Being large *per se* is, therefore, no guarantee of safety from being taken over. Second, it has become easier, through leveraged buyouts, to take over a large diversified conglomerate, to sell off parts of it, and then to re-focus the company on its 'core' activity. There has been a tendency in recent years for such 'deconglomeration' to be used in order to increase the cash flow of an acquiring company, thereby helping to service the larger debt created by the takeover, while also increasing the competitiveness of the company in its core activities, to the benefit of shareholders.

A classic example of this type of activity was the unsuccessful attempt in 1990 by the Hoylake consortium (led by Sir James Goldsmith, Jacob Rothschild and Kerry Packer) to take over British and American Tobacco (BAT) of the UK, the ninth largest company in Europe. BAT had grown to be a large conglomerate through various acquisitions in the 1980s and had diversified into retailing and financial services in addition to its original tobacco interests. The aim of the Hoylake consortium was to take over the conglomerate and then to sell off many of its parts in order to concentrate on the cash generating core, mainly around the tobacco activity. In this way the companies earnings would rise and earnings per share for the shareholders would be increased. Although the takeover bid failed, it forced BAT to restructure its business in order to concentrate more on its core activities and to think more closely of the rewards it was offering to its shareholders. The collapse of the 'junk' bond market and the demise of Drexdel Burnham Lambert in the US during early 1990 has temporarily restrained the drift towards corporate restructuring through high leveraged buy outs, but this may be a temporary decline which may be reversed when interest rates fall during the early 1990s.

Conclusion

Corporate restructuring through mergers and acquisitions became increasingly important during the 1980s, as it had been during particular periods between 1958 and 1972. The growth of conglomerate type mergers has accelerated, although in recent years 'deconglomeration' has also been in evidence. Economic theory and statistical analysis do little to suggest that there are substantial benefits from merger activity, although such activity does appear consistent with managerial motives, such as higher status and remuneration.

UK legislation on Mergers and Takeovers has required some modification in order to tighten controls and to clarify the relationship between the Secretary of State and institutions such as OFT and the MMC. The Guinness and House of Fraser affairs have reflected both the undesirable aspects of merger 'mania' and the need for more vigilance from the regulatory institutions. On a more global scale, the chapter has looked at merger regulation in the US and in the EC in order to enquire how control of mergers is being exercised outside the UK framework.

Notes

1. This refers to the fact that a higher level of output may be required before the separate processes involved in producing the good 'dovetail' so that there is no idle capacity. Suppose two processes are required to produce good X. Process A needs a specialized machine which can produce twenty units per hour and Process B needs a machine able to produce thirty units per hour. Only when output has risen to sixty units per hour will there be no idle capacity. For smaller output than sixty at least one machine cannot be fully used.
2. This figure combines two sets of different data on mergers. The first series (dashed line) is derived from consolidated company accounts and is published annually by the DTI. The second series (continuous line) is collected by the DTI from public announcements of bids and is published quarterly in *Business Monitor* MQ7. The break in the diagram occurs where the two series overlap.

3. The IRC was formed in 1967 by the Labour Government. Its aim was to promote or assist the reorganization or development of any industry or enterprise in order to increase efficiency and profitability of the UK economy and to help the export drive. Between 1966 and 1971 it was associated with a number of major mergers, including those between Leyland/BMC and AEI/GEC–English Electric.

4. The decision to overturn the MMC decision was actually made by the Minister for Trade, to whom the decision was delegated by the secretary of state, the latter having declared himself an interested shareholder. This delegation resulted in Anderson Strathclyde taking the Government to court on February 1983 on the grounds that the minister had exceeded his powers. But a ruling on 3 February 1983 found that the Minister for Trade *has* power to act on behalf of the Secretary of State for Trade in deciding whether a merger should proceed after the MMC has ruled against it. The 3 February decision also ruled that the minister is not bound to adopt the commission's majority view but is entitled to take the view of the minority into account.

5. Of course, an additive procedure on these lines would not be used since in all market cases the index would equal 100. We merely use this example for purposes of illustration.

References

Aaronovitch, S. and **Sawyer, M.** (1975) Mergers, growth and concentration, *Oxford Economic Papers*, **27**, 1, March.

Cosh, A. D., Hughes, A. and **Singh, M. S.** (1980) The causes and effects of takeovers in the UK: an empirical investigation for the late 1940s at the microeconomic level in D. C. Mueller (ed), *The Determinants and Effects of Mergers*, Gelschlager, Gunn and Hain.

Cosh, A. D., Hughes, A. and **Singh, M. S.** (1985) Institutional investment, company performance and mergers: Empirical evidence for the UK: *A report to the Office of Fair Trading*. Mimeo, Cambridge.

Cowling, K. *et al.* (1980) *Mergers and Economic Performance*. CUP, Cambridge, Ch. 5.

Elliot, D. and **Gribbin, J. D.** (1977) The abolition of cartels and structural change in the United Kingdom, in: Jacquemin, A. P. and de Jong, H. W. (eds) *Welfare Aspects of Industrial Markets*. Leidin Nijhoff, The Hague.

Fairburn, J. and **Kay, J.** (1989) *Mergers and Merger Policy*. OUP.

Financial Times (1990a) Chain reaction leads to lower prices, 24 May, p. 2.

Financial Times (1990b) Insider dealing in the UK, 1 February.

Firth, M. (1979) The profitability of takeovers and mergers, *Economic Journal*, **89**.

Firth, M. (1980) Takeovers, shareholders' return and the theory of the firm, *Economic Journal*, **82**.

Gort, M. (1969) An economic disturbance theory of mergers, *Quarterly Journal of Economics*, **82**.

Gressle, M. (1990) A theme for the 1990s: Corporate Restructuring, *Acquisitions Monthly*, Jan.

Hannah, L. (1976) *The Rise of the Corporate Economy*. Methuen.

Kuehn, D. A. (1975) *Takeovers and the Theory of the Firm*. Macmillan.
Kumar, M. S. (1985) Growth, acquisition and firm size: evidence from the United Kingdom, *The Journal of Industrial Economics*, **33**, March.
Meeks, G. (1977) *Disappointing Marriage: a study of the gains from merger*. University of Cambridge, Department of Applied Economics, Occasional Paper 51, CUP, Cambridge.
Meeks, G. and **Whittington, G.** (1975) Director's pay, growth and profitability, *Journal of Industrial Economics*, **24**, 1, Sept.
Newbold, A. (1970) *Management and Merger Activity*. Guthstead, Liverpool.
Prais, S. J. (1976) *The Evolution of Giant Firms in Britain*. CUP, Cambridge.
Singh, A. (1971) *Takeovers*. CUP, Cambridge.
Singh, A. (1975) Takeovers, economic natural selection and the theory of the firm: evidence from the post-war United Kingdom experience, *Economic Journal*, **85**, Sept.
Smith, M. (1983) Make merger policy mechanical. *Accountancy Age*, 12 May.
Utton, M. A. (1974) 'On measuring the effects of industrial mergers', *Scottish Journal of Political Economy*, **21**.
Whittington, G. (1980) The profitability and size of UK companies, *The Journal of Industrial Economics*, **28**, 4, June.

6   Oligopoly

In this chapter we first record the growth of market domination by the few, using the most recent statistics on the size distribution of firms, on concentration ratios, and on advertising expenditures. We then consider attempts to explain and predict behaviour in oligopoly markets, closely relating theory to actual practice. Attempts to explain firm behaviour when there is no collusion have involved various reaction curve models (including kinked demand), and more recently game theory. However, collusion can and does take place, sometimes formally, as in cartels, or more often tacitly, under various types of price leadership.

Definition and measurement of oligopoly

Oligopoly may be defined as an industry in which there are few firms and many buyers. However, this definition begs two important questions. First, how many is 'few'? Broadly speaking, the number of firms should be sufficiently small for there to be 'conscious interdependence', with each firm aware that its future prospects depend not only on its own policies, but also on those of its rivals. Second, what is an industry? In theory, an industry is defined as a group of firms whose products are close substitutes for one another (i.e. the products have high and positive cross-elasticities of demand).[1] In practice, precise calculations of cross-elasticities of demand are impossible to make, and an industry is defined either by approximate similarity of output (such as the confectionery industry), or by similarity of the major input (such as the rubber industry, which makes a wide variety of goods from shoe soles to tyres).

Bearing in mind these problems of precise definition, the rise of oligopoly can be charted in a variety of ways.

The size distribution of firms

The progressive domination of manufacturing industry by a smaller number of large firms is shown in Table 6.1. The firm unit of most interest to our analysis is the business unit (enterprise) which may, of course, contain more than one productive unit (plant or establishment). Between 1958 (when data for the enterprise were first available) and 1968, larger firms captured a dramatically increased share both of total employment and total output in manufacturing. In fact, the share of firms with over 20,000 employees increased by 50% in terms of employment and over 40% in terms of output. Since then, this tendency towards increased concentration has not only eased but gone into reverse (see Ch. 3), with the figures for the latest year of data, 1987, below those for 1958 for firms with over 20,000 employees. Indeed, in

Table 6.1 Size distribution
of private manufacturing
firms by employment size

Employment size of enterprise (greater than)	Total employment (%)			Total net output (%)		
	1958	1968	1987	1958	1968	1987
2,000	45.8	58.6	44.0	50.6	63.0	50.7
5,000	34.3	46.8	32.4	38.3	50.7	37.4
10,000	24.8	37.0	22.7	28.2	40.0	24.5
20,000	17.3	26.6	13.3	20.0	28.5	14.5

Source: Business Monitor (1989) and earlier dates.

1987 the share of firms with over 2,000 employees was actually *smaller* in terms of employment and showed no increase in terms of output, as compared to 1958, clearly indicating the resurgence of the small firm.

Concentration ratios

Perhaps the most usual method of measuring the degree of oligopoly is through concentration ratios. These show the proportion of output or employment in a given industry, or product grouping, accounted for by, say, the five largest firms. Table 6.2 shows that concentration has increased substantially since 1963 for the majority of products presented. Take flour production; in 1963 the five largest firms contributed only 51% of UK output, by 1977 that contribution had risen to 85.7%. Table 6.2 presents the only data available for *product groups*. However, we can obtain more recent data if we use *industrial groups*. This is reflected in Table 6.3 which presents five-firm concentration ratios for both net output and employment.

Table 6.2 Five-firm
concentration ratio for
selected product groups
1963–77

Product	1963 (%)	1977 (%)
Beer	50.5	62.2
Biscuits	65.5	79.7
Bread	71.4	81.2
Cars	91.2	98.4
Cotton cloth	19.3	46.1
Flour	51.0	85.7
Optical instruments	50.7	67.3
Pharmaceuticals	53.9	63.2
Raincoats	22.3	54.7
Refrigerators	71.9	98.8
Wallpapers	95.6	79.7
Washing machines	85.2	96.2

Source: Business Monitor (1980).

Table 6.3 shows that some *industrial groups* are more dominated by large firms than others. In the tobacco industry the five largest firms account for 99% of net output and 98% of employment, whereas in the leather goods industry the five largest firms account for a mere 10% of net output and employment.

Table 6.3 Five-firm concentration ratio for selected industrial groups in 1987

	Net output (%)	Employment (%)
Tobacco	99	98
Cement, lime and plaster	89	89
Motor vehicles and their engines	79	84
Aerospace equipment manufacture and repair	74	73
Ice cream, cocoa, chocolate and sugar confectionery	64	54
Glass and glassware	56	45
Domestic type electrical appliances	54	54
Insulated wire and cable	52	59
Pharmaceutical products	47	35
Footwear	42	39
Brewing and malting	39	41
Textile finishing	29	29
Printing and publishing	18	15
Leather goods	10	10

Source: Business Monitor (1989).

Although three- and five-firm concentration ratios are the most useful in assessing changes in concentration for particular products and industries *within* manufacturing, the 100-firm concentration ratio is useful for the manufacturing sector as a whole (Table 6.4). This ratio can be traced back as far as 1909, and gives an indication of the progressive concentration of economic power within that sector of the economy, at least until the mid/late 1970s. Since then, the domination of the largest 100 firms has begun to recede.

Table 6.4 Share of 100 largest private firms in manufacturing net output by output size

Year	(%)
1909	16.0
1924	22.0
1935	24.0
1949	22.0
1958	32.0
1963	37.0
1968	41.0
1975	41.7
1981	41.0
1983	38.8
1984	38.8
1987	38.1

Sources: Sawyer (1981); *Business Monitor* (1989).

Overall, Tables 6.2–6.4 reveal a clear tendency for markets to be dominated by a few large firms, though with a resurgence of smaller-firm activity in recent years. The concentration ratios for product groups presented in Table 6.2 are also useful in revealing a further characteristic of oligopoly, namely the increased differentiation and branding of products. Large firms often compete with each other in *specific product groups*, so that the concentration ratios in product groups can be very high. For instance, the concentration ratio in the *product* beer is higher than that in the *industry* brewing and malting. Similarly, as we can see from Table 6.2, the five largest firms selling refrigerators and washing machines in the UK account for over 95% of the market in both product groups, but the five-firm concentration ratio for the industrial group 'Domestic electrical appliances' is much lower (Table 6.3). This is because makers such as LEC, Hotpoint and Tricity in refrigerators, and Hotpoint, Hoover and Creda in washing machines, *each produce* a variety of models themselves. To the consumer, therefore, the rise of oligopoly may not be immediately apparent. There may often *seem* to be extensive competition between a wide variety of brands of product. In fact, these are often produced by only a few major competing firms. The market for soap powders is one example, with most of the leading brands produced by Procter and Gamble and Lever Brothers. By using product groups, we can move behind the veil of branding to see the true extent of market domination by the few.

Advertising expenditure

Data on advertising are a useful, if indirect method, for gauging both the rise of oligopoly markets, and the tendency towards product differentiation. Advertising is essentially aimed at binding consumers to particular brands for reasons other than price. Recent estimates in the USA of branded, processed foods, put their prices almost 9% higher than 'private label' equivalents – similar products packaged under the retailer's own name – due solely to more extensive media advertising.[2] It is the highly concentrated (oligopoly) markets, with extensive branding, that spend most on advertising, as can be seen from Table 6.5.

Table 6.5 Top twenty brands 1989; advertising league

Rank	Brands	Expenditure (£000s)		
		Feb 89–Jan 90	TV	Press
1	Water Authorities Flotation	22482	11633	10849
2	Woolworths	20827	9437	11390
3	Sky Television	17214	5097	12117
4	Water and Sewage Businesses	16266	12019	4247
5	B & Q	14980	2209	12771
6	McDonalds	14974	14624	351
7	Tesco	14214	3700	10513
8	Currys	13784	344	13440
9	Benson & Hedges Special Filter	13764	0	13764
10	MFI Hygena	12910	1343	11568
11	Dixons	12269	580	11689
12	Texas Home Care	11642	1455	10187
13	Comet	11570	5329	6240
14	Rover Group Rover 2000	11546	6146	5400
15	Fiat Uno	11024	5402	5622
16	Ford Fiesta	10702	5961	4741
17	British Telecom Call Stimulation	10172	10105	67
18	NDC/MMB Milk	10122	8055	2067
19	Asda	10093	1745	8349
20	Yellow Pages	9851	9851	0

Source: Campaign Report (1990).

Oligopoly

Table 6.5 shows advertising expenditure figures for the top twenty UK *brands* between February 1989 and January 1990. The table is dominated by three sectors, the retail sector, the automobile sector, and advertising related to the privatization of water. The spread of such expenditure between television and the press depends on whether the advertiser wants to strive for a high profile image (in which case the brand needs the immediacy of television), or whether advertisers want to communicate rather more complex messages, which tends to favour a greater usage of the press.

Another way of understanding the impact of advertising on oligopolistic markets is to study the total advertising expenditure of the top twenty *companies*, as listed in Table 6.6.

Table 6.6 Top twenty companies 1989; advertising league

Rank	Advertiser	Expenditure (£m)	
		Feb 89–Jan 90	Jan–Dec 88
1	Procter and Gamble	61.54	65.07
2	Kellogg Company of Great Britain	50.20	44.08
3	Lever Brothers	45.17	31.88
4	British Telecom	44.87	43.80
5	Water Authorities Association	39.11	0.01
6	Ford	37.86	29.50
7	Nestlé	35.14	37.77
8	Rover Group	32.81	29.31
9	The Electricity Council	32.26	30.61
10	Mars Confectionery	31.89	32.92
11	Halifax Building Society	30.22	18.70
12	Gallaher Tobacco UK	29.36	28.39
13	Pedigree Petfoods	27.55	36.02
14	H. J. Heinz Co	25.93	19.91
15	Renault UK	25.72	21.15
16	Volkswagen Audi Group (VAG UK)	25.67	17.24
17	British Gas	25.34	21.35
18	Elida Gibbs	24.88	25.62
19	Midland Bank	24.66	22.94
20	Procter and Gamble (Health and Beauty)	24.64	20.41

Source: Campaign Report (1990).

Here we see the presence of rival companies much more clearly. For example, two companies which compete aggressively with each other in the *household stores and toiletries* sectors are Procter and Gamble and Lever Brothers, and in the year ending January 1990 they were first and third in the advertising league. If we take the clothes washing market, Procter and Gamble's products (such as Ariel automatic washing powder) are in competition with Lever Brothers' products (such as Persil automatic and the more recent Radion automatic introduced in the early 1990s). In the *automobile industry*, companies such as Ford, the Rover Group, Renault UK and Volkswagen Audi Group (VAG UK) are all included in the top twenty advertisers. Indeed, if we take the top thirty-two advertisers, then Peugeot Talbot, Citroen UK and Fiat Auto UK are also included. In the small car market, for example, there was intense competition between Ford and Fiat, with the newly designed Ford Fiesta and the Fiat Uno competing fiercely for share of the UK market. Finally, it is also worth noting the presence of two very large *confectionery* groups in the top twenty advertisers. Although Nestlé and Mars confectionery dominated the sector's advertising in this period, they were also in competition with two other giants, Rowntree Mackintosh and Cadbury Schweppes, which were twenty-sixth and twenty-eighth in the advertising league, respectively. These confectionery companies all sell extensive branded goods and compete intensely with each other.

Not only is UK advertising dominated by companies promoting product differentiation, but the market itself is also growing rapidly. The MEAL research company estimated that the top 100 advertisers in the UK increased their expenditures by over 50% between 1984 and 1987, and a further 16% between 1988 and 1990. The rise of oligopoly markets – dominance of a few large firms producing differentiated products – is therefore reflected in both the structure and rapid growth of UK advertising. Moreover, if extra advertising is 'successful', raising the attachment of consumers to particular brands, then the rapid growth of UK advertising is itself a useful index of increasing product differentiation, at least in the minds of consumers.

Oligopoly in theory and practice

The central task of market theory is to predict how firms will set prices and output. In perfect competition and pure monopoly we can make definite predictions. In perfect competition it can be shown that in the long run price will be equal to the lowest possible average costs of the firm – what Adam Smith called 'the natural price'. In pure monopoly the firm seeking to maximize profits will restrict output and raise prices until marginal revenue exactly equals marginal cost.

In oligopoly, where there are few firms in the market, and where there is product differentiation, there can be no such precision. Where the number of firms is sufficiently small for each firm to be aware of the pricing policy of its rivals, it will have to try to anticipate its rivals' reactions to its own pricing decision. Further, where products are differentiated, the firm will have to estimate the degree of brand loyalty customers have for its products – the greater that loyalty, the smaller the effect of price changes on consumer demand. This constant need to anticipate the reaction both of rivals and consumers, creates a high degree of uncertainty in oligopoly markets.

Despite this uncertainty, the importance of the oligopoly-type of market structure in modern economies has encouraged the quest for theories to explain and predict firm behaviour. Although little progress seems to have been made in devising a general theory of oligopoly behaviour, some progress has been made in understanding the behaviour of *particular* firms in *particular* oligopoly situations. We might usefully review a number of such theories, keeping a close eye on firm practice.

Non-collusive oligopoly

First, we consider situations in which each firm decides upon its strategy without any formal or even tacit collusion between rivals. There are essentially three approaches the firm can adopt to handle interdependence when oligopoly is non-collusive:

1. The firm could assume that whatever it decides to do, its rivals *will not* react, i.e. they will ignore its strategies. This assumption may reasonably be valid for day-to-day, routine decisions, but is hardly realistic for major initiatives. The Cournot duopoly model[3] is, however, of this type. Each firm simply observes what the other does, and then adopts a strategy that maximizes its own profits. It makes no attempt to evaluate potential reactions by the rival firm to its own profit-maximizing strategy.

2. The firm could assume that rivals *will* react to its own strategies, and use past experience to assess the form that reaction might take. This 'learning' process underlies the reaction-curve model of Stackleberg.[4] It also underlies the kinked-demand model (see below), with firms learning that rivals do not match price increases, but certainly do match any price reductions.

3. Instead of using past experience to assess future reactions by rivals, the firm itself could try to identify the *best possible* move the opposition could make to each of its own strategies. The firm could then plan countermeasures if the rival reacts in this (for the rival) optimal way. As we see below, this is the essence of game theory.

Approaches (2) and (3) might lead us to expect a considerable amount of price movement, as rivals incessantly formulate strategy and counter-strategy. In practice, however, the oligopolistic industries experience *short bursts* of price-changing activity (often linked to price warfare), together with longer periods of relatively stable or rigid prices. We briefly review these two types of situation, noting the relevance of kinked-demand theory to stable prices, and conclude our discussion of non-collusive behaviour with an outline of game theory.

Price warfare   Price-cutting is a well-attested strategy for oligopoly firms, both for raising and defending market share. This can, of course, lead to a competitive downward spiral in firm prices, resembling a 'price war'. Examples of this abound. We will see, in Chapter 9, how price warfare developed in the late 1970s and early 1980s amongst petrol retailers. This was largely due to a change in strategy by the major oil-refiners. In a static total market, the majors began to compete amongst themselves, each hoping that by raising market share it could more fully utilize expensive refining capacity. Instead of offering similar discounts to retailers who sold their petrol exclusively, the majors now sought to outstrip one another in size of discount. The monthly cost of discounts in 1983 was around £7m. for Shell, and £6m. for BP. Price warfare between petrol retailers was therefore largely subsidized by the major oil-refiners.

In the grocery trade, Tesco's price cuts in June 1977 (Checkout 1977) and again in May 1982 (Checkout 1982), both led to periods of price warfare. Tesco, Asda and Sainsbury's are the three largest firms in the grocery trade, with nearly 40% of total sales. Tesco launched Checkout 1982 with 1,500 new price cuts of between 3% and 25%, and spent £7m. on television advertising. In the short run Tesco raised its market share by 12% in eight weeks, though competitive price reactions by both Asda and Sainsbury's subsequently modified these gains.

With European competition increasing, it is possible that price warfare situations may be induced by foreign firms entering the UK market for the first time. For example Aldi, a major German food retailer, set up its first two supermarkets in the suburbs of Birmingham in 1990 with the intention of selling a narrow range of products but at a large discount (*Marketing Week*, 1990). Their policy was not only to sell familiar *brands* (such as Kellogs and Mars bars) cheaper, but also to lower prices on a large range of their *own products* by keeping staffing, advertising and design costs to a minimum. If such new competition is successful then it is possible that price wars could once again spread from the discount stores such as Aldi, Kwik Save and Lo-Cost to the big food retailers. Whatever the outcome of this new foreign competition, it is certain that the main casualties will be the small corner shops.

In the holiday business, 1985 saw the most fierce outbreak of price warfare for a decade. The holiday business was dominated by five firms, who together accounted for 44% of the market. Thompson Holidays reacted to a price cut by the smaller Enterprise Holidays Ltd by cutting the price of its holidays by an average of 17%. Intasun, Thompson's closest rival, responded with a similar price cut, as did Horizon. As a result of price warfare, Thompson estimated that they would earn only £2.50 on an average £300 holiday. However, they anticipated that the strategy may yield future benefits, by raising their market share to 30% by the late 1980's, with some 100 smaller tour operators being unable to match the price cuts and being forced out of business.

Clearly in oligopolistic markets, where only a few firms dominate, a price-cutting strategy by one is likely to be followed by others. After short bursts of price warfare, the market may settle down into prolonged periods of price stability, although the fact that firms no longer compete in price may not mean an absence of competition. In periods of price stability, non-price competition often becomes more intense, with advertising, packaging and other promotional activities now used to raise or defend market share. For example, Asda has advertised intensively since 1982, spending more than Tesco and Sainsbury's on this form of competition. These three companies continued to use advertising as an important form of non-price competition into the 1990s, with Tesco spending £14.2m on advertising followed by Sainsbury (£10.5m) and Asda (£10.1m) in the year ending January 1990. Coupled with this overall advertising strategy, there have been other efforts at product differentiation. For example, there has been the increasing use of the environment as a marketing tool. Tesco, Sainsbury and others have become linked into competitive 'green grocer' campaigns to promote environmentally friendly products.

Interestingly, the intense price competition in the holiday industry during the middle of the 1980s and the slump in the market a few years later, left the industry with falling profit margins. As a result, Thompson Travel became increasingly engaged in non-price competition in order to increase its market share. It did this by increasing its advertising of 'quality destinations and resorts' and by providing better holiday insurance cover than its rivals.

At the same time these non-price strategies increase product differentiation, real or imagined. We might note that any extra brand loyalty induced by non-price competition, by making demand curves less elastic, gives the firm more opportunity to raise prices at a later date.[5]

Price stability　　That price in oligopoly will tend to have periods of stability is, in fact, predicted by economic theory.

Kinked demand.　　In 1939 Hall and Hitch in the UK and Sweezy in the USA proposed a theory to explain why prices often remain stable in oligopoly markets, even when costs rise. A central feature of that theory was the existence of a kinked-demand curve.

　　To illustrate this we take an oligopolistic market which sells similar, but not identical products, i.e. there is some measure of product differentiation. If one firm raises its price, it will then lose some, though not all, of its custom to rivals. Similarly, if the firm reduces its price it will attract some, though not all, of its rivals' custom. How much custom is lost or gained will depend partly on whether the rivals follow the initial price change.

　　Extensive interviews with managers of firms in oligopoly markets led Hall and Hitch to conclude that most firms have learned a common lesson from past experience of how rivals react. Namely, that if the firm were to raise its price above the current level (*P* in Fig. 6.1), its rivals *would not* follow, content to let the firm lose sales to them. The firm will then expect its demand curve to be relatively elastic (*dK*) for price rises. However, if the firm were to reduce its price, rivals *would* follow to protect their market share, so that the firm gains few extra sales. The firm will then expect its demand curve to be relatively inelastic (*KD'*) for price reductions. Overall the firm will believe that its demand curve is kinked at the current price *P*, as in Fig. 6.1.

Fig. 6.1 Kinked demand curve and price stability

Notes: d–d' = Demand curve when rivals *do not* follow price changes
D–D' = Demand curve when rivals *do* follow price changes
dKD' = Kinked demand curve
dLMN = Associated marginal revenue curve

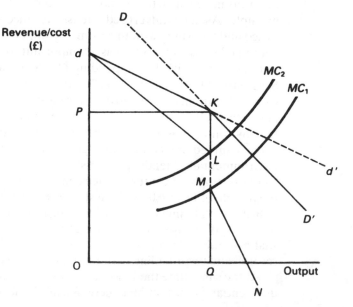

One can intuitively see why this belief will lead to price stickiness, since the firm will rapidly lose market share if it raises price, and gain little from reducing price. A kinked-demand (average revenue) curve of the form dKD', will have a discontinuity $(L - M)$ in its associated marginal revenue curve below the kink point K.[6] The marginal cost curve could then vary between MC_1 and MC_2 without causing the firm to alter its profit-maximizing price P (or its output Q).

A number of industries have exhibited price stability, despite rising costs. The confectionery industry, presently dominated by Mars, Rowntree Mackintosh and Cadbury Schweppes, is a good example of this tendency. During some periods in the 1980s, price wars were often avoided, though competition between these companies still continued in other forms. For example, in the mid 1980s non-price competition took the form of product weight. In one such period, Mars raised the weight of Mars bars by 10%; Cadburys raised the weight of its Fruit and Nut by 14% and Rowntree Mackintosh raised the weight of Cabana by 15% and increased the chocolate content of KitKat by 5%. In all of these cases the firms accepted rises in their costs, i.e. more ingredients per bar, *without changing price*.

Similarly in 1990, competition in the UK snacks market increased as the three major companies, KP Foods, Smiths and Walkers (owned by the US company, PepsiCo), and Golden Wonder (the Dalgetty subsidiary), looked for new ways of competing. KP foods introduced its new crisp-like snack called 'Frisp' and spent £4.4m on marketing it in the first three months alone. To prevent being squeezed out by its two big rivals, Golden Wonder planned to launch a few new products in the middle of 1990 and in the meantime increased the packet size of all its crisps and snacks from 28 gm to 30 gm *without raising prices*. In terms of our kinked oligopoly model, the companies noted above preferred to accept the higher costs of non-price competition (which can be illustrated by the upward shift in the MC curve), rather than engage in price warfare, in order to gain market share. The reason for this is that companies sometimes believe they have a better idea of the costs and benefits involved in *non-price competition* as compared to the unknown risks of getting involved in price-competition. When a company becomes involved in price-competition, gains and losses are more difficult to assess because they depend on the *reactions* of competitors to the initial company's pricing strategy.

Despite the usefulness of the kinked oligopoly model as a descriptive tool in the understanding of oligopoly behaviour, it still faces a number of problems:

1. The theory does not explain how oligopolists actually *set* an initial price; merely why a price, once set, might be stable. Kinked demand is *not* a theory of price determination.

2. The observed stickiness of prices may have little to do with the rival-firm reaction patterns of kinked-demand theory. It is, for instance, administratively expensive to change prices too often.

3. The assertion, implicit in kinked-demand theory, that prices are more 'sticky' under oligopoly than under other market forms, has not received strong support from empirical studies (Wagner 1981). For instance,

Oligopoly

Stigler, in a sample of 100 firms across 21 industries in the USA, had concluded as early as the 1940s that oligopoly prices hardly merited the description 'sticky'. Domberger, in a survey of twenty-one UK industries, found that the more oligopolistic the market, the *more* variable was price (Domberger 1980).

Game theory   One of the more recent attempts to assess non-collusive behaviour by oligopolists has involved game theory.[7] The intention is to go beyond the rather general reaction patterns of earlier theory, to more explicit assessments of strategy and counter-strategy. We might usefully illustrate the principles involved by a simple two-firm (duopoly) game, involving market share. By its very nature, a market share game must be 'zero sum', in that any gain by one 'player' must be offset exactly by the loss of the other(s).

Suppose Firm A is considering two possible strategies to raise its market share, a 20% price cut or a 10% increase in advertising expenditure. Whatever initial strategy A adopts, it anticipates that its rival, Firm B, will react by using either a price cut or extra advertising to defend its market share. Firm A now evaluates the market share it can expect for each initial strategy and each possible counter-strategy by B. The outcomes expected by A are summarized in the pay-off matrix of Table 6.7.

Table 6.7 Firm A's pay-off matrix

		Firm B's strategies	
		Price cut	Extra advertising
Firm A's strategies	Price cut	60*†	70†
	Extra advertising	50*	55

* 'Worst' outcome for A of each A strategy.
† 'Worst' outcome for B of each B strategy.

If A cuts price, and B responds with a price cut, A receives 60% of the market. However, if B responds with extra advertising, A receives 70% of the market. The 'worst' outcome for A (60% of the market) will occur if B responds with a price cut. If A adopts the strategy of extra advertising, then the 'worst' outcome for A (50% of the market) will again occur if B responds with a price cut. If A expects B to play the game astutely, i.e. choose the counter-strategy best for itself (worst for A), then A will choose the price-cut strategy as this gives it 60% of the market rather than 50%. If A plays the game in this way, selecting the best of the 'worst possible' outcomes for each initial strategy, it is said to be adopting a 'maxi–min approach' to the game.

If B adopts the same maxi–min approach as A, *and* has made the same evaluation of outcomes as A, it also will adopt a price-cut strategy. For instance, if B adopts a price-cut strategy, its 'worst' outcome would occur if A responds with a price cut – B then gets 40% of the market (100% minus 60%), rather than 50% if A responds with extra advertising. If B adopts extra advertising, its 'worst' outcome would again occur if A responds with a price cut – B then receives 30%. The best of the 'worst possible' outcomes for B occurs if B adopts a price cut, which gives it 40% of the market rather than 30%.

In this particular game we have a stable equilibrium, without any resort to collusion. Both firms initially cut price, then accept the respective market shares which fulfil their maxi–min targets – 60% to A, 40% to B. There could then follow the price stability which we have seen to be a feature of some oligopoly situations. In some games the optimal strategy for each firm may not even have been an initial price cut, but rather non-price competition (such as advertising). Game theory can predict both price stability and extensive non-price competition.

The problem with game theory is that it can equally predict unstable solutions, with extensive price as well as non-price competition. An unstable solution might follow if each firm, faced with the pay-off matrix of Table 6.6, adopts entirely different strategies. Firm B might not use the maxi–min approach of A, but take more risk.[8] Instead of the price cut it might adopt the 'extra advertising' strategy, hoping to induce an advertising response from Firm A and gain 45% of the market, but risk getting only 30% if A responds with a price cut. Suppose this is what happens. Firm A now receives 70% of the market, but B only receives 30%, which is below its initial expectation of 45%. This may provoke B into alternative strategy formulation, setting off a further chain reaction. The game may then fail to settle down quickly, if at all, to a stable solution, i.e. one in which each firm receives a market share which meets its overall expectation. An unstable solution might also follow if each firm evaluates the pay-off matrix differently from the other. Even if they then adopt the same approach to the game, one firm at least will be 'disappointed', possibly provoking action and counteraction.

If we could tell *before the event* which oligopoly situations would be stable, and which unstable, then the many possible outcomes of game theory would be considerably narrowed. At present this is beyond the state of the art. However, game theory has been useful in making more explicit the *interdependence* of oligopoly situations. Here we have used game theory in a situation in which the firms did not collude. Game theory can also show (in games which are *not* zero sum) that collusion between firms may sometimes improve the position of all.[9] It is to such collusive behaviour that we now turn.

Collusive oligopoly

When oligopoly is non-collusive, the firm uses guesswork and calculation to handle the uncertainty of its rivals' reactions. Another way of handling that uncertainty in markets which are interdependent is by some form of central co-ordination; in other words, collusion. At least two features of collusive oligopoly are worth emphasizing. First, the objectives that are sought through collusion. Second, the methods that are used to promote collusion – these may be formal, as in a cartel, or informal, via tacit agreement.

Objectives of collusion   *Joint profit maximization.*   The firms may seek to co-ordinate their price, output and other policies to achieve maximum profits for the industry as a whole. In the extreme case the firms may act together as a monopoly, aggregating their marginal costs and equating these with marginal revenue for the whole market. If achieved, the result would be to maximize joint profits, with a unique industry price and output (P_IQ_I), as in Fig. 6.2.

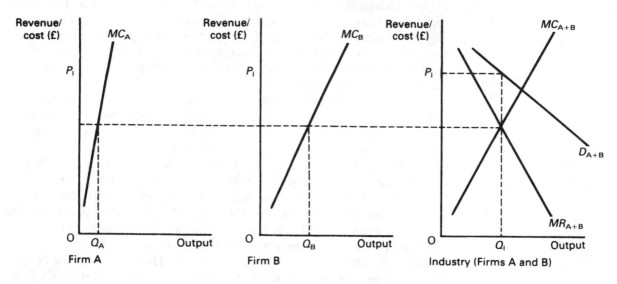

Fig. 6.2 Joint profit maximization in duopoly

A major problem is, of course, how to achieve the close co-ordination required. We consider this further below, but we might note from Fig. 6.2 that co-ordination is required both to *establish* the profit-maximizing solution for the industry P_IQ_I, and to *enforce* it once established. For instance, some agreement must be reached on sharing the output Q_I between the colluding firms. One solution is to equate marginal revenue for whole output with marginal cost in each separate market,[10] with Firm A producing Q_A and Firm B, Q_B. Whatever the agreement, it must remain in force – since if any firm produces above its quota, this will raise industry output, depress price and move the industry away from the joint profit-maximizing solution.

Deterrence of new entrants – limit-pricing.   Firms may seek to co-ordinate policies, not so much to maximize short-run profit but rather some longer-run notion of profit (see Ch. 3). A major threat to long-run profit is the potential entrance of new firms into the industry. Economists such as Andrews and Bain have therefore suggested that oligopolistic firms may collude with the objectives of setting price below that which maximizes joint profits, in order to deter new entrants. The 'limit price' can be defined as the highest price which the established firms believe they can charge without inducing entry. Its precise value will depend upon the nature and extent of the 'barriers to entry' for any particular industry. The greater the barriers to entry, the higher the 'limit price' will be.

Substantial economies of scale are a 'barrier to entry', in that a new firm will usually be smaller than established firms, and will therefore be at a cost disadvantage. Product differentiation itself, reinforced by extensive advertising, is also a barrier – since product loyalty, once captured, is difficult and expensive for new entrants to dislodge. Other barriers might include legally enforced patents to new technologies in the hands of established firms, and even inelastic market demands. This latter is a barrier in that the less elastic the market demand for the product, the greater will be the price fall from any extra supply contributed by new entrants.

The principle of 'limit-pricing' can be illustrated from Fig. 6.3.

Fig. 6.3 Limit pricing as a barrier to entry

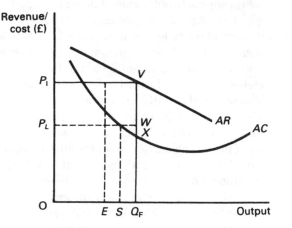

Let us make the analysis easier by supposing that each established firm has an identical average cost (AC) curve, and sells an identical output, Q_F, at the joint profit-maximizing price P_I set for the industry. Suppose a new firm, with an identical cost profile, is considering entering the industry, and is capable of selling E units in the first instance. Despite the initial cost disadvantage the new firm believes it can survive. One way of preventing the survival of the new firm, perhaps even deterring its entry, would be for the colluding established firms to reduce the industry price to P_L. Although this would reduce their own excess profits in the short run (by VW per unit) the new entrant would make a loss selling E at price P_L, since price would be less than average cost at that output. It would have needed to produce as much as output S *immediately* at the price P_L, even to have just covered its average costs.

The greater the barriers to the entry of new firms, the higher the 'limit price', P_L, can be, i.e. the closer P_L can be to P_I. The most favourable situation for established firms would be if barriers were so great that P_L were at, or above, P_I. In other words, established firms could set the joint profit-maximizing price without inducing entry.

Occasionally a limit-pricing policy is explicitly adopted, as in the early 1960s when the three major petrol wholesalers, Shell/BP, Esso and Regent were threatened with new entrants. In 1963 Shell announced a price reduction 'to make the UK market less attractive to newcomers and potential newcomers'. Again, in 1973 the Monopolies and Mergers Commission (MMC) found evidence of limit-pricing by Kellogg concluding that 'when fixing its prices, therefore, Kellogg has as an objective the preservation of its share of the market against potential competitors'.

Although limit-pricing can be seen as imposing a further barrier to entry, it has often proven ineffective. As we will see in Chapter 9, limit-pricing by Shell and the other majors did not deter new entrants – in fact, there were as many as nineteen new entrants to the petrol wholesale market during the 1960s – and the combined market share of the majors continued to fall throughout the 1970s and early 1980s.

An obvious constraint to limit-pricing is that prices cannot be set below X in Fig. 6.3, the level at which the established firms begin to make excess profits (normal profit included in average cost), at least not for any length of time. The established firms may therefore resort to non-price competition to reinforce barriers against new entrants. For instance, the petrol companies sought extensive 'solus' agreements, giving discounts to retailers dealing exclusively with them, and sought to buy up retail outlets directly. In the detergent industry, Lever Brothers, by introducing new brands, have increased product differentiation and raised barriers to entry. As much as 58% of their turnover comes from new brands introduced in the past thirteen years. Extensive advertising (as shown by Tables 6.5 and 6.6) is yet another way of increasing barriers to entry into a market or industry. Advertising can be used to increase brand loyalty, thus making it difficult for new firms with a new product to enter a market. Increased advertising can be used by firms already in the industry not only to keep other firms out, but also to drive out existing firms which have newly entered the industry.

To investigate this latter proposition, a study was undertaken into the behaviour of forty-two companies operating in various consumer goods markets, such as electric shavers, deodorants, washing up liquids and kettles, over the period 1975 to 1981. The study investigated the advertising strategy of companies *already in* these oligopolistic markets after new firms with new products had managed to enter those markets (Cubbin and Domberger 1988). The results of the study showed that increased advertising was used as a weapon in an attempt to drive out new entrants in 38% of markets studied, and that the response of the firms already in the market to the new entrants depended on the *structure of the oligopoly* and the *nature of the market*. For example, in a tightly competitive oligopoly situation, where a dominant firm controlled more than 30% of the market, it was more likely that the new entrant would be exposed to increased advertising competition than in a looser oligopoly where there was no clear dominance by one firm. Similarly, increased advertising competition was more likely to face new entrants in static markets, i.e. those in which demand is not growing. This is partly because growing markets tend to be dominated by new consumers with less attachment to the products of existing firms. Advertising in this situation is therefore a less-certain weapon for driving out a new entrant, as compared to a market in which demand is static.

We now turn briefly to the methods which firms have actually used to promote collusion in oligopolistic markets.

Methods of collusion   *Formal collusion – cartels.*   Formal collusion often takes the form of a cartel – in other words, the establishment of some central body with responsibility for setting the industry price and output which most nearly meets some agreed objective. Usually it also has the responsibility for sharing that total output between the members. Cartels are against the law in most countries, including the UK. However, in the UK the Cement Makers' Federation was an exception. Up to 1987 it still held monthly meetings in which deliveries, prices and market shares were discussed. The three main companies sharing the market were Blue Circle (60%), Rio Tinto Zinc (22%) and Rugby Portland (18%), with their common price calculated on a formula which averaged the costs of different producers. The Restrictive Practices Court permitted the cartel to continue on the basis that a common price agreement enables cement capacity to be controlled in an orderly way. Nevertheless, increased concentration of the cement industry in the last few years raised the possibility of intervention by the MMC and this, together with international competition from cheap European imports (especially from Greece), caused the cartel to be abandoned in 1987.

Various cartels operate internationally. The most famous is OPEC, in which many, but not all (the UK is not a member) oil-exporting countries meet regularly to agree on prices and set production quotas. Whilst OPEC worked successfully in the mid-1970s in raising oil prices, in the worldwide economic slump of the early 1980s co-ordination has proved increasingly difficult. As demand for oil has fallen, exporters have been faced with the necessity of cutting production quotas to maintain prices; and some, such as Iran and Nigeria with major internal economic problems, have been unwilling to do this, preferring to cut prices and seek higher market share. Of course the Iraqi pressure on OPEC countries to curtail production and raise prices, and the subsequent Kuwait invasion, contributed to higher oil prices in the early 1990s. The International Air Transport Association (IATA) is the cartel of international airlines, and has sought to set prices for each route. During the 1970s it was seriously weakened by price-cutting competition from non-member airlines, such as Laker Airways. It has been further weakened by worldwide recession, with lower incomes causing demand for air travel, with its high-income elasticity, to fall dramatically. To fill seats, the member airlines began to compete amongst themselves in terms of price, often via a complex system of discounts. The experiences of OPEC and IATA suggest that cartels are vulnerable both to price-cutting amongst members when demand for the product declines, and to competition from non-members.

A more recent example of an international cartel has been brought to light by investigations during 1990 into the activity of the International Telegraph and Telephone Consultative Committee (CCITT), a Geneva based 'club' consisting of the main international telephone companies of the major industrial countries (*Financial Times* 1990a). Major international telephone companies such as AT&T (USA), British Telecom (UK), Deutsche Bundespost (Germany), France Telecom (France), Telecom Canada (Canada) and KDD (Japan) belong to the group. The CCITT had a book of 'recommendations' for its member companies which included two important features. First, it suggested a complicated method of sharing the revenues received from international telephone calls. When international phone calls are made from the UK to Japan, for example, BT receives the money for the call but it has to pay KDD in Japan for delivering the call to its final destination in that country. The particular method used to calculate the distribution of the revenue received for the call between the various international telephone companies tended to penalize any company that attempted to cut its telephone prices. This in turn made it difficult for both existing or new companies to decrease prices because their profits would also fall. Second, it suggested that members of the group should not lease too much of their international telephone circuits to other private companies, since this could increase potential competition.

The effect of the first 'rule' was to provide high profit margins for telephone companies because prices were kept artificially high by the peculiar revenue sharing scheme. Meanwhile, new technological advances had decreased the *real* costs per minute of using a transatlantic cable from $2.53 per minute in 1956 to $0.04 in 1988. While costs had fallen drastically, the price charged for a peak call from the US to the UK and Italy remained at $2 and $4 per minute respectively! As a result profit margins on international calls (i.e. profits divided by revenue) of some of the top earners were as follows: Japan (75%), Canada (68%), US (63%), Britain (58%), W Germany (48%) and France (43%). British Telecom earned a profit of between £600m and £800m on its international business during the 1988/9 financial year, depending on the accounting definitions used. The second 'rule' made it difficult for new companies to enter this market because most of the international cables were built by members of the CCITT and new operators had to get permission from these companies in order to lease cable space from them. If they were not allowed more space on international cables, then new companies had to use satellite links which were more expensive and of lower quality than cable links. By the middle of 1990 the European Commission had decided to investigate this cartel-type arrangement to see whether it prevented competition in the international telephone business.

Tacit collusion – price leadership.   Although cartels are illegal in most countries, various forms of tacit collusion undoubtedly occur. In 1776, Adam Smith wrote in his *Wealth of Nations* that entrepreneurs rarely meet together without conspiring to raise prices at the expense of the consumer. Today the most usual method of tacit collusion is price leadership, where one firm sets a price which the others follow.

1. Dominant-firm leadership. Frequently the price leader is the dominant firm. In the late 1960s Brooke Bond controlled 43% of the market for tea, well ahead of the second largest firm Typhoo with only 18% of the market. Brooke Bond's price rises were soon matched by those of other firms, bringing the industry to the attention of the Prices and Incomes Board in 1970. Sealink, with 34% of the cross-Channel market, seems to have been the price leader in ferry travel to the Continent. In the car industry, Ford has frequently acted as the dominant market leader by being first with its price increases. In 1990, companies who bought fleet cars from Fords, Rover, Vauxhall and Peugeot Talbot, accused the big car manufacturers of operating a price cartel led by Ford. By initiating two separate price rises (amounting to a total of 8.5% by the middle of 1990), Ford was seen as the dominant leader of a 'cartel' by the fleet car buyers.

2. Barometric-firm leadership. In some cases the price leader is a small firm, recognized by others to have a close knowledge of prevailing

market conditions. The firm acts as a 'barometer' to others of changing market conditions, and its prices are closely followed. In the mid-1970s Williams and Glyn's, a relatively small commercial bank, took the lead in reducing bank charges in response to rising interest rates. Maunder also found this sort of price leadership in the glass bottle and sanitaryware markets of the 1960s and early 1970s (Maunder 1972). Since the mid-1970s there have been signs that the 'minor' petrol wholesalers have had an increasing influence on petrol prices (see Ch. 9).

3. Collusive-price leadership. This is a more complicated form of price leadership; essentially it is an informal cartel in which prices change almost simultaneously. The parallel pricing which occurred in the wholesale petrol market (noted in Ch. 9) until the mid-1970s, suggested this sort of tacit group collusion. In practice it is often difficult to distinguish collusive-price leadership from types in which firms follow price leaders very quickly.

Sometimes it is difficult to prove that this sort of collusion is present when all the firms in an industry are influenced by a third factor outside their control but which they all have to respond to quite rapidly, thus *appearing* to show collusion. For example, the Office of Fair Trading investigated parallel pricing and excess profits in the petrol wholesaling business in 1989/1990. Although the sector comprises 69 petrol wholesalers, it is still dominated by Esso, Shell, BP, Texaco and Mobil who account for 65% of the market. The report found that there was no evidence of price collusion by the wholesalers because they seemed to adjust their prices fairly simultaneously to the common world oil price reflected by the Rotterdam spot market. Also the allegations that the oil companies implemented price rises more quickly than price falls were rejected by the report. They found that when Rotterdam prices rose, UK wholesalers delayed price rises to avoid losing market share, and when Rotterdam prices fell, the wholesalers' price fell after a short delay, but in smaller steps. Over time it is sometimes difficult to distinguish between periods of actual collusive price leadership from periods of 'apparent' collusive price leadership.

Conclusion

That oligopoly has become a progressively more important form of market structure in the UK is clear from the data, particularly from concentration ratios. Interdependence is a key feature of such markets, which makes the outcome of any strategy by a firm uncertain, depending to a large extent on how the rivals react. Price competition may be a particularly hazardous strategy, perhaps leading to a 'price war'. In any case, to the extent that kinked-demand theory is valid, the profit-maximizing price may not change even for wide variations in cost. For both these reasons there may be extensive periods of price stability. Even so, there may still be close competition between firms for market share, though this will be mainly of the non-price variety – advertising, packaging, new brands, etc. Non-price competition, by increasing product differentiation, real or imagined, may benefit firms not only by raising market share, but by providing greater future control over price – extra brand loyalty making demand curves less price-elastic.

The uncertainty of rival reactions, whether price or non-price, can be mitigated by guesswork, based on past experience (reaction curves), or by trying to evaluate the rivals' optimal counter-strategy (game theory). Collusion between firms may be a still more secure way of reducing uncertainty, and avoiding mutual damage. This could be arranged formally, as in cartels, or informally by some form of tacit collusion (information agreements, price leadership, etc.). Although we may be no nearer a general model of oligopoly behaviour, we have made some progress in predicting how firms react under particular circumstances at particular times.

Notes

1. Cross-elasticity of demand is defined as the percentage change in quantity demanded of X, divided by the percentage change in price of Y. If X and Y are close substitutes, then a small fall in price of Y will lead to a substantial decrease in demand for X. This gives a high positive value for the quotient.
2. See, for instance, Jump (1982).
3. For further detail see, for instance, Koutsoyiannis (1979).
4. Ibid.
5. We have already noted that brand loyalty permitted prices to be 9% higher for branded processed foods in the USA than for supermarket own-brand equivalents. See Jump (1982).
6. This is because each demand curve, *dd'* and *DD'* respectively, will have its own separate marginal revenue curve, bisecting the horizontal between the vertical axis and demand curve in question.
7. See, for instance, Murphy and Edwards (1981).
8. The maxi–min approach is a rather conservative strategy in that it assumes that the rival reacts to your strategy in the worst possible way for you.
9. As in Note 7.
10. A distribution of the joint profit-maximizing output such that aggregate $MR = MC$ in each separate market, is often called the 'ideal' distribution. From Fig. 6.2 we can see that there is no other distribution which will raise total profits for the industry. For instance, one extra unit produced by Firm B will add more to cost than is saved by one less unit produced by Firm A (i.e. $MC_B > MC_A$). Whether the firms will acquiesce in such a share-out is quite another matter.

References

Business Monitor (1980) PO 1006 Statistics of product concentration of UK manufacturers.
Business Monitor (1989) PA 1002 Report on the Census of Production.
Campaign Report (1990) 'Top Advertisers and Brands', 4 May.
Cubbin, J. and **Domberger, S.** (1988) Advertising and Post-Entry Oligopoly Behaviour, *The Journal of Industrial Economics*, Vol. 37, Dec.

Domberger, S. (1980) Mergers, market structure and the rate of price adjustment, in: Cowling, K. *et al. Mergers and Economic Performance.* CUP, Cambridge, Ch. 13.

Financial Times (1990) Reconnecting charges with costs, 3 April.

Jump, N. (1982) Corporate strategy in mature markets, *Barclays Bank Review*, **57**, 4, Nov.

Koutsoyiannis, A. (1979) *Modern Micro Economics* 2nd edn. Macmillan, Ch. 9.

Marketing Week (1990), 15 June, p. 22.

Maunder, P. (1972) Price leadership: an appraisal of its character in some British industries, *The Business Economist*, **4**.

Murphy, T. and **Edwards, V.** (1981) Using game theory in introductory micro-economics courses, *Economics*, **17**, Part 4, Winter.

Sawyer, M. C. (1981) *The Economics of Industries and Firms.* Croom Helm.

Wagner, L. (ed.) (1981) *Readings in Applied Micro-Economics* 2nd edn. OUP, Oxford.

7   The multinational enterprise

In this chapter we look at the multinational enterprise, the fastest-growing type of productive unit in Western economies. We consider the way multinational activity is measured, and the changing pattern of that activity in recent years. The industrial and spatial features of multinational activity in the UK are examined, and our observations related to current economic theory. We conclude by assessing the overall impact of multinational activity on UK employment, the balance of payments, technological change, and international competitiveness.

Definition of the multinational

A 'multinational' company or enterprise is defined as an enterprise which owns or controls production or service facilities outside the country in which it is based. In other words, multinationals are not simply companies which trade abroad by exporting their products, they are companies which actually own (via a wholly or partly owned subsidiary), or control (via branch plant, joint venture, or minority interest), productive facilities in other countries. They have either acquired already-existing foreign enterprises or have themselves built productive facilities abroad. We shall use the term 'affiliates' to refer to all these types of ownership or control.

Multinationals normally have interests in at least four or five countries. However, definitions fail to give any real idea of the scope and diversity of multinational business enterprise; it covers everything from the thousands of medium-sized firms which have a few affiliates abroad, to the giants whose activities are the subject of international interest and concern.

One of the most striking features of multinational companies is their size. The largest multinationals are formidable business machines which have annual turnovers larger than the GNP of most of the countries in the developing world. The very largest, Exxon, Ford and General Motors of the USA, each have a turnover which is larger than the GNPs of all but fourteen countries. The largest European multinationals rank with the US companies in terms of size and power – they include such household names as Royal Dutch Shell, BP, Unilever, Philips, Volkswagen, British American Tobacco (BAT), and Daimler Benz. Multinational business is growing fast. Every year new companies appear in the list of world multinational enterprises – many of the recent additions coming from the fast-growing 'middle-income countries', such as Singapore. The output of existing multinational companies is growing at an annual rate of 10–15%, which means that multinational output is growing faster than the output of major economies such as Japan or Germany.

The activities of these companies are therefore sufficiently extensive to raise important issues for both national and international economic policy. One of the major problems is the relative powerlessness of national governments against the actions of companies which can switch production from country to country, evade taxation by pricing policies which declare profits in countries where company taxation is lenient, and use their political 'muscle' to affect decision-making at every level of government. The long-term solution to this problem is undoubtedly to institute some form of international control over the activities of these companies. Tentative steps have already been taken in this direction (see below). Codes of behaviour need, however, to be enforced, and existing enforcement mechanisms are not always adequate. Poorer countries in particular may lack the judicial, political and economic resources needed to contain the activities of the multinationals.

The measurement of multinational activity

There are two separate elements in the measurement of multinational activity. One is the size of the company involved, and the other is the degree of 'foreign participation', i.e. the extent to which the company really is 'multinational'.

When measuring the size of domestic companies, we usually use one or more of several indicators: annual sales, size of assets, or numbers employed. In the case of the multinational, the usual practice is to measure size by annual sales data.

However, the problem of measuring foreign participation is more complex. Companies differ in the ways they choose to sell abroad. All large companies export directly as well as sell abroad through affiliates. Large companies also differ in the proportion of their income earned overseas, and in the number of foreign personnel they employ.

Table 7.1 gives some indication of how the assessment of 'foreign participation' varies with the measure used. The figures relate to five representative UK multinationals in an illustrative year. BP is a worldwide organization concerned primarily with the exploitation and production of oil and gas. Eleven British wholly owned BP companies deal with various aspects of the business, including the marketing of oil, the production of chemicals and plastics, and the processing and marketing of minerals as a by-product from the main company operations. In addition, however, there are over sixty subsidiaries and related companies in other countries.

ICI is one of the world's major chemical groups. As well as being one of the largest manufacturing and exporting companies in the UK it operates worldwide through a network of subsidiaries. It operates four divisions – consumer and speciality products, industrial products, oil and gas, and agrochemicals. It has affiliates in every corner of the globe in sixty separate countries.

Grand Metropolitan is a group of companies operating in the area of consumer products and services in the food, drink and personal service sectors. The stated company objective is to derive revenue equally from the domestic market in the UK, the domestic market in the USA, and the

Company	BP	ICI	Grand Metropolitan	Allied Lyons	United Biscuits
Major industry	Oil	Chemicals	Food	Food	Food
Sales (1986 £bn)	40,986	10,136	5,291	3,301	1,907
Foreign sales as % of home sales	44	76	38	28	47
Foreign assets as % of home assets	15	51	40	22	—
Foreign earnings as % of home earnings	24	38	38	—	35
Foreign employment as % of home employment	77.3	50	40	—	26

Source: Company reports.

Table 7.1 Foreign content of five UK multinationals

international market, in order to spread risk. Products range from beer to dog food, services range from casinos to health care.

Allied Lyons is organized into three divisions – beer, wines and spirits, and food. Overseas affiliates are active primarily in the food division, but it is the aim of all sections of the group to develop and maintain the lead in international markets by marketing international brand leaders. United Biscuits owns such brand leaders as KP Foods, Pizzaland and Wimpy. Their multinational involvement is primarily in the North American market.

How can we measure the 'foreign participation' of these companies, i.e. the extent to which they can be called 'multinational'? Different measures give different information. For instance, in the case of BP the vast majority of employees work in non-UK companies, but only 15% of assets are held abroad. Nearly 50% of United Biscuit sales are made by foreign affiliates, but only 35% of company profits are made abroad. There is clearly no one measure of 'multinationality'; the pattern of foreign participation is different for every company.

Multinationals and the changing pattern of direct foreign investment

Investment by multinational companies usually entails the building or acquisition of productive assets (e.g. plant, equipment and buildings) in another country. This is termed 'direct foreign investment' (d.f.i.), to distinguish it from 'portfolio investment' – the buying of shares in a foreign concern which does not result in direct control of that business.

It is worth noting that the majority of world d.f.i. takes place between developed countries – investment in LDCs only accounts for less than a quarter of the total. The first substantial influx of foreign direct investment came from the US to Europe after the Second World War. This was not only in response to the European need for recovery, but was made possible by the growth of improved communications and more efficient company organization. Since then the picture has changed considerably; Europe has become an increasingly active overseas investor, as has Japan.

Table 7.2 looks at the current importance of direct foreign investment for five major countries. It demonstrates that the dominant position of the US as an exporter of capital has waned. In fact, alone of the major industrialized countries, the US has become a net importer of capital. The other four countries have, however, become net exporters of capital. The so-called middle income countries in particular, such as those in South-East Asia, now account for nearly a tenth of the world total in d.f.i.

Table 7.2 Direct foreign investment

| ($ billion) | Direct foreign investment (1980–88) | |
	Inward	Outward
US	251.7	157.3
UK	64.7	133.2
Japan	2.9	96.0
Germany	9.1	52.5
France	27.9	43.3

Source: Julius 1990.

We can identify other changes in the pattern of d.f.i.

1. The *destination* or locus of multinational investment has changed. When the USA was the major investor, most industrial capital flowed into Canada or Latin America. Now, with the growing importance of companies from Japan and the LDCs as investors, the countries of South-east Asia have become major recipients of direct investment. However, the share of investment going to the LDCs *as a whole* has fallen over time. The majority of investment going to the LDCs is now destined for a select few, such as the Philippines, Taiwan, South Korea, Brazil and Mexico, which together form a group known as the 'newly industrializing countries' (NICs). Foreign penetration in these countries is high; for instance in Taiwan, all five leading electronics exporters are US owned.

2. The *rationale* of d.f.i. has changed. In the past the emphasis was on the need to invest abroad in order to supply local foreign markets, or in order to exploit natural resources located in the 'host' country, such as oil, rubber or minerals. Today, companies invest abroad as part of a worldwide company strategy which takes into account both cost and revenue factors. The emphasis is now on regional or global specialization both in process and product.
    Process specialization has been helped by the fact that products have become more standardized, yet at the same time more complex, requiring extra stages in the production process. This has created opportunities for locating such stages in the most profitable geographical area. For instance, companies can locate labour-intensive processes in low-wage countries, with the final stage of the production process (e.g. assembly) located nearer to the intended markets of the developed countries.
    Product specialization occurs when companies produce standardized products in their entirety in specific geographical locations, before distributing them to their intended markets. Although standardized,

each product is differentiated according to market requirement, such as taste, or safety specification. For instance, the car industry in Europe concentrates the production of a particular model in a particular country, and then ships the finished product from country to country. Johnson Wax was able to trim production costs by 15% by rationalizing its product range across countries, thereby simplifying production and reducing inventories. A slightly different example of product specialization is provided by Guinness, which brews forty-three different varieties of the product in as many countries, each one carefully blended to suit local taste. Sometimes the product stays the same; only the name changes. For example, when surveys showed that in some European countries and Japan the name 'Diet Coke' had medical connotations for consumers, the company changed the name of the product to 'Coca Cola Light'.

3.   The *control* of overseas production has become more centralized. This has resulted in part from the *need* to manage global resource allocation and production planning, and in part from the new *opportunities* actually to do so created by computer/telecommunication systems (see Ch. 10). For instance global marketing strategies have become increasingly important as determinants of multinational investment decisions. Philips' consumer electronics division, threatened by Japanese competition in colour television, centralized its production in Europe and standardized its models. The new automated production system reduced the time taken to produce a set from 22 hours to half an hour (Kashari, 1990).

The last twenty years have therefore seen changes in the source, destination, rationale and control of multinational activity. We now look at the way in which these trends have been reflected in the UK.

Economic theory and direct foreign investment

We have now seen how the investment activities of multinational companies have led both to a growth of world d.f.i. and to a change in its pattern. We now need to ask whether there is any theoretical framework which will help us to explain and predict the growth of d.f.i.

Conventional economic theory has run into difficulties in trying to explain the changes that have occurred in world d.f.i. For instance, neo-classical theory, in dealing with factor location, predicts that productive capital will move to capital-scarce regions. This prediction is totally at variance with the fact that post-war d.f.i. has flowed mainly into capital-rich countries. In the late 1970s and early 1980s something like 74% of such investment was located in the developed countries, and only 26% in the capital-scarce LDCs. Nor can traditional international trade theory shed much light on the existence of d.f.i., since it relies heavily on the assumption of international immobility of factors of production, including capital.

Since standard theory has been unable to explain these investment flows, alternative theories have been sought. The most promising have attempted to link d.f.i. to the growth of industrial enterprise in situations of uncertainty, imperfect markets, and open economies.

These theories are based on a perspective which no longer views the company as the profit-maximizer of neo-classical theory. Instead, it is viewed as an organization with a variety of possible objectives, both in the short and the long term (see Ch. 3). The relevant objectives in the case of d.f.i. are clearly long-term ones, since investment is a long-term company decision. The major long-term company objective is seen here as being growth, whether of output, sales or assets.

Ownership-specific advantages

Companies which choose growth as an objective have a number of alternative strategies open to them. They can diversify laterally into new products, or vertically into new activities. They can expand by acquisition or merger, or can choose to exploit foreign markets by setting up new affiliates abroad. All these are possible courses of action, depending for their feasibility on the business opportunities which present themselves in each particular case. However, the option of expanding abroad is probably a less comfortable one than other alternatives. There is the distance factor, there are language barriers, potential difficulties with supplies, with personnel, with government regulations, and a host of other uncertainties. Any company which chooses to grow by investing abroad must therefore believe that it is an easier or more profitable option than home-market expansion. This must in turn imply that the company has some kind of competitive advantage *over firms already serving foreign markets*. We can think of such advantages as 'ownership-specific', i.e. particular advantages possessed by a company over its competitors which derive in some way from the characteristics peculiar to that company. In other words, the company must possess some degree of monopolistic or oligopolistic market power. The typical multinational company fits this picture, with empirical evidence showing it to be larger, more profitable, more research-orientated, and more diversified than equivalent companies which do not produce abroad (Buckley and Casson 1976).

It is useful to list some of the characteristics which give the multinational company advantages over indigenous firms when selling in the country in which those firms reside:

1. Possibilities of extracting raw materials or of developing markets not available to indigenous firms. The exploitation of complex natural resources such as oil, and their subsequent sale in overseas markets, is a clear example of this.

2. Advantages of size. These can result in lower costs, via scale economies; cheaper and easier access to capital; and greater opportunities for research and development (R & D) than is available to indigenous firms.

3. Possession of assets such as patents or trademarks.

4. Managerial skills. Often the most crucial assets which multinationals possess are human, i.e. the technological and managerial skills needed to exploit the potential created by access to foreign markets.

Location-specific advantages

Ownership-specific advantages therefore explain the 'why' of foreign *sales* activity. But they do not explain why a company should choose to *invest* in productive capacity abroad, rather than sell into the foreign market from the home production base. This can only be explained by the fact that foreign locations must have some kind of advantage over home production locations, so that firms for some reason or other find it easier or cheaper to *produce* abroad. We refer to these as 'location-specific' advantages – advantages which belong not to the company, but to the geographical location. Examples of these include:

1. Resources which can only be used where they are actually located, i.e. abroad.
2. Low labour costs and/or incentives offered by host governments.
3. The possibility of product specialization for local market needs.
4. The necessity to provide after-sales service.
5. The possibility of evading tariff or non-tariff barriers.

Even if ownership and location-specific advantages exist, they are not in themselves *sufficient* to explain d.f.i. It would still be possible for the company to exploit them by, say, producing abroad under a licensing arrangement.

Market imperfections

The fact that companies do prefer to *invest* in productive capacity abroad, rather than merely to license production of their products, must be explained by other reasons. The key to these may lie in the fact that markets are imperfect. Multinationals must function and trade abroad in markets some distance from their home base. They must buy materials and supplies on local goods markets, and labour and technology on local factor markets, and they must sell the final product on markets where there may be a high degree of non-price competition. Multinationals invest abroad by horizontal or vertical integration because they prefer to reduce the uncertainties which they face on these foreign markets by 'internalizing' them, i.e. incorporating them within the company structure. Investment abroad can therefore help:

1. Ensure regularity of supplies of materials in LDCs where conditions of supply are often unstable.

2. Eliminate bilateral monopoly, e.g. in situations where there is only one supplier of a raw material to the multinational.

3. Reduce risk in situations where financial commitment is heavy, e.g. by securing greater control of overseas price.

4. Create or increase barriers to entry, thereby preventing potential competition.

5. Avoid the impact of government policy, e.g. getting behind tariff walls, etc.

All of these are ways in which multinationals use d.f.i. to reduce the risk of operating in imperfect foreign markets, in circumstances where company strategy dictates that growth is best served by expansion into these markets.

Investment abroad then means that the company no longer has to operate in these markets as an outsider – market operations are 'internalized' within the company. Backward or 'upstream' vertical integration ensures the quantity and quality of supplies. Forward or 'downstream' vertical integration ensures that products are marketed successfully. Horizontal integration combines the 'on the ground' expertise of a local company with the process or product technology provided by a parent company.

We now look at the picture within the UK.

Direct foreign investment and the UK

The overall situation with regard to d.f.i. in the UK is the result of decisions taken by multinationals over a period of years. The UK is historically a net creditor as regards d.f.i., with investment by UK multinationals abroad exceeding that by foreign multinationals into the UK (see Table 7.3). During the 1970s the rate of increase of outward direct investment was slower than that for inward direct investment. The pattern in the 1980s has however been one of sharply rising outward investment. (The negative 1984 figure for inward investment is due to disvestment by oil companies as the fall in oil prices reduced the profitability of opportunities for exploration.) United Kingdom companies have extended their interest in overseas companies, helped partly by increasingly buoyant international capital markets which have facilitated the raising of capital abroad. In fact, the figures somewhat understate the degree of UK company investment abroad, since a certain amount is financed by foreign currency borrowing on the Euromarkets, or locally funded acquisitions by foreign subsidiaries. Since these do not represent flows of direct investment they are not included in the above figures.

Table 7.3 Net foreign investment flows. Totals for all industries (£m.)

	Outward	Inward
1980	3,391	2,541
1981	4,671	980
1982	2,122	1,137
1983	3,460	2,063
1984	5,929	−246
1985	8,836	4,123
1986	11,641	4,078
1987	19,041	8,508
1988	20,758	8,990
1989	19,164	15,848

Source: British Business, 17 May 1985, 11 March 1988; *Business Bulletin* 1990.

Inward investment has remained relatively static, though rising in the late 1980s with the prospect of a single European market in 1992. On the face of it, it would appear that foreign investors do not find the UK a particularly attractive location. However, the information given by the figures has to be seen in the light of the fact that they include net retentions. In 1986, for instance, earnings on overseas direct investment in the UK fell by 31%, but dividend payments to foreign shareholders rose exceptionally. This meant that the figure for retentions in that year was small. The overall figure for inward investment thus hides the fact that foreign acquisitions in the UK actually doubled in 1986.

The most recent figures reflect a high level of cross-border acquisitions and mergers in 1988. Despite a rise in inward investment, UK companies were still more active in acquiring foreign companies than were overseas companies in investing in the UK. Some of the transactions were very large; the UK company BAT acquired the US insurance company Farmers for £2.8bn, and the Swiss company Nestlé acquired Rowntrees for £2.5bn.

The figures quoted in Table 7.3 are useful on an individual basis. However, they cannot be used to demonstrate the trend of d.f.i. – i.e. the way in which direct foreign investment is changing. The reason for this is that direct investment can be done in many different ways. It can involve building plant and purchasing equipment, but it can also involve the purchase of all, or part, of already-existing companies. In this latter case the transaction is in *financial assets*, and there is then no possibility of comparing one transaction with another, because no suitable price indices for these assets exist. In 1988, for instance, over half of all outward d.f.i. was accounted for by the acquisition of overseas companies' share and loan capital.

What we must then do in order to get a picture of the underlying trend is to compare flows of inward and outward investment with GDP at current market prices. We can see from Fig. 7.1 that the ratio of both outward and inward investment to GDP was low in the sixties, but peaked rapidly in the early seventies, due primarily to companies' response to Britain's entry into the EC. After that the ratios were depressed as a result of the oil crisis, but began to grow in the late seventies and again in the eighties due to the search in all countries for greater profitability abroad. In the mid and late eighties there has been a major move by UK companies towards globalization in ownership and operational terms, and this is reflected in the rapidly rising outward d.f.i./GDP ratio. The major influence on inward d.f.i. in the seventies was the development of oil and gas exploration in the North Sea, since when, apart from the dip in 1984 which was due to special factors, the trend rate has remained roughly constant.

Investment into the UK

Although the UK remains a net investor abroad, it is the implications for the UK economy of inward investment which are of immediate significance; this is particularly relevant as the figures for 1989 show a surge in investment by foreign companies. We now look at this in more detail. In doing this, we must be careful to distinguish between stocks and flows – i.e. between investment which has already happened and thus determines the volume of assets held, and current investment decisions which may show quite a different pattern.

The UK is not the most popular destination for companies seeking to expand abroad – some of the reasons for this will be discussed presently. Table 7.4 shows that other countries, particularly European countries, have experienced faster annual rates of growth of inward d.f.i. in recent years, even though in some cases foreign investment has not hitherto been significant for those countries in terms of the d.f.i./GDP ratio.

Fig. 7.1 Inward and outward
direct net investment as a %
of UK GDP (*)
(*Sources: British Business*
(various), *Business Briefing*,
1990)

Table 7.4 Foreign
investment inflows: size of
flow 1988

Country	Inflow $bn 1988	Inflow % of GNP	Nominal growth % 1983–88
USA	58.5	1.2	37
UK	13.9	1.9	22
France	8.5	1.0	37
Spain	7.0	2.3	34
Italy	6.8	0.9	42
Australia	5.4	2.6	13
Benelux	5.1	3.4	32
Canada	3.9	0.9	18
Netherlands	3.6	1.7	21
W. Germany	1.6	0.2	4

Source: Lloyds Bank Economic Bulletin (June 1990).

The US is the largest single investor in the UK in terms of assets held, as Fig. 7.2 shows. This shows the 'stock' position. However, the picture is in the process of change. The majority of inward investment in the UK now comes from Europe, as Fig. 7.3 shows, and this fact will reduce the historical dominance of US companies in time. The other factor which will change the historical position is the increase in Japanese investment. Japan was only the seventh largest investor in 1988 in terms of assets held, but this figure is probably understated to the extent that Japanese investment is financed in the UK.

In sectoral terms it can be seen (Fig. 7.4) that manufacturing investment accounts for only 34% of inward d.f.i. This figure is part of the downward trend in foreign investment into the manufacturing sector over the last twenty years. In 1976 manufacturing investment in the UK accounted for 73% of the total, whereas in 1982 that figure was only 42%. It has to be remembered,

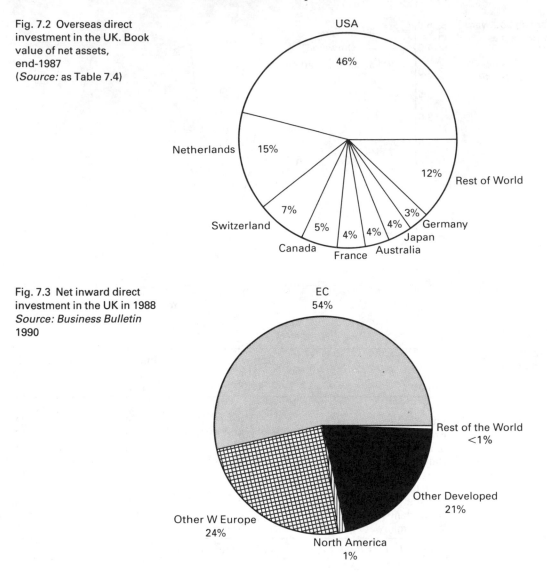

Fig. 7.2 Overseas direct investment in the UK. Book value of net assets, end-1987 (*Source:* as Table 7.4)

Fig. 7.3 Net inward direct investment in the UK in 1988 *Source: Business Bulletin 1990*

however, that total investment is growing, but growth is almost all accounted for by investment in insurance, banking and property, sectors which themselves are growing rapidly. In 1987 foreign investment accounted for 16.5% of total assets in the banking sector and 10% of other financial institutions; this growth is undoubtedly related to the advent of deregulation in that sector, as foreign companies have come to take advantage of the growth of newer financial markets.

Manufacturing investment, both inward and outward, has shown a particular pattern over the years. If we divide manufacturing industry into 'more technology-intensive' and 'less technology-intensive' sectors, we find that the UK, unlike her competitors, has tended to invest in 'less technology-intensive' sectors abroad, and to play host to companies which are in the 'more technology-intensive' sectors.

Fig. 7.4 Overseas direct
investment in the UK. Book
value of net assets,
end-1987
(*Source:* as Table 7.4)

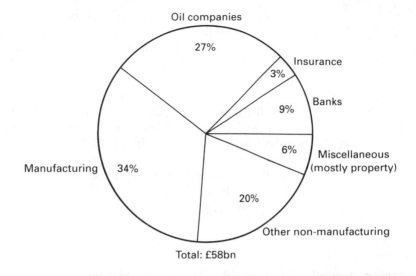

Total: £58bn

The largest UK investors overseas (outward investment) have been biased towards the 'less technology-intensive' sectors, such as food, drink and tobacco, textiles, etc. On the other hand, the largest overseas investors into the UK (inward investment) have a strong bias towards the more technology-intensive sectors, i.e. pharmaceuticals, engineering products, motor vehicles, etc. (Dunning 1981).

It might be argued that one of the problems associated with this sectoral pattern of inward investment is that in terms of productivity gains the UK might do better if there were more investment in the manufacturing sector. However, against this has to be set the fact that foreign companies outperform their UK counterparts in the sectors where foreign investment does happen. Statistics on foreign company performance are collected only for the manufacturing sector, and they show that whereas foreign firms accounted for 20% of manufacturing output in 1987, they accounted for only 13% of employment (*Lloyds Bank Economic Bulletin* 1990). The implication is that productivity in those firms was of the order of 50% higher than UK firms in the same sector, and that this was due primarily to a much higher level of per capita capital investment in those companies than in UK companies in those sectors. Furthermore, productivity gains are not the only gains. One might for instance expect employment creation to benefit from foreign investment in the service sector. The huge expansion of jobs in the financial sector in recent years owes much to the activities of multinational banks and finance companies.

Future prospects for inward investment are hopeful. Although over the last two decades the growth rate has been no more than 7% per annum, the trend has now begun to accelerate and there are reasons to predict that the rate of inward investment will now be higher. The most notable change which will trigger this is the advent of the single European market in 1992. Companies from countries outside the Community will almost certainly find it advantageous to locate within that market. The US and Japan, the two major non-EC countries, already each have one third of their European investment in the UK. We might therefore assume that they will choose the

UK for future expansion. It has been estimated (*Lloyds Bank Economic
Bulletin* 1990) that annual inward investment flows into the EC as a whole
might average 12% growth by 1995; such a figure would imply that the stock
of foreign investment in the UK would rise from 14% of GDP to 27% of
GDP by 1995, and that the annual flow of inward d.f.i. would rise from 1½%
of GDP (see Fig. 7.1) in 1988 to 3% of GDP in 1995. This might mean that
something like 40% of UK manufacturing capacity was foreign-controlled.

As well as attracting investment from outside the EC, we might also
expect the EC investment into the UK to increase due to the necessity for
companies in the single market to achieve market-wide economies of scale,
and the relative ease of arranging acquisitions in the UK. In fact, worldwide
d.f.i. as a whole is likely to feel the impact of the resultant wave of intra-
European mergers, acquisitions and new investments.

UK investment abroad

We now look at the way in which outward d.f.i. has changed in recent years.
Fig. 7.5 shows that the US is by far the most popular destination for outward
UK d.f.i., and has attracted a rising share of investment in the eighties. The
trend rate of growth of UK investment in the US has increased steadily since
1983, but it accelerated sharply in 1986 and 1987. This can be explained by
the continuing profitability of UK company subsidiaries in the US, which
provided one-third of all earnings from d.f.i. in 1986. This was the case in
spite of the fact that the relative appreciation of sterling against the US dollar
depressed the sterling value of company earnings denominated in dollars.

Fig. 7.5 Net outward direct
investment by UK
companies in 1988
Source: Business Bulletin
1990

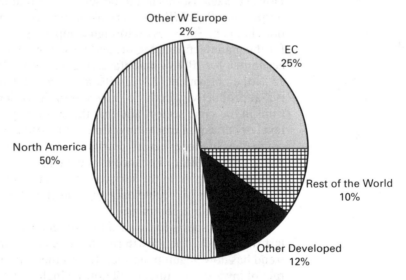

However, in 1988 investment in the US fell back, whereas investment in
the EC, notably in France and the Netherlands, increased sharply. This does
not necessarily denote a change in the attractiveness of the US as a
destination for UK investment, because the information conveyed by the

figures may be misleading. About half of all outward d.f.i. in 1988 was done by the acquisition of foreign companies' share and loan capital. This appears in the figures if it is funded in the UK. However, in the case of the US such transactions have sometimes been funded on US capital markets, and in that case they do not appear in the figures. The real figure for UK investment in the US may therefore be higher.

As in the case of inward d.f.i., we might expect the advent of 1992 to result in an increase in UK investment into the EC. In 1988 this was twice as high as in 1987, and this trend is expected to continue as UK companies move to take advantage of liberalized markets in these countries. In the financial sector in particular we can expect to see substantial investment in, for instance, the insurance market, where UK companies can take advantage of ownership-specific advantages in terms of product development.

Explanation of UK direct foreign investment

We have attempted to explain the existence of the investment activities of multinationals in terms of ownership advantages possessed by the companies, location advantages possessed by the countries, and the desire to eliminate uncertainty by internalizing markets within the company structure. To what extent can this kind of analysis explain the changing pattern of UK d.f.i.?

Ownership-specific advantages of foreign multinationals in technology-intensive sectors may help explain the prevalence of this type of investment in UK inward investment. This argument gains credibility when we examine trade statistics, and note that the import of high-technology goods into the UK is an *even higher* proportion of total imports than high-technology inward investment is of total inward investment. In other words, the success of foreign multinationals in selling high-technology goods to the UK may be evidence of their greater competitive ability in the production of such goods; that is to say, they may possess ownership-specific advantages in high-technology sectors. Their investment in such sectors in the UK may therefore be aimed at exploiting these advantages.

Professor Dunning (1981:159) has used location-specific advantages to explain the reduced manufacturing share of inward investment flows. He suggests that the location advantages of the UK as a base for manufacturing activity have deteriorated relative to those of other countries, for a number of reasons which include:

1. The high comparative rate of UK inflation over recent years.
2. The lack of long-term industrial policy.
3. The better growth prospects of other European countries.
4. Restrictive practices of trade unions.
5. Low levels of profitability.

Even the liberal attitude of the UK Government to d.f.i., combined with investment incentives and the availability of satisfactory labour, has not succeeded in making the UK more attractive than other locations for manufacturing investment.

It would appear that both ownership-specific advantages and location-specific advantages can play a part in explaining recent trends in UK d.f.i.

The globalization of multinational company operations makes this type of explanation even more persuasive.

Effects of multinational investment on the UK

The economic effects of d.f.i. by multinationals are both short and long term. In the case of the UK we examine the short-term impacts of multinational investment on employment, the balance of payments, technology and international competitiveness.

We could have chosen to look at other variables. The Steuer Report (Steuer 1973), also examined the effects of foreign investment on regional development, on monopoly, and on industrial relations. In addition we could have considered non-quantifiable effects, such as the implications of d.f.i. for the exercise of economic policy, or for the future of national sovereignty, or for environmental pollution. However, for the purposes of this chapter we limit our analysis to the topics mentioned above.

Effects on employment

There are two ways in which such companies can be responsible for unemployment: first, by 'disvestment' policies of the foreign multinationals; second, by 'rationalization' decisions taken by the UK multinationals to locate production outside the UK. The unemployment which results from either of these, whilst perhaps small from a company perspective, can be devastating for the geographical area in question.

The extent of the employment effects of investment or disvestment will depend on:

a)   whether, and to what degree, these companies are skill- and technology-intensive;
b)   the way in which the investment (disvestment) has indirect effects on employment in other companies;
c)   whether investment is undertaken by 'greenfield' expansion or by takeover; in this latter case investment may actually reduce employment.

Between 1975 and 1978 there was little evidence of 'disvestment' by the foreign multinationals, since the number they employed in the UK *rose* by 3%. In the same period UK-owned companies *reduced* employment by 4% (Killick 1982). After the recession of 1979 the rate of labour shake-out in manufacturing was similar in both foreign multinationals and UK companies (both around 15%, 1978–81). It may be that in periods of economic stability the foreign multinationals add to employment opportunities, but that in periods of recession they are no more reliable than UK companies in retaining employment.

Rationalization in this country by both British and foreign multinationals was accompanied by expansion elsewhere – both Dunlop and ICI expanded production abroad at the same time as they reduced labour in the UK. When ICI closed its Mond division in Merseyside in the late 1970s it immediately opened a similar plant in Wilhelmshaven in West Germany. This is not surprising in view of our earlier observation that multinationals are constantly reappraising the pattern of specialization of both process and product on a worldwide basis. Multinationals may then leave the UK not only because the UK becomes a less attractive location, but because other locations become, for whatever reason, more attractive. Figure 7.6 details

Fig. 7.6 Restructuring and rationalization within selected MNE subsidiaries in the UK engineering and vehicle industries.

Company	Impact of rationalization on UK operations
Caterpillar	Closure of Newcastle plant in 1983 with loss of 2,000 jobs; significant job losses at Glasgow plant, with employment falling from 2,300 in 1981 to 1,200 by 1986. £62m investment in Glasgow plant announced in 1986 with new products and component manufacturing to be introduced; but no new investment transpired, and complete closure of Glasgow plant announced in early 1987
Massey-Ferguson	Substantial reduction in UK employment from 21,000 (1978) to 11,867 (1985) following reorganization of UK operations. New financing package negotiated in May 1986 at both corporate and UK subsidiary levels. Future remains uncertain
Vauxhall (GM)	UK subsidiary has become an assembly operation only, with no design or product development, limited export propensity and high volume of imports following centralization of European operations at Opel (W. Germany). Employment losses in excess of 12,000 since the early 1970s. Additional job losses (1,700) announced at Bedford Commercial Vehicle division in 1986
Ford	Cost cutting measures introduced at all UK plants; closure of foundry works at Dagenham announced in 1984. UK employment fallen by approximately 20,000 since 1979. Turnover, profits and exports, however, remain buoyant and the company has announced several large scale investments in recent years, including £65m at Halewood, £25m at Basildon, and £45m at three UK component plants
Chrysler/Peugeot	Significant rationalization measures introduced following takeover by Peugeot of France, including closure of Linwood plant. Job losses approaching 20,000 since 1979, while turnover and exports have fallen rapidly. Exports totally dependent on supply of kits to Iran
Firestone	Company has ceased manufacturing in the UK following substantial rationalization since 1978
Uniroyal	Tyre production has ceased in the UK, although a limited range of rubber and plastic products is still produced
Goodyear	Company continues to manufacture tyres in the UK, although on a much reduced scale following closure of Clydebank plant in 1981. Total UK employment fallen from 11,000 (1977) to less than 3,000
Michelin	Tyre production remains in UK but on a slightly reduced scale; 4,000 redundancies announced in 1982, including closure of Belfast plant. Additional 2,600 redundancies announced in 1985, mainly at Stoke

Source: Taken from Young, Hood and Hamill (1988: 175).

some examples of such rationalization.

Any attempt to evaluate the welfare effects of multinational activity in terms of employment, should take into account not only the number of jobs created (or lost), but also the effects on the stability of employment of the activities of these companies. There is no doubt that one particular characteristic of these companies is their very high degree of international geographical mobility; another is that wherever they go they are responsible for employing large numbers of people due to the sheer size of their operations. The social effects of the instability that this introduces into the labour market can best be seen by looking at the case of Northern Ireland, whither companies such as DuPont and Courtaulds moved in response to government incentives, and from whence they divested as soon as operations became relatively unprofitable. Alternatively, one could look at the position of new towns such as Skelmersdale in Lancashire, where whole populations relied for employment on a few large multinational companies. Divestment by Courtaulds, Thorn and other companies made Skelmersdale in the 1980s a town without work.

Effects on the balance of payments

Here we must evaluate both inward and outward flows of d.f.i. The balance of payments effects of d.f.i. can be broken down into:

1. A 'capital account' effect, i.e. the annual sum of inward and outward investment flows. As we have seen, the UK is normally a net creditor, with outward direct investment greater than inward. This means that the capital account effect is normally 'adverse' for the UK.

2. An 'invisibles' effect, i.e. foreign companies in the UK remit or 'repatriate' profit and dividends to the parent company abroad, and UK companies receive such payments from affiliates abroad. As regards total dividends, receipts by UK companies and individuals outweigh remittances, so that the 'invisibles' effect is normally 'favourable' for the UK.

3. An 'export' effect, i.e. the increase in exports as a result of sales abroad by foreign multinationals located in this country, and the loss of exports as UK multinationals choose to produce abroad rather than to export.

4. A 'trade' effect, i.e. intra-firm trade generated by the purchase of spares, parts and semi-finished goods by affiliates from parent companies.

Evidence suggests (e.g. Panić and Joyce 1980) that although (3) and (4) above are difficult to quantify, there is an important connection between the degree of foreign participation in an industry and the 'export' and 'trade' effects. UK industries with a high degree of multinational participation tend also to be those which export a high proportion of their sales. However, it is also the case that there is a significant degree of import penetration in those industries where foreign participation is highest, although the correlation here is not as significant as in the case of exports. The net effect is that those industries in which foreign participation in the UK is high, tend to have a relatively favourable balance of trade. In more general terms, Table 7.5 suggests that foreign-owned firms are responsible for a greater share of host country exports and imports than sales and investment. Foreign owned firms would therefore appear to be more active traders than domestic firms.

Reasons for this are not hard to find. Multinationals possess the very characteristics which ensure success in trade, such as process and product specialization, economies of scale, and technological expertise.

In the UK, the sourcing policies of multinationals have often increased imports and made exports less relevant in terms of company strategy. Figure 7.7 shows that import penetration in the car industry has increased mainly because of 'tied imports', i.e. the import of finished cars built elsewhere by multinational car companies (Ford Fiestas in Spain, Vauxhall Cavaliers in Belgium). The figure for 'tied imports' also includes the import of components. Exports have fallen dramatically because the multinationals no longer export built-up cars from the UK.

Overall, the experience of the UK seems to suggest that sectors with high

Table 7.5 Foreign owned
firms (FOFS]

(% of FOFs in total)	Foreign-owned firms (FOFs)				
	US	Germany	UK	Japan	France
Sales	10[c]	19[b]	19[d]	1[a]	27[f]
Value added	–	–	17[d]	–	24[f]
Employment	4[a]	8[a]	13[d]	0.4[a]	20[f]
Assets	9[b]	17[b]	14[c]	1[a]	–
Investment	8[b]	–	13[c]	–	19[f]
Exports	23	24	30	2	32
Imports	23	–	–	15	–

[a] All industries.   [b] All non-financial sectors.   [c] All large companies.
[d] Manufacturing.   [e] Manufacturing, wholesale and retail.
[f] Manufacturing and petroleum.

Fig. 7.7 UK car trade and the
multinationals: (a) import
penetration in the UK car
market; (b) car exports by
manufacturer
Source: Jones (1985)

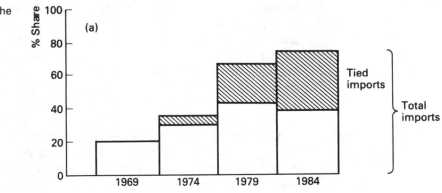

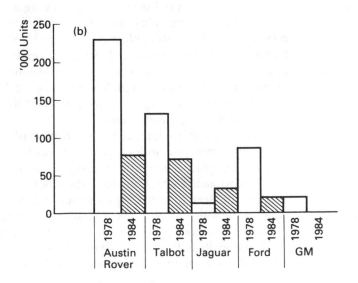

foreign participation have shown the biggest deterioration in trading performance. As well as the purchase of 'tied imports' by UK based multinationals, there has been considerable geographical relocation of productive capacity by UK and foreign owned multinationals in pursuit of disvestment strategies. This has robbed these industries and sectors of the very companies that previously accounted for their successful trading performance.

Effects on technology   The issue of 'technology transfer' is not at all clear-cut. Multinational companies transfer technology from one country to another by investing abroad; this may be product technology, in so far as they introduce new products to other countries, or it may be process technology, if the methods of production used were previously unknown in the host country. In the case of a developing country it is clear that technology transfer introduces into the host country something which was not already there. The benefits of this can be evaluated in terms of increased production or productivity. These benefits must then be weighed against the costs in terms of whether or not the technology is considered 'appropriate' in the light of other objectives such as employment, resource use, or development strategies. In the case of a developed country such as the UK the issue is even more complex. Since knowledge is a 'public good', i.e. freely available to all firms (except where patented), not only is it difficult to measure the effects of technology transfer, it is often even difficult to assess whether any such transfer has taken place!

Some see the existence of technology transfer being evidenced by the way in which d.f.i. in the UK has caused a sectoral shift from less technology-intensive to more technology-intensive production. The benefits of this shift might then be assessed in terms of increased productivity, a faster rate of growth, and the stimulus given to local firms to increase their R & D effort. The costs of this shift might be felt in a number of ways. If high-technology sectors become dominated by foreign companies it can prove impossible for indigenous firms to enter the industry. Solomon (1978) points out that high-technology industry in Europe is largely dominated by US technology. In Italy the ball-bearing industry is 100% foreign owned, in France 80% foreign owned; in the UK carbon-black production is 75% foreign controlled. Other European industries dominated by foreign multinationals include tyres, office equipment, magazines, rubber, agricultural equipment, computers, electronics and space research. The effects of technology transfer will hardly benefit home companies in industries in which they play little role, and into which they find it difficult to enter.

Another possible approach to the problem of assessing the effects of technology transfer is to look at the extent to which the foreign companies' R & D takes place in the host country. The assumption might be that exposure to such research will raise the stock of 'human capital' in the host country, and lead to technological progress in appropriate fields for the host country. In both ways R & D could then be thought of as adding something to available technology which was not there before.

Traditionally R & D is an activity which is undertaken centrally within companies, though there is increasing evidence that this is becoming less the case, and that more and more companies are decentralizing their R & D activities, i.e. locating them in host countries. In a sample of fifty-five US firms, Mansfield, Teece and Romeo (1979) found that an increasing proportion of R & D expenditure by companies took place abroad, rising from 2% in 1960, to an estimated 10% in 1979/80. However, such figures conceal substantial differences, with some firms spending nothing abroad, and some spending 30 or 40% of their total R & D budget overseas. The greater the prominence given by the company to the design needs of the overseas market, the greater the proportion of R & D that tends to be undertaken abroad. For instance, pharmaceutical companies undertake much of their R & D abroad because of the necessity to conform to the variety of standards and regulations imposed by different countries.

Although the UN recommended in 1974 that host countries should require multinational enterprises to undertake R & D in their affiliates in order to stimulate innovation (UN 1974:70), no clear empirical link was established between the two. In fact, no such link may exist; for instance, about three-quarters of overseas R & D expenditure is aimed at improvements in *production flow and process control*, with the results mainly of benefit to the firms which actually spend the money. A much higher proportion of *overseas* R & D is aimed in this direction than is true of R & D in general.

It may therefore be that much of overseas R & D brings little if any benefit to the host country. In fact, there are arguments which appear to indicate that the opposite may be the case. Indigenous R & D may be choked off by the R & D dominance of foreign firms, which results in barriers to new firm entry, and the monopolization of scarce technical expertise. Taken together, this evidence suggests that the welfare effects of technology transfer are perhaps as ambiguous in the case of a developed country such as the UK as they are in the case of an LDC.

Effects on international competitiveness

International competitiveness depends on being able to export the right products at the right price. For the UK this has traditionally meant the ability to export capital-intensive goods at relatively low price. We have seen that the inflow of manufacturing investment has been biased in the direction of the more technology-intensive sectors, which one might expect would help reinforce the UK export of capital- (technology-) intensive goods. However, there is some evidence that these multinational investment flows merely reflect the fact that foreign firms are more technologically advanced than their UK counterparts. In other words, foreign multinationals possess ownership-specific advantages which they use to exploit the UK market in more technology-intensive goods, rather than to reinforce the ability of the UK to export in these traditional sectors. Katrak (1982) shows that the skill and R & D intensity of both UK imports of goods and inward investment flows, have increased over time relative to those of UK exports and outward investment flows. If this is true, then there are important consequences for UK competitiveness and for her long-term trading position. If exports increasingly consist of mature standardized products with low skill and R & D content, then the gains from trade will eventually diminish as these products face increasing competition on world markets, not least from the newly industrializing countries of the Third World. Furthermore, since the rate of growth of these markets is slower than the growth of demand for new, technology-intensive, products, the UK's share of world trade may decline even further than it already has in the last twenty years.

It may be the case, therefore, that although the UK may seem to benefit in resource allocation terms from the inflow of technology-intensive investment, this inflow merely reflects and perpetuates the technological gap which is the root cause of the failure of the UK to compete successfully on world markets.

Control of multinationals

Finally we consider the issue of control. There was no formal attempt to control the activities of multinationals until the 1970s. The guidelines proposed in 1972 by the International Chamber of Commerce, and in 1976 by the OECD's Declaration on International Investment and Multinational Enterprises were no more than codes of behaviour without any legal status. Various individual organizations have attempted to implement agreements relating to specific problems such as labour relations and technology transfer, but the most comprehensive code, which is still under negotiation, is the UN Code of Conduct on Transnational Corporations. Difficulties in the way of agreement stem mainly from the conflict of interests between parent countries, which are generally advanced capitalist countries, and host countries, which are often the relatively less powerful Third World countries.

Because of the lack of an effective code of conduct, a number of countries have imposed their own regulations on the activity of incoming multinationals. Some countries, such as Brazil, exclude foreign firms from 'sensitive' industries such as microcomputers. Others, such as India, seek to control the remittance of profits or royalty payments. Yet others make the granting of such concessions as tax holidays contingent on the employment of a certain proportion of home labour. A frequent requirement, particularly in advanced countries, is that the company involved do some local R & D. Some governments, again such as Brazil, feel powerful enough to enter into negotiation with individual companies with a view to setting up appropriate patterns of conduct. Weaker countries, such as those which need multinationals to produce cash crops for export, do not have this option.

References and further reading

Buckley, P. J. and **Casson, M.** (1976) *The Future of the Multinational Enterprise*. Macmillan.
Business Briefing, 12 April, 1990.
Dunning, J. M. (1981) *International Production and the Multinational Enterprise*. Allen and Unwin.
Jones, D. T. (1985) *The Import Threat to the UK Car Industry*. Science Policy Research Unit, University of Sussex.
Julius, D. (1990) Changing the meaning of trade, *Eurobusiness*, July/Aug.
Kashari, K. (1990) Global marketing: pathways and pitfalls, *Management Reviews and Bibliographies*, 16, 2, pp. 3–6.
Katrak, H. (1982) Labour skills, research and development and capital requirements in the international trade and investment of the UK 1968–78, *National Institute Economic Review*, 101, Aug., pp. 38–47.

Killick, T. (1982) Employment in foreign owned manufacturing plants, *British Business*, 26 Nov.

Lloyds Bank Economic Bulletin (1990) UK open for business, June.

McAleese, D. and **Counahan, M.** (1979) 'Stickers' or 'snatchers': employment in multinational corporations during the recession, *Oxford Bulletin of Economics and Statistics,* **41**, 4, pp. 345–58.

Mansfield, E., Teece, D. and **Romeo, A.** (1979) Overseas research and development by US-based firms, *Economica*, **46**, pp. 187–96.

Panić, M. and **Joyce, P. L.** (1980) UK manufacturing industry, international integration and trade performance, *Bank of England Quarterly Bulletin*, **20**, 1, pp. 42–50.

Solomon, L. D. (1978) *Multinational Corporations and the Emerging World Order*. National University Publications, New York.

Steuer, M. (1973) *The Impact of Foreign Direct Investment in the UK*. HMSO.

UN (1974) *The Impact of Multinational Corporations on Development and on International Relations*. United Nations, New York.

UN (1978) *Transnational Corporations in World Development*. United Nations, New York.

UN (1982) *Transnational Corporations in World Development – A Re-examination*. United Nations, New York.

Young, S., Hood, N. and **Hamill J.** (1988) *Foreign Multinationals and the British Economy*. Croom Helm.

8   The nationalized industries and privatization

There is no political consensus on the desired size and role of nationalized industries in the UK economy. This chapter summarizes some aspects of the debate, beginning with the case for nationalization. Issues concerning finance and pricing are analysed, showing that the constraints imposed by governments on the nationalized industries often leave them with little independent room for manœuvre. We attempt to evaluate the performance of the UK nationalized industries, using both overseas and domestic companies for comparison. We conclude with the case for and against privatization.

Nature and importance

Nationalized industries are owned and run by public corporations. These are trading bodies whose chairmen and board members are appointed by the secretary of state concerned. The nationalized industries are quite separate entities from the Government itself. They run their businesses without close supervision but within the constraints imposed by government policy.

Not all public corporations are, however, nationalized industries. The National Economic Development Office (NEDO 1976) has excluded from its definition of the nationalized industries those public corporations whose members are Civil Servants, e.g. Her Majesty's Stationery Office (HMSO), and also those whose revenue is not primarily earned through trading in the market, e.g. the National Enterprise Board (NEB). Also excluded from the nationalized industries, even though the Government holds shares in them, are companies such as British Telecom (since 1984) and Rolls-Royce because they are *not* run by public corporations.

Since 1979 many nationalized industries have been privatized. Their share of GDP has fallen from 9% in 1979 to about 4% by 1989/90; their share of annual investment from 11½% to 3.8% and their share of employment from 7.3% to just under 3.5% (1988/9). Table 8.1 presents some indicators of the scale of the remaining major nationalized industries, to which should be added Nuclear Electric.

Reasons for nationalization

This has been one of the most contentious issues in politics, both between Labour and the other major parties, and also within the Labour Party, where it contributed to the split which led to the formation of the Social Democratic Party. Although it raises economic issues, there are deep divisions of opinion

	Output	Turnover £m	Employment	Capital expenditure £m
British Coal (1987/88)	103.5 million tons	4,388	117,355	555
British Rail	21,327 million passenger miles 11,249 freight tonne miles	2,557	123,761	590
London Regional Transport	10,780 million passenger kilometres	775	38,906	312
Civil Aviation Authority	3,295,000 aircraft movements	301	6,551	32
The Post Office Group (inc. Girobank)	53 million letters per day delivered	4.459	206,856	242

Sources: Reports and accounts of British Coal and The Post Office Group. HMSO 1990 (Cm. 1004, 1005, 1007, 1021).

Table 8.1 Indicators of the major nationalized industries 1988/89

Party. Although it raises economic issues, there are deep divisions of opinion based on differing political philosophies which economic arguments alone will not resolve. Here we consider the whole range of arguments advanced in favour of nationalization.

Political

The political case for nationalization is that private ownership of productive assets creates a concentration of power over resources which is intolerable in a democracy. Clause 4 of the Labour Party's constitution promised public ownership of the means of production, distribution and exchange which, if taken literally, means the whole economy. The founders of the Labour Party saw public ownership as a necessary step towards full-scale socialism and one which would aid economic planning. This developed into a policy of nationalizing the 'commanding heights' of the economy. The 1945–51 Labour Government could claim to have achieved this by nationalizing the transport industries, the power industries and the iron and steel industries, but could be criticized for failing to include important sectors such as banking, insurance, chemicals and electrical engineering. Those in favour of a literal interpretation of Clause 4 have been in a minority within the Labour Party, the majority believing that there are other means of controlling economic activity besides outright public ownership.

Post-war reconstruction

After the Second World War some industries, e.g. the railways, were extremely run-down, requiring large-scale investment and repair. For these, the provision of state finance through nationalization seemed a sensible solution. In other industries, e.g. steel, nationalization was a means of achieving reorganization so that economies of scale could be fully exploited. In still other industries, e.g. gas and electricity, reorganization was required to change the industry base from the local to the national.[1] A different government might, of course, have used policy measures other than nationalization, such as grants and tax reliefs, to achieve these objectives.

The public interest

There are many situations where commercial criteria, with their focus on profitability, are at odds with a broader view of the public interest, and in such cases nationalization is one solution. For instance, the Post Office aims to make a profit overall, but in doing so makes losses on rural services which are subsidized by profits made elsewhere – a 'cross-subsidy' from one group of consumers to another. Some object to cross-subsidization in that it interferes with the price mechanism in its role of resource allocation when some consumers pay less than the true cost of the services they buy, whilst others pay more than the true cost. However, in the case of the Post Office cross-subsidization seems reasonable, if only because we may all want to send letters to outlying areas from time to time, and all derive benefit from the existence of a full national postal service. A private sector profit-orientated firm might not be prepared to undertake the loss-making Post Office services.

In the electricity industry the present government has, controversially, decided that the continued generation of electricity by nuclear power is in the public interest and is establishing Nuclear Electric as a public corporation whilst privatizing the rest of the industry. In taking this decision it rejected the verdict of the markets which, all over the world, have baulked at both the safety risks and the full financial costs of the nuclear industry. The Government's view is that nuclear power offers strategic advantages as an alternative to fossil fuels and also environmental benefits in that it does not contribute to the greenhouse effect. The safety risks are said to be acceptable. Chernobyl, it is argued, could not happen in the UK.

Nationalization may also be a means of promoting the public interest when entire businesses are about to collapse. The state has sometimes intervened to effect a rescue, as in 1970 when the Conservative Government decided to nationalize Rolls-Royce rather than see the company liquidated. Prestige, strategic considerations, effects on employment and on the balance of payments all played a part in the argument, as the judgement of the market was rejected in favour of a broader view of the public interest. In the long run the markets were proved wrong and the decision to intervene commercially correct, as the company is a world leader in aero-engine technology and has been successfully returned to the private sector.

State monopoly

The 'natural monopoly' argument is often advanced in favour of nationalization of certain industries. Economies of scale in railways, electricity and gas industries are perhaps so great that the tendency towards monopoly can be termed 'natural'. Competing provision of these services, with duplication of investment, would clearly be wasteful of resources. The theory of the firm suggests that monopolies may enjoy supernormal profits, charging higher prices and producing lower output than would a competitive industry with the same cost conditions. However, where there are sufficient economies of scale, the monopoly price could be lower and output higher than under competition (see Fig. 9.1). Monopoly might then be the preferred market form, especially if it can be regulated. Nationalization is one means of achieving such regulation.

Presence of externalities

Externalities occur when economic decisions create costs or benefits for people other than the decision-taker; these are called social costs or social benefits. For example, a firm producing textiles may emit industrial effluent, polluting nearby rivers and causing loss of amenity. In other words, society is forced to bear part of the cost of private industrial activity. Sometimes those who impose external costs in this way can be controlled by legislation (pollution controls, Clean Air Acts), or penalized through taxation. The parties affected might be compensated, using the revenue raised from taxing those firms creating social costs. On the other hand, firms creating social benefits may be rewarded by the receipt of subsidies. In other cases nationalization is a possible solution. If the industry is run in the public interest, it might be expected that full account will be taken of any externalities. For instance, it can be argued that railways reduce road usage, creating social benefits by relieving urban congestion, pollution and traffic accidents. This is one aspect of the case for subsidizing British Rail through the passenger service obligation grant which, in 1988/9, amounted to £533 million. The grant enabled British Rail to continue operating some loss making services. Nationalization is one means of exercising public control over the use of subsidies when these are thought to be in the public interest.

Improved industrial climate

There was hope after 1945 that the removal of private capital would improve labour relations in the industries concerned, promoting the feeling of co-ownership. The coal industry in particular had a bitter legacy of industrial relations. From nationalization until the strike of 1973, industrial relations in the coal industry, judged by days lost in disputes, seemed to have dramatically improved over pre-war days. Nevertheless, for the nationalized industries as a whole, it is fair to say that the hopes of the 1940s have not been fulfilled, perhaps because the form of nationalization adopted in the UK has done little to involve workers in the running of their industries. Participation in management, worker directors, genuine consultation and even an adequate flow of information to workers are no more common in the UK public sector than they are in the private sector.

Redistribution of wealth

Nationalization of private sector assets without compensation is a well-tried revolutionary means of changing the distribution of wealth in an inegalitarian society. Nationalization in the UK has not, unlike the Soviet Union in 1917, been used in this way; in the UK there has almost always been 'fair' compensation. Indeed, the compensation paid between 1945 and 1951 was criticized as over-generous, enabling shareholders to get their wealth out of industries which, in the main, had poor prospects (e.g. railways, coal), in order to buy new shareholdings in growth industries (e.g. chemicals, consumer durables). Once 'fair' compensation is accepted in principle in state acquisitions of private capital, then nationalization ceases to be a mechanism for redistribution of wealth.

An alternative to 'fair' compensation is confiscation. However, it would have serious consequences for UK capital markets. Ownership of assets in the UK would, in future, carry the additional risk of total loss by state confiscation, which could influence decisions to invest in new UK-based plant and equipment, and to buy UK shares. The ability of UK companies to invest and to raise finance might therefore be undermined. The transfer of assets might also prove inequitable, since shares are held by pension funds and insurance companies on behalf of millions of small savers who would then be penalized by confiscation.

Issues facing nationalized industries

One of the important sources of finance for any industry is internally generated profit. The public and the Press have ambivalent attitudes to the profit performance of the nationalized industries. If profits are high there are allegations of exploitation of captive consumers, but if there are losses there are cries of waste and inefficiency. The vastly differing market and cost conditions faced by the different industries make comparisons of their profitability a difficult exercise. For example, British Coal is increasingly facing fierce competition from low cost producers, so price rises may result in loss of business or revenue. In stark contrast, British Rail enjoys a monopolistic position with low price elasticity on many routes, creating the opportunity to raise prices in order to boost revenue.

Sources of finance

Profits contribute to the financing of investment, and industries which do not make adequate profits must seek other sources of finance, either internally or externally. The overall position of the industries still nationalized in March 1988 is shown in Table 8.2. Of a total capital requirement of £4,909m. in 1989/90, £4,459m. (around 90%) was raised internally. Internal sources include provisions made for depreciation as well as profits, but are reduced by payments of interest, dividends and tax. External sources of finance include Government (grants, subsidies, loans and equity), borrowing from the financial markets and some leasing of capital assets. Attention focuses on total external finance because it is included in the planning total for public expenditure; the trading activities of nationalized industries are not counted as part of public expenditure. It has been an objective of government policy since 1979 that the industries should raise an increasing proportion of their finance internally, enabling a reduction in the planning total for public expenditure and the Public Sector Borrowing Requirement (PSBR). Privatization and reduced levels of support for the remaining industries have cut external financing from £3,000 million in 1979/80 to only £449 million in

Table 8.2 Total nationalized industries financing 1989/90 (estimated out-turn) and 1992/93 plans (£m.)

	1989/90 (est. out-turns)	1992/93 plans
Total capital requirements	4,909	3,060
Total *internal* resources	4,459	1,540
of which:		
Current cost operating profit	689	
Other	3,770	Not published
Total *external* finance	449	−1,510
of which:		
Borrowing (net)	−960	330
Subsidies	1,168	750
Capital grants	242	430

Source: HMSO (1990: Cm. 1021).

1989/90. The figures for 1989/90 include £1,900 million *negative* external financing from the electricity industry, meaning that the industry contributed £1,900 million to the Treasury from its profits. External financing is planned to rise to £1,510 million by 1992/3, partly because the privatization of electricity will end that industry's contributions to the Treasury and also because British Rail and London Transport have increased investment programmes.

	Expenditure on fixed assets in the UK	Current cost operating profit	External grants and subsidies	Total external financing 1989/90	Planned EFL 1992/93
British Coal	520	−285	564	1,175	280
British Railways Board	721	−536	487	655	760
British Shipbuilders (Merchant)	–	1	12	35	−20
British Waterways Board	12	−45	48	47	50
Caledonian MacBrayne Ltd.	2	−6	7	1	10
Civil Aviation Authority	54	20	3	47	70
London Regional Transport	393	−160	287	287	430
Post Office	242	−8	–	−34	−76
Total	1,944	−1,018	1,408	2,213	1,510

Source: HMSO (1990 Cm. 1021).

Table 8.3 Financing requirements of nationalized industries; 1989/90 estimated out-turn (£m) [excluding those planned to be privatized by March 1993]

Table 8.3 gives data at the industry level on investment and its financing for those industries which are planned to stay nationalized until 1993. As a group, these industries required external financing of £2,213 million in 1989/90. Only the Post Office made a positive contribution to the Treasury (shown by negative external financing), although making an operating loss. The Civil Aviation Authority was the only profit maker. British Coal and British Railways are the two major industries responsible for the burden on the Exchequer, requiring external finance of £1,830 million. They are loss making and also have large investment programmes.

The nationalized industries arrange their borrowing either through the Government's National Loans Fund (NLF) or by the issue of bonds to overseas lenders. Since 1982 there has also been provision for direct use of the domestic capital market. A further source of finance is the issue of public dividend capital (PDC), by which the Government takes up stocks in the public corporation and becomes entitled to receive dividends. In general this has been a cheap form of finance; the dividends paid have been low or non-existent.

Pricing

Prices are of key importance to any trading organization. The pricing decision determines the quantity of output the market will take and therefore the total revenue of the firm, since total revenue equals price multiplied by quantity. Costs also vary with output so that they, too, are influenced by the pricing decision. With total profit defined as total revenue minus total cost, it is clear that total profit is affected by price. Determination of price is therefore important for all organizations, although for the nationalized industries there are a number of important constraints.

The public interest   Nationalized industries are expected to bear in mind their public service obligations in fixing prices. It would, for example, be seen as socially unacceptable and an abuse of monopoly power if the Post Office's sole criterion was to charge prices which the market would bear. The process of consultation with consumer representatives on user councils, such as the Post Office Users' National Council (POUNC), is one means of protecting the public interest.

Government macroeconomic objectives   Governments often intervene in nationalized industry pricing in pursuit of their macroeconomic policy objectives. Between 1970 and 1973 nationalized industry prices were held down as part of a government anti-inflation strategy. It was thought that if the public sector restrained price rises then the rate of increase of the Retail Price Index (RPI) would be reduced, and wage claims would be moderated. At the same time industries using inputs of goods and services produced by the nationalized industries would find their costs increasing at a reduced rate and consequently would be able to moderate their price increases.

However, the effect of restraining price rises is to raise the real income of consumers, who may then increase their demand for other goods and services, further fuelling inflation. The nationalized industries also found their costs increasing more rapidly than their prices and as a result ran into deficits. These deficits were funded by borrowing, which raised the PSBR and contributed to growth of the money supply. This may in turn have further stimulated inflation.

In 1976 the then Labour Government introduced the system of cash limits, or external financing limits, as part of its programme to control and cut public expenditure (see Table 8.3 and the discussion below). If external borrowing is limited in this way then the nationalized industries are forced to generate additional investment funds from their own revenues. Since demand for the output of the nationalized industries is generally price-inelastic, prices often have to be raised to create more revenue. In the case of the gas industry, prices had to be raised by 22% during 1982/83 in order to pay a levy to the Government of £704m., and to create a planned current operating profit of £542m. Between 1980 and 1983 gas prices rose by 100%, bringing them much closer to electricity prices which rose by only 60% in the same period. This was presented as a measure to encourage energy conservation but it was also a convenient means of reducing the PSBR and of preparing the industry for privatization.

Government microeconomic objectives   The microeconomic objective of achieving an efficient allocation of resources has placed a third constraint on the pricing policy of nationalized industries. Prices are signals to consumers, indicating the resource costs of goods and services. Where costs are high, standard welfare theory would suggest that prices should also be high so that consumers can judge whether the benefits to be derived from consumption are greater than the costs incurred. Even if we accept that the prices of nationalized industries should be constrained by microeconomic objectives, there still remains the problem of deciding which costs to include in the pricing decision.

Marginal cost pricing – theory

Under the assumptions of perfect competition, price for the profit-maximizing industry (and the firm) is always equal to the marginal cost (MC) of production. The marginal cost is the extra cost of producing the last unit of output, and if there are no externalities then marginal cost represents the value of the output which the resources could have produced in their best alternative use. The price consumers pay represents their valuation of the benefits of consumption, i.e. their 'willingness to pay' (WTP). This is indicated by the demand or average revenue curve.

Fig. 8.1 Marginal cost pricing and consumer welfare

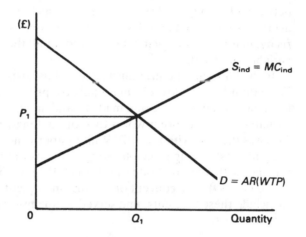

In Fig. 8.1 we have a perfectly competitive industry. The reader familiar with the theory of the firm will know that the supply curve of the perfectly competitive industry is the marginal cost curve of that industry. Price will be set at P_1, and output at Q_1, by the intersection of supply, MC, and demand, AR (WTP). This is the price and output at which consumer welfare is a maximum. If output is less than Q_1, $WTP > MC$, so that there is more consumer benefit than resource cost in producing additional units of output. Above Q_1, $WTP < MC$, i.e. consumer benefit is below the resource cost of producing each extra unit beyond Q_1. Clearly, at Q_1, with $WTP = MC$, we have a welfare maximum. It is this kind of theoretical analysis which has led governments to impose marginal cost pricing techniques on the nationalized industries.

Marginal cost pricing – practice

The principle of setting price equal to marginal cost was first explicitly introduced in the 1967 White Paper on the nationalized industries. Putting the principle into practice is not, however, without its difficulties.

One particular problem is that marginal cost pricing may result in losses. This is the case when average costs are falling. In Fig. 8.2 when average variable cost (AVC) is falling, marginal cost (MC) must be below it.[2] Setting price equal to marginal cost for output levels below Q_1 will result in a price which is below AVC. Setting price equal to marginal cost for output levels

Fig. 8.2 Problems for
marginal cost pricing

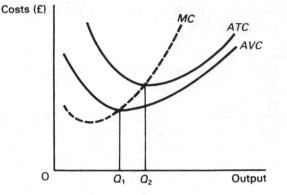

between Q_1 and Q_2 will result in a price which, whilst above AVC, is below average total cost (ATC). Except where output is above Q_2, when ATC is rising, marginal cost pricing does not cover all the costs incurred, both variable and fixed.

In the long run, the firm must cover all its costs, both variable and fixed. For output levels below Q_2, marginal cost pricing fails to do this. In practice, therefore, attempts are often made to add an element of capital or fixed costs to marginal cost, in other words to adopt a 'long-run' view of marginal costs. This was the case with the 1978 White Paper which, whilst retaining the marginal cost pricing principle, sought to cover the capital costs of projects, together with a 5% real rate of return (RRR) on the capital invested (raised to 8% in 1989). The concept of average incremental cost (AIC) was defined to include these elements, and served as an approximation to long-run marginal cost.

The theory of the second best

The case for the nationalized industries following a marginal cost pricing policy is that by so doing they will raise economic welfare. However, this is only necessarily true in a 'first-best' economy. In such an economy there is perfect competition everywhere, no uncertainty, no externalities, and no government intervention in the form of taxes and subsidies. The real economy is far removed from this, characterized by many market imperfections. In such a second-best economy the pursuit of marginal cost pricing by the nationalized industries may not, in fact, raise economic welfare; it may even reduce it. To raise economic welfare may now require the nationalized industries to set prices which diverge from marginal cost. This is the so-called theory of the second best. For example, if a rail service reduces road congestion and traffic accidents in a city, then these external benefits may make it possible to justify a lower price for the rail service. The real costs of the rail service are in this case overstated, because the money costs of operating the service do not take into account the benefits of reduced congestion and fewer accidents. Any commercial losses on rail should then, on economic grounds, be subsidized to the value of the congestion and road accidents which have been avoided. In this case price should be lower than marginal cost alone would have dictated.

In practice there are further complications in multi-product firms, which means most of the nationalized industries. The Civil Aviation Authority, for example, may be seen as supplying a different product at different times of the day, since a flight 'slot' supplied at one time is usually a poor substitute for one supplied at any other time. It may then be very difficult to estimate marginal costs accurately as each 'product' shares the same capital stock and there is a high degree of interdependence between the products. It becomes much easier to adopt an 'average cost plus' approach to pricing even if this does result in some arbitrary cross-subsidization. Further pressures away from marginal cost pricing are created by the financial targets set by the Government. Once profit and investment targets, together with cash limits, are established there remains little leeway for setting prices.

In some instances the prices are market determined; for example British Coal's contracts with the new electricity companies. Where there is scope for price setting then the 'financial target will determine the general level of prices in the light of general objectives and the need to cover continuing costs of supply including an adequate return on capital' (HMSO Cm 1021, 1990). Once profit and investment targets, together with cash limits, are set there remains little leeway for setting prices.

Control of nationalized industries

Each industry agrees strategic objectives with its supervising ministry. The basic objective of British Coal, for example, is 'to earn a satisfactory rate of return on its net assets and achieve full financial viability without Government support'. This objective is to be reached subject to external financing limits (EFLs) and financial performance targets introduced in the 1978 White Paper. Additionally, since the 1980 Competition Act, the industries are subject to investigation by the Monopolies and Mergers Commission.

1. *Cash limits*. Control under the policy of cash limits involves setting an external financing limit (EFL) for each industry – see Table 8.3, last column. As the term suggests, the figure set is the upper limit on all funds which may be raised from outside the industry in the year in question and it is this total which enters the planning total for public expenditure.

Once the EFL is established, then there are clear implications for the level of capital investment in the industry, given its profitability. Any action which reduces profits then jeopardizes investment plans in the industry and perhaps employment, an important negotiating point in industrial disputes.

External financing limits are negotiated between ministers and boards, and it is then the task of the boards to run their industries so that they remain within the EFL. If this proves impossible then the EFL may be relaxed for the year in question, but consideration will be given to adjusting the following year's EFL to recoup the overspend. The consequence is that financially sound corporations (e.g. BT when nationalized) have been prevented from borrowing on the scale they would like to develop their business – all in the cause of restricting PSBR and achieving monetary control.

2. *Financial targets: medium term*. A financial target for the medium term (usually three years) which should be decided in the light of all factors affecting the industry. Examples of financial targets and outcomes are as shown in Table 8.4(a).

3. *Financial targets: new programme*. In addition to the financial target for the industry as a whole, all *new programmes* should show a return on capital of 8% (also known as the required rate of return – RRR). This rate has been chosen on the basis of the opportunity cost of capital, in that it represents what capital might have earned if invested in the private sector. It appears on that basis a rather high rate and is more than the industries have normally paid for their capital to the NLF. Consequently, one result of the White Paper is for nationalized industries to seek higher profits (and prices) than they otherwise would have done. Notice that it is *programmes*, not projects, which are being considered. Subject to the constraint that broad programmes of investment yield 8% in real terms, management retains the right to appraise *individual projects* in accordance with its own criteria.

4. *Performance targets*. Industries are also set performance targets which can be seen as moderating any tendency to achieve the financial targets at the expense of the consumer through the use of monopoly power. Examples of performance targets and outcomes are shown in Table 8.4(b).

Table 8.4(a) Financial targets

	Target	Achievement
British Railways Board	By 1992–93 Public Sector Obligation (PSO) grant down to £345m	1988–89: PSO grant £549m
British Coal	1988–89: breakeven	1988–89: deficit of £203m
Post Office	1989–90 to 1991–92: 6.4% return on capital employed after interest and before tax	1988–89: 2.5%

Source: HMSO (1990 Cm. 1021).

Table 8.4(b) Performance targets

	Performance target	Achievement
British Railways Board	90% of Inter-City trains to arrive within 10 minutes of scheduled time	1988–89: 87%
British Coal	To reduce operating costs by at least 20% in real terms between 1985–86 and 1989–90	20% reduction achieved 1988–89
Post Office	To reduce real unit costs of handling letters by 6% over the 3 years to March 1989	5.4% reduction

Sources: HMSO (1990 Cm. 1004, 1005, 1007).

These criteria for performance may conflict. In particular, many of the measures necessary to improve the non-financial performance may require investment of a type which might not satisfy the financial criteria in (2) and

(3) above. For example, rail operating costs per mile can be reduced by investing in new, more economical rolling stock, but it may not yield an RRR of 8%. In addition, the choice of a common RRR on all new investment programmes, irrespective of industry, ignores the differences in risk between industries.

Performance of the nationalized industries

There are major difficulties in judging the performance of nationalized industries. As monopolies, many of them have no direct competitors with which to make comparison. Comparison with private sector companies in other industries is not very helpful because conditions differ so much between industries. It is then tempting to make comparisons with the same industry in another country, but again conditions are very dissimilar.

Table 8.5 Nationalized industries labour productivity[1]

		Annual percentage change		
		Nationalized industries[2,3]	Manufacturing industries	Whole economy[4]
	1979–80	0.8	1.0	0.7
	1980–81	−1.8	−5.3	−2.1
	1981–82	2.0	6.9	3.2
	1982–83	2.0	6.3	3.2
	1983–84	4.5	8.5	3.5
	1984–85	5.5	4.9	1.1
	1985–86	8.4	1.8	1.7
	1986–87	8.6	4.8	3.4
	1987–88	7.3	6.4	3.0
	1988–89	6.4	5.6	2.2
Average to	1979–80 1988–89	4.4	4.0	2.0

[1] Output per person employed.
[2] Adjusted for the coal strike.
[3] Industries in the public sector at 31 March 1990.
[4] Excluding North Sea sector.

Source: HMSO (1990: Cm. 1021).

Table 8.5 presents data for the growth of labour productivity (in the form of output per person employed) in the industries still nationalized in March 1990. The table shows that labour productivity grew at an annual rate of 4.4% in the nationalized industries over the period 1979/80–1988/89, greater than the average for manufacturing and more than twice the average for the whole economy. This is a remarkable performance because this set of businesses is, in the main, what is left after the privatization of the best performers. However it is not unambiguous evidence of the success of public ownership because we do not know what the *potential* for labour productivity improvement was and we do not have data for productivity of *capital*. Increased labour productivity could be a result of massive capital investment, which might be accompanied by falling output per unit of capital and even falling total factor productivity. Molyneux and Thompson (1987) have shown that between 1978 and 1985, *total factor productivity* was actually rising at 2.8% per year in British Rail and 1.9% per year in the Post Office, but was unchanged in British Coal. It seems likely that capital investment has made a contribution to rising productivity as fixed investment in the industries rose from £918 million in 1984/85 to £1,682 million in 1988/89. There has also been a contribution from changed working practices.

Industries with good productive performance can still fail the consumer if they produce a range of products which do not maximize consumer welfare; they will then be 'allocatively inefficient' even if 'productively efficient'. As explained earlier, allocative efficiency is achieved under the assumptions of perfect competition if prices are set in accordance with marginal cost. If there are *social* costs or benefits, then prices may be adjusted accordingly. Molyneux and Thompson conclude that, typically, nationalized industries are *not* applying marginal cost pricing and often lack the necessary information about costs and consumer preferences in different sectors of their markets. The standard national postal charges, quoted earlier, are a good example of a situation resulting in haphazard cross-subsidization among customers. So despite apparently good productive efficiency, the nationalized industries have often failed to achieve allocative efficiency, a conclusion supported by an OECD report (1988/89). Many of the pricing practices in the private sector would, however, lead to exactly the same criticism.

Consumers themselves are the most appropriate judges of any business's performance. The remaining nationalized industries include several which have a poor image among consumers, for example London Regional Transport, which is responsible for the overcrowding and poor facilities on the Underground. In 1989 the Consumer Association did a survey of 431 British Rail Network South-East commuters and also 500 Inter-City passengers. Of the commuters, two thirds thought the quality of the service had declined over the previous three years and 40% thought the quality was poor value for money. In contrast, over 80% of the Inter-City passengers said that the service was 'fairly or very good'. Some of the problems of the Underground and Network South-East are the result of underinvestment which follows from the reduction of subsidies. The Consumer Association has shown that the UK provides only one third as much subsidy to British Rail as a proportion of GDP, as the average for a sample of eight European countries.

Privatization

Privatization means the transfer of assets or economic activity from the public sector to the private sector. It is more than just a synonym for denationalization and has many facets. Sometimes the Government has kept a substantial shareholding in privatized public corporations (49.8% in BT). In other cases a public corporation has been sold in its entirety (e.g. National Freight Corporation). Government-owned shares in companies which were not public corporations have also been sold (e.g. British Petroleum, Amersham International). Where public sector corporations and companies are not attractive propositions for *complete* privatization then profitable assets have been sold (e.g. Jaguar Cars from the then British Leyland and also British Rail Hotels). The divide between public and private sectors may be broken down by joint ventures such as the formation of Allied Steel and Wire by British Steel and GKN. In the local authority sector, in the period 1982/83–1987/88 a total of 673,000 dwellings have been sold to tenants, whilst only 136,800 new dwellings have been built. Throughout the public sector many activities have been opened up to market forces by inviting tenders. British Rail catering, local authority refuse collection and hospital cleaning are all examples of formerly 'in house' services which are now contracted out. British Rail has benefited from an injection of private capital in its rolling stock; about 40% of the freight wagons running on its tracks are privately owned. There is even serious discussion of prisons being financed and run by the private sector. The British Government was insistent that the Channel Tunnel be privately financed and operated, and has also allowed the private sector to finance and operate the new bridge across the Thames at Dartford.

All over the world privatization seems to be an idea whose time has come, nowhere more so than in Eastern Europe where the new Governments installed after the political upheavals of 1989 are urgently looking for ways of increasing the role of the private sector of their economies. Advice is often sought from the UK. State assets have also been sold in other Western European countries. In the Third World, privatization appeals to Governments as a way of raising finance without increasing their debt burden.

Table 8.6 shows central Government receipts from privatization and the businesses which have been sold over 11 years of Conservative administration.

In addition to the proceeds to the Government, some public sector businesses *retained* their own receipts. These include the businesses shown in Table 8.7 (receipts shown in £ million).

Looking forward from 1990/91 to 1992/93, the public expenditure plans estimate privatization receipts of £5 billion for each of the three years. The Government's objective for the remaining nationalized industries is:

'to ensure their effectiveness and efficiency as commercial concerns and to strengthen them to the point where they can be transferred to the private sector, or where necessary, remain as successful businesses in the public sector'.

The biggest privatization of the early 1990s was that of the electricity industry, which raised around £10 billion. There will be further receipts from the water privatization. Opportunities will be taken to involve more private capital in British Rail and, possibly, British Coal but neither business is financially sound enough for a quick full privatization. Although the Conservative government indicated that the Royal Mail would not be privatized, there is still the possibility of hiving-off parts of the Post Office Group. For instance there is the precedent of Girobank, which the Post Office sold to the Alliance and Leicester Building Society in 1990.

The case for privatization

In the Conservative Party there is now a commitment to 'privatize' wherever possible, as the following statement by Mr Nicholas Ridley, then Financial Secretary to the Treasury, illustrates:

The nationalized industries and privatization

£ million

	1979–80 outturn to 1981–82 outturn	1982–83 outturn	1983–84 outturn	1984–85 outturn	1985–86 outturn	1986–87 outturn	1987–88 outturn	1988–89 outturn	1989–90 estimated outturn
Amersham International	64								
Associated British Ports Holdings plc		46		51					
British Airports Authority							534	689	
British Aerospace plc – sale of shares	43				347				
British Airways plc – sale of shares						435	419		
British Gas plc – sale of shares						1,820	1,758	1,555	
British Gas plc – redemption of debt						750		250	400
British Petroleum plc – sale of shares	284		543				863	3.030	1,370
British Steel plc – sale of shares								1,138	1,280
British Sugar Corporation	44								
British Telecommunications plc – sale of shares				1,358	1,246	1,081			
British Telecommunications plc – loan stock				44	61	53	23	85	
British Telecommunications plc – redemption of preference shares						250	250	250	
Britoil plc – sale of shares		334	293		426				
Cable and Wireless plc – sale of shares	181		263		577				
Enterprise Oil plc – sale of shares				384					
Forestry Commission		14	21	28	17	18	15	15	10
General Practice Finance Corporation								67	
Land Settlement			2	12	5	2			
Motorway Service leases		4	1			2	1		
National Enterprise Board Holdings	122			168	30	34			
Plant Breeding Institute							65		
Rolls-Royce							1,028	3	
Royal Ordnance							186		
Water plcs – sale of shares									500
Miscellaneous	342	57	15	4	−2	15	−2	−7	20
Total		455	1,139	2,050	2,707	4,460	5,140	7,073	3,580

Source: HMSO (1990).

Table 8.6 Privatization proceeds, 1979–80 to 1989–90 (excluding proceeds from sales of subsidiaries)

It must be right to press ahead with the transfer of ownership from state to private enterprise of as many public sector businesses as possible. . . . The introduction of competition must be linked to a transfer of ownership to private citizens and away from the State. Real public ownership – that is ownership by people – must be and is our ultimate goal. (Treasury 1982)

The policy stems from the traditional Conservative antipathy to the state and the new emphasis on markets which has come from 'supply side' economics. Public corporations are seen as producer led, serving the interests of their managements and workers first and never fully subjected to the test of the market if their losses are written off by the state. Privatization exposes the industries to market forces. If a state monopoly is broken (e.g. Mercury competing with BT) then consumers may choose the more satisfactory

Table 8.7 Privatization of companies retaining their own receipts and the value of those receipts (£m)

		£m
1982–83	British Rail Hotels	30
	International Aeradio Ltd	60
1983–84	British Rail Hotels	15
1984–85	Jaguar Cars	297
	British Gas onshore oil assets	82
	Sealink	40
1985–86	British Shipbuilders warship yards	75
	Sealink (further receipts)	26
1986–87	BA Helicopters	14
	Unipart (Rover) up to	52
	Leyland Bus (Rover)	4
	British Coal subsidiaries	1
1987–88	British Transport Advertising	40
	Istel (Rover subsidiary)	48
1988–89	National Bus Company Subsidiaries	36
1989–90	Scottish Bus Group	18

Source: HMSO (1990).

service, which will generate profits and expand, thus resources are allocated in response to consumer demand. The pressure to meet market requirements should improve internal efficiency (X efficiency). The stock market provides a further market test for privatized companies. Poor performance in meeting consumer preferences or in utilizing assets should result in a share price which underperforms the rest of the market and undervalues the company's assets, ultimately leaving it vulnerable to takeover by a company able to make better use of the assets. Supporters of privatization place more faith in these market forces than in the monitoring activities of Departments of State and Parliamentary Committees.

The Conservative Party also emphasizes wider share ownership. By 1990, share ownership in the UK had extended to 24% of the adult population, having been only 5% as recently as 1983. The total number of UK shareholders is about the same as the number of trade-unionists. This increase is largely due to privatization. A new group of shareholders has been attracted and become participants in the 'enterprise culture'. Additionally 90% of the employees in the privatized companies have become shareholders in the companies they work for (HMSO 1988: vol. 1). Worker share ownership is advocated as a means of involving workers more closely with their companies and achieving improved industrial relations. This has been taken further by selling companies to their managers (e.g. Leyland Bus 1987) or to consortiums of managers and workers (e.g. National Freight 1982). The latter is regarded as a highly successful example, profits having grown more than tenfold since privatization.

Privatization has also been seen as a way in which the PSBR can be cut, at a stroke! The finance of external borrowing by the nationalized industries is part of public expenditure, which then ceases when these industries become privately owned. Sale of assets or shares also increases government revenue, again reducing the PSBR in the year of the sale. Over the period 1979/80–1989/90 the Treasury gained £27.7bn from asset sales. In the three years on from 1990/91, asset sales of £5.0bn are planned for each year. Privatization made a very significant contribution to the budget surpluses of the late 1980s.

The activities of state-owned organizations are constrained by their relationship with the Government. They lack financial freedom to raise investment capital externally because the Government is concerned about restraining the growth of public expenditure (see Ch.15). Privatization is then seen as increasing the prospects for raising investment capital, thereby increasing efficiency and lowering prices.

In addition to increased financial freedom, privatization may provide the enterprise with a number of other benefits. For instance, it removes the enterprise from interference by Whitehall in investment decisions. During 1985, for example, the Department of Industry exerted heavy pressure on the then British Leyland (now Rover) to save £250m. by abandoning the development of a new engine in favour of buying in units from Honda. In this case British Leyland won and have developed a highly acclaimed new engine for the revised Metro introduced in 1990. Supporters of privatization argue that civil servants are not the best people to participate in this kind of commercial decision-making and that the process is unwieldy and time-consuming for top managers. A further limitation on nationalized industries is the political near-impossibility of diversification. In many cases this would be the sensible corporate response to poor market prospects but it is not an option which is open. So, for example, British Gas whilst nationalized was prevented from diversifying into oil production. Similarly, there are political constraints which make it impossible for UK nationalized industries to develop international strategies and become multinational companies. In the energy sector, for example, no oil company would follow British Coal and confine its activities to one country where it happened to have reserves, especially if those activities were loss making.

Again, privatization provides an opportunity for breaking with, or at least challenging, customs and work practices agreed by the nationalized industries with powerful public sector unions. An indication of this change in approach was an offer by the newly privatized BT of a lump-sum payment of £1,000 per head to each of its existing 1,150 factory workers in return for an agreement that 700 of them, and all new recruits, would take a cut in their basic wage from £117 to £90 per week.

The case against privatization

Privatization may be opposed for all the reasons that nationalization was originally undertaken (see p. 150). Additionally both the rationale of the policy and its implementation may be criticized.

Some state-owned industries, e.g. British Shipbuilders, have always faced stiff competition in their markets. It has been the public utilities which have had monopoly power. So far privatization has done little to encourage competition; rather it has transferred monopolies intact to the private sector. This was certainly the case with British Gas and also BT in its dealings with domestic consumers. The Government has gone a long way towards meeting this criticism in its arrangements to privatize the electricity industry. The

Central Electricity Generating Board (CEGB) will be broken up, ending its monopoly over the generation and transmission of electricity through the National Grid. The generating business of the CEGB will be split into three new businesses; National Power and the smaller PowerGen, which will both be privatized in February 1991, and Nuclear Electric, which will be retained in public ownership. The National Grid itself will be transferred to a new company jointly owned by 12 regional supply companies, the latter having been privatized in November 1990. The Grid will be open to National Power, PowerGen, Nuclear Electric, Scottish Power and Scottish Hydro-Electric (the Scottish companies being privatized in mid-1991). In addition new entrants to the industry and imports (for example from France) will have access to the Grid. Any organization, including the regional supply companies, will be free to generate their own supplies which can also be offered to the National Grid. The regional supply companies will buy electricity from the National Grid at prices determined by a bidding process among the competing suppliers, a process conducted at half hourly intervals. Most consumers will still be supplied by monopoly regional companies but the larger industrial users will be able to buy their electricity from any supplier. This has already spurred the regional supply companies into price cuts to keep their customers.

The ingenuity which has gone into this extremely complex privatization is in complete contrast with earlier simple transfers of monopolies to the private sector. In the case of public utility privatizations, the Government faces a dilemma; breaking up monopolies to increase competition reduces the market value of the share offer. Monopolies are worth more as share floatations because they reduce uncertainty.

The extension of share ownership does not in itself attract much criticism. The issues are the prices and the marketing of the shares. It is argued that valuable national assets have been sold at give-away prices. This criticism is made of both privately negotiated deals and the public share offers. An example of the former is the offer for Austin Rover made by British Aerospace in March 1988 which valued a company which has received a total of £2.9bn of public funds at only £150m. and this on condition that the Government wrote off £1.1bn of accumulated losses and injected a further £800m. The deal could be presented as giving away £650m. and a company with net assets of more than £1.1bn. The generosity of the government's approach was confirmed when the European Commission ruled that the £800 million Government injection of capital must be reduced to £572 million, in the interests of fair competition in the EC motor market. The Commission has also insisted that British Aerospace repay £44.4 million which it received from the Government as 'sweeteners' during the deal. Beyond that there is the further question of whether British Aerospace can use £1.1 billion of accumulated Rover losses to offset its own tax liabilities. The Government's prime objective was to return Rover to the public sector as quickly as possible in the belief that the benefits would soon outweigh any losses on the deal. There were also the provisos that the company remain under British ownership and that employment be maintained. These provisos severely restricted the number of potential buyers.

In most cases public share offers have been heavily over-subscribed and large percentage profits have been made by successful applicants. Rolls-Royce shares, for example, were issued part paid at 85p on 20 May 1987 and moved to 147p by the close of business that day, a profit of 73% before dealing costs. British Telecom shares reached a premium of 86% on the first day. The electricity privatization is expected to raise about £10 billion, but the assets involved have a value of £28 billion, according to the shadow energy secretary. Underpriced issues have cost the Treasury substantial revenues but also conditioned a new class of small shareholders to expect quick, risk-free capital gains. These expectations were encouraged by barrages of skilful advertising. Not surprisingly many of the new shareholders cashed in their windfall gains by selling their shares. As a result share ownership in the new companies quickly became more concentrated. For example the 1.1 million BA shareholders at the flotation in February 1987 had reduced to 0.4 million by early October (*Observer* 1987). Despite this there is no doubt that there has been a dramatic extension of share ownership, although the majority of shareholders have shares in only one company.

Many of the new shareholders must have been shaken by the stock market crash of October 1987 when the FTSE 100 Share Index fell 29% in a week. The crash coincided with the sale of the Government's remaining 31.5% stake in BP. The sale went ahead despite the crash, leaving the underwriters with losses estimated at £1bn (*Financial Weekly* 5/11/87) and the Bank of England putting a floor under the shares by offering to buy back partly paid shares at 60p, against the issue price of £1.20. The losses of the underwriters provided some counter to the argument that the City had received excessive fees and commissions on privatization issues. The stock market crash and the difficulties of the BP offer did not, however, prevent the successful privatization of both British Steel and the water industry.

The discipline of the capital markets may prove a very mixed blessing for some of the privatized companies if they become subject to the City's alleged 'short termism'. The large investment fund managers are often criticized for taking a short-term view of prospects. This would be particularly inappropriate for the public utilities where both the gestation period for investment and the pay-back period tend to be lengthy. The freedom with which ownership of assets changes hands on the stock market is not always in the public interest. The acquisition of B Cal in 1987 by the newly privatized BA, for example, was investigated by the Monopolies and Mergers Commission (MMC) and approved on condition that BA gave up some of the routes acquired. There was also concern at the 22% holding in BP which the Kuwait Investment Office acquired very cheaply in the aftermath of the stock market crash. The MMC ruled that the Kuwait holding be reduced to 11%. In many of the privatizations the Government has taken steps to retain some control over the new companies. This may be by retaining a proportion of the shares (British Aerospace, BT, British Gas) or by limiting the size of individual shareholdings (15% maximum in Jaguar and British Gas) or by setting an upper limit on the total foreign shareholding (15% in British Aerospace and Rolls-Royce).

The flow of funds into privatization offers has been diverted from other uses. It is reasonable to suppose that applicants for shares are using their savings rather than reducing their consumption. Large sums of money leave the building societies during privatizations, and other financial institutions are also deprived of funds. This raises the possibility that what is merely a restructuring and change of ownership of state industry may be reducing the availability of funds for other organizations which would use them for real capital investment. The effects of privatization issues on the financial markets are much the same as the effects of government borrowing, raising the same possibilities of 'crowding out'.

The contribution of privatization to reducing the PSBR has been widely criticized as 'selling the family silver'. The sale of capital assets to fund current expenditure is a practice few households would happily extend to their own finances! The planned sales of £5bn per year from 1990 to 1993 will be of profitable assets and so the Exchequer will lose the returns which would have been available.

The argument that privatization gives greater commercial freedom is clearly correct given the current arrangements in the public sector. It could well be argued, however, that many of the current constraints arise out of a prejudice against public sector activity and unnecessarily tight borrowing limits. It would be possible to give public sector organizations much more commercial freedom whilst retaining the benefits of public accountability and traditions of public service which are particularly important in the 'natural monopolies' like gas and electricity. It is also questionable whether commercial freedom is appropriate for some of the privatized companies, especially the public utilities. The Government have recognized this by setting up regulatory bodies (such as OFTEL) and establishing constraints on the privatized companies. It will be interesting to see if the privatized electricity industry is as output-oriented as the old nationalized industry, or whether it improves its contribution to conservation of energy and a cleaner environment.

A final criticism of privatization is a moral one, that the public are being sold shares which, as taxpayers, they already collectively own. The purchasers of the shares benefit from the dividends paid by the new profit seeking enterprises, at the expense of taxpayers as a group. Those taxpayers who do not buy the shares, perhaps because they have no spare cash, are effectively dispossessed.

The performance of privatized companies

Table 8.8 shows simple indicators of financial performance for a sample of seven privatized companies. All have seen healthy increases in sales per employee, Jaguar being the exception with an increase little ahead of inflation. The returns on capital employed have all fallen since privatization, except for Associated British Ports. The slump in Britoil returns is partly a result of the collapse in the price of oil after 1986. Jaguar is very dependant on the USA market and found it difficult to stay competitive as the £ rose against the $. Both Jaguar and Britoil have been victims of takeovers, Britoil by BP and Jaguar by Ford. Whilst this might be said to show failure of privatization, the supporters of the idea would argue that it is a necessary part of the working of the market economy and will result in a better use of assets. No firm conclusion can be drawn from comparisons such as this because the outcomes are not necessarily the result of privatization. There are so many other determinants of company performance. The general economic environment has been good for most of this period, on the other hand the companies were very carefully prepared for privatization and some of the initial levels of return were almost artificially high. Finally we should remember that the remaining nationalized industries have performed well in terms of productivity growth if not always in terms of financial results.

Company	Year privatized	Return on capital employed %		Sales per employee £	
		In year of privatization	1989/90	In year of privatization	1989/90
Amersham International	1982	20.16	16.49	29,961	64,644
Assoc. British Ports	1983	8.96	9.87	17,235	47,647
British Aerospace	1981	8.62	7.31	26,683*	71,255
British Telecom	1984	17.69	16.15	32,114	45,612
Britoil	1982	71.17†	15.81‡	472,388†	530,228‡
Cable and Wireless	1981	20.72	15.67	32,990	61,471
Jaguar	1984	48.36	14,16‡	65,628	83,794‡

* 1982 data.   † 1983/84 data.   ‡ 1988 data.

Source: Observer (1987) and Jordan's Database of Accounts of Major Public and Private British Companies version 3.0. FAME Retrieval Software. Copyright Bureau van Dijk 1990.

Table 8.8 Performance of some privatized companies

We may also assess the privatized companies by their performance in meeting consumer demand. Where companies are in competitive markets their financial performance is likely to be a good indication of their ability to satisfy consumers. Jaguar, for example, dramatically improved its reputation for quality and reliability in the early 1980s helping the company towards very high returns on capital. In the monopolistic public utilities good financial results can often be achieved through monopoly power. Here there is mixed evidence that privatization has done much to create new attitudes or to improve service to consumers. Ofgas, the regulatory body for the gas industry, was driven to the extreme of legal action against British Gas to gain access to adequate information about pricing policies. British Telecom's performance since privatization has been monitored by the Consumer Association (CA) in their magazine *Which?* (June 1988). Using a panel of 647 consumers the CA concluded that by 1988 service to phone users was worse than in 1983, before privatization. There were more wrong numbers, more phones out of order and almost twice as many customers had difficulty in getting BT to respond to queries about bills. By 1990 the Consumer Association was able to report some improvement in BT performance. Almost 90% of new lines were installed within four weeks of the order being placed, compared with only just over 50% in 1983, on the other hand there was no reduction in the need for repairs to phones or in the time taken to make them.

Conclusion

The extent of state intervention in the economy and the form it should take remains a controversial issue going beyond the scope of economic enquiry. There is a strong case for some form of government intervention in selected industries, to protect the public interest, prevent abuse of monopoly power and compensate for externalities. It does not follow that nationalization is the best form of government intervention. The extent of privatization since 1979 has radically changed the role of the state in the economy and makes it very unlikely that there will ever again be the range of state industries which existed in 1979. The performance of both state-owned and privatized industry is difficult to evaluate. It has not been convincingly demonstrated that the form of ownership of an organization is the most important influence on its performance. Of much greater importance would seem to be the degree of competition and the effectiveness of regulatory bodies.

Notes

1. For example, the transition from private to public ownership meant the takeover of some 550 separate local concerns in the electricity industry and over 1,000 local concerns in the gas industry.
2. A useful illustration is in terms of scores in a game. If the last (marginal) score is below the average of all previous scores, then the average must fall. As soon as the marginal score has risen above the average, the average begins to rise. If we plot the scores as a curve, the marginal curve must intersect the average curve at its lowest point.

References and further reading

Consumer Association 'Which?' March 1990 and July 1990.
HMSO (1990) *The Government's Expenditure Plans 1990–91 to 1992–93*, Cm. 1004, 1005, 1007, 1021.
Jordan's Database of Accounts of Major Public and Private British Companies, version 3.0. FAME Retrieval Software. Copyright Bureau van Dijk 1990.
Molyneux, R. and **Thompson, D.** (1987) 'Nationalized Industry Performance: Still third rate?' *Fiscal studies*, **8**, 1, February.
Observer (1987) Privatization survey.
OECD (1989) 1988/89 *The United Kingdom*. Chapter V. Public Sector Efficiency, Economic Survey.
Treasury (1982) Economic Progress Report, 145, May.

9   Pricing in practice

The first part of this chapter briefly illustrates how economic *theory* can predict a variety of prices for a product, depending on the structure of the market and the objectives of the firm. The second and major part looks at pricing in *practice*, using recent research findings to illustrate how firms actually price their products. Costs clearly play a role in price-setting, although a variety of other factors must also be considered, including market-share strategies, the phase of the product life cycle, the degree of product differentiation, and the role of distributors. Chapter 3, 'Firm objectives and firm behaviour', could usefully be read before beginning this chapter.

Pricing in theory

Price and market structure

For simplicity we shall initially assume that the firm's objective is to maximize profits. Given this objective the price charged may still vary depending on the type of market structure within which the firm operates. This is well illustrated by a comparison between the extreme market forms of perfect competition and pure monopoly.

Perfect competition vs pure monopoly   Under perfect competition, price is determined for the industry (and for the firm) by the intersection of demand and supply, at P_C in Fig. 9.1. As the reader familiar with the theory of the

Fig. 9.1 Price under perfect competition and monopoly

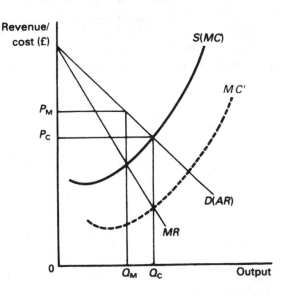

firm will know, the supply curve, S, of the perfectly competitive industry is also the marginal cost (MC) curve of the industry. Suppose now that the industry is taken over by a single firm ('pure monopoly'), and that costs are initially unchanged. It follows that the marginal cost curve remains in the same position; also that the demand curve for the perfectly competitive industry becomes the demand (and average revenue (AR)) curve for the monopolist. The marginal revenue (MR) curve must then lie inside the negatively sloped AR curve. The profit-maximizing price for the monopolist is P_M, corresponding to output Q_M, where $MC = MR$. Price is higher under monopoly than under perfect competition (and quantity, Q_M, lower). This is the so-called 'classical' case against monopoly.

Our intention here is merely to point out that price will tend to *differ* for firms depending on the type of market within which they operate. In our comparison of extreme market forms, the final outcome for price may or may not be higher under monopoly than under competition. It is in part an empirical question. If economies of scale were sufficient to lower the MC curve below MC' in Fig. 9.1, then the monopoly price would be below that of perfect competition. Price will however, except by coincidence, *be different* under these two market forms, as it would under other market forms, such as monopolistic competition or oligopoly.

Price and firm objective

So far we have assumed that the firm has a single objective, i.e. profit maximization. If there are other objectives then there will tend to be a still wider range of possibilities for price. We saw in Fig. 3.4 that a sales-maximizing objective would usually lead to a lower price than would a profit-maximizing objective. The situation becomes even more complicated when we examine behavioural or non-maximizing objectives, as these yield not a unique price, but a range of price outcomes for any given market structure. Clearly firm price depends also on firm objective.

Price, market structure and firm objective

Price thus depends on both market structure and firm objective. Since there are many possible combinations of these, any given product or service can experience a wide array of possible prices.

From Fig. 9.2 we see that the four market structures can lead to at least

Fig. 9.2 Market structure, firm objective and price

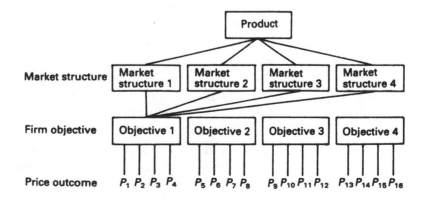

four different price outcomes (P_1-P_4) for objective 1. A further four prices (P_5-P_8) might result from objective 2, and so on, giving at least sixteen prices[1] for the four market structures and the four firm objectives. To derive guidelines for price-setting from theory, which will have general validity, is clearly a daunting if not impossible task.

Pricing in practice

We now turn to practice to see whether observation will give us more help than theory in determining price.

Cost-plus pricing

We first examine the influence of cost on price. The suggestion here is that it is not so much the demand side of the market that affects price, but rather the supply side, via costs of production.

Cost-plus pricing is a description given to a number of practices whereby price is closely related to costs of production. Costs are usually separated into two categories. First, there are costs which vary directly with output, such as wages and raw materials. Within the normal capacity range these costs bear a roughly linear relationship to output, and are called 'variable costs', though also known as prime, or direct costs.[2] Second, there are costs which do not vary with output within the normal capacity range. These costs may include rent, rates and depreciation on capital equipment, and are called 'fixed costs', though also known as overhead or indirect costs.

Most cost-plus pricing strategies add a certain percentage profit mark-up to the firm's costs, in order to arrive at a final price. The precise outcome for price will vary from firm to firm for three main reasons:

1. There is the problem of selecting which costs to include in the pricing decision. Some firms may include only variable costs in the base for the mark-up. Interestingly this is called 'marginal costing' by accountants even when the base is average variable cost.[3] Other firms may include both variable and fixed costs in the base (full-cost pricing). When the firm is producing more than one product, full-cost pricing faces the problem of apportioning total fixed costs between the various products. For instance, if a factory was already producing Product A, and a new Product B was introduced using the same machinery, what part, if any, of the unchanged capital costs should be allocated to B? Product B may be asked to 'absorb' some proportion of the fixed costs already included in the price of A. Different firms will make different decisions on how to absorb fixed costs across their various products.

2. Whatever the costs to be included in the base, there is the problem of estimating the 'normal' level of output at which the firm will operate. This estimate is important since *average cost* (both the variable and fixed elements) and therefore the size of the cost base, will vary with output, i.e. with capacity utilization.

3. Whatever the costs included, and the estimate of capacity utilization, there is the problem of calculating the percentage mark-up to be added to costs. Some firms may set a relatively constant percentage mark-up,

whilst others may vary the percentage according to firm objective and market circumstance.

An array of price outcomes is therefore possible for a firm, depending on the practices it adopts in dealing with each of the three problems outlined above. Although cost-plus pricing cannot therefore yield precise predictions for firm price, it does put price-setting in a particular perspective. The emphasis is upon *costs* influencing price, and then producers selling what they can at that price. Demand has little influence on price-setting in cost-plus theory, except perhaps in affecting the size of the mark-up to be added to costs. Any extra demand is met from stocks, or by lengthening the order book, rather than by the immediate price rise predicted by market theory.

Empirical evidence   The empirical evidence for cost-plus pricing, in one firm or another, is rather impressive. Hall and Hitch (1939), in their survey of entrepreneurs in the 1930s, found that most adopted a full-cost pricing approach. Hague (1948) came to a similar conclusion in his study of twenty firms in the Midlands, finding that price was set by adding a largely conventional profit margin to average total cost. A more recent intensive study by Coutts, Godley and Nordhaus (1978) of seven UK industries, also lends support to cost-plus pricing. Their study set out to test the relative importance of costs, demand, taxes, government intervention, and international trade, on the price of manufactured goods in the UK over the period 1957–73. The results suggest that firms have very limited and specific rules about the process of price determination and that costs of production are the most important single influence on price. Hazeldine (1980) used North American data to identify the factors affecting the price of internationally traded products. He found the major influence on their price to be domestic costs of production, though the degree of international competition faced by those products would also affect price. Sawyer (1983) found that as a first approximation price changes depend on input prices, i.e. costs. In his sample, it was employment and output which changed relative to demand, rather than price.

Clearly, prices of both domestic and internationally traded products are related to cost though, as with Hazeldine, market factors can still play a part. The influence of the market on final price has also been emphasized by studies on the profit mark-up. Hawkins (1973) in reviewing the evidence, concludes that the mark-up seems to be higher when demand is inelastic, when there are barriers to the entry of new firms, and when real incomes are rising. These are obviously situations in which higher profits can more easily be made. Some therefore see cost-plus pricing as being less divorced from market factors than might at first appear. Eichner (1987) supports this view, finding the mark-up to be higher when fewer substitutes are available, when new entrants are less likely, and when there is little chance of government retaliatory action (e.g. anti-trust legislation, referrals to Monopoly Commission, etc.). In fact it has been suggested that cost-plus pricing is actually a rule of thumb for setting the profit-maximizing price. Firms rarely have detailed knowledge of marginal revenue and cost, and even if they had would find it administratively too difficult to change to the profit-maximizing price ($MC = MR$) with every market fluctuation. Nevertheless, they do respond to major shifts in the market, varying the percentage mark-up according to the ease or difficulty of making profit.

Dean (1978) also argues against too heavy a reliance on cost in the determination of price. He suggests that costs are only useful in setting the 'floor' below which price cannot fall if the firm is to stay in business. Beyond this, actual price may vary independently of costs. We now turn to price-setting practices that are more broadly based than cost.

Market-share strategies

Price changes may, in fact, be made for reasons of strategy rather than variations in cost. For instance, prices may be reduced to raise market share, or to defend existing market share in the face of greater competition. Grant's study of the oligopolistic *wholesale* petrol market (Grant 1982; see also MMC 1990) is a clear case of market-share strategies exerting a dominant influence on price-setting. As we see from Table 9.1, four firms accounted for over 78% of the volume of petrol sold in the UK in the early 1970s and five firms for over 65% by the late 1980s.

Table 9.1 Wholesalers' share of the UK retail petrol market (by gallonage)

	Market share (%)				
Major oil companies	1970	1975	1980	1985	1988
Shellmex and BP Ltd	39.6	35.0			
BP Oil			15.1	12.0	12.6
Shell UK			22.6	19.1	16.5
Texaco	8.0	9.2	8.2	9.7	9.5
Esso Petroleum	23.4	19.2	19.6	19.5	19.2
Mobil Oil Company	7.1	6.6	7.1	7.4	7.7
Total Majors	78.1	70.0	72.6	67.7	65.5
Others	21.9	30.0	27.4	32.3	34.5
	100.0	100.0	100.0	100.0	100.0

Sources: Grant (1982); MMC (1990).

Fig. 9.3 shows that the major firms have followed a pattern of parallel pricing since the early 1970s, charging roughly the same wholesale price within a geographic region. They also offered similar discounts for 'solus' agreements, where the retailer takes all his petrol from the one company. As a result the relative market share of the 'majors' remained almost static.

In the mid-1970s world petrol prices fell – the Rotterdam spot price fell by as much as 40% in 1974/75. Rotterdam was an important source of supply to the smaller UK companies which did not possess their own refineries. This fall in price allowed these 'other' smaller wholesale firms, such as Gulf, ICI, Elf and Amoco, to provide much cheaper petrol than that of the majors. Up to 1979, as we see from Fig. 9.3, the response of the majors was 'collective'; they did not reduce scheduled prices but rather introduced almost identical temporary discounts to retailers. Although this did not protect them from the continuing loss of market share to the smaller companies (see Table 9.1), it did protect their *relative* shares within the reduced total.

By the end of 1979 the picture had changed, with the UK majors for the

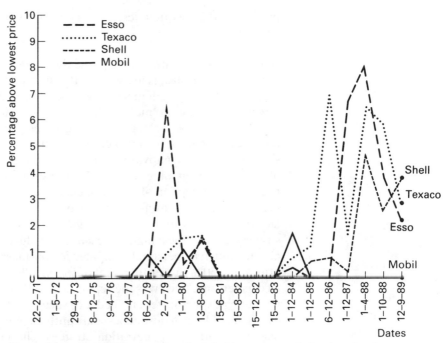

Fig. 9.3 Relative price differences in wholesale petrol from four major suppliers 1971–89
Sources: Petroleum Times incorporating the *Price Report*

Notes: Percentage *differences* in scheduled inner zone wholesale prices between four major oil companies for four-star motor spirit. In 1971 prices were equal at 31.75p per gallon. In 1988 the cheapest Mobil was 33.14p per litre.

Time shown on the horizontal axis is not to scale.

first time seriously attacking each others' market share. Prices were cut in a non-uniform manner as each major sought an increase in retail sales to absorb under-utilized refining capacity. However, the loss of revenue resulting from this price war caused the majors to restore quickly some price stability and by mid-1981 (see Fig. 9.3) prices were once again moving roughly in parallel. Between 1985 and 1990 the oil price fell sharply. This again induced some volatility in price as the majors sought to gain a greater share of a declining market by using price competition against each other. Of course the oil price has risen again since the Gulf crisis in 1990, and the majors have ceased to compete so much in terms of price, raising prices more-or-less together.

From this case we can see that short-term pricing policy can be dictated by market-share strategies. Parallel pricing has been used by the majors to avoid mutually damaging encroachment on their respective market shares. However when times get difficult, price wars can still break out. When prices *are* dictated by market-share strategies they may bear little relationship to costs of production, at least in the short run.

Life-cycle strategies

The pricing strategy of the firm will not only be affected by considerations of market share. The position of the product in its life cycle will also influence price. It is recognized (see for instance Sizer 1981) that products frequently have a finite market life, and that within that life they change their strategic role (see also Ch. 3 on portfolio planning). The three broad phases of the life cycle which products go through after their successful introduction (most products fail!) are often described as the growth phase, the maturity phase and the decline phase.

Growth phase   In the growth phase the product's market share, and possibly the total market size, is increasing. It is normal for those first into a market to support growth by high marketing expenditure. Market leaders may be forced in this phase to make a choice between two types of strategy. They can adopt a 'skimming' strategy, charging a *high* price which creams off a small but lucrative part of the market. Producers of fashion products, which have a short life and high innovative value as long as only a few people own them, often adopt a skimming strategy. Such a strategy might result from the producer's perception of a price-inelasic demand for his product, with a high premium placed on exclusivity, or from the producer's awareness that he lacks the capacity to produce in large quantities. A variant on the skimming strategy is to charge a high price *and* to produce in large volume. IBM was able to launch its personal computer for business use in the mid-1980s at a price some 50% higher than that of *technically equivalent models* produced by its competitors. Such was the reputation of IBM that this, allied to extensive marketing expenditure, enabled it to secure 40% of the total market within two years of launch despite a significantly higher price. Alternatively market leaders can adopt a 'penetration' strategy, charging a *low* price and raising marketing expenditure in order to establish a much larger market presence. The penetration strategy is more likely to deter early competition and may ultimately prove more profitable if the firm can afford to wait for a return on its initial outlay. The firm can then delay raising the price of its product until *after* it has secured a substantial market presence.

How much of a role cost plays in the determination of price during the growth phase will depend on the individual firm. It is not unknown for companies who market aggressively to set prices *below* average cost in order to gain high market share, in the expectation that costs will fall as output and experience increase. This is particularly so in high-technology industries. Personal computers are an example of a product in its growth phase, with high levels of expenditure on marketing and product development. Amstrad used a penetration pricing strategy when they introduced their word processors in 1986 at one-quarter of the price of competitors. In the early 1990s the introduction of domestic satellite television into the UK was accompanied by enormous set-up and marketing costs which could only be recouped through large-scale usage. The initial prices have clearly been *less than* average costs, again in pursuit of high market penetration in the growth phase.

Maturity phase   As time passes the product reaches maturity. Both the firm and the market are then in a situation which can be expected to continue for some time. The strategic pricing decisions will in this phase depend largely on the market share that has already been established and on the quality of the product compared to that of its competitors.

For a company with a high market share and a high-quality product, the policy is often to charge relatively high prices, supported by high marketing and product development expenditure in order to maintain the position of leadership. Prices may, however, still be well in excess of average total cost, since technical costs in the maturity phase are often low as a result of scale economies. Again, prices may diverge from cost during the maturity phase of the product life cycle.

Take for example the personal stereo or 'walkman'. This is a relatively mature product, yet producers are constantly updating the concept of personal entertainment with micronization, compact disks, DAT tapes, hand-held televisions, etc. Ohmae (1985) argues that the Japanese approach to life-cycle management is to continuously invest in strategic products in order to maintain the 'mature phase' for as long as possible; i.e. to use updating-investment as a means of delaying the onset of the 'decline phase'.

Decline phase   As the product falls into 'decline', perhaps through changing social habits or because of technological innovation, market leaders will usually maintain their high price, relying on the brand loyalty and buying habits of their existing customers. Research and development (R & D) and marketing expenditure will be reduced, giving a higher cash flow which can be channelled into new products. Market followers will not have the advantage of high prices and are likely to withdraw their product from the market in the decline phase of the product life cycle.

Pricing policy may in these various ways be shaped by factors other than cost; here the phase of the product life cycle has played an important role.

Market segmentation strategies

There is a trend in advanced economies towards wider variety in consumer choice and greater specialization in industrial products. In other words the markets are far less homogeneous than had been thought; being constructed of *segments* which can be distinguished from each other. For example, snack foods (such as potato crisps and peanuts) were once considered one market, but new product development, branding and packaging have segmented this in many ways; for example Smiths Crisps 'Monster Munch' for children and Phileas Fogg's 'Mignons Morceaux' for adults. Indeed, in the early 1990s, the Phileas Fogg brand has virtually created a niche market of 'adult nibbles', with the prices about 10% higher than the common snacks. Their target market is adult buyers who are entertaining guests. This form of *life-style segmentation* is now used by many firms in preference to the social class distinctions of the previous three decades.

The price of goods and services may increasingly be related to the demand characteristics of the market segment, rather than to the actual costs of production. For example, the changing lifestyles of consumers are giving rise to changes in demand elasticity and buying habits. Bliss (1988) explores the idea that, by assembling goods in one place, a shop saves its customers 'search' costs. The *one stop shop* customers are prepared to *pay more* for the convenience of being able to buy all the household groceries in one shopping visit, than to spend time looking around several shops for the lowest prices. Price is therefore partly derived from the 'alternative' or 'substitute' costs facing the consumer (i.e. 'opportunity' cost).

The beer market provides a further example of how market segmentation can form the basis of pricing strategies, rather than the costs of producing the various products. In the Monopolies and Mergers Commission Report (MMC 1989) on the 'Supply of Beer' it was concluded that lager was more highly priced than beer but that 'the high price of lager was not justified by the cost of producing it'. Figure 9.4 shows the costs of producing four different types of draft beer. The cost of producing draft lager is less than packaged beer, for instance, yet its contribution to profits is considerably higher – the highest in fact of all the beers. Lager is attractive to younger drinkers, whose demand is apparently less sensitive to price. The demand for lager therefore displays a lower price elasticity, and in consequence a higher price can be charged.

Fig. 9.4 The price of beer (pounds per bbl) *Source:* MMC (1989)

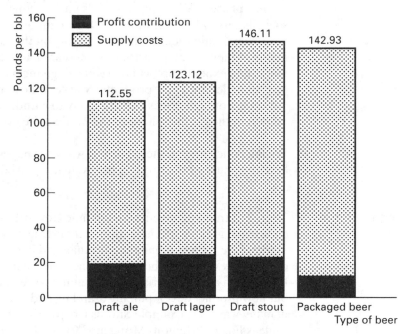

Price discrimination strategies

Price discrimination may also result in prices bearing little or no relation to cost. Conventional economic theory tells us that there are two conditions necessary for price discrimination, i.e. the charging of *different prices* for the *same product* in *different markets*. First, for price discrimination to be *possible*, there must be barriers (e.g. distance, time, etc.) preventing consumers switching from the dearer to the cheaper market. Second, for price discrimination to be *profitable*, there must be differences in price elasticity of demand between the markets. The profit-maximizing condition would then be that marginal cost for whole output be equal to marginal revenue *in each separate market*. In this way economic theory would predict higher prices in markets for which demand was less elastic, irrespective of cost conditions.

The market for motor vehicles has provided a clear example of price discrimination. Cars produced in a given location have been sold at substantially higher prices in the UK than in the rest of Europe. United

Kingdom import legislation and the fact that European models were left-hand drive made it difficult to transfer cars across markets, so that the price differential persisted for many years. Recent EEC regulations have made it easier for UK residents to order right-hand drive models in Europe, at European prices, and import them into the UK without levy. The result has already been to reduce substantially the price differential between a particular model purchased in the UK and the same model purchased in Europe. Another example is the price of telephone calls. The increase in demand for lines during business hours means that a premium can be charged over this period. Price sensitive users will wait for 'cheap rate' periods before making calls. This illustrates how demand affects the *price* of a service which *costs* virtually the same to provide, whatever time of day it is used.

Product differentiation strategies

Product differentiation refers to attempts by the firm to make its product different from other products. This may be achieved by changing the characteristics of the product, through R & D expenditure, or by changing consumer perceptions of the product, through additional marketing expenditure. Product differentiation enables the firm to lessen the prospect of facing direct competition, and to move towards a more monopolistic position, with greater control over price.

In some cases product differentiation is becoming more difficult. Petrol companies, for instance, found product differentiation virtually impossible after the star/octane ratings were made public. Similarly, packaged food manufacturers with well-known brands such as Birds Eye and Heinz are being put under increasing pressure from retailers' own brands, some of which are now perceived as being of higher quality. Despite these difficulties many manufacturers are successful in differentiating their products and in gaining premium prices because of it.[4] Their success would seem to lie in extensive market research to discover consumers' perceptions, interests and needs. From the results of this research, new products can be launched with the appropriate 'image' for conveying uniqueness.

An example of this was the introduction of Krona margarine by Van Den Berghs in the UK market. The Krona image was that of a direct substitute for butter at a lower price, although it was in fact a high-priced margarine. Despite the fact that there are already many margarines on the market, each slightly different from the next, Krona became brand leader in the test market (10%) area within two years of launch. This was achieved through extensive advertising, an appropriate 'image' and presumably a credible product! Although Krona was more expensive than other margarines it sold more than double its nearest rival (Broadbent 1981), which is clear evidence of 'successful' product differentiation giving a firm control over the price it charges. The result of such control is to give the firm greater discretion to vary price for reasons other than cost.

It is in the firm's interest to establish the *extent* to which product differentiation gives it control over price, i.e. what the customer is prepared to pay. Kraushar (1982) describes how market research helps solve the problem of discovering exactly what the market will bear. Two techniques are frequently used: buy–response questions and multi-brand choice.[5]

Buy–response and multi-brand choice   The buy–response test is where a large sample of respondents are shown the product and asked 'If you saw this product in your local store, would you pay £x, £y, £z . . . etc. for it?' The list will typically contain ten prices. A large number of responses makes it possible to construct a buy–response curve, giving the percentage of buyers at different price levels. In the example shown in Fig. 9.5, 90% of those willing to buy would pay up to 40p for the product, and 35% would pay up to 56p. The flatter the buy–response curve the more control the firm has over price.

Fig. 9.5 A typical
buy–response curve

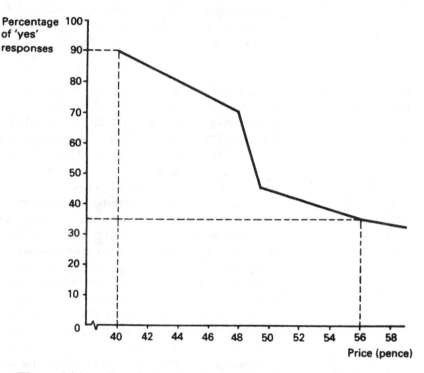

The multi-brand choice test is where respondents are asked to rate the product in question against similar products. The question may take the form 'If we add this feature to our product, making it different from our competitors', would you pay an extra £x, £y, £z . . . etc. for it?' The aim is to establish a *relative* price for the product.

Kraushar cites a number of examples where these two approaches to price determination have been used successfully. Using buy–response curves, a manufacturer's undercoat paint was found to be more price-sensitive than his gloss paint. The manufacturer decided therefore to keep the price of his undercoat paint at the same level as that of cheaper competitors' 'own brands'. However, with gloss paint being less sensitive to price, the manufacturer was able to raise the price of this product relative to his competitors'. Using the multi-brand choice test, pre-pasted wallpapers were investigated in order to discover what the perceived additional value was of having the paste already on the paper. It was found to be highly valued and as a result the product was priced more highly than other wallpapers, and still sold well.

Influence of retailers on price

Whatever lengths manufacturers go to in establishing the retail price for a product, they have to take account of the profit margins of the intermediaries – the distributors, both wholesalers and retailers. The power to control prices would in some markets appear to be moving out of the hands of producers and into the hands of distributors. Whilst oil producers and refiners still largely control the pump prices of petrol, the same control is not always available to producers in the grocery trade, as we shall see below.

Most studies of pricing have focused on the producer because, historically, retailers have had little influence on the market. Indeed, in the extreme, the producer may have such control that the retail mark-up may even be zero; many petrol sales in the USA are made at zero retail profit margin. The retailer's profits are made on sales of other 'convenience' goods such as greeting cards, barbecue charcoal, video hire, etc. This trend is apparent too in the UK; for example a Jiffy (Jet petrol) convenience store on a petrol forecourt can generate sales of £25 per square foot, which is similar to specialist retailers such as Tie Rack and Sock Shop. We can see from this that the supply of petrol is highly controlled and that the full cost of retailing the petrol may *not* be taken into account in pricing the petrol.

Brewers distribute their beers to a number of different types of trade channels. A Monopolies and Mergers Commission report in 1989 stated that the price, and the amount of contribution to profits, varied according to the channel used. In *Managed Houses*, where they have most control, the wholesale price of draft lager averaged £128.23 per bbl (a beer barrel (bbl) is 36 gallons or 288 pints). In *Free Houses* the price averaged £116.49 per bbl. However, in Free Houses where a low interest loan had been provided by the Brewery (giving the Brewery more control), the price was £126.11 per bbl. These differences are illustrated in Fig. 9.6. Prices of beer are influenced by demand (as we saw earlier) and, as we can see here, by the extent of control of the brewer over the retailer.

Brewing is another example of the producer successfully exerting control on price. However, as *retailers* become more powerful, they may be able to wrest control of prices from the producer. Bulk buying and a large share of the premium price grocery market makes such retailers as Tesco, Sainsbury and Marks and Spencer formidable buyers who can significantly influence price. Furthermore such companies as these develop *strategic alliances* with suppliers. The powerful buyers provide technical and marketing expertise to the supplier and are willing to make long term commitments to the supplier in return for price and quality performance targets. As early as 1981, the major multiples were found to be enjoying lower costs and charging customers lower prices. Since then have further increased market share, enlarged the ranges of 'own brand' goods and increased the dependence of suppliers upon them through computerised ordering and stock systems. One particular way in which retailers demonstrate their power is through the use of loss leaders.

Loss Leaders   A loss leader is a low priced item used to attract customers. For example, a well known branded product, which the customer uses for a reference price, might be subject to *deep discounting* by the retailer; here the retail price may be at, or even below, the invoiced cost. Such pricing can

Fig. 9.6 The price of lager by
type of trade channel
Source: MMC (1989)

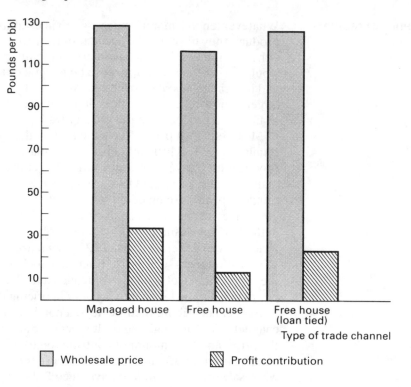

create, in the mind of the customer, what the John Lewis Partnership has described as a 'convincing aura of good value'. For suppliers of well known brands, however, this action by retailers can be damaging. It can reduce the perceived value of the product and discourage other retailers from selling it. When B&Q (DIY superstores) reduced the selling prices of Black and Decker power tools in 1989, Black and Decker retaliated by withholding supplies. This was illegal under the Resale Prices Act 1976 unless there was reasonable cause to believe that the retailer had been using them as loss leaders. Black and Decker normally gave a 15% margin to the retailer and decided that any retailer charging a price which reduced that to 12.5% or below was cutting the price by too much. The Monopolies and Mergers Commission disagreed, saying that a general rule of this type was too sweeping, and that individual cases need to be looked at (MMC 1989). They therefore disallowed Black and Decker's bid to withhold supplies, saying that it was 'anti-competitive'. Again we have an example where the retailer (here supported by statute) influenced the price despite the wishes of the producer, causing the final price to deviate from cost.

Discounts and price reductions   There are various methods by which the large retailers[6] obtain reductions in the price of goods purchased from manufacturers and wholesalers. Manufacturers and wholesalers often have published price lists but these only give an indication of what is actually being charged. Some suppliers do not publish price lists, others have different lists for different types of retailer. Prices, especially prices for large retailers, are a matter for negotiation, and reductions from stated prices come in a number of ways. The MMC report (1981: Ch. 4) describes some of the more common ones, which include:

Discounts for bulk delivery. Depending on quantity delivered in a 'drop'.
Special discounts. Negotiated discounts which take account of the overall relationship with the retail customer.
Retrospective discounts or rebates. Discounts made on the basis of quantities actually sold, sometimes called 'over-riders'. These are negotiated at the beginning of a contract, and if the quantity sold reaches an appropriate level, then the discount becomes operative, and is given at the end of the contract period.
Favourable credit terms. Allowing some retail customers longer to pay, thereby reducing their costs.
Special promotions. In this case wholesalers and manufacturers pay for the price reduction passed on to the final customer, so that the retailer's short-term profit does not suffer.

In addition to these price benefits, other non-price incentives may be given to retailers. These include payments to cover the costs of shelf-filling, point-of-sale advertising, staff training, etc.

When retailers have substantial buying power, the producers are far less able to set prices purely on a cost-plus basis. Although producers may not formally *change* their percentage mark-up on cost, they often do so in practice by varying the discounts permitted to retailers in the light of market conditions.

Conclusion

Pricing decisions depend both on the structure of the market in which the firm operates, and the objectives it pursues. There are, in fact, a variety of market structures and a variety of firm objectives, so that theory predicts a wide range of price outcomes. Can observation of firm practice lead us to more definite conclusions? Costs certainly determine the price floor, since in the long term price cannot fall below average total cost if the firm is to stay in business. However, those who support cost-plus theories would argue that everyday prices are closely related to cost. There is a considerable body of empirical support for cost-plus price-setting, though there is also evidence that the percentage mark-up on cost varies with both market circumstance and with firm strategy. The phase of the product life cycle may also influence price, as may the firm's degree of 'success' in setting prices which discriminate between markets, or in establishing product differentiation. Finally, the nature of the retail outlets used by the firm will affect the price, with the producer having less freedom to dictate price where retail outlets themselves have a large customer base.

Notes

1. For instance, it is assumed in Fig. 9.2 that the four firm objectives are of the maximizing type, with only a single price outcome for each objective. Equally, Fig. 9.2 assumes that for each objective and market structure

there is a single price outcome covering both short- and long-run time periods. If either of these assumptions is relaxed, there might be more than sixteen different price outcomes from our figure. See also Eichner (1987).

2. The terms 'prime' and 'direct' costs are not entirely synonymous with 'variable'. The first two relate to measurable costs entering directly into a cost unit or cost centre whereas the term 'variable' is concerned with the behaviour of the cost. In fact most direct costs are also 'variable'. Similarly many overhead or indirect costs are 'fixed'. Further clarification may be sought from the ICMA's (Institute of Chartered Management Accountants) *Terminology* (1982) section 4.

3. Cost-plus pricing based on *variable* cost is usually known in the distributive trades as mark-up pricing.

4. Jump (1982) points out that brand loyalty permitted prices to be 9% higher for branded processed foods in the USA than for own-brand equivalents.

5. A comprehensive discussion of various pricing research techniques is given in the *Journal of the Market Research Society* (1988).

6. Retailers were defined as follows:

   (a) Four major   Associated Dairies
                                 Fine Fare
                                 J. Sainsbury
                                 Tesco Stores

   (b) Other multiples   Retailers with ten or more branches excluding the 'major' multiples and co-operatives

   (c) Independents   Retailers with less than ten branches

   (d) Co-operatives   Co-operative Retail Societies

References

Broadbent, S. (1981) *Advertising Works*. Holt, Rinehart and Winston.

Coutts, K., Godley, G. and Nordhaus, W. (1978) *Industrial Pricing in the UK.* CUP, Cambridge.

Dean, J. (1978) Techniques for pricing new products and services, in: Britt, S. H. and Boyd, H. W. (eds) *Marketing Management and Administrative Action*, 4th edn. McGraw-Hill, Maidenhead.

Eichner, A. S. (1987) Prices and Pricing, *Journal of Economic Issues*. Dec.

Grant, R. M. (1982) Pricing behaviour in the UK wholesale market for petrol 1970–80: a 'structure-conduct analysis', *Journal of Industrial Economics*, **30**, 3, March.

Hague, D. C. (1948) Economic theory and business behaviour, *Review of Economic Studies*, **16**.

Hall, R. L. and Hitch, C. J. (1939) Price theory and business behaviour, *Oxford Economic Papers*, 2, May.

Hawkins, C. J. (1973) *Theory of the Firm*. Macmillan.

Hazeldine, T. (1980) Testing two models of pricing and protection with Canada/US data, *Journal of Industrial Economics*, **29**, 2, Dec.

Journal of the Market Research Society (1988) **29**, 2.

Jump, N. (1982) Corporate strategy in mature markets, *Barclays Bank Review*, **57**, 4, Nov.

Kraushar, P. (1982) How to research prices, *Management Today*, Jan.

MMC (1981) *Discounts to Retailers.* House of Commons Papers, 311, HMSO.

MMC (1989) *Black and Decker*, House of Commons Papers, Command 805.

MMC (1989) *The Supply of Beer*, House of Commons Papers, Command 651.

MMC (1990) *The Supply of Petrol*, House of Commons Papers, Command 972.

Ohmae, K. (1982) *The Art of Japanese Business.* McGraw Hill, New York.

Ohmae, K. (1985) *The Mind of The Strategist.* Penguin Books.

Sawyer, M. (1983) *Business Pricing and Inflation.* Macmillan.

Sizer, J. (1981) *Perspectives in Management Accounting.* Heinemann.

10 Microelectronics and information technology

This chapter considers how the new microelectronic-based technologies are affecting the UK economy. A major issue is whether job opportunities will be eroded not only by economic recession, but also by the new technologies. Predictions for total employment have, however, too often been based on individual cases of employment displacement following technical change. To counter this, we apply simple economic theory to the employment issue and derive the economic circumstances which will crucially determine whether the net effect of the new technologies will be to raise or lower employment opportunities. We then consider the changes in skill profile required of those who are employed, and assess the UK's trade performance in information technology goods and services. We conclude with a review of UK Government strategies to promote the diffusion of information technology.

Information technology

The year 1982 was Information Technology Year, and we have a Minister of Information Technology. Indeed so many and varied are the references to information technology in all walks of life that few will be unfamiliar with the term. Yet its meaning is still obscure to many! In fact, information technology refers to the *convergence* of technologies in computing, microelectronics and telecommunications, helping us to produce, process, store and transmit *information*, in the form of pictures, words or numbers. Prestel Viewdata is one such example of convergence, with the television and telephone linked together, and most importantly to computer facilities, permitting a two-way flow of information from computer to television screen and back again (as with home ordering).

The prospects for any new technology depend first on its contribution to the supply of output, here 'information' in one form or another; and second, on what is happening to the demand for that output.

Supply of information

The microprocessor   Convergence of the separate technologies of computing, microelectronics and telecommunications has been due largely, though not exclusively, to the development of the microprocessor – the computer on a chip. There are at least four aspects of the microprocessor which make it worthy of close attention.

Miniaturization.   The microprocessor is essentially the whole of a computer – logic, memory and control – etched on to a chip of silicon about 1 cm square and 0.5 mm thick. Compare this with the first digital computer which weighed

30 tons and needed 18,000 vacuum tubes! The computer is now compact enough to be attached to typewriters, cash registers, televisions, machine tools, etc.

Cheapness.   Miniaturization techniques, such as very large scale integration (VLSI), permit up to 100,000 components per chip. Further progress suggests that as many as 1 million components may soon be etched on to a single chip – the American company Hewlett-Packard has recently announced that its latest chip contains 600,000 components. The scale economies are such that the cost per component (and therefore computer function) is less than 0.01% of what it was fifteen years ago. Cheapness follows largely from scale economies, but also from low raw-material costs. The chip is made of silicon, essentially sand. Of course, the major costs of the microprocessor are design and set-up costs for producing the first one. After that each microprocessor can cost as little as a few pence to manufacture.

Durability.   The engineer's nightmare is moving parts. There are none in the microprocessor! If *initially* the microprocessor works, it can go on almost indefinitely.

Flexibility.   A single microprocessor can be programmed for a wide variety of tasks: controlling traffic flows, guiding aeroplanes, monitoring typing speeds, recording goods purchased. More expensive ones can be bought that can be reprogrammed rather than discarded when the initial function is no longer required.

So then, compact, cheap, durable and flexible computing power is now readily available. Add to this *increased performance* (the current Hewlett-Packard HP 9000 can perform 100 times more calculations per second than the 1972 version), advances in *memory technology* (356,000 binary digits of memory in current chips), and in speed and quality of *information transmission* (via satellites, fibre optics and cable systems), and we can readily appreciate the reasons for interest and concern over microprocessor development.

Demand for information

So far, we have looked at the *supply* side – the increased technological capability for producing, storing, processing and transmitting information. In fact, this has coincided with increased *demand* for information.

In the increasingly complex environment in which both individuals and firms operate, it is hardly surprising that the demand for information has grown. The Organization for Economic Cooperation and Development (OECD) estimated a sevenfold increase in volume of information flow 1970–85. A further reflection of increased demand has been the change in occupational structure towards 'information occupations', i.e. those primarily concerned with the creation and handling of information. Recent OECD reports have shown these to have grown substantially in all advanced industrialized countries, now averaging 40% of 'all employees'. In fact if we group occupations into four sectors, agriculture, industry, services and information, the information sector has now become the largest single 'sector' for employment in all reporting countries, prompting some to speak of the coming of 'post-industrial society'.

An interesting case study on the growing importance of knowledge-intensive industry is provided by Japan (Smallwood 1988). As Fig. 10.1 indicates, in the past twenty-five years or so, Japan has moved substantially *away* from labour-intensive and even capital-intensive industries, and *towards* knowledge-information-intensive industries. This is a movement being mirrored in most advanced industrialized economies.

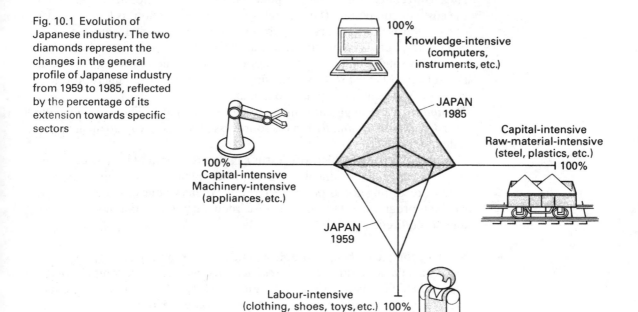

Fig. 10.1 Evolution of Japanese industry. The two diamonds represent the changes in the general profile of Japanese industry from 1959 to 1985, reflected by the percentage of its extension towards specific sectors

Economic implications

Information technology can lead to new or improved products and services (product innovation), or to new ways of producing existing products and services (process innovation).

Product innovation

A host of new and enhanced products and services is now available. New 'products' such as personal computers, calculators, electronic games and computerized search services, have largely provided new employment opportunities. Enhanced 'products', such as point-of-sale terminals instead of cash registers, word processors instead of typewriters, have both created and destroyed employment.[1] Economists have paid relatively little attention to product innovation, assuming it to be less important than process innovation, and anyway largely beneficial to the UK. A Policy Studies Institute report on UK manufacturing[2] gives some justification for this view. In their survey of 1,200 manufacturing firms, few applications of microchips (only one in five) were in product innovation. Most firms (70%) reported no change in employment, but where employment was affected three out of four firms reported an increase in employment.

Process innovation

The major concern has been with the effects of information technology in providing new processes for the production of existing products and services. Fully automated factories, and electronic offices, are but extreme examples of a general move towards microelectronics in the production process, such as the progressive use of direct numerically controlled (DNC) machine tools. Again, the Policy Studies Institute report quoted above supports this as the focus for attention. Four out of five applications of microchips in UK manufacturing were for process innovation, and where employment was affected, three out of four firms reported decreased employment. A recent report by the West German Commerzbank estimated that every robot employed in industry today replaces three workers on average, and that by the early 1990s the second generation of 'intelligent' robots, with heightened sensory powers, will each replace between five and ten workers in certain assembly jobs. However, economic analysis by no means supports the inevitability of high levels of technological unemployment following from process innovation. It is to this issue that we now turn.

Level of employment   The incentive for using information technology in the production process is higher total factor productivity, i.e. greater output per unit of factor input (labour and capital). A typist with word processor rather than typewriter, can produce more (IBM quote a 148% increase in output (Rada 1980)), better-edited, text per time period. The progressive use of integrated circuits and computerized assembly lines has more than doubled output of UK colour television sets per man-hour since 1978 (NEDC 1982). Higher output per unit of factor input reduces costs of production, provided only that wage rates[3] and other factor price increases do not absorb the whole of productivity gain. Computer-controlled machine tools are a case in point. Data from Renault show that the use of DNC machine tools implied machining costs one-third less than those of general-purpose machine tools at the same level of output (OECD 1981). Lower costs will cause the profit-maximizing firm to lower price and raise output under most[4] market forms, as in Fig. 10.2. A downward shift of the average cost curve, via the new technologies, lowers the marginal cost curve[5] from MC_1 to MC_2. The profit-maximizing price/output combination ($MC = MR$) now changes from P_1/Q_1 to P_2/Q_2. Price has fallen, output has risen.

The dual effect on employment of higher output per unit of labour (and capital) input can usefully be illustrated from Fig. 10.2. The curve $Q = F(N)$ is the familiar production function of economic theory, showing how output (Q) varies with labour input (N), capital and other factors assumed constant. On the one hand the higher labour productivity from technical change shifts the production function outwards to the dashed line $Q' = F(N)$. The original output Q_1 can now be produced with less labour, i.e. with only N_2 labour input instead of N_1 as previously. On the other hand, the cost and price reduction has so raised demand that more output is required. We now move along the new production function Q' until we reach Q_2 output, which

Fig. 10.2 Information
technology and
employment

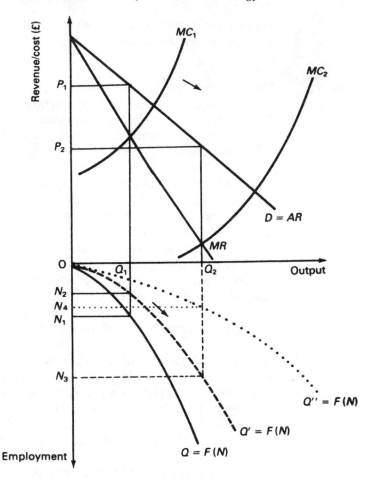

requires N_3 labour input. In our example the reduction in labour required per unit output has been more than compensated for by the expansion of output, via lower price. Employment has, in fact, risen from N_1 to N_3.

This analysis highlights a number of points on which the final employment outcome for a firm adopting the new techniques will depend:

1. The relationship between new technology and labour productivity, i.e. the extent to which the production function Q shifts outwards.

2. The relationship between labour productivity and cost, i.e. the extent to which the marginal cost curve shifts downwards.

3. The relationship between cost and price, i.e. the extent to which cost reductions are passed on to consumers as lower prices.

4. The relationship between lower price and higher demand, i.e. the price elasticity of the demand curve.

Suppose, for instance, that the new process *halved* labour input per unit output! If this increase in labour productivity (1 above), reduces cost (2 above), and price (3 above), and output *doubled* (4 above), then the same total labour input would be required. If output more than doubled, then more labour would be employed. The magnitude of the four relationships above will determine whether the firm offers the same, more, or less employment after technical change in the production process.

Although a more detailed treatment must be sought elsewhere (see, for instance, Stoneman 1983), there is in fact a fifth relationship crucial to the final employment outcome. Namely, the extent to which any higher total factor productivity arising from a technological innovation can be separately attributed to capital or to labour. An innovation is said to be capital saving when the marginal product of capital rises relative to that of labour, and labour saving when the converse applies. This whole issue is surrounded by problems of concept and measurement. We can, however, use Fig. 10.2 above to present the outline of the argument.

Suppose we take the dashed line $Q' = F(N)$ to represent a situation in which the new technology is capital saving (with only a small rise in labour productivity), so that the new and higher output Q_2 requires considerable extra labour to produce it (N_3 employment). If on the other hand the new technology were labour saving (with a substantial rise in labour productivity), then the new dotted line $Q'' = F(N)$ in Fig. 10.2 would be more appropriate. Output Q_2 would now only require employment N_4. The prospects for higher employment would therefore appear more favourable when innovations are capital saving, raising the marginal product of capital relative to that of labour.

Broadly speaking, the scenario most favourable to employment would be where a small increase in (labour) productivity significantly reduces both cost and price, leading to a substantial rise in demand.

Direct and indirect effects on the firm. So far we have examined the impacts on employment within a firm using the new technology *directly* in its production process. A number of rather more *indirect* effects may follow for other firms. For instance, firms in the capital goods producing industries which use the new technologies directly, may experience a reduction in costs, leading to a lower price for the machinery and equipment they sell. Other firms making no direct use of information technology themselves, but simply buying machinery and equipment from the capital goods producing firms, will find a change in the relative price of their factor inputs. The price of capital (machinery and equipment) will now have fallen relative to the price of labour. Figure 10.3 illustrates how standard economic theory deals with this *indirect* effect of information technology.

An *isocost* line such as $\bar{C}_1$ is a line of constant cost, showing the various amounts of capital (K) and labour (L) that can be purchased for that constant sum. The slope of any isocost line is the factor price ratio, here price of labour (w) to price of capital (r).[6] An *isoquant* such as $1x$ is a line which shows the various combinations of capital and labour technically able to produce a constant level of output – here one unit of good x.

The tangency between isocost $\bar{C}_1$ and isoquant $1x$ is the initial situation, with $\bar{C}_1$ (the isocost line nearest the origin) representing the lowest cost of producing $1x$ at the prevailing factor price ratio w_1/r_1. The process of production used to produce $1x$ in the cheapest way possible has a capital/

Fig. 10.3 Indirect effects of
information technology

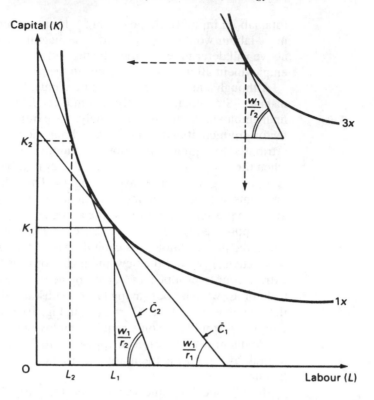

labour ratio of K_1/L_1. Suppose the price of capital now falls from r_1 to r_2; the isocost line now becomes steeper (since $w_1/r_2 > w_1/r_1$. The new minimum cost for producing $1x$ is $\bar{C}_2$ – i.e. tangency between the $1x$ isoquant and the nearest isocost line to the origin with the new slope w_1/r_2 – giving a capital/ labour ratio K_2/L_2. Not surprisingly, standard theory has predicted an increased use of the cheaper capital input K_2 instead of K_1, and a decreased use of the now relatively more expensive labour input L_2 instead of L_1. So, in firms simply making use of capital goods produced by the new technologies, there seems to be a prospect of less employment, with cheaper capital substituted for labour.

However, initial impressions may again be misleading. Using more of the now cheaper capital input and less labour, may well have reduced the cost[7] of producing $1x$, $\bar{C}_2$ may be less than $\bar{C}_1$, lowered price and raised output above $1x$. If demand were sufficiently price-elastic, so that output rises well above $1x$, then the new tangency solution[8] could be with an isoquant curve so far above $1x$ (e.g. $3x$ in Fig. 10.3) that more than L_1 labour is required as factor input. That is to say, employment may also rise in the firms that experience the *indirect* effects of technological change in the form of cheaper capital input.

So far we have seen that from the point of view of both firms using new processes directly, and firms using the output of such firms as factor input, there is no inevitability that unemployment must rise. It is an empirical question, depending to a large extent on the magnitude of the relationships

(1) to (4) outlined above, and on whether the innovation is broadly capital or labour saving.

The real income effect and aggregate employment.   The analysis has been essentially microeconomic in nature. We have examined the impacts of information technology on a single firm. As we know from macroeconomics, such analysis, whilst helpful, can fail to take into account interdependences which are important to the overall outcome. We turn briefly to this broader viewpoint.

Real income usually rises throughout the economy as a result of higher productivity. This can be due to higher earnings, such as wages and profits, or to lower product or service prices. This real income effect will increase the demand for a whole variety of goods and services. Those with the highest income elasticities of demand will, of course, benefit most from this effect. In terms of Fig. 10.2 above, we can now add to our initial analysis a potential rightward shift of the demand curve, creating still better prospects for output and employment.

The foreign sector and aggregate employment.   Finally, any attempt to discuss aggregate employment must consider the foreign sector of the UK economy. For a trading nation such as ours, it is of crucial importance how fast other countries adopt the new technologies. If there is any extra unemployment via the new technologies, this must be compared with the extra unemployment which might result if the UK alone abstained from information technology (general abstention being highly unlikely). British exports would then become less competitive than those produced elsewhere, and imports into the UK more competitive than home-produced commodities. Unemployment would result in export- and import-competing industries and, via the multiplier, elsewhere.

Of course, the balance of payments deterioration might lower the exchange rate (see Ch. 22), making our exports cheaper and imports dearer. However, this effect cannot be relied upon. North Sea oil has kept the pound artificially high for some time and the Government has encouraged a high pound as part of its anti-inflationary strategy.

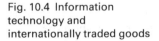

Fig. 10.4 Information technology and internationally traded goods

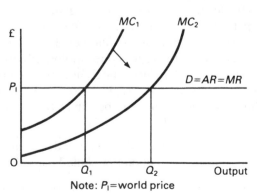

Note: P_1=world price

The impact of the 'foreign trade effect' on output and employment when the UK *does* adopt the new technology can be considered with reference to Fig. 10.4. The outcome will depend in part upon the rate of diffusion of the new technology in the domestic economy relative to that elsewhere. We assume in Fig. 10.4 that the good (or service) is internationally traded, and that domestic producers can sell as much as is available at the world price P_I. The top half of Fig. 10.2 now looks like Fig. 10.4.

We assume that our previous analysis still applies, and that as the domestic economy adopts the new technology, marginal cost falls, and output expands from Q_1 to Q_2. However, if technical progress occurs in other countries too, then the world price P_I can be expected to fall. How much expansion of output there will then be (and therefore how favourable the prospects for employment) will depend partly on *how fast* the domestic economy adopts the new technology relative to the fall in world prices.

Simulation studies and aggregate employment.   Aggregate employment must be examined in a macroeconomic framework, with all the interdependences in play! A simulation exercise by the Manpower Research Group of Warwick University sought to do just that, using a macro-model of the UK economy. Microelectronics was assumed to add an *extra* 0.5% per annum to the projected growth path of productivity between 1985 and 1990. When the various macroeconomic feedbacks through costs, prices, real income and demand are allowed to operate, 60% of the initial loss of employment from productivity gain was 'compensated'. When the extra UK competitiveness from adopting the new technologies was incorporated into the model, then over 100% of the initial employment displacement was 'compensated'. In other words, the net effect of the new technology in the UK between 1985 and 1990 was to raise employment relative to a base projection. Stoneman and Blattner (OECD 1982) reviewed a number of simulation exercises in various OECD countries, and concluded that in general such models have compensation effects close to or in excess of 100%.

Simulation studies must, of course, be treated as illustrative only. What we can, however, state with confidence is that neither micro-, nor macro-analysis suggests that unemployment must follow the progressive adoption by the UK of information technologies.

Structure of employment   Whatever the effect of information technologies upon the level of employment, it is generally recognized that there will be a new pattern of skill requirement. Of course, the change in skill profile will vary from one application to another. It will depend in part upon the characteristics of the replaced technology. If information technology replaces an earlier vintage of electronic technology, then the occupational change may be less dramatic than if it replaces, say, electromechanical technology. Although we cannot hope to be exhaustive, some broad trends are already in evidence (see OECD 1981, 1982):

1.   Within industrial production, a reduced *proportion* of blue-collar workers engaged upon low-skilled activities, such as assembly work.

2.   Within the service sector, a reduced *proportion* of the more routine,

information-handling occupations, such as lower-skilled clerical employees.

3. An increased *proportion* of occupations providing infrastructure support in the form of installing, operating and repairing the new machines and technologies.

4. Some de-skilling of certain craft occupations, with the skills of operatives being in part transferred to machine intelligence (e.g. the set-up and calibration of machine tools now being computer controlled).

Some of these points are illustrated in recent Department of Employment data on unemployment and job vacancies in the UK.[9] For every 100 unemployed in each category, there is only one vacancy for general labourers, 13 vacancies for clerical employees, but 87 vacancies for electronic engineers. Again, whereas unskilled manual employment was 46% of all vacancies in June 1979, by early 1990 it had fallen to 42%. Skilled (manual) craft occupations had similarly diminished over this time period from 24% to only 17% of all vacancies.

As a rule of thumb, higher, more general levels of skill seem to be required in both office and factory. This has important consequences for the types of training to be offered under policies to improve skill and competence for work as outlined by the Government's 'Employment for the 1990s' and 'Training for employment initiatives'.

Government policies towards information technology

The UK, along with other governments, has tried to promote electronic-based technologies by subsidizing the national computer industries. International Computers Ltd (ICL) received £30m. between 1972 and 1975, and favoured consideration when submitting contracts for computer systems in UK Government departments. The microprocessor manufacturer, INMOS, has been government-funded up to £50m., and its office equipment sister, NEXOS, has also received support. Further funds have been available in the UK to support the Microelectronics Applications Project (MAP), with the initial cost of pilot schemes borne by the Government. Similar support has been available for schemes to combine computer-aided design with computer-aided manufacturing (CAD/CAM), and for promoting information technology demonstration projects. Despite the 'computer in every secondary school' programme, UK policy has been heavily biased towards helping the equipment manufacturers, whereas other countries (e.g. France/Norway) have given rather more encouragement to consumer use. It may be important for the UK to move further in this direction, since Viewdata, cable television and other consumer items are likely to be the catalysts for more extensive use of information technology goods and services. In addition, the firms that were early recipients of government support have now ceased to exist, at least in their original form. For example, in 1990 Fujitsu of Japan acquired ICL.

One encouraging line of development has been via the National Economic Development Office (NEDO) sector working parties. Information technology is a highly interdependent sector of activity, with 'success' in one field dependent on success elsewhere, e.g. software developments require the most advanced 'chips'. Again, 80–90% of the cost of any information technology system is in the terminal hardware, so that the existence of a competitive UK terminal supply industry is essential. Through the various sector working parties (SWPs) more broadly based strategies are being pursued. The electronic consumer goods and electronic components SWPs came together to promote co-operation between users and suppliers (NEDC 1982), with the result that UK component quality has improved by an astonishing factor of 6 since June 1979. In a heavily interdependent sector such as information technology, advances have to be made on broad fronts and the collaboration of SWPs is an important development. Indeed, the dangers of *not* advancing on broad fronts in such a rapidly developing field as information technology are well illustrated by the colour television industry. By 1985, the major part of the television chassis was effectively based on silicon chips. This puts more of the set design decisions into the hands of those who supply integrated circuits. A UK presence in microprocessor design and manufacture, as with INMOS, then becomes still more important. Yet INMOS was long since sold, and the 'shell' of that company is now in overseas hands. Indeed Table 10.1 below indicates the absence of a UK owned firm in the top 10 firms of the worldwide semiconductor industry, or for that matter in the top 10 firms in the computer or telecommunications industries. Certainly scale economies make size vital for any 'player' in the semiconductor industry. The cost of developing and tooling-up to make D-ram memories – the most widely used type of chips – was estimated at about $2bn in 1991, and this cost is expected to double with each new 'generation' of chips.

Computers		Sales $bn	Telecommunications (1988)		Sales $bn	Semiconductors		Sales $bn
Company	Country		Company	Country		Company	Country	
IBM	US	62.71	AT&T	US	10.24	NEC	Japan	5.01
DEC	US	12.74	Alcatel	France	9.41	Toshiba	Japan	4.93
Fujitsu	Japan	11.88	Siemens	W. Germany	6.81	Hitachi	Japan	3.97
Unisis	US	10.10	NEC	Japan	5.82	Motorola	US	3.32
NEC	Japan	10.02	Northern Telecom	Canada	5.40	Fujitsu	Japan	2.96
Hitachi	Japan	9.84	Ericsson	Sweden	5.04	Texas Instruments	US	2.79
Hewlett-Packard	US	8.10	Motorola	US	3.02	Mitsubishi	Japan	2.58
Olivetti	Italy	7.26	Philips	Neths.	2.80	Intel	US	2.43
Bull	France	6.47	Fujitsu	Japan	2.49	Matsushita	Japan	1.88
NCR	US	5.96	Bosch	W. Germany	2.16	Philips	Neths.	1.72

Source: Dataquest, Financial Times (1990).

Table 10.1 How European electronics companies rank in the world. By total sales (US $bn) and sector, 1989.

There is some concern that efforts to support the diffusion of information technology have been withdrawn too quickly. For instance, MAP, started by the Labour Government in July 1978, spent about £50m. in helping mainly small firms get microelectronic projects started. The Policy Studies Institute was commissioned by the Government to study the effectiveness of the MAP programme. Its report in September 1985 (PSI 1985a) concluded that MAP had played a vital role in giving support to firms which had trouble raising funds from the City to develop new products and processes. Small firms had particularly benefited, with more than a quarter of the companies who received grants employing fewer than twenty people. Also, the performance of projects receiving MAP support was found to be significantly better than those which did not. It was reported by 30% of firms that their employment had increased as a result of MAP-backed projects, with only 5% reporting a reduction. In fact one in five of firms supported achieved sales of over £1m. in the first year of their new product, with sales climbing higher in later years. Yet, despite the encouraging findings of the report and its recommendation that 'it (MAP) is a form of support which in our view needs to be not only continued but expanded', the MAP programme had already been submerged in the Government's overall support for innovation programmes!

Interestingly, a major international study of microchip modernization in the UK, France and West Germany (PSI 1985b), found the same broad patterns in all three countries. Only up to a half of all factories actually used microelectronics, and direct job losses through automation were less than 0.5% per year. Perhaps surprisingly, only 7% of firms in the UK felt union opposition to be a major difficulty in adopting new technology, compared to 14% in West Germany, and 16% in France! In all three countries the lack of microelectronics expertise has been the biggest difficulty encountered: a 'very important problem' for 55% of German factories, 51% of French factories and 45% of UK factories. British firms, in contrast, found more problems in the 'general economic climate', than did France and West Germany (43, 23 and 20% respectively) and in 'raising finance' (30% UK, 19% France, 18% West Germany).

Conclusion

As regards the level of employment, new and enhanced products and services (product innovation) create, as well as destroy, jobs. Less labour-intensive processes (process innovation) may, via productivity gain, reduce costs and prices. This may so stimulate demand and output that total employment does not fall. A Policy Studies Institute report (PSI 1985c) concluded that *technological* unemployment has been barely affected by microelectronic and related technologies. The simulation study by the Manpower Research Group of Warwick University for the UK economy also revealed 'compensation effects' in excess of 100% of the initial labour displaced, i.e. more jobs created than destroyed by technology itself. However, there is the concern that information technology adopted by firms may have so raised their productive potential that each unit rise in output will now generate less new employment than in previous cycles. This concern is of course heightened at a time of curbed economic growth, as in the early 1990s. The occupational profile of employment is certainly being affected by information technology. The lesser-skilled office and factory employees, and skilled craftsmen, are amongst those most at risk from the new technologies. Retraining programmes must take into account these changing patterns of skill requirement. Government policy may need some readjustment away from equipment suppliers (increasingly giant European, US and Japanese firms) and towards final consumers, since a prerequisite for advanced information technology goods and services may be the possession of cabled, videotex systems or satellite receivers in the home, as well as in the office. The 'general economic climate' may be a key factor in promoting further diffusion of the new technologies, as may the availability of microelectronics expertise and sources of venture capital. The Government will have to monitor carefully whether withdrawal of explicit support for information technology projects can be undertaken without seriously setting back the diffusion process.

Notes

1. As with the closure of the electromechanical National Cash Registers (NCR) plant at Dundee.
2. See PSI (1985b). Forty-eight per cent of the manufacturing establishments surveyed were found to make use of microelectronics.
3. Wage rises offered to workers for accepting technical change are often termed 'featherbedding'.
4. Not, of course, under *all* market forms. For instance, in perfect competition firm price may be unaffected (via a horizontal demand curve), though firm output would still increase.
5. Remember MC intersects ATC at its lowest point. A fall in ATC must, therefore, also lead to a fall in MC.
6. For instance, if $w = 10$ per unit and $r = 5$ per unit, a constant sum of £60 could buy six units of labour and no capital, or no labour and twelve units of capital, giving a slope of $12/6 = w_1/r_1$ for the isocost line $\bar{C}_1$.
7. From Fig. 10.3 we cannot say definitely that $\bar{C}_2$ is less than $\bar{C}_1$, because $\bar{C}_2$ is *not* nearer to the origin than C_1 at all points. However, the usual reason for adopting a new process of production K_2/L_2 is to lower costs.
8. That is, tangency between an isoquant curve above and to the right of $1x$ in Fig. 10.3, and an isocost curve above and parallel to $\bar{C}_2$ (reflecting the new factor price ratio w_1/r_2,.
9. See *Department of Employment Gazette* (latest available edition).

References and further reading

Financial Times (1990) *Shadows over the sunrise sector*, 25 July.
Henry, M. (1983) The UK electronics industry, *Barclays Review*, **58**, 3, Aug.
Large, P. (1984) IT industry in grave danger says Neddy, *Guardian*, 21 June.
NEDC (1982) Sectoral Report No. 27, *The Electronic Consumer Goods Industry*, April.
OECD (1981) *Information Activities, Electronics and Telecommunications Technologies*. Paris, Sept.
OECD (1982) *Information Technology, Productivity and Employment*. Stoneman, P. and Blattner, N. Paris, May.
PSI (1985a) *Promoting Innovation: microelectronic applications projects*. London.
PSI (1985b) *Microelectronics in Industry: an international comparison*. London.
PSI (1985c) *Chips and Jobs*. London.

Rada, J. (1980) *The Impact of Microelectronics*. ILO, Geneva.
Smallwood, C. (1988) Know-how is a must to keep the miracle alive, *Sunday Times*, 12 June.
Stoneman, P. (1983) *The Economic Analysis of Technological Change*. OUP, London.
Wall, S. (1985) Information technology and employment, *The Economic Review*, **3**, 2, Nov.
Whitely, J. *et al.* (1981) *Employment in the late 1980s: a provisional study*. Manpower Research Group, Warwick University.

11 Consumption and saving

Consumption is the most important single element in aggregate demand, so that its accurate estimation is essential to the management of the economy. Keynes (1936) related consumption to current disposable income, and for many years this was widely accepted. However, in the 1950s evidence began to appear of a discrepancy between the consumption function estimated from long-run time-series data, and the much flatter consumption function estimated from short-run time-series and cross-section data. The Keynesian consumption function could not resolve this discrepancy, and it was this, together with the need for more accurate forecasts of consumption, that led to the development of the Permanent Income, Life-Cycle and Relative Income Hypotheses. In this chapter the Keynesian and alternative theories of consumption are considered in detail, their predictions are compared with actual fact, and their different implications for policy analysis are noted. We also look carefully at the mirror image of consumption, namely the savings ratio, and try to explain its unexpectedly sharp rise in the 1970s when inflation and unemployment were increasing, as well as its collapse to historically low levels in the late 1980s. We conclude with a brief discussion of consumer forecasting.

Consumption

The consumption function – the relationship between consumer expenditure and income – is probably the most widely researched relationship in macroeconomics. The impetus to this research was given by Keynes's initial conceptual breakthrough in the *General Theory of Employment, Interest and Money* of 1936 (Keynes 1936). In the Keynesian view of the economic system, both output and employment are determined by the level of aggregate demand. As consumer spending is by far the largest element in aggregate demand, being approximately 50% of total final expenditure on goods and services in 1990, it is essential that the factors influencing consumer spending be identified in order that it may be forecast accurately. This forecast for consumer spending can then be added to forecasts for the other elements of aggregate demand, namely investment, government spending, and net exports (exports minus imports), to derive an overall forecast for *total aggregate demand*. Policy-makers can then decide whether this projected level of demand is appropriate for the economy, and if not, what corrective fiscal or monetary action should be taken.

The central position of the consumption function in Keynesian economics has therefore led to many attempts to estimate an equation that would indeed predict consumer expenditure. Unfortunately, most of the early Keynesian types of equation failed to explain some of the more interesting features of aggregate consumer behaviour. Alternative theories were therefore developed in the 1950s and 1960s which, it was claimed, fitted the facts rather better than the simple Keynesian view of consumption.

The development of these new theories, and the relative economic stability of the 1950s and 1960s, led economists to believe that consumer spending was probably one of the best-understood and best-forecast variables in economics. We see from Table 11.1, however, that there was a sharp fall in the proportion of personal disposable income consumed (the average propensity to consume (a.p.c.)) in the early and late 1970s, which was *not* predicted by the existing equations. This fall in the a.p.c. was reflected in the sharp rise in the savings ratio, and we return to this, along with the subsequent fall in the savings ratio in the 1980s, later in the chapter.

The Keynesian consumption function

In the *General Theory*, Keynes argued that 'The fundamental psychological law . . . is that men are disposed, as a rule and on the average, to increase their consumption as their income increases, but not by as much as the increase in their income' (Keynes 1936: 96). From this statement can be derived the Keynesian consumption function[1] which is usually expressed in the following way:

$$C = c_0 + bY$$

where C = consumer expenditure;

c_0 — a constant;

b = the marginal propensity to consume (m.p.c.), which is the amount consumed out of the last pound of income received; and

Y = National Income.

The Keynesian view is that when income rises, consumption rises, but by less than income, which implies that b, the m.p.c., is less than 1. Keynes also argued that 'it is also obvious that a higher absolute level of income will tend, as a rule, to widen the gap between income and consumption' (Keynes 1936: 97). This is usually taken to mean that he thought that the proportion of income consumed, C/Y (i.e. a.p.c.), will tend to fall as income increases. In fact the positive constant c_0 in the above equation ensures that this will happen, since

$$\text{a.p.c.} = \frac{C}{Y} = \frac{c_0}{Y} + b$$

and this will decrease as Y increases if, and only if, c_0 is positive. This also implies, of course, that the a.p.c. is greater than the m.p.c. by an amount c_0/Y.

Drawing the consumption function as a straight line, as in Fig. 11.1, means that we are assuming that the m.p.c., b, is a constant, as it is the slope of the consumption function. The a.p.c. is found, for any level of income, by measuring the slope of the radian from the origin to the appropriate point on the consumption function. For example, if income is Y_1, then consumption would be C_1, and the a.p.c. would be C_1/Y_1, which is the tangent of the angle α. It can be seen that as Y increases, the slope of the radian from the origin to

Fig. 11.1 The consumption function

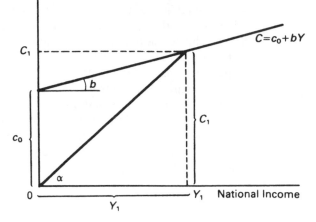

the consumption function falls, which means that the proportion of income consumed (a.p.c.) falls.

For Keynes, the main influence on consumption in the short run was current disposable income, i.e. income minus direct taxes. When this fluctuated, so would consumption, but because the m.p.c. was less than 1, consumption would change by an amount less than the change in disposable income. If we look at the actual data for the UK and plot consumption against disposable income, both measured in real terms (using 1985 prices), we can see from Fig. 11.2 that over the period 1960–89 there appears to be a close positive relationship between consumption and disposable income.

Fig. 11.2 The consumption–income relationship 1960–89

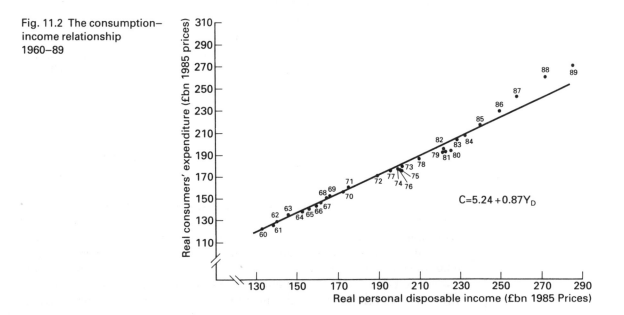

In order to find numerical estimates for c and b for our consumption function, we can fit a regression line, or line of 'best fit',[2] to the data in Table 11.1 below. Using linear regression we can derive the following equation:

$$C = 5.24 + 0.87Y_D$$

where Y_D is real disposable income (£bn).

This consumption function (1960–89) not only appears to fit the data well, as can be seen from Fig. 11.2, but also seems to support the Keynesian view that the m.p.c. is less than 1 (in our case 0.87). Further, because we have a positive intercept of 5.24 (£bn), it implies that the a.p.c. falls as income rises:

$$\text{a.p.c.} = C/Y_D = 5.24/Y_D + 0.87$$

As a first attempt, therefore, the above equation, which explains changes in consumption in terms of changes in current disposable income, seems to fit the facts and the Keynesian theory rather well. To take an example, in 1985 real disposable income was £239.78bn; fitting this into our equation gives predicted consumption of £214.71bn. Actual consumption was £217.02bn, an error of only 1%. The equation also gives an estimated a.p.c. of 0.89 for 1985 whereas the actual a.p.c. was 0.91, again only a very small error.

Closer examination of the data, however, indicates that using changes in current disposable income to explain changes in consumption may be less than satisfactory. If the only influence on consumption was current income then we would expect the m.p.c. to be fairly constant. Column 6 in Table 11.1, which shows the annual change in consumption divided by the annual change in disposable income, indicates apparently random fluctuations in the m.p.c. If we ignore the years when income and consumption moved in opposite directions (giving a negative m.p.c.)[3] then the m.p.c. has ranged in value from 0.00 to 2.20. If disposable income rose by £1bn the first figure would predict no rise in consumption, whereas the latter would predict an increase of £2.20bn. Obviously we cannot explain changes in consumption solely by changes in current disposable income; other factors must be taken into account.

The simple Keynesian consumption equation implies that the a.p.c. will fall as current disposable income increases. The evidence for the period 1960 to 1980 appears to support this, with the a.p.c. falling from 0.93 to 0.86. However whilst the overall trend was downwards, there were marked fluctuations around this trend. This can be seen clearly from Fig. 11.3. In the years of peak economic activity (such as 1961 and 1964–65) the a.p.c. was below trend, whereas in the years of depressed economic activity (such as 1963 and 1972) the a.p.c. was above trend. It appears that over this period there was a tendency for the a.p.c. to behave in a *contra-cyclical* manner. Unfortunately the behaviour of the a.p.c. does not follow this pattern during the two recessions of late 1973 to mid 1975, and mid 1979 to early 1981, since the a.p.c. remained below trend. It should however be noted that these two recessions were associated with rapid inflation, the influence of which on consumption and saving will be the subject of a later section.

Finally, from 1980 to 1988 there was a strong upward trend in the a.p.c. This too needs further explanation as disposable incomes were increasing

Year	1 Real personal disposable income	2 Real consumers' expenditure (1985 prices)	3 Average propensity to consume (a.p.c.)*	4 Change in real personal disposable income	5 Change in consumer expenditure	6 Marginal propensity to consume (m.p.c.)†	7 Personal savings ratio (%)
1960	132,910	123,119	0.93	8,216	4,572	0.56	7.4
1961	138,462	125,848	0.91	5,552	2,729	0.49	9.1
1962	139,964	128,690	0.92	1,502	2,842	1.89	8.1
1963	146,279	134,838	0.92	6,315	6,148	0.97	7.8
1964	152,504	138,985	0.91	6,225	4,147	0.67	8.9
1965	155,660	141,107	0.91	3,156	2,122	0.67	9.3
1966	159,072	143,617	0.90	3,412	2,510	0.74	9.7
1967	161,455	147,162	0.91	2,383	3,545	1.49	8.9
1968	164,266	151,271	0.92	2,811	4,109	1.46	7.9
1969	165,769	152,112	0.92	1,503	841	0.56	8.2
1970	172,246	156,336	0.91	6,477	4,224	0.65	9.2
1971	174,463	161,208	0.92	2,217	4,872	2.20	7.6
1972	189,069	171,052	0.90	14,606	9,844	0.67	9.5
1973	201,034	179,852	0.89	11,965	8,800	0.74	10.5
1974	199,421	177,233	0.89	−1,613	−2,619	1.62	11.1
1975	200,353	176,273	0.88	932	−960	−1.03	12.0
1976	200,029	176,853	0.88	−324	580	−1.79	11.6
1977	195,606	176,016	0.90	−4,423	−837	0.19	10.0
1978	209,894	185,950	0.89	14,288	9,934	0.70	11.4
1979	221,673	193,794	0.87	11,779	7,844	0.67	12.2
1980	224,885	193,806	0.86	3,212	12	0.00	13.5
1981	222,254	193,832	0.87	−2,631	26	−0.01	12.6
1982	221,709	195,561	0.88	−545	1,729	−3.17	11.6
1983	227,931	204,318	0.90	6,222	8,757	1.41	9.8
1984	232,426	207,927	0.89	4,495	3,609	0.80	10.2
1985	239,781	217,023	0.91	7,355	9,096	1.24	9.5
1986	249,272	228,951	0.92	9,491	11,928	1.26	8.2
1987	257,639	242,963	0.94	8,367	14,012	1.67	5.7
1988	271,439	259,656	0.96	13,800	16,693	1.21	4.3
1989	284,947	270,759	0.95	13,508	11,103	0.82	5.0

* Column 3 = column 2 divided by column 1.
† Column 6 = column 5 divided by column 4.
Source: CSO, Economic Trends, various editions.

Table 11.1 Personal
disposable income,
consumption and saving
ratio (£m at 1985 prices),
1960–89

over much of this period. It appears, therefore, that a Keynesian consumption function based only on *current disposable income* is insufficient to explain fully the short run changes in consumer expenditure.

Dissatisfaction with the simple Keynesian consumption function emerged soon after World War II. There were several reasons for this. Firstly, forecasts of post-war consumption, based on current income, underestimated the actual spending on consumption. This was largely due to the fact that such forecasts ignored the role of liquid assets accumulated during the war. Secondly, Kuznets (1946) showed that if decade averages were taken, then the long run a.p.c. in the USA was more or less constant. This implies that the long run consumption function passes through the origin and is steeper than the short run consumption function (i.e. the m.p.c. is larger in the long run than in the short run, as can be seen in Fig. 11.5).

It was felt by economists that any adequate theory of consumption must be

Fig. 11.3 The a.p.c. 1960–89
Source: CSO, *Economic
Trends*, various editions

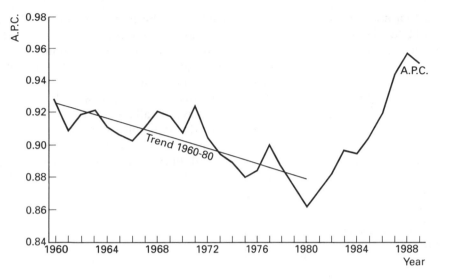

able to reconcile the differences between the short run and long run consumption functions. It should also be able to explain the role of wealth on consumption, and why, in *cross-section data*, high income earners have a lower a.p.c. than low income earners. The Keynesian function had been tested against the available evidence and been found wanting. Therefore the search for new theories began, and it is to these theories that we now turn.

Post-Keynesian theories of the consumption function

The newer theories of the consumption function differed from that of Keynes in that they were more deeply rooted in the microeconomics of consumer behaviour. Two of the theories, Friedman's Permanent Income Hypothesis (PIH) and Modigliani's Life-Cycle Hypothesis (LCH), start from the position that consumers plan their consumption expenditure not on the basis of income received during the current period, but rather on the basis of their long-run, or lifetime, income expectations. The third theory, Duesenberry's Relative Income Hypothesis (RIH), is different again, assuming that consumption is influenced by the consumer's relative income; both current income relative to previous income, and current income relative to other people's income. Unlike the PIH and LCH, Duesenberry's RIH is, in fact, at odds with traditional microeconomic theory of consumer behaviour, which assumes that each individual's preferences are independent of the consumption behaviour of others. Duesenberry differs in assuming that the utility a consumer derives from a given bundle of consumer goods depends to some extent on what others around him are consuming. In his theory, consumer preferences are 'interdependent' and consumption is influenced by the 'demonstration effect' of other people's consumption, i.e. 'keeping up with the Joneses'.

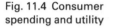

As mentioned above, both these hypotheses break the link between
consumption and current income by arguing that the consumer plans his
expenditure not on the basis of current income, but on a longer-term view of
income. As Friedman points out, the Keynesian view that consumption is a
function of current income, if taken to the extreme, would mean that
someone who was paid monthly, would on the day in which income is
received (pay-day), do all his consuming on that day. In contrast these
theories argue that if people can borrow and lend freely, then consumption in
any one time period should not be tied too closely to the income received in
that time period. Further, individuals not only have the ability to even out
consumption in the face of fluctuating income, but the desire to do so. This is
illustrated in Fig. 11.4.

Fig. 11.4 Consumer
spending and utility

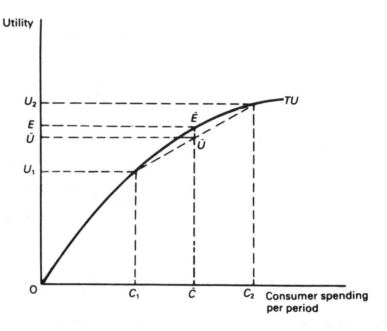

Figure 11.4 presents a total utility (TU) curve, which is drawn on the
assumption that extra units of consumer spending give progressively smaller
additions to total utility (diminishing marginal utility). If income now
fluctuates so that consumer spending in Period 1 is C_1, and in Period 2 is C_2,
then the average level of utility over the two periods would be $\bar{U}$. If,
however, the consumer could borrow in the period of low income, Period 1,
and repay this loan in the period of high income, Period 2, then consumption
could be stabilized over the two periods at $\bar{C}$ per period, and the average
level of utility would be raised to $\bar{E}$. The reason for this is, of course, that the
extra utility $(U_2 - \bar{E})$ gained by increasing consumption from $\bar{C}$ to C_2 is less,
because of diminishing marginal utility, than the extra utility lost $(\bar{E} - U_1)$
when consumption falls by an equal amount from $\bar{C}$ to C_1.

In both these theories, therefore, the link between current consumption
and current income is broken. A consumer determines his consumption for a
given period on the basis of a longer-run view of the resources available. The
ultimate constraint on an individual's consumption is then the wealth

available to him, both in the form of non-human assets (money, building society deposits, shares, etc.) and in the form of human assets (future labour income).

The Permanent Income Hypothesis   In Friedman's PIH an individual's consumption is based on that individual's permanent income (Y_p). Technically Y_p is defined as the return on the present value of an individual's wealth, and hence it is what can be consumed whilst leaving the individual's wealth intact. More generally Y_p could be thought of as some form of long-run average income, or 'normal income', which can be counted on in the future. An individual's actual or measured income (Y) in any time period will be made up of two parts – the 'permanent part' Y_p, and the 'transitory' part (Y_t). Transitory income might be positive, if the individual is having an unexpectedly good year, or negative, if the individual is having a bad year. It follows that measured income is

$$Y = Y_p + Y_t$$

In the simplest form of the PIH, consumption is a constant proportion of permanent income, i.e.

$$C = kY_p$$

where

$$k = F(i,w,x)$$

The proportion k is determined by factors such as the interest rate (i), the ratio of non-human to human wealth (w), and a catch-all variable (x) which includes age and tastes as a major component. If i rises, then individuals are assumed to feel more secure as to the future returns from their asset holdings, so that k increases. Equally, k will increase if the ratio of non-human to human wealth (w) rises in total wealth holding. This is also thought to increase individual security, since non-human wealth, such as money and shares, is assumed more reliable than human wealth, such as expected future labour income.

If the economy grows steadily, with no fluctuations, then Y_p would be appoximately equal to Y (measured National Income), and not only would a constant proportion of permanent income be consumed, but also a constant proportion of measured National Income. A study by Simon Kuznets in the USA showed that if *long-run* data were used (ten-year averages of consumption and income) then the a.p.c. was roughly constant. Taking ten-year averages effectively eliminates short-run fluctuations in income, and so Kuznets's results are consistent with the constant proportion k in the PIH.

This long-run consumption function derived from time-series data averages over the business cycle, with its constant a.p.c., seemed, however, at odds with the short-run consumption function derived either from time-series data on an annual basis or from cross-sectional data. The short-run consumption function was flatter than the long-run function (see Fig. 11.5 below), having therefore a lower m.p.c. and an a.p.c. that was not constant, falling when incomes rose (booms) and rising when incomes fell (slumps). The answer to this puzzle, according to Friedman, is that in booms more

210 Consumption and saving

people will think that they are doing better than normal than will think they are doing worse than normal. For the economy as a whole, therefore, there will be positive transitory income (Y_t), so that measured National Income (Y) will be above permanent income (Y_p). The unexpectedly high measured income will, however, have little impact on consumer views of their permanent income unless it lasts for several years. Since consumer spending plans are based on permanent income, any boom that is not long-lived will have little effect on consumer spending. The unexpected increases in income are therefore largely saved, with the result that in a boom the average propensity to consume falls. This is seen in Fig. 11.5.

Fig. 11.5 Long- and short-run consumption functions

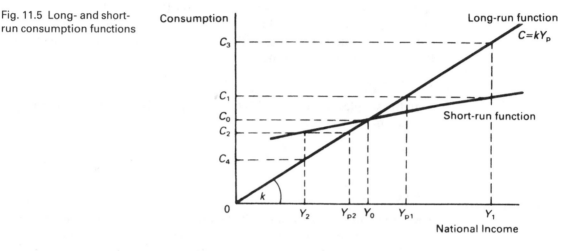

As the economy expands along its long-run trend, then consumption is a fixed proportion, k, of income. In reality, however, the economy fluctuates around this long-run trend. Suppose we start in situation Y_0, with measured and permanent income equal, consumption (kY_0) equal to C_0, and a.p.c. equal to k. The economy then experiences a boom with measured income rising to Y_1. Permanent income will, however, be less affected by the sudden increase in income, and in our figure only rises to Y_{p1}. Consumption, being based on permanent income, now rises to C_1 (kY_{p1}). Only if measured income remained at Y_1 for several years would permanent income be revised upwards to Y_1, and consumption to $C_3(kY_1)$. If this is not the case, then the proportion of income consumed will only be C_1/Y_1, i.e. the a.p.c. will have fallen below the initial level k during the boom.

In a slump, income will fall, say from Y_0 to Y_2, and although permanent income may be revised downwards a little to Y_{p2}, it will fall proportionately less than measured income. Consumption will therefore be C_2 (kY_{p2}), falling much less than if Y_2 had been regarded as permanent (when consumption would fall further to C_4). The a.p.c. will then be C_2/Y_2, which is above the initial level k.

It can be seen from this analysis that Friedman is able to explain why the short-run consumption function is flatter, with a variable a.p.c., whilst the long-run consumption function is steeper, with a constant a.p.c. Booms will, unless long-lived, cause a.p.c. to fall. There will be little upward revision of consumption plans, when higher income is largely regarded as transitory. Slumps will, unless long-lived, in a similar manner cause a.p.c. to rise.

The Life-Cycle Hypothesis   The LCH developed by Modigliani and his associates, is similar in many ways to the PIH. Consumption is again seen as being a constant proportion k of Y_p, with the same sort of variables affecting k as in Friedman's theory. Modigliani stresses, however, the age of the consumer, with the consumer trying to even out consumption over a lifetime in which income fluctuates widely. In youth and old age, when income is low, consumption is maintained by borrowing or drawing on past savings respectively, so that consumption is a high proportion of income; in middle life, when income is relatively high, a smaller proportion is consumed, with savings being built up to finance consumption after retirement.

One of the empirical facts that needed to be explained by any theory was why, from *cross-sectional* data, it was seen that low-income groups had a higher a.p.c. than high-income groups. The LCH argued that low-income groups contain a high proportion of very young and very old households, both of which have a high propensity to consume. On the other hand, the high-income groups contain a high proportion of middle-aged households, with a low propensity to consume.

The variations in a.p.c. observed using *time-series* data, when National Income rises or falls, can also be explained by the LCH. Any windfall or transitory income received in a boom is spread over the individual's remaining lifetime. For example, an unexpected increase in income of, say, £1,000 for someone with twenty more years to live, would mean that they would revise their Y_p upwards by about £50 per annum, so that consumption in the year in which the windfall is received would increase by a relatively small amount (some proportion of £50). The a.p.c. would therefore fall with higher income because consumption (the numerator) will have risen by only a small amount, based on Y_p, but measured income (the denominator) has risen by the full £1,000. An unexpected reduction in income in a recession would likewise be spread over an individual's lifetime, with borrowing and/or the running down of past savings leading to only a small cut in that individual's current consumption, thereby causing a.p.c. to rise.

The LCH has therefore been able, like the PIH, to reconcile the flatter short-run consumption function with the steeper long-run consumption function (with constant a.p.c.). It follows that both theories imply that the m.p.c., which is the slope of the consumption function, is lower in the short run than it is in the long run. In the PIH any unexpected increase in income is not consumed, but largely saved, whereas in the LCH it is spread over the consumer's lifetime.

A distinction must be made at this stage between these theories and Keynesian theory. Keynesian theory suggests that current disposable income is the main factor influencing *consumer expenditure*. This is defined as spending not only on non-durable consumer goods, such as food and clothing and personal services, but also on consumer durables, such as cars and video recorders. Both the PIH and LCH, however, explain *consumption* rather than consumer expenditure. Consumption includes, in addition to the purchase of non-durable goods and services, only the 'use' of consumer durables, as measured by depreciation. In these theories, if a consumer spent a windfall gain of, say, £5,000 on a car that lasted ten years, then only £500 of this expenditure would be classified as 'consumption', the other £4,500 would be classified as 'saving' because the consumption of this part of the car is postponed until future years. For Friedman and Modigliani therefore, windfall income, even if spent on consumer durables, is classified as being mainly saved, which further helps explain the low m.p.c. out of changes in current income predicted by these theories.

It follows that the multiplier[4] predicted by these theories will be small in the short run, because m.p.c. is low in the short run. Changes in government spending and taxation aimed at stabilizing the economy will therefore be relatively ineffective, especially if these changes are seen as being only temporary. A by-product of Friedman's work on the consumption function appears, therefore, to be an attack on the effectiveness of Keynesian short-run demand-management policies. It should be remembered, however, that both Friedman and Modigliani are explaining consumption, and not consumer expenditure. A windfall increase in income that is spent on consumer durables is largely classified as savings, which although correct from their theoretical standpoint, is still actual expenditure that will generate both income and jobs.

The PIH and LCH appear to have broken the link between current consumption and current disposable income by arguing that consumption depends not only on current disposable income but also on all future disposable income. It could be argued, however, that there are two reasons why the influence of current income may be more important than these theories imply. First, it is unreasonable to believe that all consumers will be able to borrow and lend in different periods to even out their consumption pattern. An unemployed worker is unlikely to be able to borrow money to maintain his consumption, even though he is convinced he will be able to repay the loan out of future earnings. In this case, once past savings are exhausted, the constraint on consumption will be current disposable income. Second, estimates of future disposable income, on which permanent income is based, are highly uncertain. It is reasonable to expect, therefore, that the consumer uses his recent experience, his current income, as an important basis for estimating long-run or permanent income, and hence wealth. For both these reasons, therefore, one could still argue that current disposable income is still a major influence on current consumption, even under the PIH and LCH.

The Relative Income Hypothesis

The basis of Duesenberry's RIH is that the propensity to consume does not depend so much on absolute income (Keynes's theory) but more on relative income, both through time and between groups at one point in time.

If we consider *time-series* data, then the theory argues that what matters in determining consumption is the individual's current income relative to his previous peak income. Consumers get used to a certain level of consumption and, if income falls, they resist the fall in consumption that this might imply, i.e. the a.p.c. rises in a slump.

Fig. 11.6 Relative income and consumption

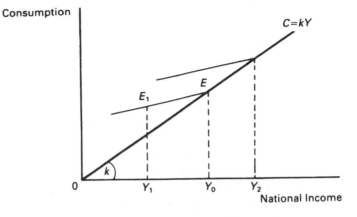

From Fig. 11.6 it can be seen that although the basic long-run consumption function is proportional to income, it still varies with the business cycle. If income is Y_0, and this is higher than the previous peak, then consumption will be at E with $C = kY_0$, and a.p.c. $= k$. If, in the next period, income falls to Y_1, then consumption contracts not along $C = kY$, but by less, say to E_1. The a.p.c. at Y_1 is greater than at Y_0, because people are reducing the proportion of income saved in order to maintain consumption out of a lower income. In a slump, a.p.c. therefore rises above k. During recovery, as income increases, consumption expands along the short-run consumption function $E_1 - E$, i.e. in recovery a.p.c. falls (though it is still above k). When the previous peak income, Y_0, is reached, and surpassed, consumption expands along the consumption function $C = kY$. If, when income has reached Y_2, there is another recession, and income falls, consumption again contracts by proportionately less than income, so that the a.p.c. rises.

The RIH also explains the empirical fact that, if *cross-sectional* data are taken, the a.p.c. falls as income rises. It does so by suggesting that low-income groups aspire to 'average' consumption patterns. The proportion of income consumed or saved, therefore, depends on the individual's income relative to average income. If an individual has a below-average income, his attempt to emulate the consumption pattern of those with average income will mean that he consumes a higher than average proportion of his income. Likewise, someone with an above-average income is likely to consume a smaller proportion of his income than average. This will again give the flatter curve observed for consumption functions using cross-sectional data.

The savings ratio

Consumer spending has clearly been one of the most widely researched areas in macroeconomics. Despite this there have been unexpectedly large movements in the proportion of income consumed, and hence saved, over the last twenty years. In the 1970s, personal savings rose as a proportion of personal disposable income, reaching a peak of 13.8% in 1980. In the 1980s the savings ratio fell, reaching a low point of 4.3% in 1988. These largely unanticipated swings in savings imply that the consumption function is less stable than Keynes had thought. The job of macroeconomic demand management is made more difficult.

Measurement of the savings ratio

The savings ratio for the personal sector is the *difference* between personal disposable income (PDI) and consumption, expressed as a percentage of PDI. Several practical and conceptual problems arise with respect to the savings ratio. Firstly, it is the difference between two large and fairly inaccurate aggregates, and hence it is inevitably inaccurate itself (up to 20% out either way, according to the government's own calculations). As a result the published figure is often revised; for example, the savings ratio for 1974 first appeared as 12.7%, was subsequently revised up to 14.4% and has since been revised down to 11.1%. Secondly, the personal sector includes not only households but also unincorporated businesses, non-profit making bodies and life assurance and pension funds. The inclusion of businesses means that PDI, and therefore personal savings, will be influenced by *stock appreciation*. Thirdly, the savings ratio is sensitive to what is included in the respective definitions of consumption and capital expenditure. For example, in 1984 the Central Statistical Office reclassified expenditure on *home improvements*, moving this item out of consumption and into capital expenditure. This increased the savings ratio for 1983 by as much as 1.5% points. Finally it must be remembered that the personal sector includes unincorporated businesses. Stock appreciation during periods of high inflation increases the income of these companies and thus may raise the savings ratio.

Post-war behaviour of the savings ratio

From Fig. 11.7, it can be seen that over the post-war period there has been a long-run upward trend in the proportion of personal disposable income saved. The period as a whole could be divided into four parts for further investigation.

Fig. 11.7 Personal saving as a percentage of personal disposable income 1950–89 *Source: Economic Trends* (various editions)

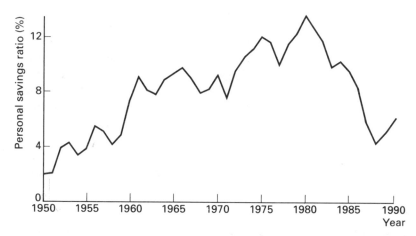

The first period, from the end of the Second World War up to 1960, saw a rise in the savings ratio, from an exceptionally low level (0.1% in 1948) to what was considered at the time a more normal level (7.2% in 1960). The explanation for this appears to be that people in the early post-war years were catching up on consumption that had been postponed during the war years, so that the savings ratio in the early post-war period was uncharacteristically low. The rise in the savings ratio after these early years can therefore be seen as a return to normality.

The second period, from 1960 to 1971, revealed no marked upward trend, with the ratio fluctuating around an average of 8%. The fluctuations in the ratio coincided with variations in the rate of growth of National Income; the savings ratio fell when the economy slowed down, and rose when the economy accelerated. This period could therefore adequately be explained by any of the post-Keynesian theories of consumption.[5]

In the third period, from the early 1970s to the early 1980s, the upward trend in the savings ratio has been re-established, reaching a peak of 15.2% in 1980. As we noted, this has been puzzling, being associated with high rates of inflation, negative real interest rates, and periods when real disposable income actually fell (1974, 1976, 1977, 1981).

A number of attempts have been made to explain why the savings ratio has risen under these conditions. For example, the Bank of England (1978) has argued that increases in contractual savings (regular contributions to pension funds and life assurance companies) have at times contributed to the high savings ratio, especially in the early 1970s. Rising unemployment and related uncertainties, in times of recession, may also have led to an increase in savings for precautionary reasons.

Savings and inflation The greater part of the research, however, has been into the relationship between inflation and the savings ratio. Most of the studies have found a positive connection between these two variables, but there is some disagreement as to why the inflation rate should affect the savings ratio.

One theory (Deaton 1977) explains the relationship in terms of consumers failing to perceive the actual rate of inflation. The suggestion is that consumers *underestimate* the average price level and are therefore unduly shocked at the apparently 'excessive' rise in the price of particular commodities. Until such time as consumers recognize the true (and higher) level of average prices, purchases of these commodities will have been cut back in response to the assumed sharp increase in individual prices. Savings will therefore rise as a result of this 'inflation surprise' effect. This theory suggests that it is unanticipated inflation that matters, so that the effect on consumption, and therefore savings, will be particularly strong in the early stages of inflation when the rate of inflation is accelerating.

A study by Bulkley (1981) has supplemented the above theory, showing that even if inflation is fully anticipated the savings ratio will still increase as long as anticipated inflation is itself increasing. Even if inflation is fully anticipated, workers' real wages will still have fluctuated throughout the year, since money wages are usually set on only one occasion in the year. Real wages will therefore be at a maximum when the money wage is first set, falling to a minimum a year later as prices progressively rise. In order to smooth out his real consumption pattern over the year, an individual will save more each week early in the contract period, and correspondingly less later in the contract period. If inflation is constant, and if wage contracts are spread evenly over the year, then the additional savings of some will cancel out the reduced savings of others, and there will be no aggregate effect on the savings ratio. However, when anticipated inflation is increasing and with it the money wage, then the extra savings by those who have recently received higher wage awards will more than offset the reduction in the savings of those nearing the end of their nominal wage contracts, and the savings ratio will rise.

Other explanations (Cuthbertson 1982) stress the impact that inflation has on the real value of an individual's liquid assets, affecting the individual's desire to save. Liquid assets include notes and coins, bank and building society deposits, National Savings and other short-term assets. Because the real rate of interest (nominal rate minus the rate of inflation) on liquid assets over this period has often been zero or negative, the real purchasing power of a given stock of these assets has fallen. If the consumer wishes to maintain the real value of his liquid assets, for reasons of security or flexibility, he must choose either to cash in less liquid assets, or to save more from current income. The real rate of return on some non-liquid assets such as housing and consumer durables has been positive over this period as a whole, and so rather than cash these in, one would expect the holdings of these to increase in inflationary times. Other non-liquid assets, such as life assurance and long-term contractual saving, are expensive to cash in, as are government bonds when the interest rate is high. Thus the desire to rebuild a given stock of real liquid assets could really only come from a reduction in non-durable consumption, i.e. saving. People have tended, therefore, during the recent inflationary times to save a higher proportion of their disposable income in the attempt to maintain the real value of their liquid assets.

Savings in the 1980s and early 1990s

The fourth period embraces 1980 to the present time. During this period the savings ratio fell from its peak of 13.8% in 1980 to a thirty year low of 4.3% in 1988. There appear to be a number of reasons for this. First, in inflationary times some savings are needed just to maintain the *real* value of assets, the values of which are fixed in money terms. As the inflation rate falls, as it did from 1980–83, the need for such saving declines. A second factor in the fall of the savings ratio seems to be the behaviour of pension funds. Conventionally, these funds are seen as the property of the personal sector and the income of these funds (including investment income and employers' contributions) is treated as part of personal income. However, movements in this element of personal income are unlikely to have much effect on consumption and for that reason are more likely to affect the savings ratio. As the earnings on the funds assets rose from the low levels of the 1970s, the savings ratio increased. But in the 1980s it became apparent that the value of these pension funds had risen above the sum needed to meet pension liabilities; as a result employers' contributions to pension funds stopped rising from 1981. Indeed in 1986 and 1987 they actually fell in *nominal* as well as real terms. This 'contributions holiday' lowered personal income and so the *personal savings ratio* fell in favour of higher company saving.

A third factor influencing the savings ratio in this period has been the increased financial liberalization of capital and money markets. The decline in the savings ratio in the 1980s has largely been the result of increased borrowing and consumption, rather than a decrease in gross savings. Easier consumer credit, and in particular mortgage borrowing (a large part of which was used to finance consumption), fuelled a consumer boom in 1986, 1987 and 1988. Not only was credit relatively easy to obtain, but the rise in equity and house prices also increased consumer wealth, providing both the collateral for further borrowing and suppressing the need for savings. Consumer confidence during this period was also buoyant due to the strong growth in real incomes and falling unemployment.

The fourth factor influencing the savings ratio has been a demographic one. Recent research carried out by the London Business School suggests that the fall in the proportion of the population in the 45–64 year age group since 1984 has influenced savings. It is the people in this age group that are the principal savers in our society; younger people are borrowing to set up home and older retired people are living on past savings. A decline in the 45–64 year age group is therefore likely to reduce the savings ratio.

Finally, it has been claimed that the official figures actually underestimate the true savings ratio. Personal income, it is argued, is underestimated in official statistics, whereas consumption is measured reasonably accurately. This would lower the level of *measured* or recorded saving.

The personal savings ratio has in fact risen since 1988. The reasons for this are thought to be a combination of the following: the up-turn in the inflation rate, higher interest rates, and possibly the upturn in the proportion of people in the 45–64 age group. Higher interest rates (bank base rate rose from 7.5% in May 1988 to 15% by October 1989) not only make saving relatively more attractive but have also depressed house prices, thereby decreasing consumer wealth and discouraging consumption. Consumer spending has been further constrained by higher interest rates raising the cost of mortgage repayments, and hence reducing disposable incomes net of such repayments.

One final point needs to be made at this stage. So far we have concentrated on the *personal* sector savings ratio. If we take a wider perspective and consider *total* domestic saving, which includes the corporate and public sectors in addition to the private sector, then domestic savings as a proportion of GDP at factor cost (current prices) has been much more stable in recent years. As Fig. 11.8 shows, the domestic savings ratio has varied between 5.3% and 8.3%, but has shown no discernable downward trend. Increased corporate and public sector saving (from 1985) have largely compensated for a lower personal savings ratio.

Fig. 11.8 Domestic saving as a % of GDP at Factor Cost (current prices)
Source: Bank of England *Quarterly Bulletin* (1990)

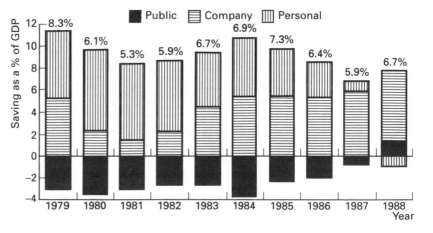

Forecasting consumer spending

The consumer expenditure equation in the Treasury macroeconomic model has been modified several times in recent years. This is not surprising given the volatile behaviour of both consumption and savings. The first published versions of the consumption function in the model simply related consumption to current and past values of consumption. This type of equation, which gave a lower m.p.c. in the short run than in the long run, was consistent with both the PIH and LCH of consumption.

The fall in the a.p.c. (rise in the savings ratio) in the early 1970s was, however, not predicted by the Treasury equation, and so a search was made for an alternative specification that could account for this behaviour. This process involved a disaggregation of consumer expenditure into expenditure on consumer durables and non-durables on the grounds that these two may be expected to behave in different ways.

Durable consumption

Consumer durables (cars, furniture, etc.) yield a flow of current services, so that expenditure on these may be viewed as current consumption. On the other hand they may also be regarded as wealth, with their acquisition therefore considered in part as a form of savings. These two characteristics have been integrated into what is called a 'stock adjustment' model. In this model consumers have a desired stock of consumer durables which is influenced by real disposable income. If, in any period, their actual stock of durables does not equal their desired stock, then part of this gap will be closed by the purchase of extra consumer durables. Expenditure on consumer durables will therefore vary positively with real disposable income, but negatively with the stock of durable goods already held in the last period.

Other explanatory variables in the Treasury equation are wealth, the change in the unemployment rate, and the cost of credit (the real rate of interest). The wealth variable has a positive sign, and to some extent captures the effects of inflation. For instance, an increase in inflation lowers the real value of personal wealth (much of which is in money forms), and this will lower expenditure on consumer durables. The change in unemployment and the real interest rate variables have, as we might expect, negative signs, so that expenditure on consumer durables falls with a rise in both unemployment and the real rate of interest.

Non-durable consumption

By 1984 most of the major UK economic forecasting agencies, including the Treasury, were using a version of the error correction mechanism (based on the work of Davidson *et al*. 1978) to forecast consumption. At its simplest this mechanism implies that consumers plan to spend in each quarter of a year the same as four quarters previously, modified by a proportion of their annual change in income and by whether the change in income is increasing or decreasing. In addition, the role of wealth, interest rates and the influence of inflation are usually included as explanatory variables.

It could be argued that the modifications that were made to consumption equations in the early 1980s enabled them to 'explain' what actually happened to the propensities to consume and save in the 1970s. Unfortunately these newly established equations apparently failed to predict the decline in the personal savings ratio after 1985. As a result the possible addition of new variables (previously mentioned in this chapter) has been suggested. For example, the influence of demographic change (Currie, Holly and Scott 1989), of interest rate changes on household finances, and a wider view of wealth (Hendry, Muellbauer and Murphy 1989), have received considerable attention. This reassessment of existing forecasting equations in the light of recent macroeconomic experience is understandable, although such reassessment may be a little hasty given that there is a strong possibility of data revisions eliminating the apparent failure of current models (see, for example, Curruth and Henley 1990).

Conclusion

The importance of having a clear idea of what factors determine consumption cannot be overestimated. Consumption expenditure is the largest element in total expenditure and so any fluctuations in consumption will have important implications for the overall level of demand in the economy. The failure to appreciate the strength of consumer demand in 1987 and 1988 was an important contributory factor to the subsequent deterioration in the inflation and balance of payments position that has posed such problems for the UK economy.

Post Keynesian theories stress that, when deciding on consumption, consumers have a longer term planning horizon than merely considering current income. The implication of post Keynesian theories being that consumption is more stable than Keynesians thought. Evidence suggests, however, that in the face of uncertainty and liquidity constraints, current income may still be a key factor influencing consumption.

The experience of the 1970s and 1980s led to an intensified search for new variables to augment the existing consumption equations. Wealth, interest rates and inflation all seem to be factors influencing consumer spending plans. The relative importance of these variables is, however, difficult to unravel given the high degree of correlation between them.

Notes

1. This is a 'generalized' version of the Keynesian consumption function as it uses total income rather than disposable income as the independent variable.
2. 'Best' in the sense that it minimizes the sum of squared deviations from the line.
3. A negative m.p.c. means that when disposable income falls, consumption actually rises. In 1982 consumption even rose by *more* than National Income fell, giving a value of -3.17 for m.p.c.
4. The simple National Income multiplier is defined as $1/1 - $ m.p.c. for a closed economy with no government sector, and indicates the extent to which National Income changes following a given change in injections or withdrawals. If m.p.c. is low, the multiplier is low.
5. Remember that a fall in the savings ratio during 'recession' is the same as a rise in a.p.c.; and a rise in the savings ratio during 'boom' is the same as a fall in a.p.c.

References and further reading

Bank of England Quarterly Bulletin (1978) Why has the savings ratio been so high? **18**, 1, March, p. 7.

Bank of England Quarterly Bulletin (1988) *Economic Commentary*. **28**, 1, Feb. p. 19.

Bank of England Quarterly Bulletin (1990) Inflation adjusted sectoral saving and financial balances. **30**, 2, May, p. 228.

Bulkley, G. (1981) Personal savings and anticipated inflation, *Economic Journal*, **91**, March.

Currie, D., Holly, S. and **Scott, A.** (1989) Savings demography and interest rates, London Business School Centre for Economic Forecasting. Discussion paper No. 01–89 (March).

Curruth, A. and **Henley, A.** (1990) Can existing consumption functions forecast consumer spending in the late 1980s? *Oxford Bulletin of Economics and Statistics*, **55**, 2.

Cuthbertson, K. (1982) The measurement and behaviour of the UK saving ratio in the 1970s, *National Institute Economic Review*, 99, Feb.

Davidson, J., Hendry, D., Srba, F. and **Yeo, S.** (1978) Econometric modelling of the aggregate time-series relationship between consumers' expenditure and income in the UK, *Economic Journal*, **88**.

Deaton, A. (1977) Involuntary saving through unanticipated inflation, *American Economic Review*, **67**, 5, Dec.

Hendry, D. F., Muellbauer, J. and **Murphy, A.** (1989) A reconsideration of the UK nondurable consumption function. Paper presented to ESRC Macroeconomic Modelling Seminar, May.

Kennally, G. (1985) Committed and discretionary saving of households, *National Institute Economic Review*, 112, May.

Keynes, J. M. (1936) *The General Theory of Employment, Interest and Money*. Macmillan.

Kuznets, S. (1946) *The National Product Since 1869*. The National Bureau of Economic Research.

Leighton Thomas, R. (1984). *The Consumption Function* in: Demery, D. *et al. Macroeconomics*. Surveys in Economics, Longman.

12   Investment

Although only around one-third as important as consumption in total aggregate demand, investment is arguably one of its most significant components. It is highly volatile, and through its impact on productivity affects both supply and demand sides of the economy. After briefly reviewing the definition and measurement of investment, this chapter considers the theory and evidence for a number of factors allegedly affecting fixed investment. The rate of interest, the Accelerator Theory, the Capital Stock Adjustment Model, profitability, 'crowding out', stop–go policies, and inadequate financial provision, are all considered. Following a brief look at inventory investment, the chapter concludes by assessing the role of investment in economic growth.

Nature of investment

Resources in an economy can be used to produce goods and services for immediate use (consumption), or to add to the stock of fixed capital or inventories (investment). This chapter concentrates on the latter two, i.e. fixed capital investment and inventory investment.

In one sense consumption and investment are quite distinct. The act of investment usually involves abstaining from current consumption in order to acquire assets, which raise the productive potential of the economy, and therefore the possibilities for future consumption. Yet in another sense they are similar, both being components of aggregate demand, i.e. types of spending which create income for others in the economic system. We noted in Chapter 11 that consumption was around 50% of total final expenditure (TFE) in 1989. Although smaller, fixed capital investment was 14.6% of TFE in 1989, with inventory investment in that year recorded as 0.6% of TFE. The figure for inventory investment can be positive or negative; positive when inventories are being added to, negative when they are being depleted.

Stock and flow concepts

The total value of both fixed capital and inventories at any time is a 'stock' concept. The rate of change of that 'stock' is a 'flow' concept. Investment in the National Accounts is entirely a 'flow' concept, as it is the addition to the stock of fixed capital or to the stock of inventories in any given year. This helps explain why purchases of shares, paintings or antiques, although often termed 'investments' in everyday speech, are not regarded as such in the Accounts. Usually they merely represent a transfer of ownership from one person or institution to another, rather than an addition to the stock of assets. The difference between stock and flow valuations is often substantial.

Whereas the total value of inventories held was 30% of Gross Domestic Product (GDP) at factor cost in 1989, the annual 'addition' was +0.9% of GDP.

Gross and net investment

'Gross' investment, though a flow concept, overestimates the change in size of the stock of capital or inventories in the year. In the course of the year some fixed capital will have worn out or become obsolete, and some inventories will have become unusable. A part of 'gross' investment will therefore be needed simply to replace these assets used up in the course of production. If we subtract this 'replacement' investment from 'gross' investment, then we are left with 'net investment'. Net investment is then the estimate of the addition, in any year, to the stock of fixed capital and inventories, having allowed for depreciation of that stock during the year.

Of course, quantifying depreciation presents a number of problems. Estimating the loss in value of a machine in a year is difficult in itself, and may be guided less by the physical state of the asset than by the possibility of tax concessions. Also different accounting conventions will yield different measures of depreciation. For instance, historical cost accounting yields much lower figures for depreciation than does inflation accounting.

The majority of investment expenditure is on fixed capital formation rather than inventories and it is to this that we now turn.

Gross Domestic Fixed Capital Formation

Gross Domestic Fixed Capital Formation (GDFCF) is defined in the National Accounts as 'expenditure on fixed assets (buildings, plant and machinery, vehicles, etc.), either for replacing or adding to the stock of existing fixed assets'. This apparently clear-cut definition turns out to be rather arbitrary in application. For instance, 'investment' in the National Accounts is restricted to the firm sector. If a household purchases a typewriter for personal use, it is classified in the National Accounts as 'consumption', yet the same purchase by a firm is classified as 'investment', even though in both cases the capital asset yields a stream of useful services throughout its life. This is because the National Accounts treat the household purchase as self-gratification, but the firm purchase as producing a flow of marketable goods and services.

The arbitrariness of this classification is well illustrated when an individual chooses, for tax purposes, to be regarded as self-employed. The purchase of a car by a teacher for travel to work as an employee is classed as 'consumption' expenditure. Should the teacher change his designation to self-employed and engage in privately contracted teaching, then the purchase of that same car could be classed as 'investment' expenditure.

Despite problems of classification, it is important to gauge changes in GDFCF through time, both in total, and by sector and type of asset. Table 12.1 presents data for selected time periods since 1979. Given the problems we noted in measuring depreciation, the 'gross' concept is perhaps the most useful for purposes of comparison, whether through time or across countries. In fact, GDFCF has grown by more than £23bn in real terms since 1979.

| | | Sector | | | | Types of asset | | | | | |
| | | Private | | Public | | Dwellings | | | Other new buildings & works | Vehicles, ships & aircraft | Plant and mach. |
	Total	Total	Manu-facturing	Central govt	Public corp.	Total	Private	Public			
1979	56,450	40,268	10,136	7,349	8,677	13,363	3,615	9,665	16,172	7,514	19,736
1981	48,298	35,990	6,579	4,632	7,775	10,247	2,155	8,149	14,859	4,895	18,269
1984	58,053	43,872	7,818	6,613	7,573	12,562	2,825	9,737	18,144	6,132	21,220
1987	66,890	55,536	9,178	6,978	4,376	13,732	2,741	10,991	21,164	6,518	25,476
1989	79,702	68,063	10,480	7,289	4,350	14,156	2,803	11,353	22,368	7,815	33,363

Source: CSO, *Economic Trends* (various editions).

Table 12.1 Gross Domestic Fixed Capital Formation by sector and by type of asset (£m. at 1985 prices)

Closer examination of the data does, however, indicate that with the onset of recession in 1979/80, GDFCF actually fell for two years before an upturn in world economic activity led to the recovery of investment.

The components of GDFCF have changed substantially over the last decade. There has, for example, been a significant shift in investment from the public to the private sector. Since 1979, public sector investment has fallen by around £4.5bn. This is partly due to the privatization programme which has been implemented in recent years and has reduced the number of public corporations. However, it also reflects the desire of government to cut back on spending initiatives. Because of difficulties involved in cutting back on current expenditure plans, capital projects have been sacrificed in a bid to fulfil this objective. In contrast private sector investment has risen by almost £30bn. The public sector now only contributes around 15% of GDFCF, yet as recently as the late 1960s, it accounted for over 50%.

Investment by type of asset has also changed since 1979. Investment in plant and machinery has grown most rapidly, increasing by nearly 70%. It now accounts for around 42% of total GDFCF. There has also been a healthy rise in the real level of investment in new building and work which in 1989 contributed 38% of GDFCF. The increase in the level of investment in dwellings and in vehicles, ships and aircraft has been rather more modest. The growth of 6% in dwellings masks a significant transfer of resources from the public to the private sector. Investment in public sector housing has fallen by 22% in real terms since 1979 while in the private sector it has risen by 17%.

If we disaggregate further to the *industrial sector*, we find that it is investment in manufacturing that has been most volatile. In real terms, gross investment in manufacturing fell by more than a third between 1979 and its lowest point in 1983. For much of the 1970s investment in manufacturing had remained fairly constant, but with the onset of recession in 1979 it declined sharply, making the largest single contribution to the overall fall in GDFCF. Although the economic recovery has led to a resurgence in manufacturing investment since 1983, it was only in 1988 that it finally surpassed the level achieved at the end of the previous decade. In 1979 manufacturing investment accounted for around 18% of GDFCF. By 1989 its share had fallen to 13%, reflecting the diminishing importance of the manufacturing sector to the UK economy.

Factors affecting fixed investment

Gross Domestic Fixed Capital Formation is so heterogeneous that any explanation must address itself to particular components. For instance, investment in dwellings is influenced by population trends, expected lifetime income, the availability and cost of mortgage finance, etc. Most attempts at theory and empirical work have, however, tended to concentrate on investment in plant and machinery, particularly in the manufacturing sector. Here we review the factors which allegedly affect this type of fixed investment.

The rate of interest   The earliest theories of investment placed considerable emphasis on the importance of the rate of interest, seen here as the compensation required for forgoing current consumption. Fisher used the rate of interest to derive the present value (PV) of an expected future stream of income. By calculating the PV of various alternative investment projects they could then be ranked against each other.[1]

This approach can be taken a stage further by introducing the marginal efficiency of investment (MEI). The MEI was defined as that rate of discount which would equate the PV of a given stream of future income from a project, with the initial capital outlay (the supply price):

$$S = PV = R_1/(1 + i) + R_2/(1 + i)^2 + R_3/(1 + i)^3 + R_n/(1 + i)^n$$

where S = the supply price;
PV = the present value;
R = the expected yearly return; and
i = that rate of discount necessary to equate the present value of future income with the initial cost of the project.

Fig. 12.1 The investment demand schedule

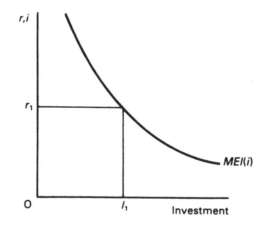

The curve relating the marginal efficiency of investment (i) to the level of investment in Fig. 12.1 is negatively sloped, for two main reasons. First, the earliest investment projects undertaken are likely to be the most profitable, i.e. offering the highest expected yearly returns (R), and therefore having the highest marginal efficiencies of investment (i). As more projects are initiated, they are likely to be less and less profitable, with lower expected yearly returns, and therefore lower MEIs. Second, a rise in the level of investment undertaken is, at least in the short run, likely to raise the supply price (S), which in turn will reduce the MEI. This could follow if the capital goods producing industries faced capacity constraints in their attempt to raise output in the short run.

The decision on whether to proceed with an investment project will depend on the relationship between the rate of interest (r) and the marginal efficiency of investment (i). If r is less than i, then the annual cost of borrowing funds for an additional project will be less than the expected annual return on the initial capital outlay, so that the project will be profitable to undertake. In Fig. 12.1, with interest rate r_1, it will be profitable to invest in all projects up to I_1, with I_1 itself breaking even. The *MEI* schedule is therefore the investment demand schedule, telling us the level of investment that will be undertaken at any given rate of interest. Expectations play an important role in this theory of investment. If, as is often the case, expectations are volatile, then the expected yearly returns (R) on any project will change, causing substantial shifts in the *MEI* schedule. At *any given rate of interest* investment demand will therefore be changing, which will reduce the closeness of any statistical fit between the interest rate and investment. In fact, it may be via expectations that interest rates exert their major influence on investment. A fall in rates is often a signal to investors of better times ahead, raising expected returns, shifting the *MEI* curve to the right, and raising investment (and conversely). Although this may dilute the statistical fit between r and I, there may still be an underlying linkage between the two variables.

Evidence One problem in testing the influence of interest rates on investment is the selection of an appropriate interest rate. The average yield on debentures is a rate frequently used, as this broadly indicates the cost of new borrowing for a company at any point in time.

Most UK studies have failed to show any close connection between interest rates and investment, suggesting that the latter is interest-inelastic. Feldstein and Flemming (1971) carried out a study of investment in all the major industrial sectors of the UK, using as their interest rate variable a weighted average of equity and debenture yields. They found that a tax allowance variable played a far more important role than the interest rate in affecting investment. The interest rate variable turned out to be statistically insignificant with a positive rather than a negative sign. In fact, Savage (1978) in reviewing econometric evidence over a wide range of studies, concludes that the interest rate has been found to have little significance in influencing UK fixed investment. The few studies which found some relationship had to resort to extensive and differing lag structures, using interest rates which hardly reflected the rates most companies have to pay for borrowing. Hines and Catephores (1970) and Nobay (1970) both found a significant link between manufacturing investment and interest rate. However, the former lagged the change in interest rate by six quarters and the latter by five quarters, and both used the (perhaps unrealistic) rate on long-term government bonds.

More recent data on aggregate investment and the average yield on debentures again show little correlation during the 1970s and 1980s. For instance, GDFCF rose steadily between 1978 and 1979 despite upward movements of interest rates during these years. Even when we use 'real' rates of interest, i.e. the nominal rate adjusted for inflation, the correlation is still far from clear. In 1975, when the real rate of interest was around -10%, investment fell, yet in 1984 and 1985, when the real rate of interest was around $+8\%$, investment rose by more than 11%. A more recent analysis of the relationship between the real rate of interest and gross fixed investment in plant and machinery in manufacturing was conducted by Turner (Turner 1989). He found only a weak negative relationship between the two variables.

In contrast to the rather weak relationships noted above, the Bank of England's most up to date model suggests a much stronger impact of the interest rate on gross fixed investment (Easton 1990). It appears to show that a rise in interest rates of 1% would result in a fall in investment by 1.3% after four months, and 2.8% after twelve months. However most of the impact of the interest rate rise was on the residential investment (housing) component of gross investment, which fell by 3.2% and 4.1% over the same lagged periods.

The rate of change of output – the Accelerator Theory

The Accelerator Theory relates net investment to the rate of change of output. If the capital stock K is fully utilized, and the capital/output ratio v is a constant, then net investment (I) can be expressed in the following way:

$$K_t = v\,Y_1$$
$$K_t - K_{t-1} = v(Y_t - Y_{t-1})$$
$$I_t = v\,(Y_t - Y_{t-1})$$
$$I_t = v\,\Delta\,Y_t$$

where Y is output and t and $t-1$ are time periods.

Net investment in year t is then a constant proportion of the change in output during that year. For example, if output rose by £2m. for the economy (ΔY_t = £2m.), and each extra £1 of output needed an average of £5 of capital equipment to produce it ($v = 5$), then $I_t = 5.2m. = £10m.$ A number of criticisms have been levelled at the Accelerator Theory. First, the assumption that there is no excess capacity is particularly suspect. If there is spare capacity then a rise in output ΔY_t can be met from the existing capital stock, with no need for new investment. It has been estimated by the CBI that in the period 1980–89 an average of only 42.5% of firms were working at full capacity. Such a large amount of excess capacity must severely impair the effective functioning of the accelerator. Second, the assumption of a constant capital/output ratio, v, is becoming less and less plausible. The advent of new generations of microelectronic technology is progressively reducing capital/output ratios (see Ch. 10). Third, it is also likely that prior to making an investment the firm would want to be sure that any upsurge in demand and in output is not a temporary phenomenon. *Expectations* of future demand, and therefore future changes in output, will then be important.

Evidence   Even when varying lag structures are introduced into more refined versions of the Accelerator Theory, the evidence in its support is far from convincing. McCormick *et al.* (1983) found that changes in real GDFCF by firms between 1962 and 1980 were not strongly related to the previous year's change in real consumer spending or demand. Black (1982) related changes in net fixed investment to changes in GDP over the previous three years. Again, the results were rather disappointing, with only 39% of the observed variation in net investment 'explained' by his equation. Black had already excluded investment in dwellings, in the social services, and in North Sea oil, on the grounds that investment in these sectors was unlikely to be affected by an accelerator principle.

The level of output and capital – the Capital Stock Adjustment Model

This was developed to overcome some of the problems of the simple Accelerator Theory. It states that investment is positively related to the expected level of output and negatively related to the existing capital stock. Any rise in investment will consequently depend not only on the expected level of output (demand) but also on the current size of the capital stock. Specifically,

$$I_t = b \, Y_{t-1} - cK_{t-1}$$

where I_t = gross investment in the current year;
b and c = constant coefficients;
   Y_{t-1} = last year's level of output;
   K_{t-1} = the capital stock at the end of the preceding year.

If it is assumed that the expected volume of output is roughly equal to that experienced in the previous year, Y_{t-1}, then the higher is Y_{t-1} the greater will gross investment tend to be. However, the greater the inherited capital stock, K_{t-1}, the less need there will be for adding to the capital stock, or even replacing worn-out equipment.

Evidence   A variety of studies have introduced capacity utilization variables on the lines of the Capital Stock Adjustment Model, with encouraging results. Panić and Vernon (1975) ran a series of tests in the mid-1970s relating GDFCF in six manufacturing industries to a number of variables. Their results confirmed the importance of capacity utilization in determining investment, in that investment tended to take place only when output increased sufficiently to stretch current capacity. Nobay (1970) came to a similar conclusion, and found a relationship between the change in output beyond 'capacity' and manufacturing fixed investment. Kennedy (1986) notes that the Capital Stock Adjustment Principle was useful in explaining manufacturing investment in the UK between 1955 and 1970, though less so since then.

Profitability

There are at least three reasons why changes in profitability might be associated with changes in private sector investment:

1.   Higher profits indicate a more favourable return on capital, which may encourage companies to reinvest any surplus rather than devote it to alternative uses.

2.   Higher profits may improve business confidence and raise the expected future return on any project. An outward shift of the *MEI* schedule (see Fig. 12.1 above) might then raise investment at any given rate of interest.

3.   Higher profits may raise investment by reducing its cost, as funds generated internally are cheaper than those obtained from the capital market, whether equity or debenture.

Evidence   Table 12.2 indicates a progressive fall in the rate of return on

Table 12.2 Rates of return on capital in the business sector (Averages)

	USA	UK	Germany	France	Japan
1960–73	22.8	14.1	20.1	21.1	33.1
1974–79	20.3	11.2	17.1	17.9	23.2
1980–86	19.7	11.7	16.3	16.1	21.6
1987–91*	23.2	13.5	18.0	18.2	21.0

*– projected figures
Source: OECD Economic Outlook, Dec., 1989

capital in the business sector in all five countries. However in the latter part of the 1980s a measure of recovery was experienced in all but Japan. The table also shows that since 1960 the net rate of return has been consistently lower in the UK than in the other countries.

Glyn and Sutcliffe (1972) argued that declining profits have been a major factor in low levels of investment in the UK. In their view a major cause of the decline in profits has been the ability of labour, during the post-war years of high employment, to increase its share of value added at the expense of profits. Panić and Vernon (1975) also found the rate of return on capital employed to be a significant variable in affecting investment in five of the six manufacturing industries studied.

The size of the public sector – the 'crowding out' debate

Bacon and Eltis (1976) pointed to the growth of the public sector during the 1960s and early 1970s as a major cause of decline in UK investment. Central to their approach is a sharp distinction between the 'marketable' sector of the economy, such as manufacturing industry, and the 'non-marketable' sector, such as state provision of many services. The 'marketable' sector produces goods and services which are sold on established markets, generally makes a profit, and can therefore be regarded as self-financing. On the other hand, the 'non-marketable' sector provides a range of social and administrative services which are not sold on markets, and which therefore must be financed 'externally', the necessary revenue for this having then to be raised by taxing the output of the marketable sector via taxes on both profits and wages.

The growth of the non-marketable state sector has, in this view, required progressively more finance, increasing the pressures on the marketable sector. This can be well illustrated through the following identity. For simplicity we assume a closed economy (no trade):

$$I_m + C_m + I_n + C_n \equiv 1$$

i.e. the shares of investment (I) and consumption (C), in both marketable (m) and non-marketable (n) sectors, must absorb the whole of national output. It follows that:

$$I_m \equiv 1 - C_m - I_n - C_n$$

i.e. that investment in the marketable sector I_m will depend on the level of consumption in the marketable sector C_m, and the levels of investment and consumption in the non-marketable sector I_m, C_m. The growth in non-marketable state expenditure is represented by increases in both I_n and C_n. Its 'finance' must then come from a reduction in C_m and/or I_m.

Bacon and Eltis go on to suggest that labour has been successful in protecting itself from erosion of C_m, so that adjustment has fallen largely on I_m, i.e. investment in the marketable sector. The only difference when we open the economy to foreign trade is that some relief for I_m could occur if an additional part of C_m now comes from abroad. In other words, imported goods and services help maintain consumption levels in the marketable sector. The pressure then is on the balance of payments, via extra imports, as well as on private sector investment.

Evidence   Bacon and Eltis provide considerable empirical evidence to support their argument. Prior to 1969, non-marketable consumption C_n and investment I_n grew from around 34% of the value of marketed output in 1961, to around 37% in 1969. This growth in the non-marketable sector was largely financed by workers in the marketable sector. For instance, consumption in this latter sector C_m fell from 56% of marketed output in 1961 to around 52% in 1969. Productivity of market sector workers was rising at about 3.7% per annum, but the extra taxes required to finance the growth of the non-marketable sector meant that the increase in their real incomes was much less, only 1.2% per annum.

It was around 1969 that Bacon and Eltis allege that the situation changed, with the strength of organized labour becoming more apparent. The squeeze on consumption prior to 1969 now led to trade unions adopting a more militant posture in wage negotiations. As a result, although between 1969 and 1974 the share of the non-marketable sector in the value of marketed output continued to increase (from 37 to 44%), this time consumption by the marketable sector C_m remained roughly constant at around 52%. Higher wage demands were submitted to cover any increase in tax, which consequently squeezed profits and reduced investment in the marketable sector I_m.

However, Hadjimatheou and Skouras (1979) not only reject the empirical observations of Bacon and Eltis but are particularly critical of the theoretical underpinnings of their model. They assert that the years selected for comparison of profits and investment correspond to differing points in the business cycle, making comparison misleading. In their own study, they divide the period under consideration into four cycles, and take averages within each cycle. They point to the remarkably slow growth in the share of the non-marketable sector in the value of marketed output, rising from around 31% between 1955 and 1960 to only 33% between 1969 and 1973. Although there was a small reduction in post-tax profits in the marketable sector during this period (11.6 to 10%), it was not sufficient to deter market-sector investment I_m from increasing. This analysis is therefore totally at variance with that of Bacon and Eltis.

Stop–go policies

The post-war period until the late 1970s witnessed governments playing a positive role in stimulating demand through reflation of the economy. Booms were, however, generally interspersed with balance of payments crises. This prevented the application of reflationary policies over long time periods, since deflation of demand, to reduce spending on imports, was often used to correct balance of payments deficits. The uncertainty of such stop–go policies arguably reduced business confidence and discouraged investment.

Evidence Nobay (1970) in his econometric study concluded that low profits were not so much the cause of low levels of investment, but rather the result of slow expansion of manufacturing output, accentuated by stop–go policies. Panić and Vernon (1975) also concluded that long-run instability in demand seriously undermined investment in the six manufacturing industries studied.

Inadequate financial systems

It has been suggested by Carrington and Edwards (1981) that inefficiencies in the banking system and in the capital markets have prevented industry from obtaining the finance it requires for investment. Amongst the criticisms of UK financial institutions are the allegations that UK banks place too great an emphasis on lending to consumers, whereas overseas banks are primarily concerned with long-term industrial finance. Another criticism is that UK banks tend to concentrate on short-term lending, causing a shortage of long-term funds for investment.

Evidence It is certainly true that UK banks have, in the past, tended to lend less to industry than their foreign counterparts. In 1980, UK bank-lending to industry was only around 22% of GDP, whereas in France the figure was 30%, in West Germany almost 34% and in Japan around 51%. However, Vittas and Brown (1982) suggest that because of the differing financial structure of comparative economies, it is necessary to compare *all* institutions involved in providing finance for industry, and not just the banks. When this is done there is little to choose between the UK, France and West Germany. In the early 1980s total lending to industry was around 35% of GDP in the UK, 36% in France and 43% in West Germany.

Vittas and Brown also defend the UK financial institutions against the criticism that their loans are of shorter maturity than those in other countries. A shorter maturity date raises the effective annual yield required to justify the investment, since it must cover capital pay-back as well as interest. They found that less than one-half of total lending to industry in the UK had a maturity of less than one year in 1980, with a similar percentage for France and West Germany, and an even higher one for Japan.

The deregulation of the financial sector over recent years has led to a significant increase in bank lending to industry. Despite this, the soothing pronouncement of the Wilson Committee on the adequacy of UK financial provision, and the counter-attack by economists such as Vittas and Brown show, that the debate is still not over. Chapter 15 provides further background to this alleged cause of low levels of UK investment. Before turning to the issue of the importance of investment, and providing cross-country comparisons, we briefly consider investment in inventories.

Inventories

These include materials and fuel, work in progress, and stocks of finished products. Investment in inventories, or stocks, is the change in the value of all stocks held during the period. In any single year investment in inventories can be negative or positive, and can have an important effect upon national output. The change in inventory investment was −1.2% of GDP in 1981, but +1.1% of GDP in 1989.

Firms hold stocks for a variety of technical reasons, some intended, such as promoting the smooth flow of production, and some unintended, such as unplanned deviation between actual and expected sales. To pinpoint single factors affecting inventories has proved difficult, although Kennedy (1986) notes that a modified stock-adjustment principle on the lines above helps explain changes in manufacturers' inventories during much of the 1960s and 1970s.

The importance of investment

Investment has a dual role to play within any econony. In the short run, investment may be seen mainly as a component of aggregate demand which, if increased, will have the effect of stimulating the economy and, through the multiplier, substantially raising the level of National Income. Fixed and inventory investment together made up over 15% of TFE in 1989.

In the long run, investment will also affect the supply side of the economy, raising its productive potential and thereby pushing outwards the production frontier. Economic growth is sometimes strictly defined in this way, being that increase in GDP which results from raising productive potential. More usually it is loosely defined as any increase in GDP, even when that is within the existing production frontier.

There have been a number of studies into the importance of investment as a generator of growth, though the results have not been conclusive. For example, Kuznets (1961), using time-series data for a number of countries, found little relationship between the *share* of investment in GDP, and the growth in output over time. Similarly, a 1970 OECD survey based on cross-sectional data found no clear well-defined relationship between investment shares and growth in output. Table 12.3 suggests that there may be some linkage between *growth* of investment (GDFCF) and growth in output. It could, of course, be argued that the growth in output is the *cause*, rather than the *effect*, of the growth in investment. To expand production may require additional capacity, giving rise to extra investment!

Whatever the validity of these arguments, Table 12.3 clearly shows the dramatic improvement that has taken place in the growth of investment in the UK over the last five years. From a modest performance in the early 1980s, GDFCF has grown on average by over 6½% a year since 1985. Accompanying this change has been a considerably better growth performance by the UK economy.

It was not so long ago that it was being argued that the UK's capital stock

Table 12.3 Investment and the growth of output 1980–89

| | Average annual growth (vol.) | | | | |
| | 1980–84 | | 1985–89 | | Share of GDFCF (av. 1985–89) |
	GDFCF	GDP	GDFCF	GDP	
Japan	3.0	3.9	11.4	4.5	25.7
Canada	2.4	2.3	10.0	4.0	21.1
USA	1.7	1.9	3.2	3.4	17.1
Italy	0.8	1.9	3.7	3.0	25.5
W. Germany	−0.7	1.1	3.7	2.7	20.5
France	−1.4	3.6	4.4	2.6	20.8
UK	0.8	0.8	6.6	3.7	17.9

Source: OECD (1989) and National Accounts.

was older in 'vintage' than that of its competitors, restricting the possibilities for achieving lower cost and greater competitiveness. However, the severe recession in 1980/81 saw a major contraction in production potential which hit less efficient enterprises particularly badly, but resulted in a higher level of efficiency in the remainder of the economy.

Not all economists accept that investment in the UK was sluggish even in the 1970s. Vittas and Brown (1982) reject the use of GDFCF as an appropriate measure of productive investment. The OECD (1985) country report on the UK adopted a similar argument, i.e. that GDFCF includes forms of non-productive investment which are irrelevant to economic growth, residential investment being a prime example. Table 12.4 shows the situation for seven of the countries in Table 12.3 when residential investment is excluded from private sector GDFCF. In terms of annual average growth rates, the UK fares reasonably well throughout the period, contrary to some of the arguments put forward earlier.

Table 12.4 Annual growth in private sector non-residential investment

| | Annual average | | | |
Country	1967–73	1974–80	1981–84	1985–88
Japan	15.7	2.1	5.5	10.6
Italy	7.8	1.3	−2.8	5.8
France	7.5	0.5	−2.2	5.8
West Germany	4.6	2.4	−0.6	5.4
UK	4.5	2.7	4.0	11.3
Canada	3.0	8.2	−0.7	9.2
USA	3.6	2.9	3.3	3.6

Source: OECD, *Economic Outlook*, Dec. 1989.

Efficiency and investment

The level of investment is not the only factor contributing to growth. Peaker (1974) sees investment as a *necessary*, but by no means *sufficient* condition for economic growth. Growth also depends on the efficiency with which any investment is utilized. One method of measuring the efficiency of investment is through the gross incremental output/capital ratio.

Table 12.5 presents incremental capital/output ratios for the 'whole economy' and for 'manufacturing' industry. It demonstrates what appears to have been a major weakness of the UK economy, namely that the UK required in the 1960s and 1970s *a higher rate of net investment* to produce a *given increase* in output, than did West Germany, the USA or Canada.

Table 12.5 Incremental capital/output ratios

	Whole economy		Manufacturing	
	1964–73	1973–79	1964–73	1973–79
UK	3.8	5.0	2.2	Negative*
West Germany	2.9	3.1	1.1	0.2
USA	1.6	1.7	0.6	1.5
Canada	1.7	2.6	1.1	1.9

* Manufacturing output fell in the UK, 1973–79.
Source: OECD (1985).

If we move from the *marginal* to the *average*, a similar picture still emerges. We can see from Table 12.6 that the UK produced *less* output *per unit of net capital stock* than either West Germany or the USA.

Table 12.6 Output/unit of net capital stock in 1980 index numbers, UK = 100

	Whole economy	Manufacturing
UK	100	100
West Germany	105	195
USA	160	210

Source: OECD (1985).

Tables 12.5 and 12.6 suggest that increased capital intensity within the UK may not necessarily lead to proportionate increases in output. An example of this at the level of the firm was provided in Chapter 1 where, despite having similar plant and equipment in both Halewood and Saarlouis, the Ford Motor Company's productivity in the latter plant was much higher. It was pointed out by Wragg and Robertson (1978) that *total* factor productivity must rise if growth is to be sustained. It follows that increasing the efficiency of labour, and improving the organizational structure of UK firms, may be at least as important in generating economic growth as raising the level of investment.

Recent evidence does indeed suggest that total factor productivity has increased during the 1980s. For much of the decade, it has comfortably exceeded its pre-1973 average level of around 2.5% per annum. Moreover, in a study by Smith-Goosne and Bennett (1988), it was suggested that there has been a major rise in *work-effort* in recent years. Hourly work effort has increased by some 5% compared with the average between 1973–79, and by more than 7% when set against the recessionary years of 1980/81.

Conclusion

Investment occurs in so wide a variety of assets and sectors that it must be disaggregated substantially if any close statistical fit is to be found. However, even when we concentrate on fixed investment in manufacturing, no single theory 'explains' much of the variation in investment. What evidence there is certainly suggests that UK investment is relatively interest-inelastic, reducing the effectiveness of the interest rate as a policy instrument. Nevertheless, in so far as changes in interest rates affect expectations, lower interest rates may still contribute to higher investment.

Although much less important than consumption in aggregate demand, investment has, through the multiplier, a significant effect on National Income, and is the most volatile element in aggregate demand. It also affects the productive potential of an economy. Even though the link between investment and growth is in some ways tenuous, it is interesting that the increased level of fixed investment in the UK in the 1980s has been accompanied by a much stronger growth performance. The sharp rise in productivity over the last couple of years also suggests that investment is now being more efficiently utilized.

Note

1.   For a fuller treatment of present value, see for instance R. G. Lipsey (1983) *An Introduction to Positive Economics*, 6th edn. Weidenfeld and Nicolson.

References

Bacon, R. and **Eltis, W.** (1976) *Britain's Economic Problem – Too Few Producers*. Macmillan.

Black, J. (1982) *The Economics of Modern Britain: an introduction to macroeconomics*. Martin Robertson.

Carrington, J. C. and **Edwards, G. T.** (1981) *Reversing Economic Decline*. Macmillan.

Easton, W. W. (1990) The interest rate transmission mechanism in the United Kingdom and Overseas. *Bank of England Quarterly Bulletin*, Vol. 30, No. 2, May.

Feldstein, M. S. and **Flemming, J. S.** (1971) Tax policy, corporate saving and investment behaviour in Britain, *Review of Economic Studies*, **38**.

Glyn, A. and **Sutcliffe, B.** (1972) *British Capitalism, Workers and the Profits Squeeze*. Penguin.

Guest, D. (1990) Have British workers been working harder in Thatcher's Britain? *British Journal of Industrial Relations*, Nov.

Hadjimatheou, G. and **Skouras, A.** (1979) Britain's economic problem: the growth of the non-market sector, *Economic Journal*, **89**, June.

Hines, A. G. and **Catephores, G.** (1970) Investment in UK manufacturing industry, in: Hilton, K. and Heathfield, D. F. (eds) *The Econometric Study of the United Kingdom*. Macmillan.

Kennedy, M. (1986) in: Prest, A. R. *The UK Economy: a manual of applied economics*. Weidenfeld and Nicolson, Ch. 1.

Kuznets, S. (1961) The economic growth of nations: long term trends in capital formation proportions, *Economic Development and Cultural Change*, July.

McCormick, B. *et al.* (1983) *Introducing Economics*. Penguin.

Nobay, A. R. (1970) Forecasting manufacturing investment – some preliminary results, *National Institute Economic Review*, 52, May.

OECD (1985, 1988, 1989) *Country Reports*, UK.
Panić, M. and **Vernon, K.** (1975) Major factors behind investment decisions in British manufacturing industry, *Oxford Bulletin of Economics and Statistics*, **37**, 3, Aug.
Peaker, A. (1974) *Economic Growth in Modern Britain*. Macmillan.
Savage, D. (1978) The channels of monetary influence: a survey of the empirical evidence, *National Institute Economic Review*, 83, Feb.
Smith-Goosne, S. A. N. and **Bennett, A. J.** (1988) Index of Percentage Utilisation of Labour, *Bulletin to Co-operating Firms*, No. 49.
Turner, P. (1989) Investment: Theory and Evidence, *Economic Review*, Vol. 6, No. 3.
Vittas, D. and **Brown, R.** (1982) *Bank Lending and Industrial Investment*. Banking Information Service.
Wragg, R. and **Robertson, J.** (1978) Britain's industrial performance since the war: trends in employment, productivity, output, labour, costs and prices by industry 1950–1973, *Department of Employment Gazette*, **86**, 5, May.

13   Public expenditure

The 1979 Conservative Government was returned on two major policy platforms. The first was to cut public expenditure as part of a monetarist approach to inflation control, and the second was to reduce the apparently deadweight burden of (income) tax upon incentives. These policy objectives were regarded as inseparable, with excessive public expenditure allegedly leading to high levels of taxation, borrowing and (via money supply growth and high interest rates) inflation. In this chapter we consider the first of these problems: the growth of public expenditure and the difficulties surrounding its control. The next chapter will examine the burden of taxation.

Here we look at public expenditure, its form, size and apparently inexorable growth. Problems of definition and calculation are considered – for instance, current estimates for the ratio of public spending to National Income vary from as little as 25% to over 60%. Resolving such ambiguities is extremely important since entire economic and political platforms rest upon the outcome. Attempts to control public expenditure are nothing new; they began long before Gladstone. However, the 1961 Plowden reforms were the watershed for modern planning, monitoring and control of public expenditure. These were initially in volume (i.e. real opportunity cost) terms, but since 1976 management techniques have increasingly been based on cash, i.e. what has to be paid out at current prices. Although the Conservative Government was pledged to cut back public expenditure, the evidence suggests that so far the Government has failed. Real public spending since 1979 will have shown an average growth rate of 1.3% per annum compared with an annual rate of 1% under the previous Labour administration. However, public expenditure has fallen as a *proportion* of GDP. In 1982/83 public expenditure was 47% of GDP; in 1990/91 it was only 39% of GDP. This fall is largely because of the high growth rates of GDP in the mid-1980s.

Components of UK public spending

Until April 1971 public expenditure included spending by central and local government and gross investment by the nationalized industries. This led to the rather strange practice of including *estimated* values for capital depreciation by the nationalized industries as public expenditure, even when neither actual expenditure nor borrowing took place.

Since April 1977 only *net* investment (new capital) by the nationalized industries, financed by actual borrowing from the National Loans Fund, has been included in public expenditure totals. This alteration brought the UK into line with OECD accounting practice. It is worth noting that current UK totals of public expenditure would have been still higher had the pre-1977 definition been retained. In recognition of this change, a new concept called 'general government expenditure' was introduced to replace the older terminology of public sector expenditure.

The 1989 Autumn Statement and the 1990/91 Expenditure Plans were the first to use a new definition of the *planning total*. This change, however, does not effect the overall definition of 'general government expenditure'. This new 'planning total' brings together all the elements of public expenditure for which central government is responsible. The change in definition does, however, affect the treatment of local authority expenditure; the old definition included all local authority expenditure, whereas the new definition covers only the *support* for this expenditure provided by central government, i.e. it excludes expenditure which local authorities finance themselves.

The new definition of *planning total* thus covers the following:
- central government's own expenditure;
- most of the grants, current and capital, that central government provides to local authorities;
- the credit approvals issued by central government authorizing local authorities to incur capital expenditure financed by borrowing and other forms of credit;
- non-domestic rate payments;
- the financing requirements of public corporations. With few exceptions this is the external finance of the public corporations;
- a reserve which provides a margin for uncertainties and is intended to cover any future additions to items within the planning total, whether these result from policy changes, new initiatives, contingencies or revised estimates of demand-led programmes such as social security; and
- privatization proceeds.

The 'planning total' of cash limits to control spending by government departments will be £178.9bn in 1990/91, up from £161.9bn in 1989/90. The 'general government expenditure' for the two periods respectively will be £212.9bn, up from £197.4bn.

Table 13.1 and Fig. 13.1 show current plans, presented in a number of ways that are helpful for policy analysis.

Public expenditure by programme

In 1990–91, central and local government intended to spend approximately £178.9bn, divided between twenty programmes (roughly equivalent to the responsibilities of the main government departments) outlined in Table 13.1.

Figure 13.1 reveals that health, personal social services and social security plans dominate expenditure by programme, with almost 36.5% of the total general government expenditure in 1990/91. The next most important item is defence with almost 10% of the total, followed by DoE Local Government with just over 9.6% of general government expenditure and 'Education' and 'Housing' each at around 3.1%. These programmes include capital spending (e.g. school buildings) and current spending on both goods (e.g. school books) and services (e.g. wages of policemen/nurses/teachers). The expenditure plans revealed in January 1990 showed that increased resources

Table 13.1 Public
expenditure by programme
or department (£bn)

	1989/90 estimated outturn	1990/91 plans	1991/92 plans
Ministry of Defence	20.3	21.2	22.4
Foreign and Commonwealth Office	2.5	2.6	2.7
Ministry of Agriculture, Fisheries and Food	1.6	1.8	2.0
Trade and Industry	1.7	1.5	1.1
Energy	−0.14	−0.2	−0.7
Department of Employment	3.8	3.8	3.6
Department of Transport	3.6	4.2	4.5
DOE – housing	2.6	6.3	6.7
DOE – other environmental services	1.4	1.4	1.3
DOE – Local government	19.5	20.5	21.3
Home Office (including Charity Commission)	4.2	4.8	5.0
Lord Chancellor's and Law Officers Departments	1.1	1.2	1.4
Department of Education and Science	5.8	6.6	6.8
Office of Arts and Libraries	0.5	0.5	0.5
Department of Health and Office of Population Censuses and Surveys	20.1	22.2	23.5
Department of Social Security	52.6	55.6	59.9
Scotland	9.0	9.6	10.1
Wales	3.9	4.5	4.6
Northern Ireland	5.8	6.0	6.2
Chancellor of the Exchequer's Departments	4.2	4.6	4.9
Cabinet Office, Privy Council Office and Parliament	0.3	0.3	0.4
European Communities	2.03	1.9	1.7
Reserve		3.0	6.0
Privatization proceeds	−4.3	−5.0	−5.0
Adjustment	−0.2		
Planning total*	161.9	178.9	192.3
Local authorities self-financed expenditure	14.0	13.5	14.0
Central government debt interest	17.5	17.0	15.5
Accounting adjustments	4.0	3.5	3.5
General government expenditure	197.4	212.9	225.3

* Planning total refers to the public expenditure plans and does not include 'debt interest'. This latter must be added to the total in order to establish how much the Government needs to find from all sources, including taxes and borrowing, in order to finance its total outlay.
Source: Treasury (1990a, Cmnd 1021)

had been made available for health, housing, education, and law and order. At the same time estimates of demand-led expenditure on social security have been increased. The defence budget was tightened in 1986/87 with the end of the Government's NATO commitment to raise defence spending by an annual 3%. Political developments in Eastern Europe have increased pressure to cut defence further. The phrase 'peace dividend' (see Johnson, 1990b) has been coined to express the hope that a new era of disarmament and détente will result in major savings in defence expenditure. The Gulf crisis, of course, quickly dampened 'excessive' hopes on this count.

Fig. 13.1 Public expenditure
by department 1990/91 (£bn)
Source: Treasury (1990a)

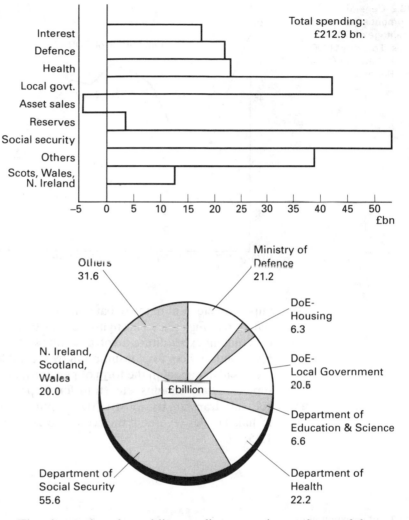

The above plans for public spending are an integral part of the
Government's medium-term financial strategy aimed at reducing inflation
and maintaining the conditions for sustained growth, the creation of jobs and
higher living standards. Within that framework, the Government's objective
for public spending is to hold its rate of growth at some 1.25% per annum
below the growth of the economy as a whole and thus to reduce public
spending as a proportion of National Income (see Fig. 13.2 below). The
Government believes that the result of this will be lower borrowing which,
combined with lower taxation, will mean that enterprise and efficiency will be
encouraged and output and employment will grow. With the fall in growth
rates for the economy, public expenditure has risen slightly as a proportion of
GDP in recent years (again see Fig. 13.2).

**Public expenditure by
demand or economic
category**

A further way of presenting the above data is to divide public spending
between goods and services (purchased by the state) and cash transfers (to
individuals or industry). This particular classification is, as we note below, an

Fig. 13.2 General
government expenditure as
a percentage of GDP
Sources: Treasury (1990a);
Financial Statements and
Budget Reports

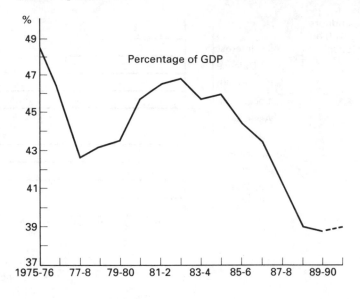

important element in the debate on the size of the public sector and is
reflected in Fig. 13.3. This figure reveals that around 36% of general
government expenditure involves public sector pay plus the purchase of
goods and services for consumption by the public. Over 35% is absorbed by
the 'disadvantaged' in the form of pensions, unemployment and
supplementary benefits, etc. (transfers to personal sector). A further 4.6%
goes into transfers to industry (the corporate sector). Capital spending is
included under several of the economic categories of Fig. 13.3 (see also Fig.
13.5).

Fig. 13.3 Public expenditure
by demand or economic
category in 1990/91
Source: Treasury (1990a)

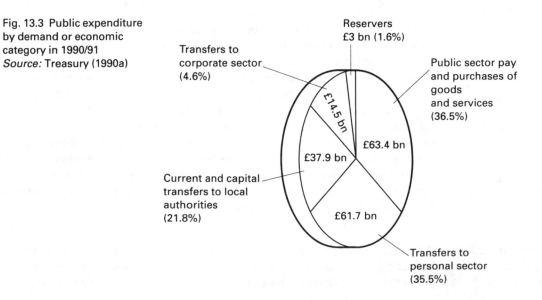

Public expenditure by source

A further way of viewing public expenditure is to look at who spends the money (see Fig. 13.4). Central and local government dominate the total, with central government responsible for almost three-quarters.

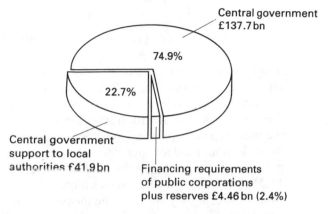

Fig. 13.4 Public expenditure by spending authority 1990/91; £bn and percentages of total
Source: Treasury (1990a)

Recent trends in UK public spending

Reduced spending on capital formation

Figure 13.5 indicates a dramatic fall in capital expenditure (including lending to nationalized industries) as a percentage of general government expenditure, compared with other components which continue to grow steadily. For instance, since 1975 capital spending has fallen by around thirteen percentage points, whereas current grants and subsidies, mainly for welfare purposes, have risen by ten percentage points and current spending on goods and services, by around two percentage points. The *Government's Expenditure Plans* acknowledge that there will be further small reductions in real terms in capital spending. This is mainly because of privatization, but the Government also notes that there is *no* clear dividing line between *capital* and *current* spending. For example, expenditure on training in the

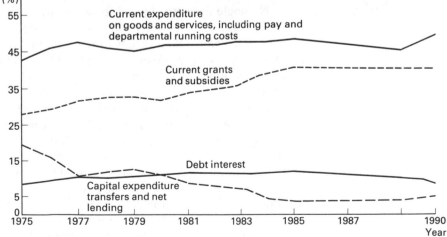

Fig. 13.5 Components of UK public spending as a percentage of general government expenditure
Sources: Economic Trends Annual Supplement No. 8, 1983, and *Economic Trends* 5 May 1985; Treasury (1990a)

employment programme, which is an investment in the future labour force and is growing rapidly, is classified as current spending. There are also other definitional problems making the line between capital and current spending hazy.

The size of public expenditure

So far we have looked at changing *shares* within total public spending, but has the *absolute* level of public spending grown as fast as critics suggest? Such people usually point to a single statistic for evidence; for instance, that the public sector employs about 30% of the labour force or, as with Milton Friedman, that public expenditure at around 60% of National Income threatens to destroy British freedom and democracy. Actually, estimates for the ratio of public spending to National Income vary widely, depending on the definitions used for each item. Figures for 1990/91 put general government expenditure at around 39% of GDP at market prices (see Table 13.2 below). If, however, transfer payments are excluded from government expenditure, as they are from the measurement of National Income, then general government expenditure falls dramatically to less than 29% of GDP at market prices. What, then, is the truth about the size of public expenditure?

An examination of data from the Central Statistical Office (CSO) suggests that as many as *ten* measures could be used for estimating the size of public expenditure. The measure selected will depend on the question at issue. If the intention is to assess the *financial resources* passing through the hands of government, then a ratio involving general government expenditure might be appropriate. However, the CSO's definition of National Income in the Blue Book excludes current grants and other transfers. Strictly, therefore, these same items should be excluded from government expenditure. They do not represent additional demand for resources, they are merely transfers of purchasing power from the taxpayer to other sectors of the community. Using this argument, a ratio of general government expenditure on goods and services of approximately 29% of National Income would appear to be the most appropriate measure.

No single measure of public expenditure has met with universal agreement, and even when one has been widely used for some time, it can be subject to change for a variety of reasons. In April 1977 general government expenditure was redefined to bring the UK into line with OECD accounting methods, and resulted in an apparent overnight reduction of some 6% in measured public expenditure. Again, what was previously tax relief may be reclassified as government expenditure, as with child tax allowances being replaced by child benefit in 1977. Public expenditure will also be affected by changes in the degree of 'privatization', or by changes in public sector pricing.

The National Income aggregate used for comparison will also influence our impression of the size of the public sector. Some ratios use domestic product, which measures resources produced *entirely within the domestic circular flow*. If, however, our interest was in the resources produced by UK nationals, *wherever they happen to be located*, then our ratio should use national product. Yet again, both domestic and national products could be valued 'gross' (including depreciation) or 'net' (excluding depreciation); at 'market prices', including the effects of taxes and subsidies, or at 'factor cost', excluding them.

For all these reasons, public spending ratios must be treated with caution when used in policy analysis.

Fig. 13.6 General government expenditure as a percentage of GDP

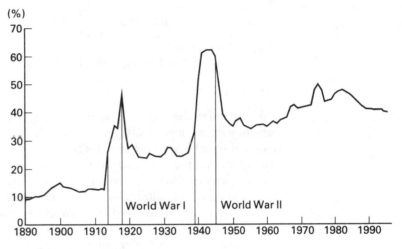

Explanations of the growth in public expenditure

No matter what the definition, statistics show that the government sector of the economy has expanded over the last 150 years (see Fig. 13.6), both in money and real terms, and as a percentage of National Income. Brown and Jackson (1982), quoting a variety of sources, show a dramatically rising trend of government spending as a proportion of GNP at factor cost up to 1976. The trend (using a different statistical series) continued upwards for data after 1976, excluding privatization proceeds. Since the early 1980s there has been a sustained fall in government spending as a proportion of National Income (see Table 13.2). By 1990/91 this ratio had fallen to 39%. The 1979 Government was returned with a mandate to cut public expenditure. Initially the results were very disappointing as public expenditure continued to grow. It was only in the late 1980s that public expenditure as a proportion of the national product fell below that which the Government had inherited in 1979. The explanation of the above trends and the difficulties involved in controlling public expenditure are based on two types of analysis: microeconomic and macroeconomic respectively.

Microeconomic analysis   Explanations based on microeconomic analysis suggest that additional public spending can be seen as the result of governments continually intervening to correct market failure. This would include the provision of 'public goods' such as collective defence, the police,

Table 13.2 Government
spending as a proportion of
National Income

(*a*) *Government spending as a proportion of GNP at factor cost* (%)

1790	1890	1910	1932	1951	1966	1970	1976
12.0	8.0	12.0	29.0	40.2	40.2	44.8	51.4

(*b*) *Government spending as a proportion of GDP at market price* (%)

1982/83	1984/85	1985/86	1986/87	1987/88	1988/89	1989/90	1990/91
46.8	46.25	44.5	43.8	42.5	39.5	39	39

Note: From 1977 onwards, an approximately 6% upward revision should be made to any government spending/National Income ratio if comparison with pre-1977 figures is to be made.
Sources: (a) Brown and Jackson (1982); (b) Treasury (1988, 1990a).

and local amenities. An extra unit of such goods can be enjoyed by one person, without anyone else's enjoyment being affected. In other words the marginal social cost of provision is zero, and it is often argued in welfare economics that the 'efficiency' price should, therefore, be zero. Private markets are unable to cope with providing goods at zero price, so that public provision is the only alternative should this welfare argument be accepted. Microeconomic analysis would also cover extra public spending due to a change in the composition of the 'market', such as an ageing population incurring greater expenditure on health care.

Macroeconomic analysis   There are also explanations of the growth of public spending based on long-run macroeconomic theories and models. The starting point in this field is the work of Wagner (see Bird 1971), who used empirical evidence to support his argument that government expenditure would inevitably increase at a rate faster than the rise in national production. Wagner suggested that 'the pressures of social progress' would create tensions which could only be resolved by increased state activity in law and order, economic and social services, and participation in material production. Using the economists' terms, Wagner was in effect suggesting that public sector services and products are 'normal', with high income elasticities of demand. Early studies in the UK (see Williamson 1961) tended to support Wagner, indicating overall income elasticities for public sector services of 1.7, and for public sector goods of 1.3, with similar results in other advanced industrialized countries. In fact, a study by the OECD (1982), found that the proportion of GNP absorbed by public expenditure between 1954 and the present day on 'merit goods' (education, health and housing) and 'income maintenance' (pensions, sickness, family and unemployment benefits) had doubled from 14 to 28%, as an average across all the advanced industrialized countries. That same report concluded that high income elasticities and low price elasticities had played a major part in this observed growth. Surveys of less developed economies were, however, more confusing, with econometric studies suggesting that little of the growth in public spending could be 'explained' by rising incomes (or low price elasticities).

Peacock and Wiseman's 'displacement theory', covering the period 1890–1953, suggested that public spending was not rising with the smooth, small changes predicted by Wagner, but that it was displaced (permanently) upwards by social upheavals associated, for instance, with depressions or wars leading to demands for new social expenditure (Fig. 13.6 above indicates the displacements of 1914–18 and 1939–45). Displacement theory has, however, been criticized for giving insufficient weight to political influences on the level of public expenditure. A further criticism of 'displacement' theory is the fact that for the UK there is little evidence that ratchet increases in public spending are long lasting. In fact, where the ratio of public expenditure to National Income has continued to rise in the 1970s and 1980s, it has been more easily explained by *downward deviations of trend National Income in recession*, with consequent increases in spending on unemployment benefits and social services, rather than through any upward revision of government expenditure plans.

The conclusion that must be drawn from reviewing such work is that there is no definite micro- or macro-explanation of the growth path for public expenditure. It then follows that there is no inevitable 'law' ensuring that public expenditure becomes a progressively rising proportion of National Income. However, should the recession continue, increased spending on unemployment and social services may indeed cause a sharp increase in the share of public expenditure in National Income. Demographic changes may also conspire to raise the share of public expenditure. There was considerable debate in the mid-1980s of the mounting 'burden' on the working population likely to result from the growing number of pensioners in the second and third decades of the next century. National Insurance reforms (such as the modifications to the State Earnings Related Pension Scheme – SERPS) were therefore introduced as part of a broader review of the Welfare State in 1985/86, with the intention of reducing the cost to the state and the taxpayer (see Ch. 14).

International comparisons of public expenditure

Given that public expenditure has grown over time in the UK, how do we compare with other countries? Conclusions based on OECD surveys indicate that UK public expenditure patterns are similar to those in most other advanced industrialized countries, although inferences drawn from international surveys must be treated with caution. The OECD definitions are frequently different from national ones, public sector boundaries vary between countries, and fluctuating exchange rates compromise any attempt at a standard unit of value.

Table 13.3 indicates that the growing share of UK public expenditure in National Income has been paralleled in other countries. If anything, public expenditure has grown less quickly in the UK; in 1964 it was joint third highest, with West Germany, of the fourteen countries shown in Table 13.3; by 1987 it was only eleventh highest of those same fourteen countries. Again, whereas the government outlay ratio averaged 48.4% across all the EC countries in 1987, the UK at 43.2% was considerably below that average. In comparative terms it would appear that there is little cause for alarm at the growth path of UK public expenditure.

Table 13.3 Total outlays* of government as a percentage of GDP at market prices. Some international comparisons

	1964	1974	1979	1987
Australia	22.1	31.6	43.2	35.8
Austria	32.1	41.9	48.9	52.5
Belgium	30.3	39.4	49.3	52.3
Canada	28.9	36.8	39.0	45.6
Denmark	24.8	45.9	53.2	58.3
France	34.6	39.3	45.0	51.8
Italy	30.1	37.9	45.5	50.7
Japan	N/A	24.5	31.6	33.2
The Netherlands	33.7	47.9	55.8	60.1
Norway	29.9	44.6	50.4	51.6
Sweden	31.1	48.1	60.7	59.9
UK	32.4	44.9	42.7	43.2
USA	27.5	32.2	31.7	36.7
West Germany	32.4	44.6	47.6	46.8

* Total government outlay = final consumption expenditure + interest on national debt + subsidies + social security transfers to households + gross capital formation.
Source: OECD (1985, 1989).

Should public expenditure be restricted?

Arguments for controlling or reducing the size of public expenditure are wide-ranging but not always convincing.

Freedom and choice

One argument is that excessive government expenditure adversely affects individual freedom and choice. First, it is feared that it spoonfeeds individuals, taking away the incentive for personal provision, as with private insurance for sickness or old age. Second, that by impeding the market mechanism it may restrict consumer choice. For instance, the state may provide goods and services that are in little demand, whilst discouraging others (via taxation) that might otherwise have been bought. Third, it has been suggested that government provision may encourage an unhelpful separation between payment and cost in the minds of consumers. With government provision, the good or service may be free or subsidized, so that the amount paid by the consumer will understate the true cost (higher taxes, etc.) of providing him with that good or service, thereby encouraging excessive consumption of the item.

Crowding out the private sector

The Conservative Government believes that (excessive) 'public expenditure is at the heart of Britain's economic difficulties' (HMSO 1979). It regards the private sector as the source of wealth creation, part of which is used to subsidize the public sector. Sir Keith Joseph clarified this view by alleging that 'a wealth-creating sector which accounts for one-third of the national product carries on its back a State subsidized sector which accounts for two-thirds. The rider is twice as heavy as the horse' (Joseph 1976).

Bacon and Eltis (1978) attempt to give substance to this view. They suggest that public expenditure growth has led to a transfer of productive resources from the private sector to a public sector producing largely non-marketed output, and that this has been a major factor in the UK's poor performance in the post-war period. Bacon and Eltis noted that public sector employment increased by some 26%, from 5.8 million workers to 7.3 million, between 1960 and 1978, a time when total employment was largely unchanged. They then alleged that the private (marketed) sector was *squeezed* by higher taxes to finance this growth in the public sector – the result being deindustrialization, low labour productivity, low economic growth and balance of payments problems.

Control of money

Another argument used by those who favour restricting public expenditure is that it must be cut in order to limit the growth of money supply and to curb inflation. The argument is that a high Public Sector Borrowing Requirement (PSBR) following public expenditure growth, must be funded by the issue of Treasury bills and government stocks. Since there are inadequate 'real' savings to be found in the non-bank private sector, these bills and bonds inevitably find their way into the hands of the banks. As we will see in Chapter 16, they may then form the basis for a multiple expansion of bank deposits (money), with perhaps inflationary consequences.

A related argument is that public expenditure must be restricted, not only to limit the supply of money, but also its 'price' – the rate of interest. The suggestion is to sell the extra bills and bonds to fund a high PSBR, interest rates must rise to attract investors. This then puts pressure on private sector borrowing, with the rise in interest rates inhibiting private sector investment and investment-led growth. A major policy aim of the Government has, therefore, been to reduce public sector borrowing.

Incentives to work, save and take risks

There are also worries that increased public spending not only pushes up government borrowing to fund a high PSBR, but also leads to higher taxes, thereby reducing the incentives to work, save and take risks. The evidence linking taxes to incentives is reviewed in Chapter 14. Suffice it to say here that the evidence to support the general proposition that higher taxes undermine the work ethic is largely inconclusive.

Balance of payments stability

A further line of attack is that the growth of public expenditure may have destabilized the economy in the 1970s and early 1980s. This was implied by the Cambridge Economic Policy Group (CEPG), who used an accounting identity (see Ch. 25) to demonstrate that a higher PSBR must lead to a deterioration in the balance of payments. The common sense of their argument is that higher public spending raises interest rates and attracts capital inflows, which in turn raise the demand for sterling and therefore the exchange rate. A higher pound then makes exports dearer and imports cheaper, so that the balance of payments deteriorates.

These various lines of reasoning have been challenged by, amongst others, the New Cambridge School which suggests that the relationships between the public sector and economic management may by no means be so simple. In fact, one adherent of the New Cambridge School, Lord Kaldor (1980), went so far as to say that there is no empirical support for a high PSBR leading either to substantial growth in money supply or to high rates of interest. Similarly, the claim that resources liberated by the public sector will automatically find their way into the private sector was hardly supported by the rising unemployment trend of the early 1980's. Another criticism is that public expenditure cuts, rather than helping to control unemployment (by cutting inflation in a monetarist model), have either caused or exaggerated current unemployment (see Ch. 18).

The debate on the role of public expenditure continues. Nevertheless, the present Conservative Government believes, as a cornerstone of its medium-term financial strategy, that it should squeeze inflation progressively out of the economy, through cuts in both the level of the PSBR and the rate of growth of the money supply. Reductions in public expenditure are seen as essential for achieving each of these financial targets (indeed, by the end of the 1980s, the government had achieved a switch from PSBR to PSDR, i.e. public sector debt repayment). This inevitably brings into focus the procedure for the planning, monitoring and control of public expenditure.

Public expenditure planning, monitoring and control

Early history

Public expenditure control has a long history dating back to the early eighteenth century. Restraint was initially the responsibility of the parliamentary opposition using a system of procedural checks on estimates and expenditure payments. In the nineteenth century, Gladstone introduced auditing through the Office of the Comptroller and Auditor-General, a Crown appointment independent of Parliament. The comptroller's scrutiny of items of expenditure helped promote Treasury and parliamentary control of public expenditure. Subsequent developments of importance included the establishment, in 1924, of the Commons Public Accounts Committee (PAC) to investigate abuse. This gave Parliament still more control in that the comptroller's report need no longer be taken at face value, but could be subjected to detailed investigation by the PAC.

Prest (1967) concluded that this system was successfully grounded in procedural tradition dating back to the 1860s. It provided a full and comprehensive check against dishonesty and speculation as, for example, with the existence of a single Exchequer account into which all receipts were paid and from which all payments were drawn.

Criticisms within and without Parliament made it clear that this audit model of control was beginning to falter in the post-war period. Since 1945, the traditional functions of Parliament had expanded rapidly and had become more technical and complex. The PAC uncovered many scandals, but as its investigations were post-mortems it was accused of 'only shutting the stable door after the horse had bolted' (see Pollitt 1977). The quality of government and parliamentary information and expertise in both monitoring and control was clearly inadequate. It was as a result of such criticisms that the Plowden Report was published in 1961 (Plowden 1961).

The Plowden Report – establishment of the Public Expenditure Survey Committee (PESC) system

Plowden inaugurated modern public expenditure management. It was intended to provide a comprehensive view of public expenditure planning and control. Previously the framework had been rather piecemeal, with departments presenting separate estimates at different periods of the year. Often, when out-turn was greater than planned expenditure, Parliament had meekly acquiesced to supplementary estimates. There was neither a global view of spending, nor effective control, in the system prior to Plowden.

Plowden established the principle that decisions involving substantial future expenditure should always be taken in the light of surveys of public expenditure over a number of years, and in relation to the prospective resources. The model adopted was a largely Keynesian one, concerned with the opportunity cost of resources used, rather than with the monetary value of spending. The new system depended upon annual surveys being published each year,[1] together with five-year plans, rolled forward one year at the next annual planning round.[2] In this pattern of five-year plans, the first two were to be in detail, and the next three in outline.

A critical element in these surveys was that data for past and future plans were to be presented at constant prices, as it was almost impossible to interpret a time series of expenditure for a period in which prices fluctuated significantly. This meant that planned changes were presented in real or volume terms (i.e. the number of roads or teachers), an important point in subsequent criticism of Plowden. Another feature of Plowden was that expenditure had to be presented by function (i.e. by programme, so that social and political priorities could be debated), by type of expenditure (current and capital), and by relevant spending authority (central/local government).

The system of control established by Plowden was to be known as the PESC system, since the Public Expenditure Survey Committee was to be its centrepiece.

Public Expenditure Survey Committee

Plowden was seen as providing a medium-term strategy for economic control, though to function satisfactorily it required an adequate institutional structure. The PESC, a body of high-ranking finance officers from the spending departments, was to be at the heart of this structure. They, together with the Treasury, were to be responsible for presenting an 'up-to-date' costing of existing programmes. However, one year's public expenditure was heavily predetermined by previous decisions, so that changes were by and large only possible at the margins. The full circle of control might start up to eighteen months prior to the beginning of the financial year in question and involve discussions between the PESC and the government departments over initial estimates, and present them to Cabinet in the November preceding the start of the financial year (April). Policy changes and 'horse-trading' could then be considered in Cabinet on the basis of firm figures.

Criticisms of the PESC system

A curious but important feature of the PESC system was to define 'constant prices' as being those prevailing *at the beginning* of the exercise: they were not updated in the light of subsequent price changes. Thus the 1981–82 White Paper on Public Expenditure (the last year for this procedure) used the prices prevailing in autumn 1979. Such a definition of 'constant prices' meant that no effective financial control was exercised in the inflationary 1970s. Departments, having planned the number of schools, hospitals, etc. at 'constant prices', could purchase these even if inflation in the current year was higher than anticipated. The Treasury recognized the additional expenditure implications of this planning defect by including in the White Paper a financial allowance (normally positive) called the relative price effect

(RPE). They did not, however, attempt to restrain this extra spending, although to highlight the use of what became known as 'funny money' in the planning process, the PESC at least monitored the amounts spent in terms of 'current money'.

Effectively, therefore, the PESC system used three types of money, i.e. constant (or survey prices) for planning, constant prices plus RPE for spending, and current prices for monitoring. This system taxed the intelligence and understanding of all but a few. It helped to bring the system into disrepute and played a major part in the eventual breakdown of the Plowden structure.

There were other criticisms of the system. Volume analysis did not encourage economic efficiency; for example, it avoided the question of substitution between individual programmes when cash was short. Nor did it assist macroeconomic management. Volume targets were planned partly on the basis of growth projections for National Income, and partly on political judgement as to how much of National Income should be absorbed by the state. Government growth projections for National Income have been notoriously unreliable, often excessively optimistic. Despite this, public expenditure programmes were rarely revised downwards (see Pliatisky 1982), creating inevitable economic problems. As Wynn Godley pointed out, public expenditure during 1971–75 increased by £5.5bn more than could be accounted for by announced policy changes, i.e. by an extra 5% of GDP. He alleged that at least £4.75bn had occurred because of inflation.

Individual government departments also created problems for the use of volume analysis. Most notorious were the cost overruns in defence and civilian aircraft R&D. The estimated government cost for Concorde in 1962 was £160m., but by 1982 it had soaked up over £1bn (around £250m. at 1962 prices). Nationalized industries created additional difficulties; volume planning often led to overcapacity and excessive output, with huge losses having to be written off. The most dramatic difficulties have, however, been created by local authorities. In 1982–83 they spent around £1.5bn in excess of central government plans, i.e. an extra 7% on the planned total. In defence of their position, local authorities have pointed out that much of the upsurge in their expenditure has occurred because of statutory demands for new or expanded services placed on them by central government. The local authority increase in manpower, particularly ancillary and health workers, can largely be explained by such statutory obligations.

In retrospect, the public expenditure crisis of the early and mid-1970s appears to have been mainly due to high inflation exposing weaknesses in the Plowden structure of volume planning. Modifications to the system of planning and control of public expenditure became inevitable.

Reform of the PESC system

Microplanning – programme analysis and review   The 1970 White Paper on Public Expenditure argued that the PESC system needed strengthening. Its conclusions were based on the Fulton Report (1968). This argued that micromanagement of spending projects had developed on an *ad hoc* basis, and was failing to provide enough information for a detailed analysis of the efficiency with which resources were being used in existing programmes and policy options. The Fulton Report therefore suggested that the PESC system should adopt programme analysis and review (PAR) – a technique by which individual programmes selected by Cabinet could be systematically analysed. Programme analysis and review was really nothing more than a method of asking basic questions about programme resources and outputs, such as what is being done and why? What methods are being used, and what results are being obtained?

The success of this technique has been limited. Governments have tended in the main to be more interested in macro- rather than micro- (individual programme) problems. Allegedly, most PAR reports have been too long and complicated, suffering from data and conceptual problems. The Civil Service mandarins have often refused to allow their publication, even when they concerned such 'innocuous' subjects as road safety, rural depopulation or fertilizers. In the end only one or two small sub-programmes have been investigated each year. It has been alleged that at this rate it would take 300 years to examine all the programmes outlined in Table 13.1 above. By 1979 *The Economist* was implying that the Government's new cost control team under Sir Derek Rayner (Head of Marks and Spencer) had effectively killed PAR, though it was anticipated that this body would do similar work by introducing business methods of accounting into government. However, even this cost control team was subsequently absorbed by the Treasury in 1983 because it was politically unpopular and had met with mixed success. The Treasury team still exists and has continued to have some 'success'.

Planning and control in 'real money' – cash limits   The first significant change from PESC volume control, which was broadly recognized as having failed, came with the widespread introduction of cash limits. Initially these had applied to some building programmes in 1974/75, but the new controls were extended and grafted on to volume control in 1976. The Treasury hoped that they would be an answer to inappropriate volume targets, and to criticisms that PESC allowed the cash content of public expenditure to rise too fast; often even faster than the general rate of inflation, since public sector inflation usually exceeded that in the private sector. Cash limits were initially fixed to reflect volume decisions, but once set they, not the volume decisions, were to be the determinants of expenditure. In other words, cash limits were not expected to be adjusted during the subsequent year to take account of inflation. Cash limits now cover directly some 60% of public expenditure and have been used in different ways throughout the public sector.

Central government generally has cash limits imposed on clearly defined blocks of expenditure. However, there are some major exceptions, such as 'demand-related services', specifically social security, together with debt interest and a few subsidies. These exclusions have restricted the overall effectiveness of cash limits as a device for controlling public expenditure. This was particularly true during the economic recession of the early 1980s, when rapidly expanding social security payments, high interest rates and substantial debt interest payments meant that public expenditure totals continued to rise as a proportion of National Income.

Local government *capital* expenditure is 'cash limited', but current expenditure is cash limited only as far as the *overall total* of the Rate Support Grant (RSG)[3] is concerned. Local authorities still have the right to decide individual items of expenditure within this overall block, and also to resort to local sources of finance. These loopholes stretched government control of local spending, so that the 1981 'local government reforms' were introduced. Whilst retaining the right of local authorities to allocate the overall block between individual programmes, block spending grants were now related to 'optimum' levels of expenditure, with financial penalties imposed on errant authorities.

A cash limit is also applied to nationalized industries to restrict their ability to borrow from sources other than the Government. The technical term used for this cash limit is the external finance limit (EFL), reflecting its rather different status. The EFL is not directly imposed on wage and industrial costs, so that these have sometimes risen within the total EFL at the cost of lower investment, higher prices or a reduced quality of service.

Cash limits are expected to encourage cost-cutting and to make managers think about the quality and the quantity of the service they provide. Cash limits have had some 'success', even leading to an undershooting of the limits, as financial managers treat the new system with excessive caution and spend well below their targets. However, there are still problems: cash limits will only be 'successful' if the Government has the political will to set effective limits in the first place, and subsequently to keep to them. A number of public sector pay awards have been treated leniently through supplementary estimates being granted, or have even been placed outside the limits. Other pay settlements for powerful groups of workers have been preceded by promises to adjust the limits if necessary. Again, the contingency reserve and the block method of funding of grants provide means by which it is possible to accommodate limited extra calls, as in the case of the Falklands war. A further weakness in the system is that the Government, when setting limits for expenditure which can be as far as two years in the future, has to make realistic assumptions about projected inflation. Usually these projections for inflation have underestimated the out-turn so that 'unintended' cuts have been imposed in programmes. We have already noted in Chapter 8 that nationalized industries have often side-stepped their 'cash limit' (the EFL) by actually cutting investment and the quality of service rather than by cutting costs. Finally, there is the criticism that cash limits tend to ignore the fact that specific volumes of goods and services may be required to meet specific needs.

Cash planning   Cash limits did constrain most spending programmes, but PESC *planning* was still undertaken in volume terms ('funny money'). The logical step, agreed in 1981, was therefore to shift *planning* itself away from volume and into cash. The year 1982/83 was the first in which public expenditure was planned, monitored and controlled in cash. Although the advantage of real volume planning, an assured outcome, is lost by the new technique, it was expected that cash planning would mean that government expenditure could more easily be related to expected government revenue. This would mean that the PSBR could be more accurately forecast, to the benefit of macroeconomic control. The clear implication is that greater weight is being given to macro-planning, in the hope that greater effectiveness here will indirectly benefit individual projects.

Has the Conservative Government controlled public spending?

In 1979 the Government announced that it was determined, unlike the previous Labour administration, to control and reduce public expenditure. In practice this has not been achieved, even allowing for the fact that the Conservative Government inherited from Labour plans entailing growth in expenditure of some 2% per annum. Since 1979, the Thatcher administration has announced wide-ranging cuts, yet the ratio of general government expenditure to GDP increased from 41% in the last year of the Labour Government to 46.8% in 1982/83. Since then, as indicated in Table 13.2 above, the Government has reduced government expenditure as a percentage of GDP. By 1992/93, provided government plans remain on course, public expenditure will comprise only 38.5% of GDP, the lowest ratio since 1965/66.

The Government's initial failure to hold spending down in the early 1980s was not for lack of trying. The recession was much deeper than forecast, so that social security payments expanded as unemployment rose to over 3 million. In addition, high interest rates raised debt interest, policy decisions raised grants to individuals, as with child benefit replacing family allowances, and demographic pressures increased expenditure on retirement pensions.

Cuts in subsidy forced the nationalized industries to increase prices more than the going rate of inflation and pressure was put on them to restrain borrowing. The Government was heavily criticized for allowing cuts to fall more heavily on 'productive' capital investment rather than current spending (see Fig. 13.5 above). The Treasury sought to justify itself, arguing that some of the alleged cuts in capital spending are more apparent than real. Definitional convention means that many items are classified as current expenditure (e.g. R & D and industrial training) when they are, in fact, capital items. In any case, the Treasury has argued against any a priori assumption that capital spending is 'productive'. Why should investment in prisons and unemployment benefit offices be considered productive? Why should more capital spending on hospitals make the National Health Service more 'productive' than more current spending on nurses?

Since the rise in ratio of public spending to National Income peaked in 1982/83, we have seen that the ratio has steadily declined. This does not, however, mean that all the problems of 'control' of public spending have been resolved. For instance the 1970s concern remains that public expenditure pay may neither be under control for *particular groups of workers* nor spent wisely or efficiently for others. This criticism arises from the fact that, search where you may through the White Papers, nowhere will you find detailed information about what public service workers have been paid, how their pay has changed or what they will be paid in the future. If, therefore, public spending increases we have no idea whether the rise went in pay or in improved services. This is a crucial element when debating the merits of improvements in the National Health Service or education.

As we can see from Table 13.4 the intention is a gradual return to the longer term objective of a balanced budget. Similarly re the expenditure of

Table 13.4 Public Sector
Debt Repayment

Year	1988/89	1989/90	1990/91	1991/92	1992/93
PSDR (£bn)	14.57	7	7	3	0
PSDR as % of GDP	3	1¼	1¼	½	0

Source: Treasury, (1990c).

particular departments. The Commons PAC (Hencke 1988) revealed that the post-war problems of lack of control and bureaucratic delay still remained within the Ministry of Defence. They stated that it cost taxpayers £3 to £4bn per annum in overrun defence contracts. One area where the Government can claim some success as a result of public expenditure control involves debt repayment. Public Sector Debt Repayment (PSDR) was 14.5bn in 1988/89, i.e. some 3% of GDP.

The *local authorities* spend over a quarter of public expenditure and have been a major source of control problems. In most expenditure programmes they have considerable discretion over totals and priorities. Only in one major area, capital, has Parliament or central government set detailed rules reducing this freedom. The Government has thus attempted to restrict local authority discretion by reducing the level of income received from the central government via cuts in the RSG and through rate capping. However, the Audit Commission, a government efficiency agency, has still criticized some local authorities for spending excessively and for wasting resources, e.g. some £700m. has been 'inefficiently' spent in one year on council house maintenance repairs. (See Ch. 14 for recent moves to curb local authority spending, e.g. uniform business rate, rate capping, etc.).

The Conservative Government has also used the policy of *privatization* to reduce the size of public expenditure (Treasury 1982). In 1979 the state sector accounted for 11.5% of GDP. Since then, more than one-third of that has been moved to the private sector. In total this has involved the transfer of around 650,000 employees, the majority of whom (some 90%) have become shareholders in the companies they work for. The privatization programme has reduced net lending to the nationalized industries (part of total government expenditure in Table 13.1 above) and has provided a (temporary) boost to Treasury funds. It is too early to make a full assessment of the impact of such privatization on industrial efficiency. The Government, however, believes that it has improved company performance by making public sector industry subject to market forces, and by breaking state monopolies (see Ch. 8). They also believe that their programme is working as most privatized companies are reporting increased turnover, investment and profitability. They maintained the momentum of the privatization programme in the late 1980s and early 1990s with the privatization of electricity and water.

Other minor reforms have been suggested for reducing public expenditure. The Treasury has merged the manpower division of the Civil Service into the public expenditure section of the Treasury, bringing manpower control into PESC planning. However, fundamental ways of reducing the size of public expenditure would require the Government to find new ways of charging for the services it provides, or to dismantle the Welfare State. Changes in the monitoring and control of public expenditure since

Plowden have not meant that planned levels of expenditure can be painlessly reduced.

Conclusion

The definition of public expenditure is by no means clear-cut and must depend upon the question at issue. Since National Income also has many variants, any public expenditure/National Income ratio must be treated with caution. The estimate for 1991/92 puts general government expenditure at around 38.75% of GDP at market prices. If, however, we subtract grants and transfers from public expenditure, as we do from all the National Income measures, then the figure falls substantially to around 26%. Whatever the definition chosen, the proportion of government spending in National Income has risen steadily throughout the twentieth century, including the early period under the present Conservative Government. The reduction in the growth of National Income played an important part in raising the ratio in the early 1980s; both directly, by restricting the denominator, and indirectly, by causing unplanned increases in expenditure on social security. Whether a growing public sector 'crowds out', or otherwise adversely affects the private sector, is a matter of deep controversy. Certainly in comparative terms the UK is by no means exceptional, with the share of UK government spending in National Income below the average for the EEC countries. More 'rigour' has been imposed into procedures to plan, monitor and control public expenditure. This, together with renewed growth in National Income, has helped to reduce the ratio of government spending to National Income well below its peak in 1982–83.

Notes

1. In fact, prior to 1970, these surveys were not published for public debate – a serious criticism of the PESC.
2. The pattern of five years (the first two in detail and the next three in outline) has subsequently been modified as circumstances have dictated. The Conservative Government, arguing economic planning difficulties, has usually planned in three-year blocks.
3. The RSG is a block grant provided by central government. It aims to finance a minimum level of services, to equalize taxable resources between different local authorities, and to relieve the domestic ratepayer of part of the local tax burden.

References and further reading

Bacon, R. and **Eltis, W.** (1978) *Britain's Economic Problem: too few producers* 2nd edn. Macmillan.
Bird, R. M. (1971) Wagner's Law of Expanding State Activity, *Public Finance*, **26**, 1.
Brown, C. V. and **Jackson, P. M.** (1982) *Public Sector Economics* 2nd edn. Martin Robertson.
CSO (1983) *Economic Trends*, Annual Supplement No. 8.
CSO (1985) *Economic Trends*, May.
CSO (1985) *Financial Statistics*, **280**, Aug.

CSO (1989) International Comparisons of Taxes and Social Security Contributions in 20 OECD Countries 1976–86, *Economic Trends*.

The Economist (1979) Civil Service war or wish? 20 Oct.

The Economist (1982) Thatcher's Think Tank takes aim at the Welfare State, 18 Sept.

Financial Times

Fulton Report (1968) *The Civil Service*. Cmnd 3638.

Hencke, D. (1988) £4bn defence scandal, *Guardian*, 10 March.

HMSO (1979) *Public Expenditure*. Cmnd 7746.

HMSO (1984, 1985) *The Government's Expenditure Plans 1985–86 to 1987–88*. Cmnd 9428–I. Cmnd 9143.

Johnson, C. (1990a) Naught for comfort, *Lloyds Bank Economic Bulletin*, 135, March.

Johnson, C. (1990b) Who gets the peace dividend? *Lloyds Bank Economic Bulletin*, 136, April.

Joseph, K. (1976) *Monetarism is not Enough*. Barry Rose.

Kaldor, N. (1980) Money supply and PSBR: are we worshipping false gods?, *The Times*, 6 Aug.

Lumby, S. (1981) New ways of financing nationalized industries, *Lloyds Bank Review*, 141, July.

National Institute Economic Review (1985) 113, Aug.

OECD (1982) The role of the public sector, *Economic Policy Committee Working Party Report*, CPE/WP1

OECD (1985) *Economic Outlook*, **37**, June.

OECD (1989) *Economic Outlook*, **46**, Dec.

Pliatisky, L. (1982) *Getting and Spending*. Blackwell, Oxford.

Plowden (1961) *The Control of Public Expenditure*. Cmnd 1432, HMSO.

Pollitt, C. (1977) Public expenditure survey, 1961–72, *Journal of the Royal Institute of Public Administration*, **55**, Summer

Prest, A. R. (1967) *Public Finance in Theory and Practice*. Weidenfeld and Nicolson.

Treasury (1981) Public Expenditure: planning in cash, *Economic Progress Report*, 139, Nov.

Treasury (1982) Public sector for the public, *Economic Progress Report*, 145.

Treasury (1990a) *The Government's Expenditure Plans, 1990–91 to 1992–93*, Cmnd 1021.

Treasury (1990b) Public spending in the 1980s, *EPR Economic Progress Report*, 206, February.

Treasury (1990c) Financial Statement and Budget Report, 1989–90.

Williamson, J. (1961) Public expenditure and revenue: an international comparison, *The Manchester School of Economic and Social Studies*, **29**.

14   Taxation

This chapter looks at the existing pattern of UK taxation and the changes that have taken place in recent years. We examine the degree of progressiveness of the UK tax system and the effects of the recent switches between direct and indirect taxation. The changing burden of taxation in the UK is charted, and international comparisons presented. We then consider the effect of higher taxes on incentives to work, save and take risks, and on the rise of the 'black economy'. After a more general treatment of the direct vs indirect tax debate, we conclude with a brief look at recent tax reform.

The taxes that are collected: some taxation concepts

Taxes may be classified in a number of different ways.

The method of collection

Taxes may be grouped by the administrative arrangement for their collection.

Direct or indirect

Income tax is paid *directly* to the Exchequer by the individual taxpayer (mainly through Pay As You Earn – PAYE), on the full amount of income from employment and investment in the fiscal year. The same is true of corporation tax, paid by firms on company profits. On the other hand, value added tax (VAT), though paid by consumers, reaches the Exchequer *indirectly*, largely through retailers acting as collecting agencies. Taxes may therefore be classified as either direct or indirect, according to the administrative arrangement for their collection. From Table 14.1 we see that direct taxes – in the form of income tax, capital taxes, corporation tax and petroleum revenue tax – are expected to produce 37.5% (81.9/218.6) of total government receipts in 1990/91. Income tax is by far the most important direct tax, alone contributing almost 25% of government receipts. Strictly speaking we should add the various National Insurance contributions to the total for direct taxation. These are a compulsory levy on employers, employees and the self-employed, expressed as a fixed percentage of total earnings, and paid directly to the Exchequer. They total some £35.9bn and provide around 16.5% of government receipts. They are not, however, included in the Consolidated Fund revenue tables.

    Indirect taxes – VAT, a range of excise duties on oil, tobacco, alcohol and motor cars, and import duties – were expected to produce 26% of total government receipts in 1990/91. Of these VAT (14.7% of total receipts) was the most important. The indirect taxes are collected by Customs and Excise.

Taxation

Table 14.1 How public spending is paid for. Income of central government

	Government revenue (£m)		
	1989/90 estimate	1990/91 f'cast	1990/91 %
Inland Revenue:			
Income tax	48.7	55.0	
Corporation tax	21.4	20.7	
Petroleum tax	1.1	1.1	
Capital Gains tax	1.9	2.1	37.5
Inheritance tax	1.2	1.2	
Stamp duty	2.1	1.9	
Total Inland Rev.	**76.4**	**81.9**	
Customs & Excise:			
VAT	29.7	32.1	
Petrol, etc.	8.8	9.7	
Tobacco	5.0	5.4	
Alcohol	4.6	4.9	
Betting	1.0	1.0	25.9
Car Tax	1.5	1.5	
Customs duties	1.8	1.9	
Agriculture	0.1	0.1	
Total customs	**52.4**	**56.7**	
Vehicle duties	2.9	3.0	
Oil royalties	0.6	0.7	
Rates*	20.1	12.2	9.2
Others	4.4	4.4	
Total taxes	**156.8**	**159**	**72.6**
National Insurance	33.1	35.9	16.5
Community charge	0.8	11.2	5.1
Interest	7.2	6.4	2.9
Trading Surplus	3.0	3.0	1.4
Other receipts	2.5	3.1	1.5
Total Receipts	**203.4**	**218.6**	**100.0**

NB Items may not add up to totals because of rounding.
* Local authority rates and national non-domestic rates.

Source: Treasury (1990)

    This Consolidated Fund revenue (£159bn), together with National Insurance receipts (£35.9bn), local authority and business rates (some £12.2bn) and for the first time the community charge (£11.2bn) plus other miscellaneous receipts, including those from privatization, are necessary to pay for the Government's expenditure plans of around £213bn in 1990/91.

    Details of the main items of government income are to be found in Fig. 14.1 and information on the income and expenditure in Table 14.2. Over the last few years government income has been buoyant as the economy has expanded. At the same time partial government expenditure control has meant that the Treasury, instead of being a net borrower has, since 1987/88, had a *negative* PSBR, i.e. a *budget surplus*. This PSDR (Public Sector Debt Repayment) rose to £14.5bn in 1988/89, before falling back to around £7bn in 1989/90. It is expected to remain at this level in 1990/91, before falling back in

Fig. 14.1 Total government
income: where the money
comes from

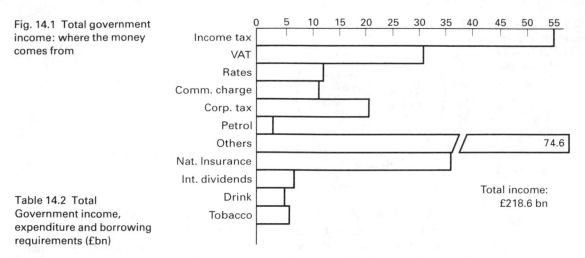

Table 14.2 Total
Government income,
expenditure and borrowing
requirements (£bn)

	Public sector debt repayment* (£bn)					
	1988–89	1989–90	1990–91	1991–92	1992–93	1993–94
General receipts	189.9	203	219	229	240	253
General expenditure	178.2	198	213	225	238	250
Fiscal adjustment	—	—	—	—	1	2
Annual adjustment[1]	—	—	—	1	1	1
GGDR	**11.5**	**6**	**6**	**3**	**0**	**0**
Pub. corp. debt. rpmt.	3.0	1	1	0	0	0
PSDR	**14.5**	**7**	**7**	**3**	**0**	**0**
Money GDP[2]	478.1	519	548	585	622	657
		(519)	(558)	(596)	(633)	(669)
PSDR (% of GDP)	**3**	**1¼**	**1¼**	**½**	**0**	**0**

* Rounded to the nearest £1bn from 1989–90 onwards.
[1] Means lower taxes or higher expenditure than assumed in lines 1 and 2.
[2] At market prices. Figures in brackets adjust for the distortion arising from the abolition of domestic rates.

Source: Treasury (1990).

subsequent years towards the Conservative government's long-term objective of a balanced budget.

The tax base

The tax base is essentially the 'object' to which the tax rate is applied. Excluding National Insurance contributions, taxes are usually grouped under three headings as regards tax bases: taxes on income (income, corporation and petroleum revenue taxes); taxes on expenditure (VAT and customs and excise duties); and taxes on capital (capital gains and inheritance tax).

Figure 14.2 shows that for 1990/91, taxes on income were expected to yield around 49% of Total Tax Revenue of £159bn; taxes on expenditure 36% and taxes on capital only 2%. In addition to these taxes (not in Fig. 14.2) there were compulsory levies in the form of National Insurance contributions on individuals and companies of £35.9bn and community charges of £11.2bn, raising the burden further on income.

Taxation

Fig. 14.2 Government
revenue 1990/91 and the tax
base (as % of Total Tax
Revenue of £159.0bn)

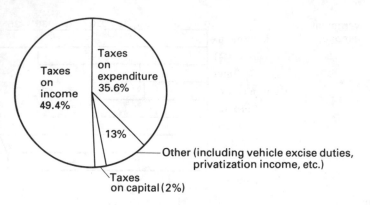

Taxes on income 49.4%

Taxes on expenditure 35.6%

13%

Other (including vehicle excise duties, privatization income, etc.)

Taxes on capital (2%)

Classifying taxes in terms of tax base, rather than method of collection, is often of more interest to economists, especially when calculating tax incidence (on whom the tax falls)! However, using the tax base does present problems of definition. For instance, Lord Wrenbury, in a legal judgment in 1925, defined income tax as being that which is 'within the Act, taxable under the Act'. National Insurance contributions, because they are based on calculations by actuaries, are not classified as a tax on income, yet they are levied as a percentage of income.

Whatever the tax base, the taxes levied can be one of two types, either specific (lump sum) or *ad valorem*.

Specific and *ad valorem* taxes   A *specific tax* is expressed as an absolute sum of money per unit of the good. Excise duties are often of this kind, being so many pence per packet of cigarettes or per proof of spirit. An *ad valorem* tax is a percentage tax, levied not on volume but on value; e.g. VAT is 15% of sales price, and corporation tax is 35% of assessable profits for larger companies and 25% for smaller companies on profits below £200,000 (1990/91).

Rate of taxation

Another useful classification is between progressive, proportional and regressive taxes. Tax is imposed as a rate or series of rates; e.g. income tax is levied at just 25% and 40% of taxable income whilst VAT items that are not exempted are zero-rated or pay 15%. These tax rates can be regarded as progressive, proportional or regressive, though such terms must be defined strictly as they are often used loosely. For a tax to be regarded as progressive, its rate structure must be such that the tax takes a rising proportion of total income as income increases; a proportional tax takes a constant proportion, whilst a regressive tax takes a declining proportion.

The pattern of UK taxation

A broadly proportional tax system

Since a progressive tax means that the rich pay more, not only in an *absolute* sense, but *as a proportion of their total income*, we need to know more than that the *marginal* rate of tax rises with income.[1] If, for instance, tax allowances and exemptions are more easily acquired by higher-income groups (as with mortgage repayments, etc.) then, despite a rising marginal rate, the individual may pay a smaller proportion of a higher total income in tax. In fact, it is the *average* rate[2] that is the best guide to whether the tax or tax system is, or is not, progressive. If the average rate is rising with income, then the tax *is* taking a higher proportion of higher incomes, i.e. the tax *is* progressive.

As we know from any game, say cricket, only when an individual scores more on his last (marginal) innings than his average for all previous innings, will his overall average actually rise. In the same way, only when the *marginal rate of tax is higher than the average rate*, will the average rate rise as income rises, and the tax be progressive. If the marginal and average rates are equal, then the average rate will be unchanged as income rises, so that the tax is proportional. If the marginal rate is below the average rate, then the average rate falls as income rises, and the tax is regressive.

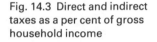 Fig. 14.3 Direct and indirect taxes as a per cent of gross household income

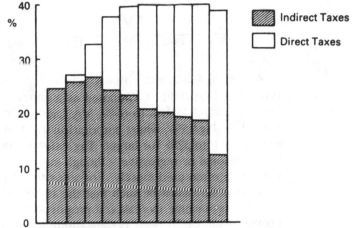

Figure 14.3 shows that, for the UK, direct taxes (the unshaded area in each bar) are progressive, taking a larger proportion of the total (gross) income of richer households. Indirect taxes are in contrast regressive, taking a declining proportion of such income. Overall, taking *both* direct and indirect taxes together, the UK tax system is mildly progressive for the bottom third of households by income, but roughly proportional to income for the top two-thirds of households.

Although indirect taxes as a whole are regressive, this is not true of every indirect tax. As we observe from Table 14.3, VAT is essentially a proportional tax, whereas other indirect taxes are strongly regressive.

Table 14.3 The regressiveness of indirect taxes

Quintile groups of households	Indirect taxes as percentage of *disposable* income per household		
	VAT	Other indirect taxes	Total indirect taxes
Bottom fifth	8.8	19.5	28.3
Next fifth	8.5	16.4	24.9
Middle fifth	7.9	14.3	22.2
Next fifth	7.6	12.8	20.4
Top Fifth	6.2	9.5	15.7

Source: CSO, *Economic Trends* (1990).

**A shift towards
indirect taxation**

We have seen that indirect taxes are more regressive than direct taxes. Here we chart the substantial changes that have taken place in the direct/indirect tax ratio during the 1970s and early 1980s.

Fig. 14.4 The ratio of central government taxes on income to taxes on expenditure
Source: Adapted from Atkinson (1979); CSO, *Financial Statistics*, Sept. 1985; Treasury (1990)

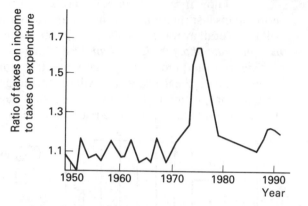

As Fig. 14.4 indicates, throughout the 1950s and 1960s taxes on income (direct) and expenditure (indirect) maintained a steady relationship, with taxes on income yielding around 10% more revenue. During the early and mid-1970s, however, the balance changed in favour of direct taxes on income as revenue providers for central government, due in part to inflation raising money incomes (and therefore direct tax receipts) and in part to fiscal drag. Fiscal drag is the extra tax yield which results from the fact that changes in both tax allowances and tax bands may not occur until *after* inflation has had its impact on money incomes. By 1975 direct taxes on income had peaked, providing some 60% more revenue than taxes on expenditure. The ratio has fallen substantially since then, and by 1986 direct taxes only provided some 10% more revenue than taxes on expenditure. Since 1986 the ratio has begun to edge upwards again as incomes have increased, with growing prosperity in the economy, raising the yield from direct taxes. However, in 1988/89 the Chancellor once more reversed the trend by permitting a substantial over-indexation of tax allowances.

Income taxes are more 'visible' to individuals than expenditure taxes, which to some extent are hidden in product prices. This may well have contributed to the *feeling* that the UK was overtaxed – for instance in a 1978 survey by *Money Which?* over 60% of respondents thought the UK to be more heavily taxed than other countries (contradicted by the facts – see Table 14.5 below).

With the slowing down of inflation in the mid–late 1970s, the ratio of direct to indirect taxes in total revenue began to fall. The new Conservative Government in 1979 then made a deliberate switch away from direct income taxation towards indirect taxation, cutting the standard rate of income tax from 33 to 30%, and raising VAT from 8 to 15%. We might have expected this switch to reinforce the downward trend in the ratio of direct to indirect tax receipts. In fact, higher inflation in the early years of that Government prevented the ratio falling. Since the early 1980s, the receipts from direct taxes on income have stabilized at around 10% above those from indirect taxes on expenditure; we have returned to the broad pattern of the 1950s and 1960s. The restored importance of indirect taxes, whatever its source, must, in the context of our earlier analysis, have made the UK tax system less progressive than it would otherwise have been.

A rise in the UK tax burden

We have seen that the *structure* of UK taxation has changed in recent years. What about the *level* of taxation? The ratio of total tax take to National Income is a frequently used measure of tax 'burden'. We can see from Table 14.4 that between 1964 and 1970 the total receipts from all taxes (including National Insurance) rose sharply as a proportion of GDP. Between 1970 and 1974 the tax ratio fell from 37% to 33.25% but has risen since then to 36.75% in 1990/91. Even the substantial income tax *reductions* of 1988/89 have left the total tax burden higher than when the Conservatives came into office in 1979. The fear that the tax burden will continue to rise rapidly, to finance growing public expenditure on a population with more old people, led to recent proposals for radical changes in the Welfare State.

Table 14.4 UK tax burden

Fiscal year	Tax as a percentage of GDP*
1964–65	29.5
1969–70	37.0
1973–74	33.25
1978–79	34.0
1979–80	35.0
1980–81	36.0
1981–82	38.5
1982–83	38.0
1983–84	37.5
1984–85	37.75
1985–86	37.0
1986–87	37.5
1987–88	37.75
1988–89	37.0
1989–90	36.75
1990–91	36.75
1991–92	36.0
1992–93	36.0

* Non-North Sea taxes, national insurance contributions and community charge as a percentage of Non-North Sea oil GDP.

1991–92 onwards are projections.

Source: Treasury (1990).

The UK tax burden: a comparative survey

Despite the rise in UK tax burden, and contrary to popular public opinion, the UK is only a middle-ranked country in terms of tax burden. From Table 14.5 we see that in 1976 the UK was only the tenth-ranked country out of eighteen in terms of tax burden, below the Scandinavian countries and close to France. OECD data in 1986 gave the UK a slightly higher ranking of ninth. Despite a rise in tax revenue as a proportion of GDP of 5.4% over this ten year period, the UK tax burden in 1986 continued to lie well below that in

Tax* as a percentage of GDP	1976		1986		GDP growth† 1978–87	
	Percentage	Rank	Percentage	Rank	Percentage	Rank
Australia	31.5	13	37.0	14	2.2	6
Austria	44.8	6	49.9	6	1.8	10
Belgium	44.6	7	49.2	7	1.3	13
Canada	35.7	11	38.5	12	2.8	4
Denmark	48.3	4	63.4	1	2.1	7
Finland	42.1	9	43.6	10	3.7	2
France	44.2	8	50.6	4	1.5	12
FR Germany	45.8	5	45.0	8	1.7	11
Greece	30.0	15	41.3	11	1.2	14
Italy	27.8	16	33.1	13	2.0	8
Japan	23.4	17	30.8	18	4.0	1
Netherlands	48.4	3	50.4	5	1.2	14
Norway	55.6	1	56.8	3	3.5	3
Spain	22.9	18	35.0	15	2.0	8
Sweden	54.2	2	61.9	2	2.0	8
Switzerland	31.9	12	32.6	16	1.9	9
United Kingdom	38.9	10	44.3	9	1.5	12
United States	30.3	14	30.9	17	2.7	5

* Including social security contributions.
† Yearly averages.

Source: CSO (1989).

Table 14.5 Comparative tax burdens and economic growth the Scandinavian countries, where over half of GDP was taken in tax and social security contributions in that year, and below other major competitors such as France and West Germany.

Tax burden and economic growth It can be concluded from the evidence of Table 14.5 that there is little relationship between low tax burdens and faster economic growth. Norway, with the third-highest tax burden in 1986, had an annual average growth rate of 3.5% in the period 1978–87, more than 50% above the OECD average of 2.06% per annum, and ranked as high as third in terms of growth rate. On the other hand, Switzerland, with the third-lowest tax burden, had only the ninth-fastest growth rate of 1.9% in that period, well below the OECD average.

Tax schedules and tax rates We should, however, bear one or two cautionary points in mind before lapsing into complacency! A study by Messere, Owen and Teir (1982) suggests that published *tax schedules* are a greater disincentive to effort than the 'effective tax rates' (i.e. the tax actually paid after all personal and other allowances have been calculated). The argument here is that it is *tax schedules* as shown in Table 14.6, widely publicized in newspapers and annual tax returns, which form the basis for the ordinary citizen's notion of tax burden.

In analysing tax schedules, the Messere study found that a higher proportion of taxpayers (over 95%) paid the basic rate in the UK than elsewhere, and that both the initial and top rates of tax on earned income

Table 14.6 UK income tax schedules 1987/88 and 1990/91

Rate of tax (%)	1987/88 Taxable income (£)	1990/91 Taxable income (£)
25	—	0–20,700
27	0–17,900	—
40	17,901–20,400	Over 20,700
45	20,401–25,400	—
50	25,401–33,300	—
55	33,301–41,200	—
60	Over 41,200	—

Note: Investment income surcharge on unearned income was abolished in March 1984.

were higher in the UK than elsewhere. Nevertheless, the taxpayer on average income in the UK paid a marginal rate no higher than in other OECD countries. The Government is clearly hoping that the reduction in the complex ladder of six different rates to a dual-rate structure since 1988/89 will encourage incentives. These changes, together with alterations in inheritance tax, will mean that the highest rate anywhere in the personal income tax system will be no more than 40%. The Treasury has claimed that the top rates in the UK 'are now broadly in line with the European average' (Hogg 1988). See Figs 14.5 and 14.6.

Fig. 14.5 Income tax before and after the Budget of March 1988

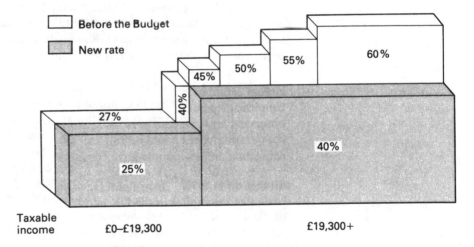

A further reason for taxpayers believing that the burden of taxation is higher than it actually is may arise from a failure to understand the method of collection of income tax. Income tax is *not* collected on the total amount of income. Each individual is granted allowances or exemptions that reduce the total amount of income liable to tax. In 1990/91 each single person was, for example, given an allowance of £3,005; married couples were given an additional allowance of £1,720 over and above the single allowance and pensioners were given even higher allowances. These allowances, plus a few others, are deducted from the total income to produce the *taxable income*. Tax rates of 25% and 40% (on taxable incomes over £20,700) are then applied to this *taxable income*. Further tax relief is also given to mortgage

Fig. 14.6 Comparative
maximum tax rates 1989
Source: Cnossen and
Messere (1989)

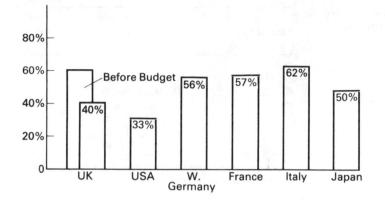

payers. Such mortgage relief on interest payments to banks and building
societies is worth some 15% of the gross monthly payments. Thus the
average burden of taxation for the average taxpayer is considerably below the
25 and 40% seen in the tax schedules.

Overall there appears little evidence that the UK has an excessive burden
of tax in comparison to other countries. Although the proportion of National
Income taken in tax has risen in the UK since the early 1970s, the UK is, in
comparative terms, only a middle-ranked country. However, particular
groups of UK taxpayers at the lowest and highest taxable income scales did
suffer unusually high marginal rates during the 1970s, as some still do in 1989.
This, together with the growing 'visibility' of the income tax and social
security payments system in the UK, may have created the impression of a
comparatively high tax burden, but this impression was, in fact, misleading
for the *average* taxpayer.

The 1988/89 reduction in tax rates and simplifications of the system have
done little to improve the tax burden on low income earners, due in part to
the continued regressiveness of National Insurance contributions (NIC). We
now have a system of direct taxation which starts with a 2% NIC falling on all
income up to £46 a week (even before any income tax is paid). Direct
taxation then rises to 7% on incomes above £46 per week, then to 32% when
income tax starts (25% income tax + 7% NIC). It subsequently increases to
34% at £105 per week (25% income tax and 9% NIC) before *falling* to 25%
at £305 a week and then *rising* again to 40% at some level of income beyond
£420 a week. We thus have the absurdity of a fall in marginal tax rates as
income rises. It is not surprising that there is confusion and disagreement as
to the specific effect of taxes on incentives (see below).

Does the level of taxation matter?

Clarke suggested in 1945, with the support of Keynes, that when taxation of
all kinds was more than 25% of National Income, damaging pressures would
follow. In fact, most industrial countries passed this figure over twenty-five
years ago, with tax ratios of over 40% for some countries in the 1970s, yet
they experienced low inflation and rapid growth of real incomes. However,
perceptions of the benign nature of taxation have begun to change in more
recent years, reverting back to those of Clarke and Keynes. Two of the major

criticisms of a high tax burden relate to its (alleged) erosion of economic incentives and its encouragement of tax avoidance and evasion. We now consider these criticisms.

Impact of taxes on incentives to work, save and take risks

As the reader familiar with indifference curve analysis will know, a higher tax on income will have two effects, which pull in opposite directions. First, an 'income effect', with real income reduced via higher taxes, which means less consumption of all items, including leisure, i.e. more work is performed. Second, a 'substitution effect', with leisure now cheaper via higher taxes, since less real income is now sacrificed for each unit of leisure consumed. The substitution effect leads to cheaper leisure being substituted for work, i.e. less work. On grounds of theory alone we cannot tell which effect will be the stronger, i.e. whether higher taxes on income will raise or lower the time devoted to work rather than leisure (where, of course, the worker has some choice).

The only general conclusions that can be drawn from indifference analysis are the following:

1. Progressive taxes have higher substitution effects, and are therefore likely to cause a greater increase in leisure consumption (i.e. less work) than if the same sum of money were raised via a proportional tax.

2. Taxes on savings create a strong disincentive to future savings via their double-taxation effect. Since saving takes place out of real disposable (net) income, to tax the returns on savings is to impose a further tax on net income.

3. Taxes on investment may discourage high-risk projects. Investment projects involve combinations of risk and yield, those with more risk usually providing more yield. If yields on investment income are more heavily taxed, then this may discourage high-risk investments, such as North Sea oil-prospecting, and encourage low-risk investments (including cash-holding).

Theory can take us little further than this general analysis. Beyond it we must look at actual behaviour to assess the impact of higher taxes on incentives. Empirical studies have taken three forms: (a) controlled experiments, usually observing how selected persons respond to higher benefits (negative taxes); (b) questionnaires based on random samples, and (c) econometric studies using data on how people have responded in the past to tax changes.

Studies up to 1970   Brown and Dawson (1969) conducted an exhaustive review of tax studies in the UK and USA from 1947 to 1968. They concluded that higher taxation had a disincentive effect on work (income < substitution effect) for between 5 and 15% of the population. These were mainly people who had the greatest freedom to vary their hours of employment – those without families, the middle-aged, the wealthy, and rural workers. In contrast, higher taxation had an *incentive* effect on work (income > substitution effect) for a rather smaller percentage of the population, who were characteristically part of large families, young, less well-off, urban dwellers. From a national viewpoint the small *net* disincentive effect on the population of higher taxes was regarded by Brown and Dawson as of little significance; over 70% appeared neutral (income = substitution effect) in their work response to higher taxes.

As regards the UK, two of the most important studies reviewed by Brown and Dawson were those based on questionnaires by Break in 1956 and Fields and Stanbury in 1968. In 1956, Break found a small *net* disincentive effect, with an extra 3% of the population claiming higher taxes to be a disincentive to further work than claimed it to be an incentive. In 1968 Fields and Stanbury updated Break's UK study and found the *net* disincentive effect to have grown to 8% of the population. In both studies the *net* disincentive effect was greater for higher-income groups, as one might expect with these paying higher marginal taxes (stronger substitution effects). This small growth in overall *net* disincentive effect between 1956 and 1968, and its being more pronounced at higher-income levels, was really all the empirical support there was in the UK for those suggesting that higher taxes discouraged work effort.

Studies after 1970   Controlled experiments and questionnaire results after 1970 gave no clearer a picture than those before 1970. If anything, they again pointed to a slight disincentive of higher taxes. For instance, Brown and Levin (see Beenstock 1979) found that an increase in marginal tax rates for 2,000 Scottish workers in 1974 reduced hours worked, at least for higher-income groups. Fiegehen and Reddaway (see Brown 1988) conducted a study on incentives amongst senior managers at board level in 94 companies in 1978, just before the large tax cuts introduced by the (then) newly elected Conservative Government a year or so later. Similarly to Break, and Fields and Stanbury (see above), they showed that 12% of managers reported an incentive effect of high taxation on hours of work, while an equal percentage reported a disincentive effect. The most common response from 41% was 'no reply or don't know'. Fiegehen and Reddaway concluded: 'it is clear that, in total, any disincentive effects that operated on senior managers had a minimal impact on the activities of British industry'. Such studies were hardly a basis for advocating that tax *cuts* would lead to an upsurge in work effort! More promising material for such an argument came from the work of Dilnot & Kell (1988) who assessed the incentive effects of top-rate tax cuts between 1978, when the highest rate of income tax in the UK was 98%, and 1988, when the top rate was 40%. Their conclusion was that the top-rate tax cuts were consistent with modest incentive effect. Still more promising material for such arguments came from the work of Professor Art Laffer.

The Laffer curve   Professor Laffer derived a relationship between tax revenue and tax rates of the form shown in Fig. 14.7. The curve was the result of econometric techniques, through which a 'least squares line'[3] was fitted to past US observations of tax revenue and tax rate. The dotted line indicates the extension of the fitted relationship (continuous line), as there will tend to be zero tax revenue at both 0 and 100% tax rates. Tax revenue = tax rate × output (income), so that a 0% tax rate yields zero tax revenue, whatever the level of output. A 100% tax rate is assumed to discourage all output, except that for subsistence, again yielding zero tax revenue. Tax revenue must reach a maximum at some intermediate tax rate between these extremes.

Fig. 14.7 The 'Laffer' curve

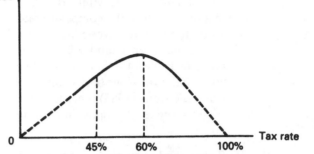

The London Business School (Beenstock 1979) has estimated a Laffer curve for the UK using past data. Tax revenue was found to reach a peak at around a 60% 'composite tax rate', i.e. one which includes both direct and indirect taxes, as well as various social security payments, all expressed as a percentage of GDP. If the tax rate rises above 60% then the disincentive effect on output is so strong (i.e. output falls so much) that tax revenue (tax rate × output) actually falls, despite the higher tax rate. The Laffer curve in fact begins to flatten out at around a 45% composite tax rate. In other words, as tax rate rises above 45%, the disincentive effect on output is strong enough to mean that little extra tax revenue results. Econometric studies of this type have given support to those in favour of limiting overall rates of tax. It is interesting to note that shortly after this study, the top rate of tax on earned income in the UK was indeed reduced from 83% to 60%.[4]

The reduction in the top income tax rate to 40% in 1988/89 was inspired by the Laffer curve and supply-side economics. The Chancellor of the Exchequer believed that the tax cuts would increase revenue. He based his tax cuts on American research by Lindsey that concluded that reductions in the top tax rates to the American Government in 1981/82 were costless as the top 170,000 taxpayers ended up paying $26.6bn under new legislation instead of $26bn under the old. Lindsey argued that the tax cuts were not only incentive creating but they also increased the *cost of tax avoidance*.

This research has been criticized partly because it is American evidence and partly because the American rates were slashed by 23% over the three years with the top personal rate being reduced from 70 to 50% whilst the UK moved from 60 to 40% in just one year. Finally, Lindsey and other tax experts have consistently argued that as tax rates are cut, economic efficiency is raised by reducing tax breaks and shelters at the same time. This was done to only a very limited extent in the UK in 1988/89 (Huhne 1988). However fresh evidence on the impact of cuts in high rates of British taxation has been provided by Minford and Ashton (see Brown 1988). The latter study concludes that the cut in the higher British tax rates to 40% will increase hours worked by 8%.

In summary, those who advocate 'supply side economics', with tax reduction a key instrument for improving economic incentives, leading to an upsurge of productive activity, receive limited support from empirical studies. Only a small net disincentive effect has been found from studies using questionnaires, such as those by Break and Stanbury. On the other hand, the Laffer curve constructed for the UK by the London Business School, and work by Minford in the UK and Lindsey in the US, do indicate that *reductions* in the composite rate of tax below 60% and down as far as around 45%, have strong incentive effects on output – the converse of *rises* in tax rate between 45 and 60% having strong disincentive effects. However, we noted in Table 14.4 that the UK composite tax rate is currently less than 40%, and reductions below this level receive little support from econometric studies. Owens (1985) regarded the empirical evidence to be insufficient to support a general proposition that the tax system is undermining the work effort.

Poverty and unemployment traps   One area where the facts do strongly suggest that the current level and type of taxation may have eroded incentives, concerns the 'poverty' and 'unemployment' traps. The families in these traps are enmeshed in a web of overlapping tax schedules and benefit thresholds, developed and administered by two separate departments (Department of Health and Social Security and the Treasury) with differing objectives in mind.

Table 14.7 How a couple with two children are affected by taxes and benefits in the current system (rent £30, rates £12 per week)

	The poverty trap, January 1989 (pounds per week)			
Gross earnings	50.00	100.00	150.00	200.00
Plus: Child benefit	14.50	14.50	14.50	14.50
Family credit	49.55	24.18	2.48	0.00
Housing benefit	25.07	12.47	4.57	0.00
Less: Income tax	0.00	5.31	17.81	30.31
National Insurance	2.50	7.00	13.50	18.00
Net income	136.62	138.84	140.24	166.19

Note: Calculations are for married men with two children aged 10 and 13, rent of £30 a week, and rates of £12 a week.

Source: Kay, J. and King, M. (1990).

The low-paid worker in the 'poverty trap' may gain nothing, or even lose, from an increase in earnings, when these cause benefits to be lost and tax to be paid. For example, a family with two children and with a gross income of £150 per week could actually be very little better off than one with only £50 per week – an implicit marginal tax rate over this range of close to 100%.

Before 1988 the implicit tax rates associated with the poverty trap were, in some cases, greater than 100%. It is now normally impossible for the rate to exceed 100%. This is because from 1988 benefits are related to net income after tax, and previous benefits paid are now taken into account. Although the reform eliminated the possibility of tax rates in excess of 100%, it did not prevent the situation depicted in Table 14.7 with rates of close to 100% over quite long ranges at low levels of income. The number of families where the head of household faced an implicit marginal tax rate greater than 70% in fact doubled after 1988 to over half a million.

The 'unemployment trap' occurs when people find they are no better off when the breadwinner is in employment than when out of employment. Table 14.8 shows that the household is only slightly worse off out of work than it would have been in work. The *replacement rate* is shown as 92%; this rate is the proportion of your net income that will be 'replaced' by the benefit system if you lose your job (or, for someone already out of work, the ratio of current income to expected net wage).

Table 14.8 The unemployment trap: net income of a married man with two children (rent £30, rates £12 per week)

In work	(£)	Out of work	(£)
Gross income	150.00	Unemployment benefit	52.95
Child benefit	14.50	Child benefit	14.50
Housing benefit	4.57	Housing benefit	0.00
Family credit	2.48	Income support	56.60
		Other benefits	4.50
Income tax	(17.81)		
National Insurance	(13.50)		
Net income	140.23	Net income	128.55

$$\text{Replacement rate} = \frac{128.55}{140.23} = 92\%$$

Note: Calculations are for a married man with two children aged 10 and 13, rent of £30 a week, and rates of £12 a week as at January 1989.

Source: Kay, J. and King, M. (1990).

Both poverty and unemployment traps may provide a disincentive to work as those caught within them find it difficult, or even impossible, to improve their position through their own efforts. They are, in effect, paying exceptionally high net marginal rates of tax (close to 100% in our poverty trap example). In 1990/91 the highest marginal rate of tax faced by recipients of social security benefits was still around 97%.

Impact of taxes on avoidance and evasion

Tax avoidance is legal; tax evasion is illegal – involving concealment in one form or another, and therefore fraud.

The black economy   The Inland Revenue in 1982 estimated that tax evasion was equal to between 6 and 8% of National Income in the UK – often called the 'black economy'. There is, however, considerable disagreement as to the size of the black economy. Estimates vary from the 2 or 3% estimated by the Institute of Fiscal Studies to the 14.5% estimated by researchers at Liverpool University. One way in which the black economy can be estimated is through the difference between National Income when measured by the income method, and when measured by the expenditure method. Apart from errors and omissions these are defined in the National Accounts in such a way that they come to the same value. If, however, people receive income and do not declare it in tax returns, it will not appear on the income side, though expenditure will increase as the unrecorded income is spent on goods and services. In recent years the 'income' valuation – based on tax returns – has fallen short of the 'expenditure' valuation by progressively larger amounts.

Clearly the black economy is growing and its size is significant. Johnson (1982) suggests that there may be as many as 1.6 million workers deriving unrecorded full-time income. The black economy causes a shortfall in government revenue, and understates estimates of economic growth. It is important, therefore, to know why the black economy has grown. One argument is that the growing burden of taxation has tempted more and more people to disregard the law by not declaring taxable income.

Direct vs indirect taxes

In Fig. 14.4 above we observed a switch from direct to indirect taxation since the late 1970s. We noted that this switch entailed a move towards a more regressive system of taxation, i.e. one which takes a smaller *proportion* of higher incomes. This must follow since we move away from direct taxes which we saw to be progressive, towards indirect taxes, which at best are proportional (VAT), and more usually are regressive (domestic rates – now the community charge or uniform business rate, excise duties, import duties, etc.). It might be useful to consider in *more general terms* the advantages and disadvantages of direct and indirect systems of taxation. For convenience we shall compare the systems under four main headings, with indirect taxes considered first in each case.

Macroeconomic management

Indirect taxes can be varied more quickly and easily, taking more immediate effect, than can direct taxes. Since the Finance Act of 1961, the Chancellor of the Exchequer has had the power (via 'the regulator') to vary the rates of indirect taxation at any time between Budgets. Excise and import duties can be varied by up to 10%, and VAT by up to 25% (i.e. between 11.25 and 18.75% for a 15% rate of VAT). In contrast, direct taxes can only be changed at Budget time. In the case of income tax, any change involves time-consuming revisions to PAYE codings. For these reasons, indirect taxes are usually regarded as a more flexible instrument of macroeconomic policy.

Economic incentives

We have already seen how, in both theory and practice, direct taxes on income affect incentives to work. We found that neither in theory nor in practice need the *net* effect be one of disincentive. Nevertheless, it is often argued that if the *same sum* were derived from indirect taxation, then any net disincentive effect that did occur would be that much smaller. In particular, it is often said that indirect taxes are less visible (than direct), being to some extent hidden in the quoted price of the good. However, Stanlake (1982) counters this, pointing to survey evidence which suggests that consumers are well aware of the impact of indirect taxes on the price level. Let us look in more detail at the direct vs indirect argument, first in relation to incentives to work and second in relation to incentives to save and take risks.

Work effort   In terms of effects on the supply of work effort, a case against the current system of direct taxes and in favour of a switch towards indirect taxes might be made in the *specific* cases of poverty and unemployment traps.

However, no *general* case can be made for such a switch. In fact, both income and substitution effects of a rise in indirect taxes are in the same direction as those for a rise in direct taxes. By raising the prices of goods, higher indirect taxes also reduce real income, and at the same time reduce the cost of leisure in terms of goods forgone. In other words, the income and substitution effects we considered above apply to higher indirect taxes as well as to higher direct taxes. Whether the *magnitude* of the income and substitution effects will be the same for indirect as for direct taxes is quite another matter. It will partly depend upon which items are taxed. If indirect taxes are levied on goods with highly inelastic demand curves, then the indirect taxes will be largely passed on to consumers as higher prices. Both income and substitution effects will then be substantial in magnitude. Of course the converse also applies – if the indirect taxes are levied on goods with elastic demand curves, both income and substitution effects will be small. We can make no general claim for 'superiority' of either type of tax with regard to work incentives.

Saving and risk-taking   With regard to incentives for saving, indirect taxes have the advantage of avoiding the 'double-taxation effect' imposed by direct income taxes. Saving takes place out of net income, i.e. income that has already been taxed. To tax the return on savings, via a tax on investment income (e.g. dividends), is to impose a type of double taxation on that income, an obvious disincentive to saving. This is, however, a weak argument in support of indirect taxes as it is quite possible to devise a system of direct taxation that avoids double taxation (as currently with tax exemptions for returns on Post Office Savings and National Savings).

The argument that indirect taxes are to be preferred because they avoid the discrimination against risky investments of a direct tax system can also be rebutted. Risky investments do usually have higher yields, and do therefore pay more direct tax than less risky investments. However, such discrimination could be reduced, perhaps by raising the value of allowances (e.g. on exploration costs, etc.) that can be set against tax.

In terms of incentives, then, there is no *general* case to be made for or against one or other types of tax system. If we are to be more specific, we must compare one *particular* type of indirect tax system with one *particular* type of direct tax system.

Economic welfare

It is sometimes argued that indirect taxes are, in welfare terms, preferable to direct taxes, as they leave the taxpayer free to make a choice. The individual can, for instance, avoid the tax by choosing not to consume the taxed commodity. Although this 'voluntary' aspect of indirect taxes may apply to a particular individual and a particular tax, it cannot apply to all individuals and all taxes. In other words, indirect taxes cannot be 'voluntary' for the community as a whole. If a chancellor is to raise a given sum through a system of indirect taxes, individual choices not to consume taxed items must, if widespread, be countered either by raising rates of tax or by extending the range of goods and services taxed.

Another argument used to support indirect taxes on welfare grounds is that they can be used to combat 'externalities'. In Chapter 8 we noted that an externality occurs where private and social costs diverge. Where private costs of production are below social costs, an indirect tax could be imposed, or increased, so that price is raised to reflect the true social costs of production. Taxes on alcohol and tobacco could be justified on these grounds. By discriminating between different goods and services, indirect taxes can help reallocate resources in a way that raises economic welfare for society as a whole.

On the other hand, indirect taxes have also been criticized on welfare grounds for being regressive, the element of indirect tax in commodity price taking a higher proportion of the income from lower-paid groups. Nor is it easy to correct for this. It would be impossible administratively to place a higher tax on a given item for those with higher incomes although one could impose indirect taxes mainly on the goods and services consumed by higher-income groups, and perhaps at higher rates.

In terms of economic welfare, as in terms of economic incentives, the picture is again unclear. A case can be made with some conviction both for and against each type of tax.

Administrative costs

Indirect taxes are often easy and cheap to administer. They are paid by manufacturers and traders, which are obviously fewer in number than the total of individuals paying income tax. This makes indirect taxes, such as excise and import duties, much cheaper to collect than direct taxes, though the difference is less marked for VAT, which requires the authorities to deal with a large number of mainly small traders.

Even if indirect taxes do impose smaller administrative costs than direct taxes for a given revenue yield, not too much should be made of this. It is, for instance, always possible to reform the system of PAYE and reduce administrative costs. The Inland Revenue is, in fact, considering a change from PAYE to an American system of income tax, with the obligation on taxpayers themselves to estimate and forward tax, subject to random checks. Also, the computerization of Inland Revenue operations may, by 1990, significantly reduce the administrative costs associated with the collection of direct taxes.

In summary, there is no clear case for one type of tax system compared to another. The macroeconomic management and administrative cost grounds may appear to favour indirect taxes, though the comparison is only with the *current* system of direct taxation. That system can, of course, be changed to accommodate criticisms along these lines. On perhaps the more important grounds of economic incentives and economic welfare the case is very mixed, with arguments for and against each type of tax finely balanced. To be more specific we must compare the particular and detailed systems proposed for each type of tax.

Tax and social security reform

The subject of tax reform is a topic in its own right and can only be touched upon here. Tax reform had been low on the political agenda before 1965, with the basic structure of taxes remaining unchanged for decades. Since then there have been more new taxes introduced than in any other equivalent peacetime period. Changes have included the introduction and repeal of selective employment tax; VAT replacing purchase tax; corporation tax replacing profits tax; the amalgamation of surtax and income tax; new taxes such as gambling and betting duties, and capital gains tax; and the replacement of estate duty first by capital transfer tax and subsequently by an inheritance tax.

Community charge and uniform business rate

Recently Conservative governments have been very active in the field of tax reform. Nigel Lawson, the Chancellor of the Exchequer in 1988, stated that his guiding principles were to reduce tax rates, abolish tax breaks, simplify the tax system and end injustice. To this end the controversial community charge (poll tax) was introduced to replace 'inequitable' local authority rates paid by 18 million *households* (Muellbauer 1987). In theory this new tax is paid (in full, or at 20% of full rate) by all 35 million adults (with a few exceptions like convicted prisoners) and therefore it is argued that this will encourage a democratic interest in local authority income and expenditure plans. This tax started in Scotland in April 1989 and was introduced in the rest of England and Wales in 1990. Businesses are treated differently, however. They are still dealt with under the existing rating system but their rateable poundage will be set by the central government instead of by local authorities. There is *one uniform business rate* (UBR) applying across the whole country. This was set at 34.8 pence per pound in England in 1990, and 36.8 pence per pound in Wales. However rateable values have been uprated to 1988 prices (instead of the 1973 property valuation prices previously existing), hardly a popular move amongst many firms which have faced substantial rate rises. To soften the financial impact of this increased burden the uniform business rate will be phased in over a five year period, with a maximum increase of 20% per annum plus inflation. Although local authorities will collect UBR, they must pay receipts into a central fund and, as we have seen, it is central government that sets the rate. This is clearly a further curbing of local authority financial control.

The unpopularity of the community charge has little to do with its shortcomings. It is unpopular because most people face an increase in their local tax bill. These facts emerge in an Institute of Fiscal Studies report (Ridge M. & Smith S. 1990). The estimated average cost of administering the charge will more than double, from 2 to 4% of the yield. The collection costs of most major taxes range from 0.5% to 2% of the yield, so the community charge will be an expensive way of raising revenue. Many of these increased costs are associated with the registration of community charge payers and the problems of chasing non-payers. The previous tax, namely rates, had registered *property* (which stayed fixed) whilst the new tax is on *people* (who move around). In 1990 the average poll tax bill was some £362; this was 35% above the average English *rate* bill of £269 per adult in 1989/90. The reason for this rise is complex. Nearly half of local authority spending is met from centrally provided grants which broadly reflect the 'needs' of the local authority area – the number of schoolchildren, miles of roads that must be maintained, and so on. Central government *obliges* each local authority to meet these needs, which are paid for out of the grant plus its share of the income from the uniform business rate plus the recommended community charge: this latter is an amount that the government believes the local authority can justifiably spend. The Government also *permits* them to provide extra services (which may be anything from municipal swimming pools to gay counselling); these may be paid for out of extra money raised by imposing a higher community charge.

The problem, of course, is that 'needs' are political footballs. What seems like a barely acceptable standard of care to a Labour councillor may look like profligate extravagance to a Conservative councillor. What was unacceptable about the rates system was that local taxpayers, including local businesses (which on average paid half the locally borne costs) had little voting power. Thus councils could 'bribe' voters by providing extra services which, in some cases, were largely paid for by businesses. The introduction of the uniform business rate has removed the latter problem, because the tax rate is set by central government, though there are other problems for local business arising from the revaluation of property values. The impact of the uniform business rate – generally accepted as sensible by experts – has been to reduce the proportion of local spending that is paid for out of locally determined taxes.

The main consequence of these complex changes is to increase the 'gearing' impact of extra local authority expenditure. Thus every percentage increase in local authority spending pushes up total taxes more than in proportion. A 1% increase in spending means that taxes, now borne entirely by voting residents, rise by 4%. So community charges in1990/91 are 30% higher because council spending is some 7–8% higher then 'needs'. In an attempt to reduce its unpopularity over the tax, the Government has attempted to rate-cap (hold down) expenditure of some high spending authorities. Other reforms to the community charge are being floated, including income banding and taking education out of local authority budgets, but the tax remains unpopular. Alternatives to the community charge have been suggested by the Labour party (a 'roof' tax) and by the Liberal Democrats (a local income tax), but these also create 'problems' of their own. Other suggestions, such as local sales tax and a return to a schedule. A type of income tax on the notional rental value of owner occupation, are considered by Johnson (1990).

Other tax changes

Other changes that have been introduced have been the abolition of unnecessary taxes, the encouragement of savings and share ownership (Treasury 1990), the reduction of tax rates with the pledge that the Government intends to aim for a 20% basic rate, the effective amalgamation of income tax and capital gains tax rates at 25% to encourage fiscal neutrality and the introduction of independent taxation for married couples. On 6 April 1990, independent taxation came into force. This measure gave married women independent status as taxpayers, that is, they are now in control of their own tax affairs. Since 1805, husbands had been legally responsible for a married couple's tax affairs and for paying any tax on their joint incomes. This usually had the effect of raising tax on the low income of wives as the husband and wife's incomes were combined, or of increasing the total tax burden on couples when their joint incomes were pushed into higher tax brackets. All individuals now receive a full single allowance whilst, in addition, married couples receive a further allowance. A man may be able to transfer any unused portion of this allowance to his spouse. The effect of independent taxation has generally been to reduce the burden of taxation on women. This tax law, however, had important implications for the savings of married women which was solved by abolishing the CRT (Composite Rate Tax).

CRT was a special rate of tax charged on interest paid by building societies, banks and some other financial institutions. It could not be repaid to savers who were not liable to tax. Therefore, since the introduction of independent taxation, some 14 million people who should not have been paying tax were drawn into the tax net. These were mostly pensioners, married women and children. From April 1991 CRT will be abolished and instead basic rate tax will be deducted from interest payments made by the financial institutions to depositors. Non-taxpayers will, on completion of a certificate, be able to receive interest gross, without any tax deduction.

In addition to these changes, the Government published a White Paper in December 1985 containing the most radical proposals for reforming the social security system for more than forty years. The measures took effect in April 1988 and fall into five categories: pensions; a new income support benefit; cuts and changes in housing benefit; a new family credit system; and the social fund.

The State Earnings Related Pensions (SERPS) was cut rather than abolished, with SERPS no longer payable on the *best twenty* years of a person's life but on *lifetime* earnings, i.e. forty-five years for men and forty years for women. There are also incentives to encourage a switch to private pensions – with an extra 2% National Insurance rebate to any company or individual who contracts out of SERPS between 1988 and 1993.

Supplementary pension and supplementary benefit and heating allowances have been abolished and replaced by a new system of income support benefit, paid at three basic rates.

As regards housing benefit, from 1988 all claimants to social security have had to pay 20% of their community charge, instead of a zero contribution as previously. *Tenants* were further hit by a 60% contribution to rents, making 80% in all. Effectively *tenants* faced a reduction of 80p in the pound on previous housing benefits from 1988 onwards.

A new family credit system replaced family income supplement, which was abolished in April 1988. The maximum credit for adults, in 1986 values, is £29.85 a week, plus amounts varying from £5.30 for each child under 11 to £19.20 for a dependent young person over 18. As earnings rise, the amount payable is withdrawn at the rate of 70p in the pound until the benefit is exhausted. The credit will not be paid to any family with more than £6,000 in savings.

Finally, a social fund was established, from which a new maternity grant will be paid to claimants on income support and family credit, and a funeral grant for the poor. Other payments and loans will be discretionary, as with loans for furniture and bedding in situations of financial hardship.

One of the intentions behind reform of the social security system was to reduce the disincentives to work widely recognized as inherent in the 'poverty' and 'unemployment' traps. However, because the proposals were also meant to be revenue-neutral, the IFS estimated that the net effect of the 1988 reforms was to *increase* effective marginal tax rates for most groups. Instead of only 2.5% of taxpayers losing between 60 and 100% of any increase in earnings in higher taxes or withdrawn benefits as at present, the IFS estimated that the figure would rise to 5.5% (1.5 million persons). Against this there was to be help for the 0.43% (100,000 persons) who previously paid effective marginal tax rates in excess of 100%. The *top* effective marginal rate was reduced from 105% under the previous system to around 96.4%.

The April 1988 reforms were also intended to improve the take-up of social security benefits and to target benefits more efficiently. Oppenheim (1990), whilst acknowledging that some people are better off with incomes higher by nearly a third in real terms, is concerned that some social security claimants have suffered badly under the new system. She asserts that even among families with children (the group targeted for extra help) many families have lost small amounts in real terms. The biggest losers, however, are single householders under 25 and people with disabilities. The Government, on the other hand, pointing to the general rise in the standard of living of all groups, would argue that targetting never meant that all groups would and should benefit from its changes.

Tax and social security reform has been introduced for a variety of reasons, not just that of improving incentives. It has often reflected more general objectives, such as simplicity, compatibility and equity. Problems abound for the would-be tax reformer as regards the first two of these objectives. There is limited room for manœuvre in the present fiscal system since any changes have to be grafted on to an existing system through complicated transitional arrangements. The problems in modifying the system are increased by the fact that an alteration in one tax has implications for others. Taxes have to be considered in groups, rather than individually. The Meade Committee (1978) went as far as advocating that the whole system be reformed. The broad lines of that reform would be to replace (direct) taxes on income and capital by (indirect) taxes on expenditure. In practice, however, piecemeal reform is the order of the day, each change adding significantly to overall administrative costs.[5]

From the point of view of equity, those in the poverty or unemployment traps could be helped by the introduction of increased welfare expenditure or a tax credit scheme, the family credit system proposed in the December 1985 White Paper being a significant step in the direction of tax credits. The idea behind the tax credit scheme is to charge tax on the whole of a person's income, but then to reduce the resulting tax liability by a series of tax credits related to circumstance (number of children, unemployment, etc.). If the credit were in excess of the tax liability, then the difference would actually be *added* to the pay packet or pension. This possibility of actually receiving income from the Exchequer is reflected in the alternative title of the tax credit scheme, namely 'negative income tax'. Equity could be further improved by treating capital gains as income and taxing at the same rate as for income, or by ensuring that those in the cash economy are taxed on *all* receipts, including fringe benefits.

Reducing the total tax burden, or lowering marginal tax rates in order to raise incentives,[6] may involve more fundamental changes, such as ending tax allowances. This would widen the tax base, so that a given total tax take could be achieved at lower rates. A similar widening of the tax base could be made by introducing new taxes such as taxes on windfall gambling gains or drawing zero-rated items into VAT. Fundamental alterations in tax burden could, however, only occur if there was less *need* for total tax revenue, as by reducing the size of the Welfare State or increasing user charges.

Conclusion

The UK tax system is broadly proportional, except for the bottom one-third of households by income, for whom it is mildly progressive. Direct taxes are, as a group, *progressive* in the UK, taking a larger proportion of the income of richer households. Indirect taxes are, as a group, *regressive*, though this is not the case for all indirect taxes. After the bottom one-fifth of income earners, VAT is broadly proportional. The movement towards indirect taxation has therefore made the UK tax system less progressive than it would otherwise have been. Although the proportion of National Income taken in tax has risen, the UK is *not* overtaxed compared to other countries. Neither does higher tax necessarily mean lower economic growth. Certainly the empirical case for higher taxes being a disincentive to effort and output is rather flimsy, whether from questionnaire or econometric study. There can be no general presumption in favour of either indirect or direct taxation, when we assess each system in terms of macromanagement, economic incentives, economic welfare and administrative costs.

Notes

1. Which it does in the UK, e.g. 25% on taxable income up to £20,700 in 1990/91, 40% on higher income.
2. The average rate is total tax paid, divided by total income.
3. That is, that line which minimizes the sum of squared deviations from the line.
4. Though the Laffer curve strictly refers only to *overall* tax level, and not that for any particular tax.
5. In the 1970s Inland Revenue staff increased by 20,000 (to 80,000) to cope with reforms, and the cost of collection rose from £1.56 to £1.80 per £100 of tax revenue. This is one of the arguments behind the suggestion that self-assessment should replace PAYE.
6. Dilnot of the IFS has estimated that the Government took 57p out of every marginal pound earned in the mid-1980s.

References and further reading

Atkinson, A. B. (1979) A tax strategy for the 1980s, *New Society*, **48**, 873, 28 June.
Beenstock, M. (1979) Taxation and incentives in the UK, *Lloyds Bank Review*, 134, Oct.

Brown, C. (1988) Will the 1988 income tax cuts either increase work incentives or raise more revenue? *Fiscal Studies*, **9**, 4.

Brown, C. V. and **Dawson, D. A.** (1969) *Personal Taxation, Incentives and Tax Reforms*. Political and Economic Planning (PEP).

Cnossen, S. and **Messere, K.** (1989) Survey and evaluation of personal income tax systems in OECD member countries. ISPE mimeo.

Crawford, M. and **Dawson, D.** (1982) Are rates the right tax for local government?, *Lloyds Bank Review*, 145, July.

CSO (1990) The effects of taxes and benefits on household income, *Economic Trends*, 439, May.

CSO *Financial Statistics* (various).

CSO *National Income and Expenditure* (various).

Dilnot, A. W., **Kay, J. A.** and **Morris, N.** (1984) *The Reform of Social Security*. Clarendon Press.

Dilnot, A. and **Kell, M.** (1988) Top-rate tax cuts and incentives: some empirical evidence, *Fiscal Studies*, **9**, 4.

Fry, V. and **Stark, G.** (1987) The take-up of supplementary benefit: gaps in the 'safety network', *Fiscal Studies*, **8**, 4, November.

Hogg, S. (1988) Chancellor slashes top income tax rates to 40%, *The Independent*, 16 March.

House of Commons (1990) Low Income Statistics, Social Services Committee, Fourth Report, House of Commons.

Huhne, C. (1988) Do tax cuts for the rich really raise revenue for the country? *Guardian*, 17 March.

Ison, S. (1990) Uniform Business Rate, *British Economic Survey*, **19**, 2, Spring.

Johnson, C. (1982) Light on the black economy, *Lloyds Bank Economic Bulletin*, 38, Feb.

Johnson, C. (1990) Pros and cons of poll tax, *Lloyds Bank Economic Bulletin*, 137, May.

Kay, J. and **King, M.** (1990) *The British Tax System*, OUP.

Meade, J. E. (1978) *The Structure and Reform of Direct Taxation*. IFS, Allen and Unwin.

Messere, K., **Owen, J.** and **Teir, G.** (1982) Tax trends and impact of taxes on different income groups, *The OECD Observer*, 25 Jan.

Muellbauer, J. (1987) The community charge, rates and tax reform, *Lloyds Bank Review*, 166, Oct.

Oppenheim, C. (1990) *Holes in the Safety Net: Falling Standards for People in Poverty*, Child Poverty Action Group.

Owens, J. (1985) Direct tax burdens: an international comparison, *The OECD Observer*, **133**, March.

Ridge, M. and **Smith, S.** (1990) Local Government Finance: the 1990 Reforms, IFS Commentary No. 22.

Stanlake, G. F. (1982) *Public Finance*. Longman Economic Studies, Longman.

Treasury (1985) *Economic Progress Report*, 176, March–April, HMSO.

Treasury (1988) *The Red Book*, 15 March.

Treasury (1990) *Economic Progress Report*, 207, The Budget and savings, April, HMSO.

The UK financial system

One of the marks of a highly developed economy is the existence of a sophisticated financial system. Any financial system exists to mediate between those who wish to lend money and those who wish to borrow it. Mediation is necessary because lenders and borrowers have different needs. Lenders want low-risk, high-return outlets for their money. They want to be able to lend without having to search for a suitable borrower, and to get their money back quickly if their own need for liquidity changes. Borrowers, on the other hand, often need to borrow money for longer periods of time, as in the case of industrial investment or house purchase. They need to be able to obtain funds quickly and easily and in return they are willing to issue IOUs such as bills or bonds which are, in effect, claims against themselves. These pieces of paper can be sold by those who hold them (i.e. lenders) on financial markets such as the Stock Exchange or the discount market if money is needed before the loan is due to be repaid. The buyers of these claims are often the financial institutions, who buy them in order to hold them as assets.

Fig. 15.1 Financial Intermediation

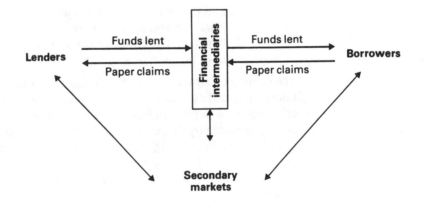

The whole process of matching the needs of lenders and borrowers is known as 'financial intermediation', and the institutions which play a part in this process are known as 'financial intermediaries' (see Fig. 15.1). Their main function is to channel funds from those willing to lend to those willing to borrow, given that lenders and borrowers often have very different needs. Paper claims can be generated either by (a) the financial intermediary issuing a claim to the lender – for instance, a certificate of deposit, or (b) the borrower issuing a claim to the financial intermediary – for instance, a bond or a share. As we shall see, these claims are then traded on the 'secondary' market, the market for already existing securities.

Role of financial institutions

Financial institutions match the needs of lenders and borrowers in many different ways:

1. They alleviate market imperfections caused by a lack of information in the market for loans and therefore reduce information and search costs (e.g. merchant banks).

2. They provide economies of scale in lending transactions, taking the deposits of small lenders and allocating them to large-scale borrowers. This reduces transaction costs (e.g. building societies).

3. They spread the risks of lending by pooling funds and allocating them over a wide range of depositors (e.g. investment trusts).

4. They bridge the gap between the desire of lenders to be able to get their money back quickly, and the desire of borrowers to borrow for a long period. The scale of their operations and their expertise enable them to provide lenders with easily marketable paper claims, denominated in small units and with relatively low yield, whilst at the same time lending to borrowers on a long-term high-yield basis (e.g. unit trusts).

5. They take advantage of people's dislike of uncertainty by providing insurance services. People will be willing to insure (effectively saving money which they may never get back) against contingencies which, if they occurred, would entail a drastic reduction in their standard of living. Insurance companies use people's savings to acquire a range or portfolio of assets which they then manage in such a way as to make profit, whilst at the same time providing cover against contingencies.

6. They can minimize uncertainty about the future by converting present income into claims on future income. Although this is to some extent true of all financial intermediation, it is particularly relevant to the operations of pension funds.

The common characteristics of all financial intermediaries are therefore as follows. First, they take money from those who save, whether it be in exchange for a deposit or in exchange for an asset. Second, they lend the money provided by those savers to borrowers, who may issue a paper asset in return. Third, in exchange for such lending they acquire a portfolio of paper assets (claims on borrowers) which they 'manage' by buying and selling them on asset markets in order to yield a profit for themselves.

The UK financial system

We therefore have three kinds of operator in the UK financial system:

1. Lenders and borrowers – persons, companies, government.

2. Financial institutions – which act as intermediaries between lenders and borrowers, and manage their own asset portfolios.

3. Markets – where money is lent and borrowed, and paper assets are bought and sold. These include the discount or bill market (the traditional London money market), the newer or parallel money markets, the gilt-edged market, and the Stock Exchange.

We shall deal in turn with financial institutions and financial markets. However, we begin by discussing financial assets.

Financial assets

Financial assets are issued by borrowers and traded by financial institutions who hold them. These assets are of two basic kinds – bills and bonds, and equities (shares). A bond is an asset signifying that a loan has been made for a fixed length of time. The borrower – usually the Government – undertakes to redeem the bond at 'par value' (£100) on a certain date, and to pay the bondholder an annual fixed sum (coupon rate) in interest each year. The bondholder will have bought the bond at a price below par value, and the annual fixed interest payment will represent a yield on his investment which will be more attractive the lower the price he originally paid. For instance, if 5% Treasury stock can be bought on the market at £50, the buyer receives £5 a year from the Government. This will give him a yield of 10% on his investment of £50. In addition he will make a further gain of £50 when the bond is redeemed by the Government at £100.

Bills are ninety-one-day assets issued by companies and the Government. The holder (i.e. whoever has lent the money) can have the bill discounted in the bill market – in other words, he can get his money back before the ninety-one days are up. The yield to the purchaser then depends on the difference between the price he paid for the bill and its redemption value.

Equities (or shares) are non-redeemable assets issued by companies. They may be ordinary or preference shares. Investors in ordinary shares may receive dividends if companies choose to pay them, but their major advantage as an asset lies in the possibility of capital appreciation. In the case of preference shares the company pays a fixed annual sum to the shareholder, and there is also the possibility of capital appreciation when the share is sold.

If financial assets were *perfect substitutes* for one another, the yields on each would be identical. Any higher yield on one type of asset would cause financial institutions to adjust their 'portfolios' in favour of that asset. The higher demand would raise the market price of the asset and thereby reduce the yield. Any variation in yields therefore represents a lack of perfect substitutability between such assets. That there is such variation is clear from Table 15.1.

Assets are imperfect substitutes because they possess different characteristics with respect to liquidity, marketability and profitability. A liquid asset is one which can be transformed into cash quickly and without loss of value. The more distant the maturity date, the less liquid is the asset likely to be. Marketability varies between assets; some assets are easily realizable, but some – such as perhaps the shares of small companies – may not find ready buyers. Profitability, too, varies between the certain but perhaps unexciting rate of return paid by fixed interest securities to the more uncertain possibility of large gains to be made on share prices. Portfolio choice will depend on how individual investors evaluate the alternatives open to them, as well as on their expectations of future interest rate movements. Yields in general will tend to be higher for longer-term investments, because lenders require to be compensated for giving up their money for long periods of time. However, if investors expect short-term interest rates to fall in the

284   *The UK financial system*

Table 15.1 Percentage
security yields, 29 Jan. 1990

Treasury bills	14.6
Commercial bills	
Prime bank bills	14.5
Trade bills	15.2
Certificates of deposit	15.0–15.2
Short-dated stock (up to 5 years)	11.6
Medium-dated stock (up to 10 years)	10.9
Long-dated stock	10.3
Debentures	12.4
Industrial ordinary shares	10.1
Base rate	15.0
Call money	14.8
Inter-bank overnight	14.8–14.9
Inter-bank 3-month	15.1–15.2

Source: CSO (1990a).

future they will wish to buy long-dated bonds today, thereby locking themselves into today's long rates. This will have the effect of driving up the price of long bonds, making their yield lower than normal, and perhaps even lower than short-term yields (see Table 15.1, short and medium-dated stock). Fig. 15.2(a) shows how this situation was the case in March 1990. Here the yield curve *falls* as the maturity date *rises*, unlike the 'normal' yield curve in Fig. 15.2(b).

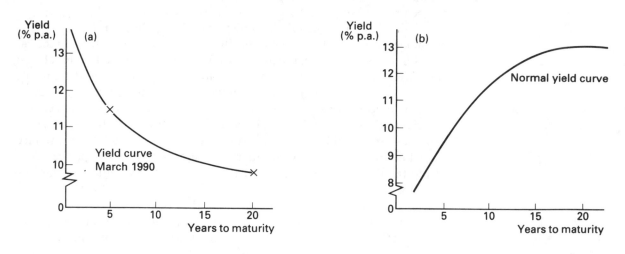

Fig. 15.2 (a) Yield curve for British Government stocks, as at March 1990.
Source: Financial Statistics, May 1990

Fig. 15.2 (b) Normal yield curve

The demand for particular assets depends not only on their characteristics but also on the institutional make-up of the financial system. The particular nature of the business of a financial institution will affect the type and proportion of assets it holds in its portfolio. Because of the need for both liquidity and profitability, banks tend to hold bills and bonds of varying maturities and yields. Pension funds may, on the other hand, choose to hold the less liquid but usually more profitable assets in their portfolios, for example company shares. All institutions will need to hold some minimum level of liquid assets to meet short-term claims, and will choose a portfolio which will yield the maximum profit subject to that liquidity constraint.

Financial institutions

Institutions within the UK financial sector are classified as (a) those which are within the monetary sector as defined by the Banking Acts of 1979 and 1987, and (b) other financial institutions, such as pension funds, investment and unit trusts, and insurance companies.

The monetary sector Until November 1981 the 'banking sector' comprised all banks in the UK which were required to observe the minimum reserve asset ratio imposed by the Competition and Credit Control arrangements of 1971, together with the discount houses and the Banking Department of the Bank of England. Inclusion in the 'banking sector' was based on an informal appraisal of a bank's size and reputation, and was usually associated with the granting of authorized bank status for exchange control purposes.

The Banking Act of 1979 defined two new entities: 'recognized banks' and 'licensed deposit-takers' (LDTs). To become a recognized bank an institution had to satisfy the Bank of England as to its reputation, the range of services it offers, and its financial status. Licensed deposit-takers had to meet the same requirements, but did not need to offer as wide a range of services. In November 1981 the Bank of England defined a new monetary sector which amalgamated the old banking sector with a number of other related institutions. The monetary sector now comprised: (a) all recognized banks and LDTs; (b) the National Girobank; (c) the Trustee Savings Bank; (d) the Banking Department of the Bank of England; and (e) those institutions in the Channel Islands and the Isle of Man which opted to adhere to the new arrangements

The National Girobank, although exempt from the provisions of the 1979 Banking Act, was included in the monetary sector. So, too, was the Trustee Savings Bank which, though again exempt, was defined by the Trustee Savings Bank Act of 1976 as being a bank. The institutions of the Channel Islands and the Isle of Man are outside the control area of the Banking Act, but were included because they voluntarily agreed to abide by the arrangements of the Banking Act.

The Banking Act of 1987, which was primarily concerned with supervisory arrangements, left the definition of the monetary sector essentially unchanged. All institutions are now known as 'authorized institutions', and the use of the word 'bank' was restricted to those institutions which had a paid-up capital of at least £5m, but in all other respects the 1981 classification remained. A major addition to this category of institution was the Abbey National, which became a public limited company in July 1989, and was authorized under the Banking Act of 1987 from that date. This change necessitated major changes to the compilation of financial and monetary statistics (see Ch. 16.)

In February 1990 there were 589 institutions in the monetary sector. Before looking at the way in which the sector has changed in recent years we examine the role of the Bank of England.

The Bank of England. The Bank of England is divided into the Issue Department, which is part of the public sector accounting system, and the Banking Department. Its functions can be divided into those which are required by its role as banker to the Government and those which it performs as banker to the banks.

As banker to the Government it must:

(a)   implement monetary policy by manipulating interest rates in the bill market, using direct controls, or restricting bank credit as necessary;
(b)   regulate the issue of legal tender;
(c)   manage both the issue and redemption of government stock;
(d)   keep the Government's accounts;
(e)   manage the Exchange Equalization Account, and when necessary use official reserves to intervene in the foreign exchange market.

As banker to the banks it must:

(a)   supervise the clearing system;
(b)   act as 'lender of last resort' to the banking system by supporting the discount market;
(c)   exercise prudential supervision over the banking system as a whole.

The Bank also acts as banker to overseas central banks, as well as to international organizations and to a small number of other institutions and private individuals.

In operational day-to-day terms the Bank of England has a major influence on three major markets, the sterling money market, the foreign exchange market, and the gilt-edged market.

1.   The Bank is a major player in the *sterling money market*, buying and selling bills on a daily basis. The object is twofold; in the first place the Bank buys and sells bills in order to ease cash shortages, or to withdraw cash surpluses, which arise in the discount market as a result of daily transactions between the government and the public. Such transactions, by affecting commercial bank clearing balances, alter the liquidity of these banks and hence their willingness to lend to, or withdraw funds from, the discount houses. Secondly, the Bank trades in bills with the government's interest rate policy specifically in mind. The buying and selling of bills by the Bank affects yields. In this way the Bank influences interest rates throughout the market. The Bank, in its daily dealings, attempts to reconcile these two separate objectives.

2.   The Bank has a major role in the *foreign exchange market* as it is responsible for carrying out government policy with regard to the exchange rate. A strong pound is essential if inflation is to be kept low. The combination in recent years of a floating pound and a weak balance of payments on current account has made it necessary to attract short term funds on capital account by maintaining high interest rates. The Bank also uses the Exchange Equalization Account to intervene in the foreign exchange market by buying up surplus sterling when necessary.

3.   The Bank is also influential in the *gilt-edged market* as it administers the issue of new stock when the government wishes to borrow money. Various methods are used, depending on market circumstances – the 'tap' method, where stock is issued gradually in order not to flood the market and depress the price; the 'tender' method, where institutions are invited to tender for a given issue; and the 'auction' method, where stock is sold to the highest bidders among the nineteen market makers in the

gilt-edged market. The Bank also manages the redemption of existing stock in such a way as to smooth the demands on the government's financial resources. For instance it buys up stock which is nearing its redemption date, so as not to have to make large repayments over a short period of time.

The Bank faces a continual problem in that its actions in each of these markets have repercussions for the functioning of the others. For instance, intervention to protect the value of sterling is often ineffective because of the size of speculative flows of short-term capital, hence interest rates must be manipulated in order to influence these flows. This often proves difficult, however, because of the way in which daily transactions between government and public affect bankers' balances, causing banks to buy or sell bills to replenish their cash balances and thus to affect their yield. Gilt market policy is also subject to the requirements of interest rate policy; this in turn places restrictions on National Debt management.

One of the most significant changes within the Bank of England during the last few years has been the improvement in arrangements for supervising the banking system. Overall supervision of any banking system is essential to protect the interests of depositors, and although there was some degree of depositor protection in the 1960s it was not until the secondary banking crisis of the 1970s that formal supervisory structures were developed and embodied in the Banking Acts of 1979 and 1987.

The Board of Banking Supervision concerns itself with three issues:

1. *Capital adequacy*. To what extent have banks sufficient reserves of capital to cover the possibility of default by creditors? This issue has become particularly important in recent years as the volume of Third World debt has grown to unmanageable proportions. There are now international proposals that banks in major countries should maintain capital reserves equal to 8% of their assets, weighted according to risk.

2. *Liquidity*. There is currently no formal requirement as to adequate liquidity holdings by banks. However, what is expected is that the Bank of England will require all banks under the Banking Act of 1987 to keep a ratio of 'primary liquid assets' to some definition of deposit liabilities. Such ratios may differ as between different types of banks, and deposits will be ranked according to their maturity. The shorter is the maturity structure, the higher will be the ratio of liquid assets required.

3. *Foreign currency exposure*. This issue relates particularly to banks which take deposits and lend in different currencies. Supervisors are concerned that banks should balance their assets and liabilities in each currency in such a way that their 'exposure' (to risk of loss on the foreign exchange market) should not exceed 10% of their capital base.[1]

Banks in the UK.   These include:

(a)   'retail banks' – banks which either participate in a UK clearing system or have extensive branch networks, viz. London, Scottish and Northern Ireland clearing banks, and the Girobank;

(b)   merchant banks, including the accepting houses;

(c)   other British banks, a general category covering banks with UK majority ownership;
(d)   American banks;
(e)   Japanese banks;
(f) other overseas banks and consortium banks (UK registered institutions owned by banks or financial institutions).
(g)   the building societies; since the deregulation permitted by the Building Societies Act of 1986 and subsequent Orders in Council.

There are two important distinctions to be made in the type of business done in the banking sector. One is the distinction between lending and deposit-taking in sterling as opposed to foreign currency, the other is the distinction between retail and wholesale business. This latter distinction refers to the size of the transaction undertaken; lending and borrowing transactions in excess of £100,000 are termed *wholesale* transactions. In the main, *retail* banks deal in smaller amounts, other banks deal primarily with wholesale corporate business.

However, this distinction is becoming increasingly blurred because of the participation of all banks in the interbank market. Retail and wholesale banks alike raise large sums of money on this market, and lend their surpluses there. This enables them to manage their liabilities more effectively, and to match the maturity of their assets and liabilities more profitably.

Table 15.2 Banks' liabilities 1976–90 (£m.)

	Sterling		Foreign currency	
	Jan. 1976	Jan. 1990	Jan. 1976	Jan. 1990
Retail banks	25,896	271,099	4,413	62,897
Merchant banks	2,270	28,295	2,822	15,213
Other British banks	8,763	39,182	9,011	11,141
American banks	3,921	18,211	32,484	94,686
Japanese banks	197	33,580	11,780	228,195
Other overseas banks and consortium banks	2,916	86,105	24,579	231,128
Total	43,963	476,472	85,089	643,259

Source: Bank of England Quarterly Bulletin (May 1977, May 1990).

Table 15.2 shows changes in the volume of business transacted by these institutions. We can identify a number of important changes which have occurred:

1.   It is clear that for the banking sector as a whole, foreign currency business predominates. However, whereas in 1976 foreign currency liabilities were roughly twice as large as sterling liabilities, in 1990 they were only 1.4 times greater. This in part reflects the recent very rapid rise in interest-bearing sterling deposits, due to high real interest rates. It also, however, reflects the effects of the growth in consumer credit in general and bank lending in particular.

2.   The figures also show the fact that the growth of foreign currency

business has been primarily located in the wholesale banking sector. Within that, the most remarkable expansion is that of the Japanese banks. In terms of numbers of banks the USA is the most heavily represented country, but in terms of market share the Japanese now account for over one-third of the market.

3. London is one of the major world banking centres, but its share of international bank lending has been falling slowly over the years, from 27% in 1980 to just over 20% in the second quarter of 1989. The major challenge to its position has come from the growth of Tokyo as a world financial centre. Over the same period, Japan's share of the world market grew from 5% to 20%. (BEQB 1989c)

4. What the overall figures do not show is the way in which the activity of banking business has changed over the last decade. The growth of the inter-bank market (see below) has meant that banks no longer have to rely on attracting deposits to cover their lending. Nevertheless, there is also much greater competition for deposits, not only with other financial institutions, but also with other and alternative forms of wealth holding, such as equities.

5. In order to make profits, banks must maintain an adequate spread between borrowing and lending rates. Profit-making is affected by the volatility of interest rates, because borrowing rates, being market determined, move more sharply than lending rates. Banks find that this introduces instability; it is therefore necessary to match maturities of assets and liabilities with great precision. They must also ensure that the riskiness of lending is kept to a minimum, since profits must be used to write off bad debts.

6. The internationalization of banking business has been made necessary by the growth of international business, the ending of exchange control, and international uncertainty in days of volatile exchange rates and interest rates. It has been made possible by improvements in communication and organizational efficiency, and by international deregulation. The response of the banking sector to these factors has been to innovate. Financial innovation can be seen in the growth of new financial instruments such as options and futures, in the diversification of banking business into new services such as personal equity plans for customers, in the use of new technologies such as automated clearing and electronic fund transfer at point of sale, and in the development of new organizational forms and procedures within the industry.

Changes in lending patterns. We have examined the changing institutional structure of the financial sector. We now look at the changing relationships between monetary sector institutions and their clients. In particular, we are interested in the way lending patterns have changed over time, and whether in fact these changes have been optimal. We look first at the changing overall pattern of lending.

Table 15.3 illustrates a number of major changes:

1. The share of total sterling bank lending to the public sector (central and

	1983	1985	1987	1989
Lending to public sector	18,389	17,274	16,025	14,692
Lending to private sector	95,009	128,222	202,200	352,667
Lending to overseas sector	18,842	27,519	38,072	44,805

Source: Bank of England Quarterly Bulletin, Feb. 1988a, May 1990.

local government and public corporations) has declined sharply. The current figure represents a dramatic retreat from the situation of the early 1970s when large government deficits were financed by the sale of public sector debt (bills and bonds) to the banking sector. Such borrowing as the government now does tends to be financed by selling debt to the non-bank private sector, or encouraging the public to lend via National Savings. Investors are attracted by the more varied and attractive securities currently available for purchase, such as index-linked stock, as well as by historically high yields. However, the situation may change if inflation rises; under those circumstances fixed yields become unattractive.

2. The share of total sterling lending to the private sector – households and businesses – has risen sharply. This is due to the huge increase in demand for credit in the last few years, primarily from the personal sector, as well as to the increased efforts of banks and other institutions to 'market' new ways of borrowing money.

3. The increase in the share of lending to the overseas sector is partly due to the ending of exchange control in 1979. But it is also due to a greater readiness by people and institutions abroad to borrow sterling as confidence in the pound has been maintained.

It is clear, then, that although bank lending has increased, lending to the public sector has declined both in relative and absolute terms, whereas lending to both private and overseas sectors has risen. We now need to look in more detail at private sector lending, particularly in the light of two criticisms which have been made of the role played by monetary sector institutions.

The first criticism is that banks in the UK have failed to provide adequately for the needs of industry. This criticism is based (a) on comparisons with other countries such as West Germany and Japan (Vittas 1986), where banks play a much larger role in industrial financing; (b) on an assumption that bad industrial performance can be attributed to a lack of finance; and (c) on a certain dissatisfaction with consistently high levels of bank profitability.

The second criticism relates to the role of the institutions in encouraging the explosion of consumer credit. The ease of obtaining credit often leads to over-borrowing and consequent personal and financial difficulties. It is often argued that the institutions put the objective of profitability before the interests of the clients when making loans. We need to examine these criticisms in the light of recent changes in corporate and personal sector finance.

Corporate sector finance.   Companies need finance for four main reasons:

1. Working capital for stocks and work in progress.
2. Cash to finance trade credit.
3. Funds to replace plant and equipment.
4. Capital for new investment.

Companies can meet these needs by internal financing – maintaining a liquidity cushion and/or retaining profits rather than distributing them to shareholders. Alternatively, they can use external financing – they can borrow from banks, issue loan stock (debt), or issue shares (equity). The choice of financing method will clearly be constrained by availability of different forms of finance, but there are other factors which have a greater influence on companies' decisions.

For instance, the choice between *internal* and *external* financing depends, amongst other things, on the sensitivity of share prices to dividend payout ratios. If shareholders object to profits being retained rather than paid out as dividends they may sell their shares, thereby increasing the likelihood of a takeover by a predator. The choice between debt and equity financing is determined by a further set of considerations. The more the company finances by means of *debt*, the greater the proportion of future profits which are committed to interest payments. In times of high interest rates, this burden will rise significantly. Debt-financed companies may then find it difficult to sell shares to shareholders who will be sceptical of the likelihood of adequate dividends. Against this has to be set the fact that in times of high inflation the real value of company debt diminishes over time. On the other hand the possibility of *equity* financing, even if it is a preferred company option, is often determined by matters external to the company, such as the state of the global equity market.

There appear to be structural differences between the major countries in the pattern of industrial financing. Retentions or ploughed-back profits are the major source of finance everywhere. In no country does equity finance contribute substantially. However, there are major differences in the use of bank finance; France, Japan and Germany fund a higher proportion of their financing needs by bank loans than do the US and the UK. But even within the UK the popularity of bank financing over time has been affected by a variety of factors.

Table 15.4 shows the changes in sources of company finance since 1970. We may note a number of points:

1. Borrowing in general, whether by loan stock or from banks, was much more significant before the inflation of the mid-1970s caused nominal interest rates to soar. Since then firms have been unwilling to expand their long-term debt, but have preferred to borrow from banks, often on a much shorter-term basis. In addition, uncertainty as to future interest-rate movements has encouraged bank borrowing rather than debt financing.

2. Borrowing from overseas has been affected by the same set of factors.

3. Companies may offset the interest on all borrowing against profits tax. In spite of the fact that in the 1980s profits have risen and nominal interest rates have fallen somewhat it is generally the case that companies have a

	TOTAL external financing	Bank borrowing	Ordinary share issues	Debentures, preference shares and capital issues overseas	Other loans and mortgages	Acquisition of financial assets	
						liquid	other
80	9.7	6.3		3.3	0.1	−3.6	−0.4
81	9.3	5.8		3.0	0.5	−4.8	−1.5
82	9.7	6.6		2.4	0.7	−2.7	−1.5
83	6.7	2.0		4.0	0.7	−6.3	−1.7
84	6.7	7.0	1.5	0.5	−2.3	−2.2	−1.8
85	12.6	7.3	3.7	1.6	−	−5.0	−0.6
86	10.9	5.3	6.0	2.2	−2.6	−11.5	−0.2
87	31.4	12.1	13.4	2.9	3.0	−8.7	−2.5
88	43.2	31.1	3.5	4.4	4.2	−5.7	1.4
89	50.0	33.4	2.3	7.0	7.3	−14.5	2.4

Source: Bank of England Quarterly Bulletin 1984, 1987, 1990b.

Table 15.4 Industrial and Commercial Companies (ICCs) external financing and the acquisition of financial assets £bn

preference for equity finance if it is possible. This is often because it may well be in the managers' interests to do so (*Bank of England Quarterly Bulletin* 1988a).

4. The possibility of equity financing depends on the state of the equity market. The rise in equity prices of the mid-1980s, has made it relatively easy to float new issues, and this gave an impetus to equity financing. Share issues were subdued in the early 1980s but rose strongly after that as the market improved.

5. Banks made a major contribution to industrial financing which is not shown in these figures, in that they facilitate the leasing of equipment. Leasing is a system whereby a financial institution purchases a piece of equipment and leases it back to the company, which then has the use of equipment it has not had to purchase. Leasing is the leading source of external finance for plant and equipment (as opposed to fixed capital).

It would appear, then, that the use of monetary sector financing by companies depends in general on the demand for such financing rather than on supply constraints as such. Nevertheless, there has always been an undercurrent of concern that the correlation between the economic performance of Japan and Germany and their bank-based financing systems might be a causal one – in which case the UK's poorer economic performance might have something to do with her market-based industrial financing system. The Wilson Committee examined this issue.

Committee to Review the Functioning of Financial Institutions (*The Wilson Committee Report* 1980). The Wilson Committee was set up to investigate the whole question of the provision of funds for industry and trade. The central question to be addressed by the committee was:

whether any failings in the level and quality of investment have been due in any important degree to an inadequate supply of finance, reflecting a failure in the functioning of the financial system, too high a price for finance, or an inability on the part of companies to find enough funds from their own resources, and if so, what can be done about it?

In answer to this question, the committee concluded that the financial sector was, in fact, providing adequately for the needs of corporate sector financing. The lack of industrial investment was attributed to a potentially low rate of return rather than to any lack of institutional financing. However, the committee was concerned about the effects on business of the high rates of interest which occur in an inflationary economy. It was also concerned about the problems of financing small businesses – in particular, the difficulties encountered by very small firms in obtaining venture capital, where the risk element is different in kind from large-scale high-risk industrial financing.

The Wilson Committee clearly felt that although there were gaps in the system, such as the provision for small firms and for high-risk finance, the fundamental problem with the financing of industry in the UK was to be attributed not to the lack of availability of external financing, but rather to the inadequacy of industrial performance. It is this which leads to low levels of profitability and to a lack of incentive to undertake new investment. In other words, the Wilson Committee shifted the focus of concern from the supply of industrial finance to the demand for such finance.

Two developments in the late eighties have proved the Wilson Committee right. The first of these is the increase in mergers and acquisitions as the preferred form of industrial growth (Fig. 15.3). The banks have played a central role in this industrial restructuring. There are several aspects to this.

1. The traditional way of financing acquisitions was by means of equity, often on a share-for-share exchange basis. However, there has been a major shift away from equity financing of acquisitions since the Stock Market crash of 1987.

2. Since 1987, acquisitions have been mainly funded by cash (bank borrowings) – see Table 15.5. Whereas in 1986, 25.6% of acquisitions were funded in this way, the figure for 1988 was 69.7%, and in 1989 around 80% of merger funding was in cash. The profitability of this type of lending is substantial in days of high interest rates.

3. Other forms of merger funding also involve the banks. Money is often raised by the issue of fixed interest stock secured against the assets of the company ('junk bonds'). But more recently banks have been providing other forms of merger funding – 'mezzanine debt', which does not rate as highly in terms of claims against the company's assets, but provides additional financial resources. Because this debt is highly 'leveraged' (see Ch. 2) and thus more risky, it yields a substantial return to the banks.

4. Banks play a central role as consultants, advisers and agents in acquisition situations. There is sharp competition between UK and American banks, in particular, in the provision of these specialized services.

The second development in which the banks have been implicated is the growth of the 'venture capital' industry. Financial institutions provide finance and specialist services to companies which are as yet unproven but have potential. Funds are used for start-ups, for expansion and second stage growth, and often for management buyouts of an existing company. Banks

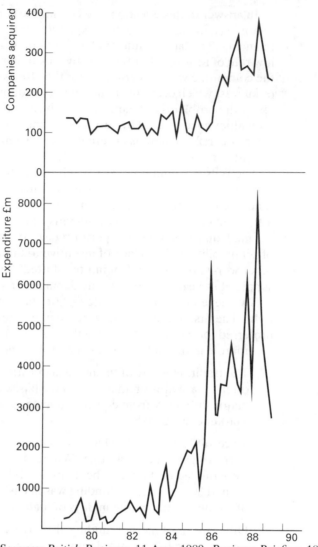

Fig. 15.3 Acquisitions and mergers: Industrial and commercial companies in the UK, 1979–89

Sources: British Business, 11 Aug. 1989, *Business Briefing*, 18 May 1990.

such as 3i, which is the largest venture capital investor in the UK and is owned by six clearing banks and by the Bank of England, raise 'independent' funds on the market and from their own retained profits. Other 'captive' funds come from pension funds, insurance companies and banks which allocate specific funds for this type of investment. The growth of the venture capital industry fulfils the need identified by the Wilson Committee, although financing gaps still remain. (BEQB 1990).

Personal sector financing.   Both the assets and the liabilities of the personal sector have been rising rapidly over the past ten years. Rising incomes have led both to an increase in wealth and an increase in borrowing. However, concern has been caused by the fact that between 1976 and 1989 the ratio of debt to personal disposable income rose from 50% to over 100% (BEQB May 1989a), and since 1980 the growth in credit has substantially exceeded

		Expenditure (£m)			Percentage of expenditure		
	Total	Cash	Issues of ordinary shares	Issues of fixed interest securities	Cash	Issues of ordinary shares	Issues of fixed interest securities
1972	2,532	493	1,459	580	19.5	57.6	22.9
1973	1,304	691	466	147	53.0	35.7	11.3
1974	508	347	114	47	68.3	22.4	9.3
1975	291	173	93	25	59.4	32.0	8.6
1976	448	321	120	7	71.7	26.8	1.5
1977	824	512	304	8	62.1	36.9	1.0
1978	1,140	654	463	23	57.4	40.6	2.0
1979	1,656	933	515	208	56.3	31.1	12.6
1980	1,475	760	669	46	51.5	45.4	3.1
1981	1,144	775	338	31	67.7	29.6	2.7
1982	2,206	1,283	701	222	58.1	31.8	10.1
1983	2,343	1,026	1,261	56	43.8	53.8	2.4
1984	5,474	2,946	1,838	960	53.8	33.6	12,6
1985	7,090	2,857	3,708	525	40.3	52.3	7.4
1986	14,935	3,822	8,642	2,471	25.6	57.9	16 5
1987	15,363	4,945	9,579	839	32.2	62.3	5.5
1988	22,123	15,425	4,852	1,846	69.7	21.9	8.4
1989	31,104	26,505	3,317	1,282	79.0	15.2	5.8

Source: British Business, 11 August, 1989.

Table 15.5 Categories of expenditure on acquisitions and mergers within the UK

the growth in income. It is clear that this is partly due to the fact that incomes have been rising in real terms, so that people feel able to take on an increased burden of debt. But it is also the case that the financial sector has encouraged people to borrow more money.

Deregulation, competition and the creation of new financial products have all served to make credit more attractive and easier to obtain. Mortgage loans in particular are now granted for higher multiples of the borrower's income, and even though incomes are heavily committed for mortgage repayment purposes, credit card debts are still mounting. Table 15.6 shows the growth of consumer credit (mortgage lending is not included in these figures).

There are two reasons why we cannot take these figures as indicative of the true size of borrowing. One is that the credit card figures include balances which are incurred and immediately repaid at the end of the month. It is estimated that the growth of credit is overestimated by about 2% because of this. The other factor to consider is that the figures do not tell us about the amount of borrowing which comes about from increases in mortgages used for purposes other than house purchase.

The Bank of England has voiced its concern at the possibility that default and arrears of debt may now increase, particularly as there is evidence that those who borrow are not necessarily those who have high incomes or a substantial cushion of assets. Nor are lenders always those institutions who are able or willing to make an adequate assessment of the creditworthiness of clients. Consumer credit, unlike mortgage borrowing, is unsecured, and changes in the financial environment, such as a rise in interest rates, might lead to a widespread incidence of default. The problem has been

	Total	Retailers	Building societies	Bank credit cards	Personal accounts	Insurance	Finance houses
1986	30,709	2,195	—	4,676	11,432	921	17,437
1987	36,341	2,590	—	5,565	13,241	982	19,533
1988	42,140	2,864	284	6,142	14,942	847	14,599
1989	46,940	2,967	577	6,606	16,255	827	11,980

Table 15.6 Consumer credit. Amounts outstanding at end Dec. 1989. £m

Market shares of outstanding credit	
Bank loans on personal accounts	34.6%
Bank credit cards	14.1%
Finance houses	41.7%
Retailers	6.32%
Insurance	2.1%
Building societies	1.2%

compounded by the rise in home ownership. In 1989 interest rates rose sharply, and consumers whose monthly mortgage repayment was already substantial found themselves in difficulties as repayments increased. The growth of new borrowing slowed, and property repossessions by mortgage lenders increased.

Building societies.   The traditional business of the building societies has been the taking of small savings deposits and the finance of house purchase. In 1984, 50% of all personal sector liquid assets were held in building society accounts, as opposed to 34% in banks and 16% in National Savings accounts. Lending was almost solely for mortgage purposes. The climate of deregulation made it necessary to remove restrictions on the ability of building societies to compete in financial markets. The Building Societies Act of 1986, and subsequent Orders in Council of 1988, have permitted societies to offer a whole range of new banking, investment and housing services in addition to their traditional savings and home loan business. They are allowed to lend amounts up to £10,000 on an unsecured basis, and to lend money on second mortgages. They can buy life assurance companies, run unit trusts and take over or start stockbroking firms. They can offer services such as tax advice, financial planning services and executorship. They no longer rely on the taking of deposits to finance their lending, because they can now borrow on the wholesale money markets.

The focus of interest here is the extent to which the building societies are likely to make inroads into traditional banking business. In practice, it is only the largest of building societies which can offer a real competitive challenge. There are two reasons for this. One is the fact that the Building Societies Act of 1986 requires that at least 90% of the society's commercial assets be devoted to mortgage lending. This leaves only 10% to finance newer activities. The other reason is that these activities must be backed by capital reserves, as in the case of banks. This effectively means that only the largest building societies, those with assets of £100m or more, can effectively compete. However, there are a number of other issues to consider in this context.

1. Banks are profit-making corporations; they measure their success in terms of profit, with client satisfaction as the constraint. Building societies are mutual organizations run for the benefit of their depositors; their success is measured in terms of growth. However, building societies are gradually moving towards the status of public companies. One, the Abbey National, has already switched to limited liability status. If this trend continues, building societies are poised to provide a greater competitive challenge to the retail banking sector.

2. Building society business is low risk because all the lending is secured and mortgage holders pay on time. This is necessarily a source of weakness for the banks in the competitive struggle against the building societies. However, as building societies enter the area of unsecured lending, they may find that the banks have the advantage of greater expertise.

3. The mutual structure of building societies means that capital resources to finance expansion can only be built up out of retained surpluses. This factor is likely to be decisive in encouraging building societies to seek corporate status at the earliest opportunity since they will then be able to raise capital on the open market.

4. Until the late 1970s, building societies provided 95% of home loans. In 1986 banks had 20% of the market, and by the beginning of 1990 they had 50% of the market. Banks have managed to attain this share by offering attractive packages. However, building societies have taken advantage of the new regulations which allow them to raise 40% (20% in the Act) of funds on the wholesale markets, and are intent on maintaining their market share by encroaching on areas of lending business which traditionally belonged to banks.

5. Building societies have been consistently successful in improving their share of personal sector deposits. This has been partly due to the new and attractive packages offered to depositors, and partly due to the increase in competition in the sector since the interest rate cartel was ended a few years ago.

6. Both types of institution have begun to acquire other institutions such as estate agents in an attempt to capture the market for home loans by offering additional services. However, this has been a costly process and it remains to be seen whether sufficient returns from these investments can be made.

Other financial institutions   We now consider the sector which comprises institutions other than those in the monetary sector. These (OFIs) are defined as institutions which 'obtain, convert and distribute available funds as their main activity'. The major institutions are life assurance and pension funds, unit trusts and investment trusts.

The institutions of this sector fulfil a number of specialist functions. Some cater for the public's need for insurance or pension provision. Still others, as in the case of unit, investment or property trusts, specialize in matching borrowers' needs for long-term finance with lenders' needs for paper assets denominated in small units which are readily saleable.

As in the case of the banks, the assets of these institutions represent paper claims against money which has been lent by them to the public sector, to industry and to persons. Decisions as to the proportion in which they hold these assets, in other words the nature of their portfolio management, determine how the sector as a whole fulfils the function of allocating the community's savings to those who wish to borrow. It should be noted that, unlike the institutions of the monetary sector, OFIs lend primarily by the acquisition of assets, rather than directly by loans and advances.

We shall examine the major portfolio holders in this sector.

Life assurance and pension funds. These are the major recipients of personal sector savings – in 1988 50% of personal savings were channelled into these institutions. This saving is used to acquire and manage a portfolio of assets which yield a sufficient return to pay pensions and insurance claims, as well as providing a working rate of return for the financial institution. Pension funds have increased thirtyfold in size over the past twenty-five years; insurance companies have grown fourteenfold over the same period (*Bank of England Quarterly Bulletin* 1986b). As investors, insurance companies and pension funds represent a major influence in the assets markets. In 1986 they held about 50% of British Government stock outstanding, and over 50% of the total shares quoted on the Stock Exchange. However, there has been a change in the relative importance of the two types of institution as recipients of savings. Individual life insurance more than doubled its share of the personal savings market in the ten years to 1988, whereas pension contributions (employers + employees) fell from 42% to around 30% over the same period (see Fig. 15.4).

Fig. 15.4 Competition for personal savings
Source: Lloyds Bank Economic Bulletin, Nov. 1989

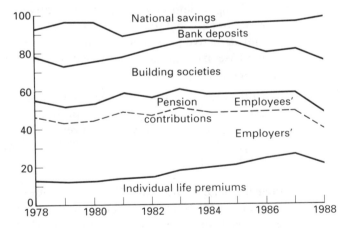

However, portfolio choice differs between the two types of institution, because the structure of their liabilities varies. Life insurance funds invest more in fixed interest securities because a large part of their liabilities is in nominal terms. Pension funds, on the other hand, are interested in the real rates of return, their liabilities are in real terms – pensions are paid in the future and are often index-linked. However, since the PSBR has shrunk, and the supply of government bonds has consequently been reduced, insurance companies are looking to other types of fixed interest stock such as corporate bonds and property. Less than 20% of life insurance funds is now held in gilts. Pension funds, too, have reduced their holdings of gilts, but in their case the reduction from 23% of total assets in 1979 to 10% in 1988 is partly explained by the attractiveness of equities in the rising market of the 80s. On the other hand, pension funds, like insurance companies, are also forced to seek alternative fixed interest investments, since for them there is an irreducible minimum of security of return, given the volatility of the equity market.

Table 15.7 shows the way in which asset holdings vary by type of institution.

Table 15.7 Asset holdings of insurance companies and pension funds

	Asset holdings at end of year 1989	
	Insurance companies	Pension funds
Total net assets	212,924	223,874
Short-term assets	5,923	14,595
British Government securities	32,169	23,804
UK ordinary shares	70,142	115,900
UK other company securities	12,245	4,499
Overseas securities	26,897	37,598
UK land and property	34,966	18,279

Source: CSO (1990b).

Perhaps the most important issue here concerns the extent to which OFIs are involved in equity finance. The fact that OFIs are responsible for over 50% of equity finance means that share prices will be predominantly affected by the portfolio preferences of these institutions. This in turn will be determined by overall 'environmental' factors such as the inflation rate, the exchange rate and the state of business expectations, as well as by the particular needs of the institutions themselves. Since institutions tend to be affected in the same way by the same set of factors, share prices will be more volatile than would otherwise be the case. This will have significant repercussions on the companies concerned: since share prices will not reflect their true valuation in terms of yield, both the decision and the ability of companies to raise funds on the Stock Exchange will be affected.

The other area of concern relates to the rise in overseas investment. In so far as institutions find it more profitable to invest abroad, UK companies may find it more difficult to float new share issues.

Financial markets

We now turn our attention to the third kind of operator in the UK financial system – the financial markets. We deal first with money markets. The term 'money market' refers to the process whereby financial institutions come together to borrow and lend wholesale funds for periods varying from one day to one year. Wholesale funds are amounts in excess of £100,000. Money markets have no physical existence; the participants in the markets are linked by telephone and computer. Money market activity has developed very rapidly in London in the last thirty years, partly due to the growth of the financial sector in general, but also because of the increasing demand for sophisticated financial services by clients both in the UK and abroad.

The oldest of the money markets is the discount market, but there are also the newer sterling and foreign currency markets. We deal with these first.

(a)   *The sterling certificate of deposit market.* CDs, as they are known, are paper assets issued by banks, building societies and finance houses to depositors who are willing to leave their money on deposit for a specified period of time. They are issued for periods ranging from 3 months to 5 years at a rate of interest which can either be fixed or floating. The holder of the CD can sell it on the market if he should want his money back before then. This system enables banks to lend longer term because they can be certain of having deposits, as lenders can realize their asset at any time. In addition, CDs are attractive to portfolio holders because the yield is competitive. They are denominated in sterling, but also in dollars and SDRs.

(b)   *The sterling inter-bank market.* Banks borrow and lend wholesale funds amongst themselves, dealing through money brokers, for periods ranging from overnight to five years. This is the largest of the wholesale markets, and its existence has revolutionized banking business. Banks can borrow to finance lending, to use unlent deposits, to balance out fluctuations in their books, and to speculate on future movements in interest rates. The London Inter-Bank Offer Rate (LIBOR) therefore represents the marginal or opportunity cost of funds to the banks and is the major influence on banks' base rates. Lending and borrowing on this market is unsecured.

(c)   *The local authority market.* This market grew up in the 1950s when the local authorities began to raise money for capital projects by issuing bills and bonds, and by raising loans. The market has now declined in importance, due to the inability of authorities to borrow and the unpopularity of the assets with investors uncertain about the future of local authority finance.

(d)   *The finance house market.* Again, this market has declined in importance because the major finance houses have now achieved the status of banks and can therefore borrow funds on the inter-bank market or by the issue of CDs.

(e)   *The inter-company market.* The fortunes of this market have varied with the ease or difficulty of borrowing from banks. In the 1960s, when bank credit was tight, companies found they could use the services of a broker to lend to one another. When restrictions on bank credit were relaxed, companies found it more advantageous to lend and borrow through banks, particularly as when they dealt directly transactions were unsecured.

(f)   *The building society market.* The new status of the building societies (see below) has made it necessary and advantageous for them to raise extra funds in the wholesale money markets. They have also begun to issue CDs.

(g)   *The sterling commercial paper market.* This is the newest of the money markets. Since May 1986 companies have been permitted to issue short-term (7–364 days) unsecured promissory notes, which can then be traded at a discount. This provides a way of raising short-term funds for general business purposes, often more cheaply than through the banking sector. In the 1989 Budget, the right to issue sterling commercial paper was extended to unlisted governments, overseas companies and certain overseas authorities; also to banks, building societies and insurance companies.

(h)   *The Eurocurrency market.* Eurocurrency is currency held on deposit with a bank outside the country from which that currency originates. These deposits are then borrowed and lent in the usual way. The Eurocurrency market is a wholesale market; it had its origins in holdings of US dollars outside the US in the sixties at a time when the US authorities were placing restrictions on capital exports. It has since grown to include dealing in all the major currencies, and become particularly important when oil price rises created huge world surpluses and deficits. London became the dominant Eurocurrency centre because the dollar was the dominant currency, and because it was strategically located half way between New York and Tokyo, so that dealing could continue round the clock. The major participants are banks, who use the market (a) for short-term interbank lending and borrowing, (b) to spread maturity transformation, (c) to match the currency composition of assets and liabilities and (d) for global liquidity transformation between branches. However, the market is also extensively used by companies, and by governmental and international organizations. Lending which is longer-term is usually done on a variable-rate basis, where the interest is calculated periodically in line with changing market rates.

There are two important factors which make Eurocurrency business attractive. The first is that the market is unregulated, so that banks which are subject to reserve requirements or interest rate restrictions in the home country, for instance, can do business more freely abroad. The other factor is that the margin between lending and borrowing rates is narrower on this market than on the home market, primarily because banks can operate at lower cost when all business is wholesale and when they are not subject to reserve requirements.

The discount market   The discount market has always played an important role within the financial system. In the last century its major function was the discounting of bills of exchange which financed the increasing volume of trade. Between the wars it provided a market for the growing volume of Treasury bills issued by the Government to meet its short-term financing needs. As the volume of Treasury bills declined in the 1970s the discount houses facilitated the rapid growth in the commercial bill market.

The prime business of the eight members of the London Discount Market Association is to buy bills and hold them until redemption date. Cash flow for this purpose is provided by overnight and short-term 'money at call' lent by the banking sector. Bills must be 'accepted' (underwritten) by a discount house or a reputable bank in order to be eligible to be traded on the market. Bills accepted by banks designated as 'eligible' banks by the Bank of England become first-class bills which the Bank of England is willing to deal in on the market. The Bank of England as well as dealing with the discount houses, now also deals with the other firms or 'dealing counterparts' on this market.

The functions of the discount houses may be summarized as follows:

(a)   They underwrite the weekly tender of Treasury bills by bidding competitively for those not sold.
(b)   They take surplus funds from the banking sector which can be recalled if banks are short of cash, thus effectively acting as a buffer between the banks and the Bank of England. Banks' daily holdings of cash fluctuate as a result of transactions between the Government and the public; bank cash held by the discount houses is used to smooth out these fluctuations.
(c)   They provide short-term finance for companies by discounting commercial bills.
(d)   They maintain a secondary market in CDs and other short term financial instruments.

Although these functions have remained essentially unchanged since the early 1970s, there have been a number of changes in the way they have been carried out, which are best examined by looking at the balance sheet of the discount market (Table 15.8):

Table 15.8 Discount market assets and liabilities as at 28 Feb. 1990 (£m.)

	Sterling	Other currencies
Liabilities: borrowed funds		
Bank of England	560	
Other UK banks	10,289	95
Other UK	4,316	150
Overseas	32	117
Total	15,197	362
Of which call and overnight	13,476	
Assets:		
Cash deposits with Bank of England	13	
Sterling Treasury bills	691	
Other bills		
local authority	4	
other bills	5,596	29
Funds lent		
UK banks	858	
Certificates of deposit	5,796	85
UK local authorities	12	
Other UK	2,209	
Overseas	75	
Investments		
British Government stocks	5	
Local authority	—	
Other	217	249
Other sterling assets	66	
Total	15,540	363

Source: CSO (1990a).

1. It will be seen that the bulk of the funding for the discount market comes from monetary sector institutions. Under the 1981 arrangements eligible banks undertook to hold not less than 2.5% of their eligible liabilities as call money with the discount houses. The purpose of this requirement was to ensure that the bill market was adequately funded. However, since October 1986 this requirement has been abolished, the Bank of England no longer deeming it appropriate in the newly deregulated capital market.

2. Traditionally the Bank of England supported the discount houses, and thus indirectly the banking sector as a whole, by lending to them at a rate of its own choosing, known since 1971 as minimum lending rate. This enabled the Bank to raise the rate when it wished to tighten liquidity in the banking sector and force the banks to recall loans from the discount houses. The current arrangement is that the Bank will support the discount market by dealing rather than lending. The Bank buys and sells daily in the market in a manner which is designed both to achieve its interest rate objectives (see Ch. 16) and to support the market. However, it reserves the right to lend direct should dealing distort market conditions. This accounts for the existence of funds borrowed from the Bank of England on the liabilities side of the balance sheet.

3. On the assets side cash deposits with the Bank of England are held to fulfil the requirement that all monetary sector institutions hold 0.45% of their eligible liabilities as non-operational deposits with the Bank of England. 'Eligible' liabilities are those deposits not originating from other monetary sector institutions; these form an insignificant proportion of total discount market liabilities. It will be seen that commercial bills form the bulk of bills held. This is partly due to the fact that the Government now prefers to fund its PSBR in other ways, and partly due to the increasing use of commercial bills by companies for short-term financing.

The capital market The capital market is concerned with the provision of long-term finance for both private and public sectors (primary market activity), as well as the trading of existing bonds and equities (secondary market activity). The Stock Exchange is the traditional centre of the capital market. Until 1986 Stock Exchange participants were either brokers, who acted on behalf of clients in buying and selling securities, or jobbers, who held stocks and shares and dealt with brokers as the market required. Restrictive rules maintained the separation of these functions and limited Stock Exchange membership and the inflow of capital into existing firms.

From the mid-1970s onwards a number of factors began to threaten the continued existence of this 'single capacity' system:

1. The Office of Fair Trading brought a case against the Stock Exchange on the grounds of restrictive practice. As a result of agreement between the Government and the Stock Exchange in 1983 the case was dropped, on condition that the Stock Exchange investigate ways to liberalize its trading arrangements.

2. An increasing amount of share trading, particularly in international

shares, was bypassing the floor of the Stock Exchange. Participants were dealing directly with one another and most transactions, particularly in Eurobonds, took place on over-the-counter markets maintained by the major banks in London.

3. The percentage fees levied on transactions were adversely affecting institutional investors.

4. Stock Exchange members began to see themselves as being at a disadvantage in the face of international competition from larger and more sophisticated international firms.

5. The fact that Stock Exchange rules limited the scope of member firms to increase their capital meant that resources for technological innovation were limited.

The pressure to deregulate came therefore not only from outside but from inside the Stock Exchange. In March 1986 outside firms were permitted to take a 100% stake in Stock Exchange member firms. The result was a large number of takeovers and mergers. Commercial and investment banks, both domestic and foreign, rapidly absorbed most of London's traditional stockbrokers and jobbers. The financial sector prepared itself for full deregulation and open competition with foreign institutions.

On 27 October 1986 the 'big bang' brought the following changes:

1. The scale of minimum commissions charged by brokers was dismantled. Commissions are now negotiable.

2. There are no further restrictions on outside ownership of member firms.

3. The distinction between jobbers and brokers – the 'single capacity system' – was abolished. There is now only one type of member, the broker/dealer. A certain number of these undertake to 'make a market' in a range of shares. All broker/dealers may deal directly with the public, but they must state in which capacity they are acting.

4. Members of the Stock Exchange have always been individuals operating in partnerships. Now the corporate member is the norm.

5. Dealing is now done electronically through SEAQ (Stock Exchange Automated Quotations), which shows the share buying and selling price, records all deals in the most traded share within five minutes, and registers the volume of trading in those shares during the day. This means that complete market surveillance is possible and investors' interests are thus protected.

The deregulation of the capital market has introduced the need for increased investor protection. The Financial Services Act of 1986 aimed to fulfil this need, as well as to abolish some of the inconsistencies which had crept into the existing regulatory system within the financial sector as a whole (excluding banks). The Act gives power to the Secretary of State for Trade and Industry to delegate powers of regulation to the Securities and Investment Board, which in turn is responsible for delegating responsibility to a number of self-regulatory bodies governing practice in the securities market, insurance broking, fund management, provision of investment advice, and activities in futures and options.

The consequences of deregulation were immediately felt. Increased competition caused a narrowing of the margins between bid and offer price, and a reduction in commissions. In spite of the fact that trade increased by 50% in the three months following the 'big bang' (*Midland Bank Review* 1987) the rise in costs associated with both increased labour and capital costs caused reductions in rates of return on capital for many firms.

It also became apparent that the real strength lay with the large financial conglomerates who had entered the market, notably those from Japan and the USA. Newly formed British competitors such as Barclays de Zoete Wedd were forced to compete in an over-capitalized market, and it was obvious that in time competitive forces would drive out the weaker competitors. The most vulnerable institutions would appear to be the middle-sized British merchant banks, who lack the resources to compete effectively.

A major worry has been the extent to which the newly structured capital market has drawn in scarce resources, notably graduates who are paid salaries far beyond their opportunity cost. This has extensive effects, not least on house prices in the South-east. It is questionable whether the value added by the increased efficiency of the capital market warrants this type of externality.

Fig. 15.5 Gilt and FTA 500 share yields
Source: Lloyds Bank Economic Bulletin (1987b); *Financial Statistics*, May 1990

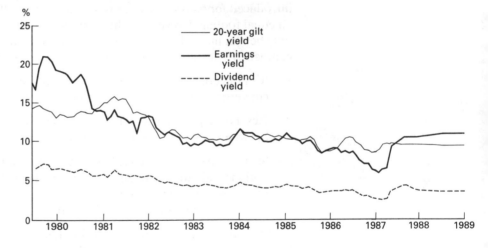

Concerns about the structure and functioning of the capital market were highlighted by the equity market crash, which began in New York on 6 October 1987. Since the 'big bang' the increased volume of trade had forced share prices up and, by reducing transactions costs, probably prolonged the equity boom which had begun in 1984 (*Bank of England Quarterly Bulletin* 1988b). In the US the Dow Jones index collapsed by 22.6%.

The immediate reasons for the market crash were not hard to find. It was clear that in the preceeding year share prices in global financial markets had risen in such a way as to force yields down several points below gilt yields (see Fig. 15.5). There had thus emerged a 'reverse yield gap' which meant that either share prices would fall sometime or interest rates had to fall. The latter was unlikely given the fact that the US was borrowing from the world on a massive scale by issuing bonds in order to finance the US deficit. Share prices had therefore to bear the burden of adjustment, and events in UK financial markets – not least in terms of job losses and company failure – continue to reflect the consequence of this.

The impact of 1992 on the financial sector

The implementation of the Single Europe Act in 1992 provides for the abolition of exchange controls and gives authorized financial institutions the right to do business anywhere in Europe. Financial sectors in other European countries are deregulating and modernizing in order to be able to compete more efficiently once the single market is in operation. Both financial institutions and financial markets are in the main more regulated and less developed than those within the UK financial sector. The implication of this is that there is more scope for innovation and change in Europe than there is in the UK, and this may present the UK financial sector with competitive challenges which currently do not exist.

However, increased freedom of competition will necessitate harmonization on a variety of fronts if enormous competitive disparities are not to result. Some of these distortions have already been foreseen and measures have been taken at Community level to eliminate them. For instance, Community-wide capital adequacy requirements are to be introduced for banks and securities firms so that all institutions compete on an equal footing. However, other distortions will inevitably remain, and will only be eliminated by agreement between individual countries as the competitive process proceeds. Examples of areas of concern include:

1. 'Conduct of business' rules, where there will have to be some convergence between stringent and lax host authorities.

2. Reserve requirements on banks will have to be standardized if some banks are not to suffer a competitive disadvantage.

3. Savings taxes, stamp duty, VAT, corporation tax, and tax treatment of options and futures are different everywhere. But it is not possible to reconcile the freedom of individual countries to tax with the freedom of capital movement within the Community.

All this has implications for the UK financial sector, and financial institutions have responded to the situation in four separate ways.

1. Banks are moving into Europe, either by share swaps (as for instance between the Royal Bank of Scotland and Banco Santander) or by the establishment of new branches, such as those by NatWest in Spain.

2. Financial institutions are extending the scope of their activities Community-wide by merging with other types of financial institution – for instance, banks have merged with insurance companies and established links with fund managers.

3. In countries where banking is small-scale and fragmented there are initiatives to promote larger banking groups. This is bound to have

competitive implications for the UK banking sector, which is already heavily rationalized and has therefore little scope for gaining economies of scale.

4. Product innovation in financial services and banking – for instance, interest-bearing current accounts and new types of credit card – is bound to spread, thus intensifying competition.

As to the impact of all this, several questions present themselves.

1. To what extent will London lose business? It is inevitable that as continental markets become more streamlined business which is now done in Eurocurrencies in London may move back to national financial markets. This is particularly likely in the case of Euro-DM business, which has to some extent been driven abroad by restrictions on the West German banking sector.

2. To what extent will business shift from banking to other types of lending? Industry might well find it easier to raise money on innovative continental securities markets.

3. To what extent will a more competitive European sector give opportunity for further expansion by competitors outside the Community? Japanese financial companies, in particular, may wish to extend the scope of their operations by acquisitions in Europe.

4. Does the future lie with diversified financial conglomerates or with highly specialized financial institutions? In terms of financial products, to what extent is standardization possible at a Community-wide level? The answers to these questions will depend on the extent to which the tendancy towards globalization of financial business is outweighed by the national character of differing market demands. Whatever the outcome, the UK financial sector is entering a period of increasing risk and uncertainty (BEQB May 1989).

Notes

1. See also *National Westminster Bank Review,* Aug. 1987, issue on supervision.
2. But see the argument in M. J. B. Hall, Deregulation of building societies; the prudential issues, *Royal Bank of Scotland Review*, Dec. 1987, where it is argued that the building societies are disadvantaged.

References

Bank of England Quarterly Bulletin (1977) **17**, No. 2, June.
Bank of England Quarterly Bulletin (1986a) **26**, No. 3, Sept. International Banking in London 1975–85.
Bank of England Quarterly Bulletin (1986b) **26**, No. 4, Life assurance company and private pension fund investment 1962–84, Dec.
Bank of England Quarterly Bulletin (1987) **27**, No. 1, Feb.
Bank of England Quarterly Bulletin (1988a) **28**, No. 1, Behaviour of industrial and commercial companies, Feb.

Bank of England Quarterly Bulletin (1988b) **28**, No. 1, The equity market crash, Feb.

Bank of England Quarterly Bulletin (1989a) **29**, No. 2, Personal credit problems, May.

Bank of England Quarterly Bulletin (1989b) **29**, No. 2, Europe, 1992 and the City, May.

Bank of England Quarterly Bulletin (1989c), **29**, No. 4, London as an international finance centre, Nov.

Bank of England Quarterly Bulletin (1990), **30**, No. 1, Venture capital in the UK, Feb.

British Business 11 Aug. 1989. Acquisitions and mergers.

British Business 7 March 1990. Consumer credit.

Carrington, J. C. and **Edwards, G. T.** (1979) *Financing Industrial Investment.* Macmillan.

CSO (1988a) *Financial Statistics.* Feb.

CSO (1988b) *Financial Statistics.* March.

CSO (1990a) *Financial Statistics.* Feb.

CSO (1990b) *Financial Statistics.* May.

Edwards, G. T. (1982) Why listening to a bank's reply matters, *Guardian*, 27 Oct.

Edwards, J. and **Mayer, C.** (1985) *An Investigation into the Dividend and New Equity Issue Practices of Firms.* IFS Working Paper No. 80, Institute of Fiscal Studies.

Lloyds Bank Economic Bulletin (1987a) Consumer credit concerns, Oct.

Lloyds Bank Economic Bulletin (1987b) Why share prices had to fall, Dec.

Lloyds Bank Economic Bulletin (1989) UK living on credit, Nov.

Midland Bank Review (1987) The economics of 'big bang', Summer.

National Westminster Bank Review (1987) Aug. Various articles on suspension.

Oxford Review of Economic Policy (1986) **2**, No. 4. Innovation and regulation in financial markets.

Royal Bank of Scotland Review (1987) Dec. Deregulation of Building Societies; the prudential issues.

Royal Bank of Scotland Review (1990) March, The Future Evolution of Financial Markets in Europe.

The Economist (1983) Buildobanking at a price, 29 Jan.

Vittas, D. (1986) Banks' relations with industry: an international survey, *National Westminster Bank Review*, Feb.

16   Money

This chapter looks at the nature of money, and its importance from both monetarist and Keynesian perspectives. The money stock must be measured before it can be controlled: we therefore look at current definitions of the money stock, distinguishing between 'narrow' and 'broad' money. We review current attempts to control the money stock, and analyse the problems which have arisen in the course of their implementation.

The nature of money

The need for money in any society arises out of the process of exchange. Anything which is used to promote the exchange of goods and services is therefore thought of as money, and its existence eliminates the need to exchange goods directly for other goods through barter. In the UK we use notes, coins and cheques to buy goods and to settle debts. Cheques represent a claim on bank deposits and can easily be converted into notes or coin (cash). We therefore define money in the UK as notes, coin and bank deposits. Recent definitions include building society deposits.

However, what is true for us is not necessarily true in general. At other times and in other places money takes different forms. Historically many different commodities have been used as money – gold is probably the most widely known of these – but even today, in some parts of the world, commodities such as shells or large stones are used as money. For any commodity to function as money it must fulfil four functions:

1. It must act as a unit of account, i.e. the unit used to express the relative values of different commodities.

2. It must act as a standard of deferred payment, i.e. a means by which spending can be deferred from the present to some future date, as in the case of contracts.

3. It must act as a store of value, i.e. a means by which today's wealth can be retained for future use.

4. It must act as a medium of exchange, i.e. a means by which the process of exchange can be separated into two distinct acts of buying and selling, without requiring that the seller should purchase goods from the person who buys his goods, or vice versa.

The relative importance of these functions will vary over time, and from place to place, depending on the nature of economic activity. In advanced economies where production is specialized, the medium of exchange function is paramount, because the surpluses produced must be exchanged. However, the store of value function is less important in these economies, partly because wealth can be held in the form of other assets such as bills or shares, but also because the existence of inflation has meant that money does not retain its value over time. In other societies, where subsistence activity is more common, the commodity chosen as money may serve primarily as a wealth holding rather than as a medium of exchange, or as a unit of account in, for instance, the calculation of bridewealth on the occasion of a marriage.

The commodity chosen as money varies depending on its major function. In societies where money is primarily used as a wealth form money can take the form of livestock – cattle, for instance – or large stones, or precious metals. The most important characteristics of these commodities are durability and stable value. In exchange economies such as the UK the commodity chosen will need to have the characteristics of portability, divisibility and homogeneity. In economies such as the UK the money stock typically comprises notes, coins and deposits, represented in transactions by cheques. All money commodities will have to be recognizable as such, and in addition, in economies where there is a lack of stability in the financial system, or where the financial system is not developed, the money commodity will need to have intrinsic value, i.e. to be useful for some purpose other than as money.

The most useful definition of money is therefore that 'money is anything which is generally acceptable as such'. This definition allows for the fact that the commodity chosen as money will vary according to the circumstances prevailing in particular economies. The acceptability of any commodity will depend on how efficiently it fulfils the functions of money required by that particular society.

Near money

We have argued that it is not always the case that the commodity chosen as money has to fulfil all the functions of money. However, the logic does not work the other way round – it is not the case that commodities which fulfil only some of the functions of money can be classed as money. Credit cards and luncheon vouchers, for instance, can be used for transactions, but they are not money because they cannot always be used, nor do they fulfil the other functions of money. Cigarettes are used in prisons as a medium of exchange, but they are not money. Paper assets such as bills serve as a store of value, but they cannot be used as a medium of exchange. However, liquid assets, i.e. those which can be easily converted into money without loss of value, form a potential addition to the money stock, and are often referred to as 'near money'. Assets normally classed as 'liquid' include time deposits, bills, and certificates of deposit (Fig. 16.1). Other assets become more liquid the nearer is their maturity date.

The importance of money

Economists have always believed that 'money matters'. In other words, it has always been assumed that as well as fulfilling the functions discussed earlier, changes in the money stock will have a significant effect on the workings of

Fig. 16.1 Liquidity spectrum

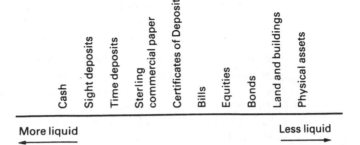

the economy. However, there has been much disagreement as to whether changes in the money stock, M, are *causally* related to changes in macro-economic aggregates. As we shall see later, recent experience has tended to cast doubt on this. Even if we do assume for the sake of argument, that there *is* such a connection, we have then to establish whether changes in the money stock will work quickly to affect economic variables which alter rapidly, such as output and employment, or whether the effects of monetary changes will have a more profound and long-term effect on variables which move more slowly, such as prices. Both the Classical economists and the more recent monetarist school are inclined to emphasize the longer-term view; Keynesian economists are concerned with short-run effects. It would, however, be a mistake to see these two points of view as diametrically opposed to one another. Keynes himself recognized the possibility that excessive monetary expansion would lead to inflation, but the focus of his attention as an economist working at a time of depression was on the short-run effects of monetary policy. Monetarism gained in stature during the 1970s at a time when inflation was the major policy problem, and when supply-side deficiencies, such as low productivity and labour market rigidities, were a clear hindrance to economic expansion.

The Quantity Theory of Money

The connection between money on the one hand and output and prices on the other can be formally stated by means of the Fisher identity known as the Quantity Theory. It states that

$$M \times V = P \times T$$

in other words, that the amount of money in the system times the velocity of circulation (the speed at which money circulates) must be identical to the number of transactions times their price.

The velocity of circulation is a measure of the speed at which money circulates in the economy, and is determined by the following.

1. The *rate* at which money is passed from one person to another. This, in turn, is primarily determined by *payments practices* – by whether wages are paid weekly or monthly, for instance, or by how quickly credit accounts are settled.

2. The *length of time* for which money is held. Money is held for transactions purposes, but also as a wealth form. The greater the fraction of the money stock held as an asset (i.e. as a wealth form), the lower is

the *overall* velocity of circulation (although that part of the money stock which is still circulating will have to circulate faster if a given volume of monetary transactions is to be maintained).

The Quantity Theory thus assumes that there is a long-term equilibrium relationship between private sector money holdings and nominal incomes. The 'theory' is of course an identity, in the sense that in the long term it must be true by definition. However, we can use it to illustrate the disagreement between monetarists and Keynesians in terms of the interrelationships between the four variables M, V, P and T. The two schools of thought differ in their views on such interrelationships, as well as on the question of the time perspective.

The monetarist view of money

Monetarism is interested in long-term relationships. Monetarist economists believe that money affects 'money things' such as prices, rather than 'real things' such as output and employment. They therefore believe that T, the volume of transactions (and therefore of output), is determined by factors outside the Quantity Theory itself – for instance, by supply-side factors operating on the labour and goods market such as productivity, production costs and profits. T, in other words, is exogenously determined.

Monetarists also hold that V is constant in the long run. If T is exogenously determined and V is constant, then there is a clear relationship between M and P. However, monetarists would argue that the relationship is not merely true in a definitional sense, but that there is a causal relationship whereby changes in M will actually cause changes in P. We must first examine how this can be the case. We then deal with some of the criticisms of this position.

The monetarist explanation for the connection between money and prices hinges on the effects of an increase in M in different markets. It would be simple to argue that an increase in the money stock, by giving people more purchasing power, causes goods market prices to rise. In fact, the early Classical economist would have argued in this way, but in those days goods prices were market determined, whereas nowadays goods prices, as Keynes pointed out, are determined by costs of production and do not vary with changes in demand. So modern monetarists do not attempt to account for the effect of changes in M on P by looking at the goods market alone. Instead, they concentrate on the labour market and the asset market in order to identify the ways in which the prices of goods are affected by changes in M.

Monetarists admit that changes in M may well be associated with temporary changes in output due to the way labour markets work and to the existence of inflationary expectations. If there is an increase in the money stock producers are likely to increase production to meet the increased demand for goods. Labour market conditions may mean that they have to pay higher wages to get the extra labour, but they know that they can pass these higher costs on in the form of higher prices. There will thus be both a rise in wages and a rise in output and employment.

Wages will rise from W to W_1 and output and employment from e^* to e^1. However, workers will quickly realize that although their wages have risen in money terms, in real terms they are no better off since prices have also risen. Because it is assumed that the supply of labour depends not on the money

Fig. 16.2 The labour market

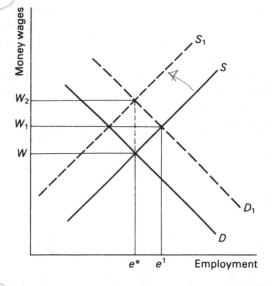

wage but on the real wage, the supply of labour will now be reduced and output and employment will return to their original level at e^*, but money wages will have risen to W_2 leading to a rise in prices and inflation.

Monetarists also point to the effect of an increase in M on asset prices. Money is regarded by the monetarist as an *asset*, i.e. a form of wealth holding as well as a medium of exchange. It is, however, just one asset within a whole spectrum of assets, of varying degrees of liquidity, profitability and marketability.

The definition of the word 'asset' used here is so broad that it includes cash at one end of the spectrum, and physical assets, including goods, at the other. All these assets will have different characteristics, not only in terms of liquidity, but also in terms of profitability and of marketability. Asset-holders will hold a portfolio, or range of assets, which will depend on their preferences for these characteristics, as well as on the prices and relative rates of return of each asset.

An increase in M may mean that money holdings in the portfolio rise beyond an acceptable level. To avoid this, asset-holders will readjust their portfolio, switching out of money towards the less liquid end of the spectrum. This will increase demand for relatively less liquid assets, raising their prices. This will be true not only for the prices of financial assets such as shares and bonds, but also for those physical goods held as assets. As a result, an increase in M will imply an increase in P.

It is important to note that monetarism changes the relationship between M and P (given V and T) from that of an identity, to a causal relationship. Although monetarism provides a theoretical rationale for doing this, a number of criticisms can be made of the view that a change in M will automatically lead to a change in prices. The first, and perhaps the most damaging, relates to the assumption of constant velocity of circulation.

The velocity of circulation has always fluctuated in the short run, often in response to sudden fluctuations in the money stock. However, monetarists have always argued that in the longer term it could be assumed stable. This no longer appears to be the case (*Royal Bank of Scotland Review* 1987). Velocity has fallen dramatically in the 1980s, reversing a trend which had been rising since 1950, although, as Fig. 16.3 shows, different monetary aggregates behave differently. Prior to 1980, the growth of deposits was restricted, and negative real interest rates made deposit-holding unattractive. Velocity therefore rose. Since 1980, however, short-term interest rates have been historically high and real interest rates have been positive. People have therefore preferred to hold their wealth in interest-bearing deposits rather than in non-monetary forms. This has decreased the velocity of circulation of the broader monetary aggregates.

Fig. 16.3 Velocity of the monetary aggregates
Source: Bank of England Quarterly Bulletin (1990b)

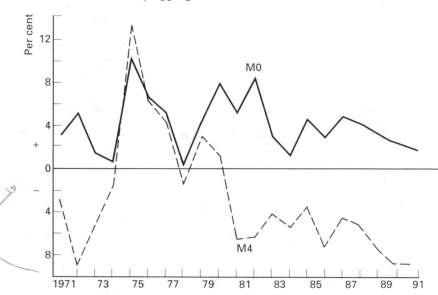

Velocity can therefore not be assumed constant, and any assessment of changes in the money stock on the economy will have to take that fact into account.

Another problem with the monetarist explanation of the effects of changes in *M* relates to assumptions made about goods and labour market behaviour. Goods prices are assumed to be demand- rather than cost-determined, changing as asset holdings change. Labour supply in the aggregate is assumed to be a function of the real wage, rather than dependent on the desire for employment. Whereas it can be argued that there may be circumstances where these assumptions might be relevant – for instance, where physical assets are goods which already exist such as houses or paintings, or where wages are so low as to be matched by social security payments, they cannot be said to be appropriate in the general case. The monetarist response to this is to point to the long-run emphasis of their argument. Of course in policy terms this perspective is unrealistic, since circumstances and policy problems are constantly changing, so that the long-run is never in fact reached.

The Keynesian view of money

The perspective of Keynesian economics is essentially short run. Keynesians believe that changes in the money stock affect 'real' variables such as output and employment rather than money variables such as prices. Keynes thought in terms of financial assets only: he thus envisaged people as holding money for speculative motives as well as for transactions purposes. Each individual would switch money holdings into bonds when he considered the price low enough and the yield high enough to warrant the loss of liquidity. An increase in the money stock would have the effect of increasing the flow of money on to the bond market, hence driving up the price of bonds. The yield, i.e. the rate of interest, would fall in consequence. Since assets were purely financial, no other prices in the economy would be affected.

The fall in the interest rate will have the effect of encouraging investment (see Ch. 12), and output, employment and incomes will rise in consequence as the multiplier effect works through the economy. We should ask ourselves why Keynes did not see this general expansion as causing a rise in prices. The answer is that, in the Keynesian view of the economy, different variables adjust at different rates. Market quantities, such as output or the number of jobs, adjust much more quickly than market prices. Prices may indeed rise as a result of an expansion in aggregate demand, but they will rise slowly, because it will take time for manufacturers to feel the effects of overall expansion on costs of production. Price rises will only accelerate when the economy nears full employment. The market is therefore in a permanent 'disequilibrium' state, because prices do not adjust fast enough to equate demand and supply.

The differences between the two positions can be summarized as follows. Monetarists believe that money affects money things (prices) through asset-switching behaviour which affects *all* relative prices, including goods prices. Real things (output and employment) are, at least in the long run, affected not by money, but by supply-side factors such as productivity, profits and costs. Their perspective is fundamentally a long-term one. Keynesians, on the other hand, believe that money affects real things because changes in M alter prices of financial assets, and hence the rate of interest, investment and consumption; this change in aggregate demand leads to changes in output and employment. Prices are largely unaffected, since markets never fully adjust and remain in disequilibrium, with quantities responding more rapidly than prices to changes in demand.

This debate between monetarists and Keynesians is not just about the role of money, and the consequent nature of monetary policy, it is also about ideology. It is about whether the market can, and should, be allowed to allocate resources in a modern economy. However, the choice of economic policy tends to be based on pragmatic rather than ideological grounds, with the control of inflation having become the overriding policy priority of all governments since the early 1970s when inflation became an endemic part of every Western economy. The control of the money supply has therefore assumed major importance even for those of a broadly Keynesian persuasion who doubt the causal link between M and P, because even if a rise in P (inflation) is not actually *caused* by an increase in M, it must be *financed* by such an increase. In other words, the money stock must at the very least play a permissive role in the inflationary process, otherwise even inflationary factors such as wage increases would be choked off by shortage of bank loans and rising interest rates. It is to the measurement and control of M, the money stock, that we now turn.

Counting the money stock

The importance of measuring the money stock derives from the fact that governments need to control the quantity of money in existence in order to achieve macroeconomic policy objectives. Estimates of the money stock have been published since 1966. However, there is no one measure of the money stock which will serve all purposes. We need firstly a measure of the money stock, such as M_0, which will approximate to the notion of a 'cash base'. Other definitions, such as M_2, are designed to reflect spending or the volume of transactions in the economy. Yet others, such as the now defunct M_3, were defined because they were operationally useful in policy terms (M_3 consisted of notes, coins and all bank deposits). Wider measures, such as M_5, include liquid assets which are theoretically available for spending in the near future.

Money stock definitions are changed frequently by the authorities not only because of changing asset-holding behaviour by the public but also because of the fact that the financial sector itself has undergone a period of rapid structural and institutional change. Money is held on deposit by the public not only for transactions purposes but also as an asset, and anything which changes the motivation for holding money will cause changes in the aggregates and hence make them less useful for explaining and predicting what happens in the economy. A good example of this is the way in which the velocity of circulation (see above) has made it difficult to be dogmatic about the relationship between the money stock and the rate of inflation. Also, structural changes and innovations in financial instruments tend to change the assets which are included in any particular category, and this in turn changes the relationship between money and spending. There is thus no constant relationship between any one definition and income or inflation. Even if it is possible to establish such a relationship, any attempt to control the aggregate will lead to attempts on the part of individuals and institutions to evade the controls (Goodhart's law), and such attempts are likely to be successful, given the wide range of substitutability between different financial assets. For these reasons, frequent changes and amendments have been made to the definitions over the last decade, and the result has been that we now have a set of definitions which are to some extent inconsistent. The Bank of England is currently undertaking a fundamental review of the whole issue with a view to rationalizing the whole structure of monetary aggregate definitions (Bank of England 1990a). The definitions which follow are therefore of necessity subject to change.

In counting the money stock, two prior questions present themselves:

1. Which deposits should be included? Some measures include only sight deposits, some also include time deposits. In measures designed to count balances available for transactions balances, only retail deposits (<£100,000) are counted, in other cases wholesale balances (>£100,000) are also included. All deposits counted are now made by the private sector as opposed to the public sector; public sector deposits were excluded in 1984. Deposits held by overseas residents are also excluded from the definitions, although in some other countries they are included.

2. Which institutions' liabilities should be taken into account? Traditionally only bank deposits have been counted, but more recently building society deposits have been included in certain measures (M_2, M_4 and M_5)

to reflect the fact that these institutions now provide a range of banking services (see Ch. 15). The most recent changes to the published money stock figures have been occasioned by the fact that, in July 1989, the Abbey National building society changed its status to that of a bank. To include their very large deposits in money stock measures which did not already include building society deposits would have involved large breaks in the statistical series of those measures. Given that these monetary measures are no longer targetted for policy purposes, and that these aggregates have therefore lost some of their relevance, it was decided to cease publication of M_1, M_3 and M_3c, and to introduce a new monetary aggregate, M_4c.

It is also possible that the inclusion of building society liabilities may not be the end of the process. The Government has always issued liabilities – e.g. Treasury bills – with some of the characteristics of money, and even the liabilities of commercial organizations, such as bank-accepted bills, are now included in M_5. Newer paper assets, such as sterling commercial paper and short bonds, may eventually be deemed sufficiently 'money-like' to be included in the broadest aggregates.

3. Which currencies should be included? Only one of the definitions includes foreign currency deposits; it may well be the case that after 1992 these deposits may be a more significant element in the definitions.

Monetary aggregates currently in use are as follows.

M_0

This consists of:

(a) notes and coins in circulation outside the Bank of England (with banks and the public); plus
(b) bankers' operational (i.e. clearing) deposits with the Bank of England.

This measure is known as the wide monetary base. It represents the cash base of the system, and is the only money stock measure which is not substantially affected by changes in the financial system.

M_0 can change for two reasons:

1. The Government can issue more notes and coins.

2. Clearing deposits can change as a result of transactions between the public and the Government. These happen all the time as a result of taxation collection, or public expenditure, or open market operations. Any transaction between the Government and the public will alter bankers' balances at the Bank of England and hence alter M_0.

It is clear therefore that M_0 can be directly affected by controlling the note issue, by keeping the growth of public expenditure in line with taxation receipts, and by manipulating transactions in the bill market and the gilt market.

However, the authorities have also taken into account the fact that the velocity of M_0 has risen steadily over time due to the fact that people's cash-holding behaviour has changed. Many more people now have bank accounts and pay by cheque, and credit cards have become more generally used.

NIBM$_1$

This consists of:

(a) non-bank private sector's holdings of notes and coin; plus
(b) sterling non-interest bearing sight deposits held by the UK non-bank private sector with UK banks.

This measure represents the non-interest bearing component of the traditional 'narrow' money stock measure, M$_1$. It was devised as a measure which would isolate the count of sight deposits from the fluctuations which occurred as people moved their money in and out of their bank accounts in order to 'shop around' for the best short-term rate of interest on their deposits. It continues to be published because it is not affected by the changing status of building societies, since these do not take non-interest-bearing deposits. However, its usefulness as an indicator of expenditure is limited by the fact that people also use their interest-bearing deposits for transactions purposes, so that NIBM$_1$ understates the expenditure potential in the economy.

M$_2$

This consists of:

(a) notes and coins in circulation with the non-bank public (including building societies); plus
(b) sterling retail deposits held by the UK private sector with UK banks, with building societies and in the National Savings Bank ordinary account;

'Retail' deposits comprise all non-interest-bearing deposits plus all sight or time deposits on which cheques can be drawn, regardless of maturity, plus other deposits (excluding certificates of deposit) of less than £100,000 and with less than one month to maturity. This is therefore the *transactions measure* of the money stock. It was introduced in 1982 to identify all balances available for immediate spending. Since it was designed to include building society deposits it is unaffected by the recent institutional changes which have taken place in that sector.

There are a number of problems with this definition from the point of view of its usefulness (Bank of England, 1990a).

1. It is inconsistent with the broad aggregate M$_4$ (see below). It could be made consistent by:

    *   eliminating the cash holdings of building societies, which are in any event small
    *   removing the National Savings Bank ordinary accounts, which no longer form a significant total of transactions expenditure

2. It includes newer types of account which are mainly savings accounts, such as high-interest cheque accounts. It is therefore no longer purely a measure of transactions balances. A 'transactions' measure would need to be defined with reference to the facilities offered by accounts and the restrictions imposed on withdrawal.

3. The definition of 'retail' balances as being limited to £100,000 is arbitrary

in an inflationary situation; some form of indexing of this limit needs to be used.

4. There is a need for an aggregate which refers to the personal sector only. M_2 includes companies and OFIs (see Ch. 15) as well as persons.

5. The assets within M_2 range along a spectrum of liquidity – i.e. some are more immediately 'money' than others. There is a need for an aggregate which *weights* the 'moneyness' of the assets it contains. This can be done by using what is called a 'Divisia' index.

M_4

This aggregate was introduced in 1987 and includes:

(a) notes and coins in circulation with the public; plus
(b) all sterling deposits (including certificates of deposit) held with UK banks and building societies by non-bank non-building society private sector.

This measure was introduced in 1987 to take account of the evolving role of the building societies. The fact that building societies now act as banks, providing cheque accounts and other services, means that their deposits should now be counted as available for transactions rather than as savings deposits, as they were in the past. One of the uses of M_4 is that the 'counterparts' of the measure can be easily identified (see below).

M_4c

This is a new monetary aggregate which replaces the old M_3c. Its purpose is to allow for the very large total of foreign currency as opposed to sterling deposits. It consists of:

(a) notes and coin in circulation with the public; plus
(b) all sterling and foreign currency deposits (including certificates of deposit) held with UK banks and building societies by the non-bank, non-building society private sector.

M_5

This measure is the old PSL_2 measure, and comprises:

(a) M_4; plus
(b) private sector holdings of bank bills, Treasury bills, local authority deposits, certificates of tax deposit and national savings instruments (excluding certificates, SAYE and other long term deposits).

M_5 is the money stock measure which includes liquid assets; again, there are a number of issues here.

1. The major problem is to know exactly which assets should be included here. A 'liquid' asset is defined as one which can be realized at short notice without significant loss of either interest or capital value. What might be termed a 'liquid' asset then obviously varies with the state of the market and with the extent of innovation in terms of new financial instruments. For instance, how should issues of sterling instruments by borrowers other than deposit-taking institutions be treated? How should we assess the liquidity of, say, eurosterling bonds approaching maturity?

2. National Savings certificates which have matured, but which are still held on extension terms, are repayable on demand. Government borrowing in the early 1980s resulted in a large stock of these instruments. However, they are excluded from M_5.

3. It is questionable whether M_5 serves any useful purpose, given that the maturity cut-off does not fully reflect the liquidity of the assets.

4. The international dimensions of liquidity would need to be taken into account for completeness. These comprise:

   - UK residents' holdings of sterling abroad (these are not large);
   - UK residents' holdings of foreign currency liquidity held at home and abroad (this includes for instance eurocurrency deposits held in the UK);
   - overseas residents' holdings of sterling at home and abroad.

Table 16.1 summarizes the relationships among the monetary aggregates and their components.

Table 16.2 shows the growth rates of the monetary aggregates. It illustrates the fact that the aggregates behave differently. The broader aggregates are more stable, but it is the narrower aggregates which respond more sensitively to changing external pressures. For instance, it will be seen that in the latter part of 1989, $NIBM_1$ began to decline, and M_2 grew at a slower rate, in response to the tightening of monetary conditions.

Monetary control

Monetary policy is undertaken by the Government in order to affect macroeconomic variables such as output, employment and inflation. It involves controlling the quantity of money in existence, or its rate of growth, either by controlling the supply of money or the demand for money via the interest rate, i.e. the price of money. Before we examine the recent history of monetary control in the UK it might be helpful to look at some of the basic principles underlying this issue.

The money supply can be defined as cash plus deposits. The Bank of England has complete control over the supply of cash in the system, and this cash is held either by the banks or by the public for various purposes – there is a constant flow of cash in and out of the banking system. This flow depends on the need of the public to hold cash for various purposes at any one time, and is not under the control of the authorities.

Bank deposits are created by bank lending. When a customer is granted a loan of £100 by his bank, his current account (deposit) is credited with the amount of the loan. Total bank deposits thus increase by £100 (see Fig. 16.4). At the same time the bank acquires an asset (the loan). Both liabilities and assets of the banking sector have thus increased, and so also has the money stock as measured by liabilities (deposits). This process can clearly not continue indefinitely; it will be limited by the extent to which the banks consider it prudent to create credit, given the cash reserves they hold, and given that a certain proportion of depositors are likely to wish to withdraw cash in any one period of time. Bank lending in a competitive environment is

Notes and coins in circulation with the public	Notes and coins in circulation outside the Bank of England
+ Private sector non-interest-bearing sterling sight bank deposits	+ Bankers' balances with the Bank of England
= Non-interest bearing M_1	= M_0*

+ Private sector interest bearing sterling sight bank deposits

+ Private sector sterling time bank deposits

+ Private sector interest-bearing retail sterling deposits with bank and building societies, and national savings bank ordinary accounts

+ Private sector holdings of sterling certificates of deposit

– M_2

+ Private sector holdings of building society shares and deposits and sterling certificates of deposit

= M_4

+ Holdings by the private sector of money market instruments (bank bills, Treasury bills, local authority deposits) certificates of tax deposit and national savings instruments (excluding certificates, SAYE and other long-term deposits)

+ Private sector foreign currency bank and building society deposits

= M_4c

= M_5

* M_0 is calculated on a weekly average basis. All other aggregates are observations at end months.

Source: Financial Statistics Explanatory Handbook (1990) June.

Table 16.1 Relationships among the monetary aggregates and their components

also limited by the amount of creditworthy customers they can attract, and by the extent to which lending is 'redeposited' (see Ch. 15). Also, banks may find it expedient to hold assets other than loans to customers – in particular, to hold liquid assets in the form of money-market loans which can be realized quickly should it be necessary to repay depositors. These 'liquid assets' can also be classed as 'high-powered money'.

The money supply is thus dependent on:

(a) the total volume of cash in existence;
(b) the proportion of cash held by the banks;

Table 16.2 12 months unadjusted growth rates of $NIBM_1$, M_2, M_4, and M_5

End quarters		$NIBM_1$	M_2	M_4	M_5
1986	2nd qtr.	9.8	14.1	15.7	14.8
	3rd qtr.	16.7	15.2	15.8	15.0
	4th qtr.	11.6	14.3	15.4	14.7
1987	1st qtr.	10.4	12.3	14.0	13.5
	2nd qtr.	13.3	12.0	13.9	13.5
	3rd qtr.	5.5	10.0	14.9	14.4
	4th qtr.	10.1	10.4	16.3	15.8
1988	1st qtr.	15.1	13.6	16.8	16.6
	2nd qtr.	10.7	15.1	16.8	16.1
	3rd qtr.	12.5	17.3	18.7	18.0
	4th qtr.	12.4	16.9	17.6	16.7
1989	1st qtr.	2.4	14.8	18.1	17.1
	2nd qtr.	−3.2	11.3	18.6	18.0
	3rd qtr.	−6.0	10.0	17.4	16.8
	4th qtr.	−5.5	9.8	18.2	17.9
1990	1st qtr.	−4.6	8.5	17.5	17.1
	2nd qtr.	−2.4	8.1	16.9	16.7

Source: Bank of England Quarterly Bulletin (1990b).

Fig. 16.4 Banks' balance sheet

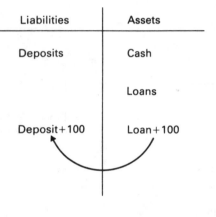

(c) the ratio of cash to deposits desired by the banks;

(d) the demand for loans. Unless people are willing and able to borrow banks cannot lend, even if they have sufficient reserves to do so.

In a fractional reserve banking system such as the one we have outlined, what possibilities exist for the monetary authorities to control the growth of the money stock?

1. The authorities may control the quantity of cash in existence. However, this will be ineffective because, as we have seen, the important focus for control purposes is not the total quantity of cash in existence but the quantity of cash held by the banks. This can be affected in two ways:

(a) The authorities can initiate transactions which affect the size of bankers' balances at the Bank of England. If, for instance, the authorities sell gilts to the public ('open market operations') there will be a transfer of cash from banks' clearing balances at the Bank of England into the government accounts as the cheques paid by the public for the gilts are cleared. The authorities can reinforce this procedure by making regulations as to the proportion of total cash to deposits which must be held by the banks – so that when banks' cash holdings are reduced by the above strategy they would be forced to reduce their lending. However, it has to be remembered that bankers' balances change constantly as a result of normal transactions between the Government and the public.

(b)   When the Government finances its borrowing requirement by borrowing from the Bank of England it issues securities to the Bank in exchange for cash (i.e. it 'prints' money). It then spends the cash, usually by writing cheques to members of the public, which are cleared through bankers' balances at the Bank of England, causing them to rise. If the Government wants to check the growth of the cash base it must therefore be careful not to borrow in this way.

2.   The authorities might impose regulations on the banks forcing them to hold a certain proportion of cash + liquid assets to total deposits. Control measures might then consist of:

(a)   keeping a tight control on the volume of suitable liquid assets available. For instance, if Treasury bills were to be defined as liquid assets, the authorities should ensure that only a limited quantity are issued;

(b)   open market operations as described above, which would force the banks to sell liquid assets in order to make up their cash ratio;

(c)   requiring the banks to deposit some of their liquid assets with the Bank of England so that they would not be available to back lending; this is known as 'calling for special deposits'.

These techniques were in wide use during the 1960s and 1970s, and formed the basis of monetary control measures at that time.

3.   The authorities may use directives – for instance, they may ask the banks to restrict the volume or the type of lending they undertake, by imposing 'credit ceilings'. Alternatively, they may attempt to enforce penalties on banks whose deposits grow faster than some predetermined rate. As we shall see, the supplementary special deposit scheme (the 'corset') of the 1970s, was such an attempt.

4.   Another line of attack might focus on influencing the demand for loans. The authorities might raise short-term interest rates in an attempt to deter people from borrowing. This is the technique currently in use. They might combine this with policies designed to make it more difficult or more expensive for the banks to raise funds, hence affecting the profitability of lending. It is also possible to use changes in the tax regulations to affect the demand for loans – for instance, the authorities might reduce or abolish tax relief on mortgage interest payments.

It would appear that the monetary authorities have an impressive battery of weapons at their disposal for the achievement of monetary policy objectives. However, post-war monetary control in the UK has been beset with difficulties. The key to understanding why this is the case is to remember that the financial system is constantly changing – perhaps never more so than in the last twenty years – and policies designed to control it have to alter accordingly. Institutions, instruments and markets evolve partly in response to outside influences and partly in order to evade controls imposed by the authorities. Also, governmental objectives change, as do beliefs about how to achieve those objectives, so that control strategies are constantly reformulated. We now look briefly at the changing nature of monetary policy over the last twenty years, before examining the way in which the current perspective has been established.

Monetary control in the 1970s

In the 1950s and 1960s Keynesian economists believed that the important monetary variable was the interest rate, because the interest rate affected the level of investment and was thus the bridge between the market for money and the market for goods. However, empirical evidence increasingly showed that investment is interest-inelastic, and that investment and other types of expenditure were influenced by the availability rather than the cost of credit. Monetary policy thus came to consist primarily of ceilings on lending, although the traditional weapons of liquidity ratios and special deposits were also in use.

Competition and Credit Control (CCC)

In 1971 the focus of monetary control was altered. Regulations were introduced which were designed to control the growth of liabilities, i.e. deposits. The price of credit, i.e. the interest rate, was to be market-determined rather than controlled by the authorities. Whereas previous arrangements had placed the emphasis on controlling the growth of lending, i.e. assets, the CCC document specified that banks should maintain a minimum ratio between 'eligible' reserve (liquid) assets and eligible liabilities. These latter were defined as total liabilities minus the deposits of monetary sector institutions. Eligible reserve assets included:

1. Balances at the Bank of England (other than special or supplementary special, deposits), to be an average of 1.5% of eligible liabilities.

2. Secured money at call with London discount market institutions.

3. British Government and Northern Ireland Treasury bills.

4. British Government stocks with a residual maturity of less than one year.

5. Local authority bills eligible for rediscount at the Bank of England.

6. Commercial bills eligible for rediscount at the Bank (up to a maximum of 2% of eligible liabilities).

If holdings of reserve assets fell below the fixed minimum, it followed that banks were in theory obliged to reduce their deposits by eight times that amount in order to retain the desired ratio. The converse would apply if reserve assets rose. Eligible reserve assets therefore functioned in this system as '*high-powered money*', i.e. assets which could generate a *multiple* contraction or expansion in the money stock (bank deposits).

There were two major ways in which the Bank of England could reduce the money supply under this system:

1. It could require the banks to make 'special deposits', i.e. to place a certain percentage of their eligible liabilities in a special deposit at the Bank of England which earned interest at Treasury bill rate. The effect of this was to remove liquidity from the banking system and cause banks to contract lending (and hence ban deposits) if they were already close to the 12.5% limit.

2. It could undertake 'open market operations'. Sales of gilts by the Bank of England on the open market caused banks' balances at the Bank of England to decline (as the cheques which pay for the gilt sales were cleared), forcing the banks to contract lending (and with it bank deposits) if near to the 12.5% limit. The banks might also seek to recall money lent to the discount houses, so that the discount houses had then to borrow from the Bank of England which acted as a 'lender of last resort'.

During the 1970s the Bank of England was prepared to function as a lender of last resort, but only at a rate of its own choosing. Minimum lending rate (MLR) was a penal rate, higher than other market rates. Through open market operations, the Bank of England could force the discount houses to borrow from the Bank, in this way placing upward pressure on interest rates throughout the system. This was sometimes referred to as making MLR 'effective'. Being forced to pay higher rates for loans, the discount houses would only lend to the Government, i.e. discount Treasury bills, at higher interest rates. In addition, the very act of selling gilt-edged stock on the open market forced their price down and raised the rate of interest. The Bank of England could, if it chose, reinforce this tendency to higher interest rates by raising MLR.

Very often, therefore, restrictive monetary policy consisted of two components – a tightening of high-powered money, as reserve assets were removed from the banking system by calls for special deposits or open market sales, and a raising of interest rates.

The CCC document placed the major emphasis on control of the money supply rather than on interest rate policy – interest rates were to be left to find their own level. In practice, however, monetary policy in the 1970s consisted of a mix of money supply control and interest rate policy.

Breakdown of the eligible reserve asset system

The eligible reserve asset system introduced in 1971 largely failed in the attempt to control the money supply. There were a number of reasons for this, which were largely outside the control of the monetary authorities:

1. It was obvious from the beginning that the authorities were not in fact willing to allow the interest rate changes necessary to achieve tight control of the money supply. It is only possible to control the quantity or the price (here the rate of interest) of money, not both.

2. The institutional focus of monetary control was too narrow. This was clearly indicated by the fact that when the clearing banks were being squeezed by the Bank of England, the secondary banking sector was still able to expand and provide alternative sources of finance.

3.   The advent of inflation in the early 1970s led to a chronic budget deficit, resulting in a large and persistent public sector borrowing requirement (PSBR). This meant a plentiful supply of government debt at the going rate of interest, much of which was bought by the banking sector. Some of this debt could be acquired by banks and used as eligible reserve assets, which meant that methods of monetary control which depended upon removing such assets from the banking sector became ineffective – banks simply replenished their holdings of Treasury bills and short-dated government bonds.

4.   As a consequence of (3) above, additional control measures, such as the supplementary special deposits scheme (the 'corset') were introduced. The corset took the form of a tax on the growth of interest-bearing deposits or eligible liabilities (IBELS). If the growth of these deposits exceeded a certain monthly percentage figure, the banks were forced to place a proportion of any excess with the Bank of England. This penalized the banks as these supplementary special deposits earned no interest at the Bank of England. Despite this restriction on the ability of the banks to expand their lending (IBELS), other sources of credit were found to take the place of bank advances. One way round the corset was the 'bill leak', whereby large firms raised money by issuing their own bills of exchange, guaranteed by the banks. These bills were used as forms of payment by the companies, acting in this way as money.

5.   The abolition of exchange control in October 1979 greatly increased flows of deposits between countries (see Ch. 22), making monetary management even more difficult. British residents were now free to open bank accounts overseas and to borrow abroad for current spending *in* the UK.

6.   Higher interest rates during the inflationary 1970s and early 1980s encouraged the growth of 'disintermediation' or 'round tripping'. This was the process whereby customers borrowed from their banks, only to relend the funds at higher interest rates in the money market. This provided additional liquidity for money-market institutions, enabling them to expand their deposits, thereby raising the money supply.

The operational difficulties experienced by the monetary authorities in the 1970s exemplified the unpredictability of the interaction between objectives, or targets, and techniques, or instruments, in a constantly changing financial environment. The authorities were uncertain as to whether the target was the quantity or the price of money, instruments of control varied in severity, and external factors, as well as the responses of the financial system itself, made it very difficult to apply monetary policy consistently. A fresh approach was clearly called for.

The medium term financial strategy (MTFS)

In March 1980 the Government unveiled its new approach to monetary control, i.e. the medium-term financial strategy (MTFS). The MTFS was designed to provide a framework of control by which the growth of the money stock could be 'targetted' over a four-year period. The emphasis of control shifted in two ways:

(a) From a short-term to a medium-term perspective;

(b) From control of the growth of deposits to control of bank *assets*, i.e. the 'counterparts' to the money stock.

Fig. 16.5 Counterparts to the money stock

Liabilities	Assets
Deposits (Money Stock)	Loans (to private sector; to public sector; to overseas)

Counterparts to the money stock   The money stock, as we have seen, is primarily defined in terms of bank deposits (liabilities). Deposits are created by lending. One line of attack on the growth of deposits might therefore be to control lending, because if lending is restricted deposits cannot be created. We shall consider for illustrative purposes the counterparts to one measure of the money stock – the now defunct M_3.

Banks lend in different ways; they lend to the Government and acquire bills and bonds in exchange, they lend to the private sector in the form of loans and overdrafts, and they lend overseas. Any such lending expands deposits and hence the money stock – the Government pays out the money it borrows to people who deposit it back in the banks, and other borrowers take loans by having their bank accounts credited (thus expanding deposits).

We can therefore present bank assets as the sum of:

(a)   lending to the Government;

(b)   lending to the private sector;

(c)   lending to the overseas sector.

In order to control these categories of lending they are quantified as follows:

1.   Bank lending to the Government is equal to total government borrowing minus what is borrowed from the private sector by means of sales of bills and bonds to individuals and institutions, or by means of National Savings.

2.   Lending to the private sector is simply the sum total of bank loans and overdrafts.

3.   Net lending to the overseas sector is calculated as follows. Firstly, sterling lending to overseas customers is counted. Secondly, any increase in sterling deposits held by foreigners is subtracted, because M_3 only includes deposits held by UK residents (these two will not cancel each other out if some of the money lent to overseas customers is used to finance payments to the UK private sector). Thirdly, account is also taken of whether the Bank of England has made net purchases or sales of foreign currency over the period. The former will increase deposits as the Bank pays sterling to foreign exchange dealers. Fourthly, any purchase of government debt by overseas residents is subtracted.

4.   Account is also taken of whether the banks themselves have increased

their own capital holdings as opposed to paying out profits – this will effectively decrease the amount of money in circulation.

All these different categories of bank assets are collectively known as 'counterparts' to the money stock, i.e. to deposits, and the monetary authorities aimed to control each one separately. In 1987/88 the figures for these counterparts were as shown in Table 16.3.

Table 16.3

Counterparts to changes in M_3 1987/1988	*£m.*
Net PSBR	−3,472
Purchases (−) of public sector debt by non-bank private sector	−4,743
Sterling lending to private sector	+44,728
External and foreign currency counterparts (−increase)	1,492
Net non-deposit liabilities	−4,582
Change in $£M_3$	33,423

Source: Bank of England Quarterly Bulletin (1988) Aug.

The inclusion of the building societies in the broader monetary aggregates has meant that the counterparts to the money stock are now formulated differently, but the basic principle is the same; account is taken not only of the wider institutional basis but also of the broader range of instruments (see Table 16.4). However, the introduction of liabilities other than those of banks and building societies inevitably makes the counterpart analysis more complex and hence less useful for discussing money stock control.

The MTFS aimed to restrict the rate of growth of the money stock by controlling each of these aggregates in the following way:

1. *Fiscal policy* was used to control the growth of the total PSBR. This involves either reducing public expenditure or increasing taxation. The PSBR has in fact been substantially reduced in recent years, partly due to public expenditure cuts (and to the sale of public sector assets such as British Telecom), but also, more recently, because of an increase in taxation receipts due to a rise in incomes.

2. The share of the PSBR funded by the non-bank private sector can be increased by *interest rate policy*. If interest rates are high enough to make yields on fixed-interest debt attractive to portfolio holders the PSBR can be funded without increasing the money stock. We may consider for a moment why this is the case. If people lend to the Government by buying bills and bonds they pay for them with money out of their bank accounts, so M_0 and the broad monetary aggregates will decline. When the Government spends the money it has borrowed it will find its way back into the banking system via payments to the public, so both M_0 and broad money will rise again. The net effect on the money stock is zero. If, on the other hand, the banks lend to the Government they acquire bills and bonds as assets which they pay for with bankers' balances. M_0 will fall, but this will be compensated for in the banks' balance sheets by the increase in holdings of public sector assets. When the Government spends the money M_0 will rise again, and so will deposits as people bank the receipts from the Government. The net effect is to increase both bank assets and deposits, and hence the money stock.

Counterparts to M_4		Counterparts to M_5
PSBR		PSBR
less		*less*
Debt sales to M_4 private sector	— *less* M_4 private sector holdings of Treasury bills, local authority deposits, CTDs, and national savings instruments (excluding certificates, SAYE, and other long-term deposits) —	Debt sales to M_4 private sector excluding those instruments included in M_5
less		*less*
External finance of the public sector		External finance of the public sector
= Public sector contribution		= Public sector contribution
plus		*plus*
Bank and building society lending in sterling to the M_4 private sector	— *plus* M_4 private sector holdings of bank bills —	Sterling borrowing by the M_4 private sector from banks, building societies plus M_4 private sector holdings of bank bills
less		*less*
External transactions of banks and building societies		External transactions of banks and building societies
less		*less*
Net non-deposit sterling liabilities of banks and building societies		Net non-deposit sterling liabilities of banks and building societies
= Change in M_4		= Change in M_5

Source: Financial Statistics Explanatory Handbook (1990).

Table 16.4 Relationship between counterparts of M_4 and M_5

An additional technique, known as overfunding, was used in the early 1980s to ensure that as little as possible of the PSBR was funded by the banking sector. Overfunding involved issuing more debt than was necessary to cover the borrowing requirement. This had the effect of reducing the cash base of the banking system as people paid for the government stock. The Bank of England then had to pump liquidity back into the system by buying large quantities of commercial bills from the bill market (the 'bill mountain'). This in turn had the effect of making the Bank of England a large lender to the corporate sector.

3. It was also planned to use *interest rate policy* to control the growth of private sector lending. As we shall see, this policy proved ineffective.

4. *Exchange rate policy* can be used to influence external and foreign currency counterparts. However, the other major influence on this element of the money stock is the interest rate, since high interest rates attract foreign capital and strengthen the pound.

The MTFS thus aimed to keep the growth of the monetary aggregates within the target ranges over a four-year period by using appropriate fiscal and interest rate policies. It was therefore important that effective day-to-day procedures be established to enable these policies to be carried out.

Monetary control procedures   In August 1981 the Bank of England announced a series of new measures which were designed to improve the functioning of the financial system in the light of some of the problems which had arisen towards the end of the 1970s, and also to form the basis for the implementation of the new monetary strategy. These measures were as follows:

1. All regulations were henceforth to apply to all institutions within the new monetary sector (see Ch. 15).

2. There was no longer to be a liquidity ratio; however, banks were asked to keep prudential stocks of liquid assets and to inform the Bank of any changes in their liquidity policies.

3. Banks were asked to deposit 0.5% (now 0.45%) of their eligible liabilities with the Bank of England as non-operational deposits. This was to provide a source of funds for the Bank. In addition, clearers were asked to maintain appropriate clearing balances as operational deposits with the Bank.

4. A category of 'eligible bank' was created. Eligible banks were asked to lend on average 5% of their eligible liabilities to discount houses and money brokers and jobbers, and not less than a daily minimum of 2.5% to the discount houses. This was to ensure that the money markets were not short of funds. In exchange for this commitment bills accepted by eligible banks were eligible for purchase by the Bank of England in the market. This arrangement was ended in 1986 after the 'big bang', although banks were asked not to make changes in their existing money-market lending policies.

5. The Bank of England announced that it would no longer act as lender of

last resort by lending directly to the discount houses at a published 'penal' rate (MLR), but would support the market by dealing in bills, responding to offers made by the discount houses. However, it reserved the right to lend directly on occasions when it judged that dealing would distort the workings of the market.

6. This support takes place within the perspective of the Bank's interest rate policy. The stated intention is to allow interest rates to be market-determined within an undisclosed band, but to deal in such a way that interest rates are affected should rates move higher or lower than the band. (Clearly, however, the Bank is in a strong position to influence rates simply by influencing expectations.)

However, the Bank of England also deals daily in the bill market in order to offset shortages and surpluses of cash in the system which can arise as transactions between the Government and the public vary one way or the other, altering bankers' clearing balances. Each morning the Bank makes an estimate of the day's position by taking into account all such transactions plus the existing state of bankers' balances. It will then offer to buy bills to relieve a shortage of cash, or sell to mop up a surplus; bankers' balances will either rise or fall as a result of these transactions. In the case of a shortage of funds, should the day's dealing not result in enough transactions at prices acceptable to the Bank, direct lending to the discount houses may have to take place.

What in fact happens is that when the cash position is adequate the Bank is prepared to allow market forces to determine the interest rate, given that it is moving within an acceptable range, provided levels of cash are adequate. However, when there are shortages or surpluses of cash the Bank will act to relieve them in such a way as to keep the interest rate at the desired level. In terms of Fig. 16.6 if we envisage the supply curve of cash (high-powered

Fig. 16.6 Monetary base control and the rate of interest

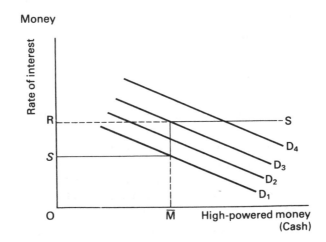

Source: Royal Bank of Scotland Review, March 1987.

money) as SS and the desired level of cash as $O\bar{M}$, the Bank will be prepared to allow the demand for cash to vary from D_1 to D_3 so long as interest rates remain between OS and OR. If demand increases to D_4 the Bank will neutralize the increase in interest rates by buying bills, thereby forcing bill prices up and yields down, and increasing the supply of cash to the system.

Assessment of monetary policy in the 1980s

We have seen that monetary policy in the 1980s has been conducted within the framework of the MTFS. Some assessment must now be made of the effectiveness of this strategy. In order to do this, we shall need to consider (a) whether the authorities have been successful in controlling the rate of growth of the money stock, and if not why not, and (b) whether the rate of growth of the monetary aggregate has borne any relation to the objectives it is supposed to affect. These questions are particularly relevant at a time when inflation has yet again begun to accelerate; the logical implication of this is that either the MTFS has been unsuccessful or that inflation is not the 'monetary phenomenon' it is assumed to be.

We saw earlier that control of the money stock was to be achieved by setting target ranges for its growth in the medium term. Difficulties of targetry relate to the choice of appropriate aggregates, the setting of appropriate target ranges, and the interpretation of developments in the monetary aggregates (*Bank of England Quarterly Bulletin* 1986). There have always been both conceptual and practical difficulties in deciding which of the money stock measures to control. Until 1982 the authorities targeted the growth of $£M_3$ as being the most representative measure. After that they began to set targets for other money stock measures (see Table 16.5) on the grounds that they wished to exert a broad influence on monetary conditions in general. However, the disappointing performance of M_1 and PSL_2 as target variables led to their abandonment in 1984. After that the authorities limited publication of targets to ranges for M_0 and $£M_3$, until 1987 when the targeting of $£M_3$ was abandoned.

M_0 is retained as a target variable. It may be asked what purpose is served by targeting M_0, given that it bears no apparent relationship to expenditure. Cynics might reply that it is psychologically expedient to have a measure of the money stock whose growth rate is predictable and easily controlled, even if it has little relevance in expenditure terms. However, the authorities have argued that changes in the growth of M_0 provides a kind of 'early warning' of growth in other monetary aggregates. Also, as we have seen, M_0 varies only in response to increases in cash by the authorities, or when transactions between the public and the Government alter. Restrictions in the growth of M_0 therefore imply a certain tightness in fiscal policy, as well as having implications for Bank dealing on the bill market and hence interest rate determination.

As Table 16.5 shows, the Government has signally failed to achieve the monetary targets prescribed, and we must now consider the reasons for this. A number of factors can be identified:

1. Private sector borrowing has proved totally insensitive to high real rates of interest in the early eighties. Both persons and companies sharply

Table 16.5 UK monetary targets 1976–90

Date target set	Target period	Monetary target	Growth range (% p.a.)	Actual outcome (% p.a.)
Dec. 1976	Apr. 1976/Apr. 1977	£M$_3$	9–13	7.7
Mar. 1977	Apr. 1977/Apr. 1978	£M$_3$	9–13	16.0
Apr. 1978	Apr. 1978/Apr. 1979	£M$_3$	8–12	10.9
Nov. 1978	Oct. 1978/Oct. 1979	£M$_3$	8–12	13.3
Jun. 1979	Jun. 1979/Apr. 1980	£M$_3$	7–11	10.3
Nov. 1979	Jun. 1979/Oct. 1980	£M$_3$	7–11	17.8
Mar. 1980	Feb. 1980/Apr. 1981	£M$_3$	7–11	18.5
Mar. 1981	Feb. 1981/Apr. 1982	£M$_3$	6–10	14.5
Mar. 1982	Feb. 1982/Apr. 1983	£M$_3$	8–12	11.1
		M$_1$	8–12	14.3
		PSL$_2$	8–12	11.3
Mar. 1983	Feb. 1983/Apr. 1984	£M$_3$	7–11	9.4
		M$_1$	7–11	14.0
		PSL$_2$	7–11	13.1
Mar. 1984	Feb. 1984/Apr. 1985	£M$_3$	6–10	11.6
		M$_0$	4–8	5.5
Mar. 1985	Apr. 1985/Apr. 1986	£M$_3$	5–9	16.5
		M$_0$	3–7	3.3
Mar. 1986	Apr. 1986/Apr. 1987	£M$_3$	11–15	20.5
		M$_0$	2–6	5.2
Mar. 1987	Apr. 1987/Apr. 1988	M$_0$	2–6	
Mar. 1888	Apr. 1988/Apr. 1989	M$_0$	1–5	7.8
Mar. 1989	Apr. 1989/Apr. 1990	M$_0$	1–5	5.8
Mar. 1990	Apr. 1990/Apr. 1991	M$_0$	1–5	–

Source: Bank of England Quarterly Bulletin, various issues.

expanded their borrowing in the 1980s. Consumer credit and mortgage finance both increased, and companies borrowed to build up their reserves.[1]

2. The growth of borrowing was paralleled by a growth in deposits, as Table 16.5 shows. What appears to have happened is that the personal sector chose to build up the liquid asset component of its total asset portfolio, attracted by interest rates driven up by competition between banks and building societies for deposits. This is partly explicable by the fact that the increase in borrowing increased the funds available for the acquisition of financial assets, and partly due to the fact that rising share and house prices enabled the personal sector to realize gains in equity markets (*Midland Bank Review* 1987). Companies, too, benefited from the competition between financial intermediaries which resulted in a narrowing of margins between borrowing and lending rates.

3. For much of the period under consideration, building societies were not included in the target money stock measures. This meant that the measures were distorted by shifts in deposits between banks and building societies as the institutions competed for funds. The money stock measures were reformulated in 1987 to take account of this problem.

We must therefore conclude that the difficulties experienced by the authorities in operating monetary targets are due both to changing financial structures and to changes in the financial behaviour of economic agents.

(This, if you remember, was the conclusion we reached in discussing the failure of monetary control in the 1970s!). However, there is also the wider issue of whether the overall strategy of monetary control embodied in the MTFS is still appropriate. Circumstances have altered since the inception of the strategy with respect to all three types of policy.

1. The technique of overfunding has ensured that FISCAL POLICY – i.e. public spending and borrowing – contributes nothing to monetary growth. As Fig. 16.7 shows, even though broad money has continued to grow rapidly, public expenditure tends to offset rather than contribute to that growth.

Fig. 16.7 Public sector contribution to M_4 growth, 1970–1990

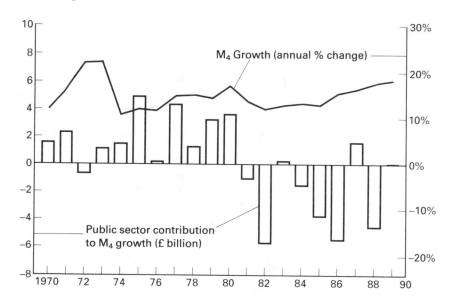

2. INTEREST RATE POLICY proved ineffective in restraining private sector borrowing in the early eighties. One of the consequences of extensive borrowing was a substantial increase in house purchase, and a rapid rise in house prices. But during the late eighties the private sector debt burden was so large that any increase in the cost of debt servicing – i.e. in interest rates – caused a fall in expenditure and hence in inflation. Interest rate policy has therefore proved an effective counter-inflation weapon, but not in the way envisaged by the MTFS; it operates on expenditure and demand rather than on the money stock in the first instance.

3. EXCHANGE RATE POLICY has become the prime anti-inflation weapon. The increase in the balance of payments deficit in the late eighties prompted fears of a decline in the value of sterling, a rise in the cost of imports, and hence an increase in inflation. The interest rate has been used to attract short-term capital flows and hence to strengthen sterling. Nominal interest rates are now substantially higher than those of our competitors.

In view of the fact that broad money aggregates are no longer targetted, and that the MTFS no longer operates in the way it was originally envisaged, it may be legitimate to argue that monetary control as such no longer exists. Turning now to our second question, we consider in what way the behaviour of the monetary aggregates has affected economic objectives – in other words, is monetary control the best anti-inflationary weapon? The objective of the MTFS, it will be remembered, was to bring about a reduction in the growth of money GDP (output × prices). However, it became clear over the eighties that what the government were trying to achieve by the MTFS was not so much a reduction in inflation in response to reductions in the money stock, as a reduction in *inflationary expectations* in response to a consistency of policy stance. Expectations are only 'rational' if outcomes can be predicted with certainty, and inflationary behaviour is only modified if people see that inflation is coming down. Inflationary predictions were never borne out in practice, and were constantly revised upwards – see Table 16.6. There is quite clearly a problem of credibility (*Barclays Bank Economic Review*, May 90) here which must inevitably defeat the government's objective of controlling inflation by influencing people's expectations with regard to policy consistency. If people see that the anti-inflationary strategy is *not* working, they will continue to behave as if inflation is going to continue.

Table 16.6 Inflation – projections and outcomes

	Inflation – projections and outcomes (GDP deflator)					
	1988–89	1989–90	1990–91	1991–92	1992–93	1993–94
1985	3					
1986	3½	3				
1987	4	3½	3			
1988	4½	4	3½	3		
1989	7¼	5½	4	3	2½	
1990		6½*	6½*	4¾	3½	3

* Adjusted for community charge effect.

Source: Barclays Bank Economic Review (1990).

Even apart from this, there is an underlying problem about the relationship between inflation and the growth of the money stock. If we remember the crude Quantity Theory formulation:

$$\text{Money stock} \times \text{Velocity of circulation} = \text{Prices} \times \text{Output}$$

it will help us to appreciate some of the dimensions of the problem.

1. The monetary aggregates include increasingly large proportions of wealth holdings. This means, as we saw earlier, that a smaller proportion of the money stock is circulating – the *overall* velocity of circulation has in fact fallen on average by 4% a year since 1980. Fig. 16.8 shows the fall in velocity of M_4, the current broad monetary aggregate. (The consequence of this is that the growth of M_4 must outstrip the growth of money GDP, since transactions must be financed.) It should be remembered that if people are holding more wealth in money form this can be because (a) it is more profitable or convenient to do so – i.e. they are holding a greater proportion of a given portfolio in liquid form AND/OR (b) they have more wealth. Both of these factors operated in the

Fig. 16.8 Velocity of
circulation of M$_4$

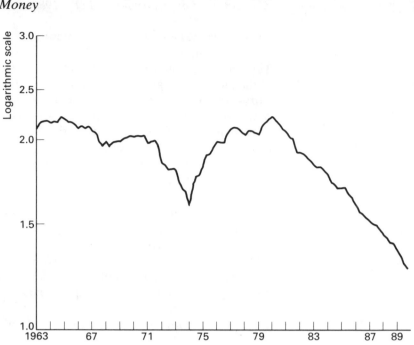

eighties – Table 16.7 shows both wealth increases and the fact that a
greater share of that wealth was held in money form. All of this clearly
renders the connection between money and inflation tenuous.

Table 16.7 Personal sector
wealth

End-year	1979		1989	
	£ billion	Share(c)	£ billion	Share(c)
(1) Tangible wealth (a)	417.2	62.8	1,392.0	55.3
of which, housing	*270.6*	*40.7*	*1,044.0*	*41.5*
(2) Gross financial wealth	246.9	37.2	1,123.0	44.7
of which:				
Equity in insurance and				
pension funds	*78.0*	*11.7*	*497.8*	*19.8*
Liquid assets (b)	*98.8*	*14.9*	*331.6*	*13.2*
Shares	*31.6*	*4.8*	*157.8*	*6.3*
Long-term public sector				
debt	*11.9*	*1.8*	*33.0*	*1.3*
Unit trusts	*2.4*	*0.4*	*23.2*	*0.9*
Other	*24.2*	*3.6*	*79.6*	*3.2*
(3) Gross financial and				
tangible wealth	664.1	*100.0*	2,515.0	*100.0*
(4) Financial liabilities	77.7		393.3	
(5) Net financial and tangible				
wealth	**586.4**		**2,121.7**	
(3) = (1) + (2)				
(5) = (3) − (4)				

(a) Bank estimate.
(b) Notes and coin, bank and building society deposits, and national savings.
(c) Shares of total gross financial and tangible wealth in percentage terms.

Source: Bank of England Quarterly Bulletin (1990b).

2. What actually happened, was that in the first half of the eighties inflation fell and output rose, as Fig. 16.9 shows.

Fig. 16.9 National output and inflation

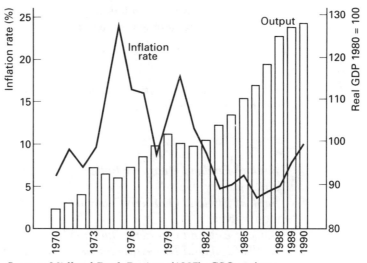

Fig. 16.9 National output and inflation

Source: Midland Bank Review, (1987), CSO various.

There was therefore an inverse correlation between the growth of the monetary aggregates, as detailed above, and inflation. In fact, there is a substantial correlation between changes in the velocity of circulation and the rate of inflation itself. If we compare Fig. 16.9 with Fig. 16.8 we see that there is a closer statistical relationship between inflation and velocity, than between inflation and the growth of overall monetary aggregates. There are several ways in which one could explain this, but it is probably not correct to look for a direct causal connection. If we look at what has happened to inflation at the end of the eighties we see that it has risen due to the factors which have little to do with the growth of the money stock, and velocity continues to fall due primarily to the profitability of holding money on deposit in days of high interest rates.

Conclusion

In conclusion, therefore, we can note that although the aim of monetary policy in the 1980s may have been consistent, i.e. to keep the rate of growth of the effective monetary aggregate broadly in line with inflation, there has been a marked change in both official pronouncements on various aspects of monetary policy and in the way policy is done. In fact, the shift has been from a doctrinaire position to one of greater pragmatism. Several things are clear:

1. The primary purpose served by the MTFS has been to demonstrate consistency in the government's policy stance and hence to affect expectations. One might also add that it gave technical credibility to the government's ideological position, based as it was on monetarism. As inflation accelerated in the late eighties the 'expectation effect' of the MTFS has been lost.

2. Targetting the money stock has proved impractical and therefore unsuccessful.

3. Anti-inflationary policy now consists solely of interest rate policy. High interest rates affect inflation (a) through expenditure and demand, and (b) by strengthening the exchange rate.

Note

1. See Ch. 15, also articles on personal sector and corporate finance mentioned there.

References

Bank of England Quarterly Bulletin (1986) **26**, No. 4. Financial changes and broad money, Dec.

Bank of England Quarterly Bulletin (1987) **27**, No. 2. Measures of broad money, May.

Bank of England Quarterly Bulletin (1988) **28**, No. 3, Aug.

Bank of England Discussion Paper **47**, (1990a) The monetary aggregates in a changing environment; a statistical discussion paper.

Bank of England Quarterly Bulletin (1990b) **30**, No. 3, The determination of the monetary aggregates, Aug.

Barclays Bank Economic Review (1990) The medium term financial strategy now, May.

CSO (1990) *Economic Trends*, July.

Financial Statistics Explanatory Handbook (1990), June.

Midland Bank Review (1987) The annual monetary survey, Autumn.

Royal Bank of Scotland Review (1987) Whatever happened to velocity? March.

17   Inflation

In this chapter we first examine a number of methods of measuring inflation, including the Retail Price Index (RPI) and the more recent Tax and Price Index (TPI). We then consider the 'costs' of inflation, both when it is fully anticipated, and when, as is usually the case, it is not. The monetarist and non-monetarist views of the causes of inflation are presented in some detail, and recent empirical evidence assessed. We conclude by outlining the implications of our analysis for current UK policy formation.

The definition and measurement of inflation

Inflation is a persistent tendency for the general level of prices to rise. In effect the rate of inflation measures the change in the purchasing power of money, i.e. how much more money you would have to have this year when faced with this year's prices to be as well-off as you were last year when faced with last year's prices. Until 1979 inflation in the UK was measured and reported almost exclusively by reference to the RPI; since then an additional measure, the TPI, has been introduced.

The Retail Price Index

The RPI, which was formerly compiled by the Department of Employment, is now the responsibility of the Central Statistical Office. It measures the change from month to month in the cost of a representative 'basket' of goods and services of the type bought by a typical household.

A number of stages are involved in the calculation of the RPI. The first stage is to select the items to be included in the index and to weight these items according to their relative importance in the average family budget. Obviously items on which a family spends a large proportion of its income are given heavier weights than those items on which the family spends relatively little. For example, in 1990 the weight given to tea in the index was 2, whereas that for electricity was 24 (out of a total 'all items weight' of 1,000). The weights used are changed annually to reflect the changes in the composition of family expenditure. The new weights are derived from the Family Expenditure Survey in which about 7,000 households, carefully chosen to represent all regions and types of household, take part each year. Each member of the household aged over sixteen years records his or her day-to-day expenditure on items over a two-week period, together with any longer-term payments, such as telephone bills, season tickets, etc. It is from these records that the weights for the RPI are based. The new weights, which begin in January each year, are largely based on the pattern of expenditure shown in the survey over the year to the previous June. For some items,

340   *Inflation*

however, such as selected consumer durables (e.g. furniture and carpets) where sales fluctuate widely from year to year, expenditure is averaged over a three-year period.

The weights for this 'general RPI' are obtained by excluding pensioner households, for which a separate RPI is calculated, and households in which the head has an income above a certain limit which in 1989 was £700 per week (this represents the top 4% of earners). These two groups are excluded because the pattern of their expenditure differs markedly from that of the great majority of households.

Table 17.1 General index of retail prices: group weights

	1987	1990
Food	167	158
Catering	46	47
Alcoholic drink	76	77
Tobacco	38	34
Housing	157	185
Fuel and light	61	50
Household goods	73	71
Household services	44	40
Clothing and footwear	74	69
Personal goods and services	38	39
Motoring expenditure	127	131
Fares and other travel costs	22	21
Leisure goods	47	48
Leisure services	30	30
	1,000	1,000

Source: Employment Gazette (1988, 1990).

The weights used for groups of items are shown in Table 17.1. It can be seen that food has been replaced as the largest item by housing (rent, mortgage interest, rates and community charge, water charges, repairs and dwelling insurance). This is part of a longer run trend associated with differing income elasticities of demand for the items in the 'basket'.

The second stage in deriving the RPI involves collecting the price data. For most items, prices are collected on a specific day each month, usually the Tuesday nearest the middle of the month. Prices are obtained from a sample of retail outlets in some 200 different areas. Care is taken to make sure a representative range of retail outlets, small retailers, supermarkets, department stores, etc. are surveyed. In all around 130,000 price quotations are collected each month. An average price is then calculated for each item in the index. For example on 10 April 1990, two hundred and ninety-three price quotations were taken for tomatoes; the prices ranged from 70p to 112p per pound, with an average of 94p.

The final stage is to calculate the RPI from all these data. All index numbers must relate to some base period or reference date. In the case of the RPI the base period was, until recently, January 1974 = 100. The new base year is January 1987 = 100. This is a presentational change (essentially a rescaling) and has no material effect upon the percentage movements in prices shown by the RPI. The old series can be translated into the new reference date by dividing by 3.945, which, in decimal form, was the level the old series had reached by January 1987. The index is calculated each month through a weighted price relative method.[1] Since the weights are revised each year to keep the index up to date, the index is calculated afresh each year with January counting as 100. Each yearly index is then linked back to the base year by means of a chain base method.[2] In April 1990 the RPI stood at 125.1, which means that average prices have risen by 25% between January 1987 and April 1990. As the index is an average, this figure conceals the fact that some prices have increased more rapidly (mortgage interest payments 108%, water rates 48% and soft drinks 33%), whilst other prices have fallen (audio-visual equipment and coffee both by 10%).

A separate index is calculated for one-pensioner and two-pensioner households. These have weights which differ from the general RPI because of the different pattern of expenditure of these households. For example, pensioners spend a higher proportion of their income on housing, fuel and food, and a smaller proportion on clothing, durable goods and transport. Despite this, 'pensioner' price indices have moved fairly closely in line with the general RPI for several years.

Once the RPI has been constructed, the rate of inflation can then be calculated, with the most usual measure being the twelve-monthly change in the RPI. For example, the RPI stood at 125.1 in April 1990. In April 1989 it stood at 114.3 and therefore the annual rate of inflation over that period is

$$\frac{125.1 - 114.3}{114.3} \times 100\% = 9.4\%$$

Inflation as measured by the RPI is shown in Fig. 17.1.

Fig. 17.1 Inflation as measured by the RPI
Source: Employment Gazette (1990)

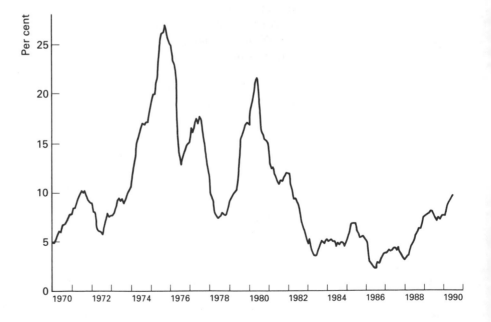

Housing costs

It has been argued that the way housing costs are treated in the RPI not only makes the RPI an unreliable indicator of the underlying inflationary trend in the economy, but also makes international comparisons of inflation invalid. The RPI includes *mortgage interest payments* as the main element in owner-occupier's housing costs. Mortgage interest payments reflect changes in both house prices (a useful estimate of the increase in debt on 'standard' mortgages) and the interest rate charged to householders on this debt. It is, however, variations in the latter, namely interest rates, which tend to be the major short-term influence on mortgage costs. Frequent changes in interest rates can therefore generate erratic movements in the RPI. Indeed the anti-inflation strategy of the Government in the late 1980s and early 1990s was based largely on high interest rates, which had the perverse effect of increasing the RPI. Inflation was then further fuelled by the fact that the RPI was the main indicator used by trade unions when formulating wage claims.

The problem is therefore how to treat housing costs in the RPI. Some European countries such as France and Italy *exclude* owner-occupation from their consumer price index. In many other countries which include owner-occupation there is a large private rented sector, and so the measurement of housing costs for owner-occupiers can be *imputed* from the actual payments made by households living in similar rented accommodation. In Britain, it has always been thought that the private rented sector was too small to allow such imputation. As a result the RPI uses the interest on a standard mortgage as part of the calculation to capture owner-occupiers' housing costs.

There are a number of arguments against including mortgage interest payments in the RPI. For example, only one quarter of the housing stock is mortgaged and therefore mortgage interest is an unrepresentative measure. Also house purchase is an investment which produces a capital gain in the long run and arguably these capital gains should be *offset* against mortgage interest. On the other hand, most mortgage payers do regard these payments as part of their cost of living and would be disconcerted if they were removed from the index.

A recent attempt to construct an alternative index has been produced by the *Sunday Times* and the Institute for Fiscal Studies. In the new index, mortage interest payments are replaced by two other measures of housing costs. The first represents the *maintenance costs of home ownership* and is calculated as a percentage of the value of the housing stock. The second component is the *net cost of housing finance* and is the difference between the mortgage rate and the building society deposit rate. The poll tax is also excluded from this index on the grounds that it is a direct tax similar to income tax. The *net* effect is to give house prices *more* weight than in the official index, but to downgrade the influence of interest rates. On the new *Sunday Times*/IFS index, inflation for the year to April 1990 was running at 6.4% rather than the official rate of 9.4%, a figure that was much closer to the inflation rate of our European partners at that time.

The Tax and Price Index

Publication of the TPI began in August 1979, after the Conservative Party had won the election of that year. One of their pre-election promises was to reduce the burden of direct taxation, in an attempt to provide greater incentives. The new TPI was constructed in such a way that it would measure changes in real spending power, which depends not only on what is happening to prices, but also on what is happening to take-home pay. The new index is therefore a composite of change in prices and change in direct taxes and National Insurance contributions (NIC). The former, as measured by the RPI, has a weight of about three-quarters in the new index. Changes in direct taxes and NIC have a weight of about one-quarter, a reflection of the direct tax burden of the average taxpayer.

It was hoped by the Government that planned cuts in direct taxation would cause the TPI to rise less rapidly than the RPI, so that workers would seek lower pay settlements than if they took the RPI as their yardstick. Initially, as can be seen from Fig. 17.2, the TPI was below the RPI. From September 1980 to April 1983, however, inflation as measured by the TPI was above that of the RPI, so that little was heard of this 'much truer guide'.[3] The main reason for the TPI being above the RPI over this period was the increase in direct taxation and employee contributions documented in Chapter 14. Since 1983 the TPI has been consistently below the RPI (except for a short period in 1989). This is the result of factors such as tax allowances rising more rapidly than inflation, cuts in rates of income tax and, more recently, the reduction in income tax arising from the introduction of independent taxation for husbands and wives.

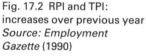

Fig. 17.2 RPI and TPI: increases over previous year
Source: Employment Gazette (1990)

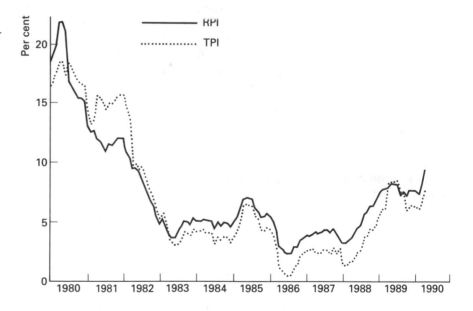

Other measures of inflation

Although the RPI and, to a lesser extent, the TPI are the usual measures of inflation, there are others. The *Index of Producer Prices* (which has replaced the old Wholesale Price Index), for example, measures the rate of inflation before it is actually felt in the shops. This index has two parts, one giving the prices of raw materials and fuel as they enter the factory, and the other the rise in 'factory gate prices' as manufactured goods leave the factory (home sales). The main use of these two indices is to give an indication of the future trend of retail prices. As might be expected, the 'materials and fuel price index' tends to be the more volatile and to precede movements in the 'home sales index' (see Table 17.2).

| Year | General index of Retail Prices | Tax and Price Index | Producer Prices | | GDP Deflator | Inflation Rate* |
			Materials and Fuels	Manufactured Products		
1980	70.6	69.78	72.6	71.2	72.3	17.9
1981	79.1	80.11	79.3	78.6	79.5	12.0
1982	85.8	88.00	85.1	84.6	85.2	8.5
1983	89.7	91.49	91.0	89.2	90.0	4.5
1984	94.3	95.05	98.9	95.0	94.9	5.1
1985	100.00	100.00	100.0	100.0	100.0	6.0
1986	103.4	101.81	92.4	104.3	102.6	3.4
1987	107.7	103.21	95.3	108.3	107.8	4.2
1988	113.0	107.50	98.4	113.2	114.8	4.9
1989	121.8	115.10	104.0	119.0	123.1	7.8

* Percentage change in the RPI over same period in the previous year.

Table 17.2 Comparison of price increases as measured by different indices (1985 = 100)
Source: National Institute Economic Review (1990)

A final measure of inflation is the *'implicit GDP deflator'*. In contrast to the RPI, which measures movements in the prices of a 'basket' of goods bought by a representative UK household, the GDP deflator seeks to measure movements in the prices of the *entire basket* of goods and services produced in the UK and can in this sense be regarded as the most comprehensive price index in the economy. It is obtained by dividing the GDP at current factor cost by the GDP at constant factor cost, and is sometimes called the 'implicit' deflator because it is derived in this indirect way. Although movements in the RPI index and the GDP deflator do not coincide perfectly, neither do they diverge excessively (see Table 17.2).

Low inflation as a policy objective

Much of the recent debate on inflation centres around how best to defeat it. Less is heard, at least in public debate, about the actual economic costs of inflation. It is important to identify these costs, and to try and quantify them, so that they can then be compared with the costs of the policies aimed at reducing inflation. These latter costs are usually seen in terms of higher unemployment, if restrictive monetary and fiscal policies are used to control inflation, or a misallocation of resources if prices and incomes policies are used. Traditionally the costs of inflation were seen in terms of its adverse effect on income distribution, as rising prices are particularly severe on those with fixed incomes, such as pensioners. However, Milton Friedman, in his Nobel lecture, shifted the focus of attention towards the adverse effects of inflation on output and employment.

In assessing the costs of inflation it is usual to distinguish two cases: that of perfectly anticipated inflation, where the rate of inflation is expected and has been taken into account in economic transactions, and that of imperfectly anticipated, or unexpected inflation. We will consider perfectly anticipated inflation first, as it provides a useful bench-mark against which to assess the more usual case of imperfectly anticipated inflation.

Perfectly anticipated inflation

Suppose we initially have an economy in which inflation is proceeding at a steady and perfectly foreseen rate, and in which all possible adjustments for the existence of inflation have been made. In this economy all contracts, interest rates, and the tax system would take the correctly foreseen rate of inflation into account. The exchange rate would also adjust to prevent inflation having any adverse effect on the balance of payments.

'Shoe-leather' costs   In such an economy the main cost of inflation would arise from the fact that interest is not normally paid on currency in circulation. The opportunity cost to the individual of holding currency would then be the interest the individual could have earned on other assets, such as deposits at the bank. Higher anticipated inflation will tend to raise interest rates, and therefore the opportunity cost of holding currency, with the rational response to this being for the individual to economize on currency holdings by making more frequent trips to the bank. The cost of these extra trips to the bank are often called the 'shoe-leather' costs of inflation.

'Menu' costs   A second cost, when inflation is fully anticipated, is that of having to change prices frequently. This is sometimes called the 'menu' cost of inflation. Presumably the more rapid the inflation, the more frequently things like price tags, cash tills, vending machines and price lists have to be changed, and this takes time, effort and money.

If these costs were the only costs arising from inflation then it would be difficult to justify a severe anti-inflationary policy. There are, however, further costs that arise from inflation when it is either not foreseen correctly, or not adjusted to fully. It is to these additional costs from imperfectly anticipated inflation that we now turn.

Imperfectly anticipated inflation

Redistributional effects   A full adjustment to inflation is far from the case in most modern economies, including the UK. For instance, some pensions in the public sector are index-linked, whereas most private pension schemes are not. Also unanticipated inflation redistributes income and wealth, both between the private sector and the Government, and within the private sector itself.

There are three basic ways in which unanticipated inflation redistributes income away from the private sector and towards government:

1.   The money value of personal income usually rises with inflation. This moves some people into higher tax brackets, with a higher proportion of their income now going to government. This is reinforced by the fact that tax allowances often fail to rise in line with inflation.

2.   Inflation reduces the *real* value of government debt, i.e. government securities held by individuals and institutions, often called the National

Debt. These securities mature at specified future dates for sums that are fixed in *money* terms, so that inflation reduces the real cost to the Government of redeeming them. In 1945 the real value of the National Debt was three times that of National Income; today it is only one-half.

3. Inflation is an implicit tax on the holding of currency. The holders of currency lose from inflation because its purchasing power falls as prices rise. Since currency is, at least nominally, a claim on the Government, the effect of inflation is to reduce the real value of such claims, i.e. it is the same as a tax on the holding of money. It is clear from Table 17.3 that in the period of rapid inflation 1974–76 and 1979–81, the personal sector consistently lost out to the public sector.

Table 17.3 Inflation losses (−) and gains (+) on the real value of net monetary assets by sector. Selected years (£bn)

	1974	1975	1976	1979	1980	1981	1986	1987	1988
Personal Sector	−10.70	−13.70	−9.30	−15.10	−12.80	−11.70	−6.80	−6.80	−9.10
Company Sector	3.00	3.30	1.50	2.20	1.70	1.60	2.50	−0.50	0.50
Public Sector	9.30	11.90	7.50	14.30	12.10	11.90	7.00	4.60	7.50
Total Domestic	1.50	1.50	−0.30	1.40	1.00	1.80	2.70	−2.70	−1.10

Source: *Bank of England Quarterly Bulletin* 1984 and May 1990.

As well as redistributing income away from the private sector and towards government, unanticipated inflation also redistributes income *within* the private sector. For example, creditors are likely to lose out to debtors if the *actual* rate of inflation turns out to be higher than the *expected* rate built into contracts (as for example through interest charges). Again, a pensioner who saved throughout his life to provide an adequate income in retirement, may suddenly find that unanticipated inflation makes his provision inadequate. In these ways unanticipated inflation is often regarded as unjust, because it falsifies 'contracts' in an arbitrary manner.

Long-term contracts are particularly at risk from unanticipated inflation, so that it is hardly surprising that the high UK inflation rates of the 1970s have limited the market in long-term securities which often yield fixed interest returns. In fact, new issues of company loan stock (debentures and bonds) were virtually non-existent in the 1970s.[4]

The pattern of monetary credits and debts is not, however, straightforward. The Government is the largest monetary debtor and is therefore, as indicated above, the major beneficiary from unanticipated inflation. But most firms and many households (e.g. those with mortgages) are also monetary debtors! The main creditors are the pension funds and life assurance companies, who in effect hold funds for households. Thus, an average household may benefit from unanticipated inflation, through reductions in the real value of mortgage payments and other debts, but may lose in terms of pension entitlements. The main problem with the redistributive effects of inflation is not so much who benefits, but rather the unplanned and arbitrary nature of the redistributive process.

Balance of payments   In the case of perfectly anticipated inflation, we assumed that the exchange rate adjusted to eliminate any adverse effect of inflation on the balance of payments. If, for example, the UK inflation rate was above that of her competitors, then the value of the pound would depreciate quickly to restore price competitiveness. Of course, in practice, exchange rates do not adjust perfectly to different rates of inflation between countries. In fact, despite relatively high inflation rates in the UK during the late 1970s and early 1980s, the pound often *appreciated* rather than depreciated. This was due to high interest rates, as the Government attempted to curb monetary growth, and to the emergence of North Sea oil, both of which made the pound more attractive to buyers. Again, the lack of full adjustment means that imperfectly anticipated inflation may impose balance of payments costs, by making UK goods relatively more expensive.

Unemployment   In recent years the emphasis has switched away from the costs of inflation expressed in terms of redistributional effects and the balance of payments, to the costs of inflation expressed in terms of lost output and employment. Friedman has given impetus to this switch by arguing that high average rates of inflation tend also to be *more variable* rates (Friedman 1977), making inflation less easy to anticipate. The uncertainty caused by high and variable inflation rates is, according to Friedman, likely to increase *unemployment* in several ways:

1. High and variable inflation increases the risk associated with any assessment of future returns on an investment project, thereby reducing both investment and employment.

2. Variable rates of inflation make it more difficult to distinguish changes in *relative* price from changes in the *general* price level. This may lead to a less efficient allocation of resources, as workers and firms find it more difficult to judge whether the increase in their wage or product price is due to an increase in the demand for *their* labour or product, or whether it is merely due to general inflation. Friedman argues that the effect of this 'on economic efficiency is clear, on unemployment less so'. He thinks it is at least plausible that the average level of unemployment would then rise, with workers and firms making mistakes more often. For example, a firm may fail to expand and create employment when the rise in price was indeed the result of demand changing in favour of *their* product, and not merely the result of general inflation.

3. High inflation may lead the Government to impose wage and price controls, thereby impeding market forces. Expanding firms may then be unable to bid resources away from declining ones by offering higher wages. The extra inefficiency introduced into the market system by price and wage controls may, according to Friedman, increase unemployment.

4. It has been argued that high inflation leads to strong trade unions (and not the reverse as the cost-push theorists might argue), as workers seek the protection of organized pay bargaining to protect their absolute and relative incomes. The argument then proceeds along the lines that strong unions are likely to reduce the efficiency of the labour market, resisting change and increasing unemployment.

5. High inflation may depress consumption. We noted in Chapter 11 that

the highest rates of inflation in the UK in the early 1970s were accompanied, somewhat unexpectedly, by an increase in the savings ratio (the proportion of personal disposable income saved), thereby reducing both consumption and aggregate demand, and raising unemployment.

Empirical evidence

The theoretical case for a positive link between the rate of inflation and the rate of unemployment appears at best uncertain. One might reasonably hope that empirical evidence would help settle the issue! Unfortunately, as is often the case in the more interesting areas of economics, the evidence is far from clear-cut and open to a variety of interpretations. Friedman examined the data on unemployment and inflation for seven major industrial countries over the period 1956–75 (Friedman 1977). He found that the rate of inflation and the level of unemployment moved *in the same direction* in only two out of the seven countries during the first two quinquennia (1956–60, 1961–65); in three out of the seven countries during the second and third quinquennia (1961–65, 1966–70); but in six out of the seven countries during the final two quinquennia (1966–70, 1971–75). Friedman therefore concludes that at least for the late 1960s and early 1970s, and at least for some countries (of which the UK, Canada and Italy are the best examples), rising inflation was indeed associated with rising unemployment.

Friedman's critics point to the fact that some of the rise in *both* inflation *and* unemployment in the early 1970s can be explained in terms of a third factor, namely the rise in the price of oil. The quadrupling of oil prices in 1973 disrupted the productive process, and raised unemployment. In addition, since the cost-push inflation induced by higher oil prices was only partially accommodated by the monetary authorities, demand deflation occurred and this too raised unemployment. Demand deflation happened because the rise in prices increased the demand for money for transaction purposes. Then, when the supply of money was prevented from increasing by as much as this extra demand, the price of money (interest rates) rose, with the result that investment and consumption fell, and unemployment increased.

Higham and Tomlinson (1982) bring forward Friedman's data on unemployment and inflation to 1980, and also extend them to include seven additional developed countries, making fourteen in all. Their conclusion is that there is *no* general support for the view that inflation and unemployment move in the same direction. However, there are some exceptions to this, with the UK, Canada and Italy again supporting Friedman's hypothesis for the period 1976–80. Nevertheless, support for the hypothesis was eroded in the UK when, over the period 1981–83, inflation fell but unemployment rose.

To summarize, it cannot be argued that inflation does not matter. It could be argued that some of the costs of inflation, though inevitable, are small, especially when it is fully anticipated. If this is accepted, then a case could be made for indexing all money contracts so that the UK economy fully adjusts to the rate of inflation. Should this happen, the rate of inflation might cease to be a major problem. The real world is, however, characterized by institutions that have not fully adapted to inflation, and is subject to inflation rates that are far from predictable. In such a world, some of the costs associated with imperfectly anticipated inflation may well apply, though their significance is still a matter of contention. Although inflation is hardly likely to be an advantage to a country, it could certainly be argued that on occasions the costs of eliminating inflation from the system, via lost output and employment, may be greater than the costs which inflation itself imposes.

Economic theory and inflation

In recent years it has become more common to talk in terms of demand side or supply side shocks, and to illustrate the arguments using aggregate demand and aggregate supply analysis. A good example of this approach can be found in Lipsey and Harbury (1988). The policy debate, in the 1980s, was dominated by the monetarist versus non-monetarist explanation and it is to this that we now turn.

The monetarist view of inflation

Monetarists essentially believe that the value of money, like any other commodity, depends upon the supply of money relative to the demand for it. If supply exceeds demand for a commodity its price will fall; if the supply of money exceeds the demand for money, then likewise the value of money will fall, i.e. the price level will rise. Sustained inflation must then be caused by an over-expansion of the money supply, and its remedy, according to the monetarists, is to control money supply growth.

The monetarist view of inflation has three foundation stones[5]: first, the Quantity Theory of Money; second, the breakdown of the traditional Phillips curve; and third, the role of exchange rates.

The Quantity Theory of Money In 1956 Milton Friedman reworked the old 'classical' quantity theory ($M.V = P.T$) we considered in Chapter 16, and turned it into a theory of the demand for money. The old quantity theory had argued that in the long run V, the velocity of circulation of money, and T, the number of transactions, were approximately constant. The implication of this was that in the long run an increase in the money supply, M, would raise the price level, P. The mechanism was that a rise in M would, with V constant, raise the value of expenditure, $M.V$, which would in turn raise the value of transactions, $P.T$. Since, in the Classical system, the economy would always return to full employment in the long run, T could be assumed fixed at the full employment level of output. The rise in M would then lead to a proportional increase in the price level, P.

Friedman reformulated this theory and argued that V, the velocity of circulation of money, although not fixed, is stable. V is a mirror-image of the demand for money! A rise in the demand for money to hold will reduce its velocity of circulation, V; similarly, if the demand for money to hold is stable, so then is V. It was by arguing that the *demand for money to hold* is a stable function of a relatively small number of variables, that Friedman sought to demonstrate the stability of V.

To Friedman, people's willingness to hold their wealth in the form of money balances, rather than other forms of assets, depends systematically on a small number of variables. A simplified version of this would be:

$M^D = f(Y, i, P)$

where Y = real national income;
　　　　i = the real return on all other assets (bonds, equities, consumer durables);
　　　　P = the price level.

If we then take the rates of change of these variables we get:

$\Delta M^D = a\Delta Y - b\Delta i + \Delta P$

where ΔM^D = the rate of change in the demand for money balances;
　　　　ΔY = the rate of change in real income;
　　　　Δi = the rate of change in the real interest rate;
　　　　ΔP = the rate of inflation;
　a and b = the income and interest elasticities of demand for money respectively (i.e. the responsiveness of the demand for money to changes in real income and interest rates).

The demand for money balances rises with Y and P, because these increase the demand for money balances for transactions purposes. It falls with i, because a higher interest rate increases the opportunity cost of holding idle money balances.

For the monetary sector of the economy to be in equilibrium, the supply of money must equal the demand for money. To restore equilibrium, a change in one of these must be matched by a change in the other, i.e. $\Delta M^S = \Delta M^D$. If we assume that the supply of money is not influenced by the demand for it (i.e. the money supply is exogenously determined by the monetary authorities) we can then write:

$\Delta M^S = \Delta M^D = a\Delta Y - b\Delta i + \Delta P$

in the new equilibrium.

Monetarists would argue that, as shown above, changes in the money supply will need to be matched by changes in money demand, if equilibrium is to be restored. To change money demand involves, at least potentially, a change in all three variables, Y, i and P. The monetarist view is that in the *short run* it is ΔY and Δi that adjust. In the *long run*, however, ΔY is determined by real forces in the economy, such as the growth of productivity or the supply of factors of production, and b is very low, approximately zero. In the *long run* therefore, it is only ΔP, the rate of inflation, which can change so that the demand for money is brought back into line with the supply of money.

The monetarist case that there is a causal link running from changes in the money supply to changes in money national income, depends upon a stable demand for money function. As already discussed, another way of making this same point is to say the income velocity of circulation (money national income/money supply) is stable and predictable. The evidence (see Ch.16) does not appear to support this proposition, and most recent studies confirm this (Healey 1987). As would be expected, there are conflicting interpretations of this evidence. There are those who see the demand as being inherently stable and who have looked for explanations for its apparent breakdown since 1980 and others who see the recent experience as confirming their view on the basic instability of money demand.

Modern versions of monetarism (Laidler 1984b) incorporate a buffer stock or disequilibrium approach to explain the falling velocity. In this view any unexpected increase in the money supply is initially held whilst individuals decide how best to reallocate their assets. Money acts as a shock absorber or 'buffer' between the real and financial sectors. During this period velocity will fall. Evidence for this comes from the early 1970s when the rapid growth £M_3 was associated with a reversal of the long-established upward trend in V. Eventually V returned to trend, bringing inflationary pressure with it in the late 1970s. The same may have happened after 1980 with the large increases in broad money storing up inflationary pressure to be released at a later date.

Other economists argue (Taylor 1987) that the effects of financial innovation operating on the opportunity cost of holding money (see Ch. 16) and the effects of inflation both influence the demand for money, and if proper account is taken of these factors the evidence for the stability of the demand for broad money is at least as strong as the evidence for instability. However, as financial innovation is unpredictable this defence is the same as saying that the demand for money (or V) is stable at any moment in time, but depends on variables which are unstable and unpredictable. This seems to imply that control of the money supply (if it can be achieved) is not going to be a very certain way of controlling money national income and the inflation rate.

Inflation and unemployment – the breakdown of the Phillips curve   The second foundation stone for the monetarist view of the inflationary process developed out of the work of Friedman (1968) and Phelps (1967) in the mid-1960s on the relationship between unemployment and inflation.

The orthodox view at the time was of a stable, inverse relationship between unemployment and inflation. If, say, the level of demand in the economy rose, unemployment would fall, but at the cost of higher inflation. This orthodox view was embodied in the so-called 'Phillips curve'. The monetarist view, as we have seen, was that an increase in the money supply will indeed increase aggregate demand, but that although this might affect output (and employment) *in the short run*, in the long run the effect will be on the inflation rate alone. It was through adapting the orthodox Phillips curve, that the monetarists were able to show how changes in the money supply would be apportioned between changes in output and changes in prices (inflation). As we shall see, they could then conclude that, in the absence of policy-induced disturbances in the money supply, the economy would operate at a 'natural' rate of unemployment, regardless of the inflation rate. In other words, lower unemployment could not be secured by accepting higher inflation, as the Phillips curve had suggested.

The traditional Phillips curve had described an inverse relationship between unemployment and the rate of change of money wages (i.e. wage inflation). This relationship is illustrated in Fig. 17.3. When presented by A. W. Phillips in 1958 the relationship was essentially an empirical one, describing what had actually happened to the unemployment rate and the rate of change of money wages in the UK between 1861 and 1957 (Phillips 1958). It was not long, however, before theoretical explanations of this inverse relationship were developed. Basically the argument went as follows.

Fig. 17.3 The Phillips curve

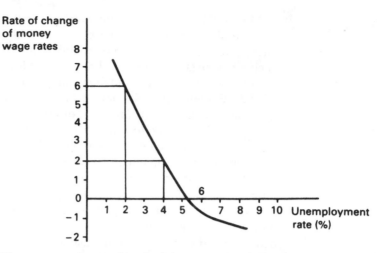

First, excess demand in the labour market is likely to be inversely related to the level of unemployment (i.e. the greater the degree of demand pressure for labour, the lower is likely to be the level of unemployment). Unemployment is therefore used as an indirect measure of excess demand in the labour market. Second, excess demand for labour will cause the money wage rate to rise, with the speed of this rise depending upon the degree of excess demand. Third, given that prices are set by adding a profit mark-up on costs, the main component of which is wages, the Phillips curve can be used to yield a theory of price inflation. Thus excess demand in the labour market will be signalled by a fall in the unemployment rate and will push up the rate of increase in money wages, which will in turn push up the rate of price inflation. The theoretical explanation of the Phillips curve was seen by Keynesians as supporting their excess-demand view of inflation.

In the 1950s, and for most of the 1960s, the evidence for the UK and other countries seemed to support the Phillips curve, with an apparent inverse relationship between inflation and unemployment. This in turn provided policy-makers with clear choices. If they were not happy with the level of unemployment, they could reflate the economy, and reduce the level of unemployment. Because this would increase the level of excess demand in the labour market, it would generate a higher rate of inflation. This 'trade-off' between unemployment and inflation could be roughly quantified, 'for *x*% less unemployment we must accept *y*% extra inflation'. Policy-makers at least knew where they were in terms of the costs of either reducing unemployment or reducing inflation.

Since the late 1960s, however, the simple relationship has broken down. The inflation rate associated with any level of unemployment has been much higher than the Phillips relationship predicted, and at times both unemployment *and* the inflation rate have increased together, as in the periods 1967–71, 1974–75, 1979–80 and 1983–85 – see Fig. 17.4. The reaction of broadly Keynesian economists to this breakdown has been to argue that the inflation rate is determined by trade unions, or socio-political factors outside the scope of economic theory. Monetarists, on the other hand, were amending the traditional Phillips curve even before it was apparent that the relationship *had* broken down.

Fig. 17.4 The relationship between the unemployment rate and the inflation rate in the UK 1966–89
Sources: Economic Trends; Employment Gazette (various)

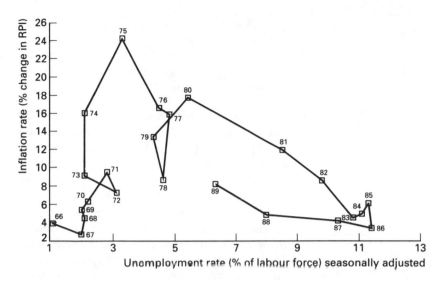

Expectations-augmented Phillips curve. In their original criticism of the Phillips curve, Friedman and Phelps argued that what workers were really interested in was real wages (i.e. money wages adjusted for the rate of inflation), rather than money wages *per se*. As wage negotiations are carried out in nominal values, the *expected* inflation rate becomes an important factor in these negotiations. Instead of there being just one stable Phillips curve, the monetarists predict an infinite number, one for each possible expected level of inflation. We can illustrate this in terms of Fig. 17.5.

Fig. 17.5 The expectations-augmented Phillips curve

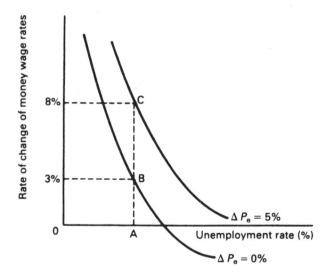

If the pressure of aggregate demand was such that we have an unemployment level of A, then if prices are expected to be stable ($\Delta P_e = 0\%$), workers may settle for, say, a 3% money wage increase, and the economy would be at B. If, however, workers expected 5% inflation ($\Delta P_e = 5\%$), to achieve the same increase in *real* wages as before they will need something like an 8% increase in money wages and so the economy would be at C. In other words, the introduction of price expectations into the analysis means that a given level of unemployment (pressure of demand) is consistent with *any* level of wage inflation, the particular level depending on the workers' expectations of inflation.

The natural rate of unemployment.   The second development of the Phillips curve by the monetarists was to introduce the concept of the natural rate of unemployment (NRU). If the demand for labour (N_D), and the supply of labour (N_S), both vary with the real wage rate, as in Fig. 17.6, then in a perfectly competitive labour market, with flexible wages and prices, an equilibrium real wage rate $(W/p)^*$ will be determined. This real wage rate will be associated with a level of employment N_F^* that might be called the 'full employment' level of employment. It is 'full employment' in the sense that all those who want to work at the going real wage $(W/p)^*$ can find employment. Even when the economy is at N_F^*, however, not all the labour force will be employed. There will still be those people who are between jobs, and new entrants to the labour force who have yet to find work, i.e. 'frictional unemployment'. In the absence of a perfectly competitive labour market, not only will there be 'frictional unemployment' at N_F^*, but with imperfect mobility of labour there will also be 'structural unemployment' (see Ch. 18). The NRU represents the amount of frictional and structural unemployment left in the economy when the supply and demand for labour are in balance. Put another way, the NRU is the *difference* between N_F^* and the amount of labour available in the economy, $\bar{N}$.

Fig. 17.6 The labour market

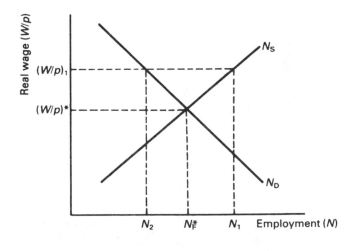

Friedman has argued that the natural rate of unemployment is not a constant, but is likely to change with time. Factors which shift the *demand curve* for labour to the left, such as a reduction in productivity due to, say, trade-union restrictive practices, are likely to reduce N_F^* and by implication increase the natural rate. Likewise, factors which shift the *supply curve* to the left, like increased real unemployment benefits which might prolong the length of time spent between jobs, are also likely to raise the NRU.

If the real wage is anything other than $(W/p)^*$ in Fig. 17.6, there will be either an excess supply of, or demand for, labour. Money wages, and hence real wages, will respond so as to re-establish $(W/p)^*$. For example, if the real wage were too high, say $(W/p)_1$, then there would be excess supply in the labour market equal to N_1-N_2 (actual employment being N_2). The surplus workers would bid down the money wage, and this would continue until the real wage had fallen to $(W/p)^*$ and employment had risen to N_F^*, the full-employment level. Unemployment will then, of course, be equal to the natural rate.

Adding the role of price expectations and the concept of the NRU to the Phillips curve helps us develop a *monetarist* version of the inflation process.

The traditional Phillips curve relationship was:

$$\Delta W = f(U)$$

i.e. the rate of wage inflation (ΔW) varied with the level of unemployment, which itself was an indirect measure of the pressure of demand in the labour market and hence in the economy in general.

The monetarist expectations-augmented Phillips curve is:

$$\Delta W = \Delta P = g(U^* - U) + \Delta P_e$$

i.e. the rate of wage inflation varies with the pressure of demand ($U^* - U$), which is the NRU (U^*) minus the actual rate of unemployment (U), and with the expected rate of inflation (ΔP_e). From the above equation it can be seen that when the pressure of demand in the economy is 'optimal', i.e. $U = U^*$, then the actual level of wage inflation ΔW (which equals ΔP if we assume zero productivity growth[6]) will exactly match the expected inflation rate which of course, could be anything.

If, on the other hand, the pressure of demand in the economy is excessive, as a result of the Government attempting to push actual unemployment below the 'natural rate' (i.e. $U < U^*$), then $U^* - U$ will be positive, and the actual rate of inflation ΔW (and ΔP) will exceed expected inflation (i.e. $\Delta P > \Delta P_e$). People will now revise upwards their expectations of inflation (ΔP_e), which will lead to even higher future rates of wage and price inflation (see Fig. 17.5). As long, therefore, as U is kept below U^* the inflation rate will *accelerate*.

Finally, if the Government deflates the economy so that U exceeds U^*, then $U^* - U$ will be negative, and the actual rate of inflation ΔW (and ΔP) will be below the expected rate. This will result in a *downward* revision of expectations and, hence, lower future rates of wage and price inflation. As long, therefore, as actual unemployment U is kept above the natural rate U^*, the rate of inflation will slow down.

Diagrammatically these points can be illustrated in Fig. 17.7. Suppose the economy is initially at point A, i.e. at the NRU U^*, with zero inflation, and zero expectations of inflation ($\Delta P_e = 0\%$). The Government, dissatisfied with this level of unemployment, then reflates the economy using monetary expansions. The increase in the money supply increases the demand for goods and services, and employers, anticipating higher prices for their goods, increase their demand for labour. This excess demand for labour causes the money wage to rise by, say, 5%. Unemployed workers interpret this as an increase in real wages (because they are expecting zero inflation), and hence

Fig. 17.7 The Natural State
Hypothesis

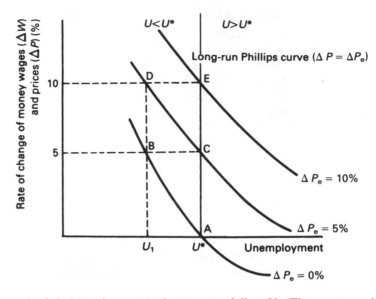

take jobs, causing unemployment to fall to U_1. The economy has therefore moved up the (short-run) Phillips curve from A to B. The 5% increase in labour cost is now passed on by firms, so that the rate of price inflation in the economy is also 5%. Real wages will therefore not have changed, and when this is realized (i.e. once expected inflation has caught up with actual inflation) the newly employed workers will no longer have the incentive to remain in their jobs, so that unemployment will rise back to U^*. The economy will now be at point C, with the same level of unemployment as before the monetary expansion, but one which is now accompanied by an inflation rate of 5% – the new expected rate of inflation.

In terms of our equation:

$$\Delta W = \Delta P = g(U^* - U) + \Delta P_e$$

the excess demand element in inflation $g(U^* - U)$ has fallen to zero as the economy returns to the NRU, and we are left with

$$\Delta W = \Delta P = \Delta P_e$$

i.e. the *actual* rate of inflation is equal to the *expected* rate.

If the Government wishes to maintain unemployment at its target level of U_1, then it has to make sure that price expectations do not catch up with actual inflation. In other words, the Government has to make sure that the newly employed do not appreciate the full neutralizing effect of inflation on their money wage rise. To do this, i.e. to avoid point C in Fig. 17.7, the Government must increase the money supply and raise aggregate demand so that wages increase by more than the expected inflation of 5% in the next time period. Suppose they increase the money supply, and raise wage and price inflation to 10%, i.e. point D in Fig. 17.7. This 10% inflation rate will be made up of the 5% excess demand inflation, plus the 5% expected inflation. Again, the position of the economy at point D will only be temporary, for if expectations catch up with actual inflation, the economy will move to point E. If the Government wishes to avoid this it must further stimulate inflation, and so on in a spiralling inflationary process.

The expectations-augmented Phillips curve therefore presents the authorities with rather painful policy choices. It can only run the economy at a level of unemployment *below the natural rate*, in the long run, if it accepts accelerating inflation. Presumably at some stage the political and economic costs of very high inflation rates outweigh the benefits of lower unemployment, and the Government will have to call a halt to the monetary expansion. Once this occurs unemployment will rise to U^*, its natural level, and the actual level of inflation will be whatever the expected rate of inflation happens then to be (i.e. $\Delta P = \Delta P_e$). In the *short run* there may be a policy trade-off between inflation and unemployment, but in the *long run* this trade-off disappears and the Phillips curve becomes vertical at the NRU, U^*. Macroeconomic policy now appears to be incapable of reducing the rate of unemployment in the economy below the level U^*, except for short periods of time when expectations lag behind reality. The only way the Government can reduce unemployment in this view of the world, is by microeconomic policies aimed at improving the workings of the labour market and thereby reducing U^*, the NRU.

Criticisms of the vertical Phillips curve. It is not surprising that this view of the unemployment–inflation trade-off has its critics. Not least amongst these are Keynesian economists who reject the idea that demand management is only able to affect the real variables of output and employment in the short run. There have been three main areas in which the monetarist view of inflation, embodied in the vertical Phillips curve, has been challenged.

First, it has so far been assumed that the implicit coefficient (c) on the price expectation variable in our inflation equation was 1.

$$\Delta W = \Delta P = g(U^* - U) + c\Delta P_e$$

If the coefficient c *does* equal 1, it means that workers are so alert that they suffer from no money illusion. It also means that workers are able to secure whatever they perceive as the expected inflation rate as a money wage increase. For example, if c were 0.7, this would mean that although workers expected, say, 10% inflation, they would be satisfied with, or be forced to accept, a 7% wage increase (assuming $U = U^*$, i.e. there was no excess demand inflation in the system). The implication of c being less than 1 is that the *long-run* Phillips curve ceases to be vertical. The Government could then keep the economy at a level of unemployment below U^* *without* accelerating inflation. Figure 17.8 helps to illustrate this point.

The monetarist version of the expectations-augmented Phillips curve (with $c = 1$) has each successive Phillips curve shifted vertically by an amount exactly equal to the level of expected inflation. If the coefficient is less than 1 then the curves do shift upwards with expected inflation, but by less than the expected inflation. This is shown by the dotted curve on Fig. 17.8. A 5% expected inflation, with $c = 0.7$, will result in an actual 3.5% wage and price increase. In this case, instead of a monetary stimulus causing the economy to move from A to B and then to C, it will move instead from A to B and then to D, where D is a long-run equilibrium (i.e. expected inflation equals actual inflation). Instead of being vertical, the long-run Phillips curve would therefore be the curve through A and D, implying both a short-run *and a long-run* trade-off between unemployment and inflation.

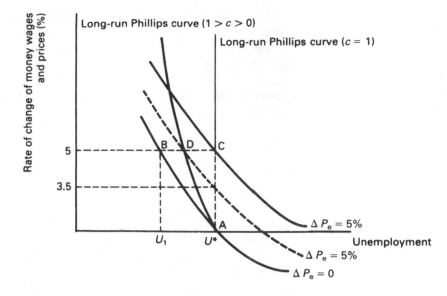

Fig. 17.8 The long-run
Phillips curve

Many studies have been carried out to determine the value of c for the UK economy (see, for instance, Parkin 1978). The earlier studies seemed to reject the extreme monetarist view of no trade-off (i.e. $c = 1$). However, in more recent studies there is evidence of c being near to 1. These later studies were conducted during a time of increasing inflation, when workers were both more likely to be aware of the impact of inflation on living standards and more concerned to ensure that wage claims fully reflect expected inflation.

A second area in which the monetarist view of inflation has been challenged concerns the process by which expectations are formed by economic agents. The less quickly expectations are revised upwards, the more likely they are to lag behind reality. This would mean that *even if the coefficient* c *was 1 and the long-run Phillips curve was vertical, it would still take a long time to move from point B to point C in Fig. 17.8. Long enough, perhaps, for the 'short-run' trade-off between unemployment and inflation to be of interest to policy-makers.

It has proved extremely difficult to assess how quickly expectations have adapted to reality. One model that provided Keynesians with some comfort was the *adaptive expectations* hypothesis. This suggests that next year's expected inflation rate will be this year's expected rate, plus some proportion of the error between actual and expected inflation this year. If we use the subscript t for this year and $t+1$ for next year, then

$$\Delta P_{et+1} = \Delta P_{et} + \lambda(\Delta P_t - \Delta P_{et})$$

where

$$1 > \lambda > 0$$

The lower the value of λ, the less quickly will expectations be revised upwards, and the more favourable will be the model for Keynesians.

There are, however, problems with adaptive expectations as a model of behaviour. For instance, economic agents do not appear to use any information other than current and past prices when forming expectations. In reality they would tend to use all the relevant information they could gather (e.g. on currency depreciation, wage freezes, future indirect tax increases) before coming to a decision about future prices. Again, if the inflation rate follows an upward trend, then expectations formed adaptively will always lag behind. Agents consistently forecast too low a rate of inflation and do not appear to learn from their mistakes in this model.

Such criticisms have led to a new alternative for modelling expectation formation. This is the controversial method of '*rational expectations*'. The rational expectations hypothesis implies that individuals base their expectations on all the relevant information available to them, including current economic *theory*, in this case the expectations-augmented Phillips curve. As soon as individuals see the Government increase the money supply they anticipate the price inflation predicted by monetarist theory and immediately revise upwards their wage and price expectations. All rational policy actions by governments are anticipated, so that price expectations no longer lag behind inflation. In Fig. 17.8 the economy moves straight from A to C, with no temporary reduction in unemployment. There is then no scope for government moving real economic variables from their natural levels even in the short run, unless its policy is to introduce purely random shocks, and this, in everyone's view, would be inappropriate.

A third area in which the monetarist view of inflation has been challenged concerns the concept of the NRU. Early estimates of the natural rate (Parkin, Sumner and Ward 1976) put it at around 2% in the UK. However, the theory itself would suggest that if actual unemployment is above the natural rate, as it was in the UK for most of the 1970s and 1980s, then prices should fall at an accelerating rate. We did not, of course, experience this. It then follows: first, that the theory is wrong; or second, that the natural rate has been inaccurately estimated; or third, that its value has increased through time. It is usually argued by monetarists that the last of these has happened (for more recent estimates see Ch. 18). Whilst this variability of the natural rate does not invalidate the theory, it does make it a rather difficult concept on which to base policy decisions.

To summarize, the breakdown of the traditional Phillips curve relationship and its replacement with the expectations-augmented version, which in the long run is vertical at the NRU, enables the monetarists to explain how changes in the money supply will, at the end of the day, influence *only* the price level, and not output and employment. If this theory is correct it further reinforces their view that inflation is a monetary phenomenon, though as we have seen the expectations-augmented version of the Phillips curve is not without its critics.

Inflation and the exchange rate   The third foundation stone for the development of the monetarist view of inflation was the incorporation, in the early 1970s, of a monetary approach to balance of payments and exchange rate problems. The view that the *domestic* rate of inflation depends on the rate of increase of the *domestic* money supply was developed from a closed economy model, and so only really applied to the USA which, under the Bretton Woods system, was the nearest approximation to a closed economy.

Monetarism therefore only came to be important to countries *outside* the USA when it developed an approach to account for the external sector.

The first step in developing a monetary approach which could incorporate the external sector took place during the period before 1971, when the world operated under the Bretton Woods system, *with exchange rates pegged* against the US dollar. Under such a system countries like the UK lost control over their domestic money supply. This followed since in order to maintain a pegged exchange rate, a country had to be prepared to sell its own currency for foreign currencies to cover any balance of payments surplus, or buy its own currency with foreign currencies to cover any balance of payments deficit (see Ch. 22). This meant that changes in *domestic* money supply could arise not only from domestic sources, but also from the *external* payments situation. Under a fixed exchange rate system a balance of payments surplus will, via sales of sterling (adding to UK foreign exchange reserves), cause the total money supply to exceed the domestic component. A balance of payments deficit will, via purchases of sterling (reducing UK foreign exchange reserves), cause the total money supply to fall below the domestic component. The following equation summarizes the argument:

$$\Delta M_s = \Delta C + \Delta R$$

where ΔM_s = the change in the total money supply;
$\quad\Delta C$ = the domestic source of monetary expansion;
$\quad\Delta R$ = the change in reserves which results from a balance of payments surplus or deficit.

The second step in developing a monetary approach which could account for the external sector, was to use economic theory to point out that under pegged exchange rates, the rates of inflation in different countries can diverge only to the extent that goods entering the price index are not freely traded. If the price increases of traded goods *did* diverge then there would be arbitrage activities which would, in effect, bring the UK inflation rate into line with that in other countries. This is the 'law of one price' which states that arbitrage will compete away all price differences between identical goods (if we assume no transport costs and no tariff barriers to trade). For example, if we assume that the fixed exchange rate is £1 = $2, then a car costing £5,000 in the UK will have to sell in the USA for $10,000. If the UK Government then tries to expand the level of demand by increasing the UK money supply, inflation will ensue. Suppose that this domestic inflation means that the car sells for £6,000 in the UK. Arbitrage will then occur, with individuals buying cars in the cheaper market (USA) and selling them in the more expensive market (UK). This profitable activity will have the effect of increasing the supply of cars in the UK, helping to push down their price, whilst at the same time increasing the demand for US cars, helping to push up US car prices. Arbitrage means that the inflation rates in different countries cannot get out of line for long, given a pegged exchange rate.

It should also be noted from monetary theory that any excessive rate of growth in the UK money supply would be brought back into line. This is because the ensuing balance of payments deficit would require the monetary authorities to purchase sterling on the foreign exchange market in order to keep it at its pegged rate. The fall in reserves (ΔR) would then restrict the growth in the UK money supply. Under a pegged exchange rate system, a small trading country such as the UK does not have the freedom to keep the rate of growth of its money supply (and hence the inflation rate) out of line with the rest of the world.

A question obviously arises. If the UK, along with others, cannot, in the long term, determine independently its own rate of growth of money supply, and thereby its inflation rate, how are these variables determined? The answer is that under the Bretton Woods system, the rate of inflation in the UK was largely determined by the rate of world inflation. The UK money supply would then adjust, as explained, according to the relationship between UK and world inflation rates. United Kingdom money supply would increase if UK inflation was lower than elsewhere (balance of payments surplus), raising the inflation towards the world 'average'. United Kingdom money supply would decrease if UK inflation was higher than elsewhere (balance of payments deficit), reducing UK inflation towards the world 'average'. What matters then is not so much UK money supply and inflation, but rather *world* money supply and *world* inflation, under a regime of pegged exchange rates. Indeed, the acceleration in the rate of world inflation in the late 1960s has often been blamed on the faster growth of world money supply at that time. This was the result of a glut of US dollars associated with the budget deficits used to finance the Vietnam War.

Under the *floating exchange rate system* which has existed in the UK since 1971, balance of payments surpluses and deficits are reflected by movements in the exchange rate, *and not so much in reserves*. Under a floating system a country has, at least in theory, control over its total money supply, so that it is the domestic country itself which is more or less responsible for its own rate of inflation. If, for example, the rate of monetary expansion in the UK is more rapid than its competitors, then it will have a higher rate of inflation than its competitors, and its currency will tend to depreciate at a rate equal to the difference in inflation rates.

The regime of flexible exchange rates came into being, therefore, largely because authorities found that they could not control domestic inflation and unemployment, whilst continuing to maintain fixed exchange rates. Flexible exchange rates allow countries to control their money supply independently, and the diversity of inflation rates amongst countries since 1971 largely reflects this independence.

To summarize, the monetarist view of inflation is based on three foundation stones. First, Friedman's reformulation of the Quantity Theory of Money enabled monetarists to argue that any change in the money supply would require a change in money national income, in the long run via prices, to restore equilibrium in the money market. Second, by adapting the Phillips curve, monetarists could go still further in explaining how an increase in the money supply will affect the components of money national income. In the short run real output will rise and employment will fall if economic agents are 'surprised' by the rate of inflation. In the long run it will only be the price level that is affected, with output and employment returning to their 'natural' rate. Third, developments in monetary analysis of the external sector have enabled monetarists to show *whose* money supply is important in determining inflation. Under a pegged exchange rate system it is the world money supply that matters, with small trading countries being more or less dragged along in tow. Under a floating exchange rate system, the onus is placed firmly in the hands of individual governments, as they now have the freedom to control their own domestic money supply and rate of inflation.

The non-monetarist view of inflation

In the 1960s most Keynesians believed that the Phillips curve showed inflation to be caused by excess aggregate demand. This Keynesian 'demand-pull' view of inflation was rather more general than that of the monetarists. In the Keynesian system, if the economy was at, or near, full employment, an increase in *any* of the components of aggregate demand could be responsible for inflation. The monetarist view, as we saw, emphasized the particular role of government spending in aggregate demand, financed by borrowing from the banking sector which increases the money supply and fuels the inflationary process. The breakdown of the Phillips curve relationship in the late 1960s led most Keynesians to abandon the demand-pull view of current inflation. Instead they proposed explanations that concentrated upon forces causing firms' costs of production to rise. This 'cost-push' view of inflation stresses either institutional features of the labour market, or the cost of imported goods, as the main factors explaining UK inflation.

Trade unions and wage-push inflation In the 'demand-pull' view of inflation, wages *react* to the level of demand in the economy. If it can be shown that in practice this is not the case, but that wages are set independently of the level of demand (say by the action of trade unions) then the 'demand-pull' view of inflation would have little credibility. This would apply both to the early Keynesian analysis of the Phillips curve, and to monetarist attempts to explain its later instability.

In its most extreme form, supporters of the wage-push view argue that the inflation rate depends almost entirely on the aggressiveness of unions in pressing for wage demands. Wiles, for instance, argues that 'we have moved from wage claims based on the actual situation in trade . . . to claims picked out of the air' (Wiles 1973: 378). In this view prices are no longer determined by the market forces of supply and demand but by trade union whim, which itself determines wages, which in turn determine prices. Prices are raised by firms in imperfectly competitive markets to retain their profitability in the face of the 'cost-push' pressure from wages. This increase in prices will in turn raise inflationary expectations, feeding into the next round of wage negotiations, so that the familiar 'wage–price spiral' continues. Wiles attributes the new cost-push inflation to social and political causes. He suggests that the national character has changed, with less emphasis being placed on self-discipline, respect for work and on restraint at the bargaining table.

Kahn (1976) presents a slightly different view of the wage-push process.

He sees it as the result of the struggle between different labour groups to maintain or improve their *relative* positions in the wages league. This is sometimes called the 'wage–wage spiral' as against the 'wage–price spiral'. If one group of workers manages to improve its position relative to others, then the disadvantaged groups react by seeking wage increases to restore the previously 'fair' pattern of wage differentials. Unilateral attempts to leap-frog other groups set in motion a chain reaction, raising both money wages and prices.

Others see the inflationary process as a result of the struggle between capital and labour for a greater share of National Income. This Marxist approach argues that whilst national income is growing both groups can acquire more real resources. However, when output stops growing, or at least grows only slowly as in the 1970s, the inherent conflict between capital and labour manifests itself in terms of higher inflation. Suppose, for example, workers secure wage increases in excess of productivity growth, then profits per unit are squeezed. Firms in imperfect markets react to this by raising their prices, in this way restoring the share of profits in national income. Workers in turn react by forcing more wage increases, and so on.

In these views of cost-push inflation, the common factor is that wage increases feed through into price increases, which in turn stimulate claims for further wage increases. Of course for this process to gain momentum, firms must accede to the wage claims they face. Why should this be more evident now than in previous times? The answer usually given is that the balance of power in the bargaining process has shifted away from firms and towards unions. Workers, it is alleged, are more prepared to strike over wage claims, due to increased welfare benefits, etc. Firms are more prepared to give in to wage rises due to the 'cost' of strikes having risen. More capital-intensive methods of production mean that periods of lost output become progressively more expensive, and more intense foreign competition means that lost output is more likely to result in lost markets. The suggestion, then, is that firms are now more likely than before to give in to higher wage demands, preferring to avoid the heavy costs imposed by strike action.

Despite such arguments the role of trade unions in the inflation process is still the subject of much controversy. It is still unclear why trade unions should have become more militant, and hence more 'pushful', since the late 1960s. Much of the evidence on wage increases and inflation could be explained just as well by workers reacting to price increases, rather than the other way round. The debate about whether unions cause inflation or merely react to it, is still an open one.

In the wage-push view of inflation, increases in the money supply are rejected as *a cause of* wage increases. However, increases in the money supply are often seen as *a consequence of* wage increases. Higher incomes, via wage increases, will raise the transactions demand for money balances. If the monetary authorities refuse to increase the money supply to *accommodate* this higher transactions demand for money, then the 'price' of money, the interest rate, will rise, reducing investment and consumption, and raising unemployment. For political reasons, therefore, governments have in the past ensured that the money supply has been adequate to support any given level of money wages, no matter how high these were, in order to avoid raising both interest rates and unemployment. The monetarist experiment in the UK is an attempt to break from this strategy by setting targets for money supply growth, though this has raised both interest rates and unemployment.

In a sense, therefore, Friedman is right when he says that inflation is always a monetary phenomenon. Even cost-push inflation, if not accommodated by an increase in the money supply, would eventually come to an end, with rising unemployment eroding the power of the unions to push for further wage increases. Monetarists do not, therefore, believe that unions cause inflation, even though their power in the bargaining process is recognized. Instead, they argue that it has been the accommodating increases in the money supply that have caused prices to rise, since it has been these that have shielded unions from the market consequences of their actions.

Import prices and real wage resistance   The previous views of cost inflation appear to be saying that the forces determining wages are in a large part non-economic, so that the causes of, and remedies for, inflation lie outside economics, in sociology and politics. Hicks (1975) objects to this view and argues that 'there is a good deal that is of an economic character' in the recent inflationary experience. He argues that cost inflation arises not so much from institutional practices in the labour market, but from higher import prices meeting real wage resistance. World commodity prices rose sharply in 1972, as did oil prices in 1973–74, and again in 1979. A rise in import prices means that the terms of trade deteriorate, so that more UK output has to be exchanged for a given volume of imports. As a result, real income in the UK is reduced, so that if an initial level of employment is to be maintained, real wages must fall.

Real wages could fall either by a reduction in money wages, which is unlikely, or by a rise in the price level that is not matched by an equivalent rise in money wages. Hicks argues that unions reacted to higher domestic prices (via higher import prices) by seeking equivalent increases in money wages, resisting a fall in the real wage. The monetary authorities then faced a dilemma. Since real wages had not fallen, the initial level of unemployment could only be maintained by 'accommodating' the price increases, i.e. allowing money supply to grow. This, of course, risked unleashing an inflationary wage–price spiral. Not to accommodate the price increases would raise unemployment. The UK did allow the money supply to rise in line with prices, and inflation rose rapidly in the mid–late 1970s. To Hicks it was the initial rise in import prices, not unnaturally meeting real wage resistance, which was the root cause of the subsequent inflationary spiral, by forcing such an unpalatable choice on the monetary authorities.

Kaldor (1976) developed this view of inflation in seeking to account for the twin problems of inflation and recession in the non-oil developed economies. Inflation arose through higher import prices, causing domestic firms to raise their own prices in the 1970s. This in turn led to price-induced rises in wages (real wage resistance) and hence further inflation. To Kaldor, the recession arose through the transfer of purchasing power from the non-oil-producing to the oil-producing countries, and the inability of the latter to spend their increased revenues on the output of the non-oil-producing countries.

The policy implications of the two views of inflation

The monetarist approach

The cause of inflation is seen by monetarists as excess monetary demand, determined by the rate of expansion of the world money supply under a fixed exchange rate system, and by the rate of growth of the UK money supply if the exchange rate is floating. Under the current floating exchange rate system, the monetarist solution to inflation is therefore a gradual reduction in the rate of growth of the UK money supply. A reduction in the UK budget deficit is seen by the monetarists as a precondition for reducing money supply growth in the UK. A budget deficit cannot entirely be financed by borrowing from the non-bank sector, as this would push interest rates too high. It is therefore always in part financed by borrowing from the banking sector. As we saw in Chapter 16, if the banking sector acquires short-dated government securities, these can be used for a multiple expansion of bank deposits, i.e. money supply.

Cutting the budget deficit in order to reduce money supply growth means a deflationary strategy, i.e. reducing government spending (injections) more than taxes (withdrawals). The resulting deflation means that the economy will be run at a level of unemployment *above* the NRU. As we have seen, this implies that the actual inflation rate will be below the expected rate so that expectations will be revised downwards. This in turn will be reflected in lower money wage claims and inflation. Eventually, once inflationary expectations and hence inflation have been squeezed out of the system, the economy will return automatically to the NRU.

Several problems are involved in this strategy. First, there is the problem of the control of the money supply. The Government has to decide which measure of the money supply it is to attempt to control. Friedman argues that it is the monetary base that should be held in check. Governments in the UK have until recently made the broader sterling M_3 ($£M_3$) the target. In the 1982 Budget the Government abandoned the idea of using a single monetary aggregate as target variable, and set targets for M_1, $£M_3$ and PSL_2 (see Ch. 16). Having set such targets, given the monetary weapons at their disposal, can the authorities achieve them? In other words, can they actually control the money supply? Recent UK experience casts some doubt upon this. Targets for $£M_3$ were first introduced in 1976, and in the financial years up to March 1985 it appears that the targets were: (a) attained five times (1976/77, 1979/80, 1982/83, 1983/84 and 1984/85); (b) just missed once (1978/79); and (c) missed three times (1977/78, 1980/81 and 1981/82). The target was therefore missed on four out of nine occasions. In his Mansion House speech of October 1985 the Chancellor suspended the use of $£M_3$ as a target variable with the current figures well over target, and placed greater emphasis on the newest and most narrow of the money supply measures, i.e. M_0. This was a step towards Friedman's argument that it is the monetary base that should be the focus of policy. By 1988, the Treasury and the Bank of England were watching three indicators closely: M_0, the exchange rate, and M_4 (a broad measure of money that includes building society deposits, see Ch. 16). In the 1990 budget, the only monetary target set was for M_0 (at 1–5%), with targets for M_4 being dropped.

A second problem concerns the speed with which expectations are revised downwards when the actual unemployment rate is pushed above the NRU. If this is a slow process, and evidence seems to suggest that it is, then the economy has to suffer a prolonged period of high unemployment as the cost of eliminating inflation from the system. Indeed, some economists, such as the new classical school, argue that because a prolonged period of high unemployment might be unacceptable politically, it might be better to execute a short, sharp reduction in the rate of monetary expansion. Although this will generate a more severe initial recession, it should cause inflationary expectations to be revised downwards more rapidly. It may, therefore, in the longer term reduce the unemployment cost of curbing inflation.

A third problem is the monetarist belief that once inflation is eliminated, the economy will return automatically to its 'full employment' rate of unemployment, i.e. the NRU. This argument relies heavily on the increasing personal savings ratio observed in the 1970s being associated with accelerating inflation. The suggestion is that accelerating inflation reduced the real value of liquid assets, so that individuals were then forced to save a large proportion of their income in order to restore the real value of their liquid assets. If this had been so, a subsequent fall in the inflation rate should then be expected to reduce the savings ratio and stimulate consumer spending. (For a fuller treatment of this point see Ch. 11.) Even if this analysis is correct, it could still be argued that the size of the effect will be too weak to restore the economy to the NRU, and that government help in terms of more spending or less taxation will also be required.

A fourth problem is that a counter-inflationary strategy that commits the economy to a prolonged period of unemployment may actually raise the natural rate. It may, for instance, raise the number of long-term unemployed, who may then be incapable of future employment. In terms of Fig. 17.6, this is equivalent to a leftward shift of the effective labour supply curve (N_S) at the market clearing real wage $(W/p)^*$, reducing N_F^* and raising the NRU. The economy may therefore stabilize at an acceptable rate of inflation but at an unacceptable level of unemployment.

The difficulties inherent in the monetarist strategy led to its abandonment in 1985. It has been argued that the January 1985 sterling crisis marked the changeover from pragmatic monetarism to mere pragmatism (Smith 1987). The 'official' end to the monetarist experiment can be dated as November 1985 when £M_3 was downgraded from a *target* variable to just a *monitored* one. Since that date monetary policy has been largely concerned with influencing the *exchange rate*. Initially it was thought that if the sterling exchange rate could be tied to that existing in a low inflation country, then inflation would be curbed in the UK. As a result sterling shadowed the Deutschmark for a period, at a rate of £1 = 3DM.

More recently, UK monetary policy has depended upon using relatively *high interest rates* to control inflation. The transmission mechanism from high interest rates to lower inflation (according to the Bank of England, May 1990) is fourfold:

1. The cost of borrowing affects the relative attractiveness of spending today as compared with spending later. A high interest rate should make spending today less attractive than spending at a later date.
2. Higher interest rates will also have an *income effect*. Borrowers will be worse off and lenders better off. If borrowers have a higher m.p.c. out of

current income than lenders, then expenditure should fall. Since borrowers are more cash constrained, in terms of consumption, than those with positive financial assets (such as lenders), they are indeed likely to have a higher m.p.c.

3. A rise in interest rates tends to cause the value of assets such as houses, shares, and government stock, to fall. This *wealth effect* should then reduce consumption and possibly investment (see Ch. 11).

4. The final mechanism is through the *exchange rate*. Higher interest rates should lead to an appreciation in the exchange rate, which should in turn lead to lower import prices. This may also force domestic firms to limit wage increases in order to remain competitive.

The non-monetarist approach

Although most non-monetarists do acknowledge the role of monetary and fiscal control in slowing down the inflationary process, they have usually argued that the unemployment cost of this monetarist solution would be politically unacceptable. Some, though not all non-monetarists, have proposed an incomes policy as the best hope of controlling inflation without incurring an excessive loss of output and employment. However, the problems involved in this sort of strategy are also severe.

Critics argue, first, that incomes policies do not work, having a maximum life of less than three years before they break down, and being followed by a catching-up phase. A second criticism is that incomes policies lead to a misallocation of resources. Expanding firms will be unable to attract the labour they need if they are not allowed to offer higher wages, and this will disrupt production. Further, by eroding differentials between skilled and unskilled workers, incomes policies lead to a reduction in the supply of skilled workers. Incomes policies, and worse still, prices and incomes policies, interfere in these ways with the workings of the market economy, resulting in a less efficient allocation of resources. A third criticism of incomes policies often made by monetarists, is that they are unnecessary. Monetarists argue that if *their* strategy is followed, the falling rate of inflation will itself cause wage claims to be revised downwards, in line with inflation. Moreover, a preoccupation with incomes policy is likely to distract the Government away from the pursuit of the appropriate monetary and fiscal policies.

Proponents of incomes policy argue, first, that although in theory this type of policy may lead to a misallocation of resources, any 'waste' is more than compensated for by the extra resources generated through being able to run the economy closer to full employment. A second argument is that even without wage and price controls, the economy is full of imperfections (e.g. monopoly unions and firms, etc.), so that in such a 'second-best world' a movement further away from perfect competition, via the adoption of wage or price restrictions, may not necessarily lead to a less efficient allocation of resources. A third argument in support of incomes policies is that even though they are often breached whilst still in force, and quickly break down altogether, they have the short-run effect of reducing the rate of wage inflation and of reducing inflationary expectations. This argument does not, of course, square with the view that there is always a catching-up phase after an incomes policy breaks down. If this were a widely held view, then expectations would have anticipated the coming breakdown, and an incomes policy would do little to reduce inflationary expectations.

Finally, it should be remembered that non-monetarists do not underestimate the danger of excess demand-generated inflation. The 'Lawson boom' of 1987/88 pushed the economy towards a high level of capacity utilization and the RPI rose from less than 4% at the beginning of 1988, to nearly 10% by mid-1990. As has already been noted, the strategy used by the Government to counter this relied mainly on high interest rates bringing down inflation. An alternative, proposed by some non-monetarists, would be to eliminate the excess demand by using *direct controls on credit*. The case put forward is that credit control would permit lower interest rates and this would in turn encourage investment and help young home owners who have large mortgage debt. It is also argued that credit controls work more speedily in cutting demand than do high interest rates. Against this, opponents argue that the financial system is so sophisticated and so international that direct credit controls, no matter how ingenious, would soon be circumvented. Further, such controls would lead to a loss of economic welfare by interfering in the free market mechanism and distort official statistics, making it difficult to assess how tight policy actually is at any moment in time.

Recent experience

The major objective of the Conservative Government's economic policy since 1979 has been the control of inflation. Judged solely on this criterion the strategy was initially successful. Inflation, as measured by the RPI, fell from over 20% in mid 1980 to below 5% by 1983. As Table 17.4 shows, this was a more rapid rate of decline than the OECD average at that time. However, the record since 1983 has been far less successful. Inflation averaged around 4–5% for the period 1983–87, began to rise in 1988 and by mid 1990 had reached 9.8%. Furthermore the initial decline in the inflation rate was associated with an unexpectedly severe recession, with a more than doubling of the unemployment rate (see Ch. 18).

Table 17.4 The UK and the world economy since 1979

	Inflation (% rate)		Unemployment (% level)		Real GDP (% growth rate)	
	UK	OECD	UK	OECD	UK	OECD
1979	13.4	8.7	5.0	5.0	2.8	3.5
1980	18.0	11.3	6.4	5.7	−2.2	1.5
1981	11.9	9.5	9.8	6.6	−1.3	1.7
1982	8.6	7.2	11.3	8.0	1.7	−0.1
1983	4.6	5.5	12.5	8.5	3.5	2.7
1984	5.0	4.9	11.7	8.0	2.1	4.8
1985	6.1	4.3	11.2	7.8	3.7	3.4
1986	3.4	2.7	11.2	7.7	3.6	2.7
1987	4.2	3.4	10.3	7.3	4.7	3.5
1988	4.9	3.3	8.3	6.7	4.5	4.4
1989	7.8	4.3	6.4	6.1	2.3	3.6

* Unemployment standardized according to international definitions.
Source: OECD Economic Outlook, June 1990.

The original 'monetarist' strategy was based on the supposed stability of the income velocity of $£M_3$ and the ability of the authorities to control their $£M_3$ targets by appropriate adjustments to the PSBR and the level of interest rates. It was hoped that by announcing targets for the money supply inflationary expectations would be revised downwards and the unemployment costs of the policy would be correspondingly low. Further the policy was also carried out without an explicit incomes policy, at least in the private sector.

It is difficult to assess how much of the fall in the inflation rate between 1980 and 1983 was due to the monetarist strategy as originally conceived by the Government and how much it was due to other factors. The targets for $£M_3$ set out in the MTFS of 1980 were consistently exceeded (see Ch. 25) and yet inflation fell to a fairly stable level. Despite the impression given by the rate of growth of $£M_3$ in 1979/80, it is generally felt that the monetary stance was too tight in this period, an impression supported by the fact that narrower measures of the money supply were growing only slowly and the exchange rate was very strong and interest rates were exceptionally high. The rise in the value of the pound has a direct impact on the inflation rate in that it reduces the cost of imports and forces domestic manufacturers to control their price increases in order to remain competitive. On top of this came the severely deflationary budget of 1981 when according to Miller (1984), the Government's structural balance (the fiscal deficit adjusted to take account of the business cycle) moved from a deficit equivalent to 4.4% of GDP in 1979 to a surplus of 2.6% of GDP in 1982. This fiscal tightening equivalent to 7% of GDP was unprecedented and took place in 1981 at the trough of the business cycle when manufacturing output had already fallen by 17.5% and unemployment was rising by around 100,000 a month. Given the overvalued pound and the depth of the recession it is not surprising that the rate of inflation should fall.

It could be argued that the apparent success of the monetarist experiment at getting inflation down owes little to the macroeconomic strategy as originally conceived. Policy turned into an orthodox deflation largely because of the difficulties of controlling economies with only the aid of simple monetary rules. The displacement of Keynesianism by monetarism proved more difficult when it came to policy implementation than it did in economic theory.

A different view of why the inflation rate dropped at this time is provided by Beckerman (1985). He argues that it can be entirely explained in terms of the fall in international commodity prices. Beckerman finds no statistical evidence for a feedback from unemployment to inflation and argues that the Government induced deflation in demand, and rising unemployment played no part in explaining the deceleration in wages since for him unemployment does not seem to have any statistically significant relationship to wage increases. He argues that the reduction in inflation originated in the goods market (wages did not lead the disinflationary process, if anything they followed it) particularly in the market for primary products.

The implication of this view is that there is no particular level of unemployment that keeps inflation at a stable rate. Thus for an individual country there is no NRU (or NAIRU). If inflation is accelerating because of rising import prices but the Government mistakenly believes it is because the actual level of unemployment is below the NRU and that they can combat inflation by reducing demand, then unemployment will rise without inflation being checked. This will then lead monetarists to rationalize the position in terms of a rising NRU and so recommend more deflation and hence higher unemployment. Given that inflation is still rising because of commodity prices, the *estimated* NRU will go on rising.

Although in Beckerman's view there is no direct relationship between unemployment and wage increases and hence no NRU for individual countries, he does not imply that this is true for industrial countries taken as a whole. A more or less simultaneous deflation would depress commodity prices, as in 1980–82. In such a situation countries are helped in their fight against inflation not by moving along their national Phillips curves but by a fall in import prices (the equivalent of a downward shift in the curve). The price of halting inflation has therefore not been confined to rising unemployment in the industrial countries; it has been borne more than proportionately by primary producers.

The aim of the Government to get inflation down even further is in this view a vain one. Apart from the impact of domestic policy on the exchange rate and hence import prices, the rate of inflation is not under its direct control. It depends on how far the industrialized world as a whole is expanding or contracting, since it is this that determines the behaviour of commodity prices.

Inflation ceased to fall after 1983. Between 1983 and the beginning of 1988 the inflation rate, as measured by the RPI, remained fairly stable (apart from the 'blip' of 1985) averaging just under 5% per annum. Although average earnings had been rising by around 8% per annum, improvements in productivity, especially in manufacturing, had helped to keep unit labour costs down at this time. Nonetheless, it proved impossible to depress the inflation rate further, even though unemployment continued to rise until June 1986. The question that might be posed is why didn't the large pool of unemployed workers exert more of a downward influence on pay claims and hence inflation? One reason could have been that a high proportion of the unemployed had been out of work for over a year. There is indeed evidence to show that the long-term-unemployed become discouraged and search less diligently for jobs than the short-term-unemployed. In effect, the excess supply of labour represented by the long-term-unemployed was not clearly signalled in the labour market. As a result they put less downward pressure on wages than would have been the case with an equivalent number of short-term-unemployed.

Other reasons have been put forward to explain why wage rates proved so insensitive to the high levels of unemployment in the mid 1980s. These include first, the fact that unemployed workers quickly become deskilled (at least in the eyes of employers) and are therefore regarded as poor substitutes for existing employees; second, that unemployed workers would be signalling 'poor quality' if they offered themselves for work at lower wage rates than existing workers, and third, that 'insiders' (the employed) have managed to exclude 'outsiders' (the unemployed) by making it difficult for firms to employ them. This may have been done by implicitly or even explicitly refusing to co-operate with 'outsiders', together with a range of restrictive practices adopted by unions in favour of existing employees.

From a low of 3.3% in January 1988, the inflation rate rose to just under 10% in June 1990. It has been argued that special factors, such as the increases in mortgage interest rates and the poll tax, have accounted for a large part of this increase in the RPI. If, however, we take *manufacturers' output prices* as a measure of 'core' inflation, then the inflation rate is still rising; up from 4% in 1987 to 5.6% in 1990.

This upturn in inflation can be linked to the strength of demand in the economy during 1987/88, together with high capacity utilization and labour scarcity. These factors caused wage settlements to edge upwards, but high demand enabled firms to raise prices to protect their profit margins. The slowdown in the economy during 1989/90 meant, however, increased cost pressures for firms as productivity growth slowed while wage settlements continued to rise. The consequent increase in unit labour costs was further compounded by the weakness of the pound during most of 1989; this led to higher import costs. The continued weakness of the economy into 1990/91, with capacity utilization falling and unemployment rising, should see inflation eventually coming down as cost pressures subside. Nevertheless, the question remains as to how far unemployment has to rise before the labour market responds with lower wage settlements.

Notes

1. If the price of an item in the index was 10p in January (P_0) and 12p in February (P_1) then the price relative would be 12/10 (P_1)/(P_0) and this would then be multiplied by the weight (W) for that item. The index for period 1 (where period 0 = 100) is given by $[\Sigma(P_1 \times W)/\Sigma(P_0 \times W)] \times 100$.
2. For example, if the index for January 1986 based on January 1985 was 120, and the index for July 1986 based on January 1986 was 110, then the July 1986 index, based on January 1985 = 100, would be calculated as follows: $120 \times 110/100 = 132$.
3. Nigel Lawson, then Financial Secretary to the Treasury, speaking at the publication of the New Tax and Price Index in August 1979.
4. The market for company bonds and debentures appeared to be reawakening. British Oxygen Company took the lead by issuing a £100m. bond in September 1982 in an attempt to take advantage of relatively low inflation and interest rates.
5. See, for example, Laidler (1984a).
6. If we assume zero productivity growth, and that firms use a cost-plus method of pricing with a constant percentage mark-up on costs of production, then a given percentage increase in wage costs produces approximately the same rate of price inflation.

References

Bank of England Quarterly Bulletin (1984) **24**, 2, June; (1990) **30**, 2 May. Inflation-adjusted saving and sectoral balances.
Beckerman, W. (1985) How the battle against inflation was really won, *Lloyds Bank Review*, 155, Jan.

Employment Gazette (1988) **96**, 8, Aug.

Employment Gazette (1990) **98**, 7, June.

Friedman, M. (1968) The role of monetary policy, *American Economic Review*, **58**, March.

Friedman, M. (1977) Inflation and unemployment, *Journal of Political Economy*, **85**, 3.

Healey, N. (1987) The UK 1979–82 'Monetarist experiment': why economists still disagree, *Banca Nazionale Del Lavoro*, 163, Dec.

Hicks, J. (1975) What is wrong with monetarism?, *Lloyds Bank Review*, 118, Oct.

Higham, D. and **Tomlinson, J.** (1982) Why do governments worry about inflation? *National Westminster Bank Review*, May.

Kahn, R. F. (1976) Thoughts on the behaviour of wages and monetarism, *Lloyds Bank Review*, 119, Jan.

Kaldor, N. (1976) Inflation and recession in the world economy. *Economic Journal*, **86**, Dec.

Laidler, D. (1984a) Monetarism: an interpretation and an assessment, *Economic Journal*, **91**, March.

Laidler, D. (1984b) The 'Buffer Stock' notion in monetary economics, *Economic Journal*, **94**, Supplement.

Lipsey, R. G. and **Harbury, C.** (1988) First principles of economics. Weidenfeld and Nicolson, London.

Miller, M. (1984) The medium term financial strategy: an experiment in co-ordinating monetary and fiscal policy, *Fiscal Studies* **2**, July.

National Institute Economic Review (1990) **126**, Feb.

Parkin, J. M. (1978) Alternative explanations of United Kingdom inflation: a survey, in: Parkin, J. M. and Sumner, M. T. (eds) *Inflation in the United Kingdom*. Manchester University Press, Manchester.

Parkin, J. M., Sumner, M. T. and **Ward, R.** (1976) The effects of excess demand generalized expectations and wage price controls, on wage inflation in the UK, 1956–71, in: Brunner, K. and Meltzer, A. H. (eds) *The Economics of Wages and Price Controls*. North Holland Publishing Co., Amsterdam.

Phelps, E. S. (1967) Phillips curves, expectations of inflation and optimal unemployment over time, *Economica*, **34**, Aug.

Phillips, A. W. (1958) The relation between unemployment and the rate of change of money wage rates in the United Kingdom, *Economica*, **25**, Nov.

Smith, O. (1987) The Rise and Fall of Monetarism. Penguin Books.

Smith, O. (1990) New 'honest' index could speed ERM entry, *Sunday Times*, 10 June 1990.

Taylor, M. (1987) Financial innovation, inflation and the stability of the demand for broad money in the United Kingdom, *Bulletin of Economic Research*, **39**, 3.

Wiles, P. (1973) Cost inflation and the state of economic theory, *Economic Journal*, **83**, June.

18

Unemployment

In his conclusion to the *General Theory of Employment, Interest and Money*, Keynes wrote 'it is certain that the world will not much longer tolerate the unemployment which, apart from brief intervals of excitement, is associated, and in my opinion inevitably associated, with present-day capitalistic individualism' (Keynes 1936). History repeated itself in the 1980s as UK unemployment again rose to over 3 million and, despite the buoyancy of the economy in the late 1980s, unemployment at the end of 1990 was still at over 1.6 million, nearly twice the level it had been for most of the post war period. Does Keynes's conclusion hold true in today's world or have we come to accept high unemployment as somehow inevitable under all forms of economic system? In this chapter we first review the changing level and pattern of unemployment in the UK, noting the new method of counting the unemployed. We then consider the contribution of economic theory to the unemployment issue, and examine a number of important issues for policy, such as whether labour has priced itself out of employment, or whether it is simply the unfortunate victim of insufficient aggregate demand or technological change. We conclude with an attempt to identify those policies which might lead the economy in the direction of higher employment.

It could be argued that the adoption, after the Second World War, of Keynesian demand-management policies secured nearly two decades of historically low unemployment (see Fig. 18.1). In recent years, however,

Fig. 18.1 UK unemployment rate (excluding school-leavers)
Sources: CSO (1990); London and Cambridge Economic Service, (1967)

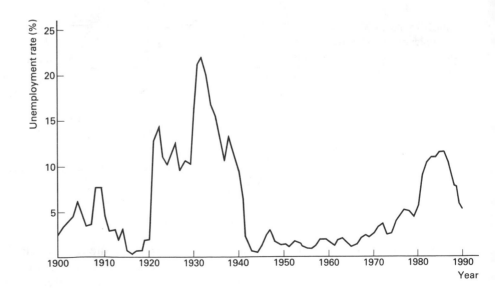

although government commitment to full employment (first stated in the 1944 White Paper on employment policy) has never been revoked, we no longer appear to have the tools with which to do the job. The traditional Keynesian solution to unemployment of reflating the economy is seen as no longer practical given its (alleged) inflationary consequences. Import controls and incomes policies, once advocated as universal panaceas, are rejected on the basis of adversely affecting resource allocation, and the current Government's emphasis on supply-side measures appears to be making little real impact. As a result a depressing number of forecasts are indicating that unemployment of around 2 million is not just a temporary phenomenon but one likely to be with us throughout the 1990s.

Unemployment in the UK

Before attempting to assess the causes of high unemployment, and to consider what, if anything, can be done, it is important to examine the unemployment statistics themselves to see what light they shed on the issue.

The level of post-war unemployment

The policy objective of a 'high and stable level of employment' (1944 White Paper on employment policy) appeared to be within reach during the 1950s and early 1960s. In this period the unemployment rate rarely exceeded 2%. However, as Fig. 18.1 shows and Table 18.1 confirms, this 'golden' period ended in the mid-1960s when an upward trend in the unemployment rate began to become established. Each successive unemployment cycle in recent years has left the UK economy with a higher unemployment rate than the previous one. Superimposed on top of this trend was the severe recession of 1980/81 which conspired to give the UK an absolute level of unemployment higher than in even the worst years of the 1930s Depression. The unemployment rate peaked in the Summer of 1986, fell sharply thereafter and showed some signs of rising again in 1990.

Table 18.1 Post-war unemployment cycles in the UK

Period	Unemployment (%)		
	Mean	Maximum	Minimum
1948–50	1.6	1.8	1.5
1951–54	1.5	1.7	1.2
1955–60	1.6	2.1	1.1
1961–65	1.8	2.3	1.4
1966–73	2.6	3.7	1.5
1974–78	4.6	5.7	2.6
1979–86	9.4	11.6	4.6

Source: CSO (1988).

Methods of measuring unemployment

Despite the frequency with which the term 'unemployment' is used, economists have problems defining it satisfactorily, both from a theoretical point of view and for statistical purposes. Being without a job is a necessary but not a sufficient characteristic to define an unemployed person. Pensioners, housewives and students would not, after all, be thought of as unemployed. Tighter criteria need to be applied and these usually include: being without work; wanting a job; seeking work; being available for work; and claiming benefit as unemployed. Different definitions of unemployment can be devised with reference to these criteria, each giving different results.

The Government's annual labour force survey uses the International Labour Office/OECD (ILO/OECD) definition: people without a job who were available to start work and who had either looked for work within the four weeks prior to interview or were waiting to start a job they had already obtained. Survey results for the 60,000 households interviewed in spring 1989 provide a useful illustration of UK practice. Unemployment for spring 1989 was given as 1.98m, a fall of over a million since the spring 1984 figure of 3.09m. The fall reflects, to a large extent, the rapid growth of the economy during the period 1986–89. However the Unemployment Unit estimates that the unmet demand for jobs was still high, there being over 1m people who would like a job but who were not counted as unemployed by the Labour Force Survey because they had not looked for work (perhaps because they thought there were no suitable jobs available, the so called 'discouraged workers'). On this basis unemployment would still be about 3m.

There are several drawbacks to the survey approach to measuring unemployment. First, the cost involved means that the frequency of surveys is limited to one a year and this, taken together with the time needed to process the data, means that the figures usually relate to the *previous* year. Second, it is not always easy to assess the accuracy of the respondents' replies to the questions asked.

An alternative approach is used for the official UK unemployment statistics. Since 1982 the official count each month has been based on the number of people eligible for, and claiming, unemployment benefits (Unemployment benefit or Income support). Collecting unemployment figures as a by-product of an administrative procedure may have its advantages in terms of cost and speed, but from an economist's point of view it is not altogether satisfactory. The main problem is that administrative and definitional changes can affect the unemployment count *without* there being any change in the underlying labour market conditions. In fact there have been twenty-nine such changes since 1979, all but one of which served to *reduce* the official unemployment count.

For example, the 1982 change from counting those *registered* at Jobcentres or Careers Offices to only counting those actually receiving benefit, is estimated to have reduced the count by around 190,000. Likewise, the 1988 Social Security Act excluded most under 18s from benefit, reducing unemployment by 90,000 at a stroke. Indeed it has been estimated, in a 1989 Bank of England discussion paper by Dicks and Hatch (1989), that up to two thirds of the fall in the jobless total between 1986 and 1989 was caused by the 'Restart' programme. Introduced in November 1987, Restart's aim was to interview, and provide guidance to, the long-term unemployed. While there may have been some success in remotivating a number of long-term unemployed, there is evidence to suggest that the reduction in the unemployment count is just as likely to have been the result of tighter 'availability for work' tests and the reclassifying of many unemployed as 'unfit for work due to long-term sickness or disability'. No doubt some of the changes to the ways in which the official unemployment statistics are counted will have improved their accuracy; however the fact that so many of the changes have led to a rounding *down* of the official count cannot help but undermine confidence in the figures and hinder the ability of economists to see what actually is happening in the labour market. Indeed it has been estimated by the Unemployment Unit that if all the changes since 1979 were stripped away, then the unemployment total would, for July 1990, be 2,494,000, nearly 900,000 higher than the official count.

Fig. 18.2 Unemployment survey and claimant measures, Great Britain
Source: Employment Gazette (1990b)

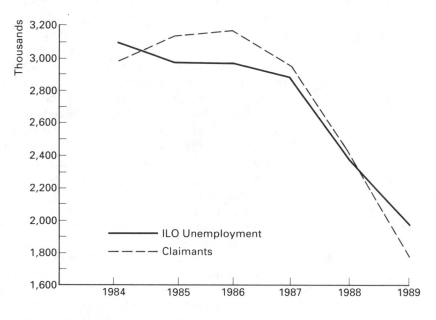

It can be seen clearly from Fig. 18.2 that the two measures of unemployment show similar *trends* over recent years. Both show unemployment in spring 1989 at more than one million lower than in spring 1984, with a particularly large fall over the last two years. Despite similar trends, there are some differences in both absolute levels and changes over time. The spring 1989 unemployment figure as measured by the ILO/OECD definition was 1.98 million, whilst the claimants count was only 1.78 million. The two methods are, to some extent, measuring different people, as Fig. 18.3 shows.

Fig. 18.3 Unemployment: Spring 1989
Source: Employment Gazette (1990b)

← — — — –ILO/OECD Unemployed – — — — →
1.98 m

ILO/OECD Unemployed but Non claimants 0.71 m	ILO/OECD Unemployed and Claimants 1.27 m	Non-ILO/OECD Unemployed but Claimants 0.51 m

← — — — — — Claimants — — — — — →
1.78 m

Most people who are 'claimant unemployed' are also classified as 'unemployed' on the ILO/OECD definition, and vice versa (the middle box in the diagram). The *difference* between the counts arises because there are *more people* who are ILO/OECD unemployed but not claiming benefit (mainly married women who are not entitled to benefit because they opted out of making National Insurance contributions and the under eighteen year olds) than there are people who are claimants but not ILO/OECD unemployed (mainly people who, for various reasons, have not looked for work in the last four weeks).

Figure 18.2 shows that the fall in the claimants count between 1986 and 1989 was about one third higher than that indicated by the Labour Force Survey. As mentioned above, evidence seems to suggest that this was largely due to the introduction of the Restart programme for the long-term unemployed. In addition, the buoyancy of the economy over that period meant that more people were attracted into the labour force. Some of these were women re-entering the job market after child rearing. Some of the re-entrants spent time looking for a job and so were classified as ILO/OECD unemployed, but because they were not eligible to claim benefit, they were not on the claimant count.

Disaggregating unemployment statistics

Further insight can be gained by breaking down the total unemployment figures into a number of components as follows.

Regional unemployment   One feature of the unemployment pattern is the great disparity between regions. This regional problem is by no means a new one; away from the South and the Midlands unemployment has been well above the national average for over fifty years, and the problem still persists despite large amounts being spent on inducements and subsidies to create jobs in depressed areas. In April 1990, when the UK average unemployment rate was 5.6%, Northern Ireland had 14.0% unemployment, Wales 6.3%, the North of England 8.5% and Scotland 8.1%, whereas in East Anglia it was 4.9% and in the South-east only 3.6%.

Traditionally the explanation of such regional variation has been in terms of the depressed regions being over-reliant upon declining industries such as coal, textiles and shipbuilding. A study by Fothergill and Gudgin (1982) suggests that this *was* true until the mid-1960s, but that since then the main problem seems to be of regions, such as the North and Scotland, being dragged down by the fact that they have a disproportionate number of big cities in which unemployment is particularly high. In other parts of these regions unemployment trends are not so bad, but what is happening throughout the UK is a massive shift of jobs from the cities to the smaller towns and rural areas on a scale that swamps most other trends in industrial location. Fothergill and Gudgin suggest that the main cause of this trend is the shortage of space in urban areas, with factories becoming less profitable than their rural counterparts because so many operate in unsuitable, old-fashioned buildings, with production organized less efficiently on more than one floor.

Industrial and occupational unemployment   Just as some regions suffered disproportionately from unemployment, so do some industries and occupations. Some industries, for example, have a cycle that is similar to that of the economy as a whole, but more extreme. Construction is a case in point, with unemployment exceeding 25% in the early 1980s, falling to 11.9% in spring 1986. As regards occupations, unskilled and semi-skilled manual workers are twice as likely as skilled manual workers to be unemployed. Manual workers as a whole are twice as likely as non-manual workers to be unemployed. In spring 1988 the unemployment rates for non-manual, manual and general labourers were 3.0, 6.5 and 14.9% respectively.

Female unemployment   Other areas of inequality in the unemployment statistics are also apparent. Since 1975 the rise in female unemployment has been about three times as fast as that for men. Various explanations have been put forward for this, including new labour-saving technology in the office, and equal pay and opportunities legislation which may have encouraged employers to substitute male labour and capital for female labour. Demographic and social factors may also have played a part. Since 1977, the birth rate has once again begun to rise, and economic recession may place more strain on a UK female labour force which has the highest activity rate of any country in the EC. However, it is worth pointing out that in April 1990 the female unemployment rate of 3.5% was still below that for the male (7.2%), and that this was still the case even when allowance is made for the *unregistered* unemployed.

Age-related unemployment   Age is an important factor in unemployment, particularly its duration. In the age-group '45 to 64', 64% of the male unemployed had been out of work for over one year in spring 1989 whereas in the under-25 age-group the corresponding figure was 26%.

Unemployment is also heavily concentrated in the 16–25 age-group, though unlike the older age-groups unemployment here is mainly of the short-term variety. None the less, it is still a serious problem and because of its political sensitivity has received much attention in recent years. The under-20s accounted for approximately 5% of the total unemployed in the 1960s; in April 1990 this figure was 8% and, of course, it would be much higher if it was not for government schemes aimed at the young unemployed. Only 2% of school-leavers failed to find a job throughout the 1960s, but in spring 1989 the unemployment rate amongst the under-20s was 10%.

The main reason why youth unemployment has risen so dramatically is that, though it follows the pattern of general unemployment, it has greater variability. The Department of Employment estimates, for example, that for every 1% increase in male unemployment there is a 1.7% increase in male *youth* unemployment, so that the proportion of young people in the total unemployed increases. A Department of Employment study (*Employment Gazette* 1978) found no systematic relationship between the proportion of young people unemployed and the earnings of young workers relative to the rest of the workforce (which in fact has not changed much since 1956). In other words, they did *not* appear to be pricing themselves out of a job. Employers' attitudes to young workers, although difficult to measure may, however, have moved in an adverse direction, and one study carried out by the Manpower Services Commission found that 31% of employers thought that there had been some deterioration in the quality of young workers.

Ethnic unemployment   One final area of inequality in unemployment statistics is its ethnic make-up, for which only irregular statistics are available. The average unemployment rates by ethnic origin in Great Britain 1986–88 were as follows:

Ethnic origin	All	White	West Indian/ Guyanese	Indian	Pakistan/ Bangladeshi	Other origins
Unemployment rate (%)	10	10	19	14	27	14

As the unemployment rate for each group expresses the unemployed as a proportion of the 'total economically active' *for that group*, it reflects to some extent the differing age structure within ethnic groups; those groups with higher proportions of both older and younger people tending to have a higher unemployment rate. Even so, people of ethnic minority origins were more likely to be unemployed than whites of the same age-group, sex and educational qualifications.

Length of unemployment   The pool of unemployed workers is a stock, the size of which at any moment depends on two things: (a) the rate of flow into unemployment; and, (b) the duration of the spells of unemployment experienced by individual workers. Not only has the unemployment rate increased because a greater number joined the register, but also because of the increase in the average time an unemployed worker spends out of work. Unemployment of all durations has increased since 1961, but this is especially true of the longer-term unemployed. In 1971 about 15% of the unemployed had been out of work for more than a year, in January 1988 this figure was 40%. This increase in the long-duration category is to be expected when the general level of unemployment rises, with fewer possibilities for leaving the unemployment register. The longer-term unemployed become progressively less attractive to employers and they engage in less job-search activity, both of which mean that the probability of finding a job falls significantly after six months out of work. Studies also show that the long-term unemployed have a high propensity to suffer a recurrence of unemployment in the future should they initially regain employment. Despite progressive falls in unemployment since 1986, and the introduction of the Restart scheme, there were still, in April 1990, over half a million people who had been out of work for over a year.

International comparisons

Table 18.2 shows recent unemployment rates in selected countries. All of these countries, apart from Japan and Sweden, experienced high and rapidly rising average unemployment over the period to the mid-1980s. The consensus explanation, outlined in more detail in later sections, was that this was a result of the adverse oil price shocks of 1973–74 and 1979–80 together with the pursuit of tight monetary and fiscal policies aimed at eliminating inflation. The rise in unemployment in the late 1970s was, however, much sharper in the UK than in most other countries.

Although the unemployment rates have been standardized to allow for differences in national definitions care must be taken in making simple comparisons. Different countries' figures reflect different labour market practices. For example, the low Japanese rate is partly the result of the jobs for life agreement between firms and workers. This system leads to a certain amount of disguised unemployment.

Table 18.2 Comparative unemployment rates (%) (standardized)

	1960–68	1969–73	1974–79	1980–85	1986	1987	1988	1989	1990*
UK	2.6	3.4	5.0	10.5	11.2	10.3	8.3	6.4	6.2
USA	4.7	4.9	6.7	8.0	6.9	6.1	5.4	5.2	5.3
France	1.7	2.5	4.5	8.3	10.4	10.5	10.0	9.6	9.4
W. Germany	0.7	0.8	3.2	5.9	6.5	6.2	6.1	5.5	5.2
Japan	1.4	1.2	1.9	2.4	2.8	2.8	2.5	2.2	2.0
Sweden	1.6	2.2	1.9	2.8	2.7	1.9	1.6	1.4	1.3

* Spring 1990.

Source: OECD Economic Outlook (1990).

Unemployment and economic theory

The traditional Keynesian way of analysing the unemployment problem has been to try and identify the various types of unemployment by cause, this being seen as the first step towards formulating appropriate policy. Economists usually distinguish frictional, structural and demand-deficiency unemployment.

Frictional unemployment

Frictional unemployment results from the time it takes workers to move between jobs. It is a consequence of short-run changes in the labour market that constantly occur in a dynamic economy. Workers who leave their jobs to search for better ones require time because of the imperfections in the labour market. For example, workers are never fully aware of all the possible jobs, wages and other elements in the remuneration package, so that the first job a worker is offered is unlikely to be the one for which he is best suited. It is rational, therefore, for a worker to spend time familiarizing himself with the job market even though there will be costs involved in this search, namely lost earnings, postage, telephone calls, etc. These 'search' costs can, however, be seen from the worker's point of view as an investment, the gain being higher future income. In principle, the economy should also gain from this search behaviour, through higher productivity as workers find jobs that are more appropriate to their skills.

Any measures that reduce the search time will reduce the amount of frictional unemployment. Improving the transmission of job information, permitting workers to acquire knowledge of the labour market more quickly, is one such measure. A more controversial issue is how the level of unemployment benefit affects search time. It could be argued that by reducing the workers' cost of searching, increased unemployment benefit will lead to more search activity and a higher level of frictional unemployment. On the other hand, a reduction in unemployment benefit, though perhaps leading (via less search) to lower frictional unemployment, could also lead to a less efficient allocation of resources, with workers having to take the first job that comes along regardless of how appropriate it was to their skills.

Structural unemployment

Structural unemployment arises from longer-term changes in the structure of the economy, resulting in changes in the demand for, and supply of, labour in specific industries, regions and occupations. It could be caused by changes in the comparative cost position of an industry or a region, by technological progress or by changes in the pattern of final demand. Examples of structural unemployment are not difficult to find for the UK economy and might include shipbuilding, textile, steel and motor-vehicle workers, i.e. workers in manufacturing industries where the UK has largely lost its comparative advantage over other countries (e.g. newly industrialized countries). On the other hand, the emerging unemployment in the printing industry and in clerical occupations has more to do with technological progress, which enables information to be processed, stored and retrieved more quickly, so that less people are required per unit of output (see Ch. 10). Yet again, structural unemployment may be due to a shift in demand away from an established product, as with the decline of the jute sacking industry in Dundee following the development of synthetic fibres.

The structurally unemployed are therefore people who are available for work, but whose skills and locations do not match those of unfilled vacancies. Structural unemployment is likely to reach high levels if the rate of decline for a country's traditional products is rapid and if the labour market adjusts slowly to such changes. Indeed, adjustments are likely to be slow since they are costly to make. From the workers' point of view it may require retraining in new skills and relocation, whilst from the firms' point of view it often means abandoning their familiar products and processes and investing in new and often untried ones. This process of adjustment is, of course, easier the more buoyant the economy.

At a broader level, one of the most important issues facing developed countries is whether they will be able to generate enough output to finance the necessary increase in service occupations required to absorb those released by the manufacturing sector. Whilst manufacturing accounted for 30.1% of employment in the EEC in 1970, it only accounted for 26.6% in 1982, and most forecasts see this structural trend continuing (see Ch. 1). In Great Britain, for example, employment in manufacturing fell by 28% between 1979 and 1990. The way in which the developed world manages this structural transition over the medium term will be one of the key determinants of future levels of employment.

Demand-deficient unemployment

The Keynesian approach Demand-deficient or cyclical unemployment is that which is associated with *too little* aggregate demand for goods and services in the economy. This type of unemployment was the focus of

Fig. 18.4 Demand-deficient
unemployment

Keynes's attention in his *General Theory* (Keynes 1936) and can be caused by a fall in any of the elements of aggregate demand, namely, consumer spending, investment, government spending or net exports.

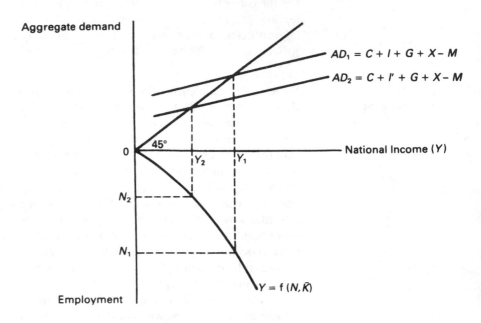

In Fig. 18.4, the economy is initially at full employment with aggregate demand equal to AD_1, National Income Y_1 and employment N_1. If then, say, investment falls, perhaps because of a deterioration in business confidence, aggregate demand falls to AD_2, causing National Income to fall to Y_2. The production function in the bottom half relates national output (income) to labour input, holding the capital stock constant at $\bar{K}$. From this it can be seen that the amount of labour required to produce Y_2 is only N_2, and so $N_1 - N_2$ is the amount of extra demand-deficient unemployment.

The division of unemployment into various types, by cause, is as we have already stated, a Keynesian approach. Its usefulness lies in the fact that it highlights the point that measures taken to alleviate one type of unemployment may leave the others relatively untouched, and if pursued too far may cause problems in other policy areas. If, for example, the Government overestimates the level of demand-deficient unemployment, and reacts by injecting too much spending into the economy, then excess demand will be generated in some labour markets with inflationary consequences. This could erode UK comparative advantages in certain industries and lead to structural unemployment as the UK prices itself out of world markets. As far as structural unemployment is concerned, its correction may require manpower and regional policies, including retraining and improving the mobility of labour and capital. In fact, both structural and frictional unemployment need measures geared specifically to correcting the mismatch between supply and demand in the various labour markets. Given that each type of unemployment requires different policies, it is important to be able to measure the contribution of each type to total unemployment.

One approach to this problem of measurement is to use the unemployment − vacancies $(U - V)$ method. When $U = V$, i.e. unemployment equals vacancies; then it could be argued that there is no demand-deficient unemployment because there are as many employment opportunities still available, V, as there are people seeking employment, U. If there is still unemployment in this situation, it must then be due to the profile of the unemployed, such as location or skill, failing to match the profile of vacancies. In other words, when $U = V$, all the unemployed must be of the non-demand-deficient type, i.e. structural and frictional.

Fig. 18.5 Unemployment and vacancies: UK 1964–87: (−) unemployment excluding school-leavers; (_ _ _) vacancies at Jobcentres (about one-third of total vacancies)
Source: Employment Gazette (1990a) and earlier editions

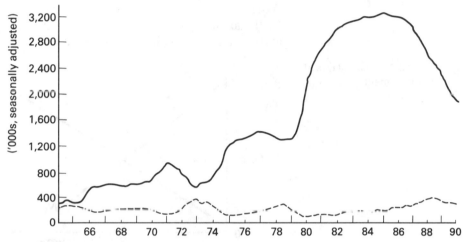

As can be seen from Fig. 18.5, the more usual situation in recent years is for unemployment to exceed vacancies. In this situation the difference $U - V$ is defined as demand-deficient unemployment, with non-demand-deficient unemployment (structural and frictional) equalling the number of vacancies. For instance, if unemployment equalled 1 million, and vacancies equalled 200,000, then of the unemployed, 800,000 would be classed as due to too little aggregate demand, and 200,000 due to structural and frictional factors.

At first sight, this method provides a useful tool for policy-makers, but like all empirical techniques it has its limitations, with two in particular worth mentioning: first, the data for both U and V are likely to be inaccurate, because not all the unemployed register and only about one-third of all unfilled vacancies are officially recorded; second, V may be a misleading index of structural and frictional unemployment. For example, when the economy moves into recession, unemployment rises and vacancies fall, so that an increasing proportion of the unemployed are classified as demand-deficient, and a smaller proportion as non-demand-deficient. Obviously any who are already structurally unemployed do not disappear during recession, they are simply being wrongly classified. One way round this problem, though far from satisfactory, is to find the level of unemployment where $U = V$ (if this has ever occurred in the labour market) and define *this* as the non-demand-deficient level, with any unemployment above this level being demand-deficient.

The monetarist approach   Unlike the Keynesians, monetarists tend not to be very interested in separating unemployment into its various types. Indeed, they argue that there is, for any economy, at any moment, a 'natural rate of unemployment' (NRU). It can be defined as that amount of the labour force which will remain unemployed even though the overall supply of labour has been brought into equilibrium with the demand for labour, through variations in the real wage rate. In Fig. 18.6 both the labour supply N_S and the labour demand N_D are functions of the real wage rate. $(W/p)^*$ is the market-clearing real wage rate and N_F^* is the equilibrium level of employment (see Ch. 17). The difference between N_F^* and the amount of labour available in the economy N will correspond to Milton Friedman's concept of the NRU. Basically, therefore, the NRU represents the amount of structural and frictional unemployment which is left in the economy when the supply of, and demand for, labour are in balance.

Fig. 18.6 The natural rate of unemployment

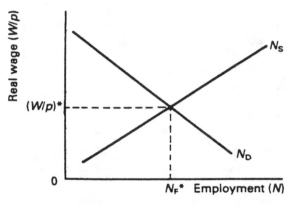

Friedman also sees the NRU as the only level consistent with a stable rate of inflation, and argues that the only way the Government can run the economy with an unemployment rate below the NRU is by perpetually stimulating the economy, causing accelerating inflation (see Ch. 17). The political unacceptability of continually accelerating inflation means that for the monetarists there is *no* long-run trade-off between inflation and unemployment (i.e. the long-run Phillips curve is vertical – again, see Ch. 17), so that there is little macroeconomic policy can do in the long run to reduce the unemployment problem. Unemployment according to this hypothesis is a microeconomic problem and policy-makers should be concentrating on improving the functioning and responsiveness of the labour market in order to reduce the NRU. Anything which increases the supply of labour at the going real wage rate (i.e. shifts N_S to the right) or increases the demand for labour at that real wage rate (i.e. shifts N_D to the right), will increase N_F^* and *reduce* NRU. Imperfections in the labour market are therefore the main determinant of the NRU, so that the Government should be attempting to improve occupational and geographical mobility, reduce trade union restrictive practices, improve job information, and provide suitable wage differentials within the labour market and between the employed and unemployed.

Whilst this hypothesis is appealing theoretically, it has so far provided policy-makers with little practical help. The main reason for this is that precise empirical estimates of the NRU have been unconvincingly low.

Laidler, for example, suggested that it might be 2%, the Treasury in 1981 suggested that it was about 5% or 1.2 million people unemployed. Until an accurate estimate of the NRU can be provided, policy-makers will be unable to judge where the *actual* rate of unemployment is in relation to the *natural* rate. This is important since it is only the *difference* between actual unemployment and the NRU which might be amenable to increased aggregate demand. Any attempt to lower unemployment below the NRU by stimulating demand will result in accelerating inflation and cannot therefore be sustained (see Ch. 17). In this view unemployment can only be reduced significantly by supply-side measures that reduce the NRU.

Probably the most influential estimates of the NRU have been provided by Layard and Nickell (Layard and Nickell 1985, Nickell 1987), neither of whom are monetarists. According to their work the NRU or NAIRU (non-accelerating inflation rate of unemployment) as they prefer to call it, was under 3% for male employees throughout the 1960s. It rose steadily after 1971 with a temporary fall at the end of the 1970s and reached a peak in 1983 at around 13.7%. Since then it has fallen to probably just under 11% in 1987.

Figure 18.7 (taken from Jenkinson 1987) illustrates the relationship between the estimates of the NAIRU for male employees and actual unemployment.

Fig. 18.7 Actual unemployment and estimated NAIRU for male employees
Source: Jenkinson (1987)

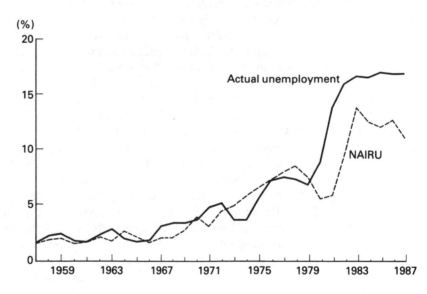

Factors affecting unemployment in the UK

Unfortunately, as in many key areas of economics, there is no consensus as to why the unemployment rate rose to such a high level in the UK in the mid-1980s. Some argue, as do the monetarists and new classical economists, that the causes are to be found in excessive wage settlements, too high a level of unemployment benefits and other labour market imperfections, causing the NRU to rise. Keynesians believe that it is the result of insufficient aggregate demand; others claim that the rapid pace of technological progress is destroying jobs. Each of these arguments will be examined in turn.

Real wages and unemployment

The argument here is that trade unions and excessive real wages are the main cause of the persistently high unemployment in the UK. This argument represents a return to the Classical view that the real wage is too high and that unemployment is 'voluntary', in the sense that it is due to the refusal of workers to accept cuts in their real wages. The Classical theory rests on two assumptions:

1.   That a theory applicable to an individual firm can be extended to the determination of employment in the economy as a whole.

2.   That the marginal product of labour (MP_L) falls as employment increases (i.e. there exists a downward-sloping demand curve for labour – MP_L – with regard to the real wage).

If these conditions hold, a fall in real wages raises employment.

Keynes rejected the first of these assumptions on the grounds that it was a fallacy of composition. Wages are, at the macro level, not only a cost of production but also an element in aggregate demand; cutting money wages would therefore probably be self-defeating unless other elements in aggregate demand were to increase. Keynes turned the Classical theory on its head by arguing that at the *aggregate level* real wages do not determine employment, rather that aggregate demand determines employment which itself determines the real wage.

It appears that Keynes reluctantly accepted the second Classical assumption which was based on diminishing returns to the variable factor, labour. It then follows that at the *micro level*, real wages and employment are inversely related, with a rise in real wages reducing employment. However, if there are increasing returns to labour, even micro-reasoning based on the firm becomes invalid. This follows since with increasing returns to labour the MP_L curve – the demand curve for labour – would no longer be downward-sloping. A higher wage could then *increase* the demand for labour. In fact Thirlwall (1981) argues that 'there is now enough empirical evidence to question seriously the orthodox assumption that diminishing returns to labour prevail in manufacturing industry over the range of unemployment relevant to policy debate'. As the economy expands from its current low base, and under-utilized capacity is brought back into use, it is unlikely that the marginal product of labour will fall; on the contrary, it is likely to rise. The point to stress, therefore, is that in the circumstances of increasing returns, a fall in real wages is no longer a prior condition, even at the micro level, for a rise in employment (i.e. less unemployment).

The main problem with the trade union/excessive real wage argument is that little convincing statistical evidence has been produced to support it. Since the proportion of the total labour force in unions declined in the late 1970s, if there were a positive relationship between trade union power and unemployment we would expect to see unemployment falling rather than rising as it did in the early 1980s.

It has been argued that perhaps the unionized sector establishes pay norms and labour market 'inflexibilities' that are adopted more generally. The evidence shows, however, that the group for which unions, it is claimed, do most, adult full-time manual workers, had an increase in real income below that of non-manual workers and below the rate of growth in overall productivity between 1979 and 1983.

Many empirical studies have been undertaken (see Standing 1986) to try and assess the impact of a given fall in real wages on employment and unemployment. The UK Government claimed in 1984 that if real wages were static for a year then half a million more jobs would be created. The Treasury paper published in 1985 which was intended to support this view (Treasury 1985) came to the conclusion that if the expected rise in money wages was cut by 3% then as many as 300,000 jobs would be created over four years. It was also estimated that if money wages fell sufficiently to give a 1% fall in real wages and that the Government cut taxes and interest rates to keep the money supply growth as fast as if there had been no cut in wages then employment might grow by between 110,000 and 200,000. Critics have argued that such effects are very modest and would not make much impact on the level of unemployment. Also in the study it was assumed that firms immediately reinvested, in the UK, the funds released by lower labour costs. If, however, firms invested abroad the employment impact would be correspondingly reduced.

The Oxford Economic Forecasting Group estimated the impact of a two-year money wage freeze. It was estimated that this would slow inflation down to about 3.5%, thus implying a fall in real wages. The impact of increased competitiveness and the real wealth effect of lower inflation would generate between 100,000 and 350,000 jobs in the long term. Again this would make little impact on unemployment and the Oxford group rejected high real wages as the primary cause of rising unemployment.

Layard and Nickell concluded that union wage push contributed only 0.3% to the rise of 7% in unemployment between 1975–79 and 1980–83. Demand factors on the other hand had contributed 5.31% and employers' labour taxes 1.29%.

The Clare Group in the *Midland Bank Review* investigated the relationship between the real product wage (RPW) and employment. The RPW was an index of wages and salaries per employee, plus employers' National Insurance and superannuation contributions divided by an index of output per employee and an index of the value added prices of manufactured goods (price minus non-labour costs). The RPW attempts to measure the effective cost of employing extra workers. A rise in the RPW is a disincentive to employment and could result from either a rise in labour costs, other things being equal, or a fall in productivity or value added per unit assuming constant labour costs. The *Review* showed that until the late 1960s the RPW and employment unexpectedly rose together; from then until the late 1970s rising RPW was associated with falling employment; since then the RPW has been stable or declined slightly whilst employment has fallen dramatically. The *Review* concluded that 'the new experience from the end of the 1970s indicates that the RPW . . . may have lost its early influence on the level of employment'. It continued: 'Something else must have been at work. Is it perhaps declining demand? . . . What has been happening in manufacturing since the late 1970s appears not to support the view that the key to higher levels of employment and output can be found in lower real labour costs alone.' The article, apart from highlighting the role of demand, also saw the slow-down in investment and technical progress as being worthy of policy concern.

The National Institute for Economic and Social Research (NIESR) used their macroeconomic model to simulate the effect of lower real wage increases; the effect of this was to lower inflation but the reduced purchasing power slowed output and employment growth. It also found that the UK had long been a comparatively low-wage low-labour-cost economy.

In 1984 the Bank of England published two papers, one by a former Chief Economic Adviser to the Treasury, Sir Bryan Hopkin (Bank of England Panel of Academic Consultants 1984), the other by Professor J. R. Sargent. Both rejected the simple view that high real wages could explain the long-term decline in manufacturing employment and the level of unemployment. Hopkin concluded: 'the case for the High Wage Induced Unemployment thesis, as a major explanation of mass unemployment in the United Kingdom, has not so far been properly made out either on theoretical or on empirical grounds'.

Unemployment benefits

It is argued by some economists that over-generous unemployment benefits, by prolonging the period over which the unemployed search for the 'right' job, increase the level of unemployment. It is also claimed that some low-paid jobs are relatively less attractive and therefore remain unfilled. Can unemployment benefits explain a substantial part of the rise in unemployment over the last twenty years? The consensus view would be no, although some economists (Minford 1983) would disagree.

The variable that is most likely to influence unemployment is the replacement ratio, that is the ratio of total benefits (unemployment and/or income support) when out of work compared to average net income in work. Over the period from the mid-1960s to the early 1970s the replacement ratio did rise; however, since then benefits relative to earnings have fallen. It is generally argued therefore that although some of the rise in unemployment (about 14% according to Nickell 1979) between 1965 and 1973 can be explained in terms of a rising replacement ratio, we cannot lay the blame for the dramatic rise in unemployment 1979–86 on unemployment benefits.

Demand deficiency

The Keynesian view of the current situation stresses demand deficiency as the main factor in reducing levels of output and employment. Certainly aggregate demand has been cut by the oil price rises of the mid- and late 1970s, and by government response to dearer oil.

In the two most serious recent recessions, 1974–75 and 1979–81, a common world factor was the rise in OPEC oil prices. The resulting balance of payments deficits of the non-oil-producing countries and their attempts to control these deficits by demand deflation, led to recession. A further deflationary factor arose from the impact of higher oil prices on the general price level, since Western governments were reluctant to allow monetary and fiscal policy to 'accommodate' these price rises. This meant higher interest rates and a further slump in demand. In the UK aggregate demand was still further reduced by an unexpected increase in the savings ratio at a time when inflation was accelerating (see Ch. 11).

The main difficulty between the 1974–75 recession and the latest one, as far as the UK is concerned, is that in 1974 the UK was still importing all its oil, as were most advanced industrial countries. By 1979, however, the UK was near to self-sufficiency in oil and so the UK should have experienced a less severe recession than her competitors, rather than the deeper one that actually occurred. Self-sufficiency meant that there was no immediate worsening of the balance of payments on current account. As a result, the authorities could have lowered indirect taxes, thereby helping to dampen the impact of higher oil prices on the general price level, and to offset the deflationary impact of higher prices on aggregate demand.

Why, then, has the recession been deeper in the UK than elsewhere? The largely Keynesian NIESR argues that the last slump (1979/81) was superimposed on an economy already in prolonged recession. Output did grow between 1975 and 1979 but at a rate below the economy's potential. The main factor which hid the underlying recession from view was the rapid growth in real wages which, despite the increase in the savings ratio, meant that *consumption* was a consistent source of demand growth up to 1979. By 1980, however, even continued real-wage growth was inadequate to offset the rise in both savings and tax propensities, so that growth in consumer expenditure largely disappeared as a source of demand growth.

The Government's restrictive monetary and fiscal policies since 1979 take a large share of the blame according to this view. In an attempt to reduce the rate of inflation, with what was thought to be only a temporary loss of jobs, the Government attempted to reduce the rate of growth of the money supply. The consequent higher interest rate, it was argued, would help in the battle against inflation by raising the value of sterling, which would then reduce the price of imports. It would also raise the price of our exports, forcing UK manufacturers to be more competitive. Firms would then realize that they could not pass inflationary wage increases on to their customers whether at home or abroad, and retain sales. This double squeeze on companies, high interest rates and an overvalued pound, has had a disastrous effect on manufacturing companies (see Ch. 1).

The chancellor's budgetary policy was also resolutely deflationary in this period. Attempts to control the PSBR, in order to restrict the growth of the money supply, have proved difficult to achieve through cuts in government spending. As a result the chancellor resorted more and more to increased taxation (a doubling of VAT in 1979, income tax increases in 1981) and 'spending cuts' that in fact increased prices, mainly nationalized industry prices, Health Service charges and council house rents.

The NIESR has estimated that by far the largest part of the shortfall of actual output from trend output between 1978 and 1980 was due to the Government's restrictive monetary and fiscal policies. The difference between actual and trend output was 4.1%, and of this 1.7% was estimated to be due to budgetary and domestic interest rate policies, with 1.3% due to the high value of the pound eroding competitiveness; so that in total 3% of the difference was due to government policy. Of the rest, 0.8% was due to the oil price rise and the world slow-down, and 0.3% was unexplained. For

Keynesians, therefore, there is no question as to the cause of the deep recession of 1979–81, and hence the dramatic rise in unemployment that took place.

New technology

This issue is considered in much more detail in Chapter 10. However, a few observations may be in order. The argument that the current high level of unemployment is due largely to technological change is against historical precedent. In 1974 registered unemployment in the UK stood at just 600,000, compared with around 3.35 million in August 1985 (on the old count). Even if technological progress is a cause of unemployment it seems unlikely to have caused almost 3 million extra unemployed in just over ten years. In the past, technology has generated more new jobs than it has destroyed, although of course these jobs may not have been in the same skills or geographical areas. Structural unemployment might, therefore, be generated by technological progress but this will mainly be short term if there are sufficient retraining programmes and if the pressure of demand in the economy is sufficiently high. In the 1950s in the USA, unemployment approached 10% and was accompanied by a heated debate as to whether it was due to automation and the computer revolution or whether it was due to deficient aggregate demand. Tax cuts and the Vietnam War stimulated demand in the early 1960s and unemployment fell to historically low levels.

Conclusions and policy recommendations

It is clear that there is no consensus amongst economists as to the cause of unemployment. Keynesians explain it in terms of demand deficiency. The Cambridge Economic Policy Group also blame demand deficiency, but specifically in terms of excessive import leakages (see Ch. 25). Monetarists explain the current position in terms both of the NRU having risen, and the actual rate of unemployment having to be above the natural rate to purge inflation from the system. The Classical school of macroeconomics tends to blame supply-side factors, such as too high a level of real wages, together with the disincentive effects of high unemployment and social security benefits and excessive taxation. These explanations differ, therefore, in the extent to which they emphasize either demand- or supply-side factors in generating unemployment. To some extent they can all account for part of the rise in unemployment since the mid-1960s but none of them appear, on their own, to give a full explanation.

One plausible account which combines some of the above explanations, bringing both supply and demand elements into play, is given by Cross (1982). Starting with the monetarist concept of the NRU, he goes on to incorporate some aspects of Keynesian demand deficiency. The NRU is the rate of unemployment consistent with an unchanging rate of inflation. As we have seen, it is generally thought to be determined by microeconomic conditions which influence supply-side factors in the labour market. For example, better information might increase factor mobility, shift the labour supply curve to the right and reduce the NRU. It could be argued, however, that demand-side factors also influence the NRU, and that current government attempts to run the economy at a level of unemployment above the NRU, to eliminate inflation, may have actually increased the NRU itself. In other words, the actual rate of unemployment may have influenced the 'natural rate'. For instance, if the economy had a recent history of low unemployment, then we would expect a more skilled and productive labour force than if our recent history had been one of high unemployment, because more people would have had on-the-job training and work experience. Low actual rates of unemployment are likely to produce a low NRU, and high actual rates of unemployment a high NRU. In other words, the actual history of unemployment is likely to influence the NRU (Phelps 1972).

Of particular importance here has been the rapid growth in the long-term unemployed who have a relatively low chance of regaining employment. This may be partly because of a fall in their productivity and partly because of employers' attitudes towards them. As Cross argues, 'the increases in unemployment since the mid-1960s have shaped a labour force characterized by an increasing number of long-term unemployed and hence by an increasing number of people whose actual or perceived productivities are lower as a result of their unemployment experience'. Potential output and employment have therefore fallen, and this has increased the NRU in the UK.

The rise in unemployment since the mid-1960s could therefore be explained partly by a monetarist type of argument, in terms of factors causing the NRU to rise. These would include further imperfections in labour and commodity markets, such as less job mobility, more militant unions, more monopoly power in product markets, and so on. The explanation could also be partly Keynesian, in terms of greater demand deficiency, due in part to the oil price increases and in part to restrictive fiscal and monetary policy. Government attempts to control the rate of inflation by restrictive monetary and fiscal policies have, as we have seen, raised long-term unemployment, causing the NRU to increase.

If this analysis is correct, then the solution to unemployment problems should be some combination of supply and demand side measures.

1. Microeconomic supply side measures are necessary to improve the working of the labour market, and thereby reduce the NRU. Some economists, such as Matthews and Minford (1987), would favour further reductions in trade union power and a further lowering in the relative level of unemployment benefits together with a tightening of the eligibility requirements.

    Others (e.g. Clark and Layard (1989)) would prefer the government to concentrate on training in order to improve the skills and flexibility of a grossly under-trained UK labour force. It is also important, in their view, to target help towards those who need it most. The long-term unemployed are an obvious case in point. As discussed in Chapter 17, the long-term unemployed do not put much downward pressure on wage deals. So absorbing them into the labour force, as the Swedish do, either through subsidised jobs or high quality training, would have little inflationary consequence. It has also been argued that cuts in National Insurance contributions for both high unemployment regions and low paid workers, would also reduce unemployment.

The housing market in the UK is also an obstacle to labour mobility and is a direct source of inflationary pressure. Residential house markets are by far the most distorted markets in the UK. The supply of building land is restricted by tight planning controls whilst the demand for land is stimulated by subsidy or tax advantages. As a consequence, house prices have been greatly affected by the financial liberalization of the 1980s. It is almost impossible for the unemployed owner-occupier from a 'high unemployment/relatively low house price area', to move to the areas of labour shortage in the more prosperous South East. Similarly, workers from the more prosperous area have also been reluctant to move, in their case for fear of foregoing substantial relative house price rises. In general, the UK preoccupation with home ownership, the lack of public sector house building and the under-developed private rented sector, all contribute to the lack of labour mobility in the UK, and so help keep unemployment high.

Finally, it has been argued that Britain's system of decentralized collective bargaining (see Chapter 20) encourages leap-frogging and stimulates wage inflation. One worker's pay increase is another's price increase; this leads to greater inflationary pressure as unions react to price increases and firms outbid each other in an attempt to attract workers. An alternative, used in some other more sucessful countries such as Sweden, Germany and Japan, is some form of co-ordinated wage bargaining to determine the 'going rate'. In Sweden, the national employers' federation bargains directly with the national trade union federation; in Germany and Japan, there is a 'pattern settlement', usually in the metal industries, which is then broadly followed elsewhere. Obviously *some* degree of flexibility is needed so that the more dynamic firms can attract the extra workers required, but with co-ordination the pointless wage–price spiral can be avoided. Arguably this would then enable the economy to contain inflationary pressures with much less unemployment than under a free-for-all system of bargaining. Fig. 18.8 tends to support this view.

2.   The above supply side measures are aimed at reducing the NRU; however it is also important to remember that policies on aggregate demand also matter. It is not enough just to rely on supply side measures. The experience of the 1980s shows that if the aggregate demand is too low, and unemployment rises well above the NRU, then the NRU itself is likely to rise. Alternatively, if aggregate demand is too high then the rate of inflation will increase.

We cannot conclude without briefly mentioning the rather appealing proposal of reducing unemployment by reducing the labour supply. This might entail some combination of a shorter working week, early retirement or job-sharing. There are, however, a number of drawbacks to this type of policy proposal. First, it may be more inflationary than the alternative of raising labour demand. Reducing labour supply has, as its main effect, an increase in 'leisure' (voluntary and involuntary), whereas raising labour demand is more likely to raise output as well. Second, if work-sharing is to be effective it must involve income-sharing. If pay is cut in line with the

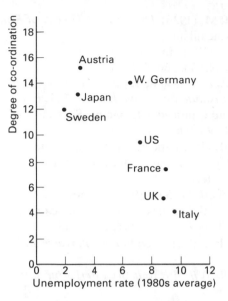

Fig. 18.8 Unemployment
and the degree of
co-ordination
Source: OECD (1990)

reduction in weekly hours, then work-sharing does have considerable potential for reducing unemployment. If, however, the working population (which is still in the majority) successfully resists a pro rata cut in pay, then the scheme would be inflationary. It may even cause more unemployment if, because of the depressed state of the economy, firms are unable to pass on the resulting higher costs in higher prices. Third, in a society where economic wants far exceed the ability to supply these wants, a reduction in labour supply could be seen as an inappropriate use of resources.

**References and
further reading**

Bank of England Panel of Academic Consultants (1984) *Employment, Real Wages and Unemployment in the UK*. Panel Paper No. 24.
Clark, A. and **Layard, R.** (1989) *UK Unemployment*, Heinemann Educational, Oxford.
Cross, R. (1982) *Economic Theory and Policy in the UK*. Martin Robertson, Oxford, pp. 96–104.
CSO (1988) *Economic Trends*, Annual Supplement, 10.
CSO (1990) *Economic Trends*, Annual Supplement, 12.
Dicks, M. J. and **Hatch, N.** (1989) The Relationship Between Employment and Unemployment, Bank of England discussion paper, No. 39.
Employment Gazette (1978) The young and out of work, **86**, 8, Aug.
Employment Gazette (1988a) **96**, 1, Jan.
Employment Gazette (1988b) **96**, 8, Aug.
Employment Gazette (1990a) **98**, 7, July.
Employment Gazette (1990b) **98**, 4, April.
Fothergill, S. and **Gudgin, G.** (1982) *Unequal Growth: urban and regional change in the UK*. Heinemann, London.
Jenkinson, T. (1987) The natural rate of unemployment: does it exist? *Oxford Review of Economic Policy*, **3**, 3.

Keynes, J. M. (1936) *The General Theory of Employment, Interest and Money*. Macmillan, p. 381.

Laidler, D. (1971) Inflation in Britain: a monetarist perspective, *American Economic Review*, **66**, 4, Sept.

Layard, R. and **Nickell, S.** (1985) The causes of British unemployment, *National Institute Economic Review*, **111**, Feb.

London and Cambridge Economic Service (1967) *The British Economy: key statistics 1960–1966*.

Metcalf, D. (1982) Special employment measures: an analysis of wage subsidies, youth schemes and work sharing, *Midland Bank Review*, autumn/winter.

Midland Bank Review (1979) Economic outlook, summer.

Midland Bank Review (1980) Economic outlook, autumn.

Midland Bank Review (1984) Economic outlook, spring.

Minford, P. (1983) *Unemployment: cause and cure*. Martin Robertson, Oxford.

NEDC (1985) *British Industrial Performance: a comparative survey over recent years*.

Nickell, S. (1979) The effect of unemployment and related benefits on the duration of unemployment, *Economic Journal*, **89**, March.

Nickell, S. (1987) Why is wage inflation in Britain so high?, *Oxford Bulletin of Economics and Statistics*, **49**, 1, Feb.

NIESR *Economic Review* (1984), 110, Nov.

OECD (1990) *Economic Outlook*, June.

Phelps, E. (1972) *Inflation Policy and Unemployment Theory*. Macmillan.

Standing, G. (1986) *Unemployment and Labour Market Flexibility*. ILO, Geneva.

Thirlwall, A. P. (1981) Keynesian employment theory is not defunct, *The Three Banks Review*, 131, Sept.

Treasury (1985) *The Relationship between Wages and Employment*, Jan.

19

Regional and urban policy

This chapter surveys the regional and urban problems experienced by the UK over the last twenty to thirty years.[1] The difficulties of defining a region are examined, together with 'convergent' and 'divergent' theories of regional development. The policies used by successive governments to alleviate the 'regional problem' are noted, and their effectiveness assessed. The urban dimension to the regional problem is then discussed and government policy outlined. The chapter ends with a brief assessment of the effectiveness of urban policy

The regions and their characteristics

Simply defined, a region is a portion of the earth's surface that possesses certain characteristics (physical, economic, political, etc.) which give it a measure of unity and differentiate it from surrounding areas, enabling us to draw boundaries around it. The commonly perceived regions of the UK, mainly counties, were formalized into 'economic planning regions' in 1964. Although certain economic criteria were used in the groupings of counties, the regions were largely established on the basis of administrative convenience.

There is nothing absolute about these planning regions. The Local Government Act of 1972 dramatically altered the county boundaries, and this led to the redrawing of the economic planning regions. These were now called Standard Planning Regions (SPRs) and they and their sub-regions are shown in Fig. 19.1.

The most crucial feature of the Standard Planning Regions and sub-regions is that they are now the units of classification for many official government statistics. In England, the eight SPRs are broken down into forty-six sub-regions, including the thirty-nine 'traditional' counties and seven metropolitan areas. Wales, Scotland and Northern Ireland constitute separate standard regions. Figure 19.2 presents each SPR in more detail, showing the sub-regions and the larger urban centres. In fact each SPR is essentially an aggregation of urban centres with their rural hinterlands. A number of other characteristics are shown for each standard region, including area, population and its urban/rural distribution, and employment by economic sector. These statistics clearly show a marked degree of variation in the resource base of each SPR.

The regional problem

Traditionally a 'regional problem' is said to exist when a region departs from the 'national average' in a number of important respects:

1. High and persistent unemployment.

Fig. 19.1 Standard Planning
Regions of the UK

2.   Low level and growth of GDP per head.
3.   Heavy dependence upon a narrow industrial base.
4.   Rapid decline in manufacturing.
5.   Inadequate levels of infrastructure.
6.   Net migration out of the region.

Table 19.1 gives some indication of the regional disparities with reference to the first two criteria.

  A number of attempts have been made to group regions in terms of common economic characteristics. For instance, the terms 'core' and 'periphery' are widely used. The 'core area' of the UK includes those regions which have experienced the most rapid economic advance in the past three decades. The South East, East Midlands and East Anglia are usually placed

Fig. 19.2 The UK: regional, sub-regional and urban Sub-regions* (Counties)

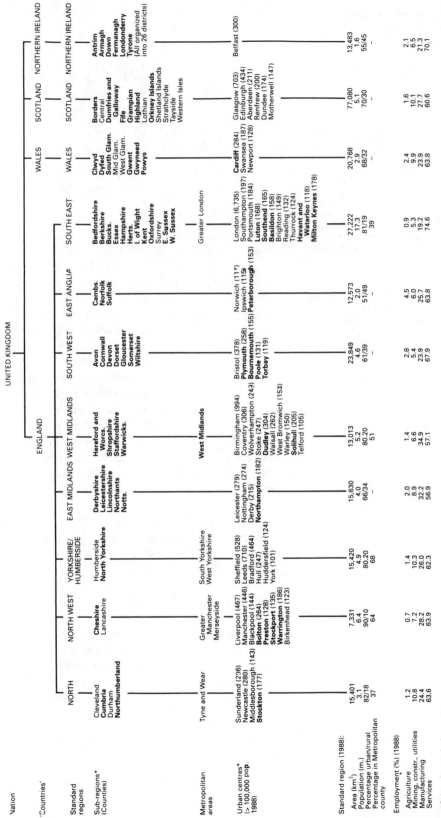

		GDP per head					Unemployment				
		1971	1975	1978	1981	1988	1971	1975	1978	1981	1990
Core	South East	113.8	112.9	112.3	114.5	119.4	59	69	70	71	63
	East Midlands	96.5	96.6	97.8	100.0	94.6	85	89	83	90	88
	East Anglia	93.8	92.2	95.6	97.3	97.1	91	84	84	81	64
Inner periphery	West Midlands	102.7	100.0	97.3	90.6	91.1	85	100	90	120	103
	South West	94.7	90.5	92.8	95.9	93.8	95	114	107	87	75
	Yorks/Humberside	93.2	95.0	95.2	93.0	91.1	112	94	97	104	120
Outer periphery	North West	96.1	96.3	97.6	94.3	93.3	113	128	122	122	131
	North	87.1	94.5	95.2	94.3	88.3	163	138	143	130	153
	Wales	88.4	89.6	88.2	86.8	84.0	128	133	136	128	115
	Scotland	93.0	96.7	95.4	98.7	93.9	170	124	132	120	145
	Northern Ireland	74.3	75.1	76.2	72.2	78.0	221	178	187	159	240

Sources: CSO (1987, 1988, 1989) and *Employment Gazette* (1990).

Table 19.1 Index of regional variation in GDP per head and unemployment (UK = 100)

in this category. In 1990, for example, unemployment in the South-east was only 63% of the national average, but the standard of living, as indicated by GDP per head, was 19.4% above the national average. The 'periphery' can be subdivided into an 'inner periphery', which contains the West Midlands, the South West, and Yorkshire and Humberside, and an 'outer periphery', which contains the North West, the North, Wales, Scotland and Northern Ireland. Regions in the 'outer periphery' are characterized by slow growth, stagnation or decline, and contain most of the old industrial areas of the UK. In 1990, unemployment in the North was 53% above the national average whilst GDP per head was 11.7% below that average. Regions in the 'inner periphery' are somewhat in between these two extremes, showing rather more signs of 'economic health' than regions in the 'outer periphery'. In 1990, for example, Yorkshire/Humberside was 20% above the national average as regards unemployment, though 8.9% below as regards GDP per head.

Attempts to group regions on these broad economic grounds are, however, becoming less meaningful. The rise of microelectronic technology (see Ch. 10), the growing importance of multinational activity (see Ch. 7), and the effects of the Single European Act (see Ch. 26) have all contributed to a more 'footloose', and therefore geographically mobile, pattern of industrial location. In today's complex and rapidly changing industrial environment, any spatial gouping of 'standard' regions into 'core' or 'periphery' may be less appropriate than hitherto. Indeed there is evidence to suggest the emergence in the 1990s of 'areas of prosperity' centred on urban regions, which are likely to grow much faster than other parts of their SPRs.[2] Nevertheless, worries continue about the widening of the North/South 'divide', so the core and periphery concepts remain useful tools of reference.

Free market or government intervention?

From Table 19.1 it is clear that regional disparities do exist in the UK in terms of both unemployment and income per head. Whether or not these disparities constitute a 'problem', requiring government intervention, depends on one's view of the economic system. Certainly changes in demand

and supply in any economy will have different effects on individual regions, since each has its own particular industrial structure. A change in the pattern of demand can cause some regions to increase production, employment and income, when they contain the industries which produce the goods and services now demanded. Similarly, regions which produce commodities for which demand has decreased, will find themselves with declining production, employment and income. As a result, growing regions will diverge positively from the national norm, while declining regions will diverge negatively.

It has been argued that in a dynamic economy regional disparities will be short run, as in time market forces will tend to equalize the situation across regions (convergence). This could occur through a movement into the high-unemployment/low-income regions of firms attracted by lower wage costs. At the same time there will be an outward migration of labour from these 'disadvantaged' regions to the relatively prosperous regions where demand, employment and wages are higher. It follows that if labour and capital are perfectly mobile, with no impediment to firms moving into and out of regions, regional differences should disappear. For example, in the disadvantaged regions unemployment would fall and wages would rise as firms relocate themselves in these areas. Similarly, in the more prosperous regions unemployment would rise and wages fall as firms move out to low-wage/low-cost areas. Given sufficient time, and no imperfections, this view suggests that there would be no need for government intervention to solve the 'regional problem', since market forces will eventually cause regions to 'converge'.

The case for intervention In practice, imperfections exist and even those who believe in the market mechanism may still advocate some form of regional policy. First, neither labour nor capital is perfectly mobile. There may be a lack of knowledge on the part of employees or employers of opportunities in other regions; or there may be high 'costs' of movement as with the need for rehousing, the breaking of social ties and the expensive relocation of plant and machinery. Second, there may be restrictions on the price of labour or capital, such as maximum or minimum wages, or limits on the dividends which firms issue. These imperfections may reduce the incentives for both labour and capital to flow out of 'disadvantaged' and into 'advantaged' regions and vice versa.[3] Under these circumstances even the free-market adherent might admit the need for government intervention to offset these market imperfections. This may take the form of policies to promote labour mobility or to coax firms to move into more disadvantaged regions. Government intervention is then seen as necessary to *enhance* the workings of the market mechanism.

Another view of the regional problem sees a still more urgent need for government intervention. Market forces are regarded as acting in a way which will aggravate rather than ameliorate regional disparities. Intervention is no longer a *supplement* to market forces but must be strong enough to *offset* them. Any fall in output and employment in a region will reduce the size of the regional market and erode economies of scale. Also labour migration from declining regions may consist of the younger, better educated, more adaptable component of the regional labour force, leaving behind a less productive labour force. New firms may no longer wish to locate production in such regions even if wages are lower. As regional output declines and unemployment rises, local authority rates may become inadequate to sustain basic infrastructure and services, further disadvantaging a region already in decline. In this view, government policy has to be strong enough to prevent regions constantly 'diverging', with poor regions getting poorer and rich regions getting richer. Such a policy might seek to inhibit the movement of labour out of disadvantaged regions by giving firms incentives to locate in these regions.

To sum up, if, as in the first view, the regions are seen as 'converging' over time, then government intervention need only strengthen the 'natural' market forces making for equality. However if, as in the second view, the regions are seen as 'diverging' over time, then a greater degree of government intervention may be needed. Otherwise market forces will cause regions to become 'polarized' into areas of very low output, employment and income on the one hand, and very high output, employment and income on the other.

Regional policy in the UK

In the UK the need for government intervention in the regions was accepted as far back as 1934, with the passing of the first of three Special Areas Acts.[4] These aimed to help the depressed areas by setting up government trading estates, subsidizing rents and providing low-interest loans. Since then legislation affecting the regions has been embodied in a variety of Industry and Finance Acts.

The Assisted Areas (AAs)

The basic principle guiding UK regional policy has been to identify specific geographical areas requiring assistance – mainly on the basis of above-average unemployment rates.

As Fig. 19.3 shows, there are currently three main types of area designated for regional assistance:

1. Development Areas (DAs) – first broadly identified in 1934, and since then redefined on a number of occasions. They remained more or less unchanged from the Industrial Development Act of 1966 until 1979, when the new Conservative Government began a review of regional aid. The review resulted in the Industrial Development Act of 1982 (revised 1984) which severely curtailed the amount of assistance for Development Areas (from £738m. in 1983/84 to only £300m. by 1987/88), and reduced the number and size of areas eligible for aid.

2. Intermediate Areas (IAs) – originated with the Hunt Report of 1969. It was recognized that some areas would, without assistance, become the Development Areas of the future. These were substantially reduced in spatial extent after the 1982 Act, but increased again in 1984 (in part, so that the areas concerned could qualify for European Regional Development Fund (ERDF) aid – see below).

3. Northern Ireland – receives special regional assistance due to the particular problems of that area.

Fig. 19.3 The Assisted Areas from Nov. 1984

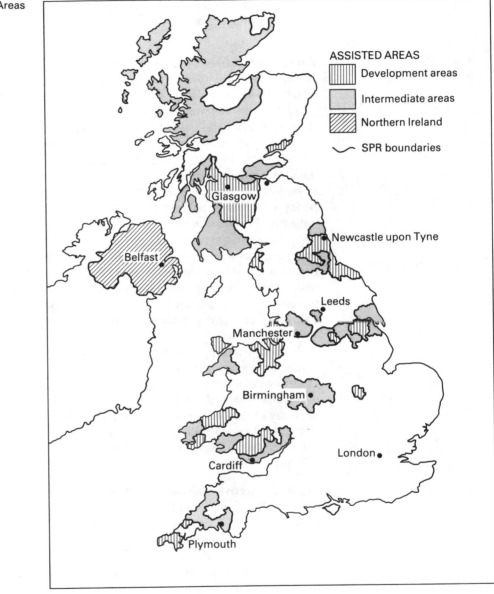

Between 1967 and 1984 certain parts of the Development Areas were designated as *Special Development Areas*. These were initially areas which had suffered severe unemployment because of colliery closures and were therefore made eligible for higher levels of assistance. This differentiation *within* the Development Areas was terminated by the Conservative Government in 1984. In January 1988 the Government reaffirmed that the definitions of the Assisted Areas would remain as shown in Fig. 19.3 until the early 1990s.

Once areas have been designated, UK policy has been of two types: first, to offer financial incentives to firms located in, or moving to, these areas; and second, to control expansion by firms outside these areas. As we shall see, the extent of financial inducement or control has varied with the type of area and with shifts in government policy emphasis.

The policy instruments

Financial incentives   In January 1988, the Conservative Government presented to Parliament a White Paper, *DTI – the Department for Enterprise*, which recommended an overhaul of the Department of Trade and Industry (DTI) in order to improve Britain's competitiveness, innovativeness and the skills of individuals, especially in AAs and inner cities. Regional financial assistance, which totalled £626m (Great Britain £553m, N. Ireland £73m) in the fiscal year 1987/88, was seen by the Government as a subsidy that was damaging industry's efficiency and therefore its ability to compete, especially in view of the 'open market' of the EC after 1992. These revisions to regional policy were predicated on a belief that payment of continuous subsidies to industries in AAs was an inappropriate way for central government to encourage an attitude of self-help and a spirit of enterprise and competitiveness. Hence, it was argued that if the regions were ever to experience *convergence*, much of the impetus would have to come from within the regions themselves, and government could only really facilitate this process – it could not legislate it, nor could it make certain areas or industries forever dependent upon the public purse (Prestwich and Taylor 1990).

A major consequence of the DTI's reorganization was to shift the focus of regional aid away from support for traditional industries and more towards encouragement of new company formation. This meant changing the balance of regional financial assistance – Regional Development Grants,[5] long the mainstay of regional policy aid, were terminated in 1988, and the emphasis shifted to Regional Selective Assistance and to a new scheme of other grants and incentives for smaller firms in both AAs and Urban Programme Areas (UPAs)

Regional Selective Assistance (RSA)   This is a discretionary grant towards capital and training costs for projects which (1) have a good chance of paying their own way, (2) create or safeguard jobs, (3) benefit the local or national economy, but (4) are unable to proceed without government money. Regional Selective Assistance (RSA) is available for service as well as manufacturing companies, and most often is administered as a Capital-related or a Job-related project grant. *Capital-related project grants* are generally used to help cover the costs of land purchase and site preparation, or the acquisition of plant and machinery. Other costs, such as those incurred because of patent rights, professional fees or machinery installation, may also be covered. *Job-related project grants* are normally used to help cover the costs of hiring and training staff.

Almost £250m was spent on RSA grants in 1988/89, and the amount will be around £265m in 1990/91.

Other grants and assistance   One of the main aspects of the Government's new regional incentives introduced in 1988 was its emphasis on schemes designed to support the wealth-creating process among small and medium-sized firms. Since April 1988 companies in Assisted Areas employing fewer than twenty-five people have been able to apply for two new Regional Enterprise Grants. The first is an *investment* grant of 15% towards the costs of fixed assets, subject to a maximum grant of £15,000. The second is an *innovation* grant of 50% which is designed to support product and process development in small companies with a maximum grant limit of £25,000. In addition, middle-sized companies employing fewer than 500 people can claim two-thirds of any costs incurred when they use outside consultancy services to help them. Services covered include marketing, design, quality management, manufacturing systems, business planning and financial and information systems, and by 1990–91 an estimated 1,250 consultancies per month were being conducted. In total, these business development initiatives, together with other grants and incentives cost the Exchequer some £334 million in 1990/91.

Industrial Development Certificate   The principal method used by successive British governments between 1947 and 1981 to try to control the regional distribution of manufacturing industry was the Industrial Development Certificate (IDC). This was first introduced in the Town and Country Planning Act of 1947. Under the Act, any proposed new industrial development in excess of 5,000 square feet (465 square metres) had to obtain an Industrial Development Certificate (IDC) from the Board of Trade before planning permission for development could be granted. The certificate could be withheld at the discretion of the Board of Trade if the development would create industrial congestion or if it was not consistent with the 'proper' distribution of industry. In practice the IDC was a *negative* form of control in that it took a restrictive attitude to new buildings in the prosperous areas in the hope that firms would then relocate in the Assisted Areas. The exemption limits for IDCs have varied over time depending on economic conditions and government policies. In the years prior to 1979 the exemption limits were 12,500 square feet (1,163 square metres) in the South East and 15,000 square feet (1,395 square metres) in other non-assisted areas. The exemption limit was increased in 1979 to 50,000 square feet (4,650 square metres) for all areas, including the South East, indicating a weakening of IDC controls. In fact, in December 1981 the use of IDCs was abandoned.

European Regional Development Fund   Since 1973 the UK has had access to a further potential source of regional assistance, the EC. It was only in 1975, however, with the establishment of the European Regional Development Fund (ERDF), that EC funds became available for regional support on a systematic basis. The ERDF is financed out of the general budget of the EC and allocates most of its funds to member countries on a quota basis rather than for specific regional projects. The funds are given directly to member governments, and are intended to be *additional to* regional aid already given by those governments. Between 1975 and 1990 the UK had received £3.6bn from the fund. Unfortunately there have been criticisms that these funds were used to replace rather than supplement regional expenditure by member governments. In an attempt to counter this, 5% of all ERDF funds have been allocated on a non-quota basis, linked to specific projects proposed by member governments.

Some 80% of the cost of the regional/social fund is now allocated to the four poorest members of the EC and the fund is encouraging designated Assisted Areas in all EC countries to construct *coherent* development programmes rather than submit large numbers of individual projects.

The effectiveness of regional policy

It is difficult to assess the effectiveness of regional policy, for a number of reasons. First, detailed statistics have only been readily available on the regions since the mid-1970s. Second, the areas qualifying for assistance have themselves been frequently redefined. For example, since 1979 the Development Areas have been 'reduced' in size to such an extent that they now only include 15% of the employed population in Britain, in contrast to 40% in previous years. Third, any assessment of the impact of regional policy involves a comparison of the actual situation with an *estimate* of what would have happened had there been no such regional policy.

Despite these problems attempts have been made to assess the effects of regional policy over the last thirty to forty years. These attempts fall into two broad categories: first, those which measure the total impact of policy on employment creation and factory/office building in AAs; second, those which assess the effectiveness of particular instruments of regional policy, such as grants, tax incentives and IDCs.

I Effects of policy on employment in, and firms relocating to, Assisted Areas. A detailed study of the impact of regional policy on job gains and firm relocations in AAs by Moore, Rhodes and Tyler (1986) came to the following conclusions –

Numbers of jobs created in AAs:
1. The total number of manufacturing jobs created in Development and Special Development Areas between 1960 and 1981 was 604,000, and 450,000 of them still remained in 1981 (i.e. 154,000 jobs were lost due to firm contraction or closure).
2. The total number of such jobs created in Intermediate Areas between 1972 and 1981 was 32,000, and 23,000 remained in the latter year.
3. Applying a medium-term regional multiplier of 1.4 (viz. for every 100 new manufacturing jobs created, 40 new service jobs are also created) to these *net* job totals yields a further 180,000 jobs in DAs and 9,000 in IAs. Added to the new manufacturing job numbers, these service jobs bring the grand total of regional policy-induced job 'creation' in AAs to 662,000 during the 1960–81 period.
4. In addition, regional policy instruments, especially Regional Development Grants, Regional Selective Assistance and various payroll subsidy schemes, had the effect of 'saving' or 'safeguarding' existing manufacturing jobs. The estimated numbers were 120,000 in DAs and 25,000 in IAs. Applying the 1.4 multiplier to these 145,000 manufacturing jobs suggests a further 58,000 service jobs 'safeguarded' –

hence a total of 203,000 jobs that would probably have been 'lost' but for regional financial assistance.

5. One further government programme which had a job impact in AAs was the Location of Offices Bureau (LOB). Through a mechanism of Office Development Permits (ODPs – modelled on IDCs), the LOB sought to restrict office development in London and other major cities (especially Birmingham) and redirect these employment opportunities to AAs. During the LOB's existence (1965 to 1979) about 35,000 government and 22,000 private sector office jobs were 'relocated' into AAs, and as with manufacturing jobs these 57,000 service jobs probably had a positive multiplier impact of almost 23,000 additional service jobs, so 80,000 new jobs in all.

Therefore, over the two decades of 'active' regional policy, 1960–81, about 945,000 jobs were created or safeguarded in AAs by government programmes, and over ninety per cent of these jobs were still in place in 1981.

Numbers of firms moving into AAs:

1. Policy-induced moves of factories from the more prosperous areas to Assisted Areas yielded a net gain for AAs of 2,085 between 1945 and 1978, with 1,218 of these moves occurring during the more active regional policy period of 1966–78.
2. At a broader scale, over 8,000 manufacturing firms moved from one county to another between 1945 and 1980, but only about one in eight of these firms appears to have been 'persuaded' to move by government policy.

As well as trying to determine the total impact of regional policy on the economies of AAs by aggregating gross and net gains in numbers of jobs and of factory moves, regional economists have also sought to demonstrate relationships between the *actual numbers involved*, and *variations in the intensity of government intervention policy* over given time periods. Figure 19.4 shows the relationship between the growth of manufacturing employment in selected regions and changes in regional policy.

In Fig. 19.4 an attempt is made to define periods when regional policy was 'active' or strong, and periods when regional policy was 'passive' or weak. Periods of 'active' as distinct from 'passive' regional policy were defined as those periods in which the amount spent on regional incentives increased significantly and in which IDCs were issued far more sparingly in the non-assisted areas.

The amount of employment in any region will depend in part on the balance of industries in that region (i.e. industrial structure), and in part on the growth of output from such industries. Given the industrial structure of an Assisted Area, the maximum employment which that region could be 'expected' to create would occur if each of its industries grew at the national average rate. This 'expected' level of employment was calculated for the four named Assisted Areas as a whole, for each year since 1950, and compared with the actual level of employment in those areas in each year. If actual

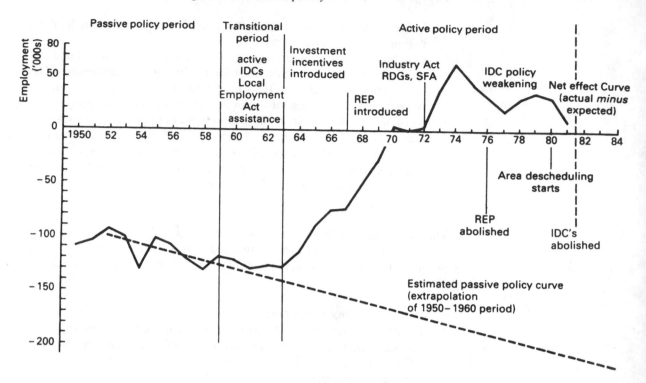

Fig. 19.4 The growth of manufacturing employment in Scotland, Wales, the Northern region and Northern Ireland relative to the UK
Source: Adapted from Gudgin, Moore and Rhodes (1982) and Moore *et al* (1986)

employment in the Assisted Areas had reached the 'expected' level, then the 'net effect' curve (actual *minus* expected) would have recorded zero on the vertical axis. The fact that in the first few years 'actual' employment was around 100,000 below that 'expected', suggests that the Assisted Areas really do have more serious employment problems than elsewhere.

During the 'passive' period from 1950 to 1959, with little or no regional assistance, actual unemployment fell progressively further behind the 'expected' level. This provides some support for the 'divergent' view of the regional problem (see earlier), i.e. that without intervention the position of the assisted regions will progressively deteriorate. The dashed line in Fig. 19.4 projects this trend during the 'passive' period through to the present time. In other words, it provides an indication of what might have happened if regional policy had not become more 'active'. However, from 1963 a variety of incentives were introduced (see above) in the Assisted Areas, together with a more stringent application of IDCs preventing expansion in the advantaged regions. We can see from Fig. 19.4 that actual employment gets closer and closer to the 'expected' level up to 1970, and after 1970 even exceeds it. 'Active' policy began to slacken in the mid-1970s, with a number of incentives abolished (e.g. Regional Employment Premium (REP) in 1976 – see below), and a less stringent application of IDCs. As a result actual employment had begun to fall towards the 'expected' level in the late 1970s, early 1980s.

II Effectiveness of policy instruments   Criticism of regional policy instruments has become part of a 'performance evaluation' procedure since the mid-1970s, particularly when it has been able to identify their 'cost-effectiveness' on a job creation basis. Research into the gross Exchequer *cost per job* in British DAs during the period 1960–81 demonstrated that the most cost effective instrument was IDC policy with its minor administrative cost. The next least expensive instrument was RSA, with a cost per job (at 1981 prices) of £17,000, followed by investment incentives at £25,000 per job and by REP, the most expensive instrument, at £73,000 per job (Moore, Rhodes and Tyler 1986). Not surprisingly, with governments determined to reduce spending from the late-1970s onwards, RSA emerged as the favoured policy instrument, while critical attention focused on investment incentives, the REP and the use of IDCs.

Investment incentives (especially RDGs) have formed a central part of regional policy since its inception in 1934. Investment grants and tax incentives were designed to encourage firms to set up in the disadvantaged regions. Surveys in the 1960s and 1970s seemed to show that capital grants may have had a significant effect on the movement of industry to Assisted Areas (Ashcroft and Taylor 1977). However, financial incentives have been criticized for being capital-biased, thus encouraging the movement of capital- rather than labour-intensive firms into the Assisted Areas. Another criticism was that these incentives, whether grants or tax allowances, were often 'automatic', being given to *all* firms in the Assisted Areas irrespective of whether they were creating new employment or not. It was this persistent criticism and the suspicion that grants were going mostly to companies who would have invested in the Assisted Areas even *without* government assistance which led to the termination of RDG schemes in 1988.

The *Regional Employment Premium* (REP) was used as a policy weapon in the UK from 1967 to 1976 and was, in effect, a direct-labour subsidy paid to all employers in the Assisted Areas to encourage the retention of existing employment and the creation of new employment. However, the benefits of a flat-rate subsidy such as the REP were eroded by inflation during the early 1970s, reducing its attractiveness to employers. Also, as with financial incentives, the REP was criticized for being available to all manufacturing establishments in the Development Areas 'whether new or old, expanding or contracting, progressive or asleep' (Moore and Rhodes 1976: 218). Another criticism was that the REP may well have encouraged firms to retain a higher labour/capital ratio than might have been dictated by economic efficiency alone.

Industrial Development Certificates (IDCs) were simple to operate and were of only minor administrative cost to the Exchequer. However, there was no guarantee that a firm refused an IDC in, say, the South-east, would actually build the factory in an Assisted Area. Projects for expansion could be shelved or moved abroad, particularly if the company refused permission to develop was a multinational. Industrial Development Certificate-type controls were more effective in redistributing employment when the economy was relatively buoyant than they were in recession when every region became desperate for jobs. In such circumstances all regions, including the relatively prosperous ones, were reluctant to accept restrictions on the expansion of firms through IDC control. It was partly as a result of this inadequacy that the use of IDCs was suspended in December 1981.

The urban problem

Urban—rural shift

One of the most striking features of the post-war period has been the shift in employment and population from London and the large conurbations towards towns and cities in more rural areas. For example, between 1960 and 1981 manufacturing employment in London fell by 51.4% and in the large conurbations by 43.2%. Total populations in these regions also fell throughout the 1960s, with falls of 6.8 and 2.1% recorded between 1971 and 1981 respectively. The areas which gained most employment and population were the industrial areas made up of smaller industrial towns, county towns with a moderate amount of industry and the largely unindustrialized rural areas. Employment in the first two areas increased by an average of 23% between 1959 and 1975, but with an even more rapid growth of 77% in the unindustrialized rural areas. Population in these areas also grew much faster than the average for the UK as a whole, as much as 10.3% in the unindustrialized rural areas between 1971 and 1981, compared to only 0.5% for the UK as a whole.[6] This process continued during the 1980s with, for example, the population of large metropolitan cities outside London falling by 5% between 1984 and 1988. In the same period the population of urban and mixed urban/rural areas rose by 7%, and in the mainly rural areas the population rose by as much as 11%.

Such shifts in employment and population away from the large urban areas have been due to a number of reasons. First, it became increasingly obvious that urban areas could not provide adequate factory floorspace for industries to expand. Automation and the adoption of new techniques led to a demand for greater floorspace per employee, causing firms to seek suitable sites outside major conurbations. Second, the cost of acquiring land in urban areas to establish new factories or to extend old ones was high compared to that in other regions. Rhodes (1980) found that rents and rates in London were double those in East Anglia, whilst on average company earnings were only 10–15% higher. As a result, profits per employee in London were 33% below those in East Anglia. Third, some surveys have shown that over 60% of UK manufacturing industry is now 'footloose', being less affected by specific locational factors. This means that factors such as proximity to the large markets of the main conurbations are now less important. Fourth, it has been noted by Fothergill and Gudgin (1982) that manufacturing plants in urban areas tend to be larger than average. For example, 68% of workers in Teesside are employed in large plants (500+ employees), with similar figures for Merseyside (64%) and Clydeside (56%). Such plants are often a part of large firms, such as multinationals, so that any company reorganization, rationalization or relocation may have a significant effect on employment in these urban areas.

All these factors have encouraged the movement of employment and population away from large urban areas, presenting a major problem for the inner core of many large cities.

The inner-city problem

During the post-war period employment and population have declined in the major conurbations, with the most serious decline occurring in the inner-city areas of such conurbations. For instance, between the early 1950s and the mid-1970s employment declined by 20% in the conurbations as a whole, but by 33% in the inner-city areas. However, in the suburban areas employment remained steady, whilst in small towns and rural areas employment rose. The decline in employment and population in inner-city areas has been aggravated by the fact that commuters have taken an increasing share of inner-city employment – from around 20% in 1951 to 33% in the mid-1970s.

Employment in inner cities has fallen in all sectors, with employment in manufacturing declining by over 50% between 1951 and 1981. The growth of public sector employment was unable to compensate for this, growing by only 8% over the same time period. Also, the concentration in inner-city areas of hotel and catering activities has further aggravated the situation, as these have high rates of labour turnover and therefore provide only intermittent employment. A study of north-west England in the 1970s (Lloyd and Reeve 1982) showed that large conurbations outside London were unable to depend on the growth of services to counter manufacturing decline.

Further evidence of inner-city problems include the fact that the share of unskilled and semi-skilled workers in the labour force is significantly higher in such areas than in outer-city areas or in the nation as a whole. Inner cities also appear to have a higher proportion of low-income racial minorities. These low-skilled, low-income groups find it difficult to move from their low-cost, council accommodation in the inner city, to high-cost, owner-occupied accommodation in suburban or rural areas. For example, the London Planning Advisory Committee in 1987 reported that there was a growing east/west divide within the city with the residents of inner and east London far more likely to be unskilled or semi-skilled and working in declining economic activities than the residents of outer and west London. The committee also reported that parts of inner London had unemployment rates of over 20%.

The severity of the urban and inner-city problem is reflected in the fact that most of the metropolitan areas or major cities shown in Fig. 19.2 have been designated as 'inner urban areas' for policy purposes (see below). The problems of inner-urban areas within the major conurbations are reflected in Table 19.2. Since 1951, only in the West Midland conurbation has inner-urban unemployment been significantly below the national average, though by 1990 even this conurbation had unemployment rates above the national average.

Table 19.2 Unemployment rates in the inner areas of the six major conurbations of the UK 1951–90 (%)

Inner area of	1951	1961	1971	1990
London	2.5	3.1	5.9	4.6
West Midland	1.2	1.4	4.8	7.6
Manchester	2.0	3.8	8.2	7.0
Merseyside	4.5	5.8	9.8	12.5
Tyneside	4.0	4.6	9.4	10.1
Clydeside	4.5	6.0	9.0	11.0
United Kingdom	2.1	2.8	5.2	5.9

Source: Gudgin, Moore and Rhodes (1982); *Dept. of Employment Gazette* (1990).

The movement of manufacturing employment away from the inner-urban areas was encouraged by the Government's *New Towns* policies in the 1950s and 1960s. This was later followed by increased availability of grants and incentives for firms locating in the Assisted Areas. Inner-urban areas also suffered from the more active use of IDC policy, which made it more difficult for firms to locate within inner-urban areas. The general improvement in communications and rising real incomes were further factors in encouraging more people to live outside inner-urban areas, in suburbs, smaller towns and rural communities.

Urban policy in the UK

Since the Second World War government policy towards the plight of urban and inner-city areas can be divided into three phases: 1945–65, 1965–77 and post-1977.

1945–65

During this phase the Government's policy was to limit the growth of major conurbations in an attempt to solve some of the pressing problems of urban congestion. *Green Belts* were established around major conurbations to prevent their expansion, and *New Towns* were built outside the major conurbations to take up any urban overspill. After 1947 the use of IDCs further restricted the growth of industries in the urban areas, whilst the Location of Offices Bureau sought to redistribute office work away from the conurbations, especially London.

1965–77

From the middle of the 1960s the Government's attitude towards the inner-city problem began to change. Attention began to be drawn to the fact that the UK non-white population had grown to some half a million and was largely concentrated in cities. Fears were expressed that race riots similar to those of the USA in 1967–68 might occur in the UK and this helped focus government attention on the urban problem. This emphasis was strengthened by the findings of the Plowden Report on children's education in 1967. This report identified deprived areas in inner cities which needed special help and led to the setting-up of *Educational Priority Areas* (EPAs) in 1969. In 1968 an *Urban Programme* was also established which, under the Local Government Grants (Social Needs) Act of 1969, was provided with a fund of £20–25m. over four years. The aim of the Urban Programme was to provide resources for capital projects and educational schemes, such as pre-school playgroups, in order to raise the level of social services in areas of acute social need. In 1969 the *Community Development Project* was established to research into new ways of solving social deprivation in large urban communities.

1977–90

During this period the focus of attention began to shift to the economic problems of inner cities. The seeds of change began with the Labour Government's White Paper *Policy for the Inner Cities* in 1977. This sought to strengthen the economies of inner-city areas, to improve the physical fabric of such areas to alleviate social problems, and to secure a new balance between inner-city areas and the rest of the region in terms of population and jobs. The White Paper also proposed the extension of local authority power to assist industry, and this was introduced through the Inner Urban Areas

Act of 1978 which empowered local authorities to declare industrial and commercial improvement areas and to give financial assistance to companies which located in such areas.

With the election of the Conservative Government in 1979 new initiatives were introduced to add to, and modify, existing legislation. Under the Local Government Planning and Land Act of 1980, Enterprise Zones and Urban Development Corporations (UDCs) were set up, in 1984 the first 'Freeports' were designated and in 1988 Simplified Planning Zones were created.

Enterprise Zones reflected the Government's desire to release the private sector from restrictive financial and administrative controls, encouraging firms to set up in the more derelict parts of inner-city areas. Initially, eleven zones were designated in 1981, with the number rising to twenty-seven by the end of 1989.[7] These Enterprise Zones enjoy a number of privileges for ten years from their date of inception; the most important being exemption from local authority rates, and 100% tax allowances on commercial or industrial buildings. Companies setting up in Enterprise Zones are also exempt from development land tax, and face fewer local authority planning regulations and controls than they would in other areas. However, in early 1988 the Conservative Government announced in a package of measures that no more zones would be created in England as it was becoming particularly worried about the consequences of the cost of the zones to the Exchequer. Despite this, the Government was obliged to consider a new zone for Sunderland in 1989 following its decision to dispose of Northeast Shipbuilders Ltd. It is worth noting that local authorities now have the power to set up 'Simplified Planning Zones' (SPZs) which do not have the financial advantages of the Enterprise Zones, but do retain the benefits of fewer planning regulations. The first two were set up in Derby and Nottingham and another eight were in the process of being designated in the early 1990s. The government has calculated that the total cost of the Enterprise Zone scheme since its inception in 1981 (including land acquisition and reclamation) was over £400m.

The role of the local authorities in allocating resources has been eroded by such legislation as Enterprise Zones. Their powers were further reduced under the 1980 Act by the creation of new agencies for urban renewal with special powers and resources, the *Urban Development Corporations* (UDCs). The UDCs were designed to undertake substantial programmes of land acquisition and reclamation in an attempt to secure the greatest possible involvement of the private sector companies in their areas. Similarly, the UDCs are involved in environmental improvement and infrastructure provision in these areas. The first generation of Urban Development Corporations were formed in the London Docklands and in Merseyside in 1980 and were given special powers to promote urban renewal in those areas. The second generation, formed in 1987, included Trafford Park, the Black Country, Teesside and Tyne and Wear. By 1988/9 these had been joined by a third generation covering Central Manchester, Leeds, Sheffield and Bristol. These corporations are financed mainly by Exchequer grants and employ 490 permanent staff in total. The London Docklands Corporation, which is the biggest of its kind, spent around £332m in 1990/1, which was a large portion of the UDCs' total spending of £542m for that year.

Six areas were designated for *Freeport* status in 1984, with work beginning on them in 1985. The six areas included Birmingham, Belfast, Cardiff, Liverpool, Prestwick and Southampton, but by 1990 only three remained in operation. Within the Freeports, goods are to be exempt from customs duties and (possibly) VAT, unless the goods are subsequently transported from the Freeport to the rest of the UK. The intention of the Freeports is to attract business and investment into the areas, particularly since goods *not destined for import into the UK* can be handled *without* tariff charges. This should help the UK gain a greater share of the rapidly growing intermediate processing and servicing activities via global specialization (see Ch. 7). The government is now reviewing the whole position of Freeports in view of the changes occurring in 1992.

In addition to such measures there has been growing concern for the inner cities, which has led to the creation of the 'Urban Programme'.

The Urban Programme   This is the main mechanism for allocating funds to the inner cities. Some £338m was designated for the programme in 1984/85, but this is to fall slightly, to a planned total of £250m by 1991/92. The aim of the programme is to coordinate the activities of governmental agencies and programmes with the private sector and local community needs in some 57 local authority areas which are facing serious economic and social problems. Of the 57 authorities which existed in 1990, 9 were *Partnership Authorities* and 48 were *Programme Authorities*. In the former, the Government has formed a close partnership with local authority bodies in order to combat urban decay. These have been specified as 'Special Areas' under the Inner Urban Areas Act of 1978 and include such areas as Hackney and Islington in London, and Liverpool, Manchester/Salford in the North West. The 48 *Programme Authorities* also receive money in consultation with the Government but there is no formal partnership.

Up to early 1988 there were two main components of the programme. These were the Inner Area Programmes (IAPs) and the Urban Development Grant (UDG). The IAPs set out local strategies and objectives based on certain Government guidelines and provide a framework for supporting projects which have already been approved by government. Expenditure by any of these local authorities which has been approved by government qualifies for a grant equivalent to 75% of such expenditure. The objectives of the IAPs are:

1. To promote the regeneration of local economies. This involves supporting projects which build new, or convert old, factory units and which create training opportunities and jobs for the labour force in those areas. In 1989/90 the programmes' expenditure on these measures amounted to £120m.

2. To improve the physical environment of local economies. This involves modernizing shops and other buildings while also improving parks, waterways and footpaths etc. The cost to the Exchequer of this aspect of policy was £44.3m in 1989/90.

3. To meet social and housing needs directly. Social needs include the

provision of community centres, sports facilities and health projects while housing needs encompass improvements in refuge accommodation and helping to improve conditions on housing estates which have environmental problems. The total cost of these policies was from £81.2m in 1989/90.

The second main component of the Urban Programme was the Urban Development Grant (UDG) which became a key instrument for funding parts of the Programme. The objective of the UDG scheme was to promote *private sector investment* in the inner cities which might not otherwise take place in the absence of the grant. The Department of the Environment normally reimbursed 75% of the amounts local authorities contribute to the approved projects. Between 1982 and 1988, 256 projects involving grants of over £130m had been approved, and some 28,500 jobs created, under the UDG scheme. However, the UDG's role as the second component of the Urban Programme was replaced by a new grant called the *City Grant* which was announced in March 1988 and became effective from the 3rd of May 1988.

Another component of the urban package although not strictly defined as being within the Urban Programme is the Derelict Land Programme. Under the Derelict Land Act of 1982, the Secretary of State for the Environment is empowered to pay grants to public bodies, voluntary organizations, private firms and individuals to enable derelict land to be reclaimed, improved or brought into use again. The grant varies between 50% and 100%, depending on the location of the site and the institutions or persons applying. By 1990/91 some £64m had been spent on the scheme. In the 57 Programme Areas, the Derelict Land Grant was replaced by the City Grant.

Action for Cities

As noted earlier in the chapter, in March 1988 the Conservative Government launched a series of new initiatives to help promote enterprise investment and employment in the inner-city areas and also published a new government booklet entitled *Action for Cities*. The main changes introduced by the new initiatives were as follows. First, the creation of a new UDC in Sheffield and the extension of the Merseyside UDC were announced. Second, a new, simplified *City Grant* noted above was introduced to replace the Urban Development Grant (UDG), the Urban Regeneration Grant (URG) and the private sector part of the Derelict Land Grant (DLG). It is designed to support capital investments undertaken by the private sector in property and business development especially in the priority areas. The total project value must be above £200,000 and the private sector must convince the Department of the Environment that the project will provide jobs, private housing or other benefits. Also, to receive the grant the Department must be satisfied that the project is unable to proceed because the costs incurred in the development (including allowance for a reasonable profit) exceed the market value of the project. If the application is successful then the grant would cover this deficit and would therefore allow projects which benefit the community to continue despite the apparent problems of covering all essential costs. The *City Grant* applications are made directly to the local offices of the DOE (instead of through the local authorities as with the UDG) and appraisals of the projects are to be made within ten weeks. These procedures will simplify and streamline the grant system. Third, measures were introduced to make more unused and under-utilized land in urban areas available for development by requiring publication of information about land held in public ownership. Fourth, the Government factory builder, the English Industrial Estates, provided £11m in the 1988/89 period for the conversion of suitable buildings for use as managed workshops. Finally, the Manpower Services Commission (now Training Agency) would be allowed to increase its staff in inner-city areas in order to advise unemployed people and also to give financial support to inner-city areas (compacts) in which groups of employers work with schools to guarantee a job with training for all young people aged sixteen to eighteen leaving school and who have met an agreed standard. By 1990, 36,000 young people, 3,800 employers and over 250 schools were involved in such compacts.

It is also worth mentioning that these new initiatives were supplemented by the investment and innovation grants introduced through the Government's regional policy and made applicable to Urban Programme areas as well as the Assisted Areas in general.

Finally, before concluding this section on inner city initiatives, it is interesting to note the creation by the Department of Trade and Industry from 1985 onwards of 8 City Action Teams (CATs). These teams consist of senior government officials from the Departments of Industry, Environment and Employment, together with representatives from their regional offices, who attempt to coordinate the work of their different government departments within inner city areas. In 1986, under the same initiative, 16 Inner City Task Forces composed of smaller teams of civil servants and people on secondment from the private sector, were formed to work directly with local businesses or local councils in an attempt to stimulate economic development, employment and training in inner city areas. By 1990 the Task Forces had supported a total of 1,700 projects with further projects planned for the 1990s.

The effectiveness of urban policy

Although greater emphasis has been placed on urban policy over the last few years, it has not been without its critics. First, it has been argued that resources directed to urban policies have been insufficient, accounting for only 14% of the Department of the Environment's spending in 1990/91. In the same period, for example, the total amount spent on the Urban Programme (£245m) was about half the government expenditure on arts and libraries. Second, it is claimed that urban policies have failed to ensure that new jobs created in the inner cities were filled by unemployed inner-city residents. Evidence suggests that higher-skilled commuters from outside the inner-city areas often 'crowd out' inner-city residents in the competition for employment. To redress the balance it has been suggested that marginal subsidies be provided for firms which recruit unemployed inner-city residents. Such schemes could also be designed to favour employers making the greatest contribution to improving the skill and job experience of inner-city residents. Third, the UDG was criticized for being more helpful in attracting renewal schemes to areas which *already* have a reasonable degree of economic activity. In a study of 41 UDG sponsored projects in operation during the mid 1980s it was found that many of the schemes would have gone ahead even without UDG grants. In fact 64% of the total employment generated by the UDG sponsored projects would have been created even without the government subsidy. In other words, companies were likely to have come to those areas even if they had not been offered subsidies (Martin 1989). In parts of the North-East and South Wales it may take more than 'pump priming' to persuade private capital to invest in areas of serious urban decay. There is, as yet, little evidence that national financial institutions such as pension funds and insurance companies are 'risking' capital by investing in projects which were eligible for UDGs. It is hoped that the new simplified grant may solve some of these problems but that awaits to be seen.

Fourth, there is a danger that programmes such as the Urban Development Corporations may not solve the unemployment problem because many of the jobs created in these areas often go to people who live outside the area. For example, a House of Commons Employment Committee (House of Commons 1988) found that although the overall increase in employment in the London Dockland Corporation area rose from 27,213 in 1981 to 36,000 in 1987, the majority of this increase represented a relocation of jobs from outside Docklands. It also pointed out that the skills demanded by the new companies entering the London Dockland Development Corporation scheme did not match the skills of the local population. Finally, the committee found that most of the new jobs created in this area tended to be in office or service work and that manufacturing employment had actually declined. As a result the unemployment level in this area was higher in 1988 than at the launch of the scheme in 1981. The Association of London Authorities claimed that for every 100 jobs lost in London between 1981 and 1986 the London Dockland Development Corporation *created* only 3 jobs. Fifth, there is a danger that urban policies could be detrimental to industrial growth as a whole. By limiting their aid to firms which locate in highly urbanized areas, governments may discourage production taking place in more suitable locations, leading to a less efficient allocation of resources. There is also the difficulty that inner cities may gain firms and employment at the expense of the suburbs, or other areas, so that there is no net gain to the economy as a whole. However, it is worth noting that in March 1989 an independent survey by PA Cambridge Economic Consultants of the Handsworth Task Force in Birmingham did conclude that 94% of the jobs created by the Task Force went to Handsworth residents.

A report on eleven Enterprise Zones produced by Roger Tym and Partners (1984) serves to illustrate some of these problems. It found that during the period 1981–83 some 769 companies were attracted into the Enterprise Zones, creating some 7,919 jobs. However, some 40% of firms were *not* totally new, but firms relocating from other areas. Of *these* firms, over 80% had moved from *within the same county* as the Enterprise Zone. Also, some three-quarters of the incoming firms would have set up firms *in the same county* even if there had been *no* Enterprise Zone. The report concluded by estimating that only between 4 and 12% of firms entering the

Enterprise Zone were *specifically* created because of the attractions of the zones themselves. Even with the Enterprise Zone, job creation figures may be misleading. For example, Botham and Lloyd (1983) point out that on Tyneside, Vickers redeveloped a site for tank production, apparently 'creating' 700 jobs, though subsequent enquiry found that these jobs had, to some extent, been transferred from another Vickers plant elsewhere in the zone. An analysis of the first five years of the Swansea Enterprise Zone indicated that its job generating function had not been impressive and that a significant amount of the employment had been in retailing at the expense of long term job losses elsewhere in the region. Employment creation in manufacturing had also been disappointing due to the superior attractiveness of Development Area incentives which tended to attract manufacturing companies to those locations (Bromley and Rees 1988). In total it has been calculated that 35,000 jobs had been created directly by the 23 zones outside Northern Ireland and a further 13,000 jobs indirectly. Their contribution to job creation has not therefore been particularly significant, with the cost to the government at about £42,000 per new job.

Finally, the effectiveness of urban policy in the UK has to some extent been undermined by government macroeconomic policies. The financial restrictions placed upon local authorities, through the Rate Support Grant system, have often made it difficult for these authorities to provide the basic infrastructure needed to attract industry and employment to the urban and inner-city areas.

Conclusion

Despite the problems of definition, it has long been recognized that some areas of the UK suffer a greater degree of economic difficulty than do others. Government policies have attempted to alleviate such problems and have experienced some measure of success, creating up to 800,000 extra jobs in the Assisted Areas since the 1960s. However, critics have commented that the 'costs' have been high, at £40,000 per job created, with much of the benefit going to companies such as ICI, Shell and BP, which often would have located plants in the Assisted Areas without financial help. This was one of the reasons which led the Government to modify the grant system in 1988.

In the 1970s the regional problem was aggravated by economic and social difficulties experienced in the large conurbations, especially within the inner cities. Policies to counteract these problems were slow to develop, though in the 1980s government policy was much more active with the development of Enterprise Zones, UDCs and inner-city initiatives such as *Action for Cities*. However, an integrated policy may be required, incorporating both government and industry views, and taking account of both the regional and urban dimension, if the UK is successfully to combat the difficulties noted above. The long-run 'costs' of *not* developing an effective, integrated, policy may far outweigh any short-term monetary 'benefits' from reduced government spending.

Notes

1. For a detailed treatment of the UK's regional and urban policy development, see Prestwich and Taylor 1990.

2. Urban regions, forming 'arcs of prosperity' cutting across SPR boundaries, which are forecast to exhibit higher growth rates than their regional average during the 1990s:

SOUTH EAST:	Ashford, Bournemouth, Milton Keynes, Reading, Salisbury
EAST ANGLIA:	Cambridge, Huntingdon, Ipswich
SOUTH WEST:	Exeter, Swindon
EAST MIDLANDS:	Kettering, Leicester, Northampton
WEST MIDLANDS:	Stoke, Telford, Walsall
YORKS/HUMBER:	Harrogate, Leeds
NORTH WEST:	Macclesfield
NORTH:	Carlisle, Newcastle upon Tyne
WALES:	Cardiff, Wrexham
SCOTLAND:	Glasgow, Inverness
N. IRELAND:	Coleraine

3. For instance, a national minimum wage might discourage employers from moving into what would otherwise have been a low-wage region.

4. For detailed discussion, see Prestwich and Taylor (1990: 116ff.)

5. Regional Development Grants (RDGs) were introduced into the policy package of financial investment incentives in 1963 and were the major instrument of regional policy until 1988. They took the form of grants and tax allowances towards the expenses of buildings and of plant and machinery, and were intended to encourage firms to establish operations in AAs. Between 1963 and 1981, the government spent £1,163m on RDGs and other investment incentives, which generated 307,000 *net* new jobs in AAs (at an average cost of £25,000 per job), over 68% of the total number of jobs created by regional policy measures.

6. For further details see Fothergill and Gudgin (1982: 16); H.M. Treasury (1985: 7–8, 18).

7. Enterprise Zones designated in the first round (Apr.–Oct. 1981) were Salford/Trafford, Wakefield, Dudley, Hartlepool, Corby, Tyneside, Speke, Swansea, Clydebank, Belfast. Designations in the second round (July–Dec. 1986) were Isle of Dogs, Middlesborough, north-east Lancs, north-west Kent, Rotherham, Scunthorpe, Telford, Wellingborough, Workington, Glanford, Delyn, Milford Haven, Invergordon, Tayside, Derry. Inverclyde and Sunderland were added in 1989.

References and further reading

Ashcroft, B. and **Taylor, J.** (1977) The movements of manufacturing industry and the effect of regional policy, *Oxford Economic Papers*, **29**, 1, March.

Botham, R. and **Lloyd, G.** (1983) The political economy of enterprise zones, *National Westminster Bank Quarterly Review*, May.

British Business (1988) *Blueprint for Enterprise*. Jan. 15.

Bromley, R. D. F. and **Rees, J. C. M.** (1988) The First Five Years of the Swansea Enterprise Zone: An Assessment of Change, *Regional Studies* **22**, 4.

Buck, T. W. and **Atkins, M. H.** (1976) The impact of British regional policies on employment growth, *Oxford Economic Papers*, **28**, 1, March.

CSO (1987) *Economic Trends*, 409, Nov.

CSO (1988) *Economic Trends*, 411, Jan.

CSO (1989) *Economic Trends*, 433, Nov.

CSO (1990) *Regional Trends*, **25**.

Department of Employment Gazette (1990) April.

Department of Trade and Industry (1980) *Guide to Regional Industry Policy Changes.*

Employment Gazette (1990) May.

Fothergill, S. and **Gudgin, G.** (1982) *Unequal Growth: urban and regional employment change in the UK*. Heinemann.

Government Statistical Service, Office of Population Census and Surveys (1982) *Census 1981: Preliminary Report for Towns*. CEN 81 PR(2).

Gudgin, G., Moore, B. and **Rhodes, J.** (1982) Employment problems in the cities and regions of the UK: prospects for the 1980s, *Cambridge Economic Policy Review*, **8**, 2, University of Cambridge, Department of Economics, Gower.

HMSO (1988) *DTI – The Department of Enterprise.*

House of Commons (1988) The Employment Effects of Urban Development Corporations HC 327–1 Employment Committee. Third Report HMSO, pp. 14–25.

Lloyd, P. E. and **Reeve, D. E.** (1982) North West England 1971–77: a study in industrial decline and economic restructuring, *Regional Studies*, **16**, 5.

Martin, S. (1989) New Jobs in the Inner City: The Employment Impacts of Projects Assisted Under Urban Development Grant Programme, *Urban Studies*, **26**, 6 Dec.

Moore, B. C. and **Rhodes, J.** (1976) A quantitative analysis of the effects of the regional employment premium and other regional policy instruments, in: Whiting, A. (ed.) *The Economics of Industrial Subsidies*. HMSO.

Moore, B. C. and **Rhodes, J.** (1977) *Methods of Evaluating the Effects of Regional Policy*. OECD, Paris.

Moore, B., Rhodes, J. and **Tyler, P.** (1986) *The Effect of Government Regional Economic Policy*. DTI, HMSO.

Prestwich, R. and **Taylor, P.** (1990) *Introduction to Regional and Urban Policy in the United Kingdom*. Longman.

Rhodes, J. (1980) Urban-rural cost differentials in manufacturing, paper given at a Department of Environment Conference on Industry and the Inner City, Sunningdale.

Secretary of State for Trade (1983) *Regional Industrial Development*. Cmnd 9111, HMSO.

Treasury (1990) *The Government's Expenditure Plans 1990–91 to 1992–93*. Cmnd 1008/1004, HMSO.

Tyler, J., Moore, B. and **Rhodes, J.** (1979) Regional policy and growth in development areas, paper presented to the Social Science Research Council Urban and Regional Economic Seminar Group, Newcastle.

Tym, R. and **Partners** (1984) *Monitoring Enterprise Zones, Year Three Report*. Roger Tym and Partners.

20 Trade unions, wages and collective bargaining

This chapter first identifies the main institutions involved in the process of collective bargaining in the UK. The structure and growth of trade unions are then traced, and the role of employers and government examined. A simple 'marginal productivity' model of wage determination is presented, before assessing the degree to which unions can use their 'bargaining power' to modify the predictions of this model. Other factors affecting the wage bargain, such as comparability, work conditions, cost of living, and productivity agreements are considered. The chapter concludes by examining the impact of collective bargaining on pay differentials, restrictive practices and strike activity.

Types of trade union

A trade union has been described as 'a continuous association of wage-earners for the purpose of maintaining or improving the conditions of their working lives' (Webb and Webb 1896: 1). Although useful, this definition does not reflect the whole range of trade union objectives. The Trades Union Congress (TUC) outlines ten general objectives of unions, with improved wages and terms of employment at the top of the list. Other aims, such as 'full employment', 'industrial democracy' and a 'voice in government' are included, but the emphasis is on the unions' 'capacity to win higher wages through collective bargaining as one of their most effective methods of attracting membership'.[1]

Despite having some objectives in common there is still a considerable amount of diversity between unions in the UK (Table 20.1). Most unions are relatively small. In 1988 just under half the unions had less than 1,000 members, but together they accounted for only 0.2% of total union membership. There has been a progressive reduction in the number of unions, from the peak of 1,384 unions in 1920, to 314 in 1988. The reduction has been particularly marked for small unions. The number of unions with less than 1,000 members has fallen by over 50% since 1971. In 1988 the ten largest unions accounted for 61% of total membership, The trend towards fewer and larger unions, largely as a result of mergers, is well established, but the 314 British unions provide a contrast with the 16 industrial unions in West Germany.

Four broad headings are often used to classify trade unions in the UK, namely craft, general, industrial and 'white-collar' unions.

					Percentage of			
	Number of unions		All membership ('000s)		No. of unions		Membership of all unions	
Members	1979	1988	1979	1988	1979	1988	1979	1988
Under 100	73	50	4	2	16.0	15.9	0.0	0.0
100–499	124	76	30	20	27.3	24.2	0.2	0.2
500–999	47	26	33	19	10.4	8.3	0.3	0.2
1,000–2,499	58	47	92	78	12.8	15.0	0.7	0.8
2,500–4,999	43	27	152	93	9.5	8.6	1.1	0.9
5,000–9,999	24	16	155	110	5.3	5.1	1.2	1.1
10,000–14,999	7	4	83	51	1.6	1.3	0.6	0.5
15,000–24,999	19	11	358	211	4.2	3.5	2.7	2.1
25,000–49,999	17	23	623	849	3.7	7.3	4.7	8.3
50,000–99,999	15	6	919	464	3.3	1.9	6.9	4.5
100,000–249,999	16	13	2,350	2,104	3.5	4.1	17.7	20.5
250,000 and more	11	10	8,490	6,237	2.4	3.2	63.9	60.9
Membership unknown	—	5	—	—	—	1.6	—	0.0
All members	454	314	13,289	10,238	100.0	100.0	100.0	100.0

Source: Employment Gazette (1981, 1990).

Table 20.1 Unions and union membership, 1979 and 1988

Rank	Name	No. of members
1.	Transport and General Workers' Union	1,312,853
2.	Amalgamated Engineering Union	793,610
3.	General Municipal Boilermakers' and Allied Trades Union	789,556
4.	National and Local Government Officers' Association	754,701
5.	Manufacturing, Science and Finance	653,000
6.	National Union of Public Employees	635,070
7.	Union of Shop, Distributive and Allied Workers	396,724
8.	Electrical, Electronic, Telecommunication and Plumbing Union	370,369
9.	Royal College of Nursing	281,918
10.	Union of Construction, Allied Trades and Technicians	250,042

Table 20.2 The top ten trade unions

Source: Annual Report of the Certification Office, 1989, Appendix 4.

Craft unions

These were the earliest type of union, and are mainly composed of workers regarded as 'qualified' in a particular craft. Most craft unions now include workers with the same skill across the several industries in which they are employed. Examples include the Electrical, Electronic, Telecommunication and Plumbing Union (EETPU) with over 370,000 members, and the Associated Society of Locomotive Engineers and Firemen (ASLEF).

General unions

These unions originated in the 1880s in the attempt to organize semi- and unskilled workers not covered by the craft unions. General unions do not restrict their membership to workers with specific skills, or to particular industries or occupations. Examples include the Transport and General Workers' Union (TGWU) with 1.4 million members, the National Union of

General and Municipal Workers (GMB) with around 800,000 members, and the National Union of Public Employees (NUPE) with around 635,000 members.

The distinction between craft and general unions is not always clear. For instance, some would classify the separate sections of the Amalgamated Engineering Union (AEU) as craft unions, yet faced with competition from general unions the Engineering Section has admitted semi- and unskilled machine operators.

Industrial unions

These attempt to place under one union all the workers in an industry, whatever their status of occupation. The National Union of Mineworkers (NUM) comes closest to this in the UK, covering most of the occupations engaged in mining operations. Other examples of industrial unions include the Iron and Steel Trades Federation (ISTF) and the Union of Communication Workers (UCW). Most industrial unions in the UK are 'a matter of degree rather than kind'. In other words, they usually cover a large number of those engaged in the industry, but by no means all. The National Union of Railwaymen (NUR) is still only one of three unions involved in that industry, with ASLEF and the Transport and Salaried Staffs Association (TSSA) playing smaller but important roles.

'White-collar' unions

These restrict their membership to professional, administrative and clerical employees. 'White-collar' unions have expanded faster than any other type of union in the post-war period. Large numbers of professions are now organized as unions, such as the National Union of Teachers (NUT) with 217,000 members, and the Royal College of Nursing of the United Kingdom (RCN) with over 280,000 members. The supervisory and managerial grades in industry have become more highly unionized with Manufacturing, Science and Finance having over 650,000 members. The National and Local Government Officers' Association (NALGO) with some 750,000 members covers a range of administrative and clerical staff in the public sector.

It is not possible to provide an accurate pattern of trade union membership by *industry*, as over 4 million members belong to unions recruiting over several industries. The fact that the UK does not have just a few industrial unions as in West Germany, or enterprise unions as in Japan, poses problems not only for classification but also for collective bargaining. The 'multi-union' structure of the UK means that many unions are involved in negotiations at both plant and enterprise levels. This can cause problems for both management and unions. Management may experience difficulties in co-ordinating negotiations with several different unions, often in the same plant. Unions may have to compromise individual aims and policies when part of a 'team' negotiating with employers. Multi-union plants or enterprises may also lead to inter-union rivalry and conflict. For instance, at BL during the 1970s there were frequent disputes over pay differentials between craft workers of the AEU and assembly workers of the TGWU. In part, this has led to the negotiation of single-union deals by many companies establishing new plants in the 1980s. The AEU and EEPTU have been at the forefront amongst unions in concluding such agreements.

The Trades Union Congress

The TUC was founded in 1868 with the aim of improving the economic and social conditions of working people, and of promoting the interests of its affiliated organizations. In 1989 there were 80 affiliated trade unions representing over 80% of trade unionists in the UK. The TUC is mainly concerned with general questions which affect trade unions both nationally and internationally, and participates in discussions relating to the national economy through its membership of the National Economic Development Office (NEDO). The General Council of the TUC represents the organization in the period between one annual Congress and another and is responsible for putting Congress decisions into effect. The General Council has no authority to call strikes, or to stop strikes called by its members, but can offer advice on disputes. Under Rule 11 the General Council can intervene in unofficial strikes and make recommendations to the unions and employers concerned.

The European Trade Union Confederation (ETUC)   ETUC was formed in 1973 out of a number of trade union organizations in the Community which had previously been divided along religious and ideological grounds. Affiliates include national trade union federations, like the TUC, and European industrial trade union groups, such as the European Metal Workers' Federations to which the relevant national organizations subscribe. At the same time as its formation, ETUC was divided into industrial committees concerned with labour affairs in their particular industrial sector, and this was expected to result in the emergence of an effective and streamlined trade union structure (Baranouin 1986). A European level of union organization may be considered essential in view of the growing economic significance of multinationals in the Community, whose power to reallocate resources transnationally cannot be effectively counteracted by a union movement fragmented by country. However, despite the revival of the idea of greater trade union involvement in Community decision-making under the Delors presidency of the European Commission (Teague 1989), the effectiveness of ETUC has been extremely limited. One explanation for this is the determined opposition of multinational companies to a European level of collective bargaining, allied to the Community-wide shift towards decentralized, company-level industrial relations. Other explanations include ETUC's lack of resources and a degree of internal conflict, with some national federations being unwilling to surrender a measure of sovereignty to ETUC.

Nevertheless, two factors may bolster ETUC's position in the 1990s, or at least European trade union bargaining power. Firstly, multinationals' international production chains have become increasingly complex, with many based on the Japanese 'just-in-time' delivery system of parts and raw materials. As a result the whole production chain has become highly dependent upon the regular, unbroken delivery of items at each stage of production. The Ford UK unions' strike in 1988 won concessions because of its threat to this system. Secondly, the European Social Charter (see below) now offers trade unions the prospect of using Community law to increase their strength in bargaining with employers.

Trade unions and change

Changes in the industrial and sectoral distribution of the UK's working population have already been discussed in Chapter 1, and these are reflected in the composition of trade union membership.

The decline of union membership in the primary and secondary sectors has, until recently, been more than compensated for by an increase in membership in the tertiary (service) sector. The tertiary or service sector now provides the largest absolute number of union members, with 44% of the total, compared to only 31.1% from the secondary sector, and 3.9% from the primary sector.[2] Although there has been continued growth in the proportion of service sector employees unionized since the Second World War, i.e. in the 'density' of unionization, the proportion for the largely 'white-collar' service workers is still below that for the 'blue-collar' industrial workers. Moreover, the density of organization is twice as high in the public sector as in the private sector.

Table 20.3 Trade union membership and density in the UK, 1979–89 (000's and %)

Year	Civilian employees in employment	Unemployed	Potential trade union membership	Trade union membership	Density* (%)
1979	23,244	1,261	24,505	13,289	54.2
1981	21,602	2,764	24,366	12,106	49.7
1983	21,170	3,079	24,249	11,236	46.3
1985	21,633	3,273	24,906	10,821	43.4
1987	22,035	2,953	24,988	10,475	41.9
1989	23,004	1,799	24,803	10,238	41.3

* Union density defined as: $\dfrac{\text{Actual union membership}}{\text{Potential union membership}} \times 100$

Source: Towers, 1989; *Employment Gazette*, 1990

Until 1980 the fall in employment, and therefore the number unionized, in the primary and secondary industries was more than compensated for by the rise in employment, and so the number unionized, in the service industries. Since 1980 this trend has been broken (see Table 20.3) and with it the sustained growth in trade union membership over the post-war period. In fact, membership fell substantially by 23.0% between 1979 and 1989, with union density declining from a peak of 54.2% to 41.3%. Even the fall in unemployment since 1986 has been unable to arrest the decline in membership, although the *rate* of decrease of both membership and density had slowed significantly by the end of the 1980s. An accurate breakdown of membership by *sex* has not been possible since 1981, but evidence suggests that females comprise about 35% of the total. Whilst opportunities for increasing female membership has increased with the rising participation rate of women in the workforce (a trend that will continue with the demographic decline in the supply of young workers), females remain under-represented in trade unions relative to their share of the total working population (around 40% in 1989).

Factors affecting union growth

Unemployment has obviously had a significant negative impact on union growth. Historically the major upswings in trade union membership have occurred in periods when unemployment has been relatively low or falling – for instance, 1901–20 and 1934–47. A study by Bain and Elsheikh (1982) found that in fifteen of the nineteen industries studied during the inter-war and post-war years, slow growth of unionization was correlated with periods of high unemployment, and vice versa. The Bain–Elsheikh model suggests that relatively high unemployment will reduce union bargaining power, and therefore discourage union membership. However, some have suggested that the *threat* of unemployment may even act as a *stimulus* to union growth. Hawkins (1981) sees this as one factor in raising union density amongst white-collar workers threatened by technological and organizational change during the 1970s. Technology is something of a two-edged sword for unions; on the one hand it may create unemployment, whilst on the other it often confers substantial industrial 'muscle' on the few key workers operating the new computer-based systems.

The level of unemployment, though important, is only one factor determining union growth or decline. Bain and Elsheikh (1980) found a positive correlation between union growth and *the average size of establishment* (*plant*) in the industry. Large establishments tend to be run on bureaucratic lines, subjecting employees to impersonal rules, which emphasize their collective, rather than individual, identity. Employees including professional and other white-collar workers, then perceive collective rather than individual bargaining as the appropriate response, with the result that union membership rises with size of plant.

Price and Bain (1976) suggest that the *rate of change of prices* and *the rate of change of wages* may also influence union growth. Rising prices have a 'threat' effect so that workers unionize to defend real wages, particularly in the early years of an inflationary period. Wage rises have a 'credit' effect for unions, in that they are attributed to their bargaining power, and this promotes membership. Bain and Elsheikh (1982) found that the real wage variable, in one form or another, had a significant and positive impact on union growth in fifteen of the nineteen industries studied. Also the desire to protect established *pay relativities* may affect union growth. For example, in advanced stages of incomes policies, when pay differentials have been substantially eroded, there is evidence that union membership increases. The suggestion here is that a series of injustices leads workers to seek greater bargaining power by joining unions in the hope of restoring differentials.

The rapid decline of both union membership and density in the 1980s clearly suggests, however, a number of negative influences on union growth. The large increase in unemployment has not only reduced the bargaining power of trade unions, and, therefore, their attractiveness to members, but it has also been concentrated in industries with traditionally high membership.

The change in industrial structure has also exercised an adverse effect on potential membership, because the growing proportion of female, part-time, temporary and white-collar workers in the labour force, are in categories where union density has been historically low. The growing importance of small firms in the national economy (see Ch. 4) may also have worked against the recovery of union membership, given the often hostile views of small businesses to union recognition.

A further threat to union growth in recent years has been the increasing incidence of companies withdrawing recognition from unions. De-recognition is a decision by an employer to withdraw from collective bargaining with trade unions in favour of alternative arrangements for regulating employment relations. The government banning trade union membership at Government Communication Headquarters (GCHQ) in Cheltenham in 1987 is a public sector example. Private sector examples include P&O Ferries' total de-recognition of the National Union of Seamen in 1988.

Unfavourable conditions for membership growth or retention have prompted many unions, notably the TGWU, AEU and the EEPTU, to design recruitment campaigns that appeal directly to women, young workers, part-time and temporary staff and even the self-employed. The increase in merger activity between trade unions in the last decade has, in part, been motivated by the need to combine dwindling memberships in order to obtain scale economies and thereby greater effectiveness in the provision of services to members.

Another consequence of the decline in union density and the growing awareness by unions to combat this trend, has been a greater willingness to concede single-union agreements under pressure from employers. Here, the employer only recognizes one union for the purposes of collective bargaining. Midland Bank has simplified its bargaining structures by recognizing only the Bank, Insurance and Finance Union at the expense of MSF, although it is more common for single-union deals to be struck at 'greenfield' sites, i.e. those of newly-established enterprises. At its new bottling plant in Wakefield, Coca-Cola Schweppes would only recognize the AEU and not the TGWU, which had historically been predominant in the company. The firm argued that the greater technical content of the work involved would more probably be provided by employees falling within the AEU's customary recruitment area. In fact the AEU, and particularly the EEPTU, have exploited the reputation of their members for skill and moderation to conclude such agreements with the growing number of Japanese firms in the UK, including Hitachi, Toshiba, Sanyo and Nissan. Moreover, these are also examples of unions winning recognition and therefore members by offering 'strike-free' deals to employers. In it, the union relinquishes the right to strike in return for a mutual commitment, in the event of a dispute and the exhaustion of disputes procedures, to binding arbitration, i.e. where both sides abide by the decision of an external arbitrator, generally appointed through ACAS (see below).

Whatever the causes of union growth, and its recent slow-down, the unions are key role-players in the area of collective bargaining, wage determination and industrial relations. Before returning to these we consider briefly the organization of another important role-player, the employers.

The employers

Employers'
associations

Many employers in the UK are members of employers' associations which seek to regulate relations between employers and trade unions. These associations are usually organized on an industry basis rather than a product basis, as with the Engineering Employers' Federation with almost 5,000 members. Their role includes negotiating with unions at industry level through joint industrial Wages Councils, the operation of procedures for the resolution of disputes, and the provision of advice to members on employment law, manpower planning and other personnel matters. In some industries there are local or regional employers' associations, combined into national federations, as with the Building Employers' Confederation. Altogether there are about 150 national employers' associations which negotiate the national collective agreements for their industry with the trade unions concerned, and most of these belong to the Confederation of British Industry (CBI). Table 20.4 presents the ten largest employers' associations.

Table 20.4 The top ten
employers' associations (in
rank order of subscription
income)

Rank	Name	Number of members
1	National Farmers' Union	112,675
2	Engineering Employers' Federation*	4,652
3	Building Employers' Federation*	9,298
4	Chemical Industries Association Limited	151
5	Motor Agents' Association Limited	14,008
6	National Federation of Retail Newsagents	31,765
7	British Printing Industries Association	3,315
8	Newspaper Society	246
9	Federation of Master Builders	21,055
10	Electrical Contractors' Association	2,268

* Comprising 16 separate associations.
Source: Annual Report of the Certification Officer, 1989, Appendix 5.

The Confederation of
British Industry

This is the largest central employers' organization in the UK, representing over 3,000 companies which employ around 12 million people. Membership includes all sizes and types of company, both private and nationalized, and covers the primary, secondary and tertiary sectors of industry, although manufacturing predominates. Policy is determined by a council of 350 members, and there are 360 permanent staff members, including representatives with the EEC in Brussels. The CBI seeks to represent the broad interests of businessmen in discussions with the Government, with national and international institutions, and with the public at large. It nominates the employers' representatives for such bodies as NEDO, the MSC and the Advisory, Conciliation and Arbitration Service (ACAS).

Union of Industrial and
Employers'
Confederations of
Europe (UNICE)

UNICE was formed in 1958 and is the European equivalent of the CBI. Its principal role is to lobby and attempt to influence the decisions of the main Community institutions. It also provides members at a national level with information on Community affairs. UNICE has hitherto proved itself to be a more cohesive and effective influence on Community proposals than ETUC. This was demonstrated, in particular, by its intensive and successful lobbying in the mid-1980s against the 'Vredeling Directive' of the European Commission, which sought to provide employees in certain companies with the legal right to formal consultation and information procedures. Multinational companies were at the forefront of the campaign against the directive, regarding the proposal as a precursor to fully developed international collective bargaining which they flatly opposed.

The Government

The Government's role in industrial relations is threefold: as an employer, as a legislator and as an economic and social policy-maker.

The Government is a major direct *employer of labour*, with central government employing almost 2.5 million persons, or 10% of the workforce. It influences not only these pay settlements but also those of the local authorities and the remaining nationalized industries. The Government can, through its position as a primary source of finance, and by using cash limits (see Ch. 13), affect wage bargaining and employment levels in the local authorities and the nationalized industries.

As a *legislator*, the Conservative administration has been particularly active, and has made extensive use of the law in an effort to reduce what it perceives as excessive union bargaining power, resulting in high UK wage cost and low labour productivity. An examination of the major legal changes introduced since 1979, mainly in the 1980, 1982, 1988 and 1989 Employment Acts, and in the 1984 Trade Union Act, reveals important changes in the context of collective bargaining. The 1990 Employment Bill represents the latest stage of the present Government's 'step-by-step' process of trade union reform.

The closed shop. This is a situation where employees only obtain or retain a job if they become a member of a specified trade union. Its advantages to unions *and* management are discussed below. The 1980 and 1982 Employment Acts provide for a regular review of closed-shop agreements by a secret ballot of employees and they give increased protection and financial compensation for those dismissed for not wishing to be union members. These provisions have been enhanced by the 1988 Act. Only a small number of closed-shop ballots have been held, covering a very small group of workers. In the absence of a ballot or one showing sufficient support for the retention of a closed-shop agreement, dismissal for non-membership of a union is automatically unfair. The 1988 Act also removed legal immunity for union action aimed to create or maintain a closed shop, i.e. unions would be made liable to pay civil damages if actions brought against them by employers and employees were successful.

A further restriction on closed shops is contained in the 1990 Employment Bill, which proposes the banning of *pre-entry* closed shops, i.e. where an individual must be a member of the specified trade union before he or she can be considered for, or commence, employment.

Strikes and other industrial action Since the end of the last century it has been impossible for a trade union to organize a strike without committing a *tort*, that is the civil wrong of interfering with the contract of employment between employer and employed. The committing of a tort enables the employer to obtain an injunction against, or claim damages from, the union. However, since 1906 Parliament has protected unions from this liability by providing them with immunity from civil action. However a major aim of the post-1979 legislation has been to narrow the scope of this immunity by rendering certain types of dispute 'unlawful'.

Industrial action is unlawful when the union is no longer covered by immunity from civil actions brought by employers or other affected parties in the courts. If successful, the employer will obtain a court injunction prohibiting the dispute, and the union will face fines or the sequestration of its assets for failure to comply. An employer can also subsequently claim damages arising from losses sustained during the action.

An important provision in the 1982 Employment Act restricts 'lawful trade disputes' to those between workers and their own employer, making 'political' strikes and inter-union disputes unlawful. Also rendered unlawful by the 1980 Employment Act is secondary action, i.e. action against an employer not party to a dispute. Picketing is now almost wholly restricted in law to the union member's 'place of work', often even excluding another plant of the same employer. Restrictions on illegal picketing are effected by making unions liable to pay damages in civil actions brought against them by employers. The 1984 Act also means loss of legal immunity in certain circumstances. Official industrial action, i.e. that approved by the union leadership, must be sanctioned by a secret ballot of the membership. The ballot must be held no more than four weeks before the event, and a majority of union members must be in favour of the action. If the action takes place without majority consent, then the union loses any legal immunity for organizing industrial action that it may have enjoyed in the past. These provisions are strengthened by the 1988 Employment Act which gives the individual union member the right not to be called out on strike without a properly held secret ballot and, most controversially, the right not to be disciplined by his or her union for refusing to strike or for crossing a picket line. The Act also established a Commissioner for the Rights of Trade Union Members to provide funds and advice to individuals wishing to take legal action to exercise these rights.

The 1990 Employment Bill took the control of union behaviour even further by proposing that the union leadership must now take positive steps to repudiate 'unofficial action', i.e. actions undertaken by union members without union consent. For instance, the union may now have to write to all members involved in such action asking them to cease their action. Failure by the union to take such steps could mean loss of immunity for the union, even though the action is unofficial.

In addition, the Bill would allow employers to dismiss unofficial strikers selectively at the place of work (e.g. the strike leaders) and deny those dismissed the right to claim unfair dismissal.

Legal regulation of wages and conditions of work   The Fair Wages Resolution, 1946, together with Schedule 11 of the Employment Protection

Act, 1975, were repealed in the early 1980s. Both provisions were broadly intended to make *non-unionized firms* observe the terms and conditions of employment established by unions and employers in the same trade or industry. Their abolition has been criticized for exposing employees to potential exploitation. The 1989 Employment Act further repealed legislation relating to the hours and conditions of the work of women and the under-18s. The intention of the Act is to raise the demand for such categories of worker by removing what the government saw as disincentives to their employment. However, it has also removed a 'Floor' of rights upon which trade unions have traditionally based adult male collective bargaining.

Trade union democracy   The Trade Union Act 1984 embodies a number of provisions for internal union democracy in addition to those pertaining to strike action. Members of the main executive committee of a trade union, who have voting power, must have been elected in a secret ballot of the union's members within the previous five years. The Employment Bill contains the right of members to a postal vote in elections for all members of union governing bodies and for key national leaders. In addition, the 1984 Act requires trade unions with political funds to ballot their members at least every ten years. Only if this is done, and majority assent for the fund achieved, can the union continue to spend money on 'political' matters, such as a campaign against new legislation or in support of a political party. To date, of all ballots which have been held on this matter, a substantial majority have been in favour of retaining the fund.

The use of the law by employers in the 1980s, specifically the seeking of injunctions to stop or prevent industrial action by unions, has been confined to a small number of disputes and industrial sectors. Over three-quarters of all injunctions sought occurred in printing, public services and shipping. In more than 90% of all cases the employer was successful in obtaining the injunction. However, this was much less likely to lead to the cessation of action in *primary* disputes, i.e. where the action is undertaken on the strikers' own behalf, compared to *secondary* disputes, where workers were taking action on behalf of other employees, as for example in cases of 'blacking'. Indeed, the current evidence suggests that resort to the law by employers can strengthen support for a strike and, where these are the subject of an injunction, lead to secret ballots showing the required majority for action. Of the 951 union ballots held between 1987 and 1989, 92% were in favour of industrial action and in the great majority of these cases the employer settled without a strike (Brown and Wadhwani 1990). So a successful ballot for strike action can be used by unions as an effective bargaining weapon, as can the threat of legal action by an employer when support for a dispute is perceived to be weak. All this suggests that ballots provide a test of each side's position short of industrial action actually occurring. In this way ballots may be said to reduce the frequency of *actual strikes*, if not the threat of them.

In its legislative capacity therefore, the Government can alter the balance of power between employer and employee. However, it is difficult to assess how far any legislation can be effectively used by employers, as this depends upon a complex array of factors, such as management style, the firm's size and position within both product and labour markets, the availability of alternative tactics and the anticipated repercussions of recourse to law on a firm's industrial relations.

The European Community and UK labour law   The European Community is discussed more fully in Chapter 26, but the current proposals of the European Commission are of potentially great significance to the UK. The most important measures are contained in the *European Social Charter* and the accompanying 'Action Programme' for its implementation. The Charter contains provisions relating to both the individual and collective rights of workers, but it is important to recognize that it is a statement of *principles* or intent and that by itself it creates no legally enforceable rights. However, the Commission plans to give legal form to the Charter's contents over the next few years, which at present enjoy majority support in the Council of Ministers.

Only a brief outline of the Charter can be given here, but measures pertaining to individual employee rights include greater freedom of movement within the Community; the right to training; protection regarding health and safety and against discrimination; provisions to safeguard the employment conditions of the young, disabled and elderly, and employees at large; minimum rules on work duration, rest periods and holidays, shift work and systematic overtime. Broadly similar rights are to be extended to part-time, casual and temporary workers. The Charter excludes a commitment to minimum wage legislation.

Measures relating to collective labour law are more limited, and the Charter does not propose any legally enforceable right to bargain for trade unions where this is not already part of a member state's law. However, the Charter does include important prospective rights to information and consultation plus the 'participation' of employees before companies make decisions on redundancies and closures. Participation by workers in company decision-making is also addressed by Community legislation. This includes a potential legal structure for multinational firms which would involve some form of board-level representation for the workforce.

The primary justification for this positive, interventionist stance of the Commission is to provide support for the move to the Single European market in 1992, which threatens major restructuring in product and labour markets. The provision of 'appropriate levels' or a 'plinth' of social rights is intended to help employees during a period of great change and to encourage greater labour mobility. Perhaps of still greater importance, by providing a 'common floor' of worker rights, the Charter seeks to equalize the terms on which member states compete for resources. A nation offering a lower level of rights, combined with low wage status, will have a considerable competitive advantage over other nations, thereby distorting competition for direct inward investment. This argument has been given still greater weight by the accession of Spain, Portugal and Greece to the Community. Indeed, the UK Government's labour law programme may be viewed as an attempt to make Britain a more attractive proposition for inward investment by multinationals (Wedderburn 1990).

As a *policy-maker*, the Government can influence a firm's labour market.

This may be 'indirect', through fiscal and monetary policy which affects the demand for the firm's goods and services, and hence its 'derived' demand for labour. Alternatively, the Government's influence on the firm's labour market may be 'direct', as in the case of incomes policies, or through various training schemes.

Perhaps 'indirect' influence has been the most significant for unions. The Government's adherence to a relatively 'tight' fiscal and monetary policy has made it more difficult for firms to pass on higher wages, and therefore costs, as higher prices to consumers. In these circumstances unions are more likely to 'pay' for favourable wage settlements in job loss, and therefore membership loss. This increased elasticity of demand for union labour reduces bargaining power and discourages industrial action, given the real threat of redundancy.

As regards 'direct' influence, a significant feature of government policy since 1979 has been the virtual disappearance of tripartism, i.e. a close involvement of trade unions and employers' organizations (primarily the TUC and CBI) in government decision-making. Also, cash limits in the public sector are a form of incomes policy, directly affecting public expenditure and therefore public sector employment.

The structure of collective bargaining

Collective bargaining refers to 'the whole range of dealings between employers and managers on the one hand, and trade unions, shop stewards and members on the other, over the making, interpretation and administration of employment rules' (Clegg 1979: 4). These rules are both *substantive*, determining pay, hours, overtime, manning levels, holidays, etc., and *procedural*, governing the way in which substantive issues are settled. The above definition indicates that collective bargaining takes place at a number of levels.

National or industry-wide bargaining

This level of negotiation predominates in the public sector in which centralized bargaining gives rise to relatively formal, fixed-term and comprehensive agreements, leaving little scope for localized or workplace bargaining. Examples of centralized bargaining include the Whitley Councils of the National Health Service and the Burnham Committee which negotiated teachers' pay until its suspension by the Government in 1987, following a lengthy dispute in schools. However there is now a clear trend towards more decentralized bargaining in the public sector. For example, in 1990 the Education Secretary announced new freedoms for local education authorities to make their own pay arrangements with teachers, within certain limits.

In the private sector national bargaining occurs on an industry level, between employers' associations and trade unions, or federations of unions. This was once the main type of collective bargaining, but has declined in importance in many industries. Today, it is mainly a 'safety net' for employees of small firms, establishing *minimum* industry levels for pay and for other substantive issues.

In fact, industry-wide and multi-company bargaining has already disappeared from a number of sectors, including the clearing banks, the cable industry, provincial newspapers and independent T.V. companies.

Single-employer bargaining

This occurs at two levels: (a) *corporate*, i.e. at the level of the company or whole organization; and (b) *establishment*, i.e. at the level of the workplace, such as the factory, plant or office.

A major conclusion of the Donovan Commission in 1968 (HMSO 1968) was that 'informal' workplace bargaining was primarily responsible for wage drift (i.e. the negotiation of bonuses and other wage premiums supplementary to industry rates), restrictive practices and unofficial strikes. Its 'informality' resided in its dependence on tacit, unwritten agreements between managers and shop stewards based on 'custom and practice', causing a fragmented bargaining system independent of corporate management or official trade union control, and often subject to conflict and renegotiation. The Donovan Commission therefore recommended the extension of 'formal' bargaining to the workplace; 'formal' in the sense of written agreements, of specified duration, on clearly delineated issues, in order to promote 'effective and orderly' industrial relations.

After the Donovan Report in 1968 there was a marked rise in formal, corporate-level bargaining. Bargaining at the company level usually integrated and formalized earlier practices at the workplace, with important consequences. First, there was a large increase in the number of full-time shop stewards involved in the negotiation of factory agreements and procedures with senior management. Rather than merely being parties to open-ended arrangements, these stewards were now joint negotiators of formal agreements, and as a result were responsible for their observance by union members. Second, by raising the level of substantive bargaining and incorporating shop stewards within it, the movement towards corporate bargaining reduced the involvement of shopfloor workers and their freedom of action. However, this shift to company agreements, largely initiated by US-owned multinationals to exert greater control over collective bargaining, has not been universal. In fact, establishment or plant-level bargaining remains important in many industries, such as clothing, and the footwear, brick and timber industries. More significantly, recent changes in managerial practice, which have devolved more responsibility to middle management for running individual establishments as separate budget or profit centres, have enhanced formal plant bargaining at the expense of company-wide negotiation. This development has been accompanied by a decline in the range of substantive issues which many managements are prepared to negotiate with unions. Instead of bargaining about planned changes and even pay deals, a growing number of employers are seeking to ensure their employees' acquiescence to them (Smith 1987). Moreover, and of perhaps greater future importance for workplace bargaining, there has been a marked increase in systems of individual assessment and reward, some linked to the profit performance of the company, which could further undermine collective representation.

In a small number of industries with fragmentary collective bargaining procedures, there are statutory wage-regulating bodies, known as Wages Councils.

Wages Councils   Employers and employees are equally represented on these councils, with a further three independent members completing the council. Wages Councils make proposals for minimum wage rates, holidays and other conditions of employment. They may, after consultation, make 'orders' which give statutory force to such proposals. Wages Councils cover 2.5 million workers in low pay industries, which include hotel and catering, retailing, hairdressing and clothing manufacture.

The Government proposed the abolition of the Councils in 1985 and 1988, arguing that they impeded flexibility and encouraged workers to price themselves out of jobs. Faced with combined employer and union opposition, the Government announced a reprieve for Wages Councils in March 1990, but repeated that they have no permanent place in the labour market. In any case, the Wages Act 1986 cut their powers significantly, restricting them merely to the setting of a single hourly and overtime rate and a maximum deduction from pay for lodging. Young workers under the age of 21 were also excluded completely from their protection.

Statutory Joint Industrial Councils   The Secretary of State for Employment may convert Wages Councils into Statutory Joint Industrial Councils (SJICs). These function in similar ways to Wages Councils, but without independent members. They are usually regarded as a half-way house between the statutory system and the development of full, voluntary collective bargaining. Whatever the arrangements for collective bargaining, in the event of breakdown in negotiations a need may arise for independent arbitration.

Advisory, Conciliation and Arbitration Service   The Advisory, Conciliation and Arbitration Service has a broad brief to promote improved industrial relations and to extend collective bargaining procedures. It conciliates in around 1,500 industrial disputes, in both public and private sectors, each year. It also provides, on request, arbitration in around 200 disputes each year, either by appointing single arbitrators or boards of arbitrators.[3]

The service is controlled by a council consisting of an independent chairman and nine others with experience in industrial relations. Three of these are nominated after consultation with the TUC, three after consultation with the CBI, and three are independent.

Wage determination and collective bargaining

The neo-classical view of wage determination is embodied in 'marginal productivity' theory. With many small buyers of labour (firms) and many small suppliers (i.e. non-unionized individuals), the wage rate would be determined by the intersection of demand and supply curves for labour.

The demand curve for any factor, including labour, is seen as being derived from the demand for the product or service it produces. Additional labour will always be required if the revenue gained from selling the output produced by the last person, the marginal revenue product of labour

(MRP_L),[4] is greater than the extra cost of employing that person, the marginal cost of labour (MC_L). In a competitive labour market (see Fig. 20.1), the supply of labour (S_L) to each firm would be perfectly elastic at the

Fig. 20.1 Wage
determination in a
competitive market

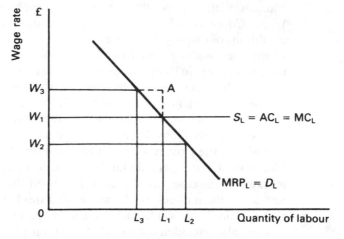

going wage rate (W_1), so that the wage rate is itself the marginal cost of labour.[5] The profit-maximizing firm would then hire people until MRP_L equalled MC_L, i.e. L_1 persons in Fig. 20.1. If more than L_1 persons were hired, then the extra revenue from their hire would fail to match the extra cost incurred.

Under these conditions the MRP_L curve becomes the demand curve for labour (D_L), since at any given wage rate the profit-maximizing firm will employ labour until MRP_L equals that wage rate. For example, if the wage rate falls to W_2 in Fig. 20.1, then demand for labour rises to L_2.

Wages and unions

If the labour force is now unionized, then the supply of labour to the firm (or industry) may be regulated. However, even though unions bring an element of monopoly into labour supply, theory suggests that they can only influence price *or* quantity, but not both. For example, in Fig. 20.1 the union may seek wage rate W_3, but must accept in return lower employment at L_3. Alternatively, unions may seek a level of employment L_2, but must then accept a lower wage rate at W_2. Except (see below) where unions are able to force employers off their demand curve for labour (MRP_L), then unions can only raise wages at the 'cost' of reduced employment. However, a *given rise* in wages will reduce employment by less, under the following circumstances:

1. The less elastic is final demand for the product.

2. The less easy it is to substitute other factors for the workers in question.

3. The lower the proportion of labour costs to total costs of production.

All of these circumstances will make the demand curve for labour, MRP_L, less elastic.

Unions and bargaining power   Unions may seek to force the employer off his demand curve for labour so that he makes less than maximum profits. It may then be possible for wages to rise from W_1 to W_3 with no loss of employment, i.e. point A in Fig. 20.1. How effective unions will be in such strategies will depend upon the extent of their 'bargaining power'.

Chamberlain (1951) defines union bargaining power as:

<u>Management costs of disagreeing (to union terms)</u>
  Management costs of agreeing (to union terms)

Although this ratio cannot be measured, as it relies on subjective assessments, it is a useful analytical tool. If unions are to exert effective influence on management the ratio must exceed unity. That is to say it must be more costly for management to disagree (e.g. loss of profits, or market share as a result of strike action) than to agree (e.g. higher labour costs and manning levels). The higher the ratio, the more inclined management may then be to agree to the union's terms.

The level of the wage demand will affect union bargaining power. The more modest the wage claim, the lower the management cost of agreement, and the higher Chamberlain's ratio, i.e. the greater is union bargaining power. This will increase the prospects for securing higher wages with stable employment.

Union density will also affect bargaining power. The greater the proportion of the industry unionized, the less easy it will be to substitute non-union labour. The management costs of disagreeing to union terms will tend to be higher, so that the ratio, i.e. union bargaining power, rises. Equally, the higher is union density in the industry as a whole, the easier it is for any particular company to pass on higher wage demands as price increases to consumers without losing market share. This is because competing firms in the industry will also be facing similar wage-cost conditions. High union density therefore reduces the management costs of agreeing to union terms, and again raises the ratio, i.e. union bargaining power. High union density will therefore also increase the prospects for securing higher wages with stable employment.

Even macroeconomic factors can be brought into this analysis. The higher the level of real income in the economy, the higher will be demand for 'normal' goods. Management will then be able to pass on cost increases as higher prices with relatively less effect on demand. This will reduce management costs of agreeing to union terms, raise the ratio, and with it union bargaining power.

However, one must recognize the existence of many other dimensions to union bargaining power, such as the degree of unanimity or conflict within unions over bargaining goals and methods. Unions will also vary in the militancy of their members and the bargaining abilities of their leaders. All this makes the assessment of bargaining power extremely difficult. It is also important to note that the 'resource' theory of the impact of trade unionism on the firm does not accept that the exercise of this power will necessarily raise production costs. Instead, the theory argues that unions can significantly increase productivity by providing an efficient means for the management and settlement of disputes. Thus, collective bargaining reduces the costs of individual expressions of grievances, which may raise the 'quit' rate of key employees and the incidence of absenteeism or poor-quality work. Further, the 'shock' effect of unions' negotiation of pay rises may force managements to increase efficiency in order to absorb higher costs (see Cameron 1987).

Wages and employers' associations

Wages are determined by a variety of factors, of which union bargaining power is but one, admittedly important, element.

Employers' associations are themselves able to create an element of monopoly on the *demand* side of the labour market (i.e. 'monopsony'). These associations bring together the employers of labour in order to exert greater influence in collective bargaining. Standard theory[6] suggests that monopsony in the labour market will, by itself, reduce both wages and employment in the labour market. When monopoly on the demand side (employers' associations) is combined with monopoly on the supply side (trade unions), the wage and employment outcome becomes indeterminate.[7]

The existence of employers' associations will clearly affect the strength of union bargaining power. The greater the density of their coverage within an industry the smaller might be the management costs of disagreement, e.g. in the case of a strike there is less likelihood of other domestic firms capturing their markets. By reducing the numerator of the ratio, union bargaining power is reduced.

Wages and other factors

Wages can be determined by institutional practices which bear little relation to market conditions.

'Spillover' and comparability   The 'spillover' hypothesis argues that wage settlements for one group of workers are transmitted ('spillover') to other groups through the principle of comparability, irrespective of product and labour market conditions. For example, the pay awards achieved by 'wage leaders' often give rise to a sequence of similar settlements in the same 'wage round' for other workers. Settlements at Ford and in the coal industry have been regarded as important targets for pay settlements in the private and public sectors respectively. The 'going rate' established by powerful trade unions becomes a 'virility symbol for those who follow' (Taylor 1989), a bench-mark against which the performance of union leaders will be measured.

Non-pecuniary advantages or disadvantages   Not all jobs have the same conditions of work. Some are hazardous, dirty, boring, require the working of unsocial hours, or receive various perquisites ('perks'). These will inevitably form part of the collective bargain, and ultimately affect the wage outcome. In some circumstances wage demands may be modified as the union places greater emphasis on non-wage factors.

Cost of living   The cost of living is an important factor in determining the wage claim, and has even been a formal part of wage settlements. In the early 1970s, as part of the Heath Government's incomes policy, cost-of-living rises beyond a certain 'threshold' would trigger additional payments to employees. Daniel (1976) found that the increase in the cost of living since the previous pay rise was by far the most important consideration for the claims of union officers in all circumstances. When inflation is accelerating, unions become still more preoccupied with securing cost-of-living increases. This can trigger off a wage-price spiral when unions overestimate future rates of inflation.

Productivity agreements   Part of the wage bargain may include the abandonment of restrictive practices, and the raising of production in return for higher wages. During the 1960s a whole series of formalized productivity agreements were concluded. The first and most celebrated of these was negotiated between Esso and the unions at the oil refinery at Fawley. A whole range of restrictive practices, including demarcation rules, excessive overtime, and time-wasting, were 'bought out' by management for higher wages. A similar agreement was signed between the British Oxygen Company and the unions covering 4,000 workers in 50 plants. Most of these productivity agreements were negotiated at plant level. In a rather less formal way it soon became accepted practice for shop stewards to 'trade' small concessions on work practices for higher wage increases. However, the statistical association between productivity and wages is less than we might expect. Wragg and Robertson (1978) in a study of eighty-two manufacturing industries between 1954 and 1973 found that changes in earnings were similar across the industries studied, but that there were marked differences in the growth of labour productivity between the industries.

The effects of collective bargaining

The process of collective bargaining has had a number of important effects on the UK labour market.

Pay differentials

Nickell and Andrews (1983) estimated that in 1979 there was a pay differential of 29% between unionized and non unionized workers, although Stewart (1981) suggested an overall trade union 'mark-up' for 1980 of only about 8%. The same author (Stewart 1987) found very little change in the trade union 'mark up' over the 1980–84 period, and this finding is supported by the work of other economists (e.g. Symons and Walker 1988). This advantage is mainly attributed to the extra payment obtained through district, local and company bargaining rather than the industry-wide settlements which they sometimes supplement.

However, the nature of the pay differential observed between union and non-union labour may be due to more than simply collective bargaining. First, union labour may be of higher quality than non-union labour, with some of the pay differential due to the higher marginal revenue product of union labour. Second, employers may raise the wages of non-union labour in an attempt to forestall unionization, thereby eroding the pay differential. Third, incomes policies imposed by governments may affect the union/non-union pay differential. Flat-rate norms which are often a part of incomes policy will compress the pay differential that union bargaining power might otherwise have secured.

In practice, the particular effect of trade unions on pay is very difficult to disentangle from those of other labour market conditions. It is interesting to note, however, that both union and non-union workers have on average been able to secure very large increases in real wages despite record levels of unemployment. This may suggest a fall in the price elasticity of demand for labour as the capital/labour ratio has increased, thereby reducing labour costs as a proportion of total costs (see above), and may also indicate a low and negative unemployment elasticity of real wages (Oswald 1986).[8] In fact, unemployed workers have perhaps ceased to exert a *permanent* influence on wage determination.

Restrictive practices and labour utilization

Flanders (1975) suggests that the process of collective bargaining reinforces the unions' perception that they have 'property rights'. These rights may include a variety of established practices which have been used to protect jobs or earnings. These practices have important consequences for labour utilization and may form part of the collective bargain. They include the closed shop, minimum manning levels, demarcation rules, seniority principles, strikes, etc. We briefly review a number of the most important 'restrictive practices'.

The closed shop   Closed shops confer a number of advantages on trade unions. First, they permit monopoly control over labour supply. This increases the unions' ability to disrupt production through industrial action, and therefore raises its 'bargaining power'. In terms of Chamberlain's ratio above, it raises the 'management cost of disagreeing', and therefore union bargaining power. Second, closed shops prevent the 'free rider' problem, whereby non-union labour benefits from union bargaining power. Third, closed shops make it easier to enforce agreements reached between unions and management. Indeed, despite restricting the freedom of employers to choose whom they will employ, the closed shop has the benefit of bringing more order and certainty to industrial relations.

The continued existence of the closed shop is threatened by existing and proposed legislation (described above). However, the fall of over 1 million workers in closed shops between 1980 and 1984 (Millward and Stevens 1987) was the result of rapidly falling employment in manufacturing industries, in which nearly a half of all union members were once covered by such agreements. About 2.6 million employees are now in closed shops, with about half of these in pre-entry closed shops (see the Employment Bill, 1990, discussed above).

Established practices   In industries such as printing, the railways, and car production, unions often have, by tradition, some control over manning levels, job speeds, the introduction of new technologies and demarcation issues. In other words, which type or grade of workers should undertake particular types of work. As a result, management decisions over the allocation of labour within an enterprise are subject to union influence.

This power has been diminished by the decline in trade union bargaining strength, including the ability of union leaders to mobilize effective action by members in support of such practices. The successful introduction of new technology and radical changes in working practices in the printing industry (as reflected in the dispute at Times Newspapers in 1986), exemplifies this weakness.

Interestingly, Daniel (1987) found that trade union opposition to investment in advanced, new technology was unusual, though highly publicized when it did occur. In fact, where there was an association between change and working practices, it was *positive*, i.e. unionized firms in the survey were *more likely* to introduce technical and other forms of change than companies where unions were not recognized.

The seniority principle   This is the principle whereby union members with the longest service in a firm are the first to be promoted and the last to be made redundant. This principle may conflict with the firm's desire to employ younger, more flexible and cheaper workers. However, companies may sometimes wish to retain senior workers having already made a substantial investment in them through specific training.

These restrictive practices may enter into the collective bargain. Unions may seek to trade them for higher wages – as in the productivity agreements noted above. Through 'buying out' restrictive practices in this way, management seeks a more efficient utilization of labour, and thereby higher productivity.

The strike weapon   One of the most powerful 'property rights' perceived by the unions is their ability to affect the collective bargain by withdrawing their labour, i.e. going on strike. This is viewed by some as the ultimate form of restrictive practice. The use of the strike weapon by unions in the UK has been the subject of much research and debate.

For much of the post-war period, stoppages in terms of their number and particularly the number of working days lost have tended to be concentrated in four broad industrial sectors: mining; engineering; shipping, transport and communications, and vehicles. However, there have been extensive and lengthy bouts of industrial action amongst white-collar workers in the public sector during the 1980s, with major disputes involving Civil Servants and teachers. Also, strikes in many industries are under-recorded because of management practice, their brevity or the small number of employees involved, and action short of strikes, e.g. overtime bans, is not adequately covered by official statistics. Nevertheless, these figures do clearly demonstrate a very substantial fall in disputes since 1979.

In 1987, there were 1,004 stoppages compared with a ten-year average for 1977–86 of 1,615. Table 20.5 shows that working days lost per thousand employees also fell significantly in the mid-1980s, but the data also indicate that this trend was widespread internationally and by no means unique to Britain. Indeed, although the *number of stoppages* has continued to fall in the UK to 770 in 1988 and 693 in 1989, the increase in the size and duration of disputes contributed to a rise in the *total number of days lost*, from 3.5 million in 1987 to 3.7 million in 1988 and 4.1 million in 1989 (*Employment Gazette*, May 1990). Working days lost per thousand employees therefore also rose, from 160 days in 1987 to 179 in 1989, prompting some commentators to claim that the late 1980s were witnessing a resurgence of industrial conflict (e.g. Beardwell 1989).

The behaviour of a number of variables has been advanced by economists as explanation for strike trends. An increase in the rate of change of unemployment is associated with the occurrence of fewer strikes, whilst increases in the rate of inflation correlate with a rise in stoppages. The level of union density is also positively related to disputes, as is increasing plant size. The relative significance of these factors varies considerably over time, but the rapid rise of unemployment combined with a fall in the inflation rate and a major decline in union density are likely to have been highly significant influences on diminished strike activity during the 1980s.

Table 20.5 Strikes: international comparisons, 1978–87 (working days lost per thousand employees)

Country	1978–82	1983–87	1978–87
United Kingdom	540	400	470
Canada	820	440	620
Denmark	120	250	190
France[1]	120	50	80
West Germany	40	50	50
Italy	1,160	510	840
Japan	20	10	10
Spain	1,110	560	850
United States[2]	200	100	150

[1] Public sector strikes excluded.
[2] Excludes strikes involving fewer than one thousand members.
Source: Employment Gazette, June 1989.

Table 20.5 demonstrates that compared to its major economic competitors the UK was marginally more strike-prone than average over the periods shown. It is often in the context of strikes that governments and employers see union 'property rights' as detrimental to Britain's economic performance, while the unions themselves perceive the withdrawal of labour as a response to the failure of management. Disputes over pay are the most common cause of stoppages, accounting for 34% of the total in 1989, followed by manning and work allocation issues (29%) and working conditions (12%), although attributing strikes to a single cause often masks the existence of other contributory factors. The threat of industrial action by a trade union may alone be sufficient to achieve its aims, but one must be careful not to overestimate its role or that of actual strike incidence in the process of bargaining. The CBI (1988) has reported that both are only rarely given as a reason for employers conceding wage increases.

Conclusion

We have seen that the trade unions play an important role in the wage-bargaining process, despite the recent decline in union density. The employers' associations and the Government are also important role-players in the process of collective bargaining. In recent years there has been a shift in the private sector from national or industry-wide bargaining to single-employer and, increasingly, establishment bargaining of a largely 'formal' nature. Wage negotiation is, however, a complex procedure, and the outcome depends upon the relative 'bargaining power' of both management and unions. Wages are also affected by a variety of 'non-market' factors, such as comparability, work conditions, cost of living, and the 'trading' of restrictive practices. Collective bargaining can have an important effect on pay differentials and may even help enshrine a variety of established (restrictive) practices which have been used to protect jobs or earnings. However, the use of the strike weapon appears to be limited to large plants in specific industrial sectors, though the fact that these are often the basic UK or export-orientated industries may still leave the UK at a disadvantage *vis-à-vis* her international competitors.

Notes

1. Trades Union Congress evidence to the Royal Commission on Trade Unions and Employers' Associations (HMSO 1968).
2. These figures exclude 21% of union members classified as covering several industrial sectors.
3. It may also refer to a Central Arbitration Committee. This is an independent national body which provides boards of arbitration for the settlement of trade disputes.
4. The marginal revenue product of labour (MRP_L) equals the marginal physical product of labour (MPP_L) times the price of output. Because of diminishing returns to labour, the MPP_L curve will eventually begin to slope downwards. This is the part of the curve reflected in Fig. 20.1, since, if MPP_L slopes downwards, so will MRP_L.
5. In Fig. 20.1 we assume the firm to be small, so that changes in its demand for labour are insignificant relative to total demand for that type of labour. As a result it can purchase all the labour it requires at the going wage rate. For this firm, the supply curve of labour can be regarded as perfectly elastic at the market wage rate. Therefore wage rate = average cost of labour = marginal cost of labour.
6. See, for example, Lipsey (1990: Ch. 27).
7. This is often called 'bilateral monopoly'. Again, see Lipsey (1990).
8. Unemployment elasticity of real wages =

$$\frac{\% \text{ change in real wages}}{\% \text{ change in unemployment}}$$

Oswald (1986: 182) estimates a coefficient of about −0.10, i.e. 'we can expect a doubling of unemployment to lower wages by (*ceteris paribus*) a little under 10%.'

References and further reading

Atkinson, J. (1984) Manpower Strategies for Flexible Organisations, *Personnel Management*, August.
Bain, G. S. and **Elsheikh, F.** (1980) Unionization in Britain: an inter-establishment analysis based on survey data, *British Journal of Industrial Relations*, **18**, 2, July.
Bain, G. S. and **Elsheikh, F.** (1982) Union growth and the business cycle: a disaggregated study, *British Journal of Industrial Relations*, **20**, 1, March.

Beardwell, I. (1989) Annual Review Article, *British Journal of Industrial Relations*, **27**, 4.

Brown, W. and **Wadhwani, S.** (1990) The Economic Effects of Industrial Relations Legislation since 1979, *NIESR Economic Review*, 131, February.

Brown, W. (ed.) (1981) *The Changing Contours of British Industrial Relations: a survey of manufacturing industry.* Blackwell, Oxford.

Cameron, S. (1987) Trade unions and productivity: theory and evidence, *Industrial Relations Journal*, **18**, 3, p. 170.

C.B.I. (1988) *The structure and processes of pay determination in the private sector.* C.B.I.

Chamberlain, N. W. (1951) *Collective Bargaining.* McGraw-Hill, New York.

Claydon, T. (1989) Union derecognition in Britain in the 1980s, *British Journal of Industrial Relations*, **27**, 2, July.

Clegg, H. (1979) *The Changing System of Industrial Relations in Great Britain.* Blackwell, Oxford.

CSO (1987) *Annual Abstract of Statistics.*

Daniel, W. W. (1976) Wage determination in industry, *Political and Economic Planning*, 563.

Daniel, W. W. (1987) *Workplace industrial relations and technical change.* Frances Pinter and PSI.

Daniel, W. W. and **Millward, N.** (1983) *Workplace Industrial Relations in Britain: Survey by the Department of Employment*, Policy Studies Institute.

Employment Gazette (1981) Feb.

Employment Gazette (1988) March.

Employment Gazette (1989) June.

Employment Gazette (1990) March.

Evans, S. (1987) The use of injunctions in industrial disputes, May 1984–April 1987, *British Journal of Industrial Relations*, **25**, 3, Nov.

Flanders, A. (1975) *Management and Unions: the theory of reform of industrial relations.* Faber and Faber.

Hawkins, K. (1981) *Trade Unions.* Hutchinson.

HMSO (1968) *Royal Commission on Trade Unions and Employers Associations 1965–8 (Chairman, Lord Donovan) Report*, Cmnd 3623.

Lipsey, R. G. (1990) *An Introduction to Positive Economics* 7th edn. Weidenfeld and Nicolson.

Millward, N. and **Stevens, M.** (1987) *British Workplace Industrial Relations, 1980–1984.* The DE/ESRC/PSI/ACAS Survey, Gower.

Nickell, S. and **Andrews, M.** (1983) Unions, real wages and employment in Britain, 1951–79, *Oxford Economic Papers* (Supplement), Nov.

Nickell, S., Wadhwani, S. and **Wall, M.** (1989) Unions and productivity growth in Britain, 1974–86. CLE Discussion Paper, Number 353.

Oswald, A. J. (1986) Wage determination and recession: a report on recent work, *British Journal of Industrial Relations*, **25**, 2, July, p. 181.

Price, R. and **Bain, G. S.** (1976) Union growth revisited, *British Journal of Industrial Relations*, **14**, 3, Nov.

Price, R. and **Bain, G. S.** (1983) Union growth in Britain: retrospect and prospects, *British Journal of Industrial Relations*, **21**, 1, March.

Smith, D. (1987) Special report, *Employment Gazette*, Dec., p. 623.

Stewart, M. (1981) *Relative Earnings and Individual Union Membership in the UK.* London School of Economics Centre for Labour Economics, University of London, discussion paper 110.

Stewart, M. (1987) Union wage differentials in the face of changes in the economic and legal environment, *University of Warwick*, mimeo.

Symons, E. and **Walker, I.** (1988) Union/non-union wage differentials 1979–84: Evidence from the FES. University of Keele mimeo.

Taylor, R. (1989) *The Fifth Estate: Britain's Unions in the Modern World.* Pan Books.

Teague, P. (1989) *The European Community: the social dimension.* Kogan Page.

Towers, B. (1989) Running the gauntlet: British Trade Unionism Under Thatcher 1979–1988, *Industrial and Labour Relations Review*, **42**, 2, Jan.

Webb, S. and **Webb, B.** (1896) *The History of Trade Unionism.* Longmans.

Wedderburn, L. (1990) *The Social Charter, European Company and employment rights.* Institute of European Rights.

Wragg, R. and **Robertson, J.** (1978) Britain's industrial performance since the war. Trends in employment, productivity, output, labour costs and prices by industry 1950–73, *Department of Employment Gazette*, **86**, 5, May.

21

Distribution of income and wealth

In this chapter we review the changes that have taken place in the distribution of income and wealth in the UK. We see that there has been some move towards greater equality in post-tax incomes, though not at every income level. We assess the usefulness of the Gini coefficient as an index of inequality, and use it to compare the income distribution of the UK with that of other countries. Income from employment is examined in some detail as this provides over 64% of all income received. Although wealth is difficult to measure, we note a progressive tendency towards a more equal distribution in the 1970s, but little change in the 1980s. This chapter concludes with a brief review of poverty in the UK.

Distribution and justice

Throughout the history of economics, the distribution of income and wealth has been a major concern. There has not only been a desire to explain the observed pattern of distribution, but also a belief that basic issues of justice and morality were involved. Positive and normative economics are therefore difficult to separate in this area.

Commutative justice

There are two main views of justice in distribution. The first may be called 'commutative justice', where it is held that each person should receive income in proportion to the value of labour and capital they have contributed to the productive process. This view underlies the ideology of the free market economy, with some economists seeking to show that commutative justice will automatically be achieved under free competition, since each factor will receive the value of its marginal product. Disparities in the distribution of income and wealth are then seen as being quite consistent with 'commutative justice'.

Distributive justice

The second view may be called 'distributive justice', where it is believed that people should receive income according to need. Given that people's needs are much the same, 'distributive justice' implies approximate equality in income distribution. This view underlies the ideology of socialism. The socialist sees the free market as a kind of power struggle, through which certain groups are exploited; hence their advocacy of various forms of social control of the economy to achieve 'distributive justice'.

Issues in distribution

In the debate about distribution, there are five specific areas of concern:

1. The distribution of income between persons, irrespective of the source of that income. Included here is income from labour (wages and salaries), and from the ownership of capital (dividend and interest) and land (rent).

2. The distribution of income between factors of production, in particular between labour and capital. Advocates of the free market believe that income accrues to labour and capital according to their relative productivity, whilst critics explain their relative shares as the outcome of a continuous conflict in which capital seeks to exploit labour, and labour to resist.

3. The distribution of earnings between different types of labour. Again, believers in the free market see differences in earnings between occupational groups as being caused by differences in relative productivity. Critics explain such differentials through the relative bargaining power of the labour groups in question.

4. The distribution of wealth. In the nineteenth century virtually all wealth was held by a small élite, who lived off the profits from it, whilst the majority lived by the 'sweat of their brows'. The injustice of this was a major spur to socialism. More recently, defenders of capitalism have argued that wealth has become progressively more evenly distributed, so that the majority benefit from profits – 'We are all capitalists now'!

5. Poverty. Free market ideologists have always acknowledged that a small minority will be unable to compete in the labour market, and will therefore be poor; so from Adam Smith onwards most economists accepted the need for some protection of the poor. Critics, however, have argued that poverty was, and remains, widespread.

In this chapter, we shall attempt to assess the facts in each of these five areas of concern, and to look more closely at the conflicting explanations. We shall start by looking at the overall distribution of income between people.

Income distribution between people

The overall picture

The most vivid illustration of income distribution is Pen's 'Parade of Dwarfs' (Pen 1971). In the course of *an hour* the entire population passes by, each person's height in relation to average height signifying their income in relation to average income. In the first minute we see only matchstick people such as women doing casual work. After ten to fifteen minutes dustmen and ticket collectors pass by, though only three feet high. After thirty minutes, when half the population has passed, skilled manual workers and senior office clerks appear, though these are still well under five feet tall. In fact we only reach the average height twelve minutes before the hour ends, when teachers, executive class civil servants, social workers and sales representatives pass by. After this, height increases rapidly. Six minutes before the end come farmers, headmasters and departmental heads of offices, standing about six feet six inches. Then come the giants: the fairly ordinary lawyer at eight feet tall, the family doctor at twenty-one feet, the chairman of a typical public company over sixty feet, and various film stars and tycoons resembling tower blocks.

This illustration demonstrates two little-understood features of the personal income distribution. First, that the mean or average income is way above median income; the median-income receiver being the person who arrives after thirty minutes, with half the population poorer and half richer. Roughly three-quarters of the population have less than the mean or average income. Put another way, the median income is only about 85% of average income. Broadly speaking, this is because at the top end there are considerable numbers of very rich people who pull the average up. Second, that amongst the top quarter of income receivers are people in fairly ordinary professions, such as teachers and sales representatives, who would perhaps be surprised to learn that the great majority of the population were significantly less well-off than themselves.

Definition of income

When we come to collect precise data about income we find various problems of definition. Should we deduct taxes and add transfer payments? Should we count capital gains as income? This latter question raises the problem of distinguishing between income which is a flow, and wealth which is a stock. Income is defined in theory, *as the amount a person could have spent whilst maintaining the value of his wealth intact*. By this definition capital gains should count as income, but for simplicity of data collection they are excluded from official tables. A further question is whether an imputed rent should be credited as income to those who own their dwelling. Again, strictly it should, as a dwelling is a potential source of income which could be spent without diminishing wealth, but for simplicity it is usually excluded. Finally, what should count as the income receiver, the individual or the household? In practice we normally use the 'tax unit' – the individual or family which is defined as one unit for tax purposes.

The problems with definitions of income were clearly seen in 1990 when the Institute of Fiscal Studies studied the whole problem of poverty, in particular those people on low incomes. The original statistics had been calculated on the *Low Income Family* (LIF) basis which uses the 'benefit unit' definition. If a household was composed of an unemployed couple and an elderly pensioner, then it was defined as *two* 'benefit' units. However the new statistics were calculated on the *Households Below Average Income* (HBAI) basis which defines the unemployed couple and pensioner as *one* unit, because the calculation is based on the household. Similarly, the new HBAI figures are based on *current* income while the old IFS used the concept of *normal* income. Finally, the ways in which the definitions of income are adjusted for family size are different. The particular definition used is very important in practical terms. The Institute of Fiscal Studies found that the newer HBAI definition resulted, in some years, in 1.13 million *fewer* people being regarded as 'poor', than would be similarly regarded using the older LIF definition.

**The Lorenz curve
and the Gini
coefficient**

The conventional means of illustrating income distribution is the Lorenz curve, shown in Fig. 21.1. The horizontal axis shows the cumulative percentage of people; the vertical axis the cumulative percentage of total income they receive. The diagonal is the 'line of perfect equality' where, say, 20% of all people receive 20% of all income.

Fig. 21.1 Lorenz curve and
Gini coefficient

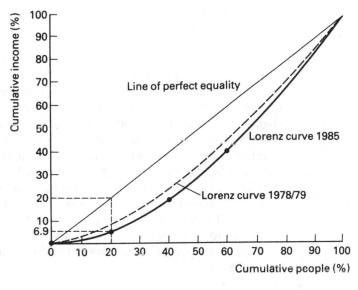

Table 21.1 presents figures for the distribution of income in the UK at selected dates since 1949. The data for 1985 are plotted in Fig. 21.1 as a continuous line, and are known as the Lorenz curve. The degree of inequality can be judged by the extent to which the Lorenz curve deviates from the diagonal. For instance, the bottom 20% only receive 6.9% of total income in 1985, so that the vertical difference between Lorenz curve and diagonal represents inequality. To assess inequality over the whole range of the income distribution, the Gini coefficient is calculated. It is the ratio of enclosed area between Lorenz curve and diagonal, to total area underneath the diagonal. If there was no inequality (i.e. perfect equality), the Lorenz

Table 21.1 Percentage
shares of income after tax in
the UK

Income receivers	1949	1970/71	1975/76	1978/79	1985
Bottom 10%	—	2.3	3.0	2.9	2.7
Bottom 20%	—	6.6	7.3	7.0	6.9
Bottom 30%	—	11.8	12.6	12.1	11.8
Bottom 40%	—	18.3	18.9	18.5	17.8
Bottom 50%	26.5	26.1	26.6	26.2	24.9
Bottom 60%	36.0	35.6	36.2	35.5	33.5
Bottom 70%	46.5	46.8	47.5	46.8	43.9
Bottom 80%	58.4	60.1	61.0	60.3	56.9
Bottom 90%	72.9	76.0	76.9	76.6	73.5
Bottom 100%	100.0	100.0	100.0	100.0	100.0
Gini coefficient	0.355	0.339	0.326	0.355	0.360

Source: CSO (1981/ 1987), Diamond Commission (1979).

curve would coincide with the diagonal, and the above ratio would be zero. If there was perfect inequality (all the income going to the last person) then the Lorenz curve would coincide with the horizontal axis until that last person, and the above ratio would be 1. The Gini coefficient therefore ranges from zero to 1 with a rise in the Gini coefficient suggesting less equality. The value of the Gini coefficient is, in fact, calculated for each year in Table 21.1.

The figures from Table 21.1, as well as confirming the conclusions we drew from Pen's 'Parade of Dwarfs', show that between 1949 and the mid-1970s the Gini coefficient consistently fell, suggesting that income distribution became progressively more equal. However, by the late 1970s, the trend was broken, with the Gini coefficient rising, i.e. less equality.

The Gini coefficient can, however, only give an overall impression. More detailed inspection shows that the bottom 20% of income receivers were slightly worse-off in 1985 with only 6.9% of income, compared to 7% in 1978/79. What has happened is that the relative position of the lower-income groups has slightly worsened, and that of some of the higher-income groups substantially improved. The top 10% received 26.5% of income in 1985 but only 23.4% in 1978/79. When one Lorenz curve lies below another *at every point* we can confidently say that a rise in the Gini coefficient must mean less equality. This appears to be the case for *all* deciles of income in 1985 as compared to 1978/79. If the Lorenz curves intersect we have to balance less equality at one part of the income distribution with greater equality at another part.

International comparisons

International comparisons are difficult to make as there are different definitions of income, and different methods of collecting data in the various countries. However, in 1975 Shail Jain, on behalf of the World Bank, compiled data from eighty nations (Jain 1975). In this study the Gini coefficient for East Germany, a Communist state, was the lowest at 0.204, suggesting that it had the most equal income distribution, with other Communist bloc states having similar figures. Japan at 0.288 was more equal than the UK (see Table 21.1); though the UK (at 0.339) was more equal than West Germany (0.394) and the USA (0.404). Indeed the UK income distribution appears to be more equal than that of almost all other Western nations. Perhaps not surprisingly India, with its Gini coefficient of 0.478, had one of the least-equal income distributions, with the top 10% of income receivers having over one-third of total income. Again the fact that the Lorenz curves intersect for many of these cross-country comparisons should make us cautious in drawing conclusions from the Gini coefficient figures.

Income distribution between factors of production

Definition of factors

In analysing the share of income between labour, capital and land there are initial problems of definition. First, under labour do we include workers and managers, thereby combining wages and salaries, since both are paid in return for work? Some argue that salaries for managers include a profit element, since they exert direct control over capital and they carry entrepreneurial risks. In practice it is impossible to separate any profit element in salaries, and payments to workers and managers are counted together. More difficult is the income of the self-employed, since this undoubtedly includes payment for both labour and capital services; a separate category is, in fact, usually made for the self-employed.

Measurement of factor shares

Table 21.2 shows pre-tax income to various factors as a percentage of total income. The share for labour has tended to increase, at least until recently. It has been estimated that at the beginning of the century labour's share was only 50%. This increase has not, however, been at the expense of profits but of rent, which has declined from about 25% to a negligible proportion (part of 'other income' in Table 21.2). This follows mainly from the decline in the relative importance of agriculture, and the rise in owner-occupation of dwellings. It is, however, of note that high levels of unemployment since 1981, and a sustained upturn in the economy, have contributed to a significant shift of income away from employment and towards corporate profit. The privatization programme has also reduced the share of public corporations and general government enterprises, and raised that of companies.

Table 21.2 Factor shares as a percentage of total income

	1973	1977	1981	1989
Income from employment	66.9	67.2	69.1	64.5
Income from self-employment	10.2	8.4	8.4	10.9
Gross trading profits				
Companies	12.5	13.0	10.9	15.2
Public corporations and				
General government enterprises	3.1	3.8	3.3	1.5
Other income	7.3	7.6	8.3	7.8
	100.0	100.0	100.0	100.0

* Rent income, and an imputed charge for consumption of non-trading capital.
Source: CSO (1983, 1990a).

One may question the importance of factor shares in overall income distribution. If it was the case that all income from self-employment, profits and rent went to a small group, the very rich, then even though only 35.4% of income could possibly come from these sources in 1989 (Table 21.2), it would still be a major cause of inequality. In fact, these sources of income are enjoyed by *all* groups, although there is a bias in favour of the very rich. The richest 1% received 28.2% of their income from self-employment, and 20.5% from investment and occupational pensions. The top 25% received 8% of their income from self-employment, and 6.3% from investment and occupational pensions. However, the bottom 25%, though receiving only 2.3% of their income from self-employment, gained as much as 10.2% from investments and occupational pensions. Thus profits, however defined, are arguably not the major cause of income inequality.

There are two main types of theoretical explanation of factor shares. The first emphasizes the role of market forces and starts with a microeconomic analysis of factor markets. If there is perfect competition in goods and factor markets, each factor will receive precisely its marginal revenue product; in other words, it will receive income in proportion to its productive value. The rising share to the factor labour would be viewed from this standpoint as reward for a greater contribution to production.

An alternative approach has been to explain factor shares in terms of power. Marx saw capitalists as exploiting labour, receiving 'surplus value' from the fact that the efforts of workers yield returns over and above their wages. Marx believed that this exploitation would increase as production became more capital-intensive and labour was displaced, creating a pool of unemployment which would depress wages, and therefore the share of labour in National Income. Eventually, the decline in people's ability to purchase the output of the capitalist factories, combined with the workers' resentment at their poverty, would cause crisis and revolution.

Neither theory is wholly adequate. Assumptions, such as perfect competition in labour markets, required by orthodox theory are clearly unrealistic (see Ch. 20). Similarly, Marx's prediction of a declining wage and factor share for labour has not been fulfilled.

The earnings distribution

Since over 64% of total income accrues to the factor labour (Table 21.2), it follows that differing returns to the various factors (labour, capital or land) are unlikely to be the main explanation of income inequality. Rather, we must turn our attention to variations in income between different groups *within* the factor labour, i.e. the earnings distribution.

Earnings by occupation

Table 21.3 shows the relative earnings of the main occupational groups, each figure representing the average earnings of that group as a percentage of overall average male earnings. Not surprisingly, non-manual workers in general receive significantly more than manual workers. But there are exceptions to this. For example, occupations involved in processing, making and repairing metal and electrical items are better paid than clerical occupations. Indeed, a more detailed analysis reveals that certain groups, such as coalminers and printworkers, receive pay approximately equivalent to that of many managerial and professional groups, such as teachers and nurses.

A hidden source of inequality between occupations is the difference in value of fringe benefits and pension entitlement. The Diamond Commission (1979) found that this typically adds 36% to the pre-tax salary of a senior manager, and 18% to that of a foreman, whilst unskilled workers enjoy little or no such benefits.

Earnings by sex

Table 21.4 shows female earnings in relation to male earnings. The position of women has improved significantly during the 1970s – a period which saw the introduction of equal pay legislation – though women continued to earn substantially less than men. The momentum towards equal pay seems to have slowed down during the 1980s, with the earnings of both manual and non-manual females making little further progress as compared to males.

Table 21.3 Earnings of occupational groups. Average (gross weekly) earnings of full-time male employees in selected occupations, as a percentage of average (gross weekly) earnings of all full-time male employees

Non-manual	
Professional, in management and administration	153
Literary, artistic, sport	125
Professional, in science, engineering and technology	120
Managerial	120
Professional, in education, welfare and health care	120
Security and protective services	103
Selling	90
Clerical	80
Manual	
Processing, making and repairing (metal and electrical)	91
Making and repairing (excl. metal and electrical)	82
Materials processing (excl. metal)	80
Transport operating	78
General labourers	68
Catering, cleaning, hairdressing	62
Farming and fishing	60

Source: Department of Employment (1990).

Table 21.4 Average female earnings as a percentage of average male earnings

	1970	1976	1989
Manual	50	62	61
Non-manual	51	61	60

Source: CSO (1988b); Department of Employment (1990).

Explanation of earnings differentials

In seeking to explain the earnings distribution there are two main theoretical approaches, similar to those we considered above for factor shares.

The first, the 'market theory', starts from an assumption of equality in *net advantages* for all jobs, i.e. that money earnings *and* the money value placed on working conditions are equal for all jobs. It also assumes that labour has a high degree of occupational and geographical mobility, so that if there is any inequality in net advantages, labour will move to the more advantageous jobs until equality is restored. Thus, differences in actual earnings must be caused by compensating differences in other advantages. Job satisfaction is one compensating advantage: enjoyable or safe jobs will be paid less than irksome or risky ones; this may partly explain the high earnings of miners. Still more important are differences in training. Training and education are regarded as investments in 'human capital', in which the individual forfeits immediate earnings, and bears the cost of training, in the prospect of higher future earnings; this may in part explain the high earnings of professional groups. Market theory therefore proposes that relative occupational earnings reflect non-monetary advantages between occupations, and the varying length and cost of required training.

Proponents of this theory agree that it is not wholly adequate, and would recognize differences in natural ability as also affecting earnings. However others, whilst still broadly advocating market theory, have suggested a more fundamental objection, namely that labour is in fact highly immobile. An extensive study by Atkinson *et al.* (1983) found a significant relationship between the earnings of fathers in the 1950s and their sons in the 1970s. On average, the sons' earnings were found to be half-way between the fathers and the national average. The more geographically mobile sons had fared best, in that their earnings were less influenced by that of their fathers. Of those who had improved on their fathers' earnings, 39% had left their home city. Of those who were doing the same or worse than their fathers, only 19% had moved away. Clearly, a combination of social, occupational and geographical immobility has a significant effect on the earnings distribution, contrary to the simple predictions of market theory.

The second theoretical approach places 'immobility' at the very centre of its analysis. This approach sees the labour market as 'segmented', i.e. one which is divided into a series of largely separate (non-competing) occupational groups, with earnings determined by bargaining power *within* each group. Some groups, especially professional bodies, have control over the supply of labour to their occupations, so that they can limit supply and maintain high earnings. Other occupational groups have differing degrees of unionization and industrial power. The relatively high earnings of printworkers and coalminers may be explained in part by their history of effective and forceful collective bargaining, whilst the fragmented nature of agricultural and catering work may have contributed to their low pay. In this approach bargaining power is held to outweigh the effects of free market forces.

These two theoretical approaches to the distribution of earnings need not be regarded as mutually exclusive. Market theory can itself be used to analyse bargaining power, with professional bodies and trade unions affecting the supply of labour, and the elasticity of labour demand determining the employment effects of their activities. More fundamentally, it may be suggested that labour, whilst fairly immobile in the short run, is highly mobile in the long run. Thus, whilst the exertion of bargaining power may affect differentials in the short run, in the long run labour will move in response to market forces, and thereby erode such differentials.

The above attempts to explain the presence of wage differentials did not explicitly seek to clarify the reasons for earnings differentials by *sex*, so clearly shown in Table 21.4. Such differentials could be due, for example, to some element of *discrimination* which might exist in the labour market between men and women, even though they were identical workers. For instance, until December 1975, when it was made illegal, collective agreements between employers and employees often included clauses which prescribed that female wage rates should not exceed a certain proportion of the male wage. The examples of wage differentials noted above were made possible because of the preponderance of males in most unions. The state has also been active in allowing this wage differential to exist. For example, up to 1970 when the Equal Pay Act was passed, the police pay structure provided for a differential wage structure for men and women up to the rank of ordinary sergeant, while the pay structure for more senior sergeant ranks included only male rates. Obviously, female policewomen were felt to be only able to achieve the lower grades and even here were not seen as of equal value to males (Tzannatos 1990).

On the other hand the observed differentials could be regarded as being due to *genuine differences* which exist (or are perceived to exist) between male and female labour. For instance it is often observed that employers make certain assumptions about the 'average' female worker, i.e. as being one who will not be working for long before leaving to have a child. As a result, employers may be more reluctant to train female workers, who are then placed at a disadvantage as compared to their male counterparts. By acquiring fewer skills, the female worker inevitably receives less pay. Again, female workers are often constrained in competing with male workers by the need to seek employment in the catchment area of their husbands' employment. Such restrictions can again result in a lower wage as compared to that received by the more mobile male counterpart.

Whatever the causes of wage differentials between males and females, there is no doubt that they still exist, even after the initial improvements in the early 1970s following the Equal Pay Act of 1970 and the Sex Discrimination Act of 1975.

Distribution of wealth

Definition and data collection

Wealth is notoriously difficult to define. The most obvious forms of wealth are land, housing, stocks and shares and other financial assets. In addition, many households hold several thousands of pounds-worth of durable goods: a car, carpets and furnishings, electrical goods and so on. All these together are known as 'marketable wealth'. But many ordinary families, whilst owning little land and few shares, may have substantial pension rights. In the case of private schemes these usually derive from contributions into a fund, which in turn is used to buy assets; whilst in the state scheme it derives from contributions which entitle people to future income from government revenues.

There are also considerable problems in obtaining information about wealth. Britain has no wealth tax, and so no regular wealth valuations are made. Attempts have been made to do this via sample surveys, but people are often reluctant to reveal their economic circumstances in sufficient detail to draw reliable conclusions. The only time that wealth *is* publicly evaluated is when substantial amounts are transferred from one person to another, usually at death, when wealth is assessed for capital transfer tax. By analysing these figures in terms of age and sex, it is possible to take the dead as a sample of the living, and so estimate the overall wealth distribution. Of course, there is an obvious likelihood of sampling error, especially in estimating the wealth of the young. The procedure also ignores certain bequests, such as those to surviving spouses, which are not liable to tax. Nevertheless, it is the best method available.

Concentration of wealth

Table 21.5 shows the Inland Revenue's estimate of the overall wealth distribution. As one would expect, wealth is much more unequally distributed than income. For example, the top 10% own 36% of wealth (Table 21.5), but receive only 26.5% of income (Table 21.1); whilst the bottom 50% own only 17% of wealth, but receive around 25% of income. If

Table 21.5 Ownership of
marketable wealth plus
occupational and state
pension rights

Percentage of wealth owned by:	1971	1976	1987
Most wealthy 1% of population	21	14	11
Most wealthy 5% of population	37	27	24
Most wealthy 10% of population	49	37	35
Most wealthy 25% of population	71	61	61
Most wealthy 50% of population	87	85	85

Source: CSO (1985, 1990b).

we *exclude* pension rights the picture becomes much more extreme: the most wealthy 1% own almost one-quarter of *marketable* wealth (i.e. excluding occupational and state pension rights), the richest 10% almost 60%, whilst the poorest half of the population have only 6%.

But perhaps more significant than the absolute figures is the astonishingly rapid reduction in inequality, especially in the early 1970s. The wealth of the richest 1% fell in five years from 21 to 14% of the total, whilst for the richest 10% it fell from 49 to 37% (Table 21.5). This reflects the high rate of inflation in those years, which rapidly eroded the value of financial assets, and also the steep decline in the prices of stocks and shares and commercial land. Over a much longer period we observe a steady reduction in wealth inequality. In 1924 the wealthiest 1% owned 60% of *marketable* wealth (i.e. excluding pension rights); this had fallen to 42% in 1951, and is now 18%. A major reason for this has been death duties, and more recently capital transfer tax (inheritance tax). This is a progressive tax, and helps break up the largest wealth holdings as they pass from one generation to another.

Despite the continuing influences of these factors, changes in the distribution of wealth have been much more modest in the 1980s, as can be observed from Table 21.5. Recently, however, it has been argued that 'new wealth' is being created in the UK as the rapid spread of home ownership and the rise in house prices means that inheriting such properties may allow both middle and working class people to benefit in the future. The percentage of UK households owning their own homes is predicted to rise from 56% in 1980 to 73% by 1995 and bequests involving land and buildings are likely to double from £7.2bn in 1990 to £14bn by 1995. Although this may improve the wealth situation of many middle and working class income earners, it will create even more problems for the children of the 25% or more parents who may never own their own homes. It may also further increase the regional disparity of wealth as a result of regional house price differentials (*Sunday Times* 1990).

Though it is an emotive issue, one may doubt that the wealth distribution is a primary source of income inequality. We have already seen that the main source of income inequality is not between capital and labour, but between different groups of labour.

Poverty

Definition

There has been much debate as to the definition of poverty. Some have tried to define it in *absolute* terms. For example, Rowntree (1901), who made a major study of poverty at the turn of the century, concluded that poverty was having insufficient income to obtain the minimum means necessary for survival, namely basic food, housing and clothing. Others have sought to define it in *relative* terms: Townsend (1973) in his survey of poverty, saw it as the inability to participate in the customary activities of society, which today might include taking an annual holiday away from home, owning a refrigerator, having sole use of an indoor WC, and so on.

On a more practical level the 'official' poverty level (defined as the minimum acceptable income level) used by many researchers in the UK is given by the level of Income Support. On the other hand, the Child Poverty Action Group has defined the 'margins of poverty' as those people whose incomes are below Income Support plus 40%. Income Support is set by governments, and may be affected not only by the needs of the poor, but also by general political policy. It also ignores other aspects of economic deprivation not directly related to money income, such as inadequate housing, schools, health care and such like. However, the Income Support level has the advantage of being definite, and figures are readily available.

The Council of Europe also has a measure of minimum income which they call the 'decency level'; this is set at 68% of the average earnings of men and women in the country in question. These various measures, together with the information on poverty which can be obtained from government statistics (such as in Table 21.1), give a good general picture of low income and poverty, but often fail to account for other forms of poverty, such as those frequently shown in statistics of homelessness or of health.

Incidence of poverty

When we look at some of these suggested measures of poverty we find some disturbing results. Table 21.6 shows that the number of people *receiving* Income Support (called supplementary benefit until 1988) has varied from 3.0m in 1978 to a very high level of 4.8m in 1987, before the fall in unemployment eased the situation to 4.2m by the end of the 1980s.

Table 21.6 Number receiving supplementary benefit (now income support)

	1978 (Feb.) ('000s)	1987 (Nov.) ('000s)	1989 (Nov.) ('000s)
Pensioners	1,735	1,735	1,729
Unemployed	678	1,817	1,036
Sick and disabled	222	376	} 1,519
Others	382	906	
Total	3,017	4,834	4,284

Source: CSO (1988a and 1990c).

If we add to these figures the people who *depend upon* these benefits, e.g. children, then the total number dependent on these benefits in 1989 was probably over 6m people, or 10% of the total population. If we take the poverty definition based on Income Support level, then we would find that in 1989 an unemployed worker with a wife and two children aged 5 and 15, would receive around £80 per week or only 33% of the average gross weekly wage in the UK. If we take the wider 'margins of poverty' definition, then the figure for the same family would be 49% of average gross income. Finally, taking the even wider 'decency' level set by the Council of Europe, we find that in 1989 the income necessary to stay above the decency line would be £162 per week, which was over twice the Income Support level shown above. In fact, as much as 30% of those actually *in work* in the UK earned less than this decency level!

More recent figures calculated from government statistics by the Institute of Fiscal Studies give a clearer picture of the problem of low income and poverty. They showed that during the recession of 1981–85, the increase in real income of the *total population* (after adjusting for costs of housing) rose by 5.4% on average. However, the real income of the *bottom 20% of income earners* increased by only 2.6%, or half that of the total population (House of Commons 1989/90). In 1990, a re-calculation of Government figures for the period 1979 to 1987 showed that, after adjusting for the cost of housing, *average* real incomes rose by 23.1%, but that the real incomes of the *bottom 10%* of earners *fell* by 5.7%. Further figures for the same period showed that in 1979, 4.9m people, or 10% of the working population, were earning *below half* the average income. By 1987 this figure had risen to 10.5m or 19.4% of the population. More disturbing still was the fact that over the same period, the proportion of UK children living in households whose earnings were less than half the average income, more than doubled, to stand at nearly 26% by 1987 (Prowse 1990).

Other indications of poverty are figures of homelessness and the figures for the 1980s are given below (Table 21.7). Homeless households in 'priority need', such as those households with dependent children, increased by 46% between 1983 and 1988, with those in 'temporary accommodation' rising by 191%. Such homelessness is often bound up with unemployment, low income and social class which, in turn, affects other variables. For example, the average infant death rate (deaths between the age of 0 and 1 yr old per thousand live births) is 10.7 for the families of partly skilled and unskilled manual workers, but only around 7 for families of professional and non-manual workers. Poverty clearly involves a complicated set of interrelated factors.

Table 21.7 Homelessness in the UK ('000's)

	1983	1984	1985	1986	1987	1988
Homeless Households in priority need	84	89	102	112	118	123
In temporary accommodation	11	14	17	22	27	32

Source: CSO (1990b).

Conclusion

There has been some move towards greater equality in post-tax incomes, though not at all points of the distribution. In fact, since the mid-1970s there has been greater inequality at both the bottom and the top of the income distribution. Income from employment provides over 64% of all income received, and must be a focus for any attempt to explain the inequality that does exist. Variations in income by occupation and by sex clearly contribute to such inequality. Wealth is more unequally distributed than income, and although there has been a progressive tendency towards a more equal distribution since the early 1970s, this process slowed down markedly in the 1980s. Poverty is a serious and growing phenomenon, no matter how we define it.

References

Atkinson, A. B., Maynard, A. K., and **Trinder, C. G.** (1983) *Parents and Children*. Heinemann.
CSO (1981) *Economic Trends*, Feb.
CSO (1983) *Economic Trends*, Jan.
CSO (1985) *Economic Trends*.
CSO (1987) *Economic Trends*, Nov.
CSO (1988a) *Monthly Digest of Statistics*, April.
CSO (1988b) *Social Trends*, 15.
CSO (1988c) *Monthly Digest of Statistics*, April.
CSO (1990a) *Economic Trends*, June.
CSO (1990b) *Social Trends*, 20.
CSO (1990c) *Monthly Digest of Statistics*, June.
Department of Employment (1987) *New Earnings Survey*.
Diamond Commission (1979) *Royal Commission on the Distribution of Income and Wealth*. Cmnd 7679.
House of Commons (1989/90) *Social Services Committee*, 4th Report, Paper 376.
Jain, S. (1975) *Size Distribution of Income*. World Bank, Washington, DC.
Pen, J. (1971) *Income Distribution*. Pelican.
Prowse, M. (1990) Why Britain's Poor Deserve a Break, *Financial Times*, 13 Aug.
Rowntree, S. (1901) *Poverty – a study of town life*. Macmillan.
Sunday Times (1990) *Families Growing Rich on Inheritance Bonanza*, 29 July.
Townsend, P. (1973) *The Social Minority*. Allen Lane.
Tzannatos, Z. (1990) *Sex Differences in the Labour Market*, Economic Review, May.

22

Exchange rates

The exchange rate is the price of one currency in terms of another. The exchange rate for sterling is conventionally defined as the number of units of another currency, such as the dollar, that it takes to purchase one pound sterling on the foreign exchange market. In the market, however, it is usually quoted as the number of units of the domestic currency that it takes to purchase one unit of foreign currency. In general terms the sterling exchange rate is perhaps the most important 'price' in the UK economic system. It affects the standard of living, because it determines how many goods we can get for what we sell abroad. It influences the price of UK exports and hence their sales, thereby determining output and jobs in the export industries. It structures the extent to which imports can compete with home-produced goods, and thereby affects the viability of UK companies. Because the price of imports enters into the RPI any variation in the exchange rate will have an immediate effect on the rate of inflation. This chapter will consider these various issues.

The foreign exchange market

The foreign exchange market is the money market on which international currencies are traded. It has no physical existence: it consists of traders, such as the dealing rooms of major banks, who are in continual communication with one another on a worldwide basis. Currencies are bought and sold on behalf of clients, who may be companies, private individuals, or banks themselves. A distinction is made between the 'spot' rate for a currency, and the forward rate. The spot rate is the domestic currency price of a unit of foreign exchange when the transaction is to be completed within three days. The forward rate is the price of that unit when delivery is to take place at some future date – usually 30, 60 or 90 days hence. Both spot and forward rates are determined in today's market; the relationship between today's spot and today's forward rate will be determined largely by how the market expects the spot rate to move in the near future. The more efficient the market is at anticipating future spot rates, the closer will today's forward rate be to the future spot rate.

The spot market is used by those who wish to acquire foreign exchange straightaway. Forward markets are used by three groups of people. There are firstly those who wish to cover themselves ('hedge') against the risk of exchange rate variation. For instance, suppose an importer orders goods to be paid for in three months' time in dollars. All his calculations will be upset if the price of dollars rises between now and payment date. He can cover himself by buying dollars today for delivery in three months' time; he thus

look see 6

locks himself into a rate which reduces the risk element in his transaction. Secondly there are *arbitrageurs* who attempt to make a profit on the difference between interest rates in one country and another, and who buy or sell currency forward to ensure that the profit which they hope to make by moving their capital is not negated by adverse exchange rate movements. And thirdly there are staightforward speculators who use the forward markets to buy or sell in anticipation of exchange rate changes. For instance, if I think that today's forward rates do not adequately reflect the probability of the dollar increasing in value I will buy dollars forward, hoping to sell them at a profit when they are delivered to me at some future date.

London is the world's largest centre for foreign exchange trading, with an average daily turnover of US $187 billion. The market is growing all the time. Some 64% of transactions are 'spot' on any one day, 24% are forward for periods not exceeding one month, and 10% are forward for longer than one month (*Bank of England Quarterly Bulletin* 1989). Increasingly, however, more sophisticated types of transactions are being done. For instance, there is a growth in the following types of transactions:

1. Foreign currency options, which give the right (but do not impose an obligation) to buy or sell currencies at some future date and price,

2. Foreign currency futures, which are standardized contracts to buy or sell on agreed terms on specific future dates,

3. Foreign currency swaps – spot purchases against outright forward currency sales.

Foreign exchange market business in London is done in an increasingly wide variety of currencies: £/$ business accounts for 27% of activity, and DM/$ for a further 22%. However trading transactions which do not involve the US dollar are becoming increasingly frequent.

Prices of currencies are determined, as on any other market, by supply of, and demand for the various currencies. Businessmen wishing to import goods will sell sterling in order to buy currency with which to pay the supplier in another country. Tourists coming to the UK will sell their own currency in order to buy sterling. Other types of transactions, too, will have exchange rate repercussions. For instance, if a German company wishes to buy a factory in the UK it will need to convert marks into sterling, as will foreign banks who wish to make sterling deposits in London, or residents abroad who wish to buy UK government bonds.

Another way of saying this is to say that in any given period of time the factors which determine the demand and supply for foreign exchange are those which are represented in the balance of payments account (Table 22.1). The demand for foreign exchange arises as a result of imports of goods and services, overseas investment (short and long term), and additions to official reserves. The supply of foreign exchange comes as a result of the export of goods and services, inflows of foreign capital and the running down of official reserves.

It will be clear from Table 22.1 that companies and individuals are not the only clients of foreign exchange market dealers. The Bank of England also buys and sells foreign currency, using the official reserves in the Exchange

Table 22.1 The balance of payments 1989 (£m.)

A. *Current account*	
1. Exports of goods	95,526
2. Imports of goods	115,638
3. Visible balance (1 – 2)	−23,112
4. Net services	3,980
5. Interest, profits, dividends	3,008
6. Net transfers	−4,727
7. Invisible balance (4 + 5 + 6)	2,261
Current balance (3 + 7)	−20,851
B. *Capital account (Transactions in assets and liabilities)*	
8. UK investment overseas	
Direct	−19,164
Portfolio	−37,023
9. Lending abroad by UK banks	−27,274
10. Other lending abroad	−5,361
11. Official reserves	5,439
12. Other external assets of govt	−942
13. Total transactions in assets (8 + 9 + 10 + 11 + 12)	−84,324
14. Overseas investment in the UK	
Direct	15,848
Portfolio	12,066
15. Borrowing abroad by UK banks	43,021
16. Other borrowing from abroad	17,428
17. Other external liabilities of govt	1,470
18. Total transactions in liabilities (14 + 15 + 16 + 17)	89,834
Capital account balance (13 + 18)	5,511
Balancing item (equal to current account balance + capital account balance)	−15,340

Source: CSO (1990b).

Equalization Account. In order to reflect on why this might be the case we have to remember that governments have an interest in the level of the exchange rate, and that they may on occasion wish to intervene in the workings of the foreign exchange market to affect the value of sterling. Historically the policy stance on this has varied. As Chapter 27 indicates, it was only after the Second World War that foreign exchange markets began to function freely on a worldwide basis. Governments then had the option of allowing exchange rates to be market-determined, i.e. to 'float', or to establish some kind of fixed exchange rate system. The decision was taken at Bretton Woods in 1945 to adopt a fixed exchange rate regime; governments thus committed themselves to continual intervention in the market in order to offset imbalances in the demand and supply for their currencies. The Bretton Woods agreement collapsed in 1972, since when currencies have been allowed to float. However, for various reasons governments continue to 'manage' the floating exchange rate system by intervening in the foreign exchange market. In the UK the Bank of England deals in this market in order to smooth out short-term fluctuations in the value of sterling as well as to influence the exchange rate as part of its overall economic strategy. Whereas in the 1950s and 1960s the exchange rate was a policy objective, it is now a policy instrument, because the price of imports enters into the Retail Price Index and hence influences the rate of inflation. However, intervention in the market alone is insufficient to affect the sterling exchange rate, simply because the size of speculative trading on the world's foreign exchange markets dwarfs the size of any one country's official reserves. Governments must therefore attempt to increase the demand for their currencies by, for instance, attracting flows of short or longer-term investment from abroad by means of high interest rates.

We have argued that in everyday terms currency prices are determined by demand and supply on the foreign exchange markets. We must now examine in more detail the forces determining any given exchange rate in the short and long term. As we shall see, all the various theoretical explanations focus on the importance of one or other of the variables outlined in Table 22.1. The theories vary only in the time perspective considered. The function of theory is to explain and predict; we shall consider later to what extent recent experience in the UK validates the different theoretical arguments.

Exchange rate definitions

Before we do this, however, we must consider what we mean by 'the exchange rate'. In a foreign exchange market where exchange rates are allowed to 'float', every currency has a price against every other currency. In order to allow for measurability economists use three separate concepts:

1. *The nominal rate of exchange.* This is the rate of exchange for any one currency as quoted against any other currency.

2. *The effective exchange rate* (*EER*). This is a measure which takes into account the fact that sterling varies differently against each of the other currencies. It is calculated as a weighted average of the individual or bilateral rates, and expressed as an index number. The weights are chosen to reflect the importance of other currencies in manufacturing trade with the UK.

3. *The real exchange rate* (*RER*). This concept is designed to measure the rate at which home goods exchange for goods from other countries, rather than the rate at which the currencies themselves are traded. It is thus essentially a measure of competitiveness. It is defined as:

$$RER = EER \times P\,(\text{UK})/P(\text{F})$$

In other words, the real exchange rate is equal to the effective exchange rate multiplied by the price ratio of home, $P(\text{UK})$, to foreign, $P(\text{F})$, goods. If UK prices rise the real exchange rate will rise unless the effective exchange rate falls. We shall return later to the question of how one might measure this definition empirically.

Exchange rate determination

We can distinguish four theoretical approaches to exchange rate determination (*Midland Bank Review* 1985). It must be emphasized that these are in no sense 'competing' theories. They are simply different ways of looking at what determines the exchange rate, depending on whether we are interested in the short run or the long run, in immediate or more fundamental determinants, and on what we consider to be the most empirically relevant factors at any given time.

Exchange rates

Exchange rates and the balance of trade

Fig. 22.1 The foreign exchange market

The *traditional* approach sees the exchange rate simply as the price which brings into equilibrium the demand and supply for currency arising from trade in goods and services and from capital transactions, as explained above. This approach was formulated in the 1950s when capital flows were small in relation to trade flows, and hence its major use is to illustrate the interrelationship between current account flows and exchange rate changes. Nevertheless, it can also accommodate capital account transactions. It is essentially a perspective which concentrates on short-run influences.

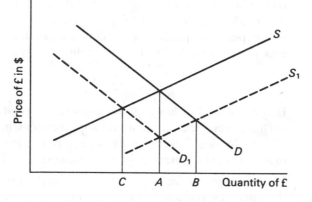

Fig. 22.1 shows that the demand for pounds will increase as the price falls. This is because customers abroad will perceive that the price of UK exports has fallen in their own currency as sterling depreciates, increasing their demand for UK exports and therefore for pounds with which to buy them. The supply of pounds will rise as the price of sterling rises because the price of imports in sterling falls as the pound strengthens. With cheaper imports, UK consumers now buy more imported items and firms exchange more pounds in order to buy these imports.[1]

Demand and supply curves can shift for a number of reasons. A shift in supply from S to S_1 might be due to a change in tastes in favour of foreign goods. A shift in demand from D to D_1 might occur because UK interest rates had fallen, leading to a decrease in the demand for pounds as investors switch their funds out of the UK money markets. In either of these cases there will be a fall in the exchange rate. In a floating exchange rate system the rate will be allowed to fall. Should the monetary authorities wish to keep the exchange rate at its original level they will be obliged to buy sterling. If the supply of sterling increases they will buy up the excess quantity AB: if the demand for sterling has fallen they will make up the shortfall by buying up quantity CA. In either case the price reverts to its original level.

This view of exchange rate determination predicts that the exchange rate will alter in response to macroeconomic policy, because the demand for imports (and hence the supply of pounds) will depend in part on the level of income. Fiscal policy will thus affect the exchange rate. It also regards short-term capital flows (and hence both demand and supply of pounds) as being sensitive to interest rate changes. Both fiscal and monetary policy will therefore have exchange rate repercussions. Expansionary policies, whether fiscal or monetary, which raise levels of income and employment, will cause the S curve to shift to S_1, as imports rise with income. Such policies will cause a balance of payments deficit and a fall in the exchange rate. The converse will be the case when policies are contractionary. In addition, in so far as fiscal and monetary policies alter interest rates (if, for instance the PSBR is reduced so that bond prices rise and yields fall, or interest rates are reduced by the monetary authorities) capital outflows will be triggered – D will fall to D_1 as investment in UK money markets is no longer forthcoming, S will move to S_1 as people move their money out of UK financial markets.

What this model does not enable us to do is to predict the overall effect of any given policy stance. In the case of an expansionary monetary policy spending will increase and interest rates will fall, the supply of pounds will increase in both cases and the exchange rate will fall. But in the case of fiscal policy, expansion may be associated with an increase in government borrowing, which will lead to a fall in bond prices (as the supply of bonds increases) and a rise in the interest rate. The effect on the exchange rate will then be ambiguous, depending on the marginal propensity to import in relation to the interest elasticity of capital flows.

We have seen how the traditional explanation of exchange rate determination is based on balance of payments flows. However, there is also a 'feedback' effect in that these flows, in particular flows of imports and exports, are themselves partly determined by the level of the exchange rate. Suppose that an exogenous disturbance, such as a change in government policy, leads to a balance of payments deficit and a consequent fall in the exchange rate. Since the demand for exports and imports is dependent on their price, will the new exchange rate level result in a further deterioration in the balance of payments and a further fall in the exchange rate, or will the balance of payments improve and the exchange rate return to its former level?

The answer to this question depends on the elasticities of demand for imports and exports. The 'elasticities' approach to balance of payments adjustment predicts that if the sum of the elasticities of demand for imports and exports is greater than 1 (the Marshall–Lerner condition) then the balance between the change in export earnings and import expenditure will be such as to improve the balance of payments, and the exchange rate will rise in consequence. In practice this principle as it stands is not empirically useful for the following reasons:

1. Trade adjustments take time. The exchange rate may adjust instantaneously, but traders take time to adjust their orders. The initial effect of a depreciation may therefore be to make the deficit larger as export demand is slow to increase at new lower prices, and importers fail to cut back their purchases. There will thus be a 'J-curve' effect as the balance of payments worsens before it improves. At the time of the UK devaluation of 1967 it was estimated that it was only in the second year after the devaluation that the gain in export volume offset the loss in revenue due to lower export prices.

2. In a floating exchange rate regime exchange rates will alter again in the time it takes for these adjustments to be made. Stability is therefore unlikely to occur.

3.   The analysis takes no account of supply conditions. In a full employment situation it may not be possible to cope with the increased demand both for exports and for import-competing goods, so that the beneficial effect of a depreciation may not be realized because of supply constraints.

4.   The fall in the exchange rate will increase home prices, because import prices have risen, and may therefore cause an inflation which will wipe out the positive balance of payments effects of the devaluation. It was estimated that by 1972 the UK had lost the gain from the 1967 devaluation because of the effect of rising inflation.

5.   It is assumed that only prices determine trade flows. In fact, there are several reasons why trade flows may be unresponsive to exchange rate changes. Quality and product differentiation are often more important in determining trade flows than prices (see Ch. 23).

6.   The analysis takes no account of the effect of exchange rate changes on capital flows. If these latter are quantitatively unimportant this does not matter, but since they currently play a very large part in exchange rate determination the usefulness of the elasticities approach is weakened.

The 'traditional' analysis of exchange rate determination, which sees exchange rates as a function of the current balance of payments position, became less useful as historical circumstances changed. Two major developments after the 1950s made it necessary to consider alternative theoretical approaches.

One of these was the growing importance of capital flows in the balance of payments accounts. These flows of international investment were partly caused by capital formation by multinational companies (see Ch. 7) but were also due to increasing preferences by asset holders for holding foreign assets as capital restrictions were eased. The last of these restrictions vanished in 1979 when the UK abolished exchange control. This development made it necessary to formulate explanations of exchange rate determination which took account of monetary factors and international portfolio choice behaviour.

The other, later, development was the advent of worldwide inflation in the 1970s. The traditional view outlined earlier took no account of internal price changes when analysing exchange rate variations. In fact, in an inflationary situation internal and external price changes are interactive.

These two developments led to the *monetary* and *portfolio* approaches to exchange rate determination on the one hand, and to the revival of the *purchasing power parity* (PPP) theory on the other. Because the monetary and portfolio approach hinges on the validity of the PPP theory, we deal first with purchasing power parity.

Purchasing power parity

This theory originated in the nineteenth century, and was used in the 1920s to discuss the correct value of currencies in relation to gold. In general terms the proposition states that equilibrium exchange rates will be such as to enable people to buy the same amount of goods in any country for a given amount of money. For this to be the case exchange rates must be at the correct level in relation to prices in the different countries. In order to state the proposition more rigorously we must assume that goods are homogeneous (or that there is only one good), also that there are no barriers to trade or transactions costs, and that there is internal price flexibility. The 'law of one price' will then ensure that the price of a good will be equalized in domestic and foreign currency terms. For instance, the price of a car in the UK in sterling must be equal to the price of a car in US dollars times the exchange rate (the sterling price of dollars). If the exchange rate is too high or too low, it will adjust if exchange rates are flexible. If they are fixed, internal prices will adjust as there is an excess of demand in one country and a shortfall in the other.

There are two versions of the proposition:

(a)   The 'absolute' version of PPP predicts that the exchange rate (E) will equalize the purchasing power of a given income in any two countries, so that

$$E = P(\text{UK})/P(\text{US})$$

(b)   The 'relative' version of the principle states that changes in exchange rates reflect differences in relative inflation rates. If internal prices rise, exchange rates will adjust to compensate.

It is easy to see how the existence of high inflation rates in the 1970s increased the attractiveness of this theory as an explanation of exchange rate determination, because the theory concentrates on showing the relationship between exchange rates and relative price movements, unlike the more traditional view which, as we have seen, had nothing to say about prices. However, what can we say about the empirical usefulness of the principle? Let us consider the problems of applying the principle first, and then look at the extent to which it was in fact successful in explaining exchange rates changes.

A number of damaging criticisms of the theory can be made:

1.   The major problem relates to the choice of price index used to give empirical content to the theory. Any overall price index includes non-traded as well as traded goods, and inflation rates may be differently reflected in these sectors, hence rendering the index unusable. Even the use of export price indices is problematic because the profitability element in export prices may vary over time. The appropriate measure would appear to be a measure of unit labour costs normalized as between countries (relative normalized unit labour costs) (RNULC) which reflects differences in wage costs per unit of output and thus includes productivity measures.[2] The RNULC measures are the most accurate way of assessing the relative competitive strength of different countries in the traded goods sector.

2.   It is difficult to discuss an 'equilibrium' exchange rate without reference to some base year. The choice of representative year can pose problems in a world where inflation rates vary constantly.

3.   Factors other than the prices of traded goods can affect the exchange rate. Barriers to trade such as tariffs can exist. Tastes can change, incomes can change, technology can change. The classic example of this latter is the effect on the exchange rate of North Sea oil.

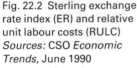

4. Although in the long run the PPP theory may have some validity, exchange rates in the short run are more likely to be dominated by the effects of capital flows, particularly short-run flows. In other words, exchange rates may 'overshoot'.

Fig. 22.2 Sterling exchange rate index (ER) and relative unit labour costs (RULC) *Sources:* CSO *Economic Trends*, June 1990

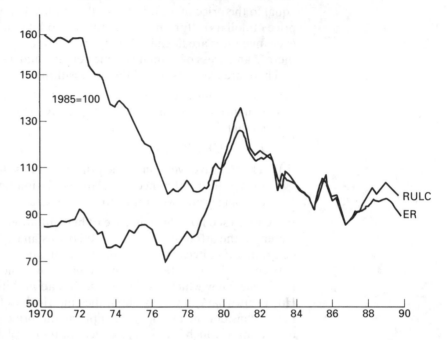

Quite apart from these particular criticisms, it is doubtful whether the PPP theory provides us with an adequate explanation of changes in the sterling exchange rate. The theory would predict that if prices rise faster in the UK than in other countries the resultant trade deficit should cause a fall in the exchange rate. We can test this by examining the relationship between the effective exchange rate and RNULC. When costs rise the UK is becoming less competitive, so we might expect to see a consequent fall in the effective exchange rate if the 'relative' version of the PPP theory holds. In other words, there should be an inverse relationship between the two measures. This is clearly not the case. As Fig. 22.2 shows, relative prices (proxied by unit labour costs) and the effective exchange rate tend to move together rather than inversely. There are various possible explanations for this:

1. Price elasticities for imports and exports may not be such as to cause the exchange rate to improve with a rise in competitiveness. In fact, with a floating exchange rate a rise in competitiveness may cause the exchange rate to fall (the J-curve effect).

2. The effective exchange rate is affected by trade in invisibles and by capital flows as well as by the relative prices of manufactured goods entering into trade.

3. Price competitiveness is not the only factor affecting trade flows. Non-

price competitiveness is also an important determinant. In other words, the crucial assumption of the 'law of one price' – that of homogeneous goods – does not hold in the real world.

We must also realize that RNULC are themselves affected by the effective exchange rate. This is because costs of production in the UK will rise faster than those in other countries if the effective exchange rate depreciates. Raw materials will become more expensive, production costs will rise, the rise in price may trigger wage demands, and RNULC will rise in consequence.

We may sum up by saying that the usefulness of the PPP theory as a theory of exchange rate determination is probably best thought of in a long-run context when changes in relative prices between countries represent the workings of inflationary forces rather than transient 'real' effects such as changes in tastes or technology. However, even in the long run it is still not possible to say whether relative price shifts determine exchange rate movements, or whether exchange rate changes influence price movements.

North Sea oil and the exchange rate   We have argued that little of the variation in the effective exchange rate can be explained by UK price competitiveness. Other factors have been more important: one of these has been the fundamental change in technological possibilities brought about by the advent of North Sea oil. North Sea oil came on stream in 1976, and the UK became self-sufficient in oil by 1980. This has been perhaps the main reason why the effective exchange rate has risen in spite of loss of competitiveness.

1976	1977	1978	1979	1980	1981	1982	1983	1984	1985	1987	1989
−3,947	−2,771	−1,984	−731	315	3,112	4,605	6,294	7,137	8,163	4,184	1,481

Source: CSO (1988a, b; 1990b).

Table 22.2 Balance on oil trading account (£m.)

There are three ways in which oil production has improved the balance of payments. First, since 1976 the UK has been an exporter of oil and has reduced its own dependence on imported oil. As we can see from Table 22.2, the oil trading balance has been steadily improving since 1976, and moved into surplus in 1980. However, since 1985 oil production has begun to decline, and this is reflected in the reduced surplus in 1987 and 1989.

Second, the inflows of capital needed to fund investment in the oil industry helped the UK balance of payments in the 1970s. However, this effect has to some extent been offset in the 1980s by outflows of interest, profits and dividends as companies remit their gains to the country of origin.

Third, the popularity of sterling has risen as an asset currency in recent years, as international asset holders have speculated on the strength of sterling deriving from the favourable oil trading balance. This explains particularly the sharp rise in sterling from 1980 to 1983, as oil trading figures became increasingly favourable. The more recent rises in sterling in 1990 were again related to the possession of oil. Problems in the Gulf raised the profile of sterling as a 'petro-currency', attractive to investors at a time of potentially higher oil prices.

The net effect of the balance of payments impact of North Sea oil is likely to have been sufficiently favourable to keep the exchange rate higher than it would otherwise have been during the eighties. This in itself had important consequences for competitiveness. A 'resource shock' can follow a higher exchange rate, as this will tend to raise the cost of other traded goods, and hence reduce competitiveness. In addition, there may be longer term structural adjustments as manufacturers find it impossible to maintain their position in world markets. This latter effect has *not* in fact happened in the UK, because the upward pressure on the real exchange rate has been counterbalanced by a fall in the rate of inflation in the 80s, as well as by a rise in domestic demand. These have enabled UK firms and exporters to become more profitable and hence to compete more effectively abroad.

The monetary approach to exchange rate determination

As we saw earlier, the growth in importance of capital account transactions led to attempts to explain the determination of the exchange rate by analysing financial flows between countries. The monetary approach to exchange rate determination, developed in the early 1970s, sees the exchange rate as the price of foreign money in terms of domestic money, determined in turn by the demand for and supply of money. If people are not willing to hold the existing stock of money there will be a shortfall in demand for it and its price will fall in relation to the currencies of other countries. What it in fact argues is that balance of payments, and hence exchange rate movements, are simply reflections of disequilibria in money markets.

Money is thought of as being an asset, the demand for which depends on income and interest rates. If the central bank in a country increases the money supply, income and interest rates remaining unchanged, people will be unwilling to hold more money and so the excess money holdings will be used to buy more goods from abroad. The result will be a balance of payments deficit and downward pressure on the exchange rate. If the authorities intervene to support the currency they will lose reserves, and so the increase in the money supply will be exactly offset by a reduction in the external component of the money stock (see Ch. 16). On the other hand, if exchange rates are flexible, the fall in the exchange rate will simply result in internal inflation (as the price of imports rises) which will exactly cancel out the original increase in the money supply.

Suppose now that there is no increase in the money supply, but that exogenous factors cause a change in the demand for money. Suppose incomes rise: the increase in demand for money balances will then lead to an appreciation of the exchange rate as less money is available for imports. Or suppose interest rates rise: the demand for money balances will be reduced, people will spend the money on imports, the exchange rate will fall and home inflation will result. (Note that the prediction here is at variance with the usual assumption that a rise in interest rates will cause an appreciation of the exchange rate because capital flows will be attracted into the country.)

The monetary approach to exchange rate determination, incorporating as it does a whole new perspective on the role of money in the balance of payments, provides a monetarist explanation of exchange rate determination. Its strength lies in the fact that it recognizes the importance of asset market changes in determining the exchange rate, as opposed to concentrating merely on the importance of current account flows in the short or long term, as the previous approaches did. That perspective allows for the possibility of introducing the question of the effect of expectations, which is essential if we are to explain exchange rate volatility. However, in evaluating the usefulness of this approach we must first of all remember that the validity of the argument rests on very limited assumptions:

1. The demand for money is a stable function of real income and interest rates.

2. Prices are determined by the world price level and the exchange rate, i.e. the PPP theory holds.

3. There is full employment domestically.

The validity of these assumptions may be criticized on several grounds:

1. The impact of a monetary disturbance on prices and hence the exchange rate may not be predictable in the short run because of the instability of the velocity of circulation (see Ch. 16).

2. Exchange rates do not conform to the naïve PPP model.

3. Changes in the money stock may produce short-run changes in output (see Ch. 16) which may make it difficult to identify ultimate effects on prices and the exchange rate.

It may help to remember the restrictiveness of these assumptions when we examine some of the implications of this monetarist view. For instance, it is clear that the theory implies that there is no need to have a balance of payments policy because deficits are self-correcting, either because increases in the money stock are reversed by exchange market intervention or by the effects of resultant price rises. Also, under a system of fixed exchange rates it will not be possible to conduct an active monetary policy since all changes in the money stock will be offset by changes in the reserves. But perhaps the major problem with the monetary approach to exchange rate determination, and certainly the central problem when it comes to any empirical testing of its usefulness as an explanatory device, is that it considers there to be only one asset – money – which affects exchange rate determination. This is clearly not the case in practice. We must therefore look to a wider interpretation of asset-holding behaviour if we are to account for the actual behaviour of the exchange rate.

Portfolio balance approach to exchange rate determination

The portfolio balance approach to exchange rate determination sees exchange rates as determined mainly by movements on the capital account of the balance of payments. However, it recognizes that there are a wide variety of assets represented by these transactions. Wealth holders will hold their assets in domestic and foreign securities as well as money, and their asset preferences will be determined by their assessment of the relationship between risk and return on these assets. Given the difference between domestic and foreign rates of return, the exchange rate will be determined by investors' assessment of the degree of substitutability between domestic and foreign assets. If domestic interest rates rise, the extent to which this will cause an inflow of capital and a consequent appreciation of the exchange rate will depend on investor expectations. If expectations change, so that the perceived relationship between risk and return alters, the exchange rate will vary accordingly.

This approach, which was developed in the mid-1970s, represents the 'state of the art' in exchange rate theory. It does not discount the influence of the current account in trend movements of the exchange rate, but it does suggest a plausible explanation for the observed short-run variability in the exchange rate shown in Fig. 22.2 above. Exchange rates may vary sharply in response to asset-switching behaviour in the face of changing rates of return and expectations.

Long-term capital flows and the exchange rate   We now look at some of the changes in the UK capital account in recent years which illustrate the importance of the 'portfolio' approach to exchange rate determination. We look first at the relationship between exchange rate movements and long-term capital flows. These flows are of two kinds, direct and portfolio investment. Direct investment consists in the main of purchases of plant and equipment in other countries by multinational companies in the UK. Portfolio investment is the acquisition of overseas securities by UK asset holders.

Table 22.3 indicates that there has been a steady rise in outward *direct* investment during the eighties, reflecting the desire of UK companies to look for production sites abroad. Their decisions may have been influenced by the fact that the strong pound of the early eighties made it difficult to sell goods abroad. In addition, although productivity levels in the UK have been rising over the period, they remain lower than in other countries (see Ch. 1). Money wage levels are also often lower abroad; this encourages companies to locate at least part of the production process in those areas. Direct investment in the UK, on the other hand, does not seem to have been particularly attractive, and the category of inward direct investment which was so buoyant in the seventies – investment in oil production – has declined in the eighties as oil production has fallen. Nevertheless, there has been a recent surge in inward *direct* investment, reflecting to some extent the desire of non EC investors such as the US to gain a foothold in the post-1992 single European market.

On the other hand, there has been no marked rise in inward flows of *portfolio* investment until 1985 and 1986. It is interesting to note that in these two years both the yields on gilts and UK equity prices were at historically high levels, and this may have caused asset switching from foreign to domestic assets. Also, deregulation in 1986 improved the attractiveness of the UK as an investment location following the 'big bang' reforms. Another factor in raising inward portfolio investment has been the stock market crash of 1987 which resulted in a repatriation back to the UK of £7bn worth of assets as financial institutions adjusted the composition of their portfolios.

Opportunities for *portfolio* investment abroad were limited for UK

Table 22.3 Long-term
international investment
(£m.)

Overseas private investment in the UK (inward)

	Direct	*Portfolio*
1983	3,386	1,701
1984	−181	1,310
1985	3,865	8,733
1986	4,945	9,365
1987	8,508	14,194
1988	8,990	11,794
1989	15,845	12,066

UK private investment overseas (outward)

	Direct	*Portfolio*
1983	−5,417	−7,193
1984	−6,033	−9,869
1985	−8,456	−19,426
1986	−11,782	−23,072
1987	−19,033	3,323
1988	−20,760	−9,849
1989	−19,164	−37,023

Sources: CSO (1988a, 1990b).

residents until exchange control was ended in 1979. After that date it was possible for major asset holders, such as financial institutions, to diversify their portfolios by the acquisition of foreign securities. Table 22.3 shows that outward flows of portfolio investment by UK residents increased dramatically in the eighties, with particularly sharp rises in 1985 and 1989. Institutional asset holders have clearly taken the opportunity to increase their rate of return and spread the risk on their portfolios by investing abroad (see Ch. 15).

Another explanation for the growth of outward portfolio investment focuses on the growth of *total* portfolios in the 1980s. Institutional portfolios – for instance, those of pension funds and insurance companies – grew at 18% per annum. This meant that there was a need for increases in suitable domestic assets, but no such increase was forthcoming. The late 1980s were a time of government buyback of debt, a shortage of new equity issues, and a reduction in the total equity base due to takeovers (*National Institute Economic Review*, 1990). The alternative for portfolio managers was investment abroad.

Short-term capital flows and the exchange rate　Here we consider the way in which the exchange rate is influenced by short-term capital flows. These consist mainly of borrowings from, and lending to, overseas residents by banks. Such short-term capital flows respond primarily to interest rate differentials. Asset switching between countries will take place so long as the interest rate differential is greater than any expected changes in the exchange rate. What happens is that if interest rates rise in, for instance, the USA, people will buy dollars in order to invest in US money markets. This will drive the dollar rate up, but as people realize their gains by selling dollars the dollar rate will come down again. It is possible to try and hedge against potential loss by selling dollars bought today on today's forward market for delivery at some future date, but that will in turn drive today's forward rate down. In a perfect market the rise in dollar spot rate and the fall in forward rates (as investors try to make sure of their future gains today) will be just sufficient to cancel out the advantages of rising interest rates. But markets are never perfect, and some *arbitrage* is always possible.

We have no firm empirical evidence for such behaviour on the part of asset holders. There should be a positive correlation between interest rate differentials and exchange rates, as people switch funds into the UK when interest rates rise relative to US interest rates, thereby driving up the sterling exchange rate. Figure 22.3, which deals with the UK/US differential, shows more evidence of negative than positive correlation. There are various reasons for this. One is that the positive effect of interest rate differentials on the exchange rate may be outweighed by exchange rate expectations. For instance, in the period 1980–82, when interest rate differentials were very low because both the UK and the USA had high interest rates, the UK exchange rate was high because people believed that a petro-currency such as sterling would remain strong.

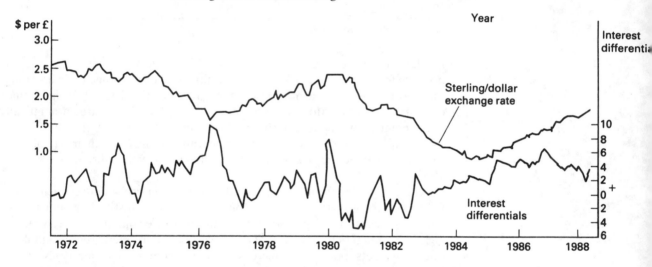

Fig. 22.3 Sterling exchange rates and interest differentials
Sources: Bank of England Quarterly Bulletin (1972–87); CSO (1990a)

Expectations about future exchange rates are formed by assessments about the potential demand for and supply of sterling. If asset holders see that the UK has a combined current and capital account deficit, they will *expect* the exchange rate to fall, and will move their money out of sterling, thereby exerting a further downward pressure on sterling. If the authorities do not wish this to happen, they must raise interest rates so that they are higher than those of other countries by a margin sufficient to attract funds into sterling. Fig. 22.4 gives an example of this; it shows the gap between UK interest rates and those in Germany. This gap has been at least 5% since 1984, and is a reflection of the strength of the mark in relation to sterling. However, it is never possible to predict the effect on capital flows, and hence on the exchange rate, of any given interest rate differential. Capital flows will be more or less responsive, depending on the strength and the nature of expectations. Lacking adequate information in an imperfect market, speculators tend to be influenced by any item of information, however

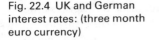

Fig. 22.4 UK and German interest rates: (three month euro currency)

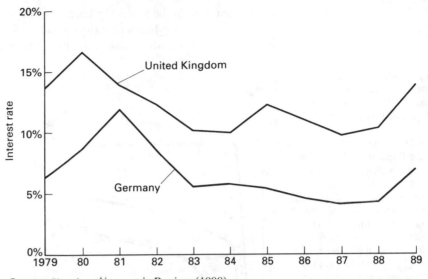

Source: Barclays Economic Review (1990).

irrelevant. Money supply figures, political developments at home and abroad, unsuccessful Summit meetings – all these tend to trigger behavioural responses in terms of flows of 'hot' money in and out of sterling. Exogenous shocks, such as the consequences of oil price rises, or the threat of international conflict, may also lead to major flows of short-term capital. It may happen that, in spite of high interest rates, the exchange rate does depreciate. In this case there will be consequent structural changes both in competitiveness and in real rates of return on long-term investment.

Economic policy and the exchange rate

We have spent some time analysing the way the level of the exchange rate is affected by a variety of factors. We now consider the relationship between the exchange rate and economic policy. Until the early 70s exchange rate stability was itself a policy objective, because the UK was committed to maintaining a fixed exchange rate. After that the importance of the exchange rate was seen primarily as a determinant of the UK's competitive position, given the existing rate of inflation. In the last few years, the exchange rate has become a policy instrument rather than a policy objective, because it has become the weapon of choice in the government's fight against inflation. The present administration began its fight against inflation when it took office in 1979 by emphasizing the primacy of monetary policy. More specifically, the government aimed to target the rate of growth of one or more of the monetary indicators in line with the rate of growth of money GDP (the rate of growth of real output + the rate of inflation). Fiscal policy was relegated to a subsidiary role within this policy framework, and there was no coherent strategy for the exchange rate. In the years since then it has become apparent that no single monetary indicator possesses a sufficiently stable relationship with nominal expenditure to be used as a control variable. In addition, it has also become clear that there is a direct relationship between changes in the exchange rate and the rate of inflation, because the price of imports enters into the Retail Price Index in different ways. We can illustrate this as follows. In Fig. 22.5 we consider in some detail the impact of a sterling depreciation

Fig. 22.5 Impact on prices of a 10% depreciation
Source: Bank of England Quarterly Bulletin (1981)
Notes:
1 A 10% depreciation of sterling against the dollar is equivalent to an increase of 11.1% in units of sterling per dollar. As it is the latter rate which is relevant in this context, the 10% depreciation leads eventually to a rise slightly greater than 11% in some import prices
2 The bank's short-term model assumes no wages response. The exchange rate is assumed to remain 10% below the level it would otherwise have been
Notes:
A = Consumer prices
B = Wholesale selling price
C = Imported foods
D = Imported finished goods
E = All imported goods
F = Imported industrial materials
G = Imported fuels

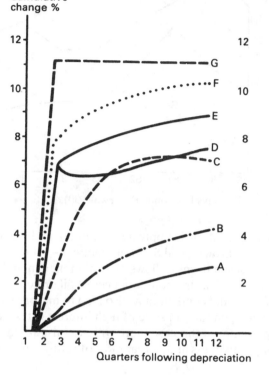

on UK import prices. Sterling depreciation will raise the cost, expressed in sterling, of imported items. However, both the magnitude and the speed of price rise will vary with type of import. This can be illustrated for the early 1980s by reference to a Bank of England short-term forecasting model. As we can see from Fig. 22.5 the full effect of the sterling depreciation on import prices will only be felt after more than two years. Imported fuel and industrial material prices will, with less elastic demands, respond most substantially and most rapidly to the depreciation. This is in part because the less elastic is demand, the easier it is to pass on cost increases to consumers. Imported finished goods' prices rise by a smaller amount, and less quickly, because some of these goods face extensive competition on home markets, i.e. face more elastic demand curves. Imported food prices will tend to be less affected, at least initially, because of the operation of the Common Agricultural Policy.

The final effect on consumer prices can be seen to be about one-quarter of the sterling depreciation, and then only after more than two years. For any depreciation, the final effect on consumer prices will depend on a number of factors:

1.   The import content of production.

2. The extent to which cost increases can be passed on to consumers, i.e. price elasticity of demand.
3. The import content of consumption.
4. The sensitivity of wage demands to cost-of-living increases.

Figure 22.5 is drawn on the assumption of no wage response, i.e. that (4) above is zero. Any such response would increase wholesale and consumer prices still further.

Whereas a fall in the sterling exchange rate will increase inflation, a rise in the exchange rate will reduce it. There is, of course, another side to the picture. A high sterling exchange rate, although helping the fight against inflation, may adversely affect output and employment. United Kingdom producers may now find it more difficult to sell their goods and services, first, because competition from cheaper imports drives them out of home markets and, second, because UK exports become expensive on foreign markets. Much of the deindustrialization of the early 1980s has been attributed to the high pound (see Ch. 1).

The adherence of governments to a policy of high exchange rates has been based on a belief that high exchange rates help fight inflation by making imports cheaper, and that on the export side reliance could be placed on the 'law of one price'. In other words, British manufacturers, seeing that they could not sell on world markets unless they observed world prices for their products, would restrain the rate of growth of labour costs, thereby raising exports and further contributing to the fight against inflation. However, the exchange rate does not stand as an isolated determinant of the rate of inflation, and exchange rate policy has therefore to be seen in the *total* policy context. There are several separate aspects of this issue.

1. As it became apparent that control of the money stock, however defined, was neither practicable nor relevant in terms of the control of inflation, the emphasis of policy shifted to *interest rates*. The basis of this strategy appeared to be the belief that high interest rates would discourage borrowing and hence slow down the growth of the credit counterparts of the money stock. Although (earlier in the 1980s) there was little empirical evidence supporting the sensitivity of borrowing to interest rate changes, the situation changed as house ownership increased and house prices rose. By the late 1980s, the average household mortgage burden had risen substantially, and this meant that any slight change in interest rates increased monthly mortgage payments in such a way as to limit other types of discretionary household spending (e.g. on consumer durables). Higher interest rates thus caused a reduction in consumer spending and a consequent recession. The way in which this might have affected inflation directly is not immediately apparent; the best guess is that a slowdown in the economy would diminish inflationary expectations. What is undoubtedly the case is that high interest rates have an indirect, but immediate, effect on inflation through the exchange rate, as explained previously.

2. The exchange rate and the stance of monetary policy are thus interlinked. However, the exact relationship will be defined by the structural characteristics of the current and long-term capital accounts

prevailing at that time. For example, a tightening of monetary conditions will involve a rise in interest rates, and hence in the exchange rate, and vice versa. In other words, a given monetary policy implies a certain level of the exchange rate. But what that precise level will be depends partly upon the basic balance on the current and capital accounts at that time, which as we have seen can in turn be influenced by rather volatile expectations.

3.   The converse of the previous argument is also true. Intervention to alter the exchange rate itself has monetary implications, because it affects bankers' balances at the Bank of England in the same way as does any other transaction between the government and the public. Both broad and narrow money stock measures are therefore affected by foreign exchange market dealings by the authorities. It is of course possible for the authorities to sterilize these effects by conducting open market operations so as to bring bankers' balances back to their original level, but these transactions affect bond prices and hence yields; sterilization thus has implications for the interest rate.

4.   The choice with regard to the appropriate combination of exchange rate and interest rate is often made more difficult by the actions of other countries. If, for instance, the US raises money market rates, funds will tend to flow out of the London money markets, and the sterling exchange rate will tend to fall. The Government will then be forced to raise interest rates to maintain the exchange rate, but this will involve an unplanned tightening of monetary policy and a consequent risk of recession.

5.   Policies which attempt to influence inflation by operating on the nominal exchange rate alone are essentially short-term 'stop-gap' policies. What is needed are policies which affect the real exchange rate through improvements in competitiveness – i.e. through reductions in costs and prices. Only by improving the basic balance by raising competitiveness will the 'balance of payments constraint' on anti-inflationary policy be removed.

6.   Exchange rate policy in the UK also has to take into account the interdependence of major currencies. During the 1980s volatility became more of a problem as global speculative pressures increased. The major five countries – the Group of Five – began a series of collaborative initiatives in 1985, to ensure that their exchange rates were correctly aligned and to present a united front against destabilizing speculation. This collaboration continues and provides the framework within which policy measures are considered.

Sterling and the ERM

In the last fifty years we have moved from a fixed to a floating exchange rate regime. With the advent of world inflation in the 70s it became impossible to maintain fixed exchange rate parities between countries because internal prices were accelerating at different rates. As world inflation subsided in the 1980s floating exchange rates became less necessary: in addition, the increased volatility of currencies led the major countries to seek some form of greater stability. The countries of the European Community had a particular problem in that it was clearly not possible to create a unified market without fixed parities. While it has not proved possible to implement any form of fixed exchange rate regime for countries as a whole, the European economies have, since 1979, operated an Exchange Rate Mechanism (see Ch. 26). This pegs currencies to the central unit, known as the 'ECU', within a permitted band of divergence. The value of the 'ECU' is based on a weighted average of the participating currencies. The ERM of the European Monetary System is seen as an intermediate step towards the inevitable European Monetary Union which must accompany the final establishment of the Single European Market.

The UK did not join the ERM when it was established in 1979, as it was feared that sterling would not be able to maintain its position within the system. After that, when sterling rose as a result of the advent of North Sea oil, it seemed inappropriate to join an exchange rate system where the dominant currency, the mark, was a non oil currency. After 1987, when the UK signed the Single Europe Act designed to create the single market by 1992, the question of joining the ERM again became a live issue. In fact, before the Chancellor, Nigel Lawson, resigned in 1989 it was clear that he was attempting to target the value of sterling at 3DM = £1. However, the UK government expressed a reluctance to join until various conditions were fulfilled. Behind what were clearly political arguments and bargaining positions lay a very real apprehension about the problems which the UK might face on entry. We now look at the short-term impact of UK entry into the ERM which took place in Oct. 1990, and the longer-term consequences of joining.

The immediate problems arise from the following:

1. The UK inflation rate is higher than those of her competitors; absolute price levels are also higher.

2. Interest rates are higher in the UK than in other European countries.

3. Wage costs and earnings exceed those in other countries.

1. INFLATION. Inflation rates in ERM countries have been reduced over the years, and have also converged (see Fig. 22.6). This has been achieved (a) by exchange rate realignments, (b) by the dominance of Germany which is a low-inflation country, (c) by the downward effect on inflationary expectations of a perceived commitment by the participating countries to co-operation in the fight against inflation. It is therefore clear that joining the ERM might still involve a sterling devaluation at some future stage in order to bring UK prices into line with those elsewhere in the system, especially since the UK appears to have an underlying inflation rate of 4–5% (*Barclays Economic Review* 1990) which is due to *structural* factors. Indeed, the fear is that a persistent tendency towards higher inflation in the UK may mean that the exchange rate band agreed on entry might be insufficient to resolve the problem.

2. INTEREST RATES. Interest rates are higher in the UK than in other

Fig. 22.6 Consumer prices

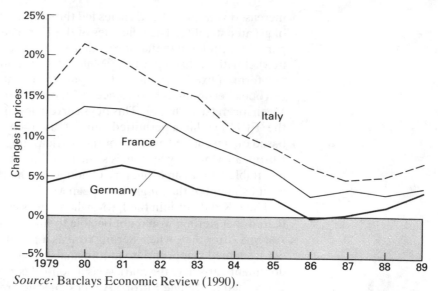

Source: Barclays Economic Review (1990).

countries because the government is attempting to fight inflation both by restricting the growth of spending and by maintaining exhange rates at a sufficiently high level. *Interest rate differentials* between countries are based, as we have seen, on expectations about *exchange rate differentials*. ERM entry might help to reduce expectations of a future fall in sterling and could therefore permit a fall in UK interest relative to those elsewhere. The problem then would be that borrowing would be cheaper in the UK, spending would rise, house prices might start to rise, and the inflationary spiral would accelerate. All this could then make it impossible for the UK to maintain the sterling rate against the ECU, again forcing a future devaluation of sterling within the ERM if the UK is to remain competitive.

3. EARNINGS. Earnings in the UK have risen about 5% more than those in Germany over the past seven years. Insofar as UK productivity has risen to compensate, there has been little net effect on *costs*. However by the late 1980s costs were rising 4% faster in the UK than in Germany. Unless productivity rises as fast as the earnings differential, there is clearly an underlying inflationary influence which may again exert a downward pressure on the value of sterling within the ERM.

All these factors could, critics argue, make it difficult for the UK to maintain the initial exchange rate established on entry into the ERM. These critics suggest that the UK will be required to undertake *progressive devaluations* of sterling within the ERM in order to maintain price competitiveness with other countries. If such devaluations are to be inhibited by UK membership of the ERM, then the UK will be at a competitive disadvantage in trade with other countries.

The real issue is whether or not membership of the ERM will help the UK to fight inflation, or whether it will make the inflationary situation worse – as a result, for instance, of lower interest rates. It is possible to argue that the discipline of the ERM will assist the fight against inflation by creating an anti-inflationary climate of expectations. The real question is whether, and how, membership might help to slow down the rate of wage increases. The fact of the matter is that the advent of the single European market in 1992 will intensify price competition, so that the problem of wage inflation will then become more acute. Membership of the ERM will, its supporters argue, be a vital element in curbing inflationary wage settlements. Since unions will be aware that the discipline of the ERM will prevent a ready resort to sterling devaluation, they will be more 'modest' in their bids for higher wages. They will no longer be able to rely on a fall in the sterling exchange rate compensating for a rise in producer costs. At the *same* exchange rate, higher costs will mean higher prices, reduced output and job losses. Supporters of entry into the ERM in 1990 regarded this 'discipline' as one of the major benefits of entry.

Notes

1. This analysis assumes that the elasticity of demand for imports is greater than 1. In the case of exports foreign buyers will demand more pounds whatever the elasticity of demand, simply because they are buying more goods as the price in their own currency falls, and the sterling price of exports has not changed.
2. The RNULC are calculated by taking indices of labour costs in the UK and dividing by the weighted geometric average of competitors' unit labour costs. 'Normalization' involves adjusting the basic indices to allow for short-run variations in productivity – so eliminating cyclical variations

References

Bank of England Quarterly Bulletin (1972–87).
Bank of England Quarterly Bulletin (1981) Sept.
Barclays Economic Review (1988) In defence of sterling – Alan Budd, Nov.
Barclays Economic Review (1990) When can sterling join the ERM – Alan Budd, Feb.
CSO (1988a) *Economic Trends*, March.
CSO (1988b) *Economic Trends*, Annual Supplement.
CSO (1990a) *Financial Statistics*, May.
CSO (1990b) *Economic Trends*, June.
Midland Bank Review (1985) Exchange rate determination: the dollar – a case study, winter.
National Institute Economic Review (1990) Why the capital account matters – Nigel Pain and Peter Westaway, Feb.

23

United Kingdom trade performance

Although the UK's balance of visible trade has been in deficit for most of the last 150 years, it has not presented a major problem as the surplus on invisible account has usually been more than able to cover any deficit on visible trade. However, since 1945, with the exception of oil, there has been a progressive and serious fall in the UK's export competitiveness on visible trade and a rise in import penetration. This chapter examines such trends, particularly those for the manufactured goods sector, and investigates in detail the problem of non-price competitiveness for the UK. The chapter concludes with an attempt to assess the importance of an adverse performance on non-oil visible trade for the UK economy.

The nature of the problem

It was observed in Chapter 22 that the UK's balance of payments has two major components: a 'current account' and a 'transactions in external assets and liabilities account'. Our main concern in this chapter will be the current account, as our trade in goods (visibles) and services (invisibles) is often used as an index of the UK's ability to compete in world markets. It should, of course, be remembered that the current account is not entirely isolated from the rest of the accounts. An adverse performance on trade in goods and services may, for instance, reflect an underlying productivity problem within the UK, which could eventually erode confidence and lead to capital outflows as investors seek safer and more productive returns abroad. In this way the current account may affect the whole of the balance of payments accounts.

Apart from the Second World War, the UK's current account has been in deficit on only thirty-one occasions between 1816 and 1989, giving the impression of a solid and consistent trading performance in both visibles and invisibles. However, a closer look at the accounts shows that, apart from times of war, there have been only six surpluses on the visible account, and only two deficits on the invisible account, throughout the whole period. It appears that the UK's weakness in her visible trade has, for the most part, been compensated for by her strength in invisibles. Table 23.1 suggests that this is basically still the case, although the picture has become more complex in the last decade following the oil price rises, and the advent of UK North Sea oil.

It would seem from Table 23.1 that had it not been for the oil shock of 1973/74, the UK current account would have remained in surplus, with the earnings on invisibles more than covering any deficit on the visible balance. With the advent of North Sea oil in the late 1970s, and with the UK becoming a net exporter of oil in 1980, the future of the current account would still

Table 23.1 Components of UK current account 1970–89 (£m.)

Year	Visible balance			Invisible balance total	Current account total
	Total	Oil	Non-oil		
1970	−34	−496	+462	+857	+823
1971	+190	−692	+882	+934	+1,124
1972	−748	−666	−82	+995	+247
1973	−2,586	−941	−1,645	+1,605	−981
1974	−5,351	−3,357	−1,994	+2,078	−3,273
1975	−3,333	−3,057	−276	+1,812	−1,521
1976	−3,927	−3,947	+20	+3,048	−879
1977	−2,278	−2,771	+493	+2,243	−35
1978	−1,573	−1,999	+426	+2,481	+908
1979	−3,497	−774	−2,723	+2,595	−902
1980	+1,177	+273	+904	+2,028	+3,205
1981	+3,360	+3,112	+148	+3,168	+6,528
1982	+2,331	+4,643	−2,312	+2,332	+4,663
1983	−835	+6,976	−7,811	+4,003	+3,168
1984	−4,101	+7,137	−11,238	+5,036	+935
1985	−2,068	+8,163	−10,231	1 5,020	+2,952
1986	8,463	+4,056	−12,519	+8,509	+46
1987	−10,929	+4,183	−15,112	7,258	−3,671
1988	−20,815	+2,797	−23,612	+5,796	−15,019
1989	−23,112	+1,481	−24,593	+2,261	−20,851

Sources: CSO (1983, 1985); *Business Briefing* (1990).

seem secure! However, the underlying trends would warn us against any such complacency. For example, the fall in the price of oil and therefore oil revenue between 1985 and 1989 weakened the visible balance significantly and further exposed the difficulties which the UK has on its non-oil account.

Visible trade

The UK's competitive weakness on visible trade can be viewed from three main standpoints: first, the deterioration in the non-oil visible balance; second, the change in the area and commodity composition of visible trade; and third, the adverse trends observed for trade in manufactures.

The non-oil visible balance   From Table 23.1 we see that the non-oil visible account has experienced alternate periods of deficit and surplus. These periods have to some extent followed the business cycle. Deficits have tended to be more pronounced during periods of recovery and boom, and surpluses during periods of recession. The relatively high incomes experienced during periods of expanding economic activity have tended to attract imports (see below), with an adverse effect on the non-oil visible balance, as in 1973/74 and in the short-lived 'boom' of 1978/79. Conversely, lower incomes during periods of recession have tended to curb spending on imports, improving the non-oil visible balance. However, since 1980 this pattern has been disturbed, with the non-oil visible balance moving sharply into deficit in 1982–85 despite economic recession. This deficit has become even worse with the growth of imports reflecting the recovery of the UK economy after 1986, fed by a consumer boom which continued unabated until 1990. All these factors suggest that the UK is facing even greater problems in becoming competitive in goods other than oil.

The area and commodity composition of visible trade   Changes in the UK's pattern of visible trade, on both an area and commodity basis, also suggest further potential problems.

An area analysis of UK visible trade, as seen in Table 23.2, shows a clear shift since 1960 towards Western Europe generally, and the EEC in particular. Both the share of UK exports to, and imports from, Western Europe almost doubled between 1960 and 1989, with most of the shift being due to increased UK trade with EEC countries. On the other hand, the share of total visible trade with North America has fallen, especially as regards imports, because although trade with the USA remained relatively steady, trade with Canada fell sharply. The share of UK trade with 'other developed countries' such as Australia, New Zealand and South Africa has also fallen, although trade with Japan, the remaining major country in this bloc, has increased (mainly on the import side). The oil-exporting countries (OPEC) now account for a higher share of UK visible exports, but with the advent of North Sea oil their share of UK visible imports has declined. The remaining significant change is the rapid fall in the importance of 'other developing countries' in UK trade, with this category consisting mainly of Commonwealth countries and Latin American states.

Table 23.2 Area composition of UK visible exports (X), and imports* (M); (% of total)

		1960		1969		1979		1989	
		X	M	X	M	X	M	X	M
1	Western Europe	32	31	40	38	57	60	59	65
	(of which EEC)	(21)	(20)	(29)	(26)	(43)	(45)	(51)	(53)
2	North America	16	21	17	20	12	13	15	13
	(of which USA)	(10)	(12)	(12)	(14)	(10)	(10)	(13)	(11)
3	Other developed countries	13	12	12	10	6	6	6	8
	(of which Japan)	(1)	(1)	(2)	(1)	(2)	(3)	(2)	(6)
4	Oil-exporting countries	6	10	5	8	9	7	7	2
5	Other developing countries	31	23	23	20	13	11	11	10
6	Centrally planned economies	2	3	3	4	3	3	2	2

* Exports are measured free on board (f.o.b.), but imports include cost, insurance and freight (c.i.f.). All figures are rounded.
Sources: Adapted from CSO (1968, 1973, 1982, 1990).

Table 23.3 shows the composition of UK visible trade over the years 1960–89. On the *export* side has been the fall in share of manufactured goods, from 84% in 1960 to 81% in 1989, and the increase in share of oil-based products from 4 to 7%. On the *import* side, there has been a significant decline in the share of food, beverages and tobacco in total visible imports, as has also occurred for basic materials, such as textile fibres, crude rubber and metal ores. In each case the volume of imports has increased, but much more slowly than total imports, so that their *share* has fallen. The opposite is true for manufactured goods, with the volume of imports growing so fast that the share of manufactured goods in total visible imports has more than doubled.

Table 23.3 Commodity composition of UK visible exports (X), and visible imports* (M); (% of total)

	1960 X	1960 M	1969 X	1969 M	1979 X	1979 M	1989 X	1989 M
(0, 1)† Food beverages, tobacco	5	33	6	23	7	14	7	9
(2, 4) Basic materials	4	23	4	15	3	9	3	6
(3) Mineral fuel and lubricants	4	10	2	11	11	12	7	5
(5–8) Manufactured goods	84	33	85	50	76	63	81	79
(5, 6) (i) Semi-manufactured goods	(36)	(22)	(35)	(28)	(31)	(27)	(29)	(26)
(7, 8) (ii) Finished manufactured goods	(48)	(11)	(50)	(22)	(45)	(36)	(52)	(53)
(9) Unclassified	3	1	3	1	3	2	2	1

* Exports (f.o.b.), imports (c.i.f.). All figures are rounded.
† Numbers in brackets relate to the Standard International Trade Classification.
Sources: Adapted from CSO (1968, 1973, 1982, 1990).

In fact, the share of *finished* manufactured goods in total visible imports has increased nearly fivefold.

Tables 23.2 and 23.3 show that the UK has shifted the geographical focus of her trade towards the industrialized countries of Europe, and in particular towards the EEC. At the same time the UK is showing symptoms of being less able to compete with these countries in the important commodity sector of manufacturing. It may therefore be useful to look at this sector in more detail.

Trade in manufactures The UK's problems as regards trade in manufactures manifest themselves in a variety of ways. Table 23.4 presents the share of selected countries in world *exports* of manufactures. The UK share fell from about 17% in 1960 to around 8% in 1989, a fall that was not matched by any of her main competitors. Whilst the volume of exports of manufactures from the developed market economies increased by nearly 48% between 1980 and 1989, the volume of UK exports of manufactures increased by only 30%.

Table 23.5 indicates the intensity of foreign competition on the *import* side. The ratio of imports of manufactures to total home demand for

Table 23.4 Share of world export of manufactures (%)

	1960	1969	1979	1989
USA	22	19	16	17
Japan	7	11	14	18
France	10	8	10	9
West Germany	19	19	21	20
Italy	5	7	8	8
UK	17	11	10	8
Others*	21	23	21	20

* All figures are rounded up, so that totals may not sum to 100. Figures for 1983 are for second quarter.
Sources: National Institute of Economic and Social Research (1970, 1983), UN Monthly Bulletin of Statistics (1990).

manufactures has risen from 17% in 1968 to 36% in 1989. Import penetration has been still more serious in vehicles and in mechanical and electrical engineering, which together have traditionally been amongst our main export earners, comprising around 50% of UK manufactured exports.

Table 23.5 United Kingdom import penetration in manufactures* (%)

	1968	1973	1979	1989
Total manufactures†	17	21	26	36
Vehicles	14	23	40	49
Electrical engineering	14	27	38	49
Mechanical engineering	20	26	32	41
Chemical and allied industries	18	22	30	41

* Import penetration is defined as imports/home demand × 100.
† Figures for total manufactures have been rounded off.
Sources: Hewer (1980); Wells and Imber (1977); CSO (1990).

Although the UK is not the only country experiencing an increase in import penetration as trade in manufactures becomes more highly specialized, the rate of increase is exceptionally fast in the UK.

The problems encountered by the manufacturing sector are also revealed in Fig. 23.1, which shows the balance of trade (value of exports/value of imports) for both finished and total manufactured goods. The ratios have fallen progressively since the early 1960s. In fact by 1982 the UK had, on an *Overseas Trade Statistics* basis, become a net importer of *finished* manufactures, and was barely in balance in its trade in total manufactures. Data for the second half of the 1980s show a continuation of this trend, with the *overall* balance of trade in manufactures as well as finished manufactures also remaining in deficit.

Fig. 23.1 UK balance of trade in manufacturers
Notes:
* Exports (f.o.b.), imports (c.i.f.)
A = finished manufactured goods
B = total manufactured goods
Sources: CSO (1968, 1973, 1987, 1988, 1990)

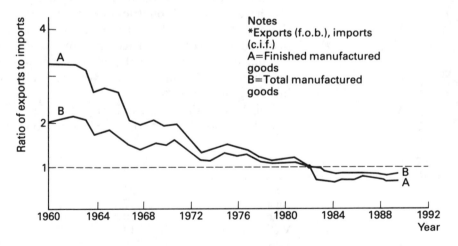

Notes
*Exports (f.o.b.), imports (c.i.f.)
A=Finished manufactured goods
B=Total manufactured goods

Reasons behind UK trade performance

This deterioration in UK performance on its non-oil account, and in particular in manufactures, may be due to a number of factors: an inappropriate trade structure, a lack of price competitiveness, or an inability to compete in terms of non-price factors such as marketing, design, delivery date and product development. We examine each of these possibilities in turn.

Trade structure

It is possible to argue that the UK's relatively poor trading performance, especially in exports, has been due to its inadequate response to the changing geographical and commodity composition of world trade. The fall in the UK's share of world trade could then be due to at least three main causes. First, a geographical composition of exports biased towards slow-growth areas. Second, an inappropriate commodity composition of exports, with the UK sluggish in shifting her exports to commodity sectors growing rapidly in world trade. Third, it may, of course, be that irrespective of area and commodity composition, the UK has basically failed to compete *within* each geographical area and *within* each commodity group. Let us examine each of these possibilities.

Evidence tends to show that the UK has *not* suffered too severely since the Second World War from a bias in the geographical composition of its exports towards slow-growth areas. It has been shown that, in the 1950s, no more than one-third of the UK's slower export growth in comparison with the other industrialized countries could be attributed to geographical differences in markets (Worswick and Ady 1962: 129). Further, Tables 23.2 and 23.3 show that since then UK exports have actually shifted *towards* the larger, faster-growing markets of the industrialized countries, Europe in particular.

Neither does an inappropriate commodity composition of exports seem a likely explanation. A survey of eleven industrial countries between 1955 and 1968 showed that the growth of UK exports was determined more by the growth of world exports than by commodity composition (Panić and Rajan 1971). Research work by Connell (1980) has shown that the commodity structure of UK exports was similar in the 1970s to that of her main competitors such as West Germany. In fact, with the exception of motor vehicles, the commodity structure of the two countries' manufactured exports retains strong similarity even into the 1980s. These studies appear to substantiate an earlier long-term analysis of the period 1954–68 by Major (1968), which showed that the area and commodity composition of trade *together* could only account for 9% of the loss of the UK's share of world trade in manufactures.

Finally, a more recent analysis of the UK's trade structure was conducted by the OECD in their annual survey of the UK (OECD 1988/9). They compared the growth rate of UK manufactured exports with that of world manufactured exports over the period 1970–87 and attempted to explain the reasons why the growth of world manufactured exports was consistently higher than the growth of UK manufactured exports. They found that variations between the two growth rate figures could be explained by a combination of three main factors – differences in both the area and commodity composition of trade, and differences in a 'residual' which measured factors *other than* area or commodity factors, e.g. the effects of price and non-price competition within each market and area. The results showed once more, that the main overall reasons why the UK's manufactured exports lagged behind world trade were due to 'residual' factors.

It would therefore seem that the main problem for the UK is her inability to compete *within* geographical areas and *within* particular commodity groupings, reflecting a decline in UK competitiveness. We now turn to an examination of UK competitiveness, both in terms of price and non-price factors.

Price competitiveness

Price elasticity of demand is a traditional measure of demand responsiveness. In the trade context it can be expressed as a ratio of percentage change in quantity demanded of exports or imports, to the percentage change in price. As regards trade, however, it is not just the absolute price of UK exports or imports which is important, but UK prices *relative* to those of its main competitors. Such relative prices often reflect differences between countries in unit costs, inflation rates or exchange rates.

International competitiveness may be assessed in a number of different ways. One is to use the UK export price divided by a weighted average of competitors' export prices. Another is to look not at prices but at costs, since even where there is no change in price, a change in costs may still affect underlying competitiveness. For instance, if price is unchanged, a rise in costs will reduce profits, perhaps reducing future investment and eventually sales. Costs, and in particular unit labour costs, are therefore often used in assessing changes in international competitiveness. Let us now examine the evidence as to whether improvements in UK price or cost competitiveness will have an important influence on trade flow.

Writers do not fully agree on the responsiveness of UK export and import volumes to changes in price. For one thing it is often difficult to identify the effect of price on quantity demanded when other factors are changing. For another, measures of price elasticity are often calculated over varying time periods, which can lead to different results. The surveys that are available suggest that the *short-run* price elasticity of demand for total UK exports varies between 0.26 and 0.46, indicating a relatively inelastic response of export demand to price change. In the *longer run*, after a time-lag of around two years, the price elasticity of demand for total visible exports rises to between 1.5 and 2.6 (Thirlwall 1980). A similar elastic response was found for exports of manufactures in the longer run (Posner and Steer 1978). As regards total visible imports, most studies reveal a UK price elasticity less than 1, and sometimes near to zero. Manufactured imports are rather more price-responsive, with estimates ranging from 0.9 to 1.6 (Panić 1975; Morgan and Martin 1975).

Despite the difficulties of measurement, it seems that after a time-lag of around two years, UK exports are much more responsive to price than are UK imports. This suggests that an improvement in UK price competitiveness, *vis-à-vis* other countries, would significantly raise the volume of UK exports, but have much less effect in reducing the volume of UK imports.

Of course, it is not just volumes of trade flow that matter, but also *values*.

The empirical measurements of UK price elasticities are encouraging in this respect in that they fulfil the Marshall–Lerner elasticity condition. This condition must be met if a fall in export prices and a rise in import prices (e.g. via devaluation) is to raise the *value* of exports relative to the *value* of imports, thereby improving the visible balance. The condition states that the sum of the respective price elasticities of demand for exports and imports must be greater than 1. Even taking the lower bands of the elasticity estimates for total visible exports and imports their sum is nearer 2 than 1, at least over the *longer-run* time period. In the *shorter run*, however, the sum may well be less than 1, so that observations in the UK of a J-curve effect, whereby an improvement in UK price competitiveness actually worsens the visible balance for eighteen months to two years, should therefore come as no real surprise.

Another way of assessing the importance of price factors in UK trade is to look at the *share* of UK exports and imports in world trade. If, for example, UK exports became relatively cheaper, one would expect other countries to substitute UK goods for their previous purchases, thus increasing UK share of world trade in these goods. We are, in effect, measuring the ease with which UK goods are substituted for foreign goods as the former become relatively cheaper. The basic question is this: will an improvement in UK price competitiveness increase our share of the world export market, and decrease import penetration as the home market switches to relatively cheaper UK goods?

For the period between the late 1950s and the mid-1960s it does seem that price competitiveness did play a part in determining the UK's share of world exports (Krause 1968). However, data for a later period (1963–75) revealed no clear link between the two (Kaldor 1978). In a statistical survey of the period 1963–90 the present author also found that changes in UK price competitiveness alone had little effect on the UK's share of world exports of manufactures. Similar results were found in other studies which used cost rather than price as an index of UK competitiveness. Featherstone, Moore and Rhodes (1977) found that changes in UK unit labour costs between 1956 and 1976 could explain only a small part of the observed UK loss of market share in world exports of manufactures. A later study by J. Fagerberg looked at the factors which determined the growth of the UK's share of world export markets between 1960 and 1983. It found that labour cost (a main determinant of price competitiveness) was much less important than non-price factors (such as the capacity to deliver goods and technological competitiveness) in accounting for the UK's relatively poor ability to compete in world markets (Fagerberg 1988).

The picture is similar for imports. One OECD survey found little link between UK price competitiveness and import penetration (OECD 1980). A statistical survey by the present author has substantiated these results for the period 1963–90. The UK's ratio of imports to home demand was barely affected by observed changes in UK price competitiveness during this period, whatever the time-lags introduced. Although price factors obviously play a part in the problems experienced by the UK on visible trade, the studies we have considered clearly show that other, presumably non-price, factors must also play a major role.

Income   The level of world income is an important factor affecting demand for UK goods, and hence her trading position. Thirlwall (1980) suggests that the income elasticity of demand for *total* UK exports (which measures the responsiveness of UK exports to changes in world income) has been relatively low over the last thirty years, being in the main less than unity. The figure for *manufactured* exports is also generally below unity, although *individual sectors and products* often have elasticity figures which vary between 1.0 and 1.5. These values tend to be lower than those for our competitors. For West Germany the income elasticity of demand for total exports is as high as 2.5, and for Japan 3.5 (Thirlwall 1978).

However, it is well known that changes in the level of UK income have a significant effect on the UK demand for imports. In other words, the income elasticity of demand for *total* UK imports is high, ranging between 1.6 and 2 (Thirlwall 1978). For *total manufactured* imports the value of income elasticity is even higher, between 2.6 and 3.0, and for *finished manufactured* imports higher still, around 4.6 (Humphrey 1976).

The UK income elasticity figure for *total imports* is not significantly different from other countries – USA 1.5, West Germany 1.8 – but for *manufactured imports* it does seem higher in the UK than elsewhere. The study by Panić (1975) found the income elasticity of demand for manufactured products to be 3.1 in the UK, but only 2.2 in France and 2.1 in West Germany. These elasticity values highlight three important points:

1.   That income elasticity of demand for total UK imports is higher than for total UK exports.

2.   That for manufactures, particularly finished manufactures, this gap between income elasticity of demand for UK imports and exports is even greater.

3.   That other countries have similar or lower (as in manufactures) income elasticities of demand for imports, but experience higher income elasticities of demand for their exports.

The implications of these figures are clear. When income (and therefore demand) in the world economy rises, UK imports will tend to grow faster than UK exports, especially for manufactures. Other countries will not however suffer to the same extent as the UK. Whilst their imports may grow steadily, their exports will grow relatively faster than UK exports, so that their visible balance comes under less strain.

Unfortunately, the effect of higher income on imports is not easily reversed. The data suggest a sort of 'ratchet effect', so that although the ratio of manufactured imports to GDP rises on the upswing of the business cycle, it does not fall to the same extent on the downswing. There is then a real danger that higher import ratios for manufactures become a permanent feature of the economy. The UK domestic appliance industry (cookers, washing machines, electric kettles, etc.) is a useful case study of a ratchet effect (Brown 1982). The share of the domestic market taken by importers doubled from 13 to 27% during the 'Barber' boom of the early 1970s, and by 1982 had risen still further to around 37%, despite economic recession. The operation of a ratchet effect ensured that the import ratio rarely fell below peak level, even in years of recession and reduced real incomes. This tendency for imports to build up during UK booms can be further illustrated by the more recent consumer-led boom of 1988–90. A survey during this period by *Which*, the monthly consumer magazine, showed that of its 21 'best monthly buys' in the consumer durables sector, only six were made in Britain; and of these six, two were produced by foreign multinationals based in the UK (*Sunday Times* 1990). With the growth of import penetration rising so strongly during the boom, it is unlikely that imports of finished manufactured goods such as these will fall when real incomes stabilize as the economy decelerates.

One reason for exports rising relatively slowly when UK and world income increases, is the tendency for firms to concentrate on the more secure home market when domestic demand is high. This shift away from the export market and towards the home market has affected our export performance, with exports progressively becoming a 'residual' market for UK producers. The UK domestic appliance industry is again a useful case illustration. In 1970 it supplied 8% of the world market; by 1982 it only supplied 5%. The first real collapse in the export market was blamed on the lifting of hire-purchase restrictions, which stimulated home demand and caused producers to neglect exports in favour of the now more buoyant home market. This trend was again seen during the 1986/8 period when domestic demand grew by 11.7% while domestic output grew by only 9.4%. As a result UK companies switched some goods destined for the export market back into the home market in order to take advantage of buoyant domestic demand and higher profit margins. The excess demand in the UK during this period also resulted in the growth of import volume by 20.3% while the volume of exports grew by only 4.3%. This fall in the volume of exports in order to meet the home demand is sometimes difficult to reverse, as it takes time to recover lost export markets. For example, in the UK truck industry it can take as long as eighteen months to secure an overseas contract.

Another reason for the slow growth of exports when UK income increases, and with it domestic demand, might be the failure of firms to increase their total capacity in order to satisfy *both* home and foreign markets.[1] For instance, an increase in total capacity may require UK companies to increase their investment in plant and equipment, and this is never easy.

Unfortunately, even if UK firms *do* manage to increase total capacity by channeling more resources into increased investment, the *composition* of this investment may be biased against export growth. For example, it has been argued that during the 1980s those UK sectors which invested most in plant and equipment were the ones which were least open to foreign competition (Muellbauer 1990). In his study, Muellbauer calculates 'tradeability' and 'investment growth' ratios for twenty-five sectors in the UK economy. The *tradeability ratio* is defined as the ratio of exports or imports to total sales (whichever is the largest). If this ratio is high, it indicates that the sector is relatively 'open' to trade, and thus to foreign competition. If the ratio is low, then the sector is less involved in trade and is not affected so much by foreign competition. The *tradeability ratio* of each sector was compared with the *growth of investment* in that sector between 1979 and 1987 (expressed as a ratio using 1979 as the base year). The general conclusion was that the investment ratio tends to be very *high* in sectors such as Distribution, Communications and Banking which have *low* tradeability ratios, i.e. which are not so open to foreign competition. In other areas (such as manufacturing) where the investment ratio is lower, the tradeability ratio is high, i.e. they are more open to foreign competition. The argument here is that investment has not grown sufficiently in those sectors most open to foreign competition. This obviously prevents many UK industries from competing effectively abroad. Similarly, too much investment may have gone into sectors such as banking, insurance, and distribution, which are not so open to foreign competition. This bias in the investment ratios may inhibit the UK's long run ability to produce goods for the world markets.

However, the UK problem is certainly more than just a shortage of capacity forcing producers to choose between home and export markets. Manison (1978) showed that even when the UK has had more spare capacity than other countries it has still experienced higher import penetration than those countries. Wragg and Robertson (1978) stress that a major problem for the UK has been to utilize *existing* capacity fully, and they conclude that raising the productivity of *existing* capacity is at least as important as increasing total capacity.

Quality, service and other effects   Price and income are not the only factors influencing UK trade performance. In the home market, competition between oligopolistic firms often takes the form of non-price competition (see Ch. 6). Since much of world trade, especially in manufactures, involves competition between domestic and foreign multinationals (see Ch. 7), it is hardly surprising that it is often non-price competition that determines which nations will be successful in the export market.

Two types of non-price competition seem particularly important for both domestic and overseas sales. First, competition in *product characteristics*, such as quality, design and ease of maintenance. Second, competition in *sales characteristics*, such as delivery date, after-sales service, marketing strategies, and the use made of agents and subsidiaries at home and abroad.

To quantify the relative importance of non-price factors, such as quality and service, is a difficult task, made more so by a dearth of regular statistics in this area. However, some *ad hoc* attempts have been made at statistical analysis. One prominent method for evaluating the importance of non-price factors is to compare the average value per unit weight of exports from different countries. This figure is obtained by dividing the total value of goods exported by a certain sector, e.g. mechanical engineering, by the total weight of such exports. We should note that the 'value per ton' that results from this calculation is simply the average price per ton. The rationale behind value per ton comparisons is that if goods are identical in non-price characteristics such as quality, then international competition will tend to make value per ton (average price per ton) similar in whichever country those goods are produced. It then follows that any discrepancy in value per ton between countries in a given export product is an indication that non-price differences exist in that product.

Research based on the years 1962–75 found that the value per ton of UK exports from the non-electrical sector (essentially mechanical engineering) was the lowest of all the major industrialized countries. Apart from Italy, the rate of growth of value per ton was also lowest in the UK between those dates. Similar results were observed in a separate study of a wide range of manufactured exports traded between the UK and West Germany (Connell 1980: Ch. 3). A number of inferences can be drawn from such evidence:

1. The lower value per ton of UK exports may reflect lower prices in the UK for *similar*-quality products. However, if UK exports were cheaper, and of the same quality, then the UK's share of the world market in such products should increase! Since the UK's share did *not* increase it is unconvincing to explain lower value per ton of UK exports in terms of lower UK prices for similar-quality products.

2. It could still be argued that the lower-priced UK exports are similar in quality to those produced abroad, but that static or falling market share is due to inadequate sales back-up. United Kingdom exporters may have lowered prices (reducing value per ton) in the hope that relative cheapness would raise sales and help compensate for an inability to market the product adequately.

3. The relatively low value per ton of UK exports could be due to differences in product mix between different countries. The UK may be going progressively 'down market', exporting 'less technology-intensive' products. The price, and therefore value per ton, of UK exports would then tend to be lower than in those countries which export a higher proportion of the 'more technology-intensive' products (see Ch. 7).

Even if the precise cause of the low value per ton of UK exports is difficult to identify it seems reasonable to assume that it must be due to factors *other than* price competition amongst export goods of similar quality. Especially since in many cases the value per ton of other countries' exports was two or three times higher than that of UK exports. Non-price factors – quality, design, marketing, after-sales service, etc. – must account for much of the substantial difference in value per ton.

The conclusion that non-price factors may be crucial is in line with other studies using entirely different methods of analysis. Krause and Lipsey found that only 28% of US and West German exporters related export 'success' to lower prices, whilst as many as 37% considered the major influence on exports to be product superiority (Stout 1977). An important NEDC report (1981) examined thirty export sectors, and concluded that factors such as marketing and the presence or absence of non-tariff barriers were much more influential than price in affecting UK exports. On the import side, a NEDC survey of machine tools in the 1960s had found technical superiority and better after-sales service the most important reasons for UK firms buying from overseas – only 5% had quoted lower price as being of major importance (Stout 1977).

Product quality. Product quality depends on many interrelated factors but it is clear that most high quality products are ones which tend to have a high research and development content, are technologically complex and are also skill intensive. A range of recent studies also supports the contention that the UK has gone 'down market' *vis-à-vis* the other advanced industrialized countries. Put another way, the UK is tending more and more to export cheaper, lower-quality products, embodying 'old' technology, and to import expensive, high-quality products, embodying 'new' technology. For instance, Katrak (1982) noted that during the 1970s UK exports contained a greater proportion of 'less skill-intensive' and 'less research and development-intensive' (and therefore less technologically advanced) products than did her imports. It has also been pointed out that there seems a clear link between the amount of effort expended on R & D and export competitiveness (Mayer 1986). United Kingdom industries with relatively *smaller R & D* as compared to their overseas competitors are *less competitive* in world trade in the products of those industries. Katrak also noted that the UK tended to export mainly 'mature' products, i.e. those which have been on the market for a relatively long period, yet to import mainly 'less mature' products. This strategy is particularly dangerous when the growth of 'mature' products in world trade is slower than that of newer products. There is also the danger that domestic and overseas markets in 'mature' products will be increasingly vulnerable to competition, such as that from the newly industrializing countries. Results from a NEDO study spanning the period 1977 to 1987 continue to indicate the UK's tendency to export lower quality products. In sectors producing machine tools and agricultural and pump machinery, it was found that UK industry was still exporting lower quality products than those sold by France, Germany and Japan. During the latter part of the 1980s it also appeared that the UK was importing lower quality equipment than its leading rivals. This latter fact is disturbing because it could affect the capacity of UK industry to produce high quality exports! (*Financial Times* 1990a).

These rather general studies on the 'down market' nature of UK production of both exports and import substitutes, may be backed up by specific industry examples. Daly and Jones (1980) in their study of the engineering industries of the UK, West Germany and France, found that the UK machine-tool industry produced and exported products which were far too standardized, and therefore open to foreign competition, whilst UK imports of machine tools tended to be composed of highly complex and advanced equipment. Similarly, a more recent study of the UK and West German furniture industry (Steedman and Wagner 1987) showed that even though the industry was far from being in the 'high technology' class, it was still obvious that the UK furniture industry continued to use technically less advanced equipment and produced for the middle- to low-quality end of the market. West German firms on the other hand used more advanced equipment and specialized in high-quality products, exporting some of these to the UK!

However, it is interesting to note that in the more dynamic sectors of UK industry, there are signs of a shift towards the higher end of the quality market. In the chemical industry, for example, there has been a trend towards the production and export of speciality chemicals and away from bulk chemical products. Bulk production of basic chemical products such as ethylene are often priced between £500 and £1,000 per tonne, while the speciality chemicals produced for the pharmaceutical industry or as a base for glue or paint production are sold at prices of up to £300,000 per tonne or more. Speciality chemicals are made in highly automated plants requiring few people and embody considerable research and engineering skills. Such speciality products, besides being of high quality and more profitable, are made in low enough volumes to be easily exported by air freight, so that UK manufacturing firms are not at a disadvantage when tackling world markets (*Financial Times* 1990b). This example serves to show that UK industry can become more competitive if it follows the quality route.

Even the UK income elasticities of demand we noted earlier could be considered symptoms of 'product inferiority'. The low income elasticity of demand for UK exports, and high income elasticity of demand for UK imports, both suggest that at higher income, goods produced by the UK export industries and by the import substitute industries are replaced by more attractive, higher-quality goods from abroad. There is some evidence to show that European exports were moving in the direction of more highly skilled, capital-intensive products in the early 1980s (UN 1981: Ch. 4, section 3) and that the UK needed to become more involved in these high-technology products to increase its export share and to reduce import penetration. In 1987 an important study (Patel and Pavitt 1987) attempted to assess the relationship between the UK's technological competitiveness in world markets with her trading performance. Measuring the UK's trading performance in certain sectors of the economy was relatively straightforward, since figures for exports and imports are easily available. However, it was more difficult to devise a measure which reflected the UK's technological competitiveness in relation to other countries. They overcame this problem by studying the *number of patents* which were granted in the USA between 1963 and 1984 and calculated an index which measured the share of those patents which had *originated* in the UK. For example, it was obvious that if one sector of US industry used a large proportion of patents which had originally been invented in the UK, then this meant that the UK was technologically very competitive in this sector. Conversely, a sector with a low ratio of US patents originating from the UK indicated a relatively lower level of UK technical competence in this particular sector. By comparing these measures of UK technological competitiveness with UK trade performance, sector by sector, it was possible to see that the interrelationships between trade and technology were very close. For example in the electrical and electronics industry, the UK's technological competitiveness was medium to low and her trade competitiveness was also low. For the chemical industry, the UK's technological competitiveness was medium to high, and so was her trade competitiveness in this sector. In other words there seemed to be a strong relationship between technological competitiveness and trading performance.

The relatively low income elasticity of demand for UK manufactured exports does tend to indicate that UK producers are unable to react promptly to world demand with good quality products. However, it has been argued recently that the value of income elasticity of demand for UK manufactured exports has increased since the late 1970s. This would suggest that UK manufacturing industry has become more responsive to changes in world demand since the recession of the early 1980s (Landesmann and Snell 1989).

The crux of this theory is that the aggregate income elasticity of demand for UK manufactured exports has risen from 0.74 in 1979 to 1.0 by 1986, and that this may be due to the shake out of inefficient exporters during the 1979–81 slump which left a core of relatively more efficient exporters. By definition, 'poor' exporters have low income elasticities and 'good' exporters have high income elasticity figures. Improvements were found in many industries, with the income elasticity figure for electrical engineering rising from 0.78 in 1979 to 1.3 by 1986, the figure for textiles and clothing rising from 0.8 to 1.3, and for transport from 0.8 to 1.0 over the same period. These figures do tend to point to an export performance from UK industry which is more responsible to world demand since the early 1980s. Despite this encouraging sign, it should also be remembered that the UK manufacturing sector needs a greater *absolute number* of firms which are responsive to the market in order to increase total exports significantly. This is difficult to achieve when the manufacturing base of the economy is being eroded, as was seen in Chapter 1 of this book.

This problem of quality has been noted in a number of official publications. Two important reports stressed the need for policy action to raise the quality of UK products (ACARD 1982; Dept of Trade 1982), both to increase exports and to decrease imports. Of course for individual firms there are costs as well as benefits in the quest for improved quality. To prevent product defect or failure, the firm may have to incur increased costs in the form of higher R & D expenditure. Even assessing the quality of existing products will incur inspection and certification costs. If quality factors are as important as we have suggested, then the benefits of product improvement (in the form of higher exports and lower imports) are likely to outweigh these costs. The ACARD report, in surveying the metal-processing, foundry and motor-vehicle assembly industries, found that the benefits derived from improved product quality far exceeded the costs incurred.

Good design, as well as product quality, is also essential if the UK is to become more competitive, but some important studies on the experience of UK graduates in design have not been encouraging! For example, a major study by Donald Verry and Kathy Pick (*Guardian* 1983) showed that between 1976 and 1982 the proportion of UK design graduates from universities and polytechnics who found 'appropriate' permanent employment was as low as 50%. Also UK design graduates were more likely to find employment overseas as compared with other types of graduates. The study concludes by stressing the need to create better opportunities for design graduates if the UK is to improve product competitiveness abroad. However, opportunities for UK designers also depend in part on UK manufacturers. For example, in 1988, UK designers in the clothing industry criticized manufacturers for not being interested in small batch production under licensing agreements with designers. As a result UK designers in this industry have turned to *overseas* suppliers, such as Italy, who have modern plants capable of dealing with *small* quantities. There may be a need in the UK for manufacturers to be more aware of the needs of a rapidly changing market in order to utilize design talents already in existence in the UK (*Financial Times* 1988a).

Encouraging the design aspects of product competitiveness is also important, because there is often a close relationship between the design of a product and its cost of production. For example, it is not always realized that a significant proportion of the cost of a finished product is often dictated by the specific design which is chosen at the outset. According to executives of General Motors in the US, some 70% of the cost of producing the transmission mechanism of its trucks is determined at the design stage. Similarly, in a study of the Rolls Royce company, John Corbett found that 80% of the final costs of some 2,000 different components were determined by the design adopted. This means that good, efficient design is an essential requirement for keeping costs at a minimum when competing in international markets (Griffiths 1989).

Product marketing and sales. Apart from quality, marketing and selling operations can have a substantial impact on market share. In a report by NEDO (1981) the UK had increased its share of total OECD exports in only nine of the thirty industrial sectors studied – with 'inadequate marketing' the single factor most often quoted as the explanation for this poor export performance. An earlier NEDO report on the UK textile industry had concluded that most of the UK's problems in competing with its EEC counterparts arose from a poor performance in packaging, delivery date and after-sales service, rather than from price. Similarly, Blackburn (1982) found that the UK was susceptible to imports of dyed and printed textiles mainly because of its inferior design, colour and after-sales service.

It does appear that other countries have devoted more sales effort to the export market than has the UK. In West Germany thirteen people are employed in the home sales department for every ten people on the export side. The figures for France are eighteen and ten respectively, but for the UK fifty-five and ten (Tessler 1982). Not only do UK competitors have larger sales forces in the export sector, but they also employ more highly skilled marketing specialists, and pay more attention to the activities of promotion, advertising, delivery date and after-sales service. Yet as early as the 1960s Steuer, Ball and Eaton (1966) had already pointed out that a delay of only one month in meeting export orders for machine tools could reduce total UK exports of such products by as much as 10%!

The importance of *early delivery* in determining export success has been stressed by many writers, such as Fagerberg previously quoted in this chapter. He found that the loss of UK market share in manufacturing exports was very closely linked to the capacity of UK companies to deliver goods efficiently. This in turn was dependent on the diffusion of technology within companies, and to the growth of UK investment in plant and equipment. It can be seen, therefore, that an efficient delivery of goods depends on many interrelated factors. However, it should be understood that even if UK companies can produce good products, there is still the problem of cutting down the time between receiving a customer's order and actual delivery. It has been calculated that between 33% and 50% of the time taken between receiving an order and final delivery is taken up by sales and distribution activities, so that any effort to cut this time period will increase competitiveness and lower costs.

The gains to be reaped from cutting this time to a minimum can be illustrated by the Japanese company Toyota. In the early 1980s the Toyota car company could manufacture a complete car in two days, but Toyota Motor Sales (the independent sales arm of the company) took between 15 and 26 days to make the sale, order from the factory and get the car delivered. Much of the delay was due to the fact that the sales company processed the orders in batches, which travelled through various levels of sales organization before reaching the manufacturing company for further processing. In 1982 the companies were merged and orders were then routed directly to the factory floor without recourse to different layers of sales and production personnel. By 1987 Toyota could supply the required car eight days after the customer had made the original order, which was half the time taken by the most efficient US or UK car makers. If the UK is to be responsive to world export demand, it will have to look much more closely at its sales and delivery techniques, so vividly illustrated by those of Toyota.

Obviously, if UK products could be made more competitive in non-price factors then the production of both exports and import substitutes would benefit. In the spring of 1982 a challenge was issued to UK industry in the form of an exhibition called *Can You Make It*. Imported products worth £100m. a year were put on show and UK firms asked whether they could produce an adequate replacement for such imports, and if so, at what price. Some 2,000 quotations were obtained from UK firms. In analysing these responses it was decided that in 32% of cases an adequate replacement could not be produced for technical reasons; in 28% of cases the replacement could not compete in price, in 13% the replacement could not be delivered on time, and in 12% the replacement was of inferior quality. Whilst price factors were important, over 70% of the firms were still unable to compete because of non-price factors (*Sunday Times* 1982). The need to *integrate* both quality and market efficiency in order to improve non-price competitiveness was recently reinforced by John Fisher, the only designer to win the Duke of Edinburgh's design award on two separate occasions, in 1978 and 1988. His designs included the first hand-held digital micrometer in 1978, and the first hand-held tonometer to measure eye pressure in 1988. He stressed the need to 'match something interesting happening in technology with marketing efficiency' (*Financial Times* 1988b).

There are signs that some UK companies have taken steps to improve marketing efficiency. British Steel Distribution, which is involved in the sales of steel products to Europe, have stressed their ability to deliver good quality steel on time and with close technical backing. The company has also promoted the use of steel more generally in the construction industry, since market research led them to learn that steel is used for only 20% of buildings in the EC. It is also supporting this policy by funding university courses to promote the use of steel. In other words, good companies are creating a market for their products by forward thinking (*Financial Times* 1990c).

The importance of visible trade for the UK

It could be argued that there is no reason to worry about the problems facing the UK on her non-oil visible trade, because oil and invisibles will rectify the financial imbalance. However, the situation is not as simple as this, involving long-term competitive problems within the UK economy which other parts of the accounts may not always be able to offset.

Problems of competitiveness for goods production in general, and manufacturing in particular, are important for a number of reasons.

1. The UK's dependence on visible trade is as high, if not higher, than many other industrial countries of comparable size. The UK ratio of exports of goods to GDP was 23.2% in 1987, compared to 26.2% in West Germany, 15.4% in Italy, 16.8% in France, 9.7% in Japan and 5.7% in the USA. Since exports are an injection into the domestic circular flow of income, any lack of competitiveness in the international markets will have a particularly important effect on economies such as the UK's in which exports are an important component of aggregate demand.

2. The importance of manufactured goods is particularly vital to the balance of payments on current account. Around 40% of all export earnings on current account (visible and invisible), and also about 40% of all expenditure on imports, derive from trade in manufactures. A less competitive performance in the manufacturing sector will, therefore, have a significant effect on the current account.

3. The rate of growth in the volume of exports of UK manufactured goods has, since 1969, been only half that of imports of manufactures. In fact by 1989, the volume of exports of UK manufactures was some 30% above its 1980 level, whilst the corresponding figure for the EEC was 49%, and for Japan 60% (UN 1989). Significantly, the UK was the only major industrial country between 1970 and 1980 to experience *both* a fall in its share of the total exports of manufactures of the 'major countries' *and* a rise in its share of the total imports of manufactures of the 'major countries'. A further erosion of competitiveness can only exacerbate these already stark trends.

4. There is evidence that trade in manufactures between the developed industrialized countries is increasing at the expense of such trade with the newly industrialized countries, at a time when it is these developed countries which are the main threat to UK trade performance. For instance, in the particularly important sector of machinery and transport equipment (49% of total UK manufactured exports) the developed industrialized countries have been the source of 86% of total world exports in this category since 1965, with 60% destined for other developed industrialized countries. Complaints about competition from 'low-wage' countries may be rather less significant to the UK than competition from these highly industrialized nations. In any case, competition from the newly industrialized countries is itself often competition from other industrialized nations through the guise of multinational company activities in those developing nations. Therefore, the fact that more and more trade is conducted between the *developed* industrial nations, and that more of that trade is in manufactures, suggests that an open economy like the UK's will encounter serious problems if it becomes progressively less competitive in non-oil visible trade (OECD 1979).

5. The import penetration ratio in manufactures has risen in the UK from

17 to 36% between 1968 and 1989. Some have argued that this loss of UK competitiveness in the production of import substitutes matters little since the ratio of exports to total sales of manufactures (the export sales ratio) has also risen in the UK from 18 to 30% over the same period. However, it has been pointed out that the export sales ratio is often artificially high in times of recession. As demand falls, and with it total sales of manufactures, the ratio becomes artificially high since the denominator falls faster than the numerator. Although UK export performance has improved, it should be understood that a higher ratio during periods of slow growth or recession may be a misleading index of long-term UK export competitiveness. Also, it is worth noting that although the exports/sales ratio did rise up to 1985, it has not changed much since that date, while the import/home demand ratio has continued to rise throughout the 1980s.

Loss of competitiveness in UK trade in non-oil visible goods *is* important for all these reasons. Although the UK oil surplus has alleviated many problems on current account (see Table 23.1), it would be short-sighted to see this as a cure for all our ills. The oil surplus has eased the immediate strains on the visible balance, but there is little evidence of improvement in UK price and non-price competitiveness. In fact oil has contributed to a high exchange rate for the pound (see Ch. 22), and in this sense has made UK producers less price-competitive in foreign and domestic markets.

Does the UK's deteriorating performance on non-oil visible trade in general, and manufacturing in particular, matter when we are still a major surplus country on invisible trade? It is quite true that the UK (see Table 23.1), along with countries like France, Switzerland and Spain, has a surplus on its invisible account. There is, however, no guarantee that this surplus on invisible account will grow fast enough to compensate for the progressive deterioration in trade in manufactures. When we convert the UK invisible surpluses into proportions of GDP (at factor cost), the ratio of 1.8% in 1987 is the same as that recorded as long ago as 1972. During the last quarter of 1989, figures for *invisible earnings* were in deficit for the first time since records on a quarterly basis were kept in 1955. This led to a fall in the ratio of invisible surplus to GDP to only 0.5% in that year. Although the fall in invisible earnings can partly be explained by unusually high payments to the EC and to losses sustained by insurers after the San Francisco earthquake, it is nevertheless true to say that the invisible account is becoming more prone to fluctuations than before. Essentially, the invisible account is made up of three elements. First, net earnings from interest, profit and dividends (IPD). Second, earnings from services such as shipping, civil aviation, general government services and financial services (such as banking and insurance). Third, transfers between the UK government and other institutions in the form of overseas aid or payments to the EC.

On average, the only element which has been in continuous deficit over the last fifteen years has been the transfer element, while IPD has, in most cases, been in surplus. Earnings from services remain in surplus, but only due to the banking and financial services component. It would be unwise for the UK to rely on the growth of such services to continue to compensate for the decline in manufactures and other visible items. The UK has already captured an 8% share of the world market in services, and further success may become increasingly difficult to achieve, especially after the 'Big Bang' of 1986 led to the arrival of a stream of foreign financial institutions in London. Other advanced countries are also concentrating on services as a means of increasing their incomes. In 1990, French earnings from the export of services had overtaken the UK figures for the first time ever, showing the growth of world competition in services. In this climate it would be rash for the UK to rely on the invisible account to support a progressive deterioration of a non-oil visible deficit.

A final point to observe is that the development of services is not necessarily divorced from manufacturing and from the visible side of the Balance of Payments. Service industries often need manufactured goods, such as computer and data processing equipment, so that a contraction of manufacturing can have adverse repercussions for services.

Apart from these reservations, it should also be remembered that the UK export of services is only 43% of the value of manufactured exports, and only 35% of the value of total visible exports. A given percentage change in exports of manufactures or of total visibles will have a larger *absolute* impact on the current account than would the same percentage change in the export of services. The same is true of imports. To concentrate on developing the invisible sector may be an inappropriate response to any loss of competitiveness experienced in non-oil visible trade.

Would a devaluation of the pound be more appropriate? We have seen that the price elasticities for manufactured exports and imports (and for total visible exports and imports) meet the Marshall–Lerner condition for a successful devaluation, in that their sum is greater than 1. As a result the value of exports will rise relative to the value of imports, though perhaps after a time-lag. However, there are fears that a lower exchange rate, whilst helping restore price competitiveness, might actually discourage the adaptive response necessary to restore non-price competitiveness. Improved quality and design have been seen to be important if the UK is to regain lost markets. Yet, ironically, firms may find it easier in the short run to sell older, more mature products, both at home and abroad, after the price advantage given them by devaluation. Mature products are generally standardized, having had a long exposure to the market. As a result they tend to be more sensitive to price changes than newer products which, being at the forefront of technology, tend to compete in terms of product characteristics such as quality and design. Devaluation, by making UK products cheaper, may therefore give a greater stimulus to the sale of mature products, at least in the short run. This will tend to erode incentives for going 'up market' into the more 'technology intensive' product areas upon which long-term UK competitiveness may depend.

Devaluation may also affect the product life-cycle strategies identified in Chapter 9, encouraging multiproduct firms to switch from newer products (early in their life cycle) to more mature products (later in their life cycle). Since it is the demand for mature products that is most responsive to the price reductions which follow a devaluation, the *multiproduct* firm may be able to increase its short-term cash flow by changing the composition of its product range towards the older, more mature products. Again, this process may also inhibit the production and export of new, more skill-intensive, high-technology products.

The net result is that devaluation, though promoting price competitiveness, may hinder non-price competitiveness by discouraging the move towards better-quality, more technology-intensive products. Brech and Stout (1981) point out that when the pound fell between 1971 and 1980, the UK machine-tool, machinery and transport equipment industries moved *less* readily towards producing more technically advanced products for export.

Conclusion

This chapter has attempted to analyse the trends in the UK balance of visible trade, with special reference to trade in manufactures. Although UK visible trade has adapted along similar lines to that of her competitors as regards both geographical area and commodity composition, her ability to compete *within* these areas and commodities has come under greater strain. The chapter also stressed the role of non-price factors, such as income, quality, design and marketing, in accounting for both UK export performance and import penetration. Although price considerations are important, they are often given too prominent a place in explanations of trade flow. The fact that UK manufactures have moved down market in quality, design and marketing, should perhaps be given more recognition as an important factor in restricting the growth of UK exports and in encouraging import penetration. The high income elasticity of demand for UK imports of manufactures is but one reflection of the growing importance of such non-price factors. In order to improve the UK's non-price competitiveness the Conservative Government introduced marketing, design and quality 'initiatives' in early 1988. These 'initiatives' are managed for the Department of Trade and Industry by the Institute of Marketing, the Design Council and the Production Engineering Research Association (PERA) respectively. Although this is a step in the right direction it should be noted that the answer to the problems of non-price competition lies as much in the boardrooms of UK companies as in the corridors of government departments.

Ironically, the UK's problem of matching other countries in terms of non-price factors has become a still more serious cause for concern over the last ten years with the progressive tendency for industrial countries to *specialize* in the production of traded goods. This has meant that countries have naturally increased their imports of specialized manufactured goods from each other, thereby increasing the import penetration ratio regardless of any change in other competitive factors (Cuthbertson 1985). Although the UK situation as regards trade in oil, and trade in invisibles is one of surplus, it would be a hazardous strategy to rely on these to 'subsidize' a progressive deterioration on trade in non-oil visible goods. The rapid fall in oil revenue between 1985 and 1989 has vividly demonstrated this point. There have been some signs that UK industry is becoming more supply responsive during the 1980s and that this has helped to increase the income elasticity of demand for UK exports, as shown by Landesmann and Snell. The question remains as to whether UK companies in general have the flexibility to follow the ebb and flow of the international market. The evidence for this remains rather elusive and patchy.

Note

1. For an analysis of the economy's failure to increase total capacity because of a labour bottleneck see, for example, Hughes and Thirlwall (1979).

References and further reading

ACARD (1982) *Facing International Competition*. HMSO.
Blackburn, J. A. (1982) The vanishing UK cotton industry, *National Westminster Bank Quarterly*, Nov.
Brech, M. J. and **Stout, D. K.** (1981) The rate of exchange and non-price competitiveness: a provisional study within UK manufactured exports. *Oxford Economic Papers*, **33**, July.
British Business (1987) Import penetration and export performance, 8 April.
Brown, M. (1982) The dark side of the boom, *Guardian*, 16 Nov.
Business Briefing (1990) Balance of Payments, 27 April.
Connell, D. (1980) The UK's performance in export markets – some evidence from international trade data, NEDO, discussion paper 6.
CSO (1968, 1973, 1982) *Annual Abstract of Statistics*.
CSO (1983) United Kingdom balance of payments in the fourth quarter and year 1982, *Economic Trends*, 353, March.
CSO (1985) *United Kingdom Balance of Payments* (1985 edn).
CSO (1988) *Monthly Digest of Statistics*, Feb.
CSO (1990) *Monthly Digest of Statistics*, May.
Cuthbertson, K. (1985) The behaviour of UK imports of manufactured goods, *National Institute Economic Review*, 113, Aug.
Daly, A. and **Jones, D. J.** (1980) The machine tool industry in Britain, Germany and the United States, *National Institute Economic Review*, 92.
Department of Trade (1982) *Standards, Quality and International Competitiveness*. Cmnd 8621, HMSO.
Featherstone, M., Moore, B. and **Rhodes, J.** (1977) Manufacturing export shares and cost competition of advanced industrial countries, *Economic Policy Review*, 3, March.
Financial Times (1988a) 12/13 March, p. 2.
Financial Times (1988b) 14 April, p. 11.
Financial Times (1990a) 16 March, p. 17.
Financial Times (1990b) 11 April, p. 20.
Financial Times (1990c) 30 April, p. 23.
Griffiths, A. (1989) Manufacturing competitiveness: new sources for old, *British Economy Survey* **18**, No. 2, Spring.
Guardian (1983) Design talent faces future on the dole, 21 Nov., p. 16.
Hewer, A. (1980) Manufacturing industry in the seventies: an assessment of import penetration and export performance, *Economic Trends*, 370, June.
Hughes, J. J. and **Thirlwall, A. P.** (1979) Imports and labour market

bottlenecks: a disaggregated study for the UK, *Applied Economics*, **11**, 1, March.

Humphrey, D. H. (1976) Disaggregated import function for UK, West Germany and France, *Oxford Bulletin of Economics and Statistics*, **38**, 4, Table 2.

Kaldor, N. (1978) *Further Essays in Economics*. Duckworth.

Katrak, H. (1982) Labour skills, research and development and capital requirements in international trade and investment of the UK 1968–78, *National Institute Economic Review*, 101.

Krause, L. B. (1968) British trade performance, in: Caves, R. E. and associates *Britain's Economic Prospects*. George Allen and Unwin Ltd, p. 222.

Landesmann, M. and **Snell, A.** (1989) The consequences of Mrs Thatcher for UK manufacturing exports, *Economic Journal*, **99**, March.

Major, R. L. (1968) Note on Britain's share of world trade in manufactures, *National Institute Economic Review*, 44.

Mayes, D. G. (1986) *Change*. Discussion paper No. 31, New Zealand Institute of Economic Research.

Manison, L. G. (1978) Some factors influencing the United Kingdom's economic performance, *IMF Staff Papers*, **25**, Dec.

Morgan, A. D. and **Martin, A.** (1975) Tariff reductions and UK imports of manufactures 1955–71, *National Institute Economic Review*, May.

Muellbauer, J. (1990) A pattern biased against trade? *Financial Times*, 19 Feb., p. 17.

National Institute of Economic and Social Research (1970) *National Institute Economic Review*, 54.

National Institute of Economic and Social Research (1983) *National Institute Economic Review*, 103.

NEDO (1981) *Industrial Performance, Trade Performance and Marketing*.

OECD(1979) *The Impact of Newly Industrializing Countries on Production and Trends in Manufacturing*. Paris.

OECD (1980) *The United Kingdom*. Economic Survey, Paris.

OECD (1988/9) *The United Kingdom*. Economic Survey, Paris.

Panić, M. (1975) Why the UK propensity to import is high, *Lloyds Bank Review*, 115, Jan.

Panić, M. and **Rajan, A. H.** (1971) *Product Changes in Industrialized Countries' Trade 1955–1968*. NEDO Monograph 2.

Patel, P. and **Pavitt, K.** (1987) The elements of British technological competitiveness, *National Institute Economic Review*, Nov.

Posner, M. and **Steer, A.** (1978) Price competitiveness and the performance of manufacturing industry, in: Blackaby, F. (ed.) *Deindustrialization*. Heinemann.

Steedman, H. and **Wagner, K.** (1987) A second look at productivity, machinery and skills in Britain and Germany, *National Institute Economic Review*, Nov.

Steuer, M. D., Ball, R. J. and **Eaton, J. R.** (1966) The effects of waiting times on foreign orders of machine tools, *Economica*, **33**, Nov.

Stout, D. (1977) *International Price Competitiveness, Non-Price Factors and Export Performance*. NEDO, Appendix C.

References and further reading

Tessler, A. (1982) The disturbing facts behind the flood of import. *Marketing*, 29 July.

The Sunday Times (1982) 28 Nov.

The Sunday Times (1990) May, p. D7.

Thirlwall, A. P. (1978) The UK's economic problems: a balance of paymei. constraint? *National Westminster Bank Review*, Feb.

Thirlwall, A. P. (1980) *Balance of Payments: theory and the UK experience*. Macmillan.

UN (1981) *Economic Survey of Europe in 1980*. Ch. 4, section 3, p. 216.

UN (1990) *Monthly Bulletin of Statistics*. March, Special Table F.

Wells, J. D. and **Imber, J. C.** (1977) Home and export performance of United Kingdom industries, *Economic Trends*, 286, Aug.

Worswick, G. D. N. and **Ady, P. H.** (eds) (1962) *The British Economy in the Nineteen Fifties*. Clarendon Press, Oxford.

Wragg, R. and **Robertson, J.** (1978) Britain's industrial performance since the war. Trends in employment, productivity, output, labour costs and prices by industry 1950–1973, *Department of Employment Gazette*, **86**, 5, May.

Protectionism

Protectionist measures are aimed at reducing the level of imports, either because of the 'damage' they cause to particular domestic industries, or because of their adverse effects on the balance of payments. In this chapter we review critically the arguments in favour of free trade, and therefore against protectionism. We examine the international institutions which have been created to foster trade, particularly the General Agreement on Tariffs and Trade (GATT). We then note the measures available to countries wishing to pursue a protectionist strategy. The extent to which such measures have been used within both the European Community (EC) and the UK is considered, together with their alleged benefits and costs.

Free trade

Free trade was given impetus by 'The Theory of Comparative Advantage', outlined by Ricardo in the nineteenth century. Essentially, Ricardo sought to extend Adam Smith's principle of the division of labour to a global scale, with each country specializing in those goods which it could produce most efficiently. Even if one country was more efficient than another country in the production of all goods, Ricardo showed that it could still gain by specializing in those goods in which its *relative efficiency* was greatest. It was said to have a *comparative* advantage in such goods. This would raise total world output above the level it would otherwise be, with the benefits shared via trade between the two countries. The degree of benefit to any one country after specialization and trade would depend upon the terms of trade, i.e. the ratio of export to import prices.

The use of protectionist measures, such as tariffs, may distort the comparative cost ratios, by raising import prices and encouraging the domestic production of goods that could otherwise have been imported rather more cheaply. In addition to disrupting the efficient allocation of *domestic* resources, such protectionist measures are likely to reduce international specialization and to lead to a less efficient allocation of *world* resources.

Figure 24.1 shows that free trade could, in theory, bring welfare benefits to an economy previously protected. Suppose the industry is initially *completely protected*. The price P_D will then be determined by the interaction of domestic supply ($S–S_H$) and domestic demand ($D–D_H$). The Government now decides to remove these barriers and to allow foreign competition. For simplicity, we assume a perfectly elastic 'world' supply curve $P_W–C$, giving a total supply curve (domestic and world) of SAC. Domestic price will then be forced down to the world level, P_W, with domestic demand being OQ_3 at this

Fig. 24.1 Free trade versus
no trade

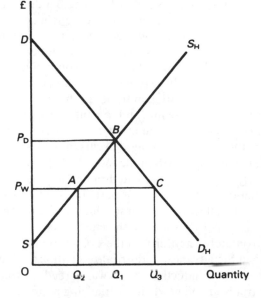

price. To meet this domestic demand, OQ_2 will be supplied from domestic sources, with Q_2Q_3 supplied from the rest of the world (i.e. imported). The consumer surplus, which is the difference between what consumers are *prepared* to pay and what they *have* to pay, has risen from DBP_D to DCP_W. The producer surplus, which is the difference between the price the producer receives and the minimum necessary to induce production, has fallen from P_DBS to P_WAS. The gain in consumer surplus outweighs the loss in producer surplus by the area ABC, which could then be regarded as the net gain in economic welfare as a result of free trade replacing protectionism.

Critics of free trade suggest that a number of drawbacks may outweigh the net gain shown above:

1. The theory is based on a 'full employment' model and fails to appreciate the problems raised by chronic unemployment. For instance, in Fig. 24.1 if domestic supply falls from OQ_1 to OQ_2 as a result of the removal of tariffs, then the reduced output may lead to unemployment. The welfare loss associated with this may more than offset the net welfare gain (area ABC) noted above.

2. It fails to analyse how the gains that arise from trade will be distributed. In practice, the stronger economies, through their economic power, have often been able to extract the greater benefits.

3. It assumes a purely competitive model of industry. If, in fact, industry includes both large and small firms, then area ABC may not represent net gain. For instance, a higher proportion of the remaining domestic output OQ_2 in Fig. 24.1 may now be in the hands of a monopoly. This growth in importance of monopoly could be construed as a welfare loss to be set against the area of net gain, ABC.

In practice a number of organizations have tried to encourage free trade in the post-war period.

General Agreement on Tariffs and Trade

This agreement was signed in 1947 by 23 industrialized nations, including the UK, USA, Canada, France and the Benelux countries. Since then the number of signatories has risen to 96 and now includes a large number of newly industrializing nations. GATT members in total account for almost 90% of the value of world trade. The objectives of GATT have been, and remain, substantially to reduce tariffs and other barriers to trade, and to eliminate discrimination in trade. In this way, GATT aims to contribute to rising standards of living, and to a fuller use of the world's resources.

Since GATT was formed, there have been seven 'rounds' of negotiations paving the way for considerable cuts in the level of tariffs being applied. In 1947, the average tariff in the industrialized world stood at some 40%, but by the early 1990s the figure had dropped to below 5%. The 'Kennedy round' of negotiations in the 1960s was particularly effective, with tariffs cut by about one-third, reducing the average duty on the manufactures to about 10% by 1972. The 'Tokyo round' in the later 1970s resulted in further reductions of approximately one-third. In the Tokyo round the negotiations favoured trade between the advanced industrialized nations, where the tariff cut was 38%; a rather smaller reduction, 25%, was agreed for trade between the advanced industrialized and newly industrializing nations.

There are a number of provisions which allow a country to deviate from the GATT strategy of reductions in tariff barriers. Article 6 permits retaliatory sanctions if 'dumping' (see pp. 514–15) can be proven. Article 18 provides a number of 'escape clauses' for the newly industrializing countries, allowing them to protect both infant industries and their balance of payments. Article 19 permits any country to abstain from a general tariff cut in situations where rising imports may seriously damage domestic production. Articles 21–25 are concerned with the protection of the national interest, permitting restrictions to be placed on imported products which might affect the nation's security.

In addition to tariff cuts, GATT has made efforts to eradicate discrimination in trade, by use of the 'most-favoured nation' clause. This requires that any trading advantage granted by one country to another must be accorded to *all* other member states. Exceptions to this are allowed in special cases, such as the creation of a free trade area or a customs union (i.e. protected free trade area).

A major drawback to GATT is its inability to apply sanctions, forcing it to rely on voluntary compliance. A further source of criticism of GATT is its allegedly excessive tolerance of restrictions on trade in agriculture. Export subsidies on agricultural products are not immediately punishable under GATT – as they are on manufactures. Members are also under no obligation to allow others access to their home markets for food. Major producers, such as Australia, are particularly anxious to have free trade in agriculture so that they can better dispose of surplus production, whereas the EC is equally anxious to preserve the regulatory framework of the Common Agricultural Policy (CAP). Another criticism of GATT, particularly from the USA, has concerned its failure to encompass trade in services, which can be, and usually are, closely regulated by member states. In fact, no headway was made in the Tokyo round as regards removing restrictions on either agriculture or services.

The latest series of multilateral negotiations, known as the Uruguay round, lasted from 1986 to 1990, but progress was slow because of the conflicting interests of GATT members. Newly industrializing countries were primarily concerned with achieving a phasing out of the multifibre arrangements and agricultural subsidies, which they saw as benefitting the advanced, industrial nations. These industrial nations on the other hand, were more interested in securing comprehensive agreements providing protection for world trade in ideas (intellectual property) and removing restrictions on world trade in services.

United Nations Conference on Trade, Aid and Development

The first United Nations Conference on Trade, Aid and Development (UNCTAD) was convened in 1964. The primary goal of such conferences is to enlarge the share in world trade of the newly industrializing countries and to raise the level of aid given by the advanced industrialized nations. UNCTAD was closely involved in the preferential tariff arrangements granted to developing countries by the EC and Japan in 1971, and by the USA in 1976

European Economic Community

As we see in Chapter 26, the EC was formed in 1957 as a customs union with the specific aim of encouraging free trade between member states. The advent of the single market in 1992 will represent the fulfilment of this particular objective. Under these conditions, all barriers to trade between the member states will be abolished. There are currently twelve members, with tariffs imposed on goods imported from non-member countries. The EC has a population of 324 million, and accounts for 31% of world exports. With a united Germany in 1990, the population rose still further, to 341 million.

European Free Trade Area

The European Free Trade Area (EFTA) was formed in 1959 with seven countries, including the UK. Since then, the UK, Denmark and Portugal have transferred to the EC, and Finland and Iceland have joined the remaining member states – Sweden, Norway, Austria and Switzerland. Free trade exists between these EFTA countries but there is no harmonization of tariffs on trade with non-members. EFTA has a population of some 40 million, and accounts for 6% of world exports.

Council for Mutual Economic Assistance

The Council for Mutual Economic Assistance (CMEA) is better known as Comecon, and was founded in 1949. Its members currently include what was, until the dramatic political transformation in 1989, the European Communist bloc as well as Mongolia, Cuba and Vietnam. In addition to encouraging trade, Comecon aims to co-ordinate economic plans, exchange scientific knowledge and to finance projects of common interest. Comecon has a population of 450 million, and accounts for 11% of world exports.

The shift in the political landscape of much of Eastern Europe has, however, left a cloud hanging over the future of this organization. Some of its members have already expressed an interest in switching allegiances to the

European Community. In addition, the early 1990s have seen the effective stoppage of multilateral co-operation between COMECON members, and its replacement by a variety of bilateral agreements.

Protectionism

There are a number of methods which may be used to restrict the level of imports into a country.

Methods of protection

Tariff   A tariff is, in effect, a tax levied on imported goods, usually with the intention of raising the price of imports and thereby discouraging their purchase. Additionally, it is a source of revenue for the Government. Tariffs can be of two types: lump sum, or specific, with the tariff a fixed amount per unit; *ad valorem* or percentage, with the tariff a variable amount per unit.

   To examine the effect of a tariff, it helps simplify Fig. 24.2 if we again assume a perfectly elastic world supply of the good S_W at the going world price P_W, which implies that any amount of the good can be imported into the UK without there being a change in the world price. In the absence of a tariff the domestic price would be set by the world price, P_W in Fig. 24.2. At this price, domestic demand D_H will be OQ_2 though domestic supply S_H will only be OQ_1. The excess demand, $Q_2 - Q_1$, will be satisfied by importing the good.

Fig. 24.2 The effect of a tariff

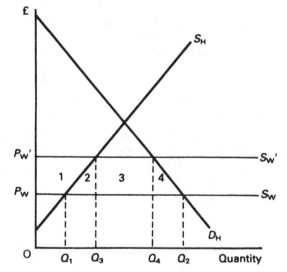

If the Government now decides to restrict the level of import penetration, it could impose a tariff of, say, $P_W - P_W'$. A tariff always shifts a supply curve vertically upwards by the amount of the tariff, so that in this case the world supply curve shifts vertically upwards from S_W to S_W'. This would raise the domestic price to P_W', above the world price P_W. This higher price will reduce the domestic demand for the good to OQ_4, whilst simultaneously encouraging domestic supply to expand to OQ_3. Imports will be reduced to

$Q_4 - Q_3$. Domestic consumer surplus will decline as a result of the tariff by the area $1 + 2 + 3 + 4$, though domestic producer surplus will rise by area 1, and the Government will gain tax revenue of $P_W' - P_W \times Q_4 - Q_3$ (i.e. area 3). These gains would be inadequate to compensate consumers for their loss in welfare, yielding a net welfare loss of area $2 + 4$ as a result of imposing a tariff.

The UK was extensively protected by tariffs until the 1850s. These were progressively dismantled in an era of free trade that lasted until the First World War. The first significant reintroduction of tariffs occurred in 1915 with the 'McKenna duties', a 33.3% *ad valorem* tax on luxuries such as motor cars, watches, clocks, etc. They were designed to discourage unnecessary imports in order to save foreign exchange, and thereby free shipping space for the war effort. In 1921, the Safeguarding of Industry Act extended protection to key industries. This was followed in 1932 by the Import Duties Act, which provided a comprehensive range of protection; a 20% *ad valorem* duty on manufactured goods in general, but 33.3% on articles such as bicycles and chemicals, and 15% on certain industrial raw materials and semi-manufactures.

Since the Second World War, the UK, along with others, has moved away from the protectionist doctrine of the inter-war period. We have already seen that considerable reductions in tariffs took place under the auspices of GATT. However, for the UK, entrance into the EC in 1972 has had a dual effect. Although tariffs on industrial products have been eliminated between member countries, permitting free trade, at the same time a Common External Tariff (CET) has been imposed on industrial trade with all non-member countries.

Non-tariff barriers In recent years there has been a considerable increase in trade that is subject to non-tariff barriers. This has been particularly noticeable with regard to trade in manufactures. In 1974 only 0.2% of UK trade in manufactures was recorded as subject to non-tariff regulation, whereas by the late 1980s, more than 10% of UK trade in manufactures was 'managed' in this way. As regards *total* UK trade, as much as 45% is still 'managed' by non-tariff regulation. As regards total *non-fuel imports* of the main industrial countries, some 22.6% are affected by selected non-tariff barriers.[2]

Let us now consider the types of non-tariff barrier in use.

Quotas. A quota is a physical limit on the amount of an imported good that may be sold in a country in a given period. Its effects are examined in Fig. 24.3.

As in the case of a tariff, we assume for simplicity that the world supply curve is perfectly elastic at P_W. Once again, if there is free trade, the domestic price will be set by the world price, P_W. Domestic production would initially be OQ_1 though demand would be considerably higher at OQ_2. This excess would be satisfied by importing the amount $Q_2 - Q_1$ of the particular good.

If the Government were now to decide that it wanted to limit the level of imports to, say, $Q_3 - Q_1$, it could impose a quota to this effect. The total

Fig. 24.3 The effect of a
quota

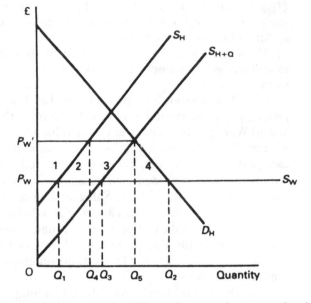

supply curve to the UK market now becomes the domestic supply curve, S_H, plus the fixed quota permitted from abroad, Q. The new domestic price rises from P_W to P_W', which in turn reduces domestic demand from OQ_2 to OQ_5. Domestic supply will expand to OQ_4, with imports reduced to the quota level $Q_3 - Q_1 (= Q_5 - Q_4)$.

As in the case of the tariff, the imposition of a quota will involve a loss in consumer surplus (i.e. area $1 + 2 + 3 + 4$). However, in contrast to the tariff, the only area of welfare gain will be the producer surplus of area 1, since the Government receives no increase in tax revenue from the quota. This leaves area $2 + 3 + 4$ as the net loss of economic welfare. For *any given price rise*, the welfare loss is then greater for a quota than for a tariff.[1] Import quotas are used fairly extensively on a whole range of products. They may be applied either unilaterally or as a result of negotiated agreements between the two parties. For instance, the EC has the authority to negotiate quota agreements on behalf of member states, including the UK, and does so on a whole range of products. One example was the quota applied to jerseys, pullovers, cardigans and waistcoats from Turkey. Between September 1985 and July 1986, 190,000 pieces were allowed to be sold in the Community. A range of products from Eastern Europe has been subject to formal quota restrictions for some time. They include jute and hemp, radio and television parts, matches, leather, gloves, headgear, ceramics and aluminium.

The import of textiles into the EC from the newly industrialized countries is controlled by the Multi-Fibre Agreement (MFA), a negotiated settlement between developed and developing countries which first came into effect in 1974. A major aim has been to provide greater scope for newly industrialized countries to increase their share of world trade in textile products whilst at the same time maintaining some stability for textile production in the developed economies. The first agreement allowed for quotas to rise by approximately 6% per annum, though a subsequent agreement began to cut back on these concessions. The MFA was renewed for a third time in 1986 although there was considerable opposition from many of the textile producers who favoured a return to normal GATT free trade rules. The new accord was widened to cover a wider range of natural fibres but also specified that the least developed countries would generally be exempt from restrictions.

An UNCTAD study in the same year concluded that the complete liberalization of trade barriers would bring substantial benefits for developing countries. It was suggested that their total export of clothing would rise by around 135% while textile exports could grow by some 80%. A more recent analysis carried out by the World Bank put the potential gains at an even greater level. These figures seem to indicate quite clearly that the export quotas work against the interest of the *producers* rather than the *consumers*. But there is an argument that the developing countries actually benefit through the MFA arrangement. This is because, it is asserted, they receive what may be termed *quota rents*, i.e. higher prices than would be guaranteed through a free market.

Looking back to Fig. 24.3, this benefit would amount to area 3. However research into this by Balassa and Michalopoulos (1985) estimated that the value of lost output to the US exceeds the quota rent by nine times and to the EC by a factor of seven.

Interestingly, a study by Professor Silberston (1985) suggested that the *developed* countries could actually gain by *relaxing* the MFA. For example, in the case of the UK, abolition of the MFA would adversely affect the UK *textile* industry, with the resulting lower textile prices squeezing profits and employment (10,000–15,000 reduction) in the industry. But the *whole economy* of the UK would benefit from the lower textile prices, with real incomes of consumers increasing and boosting aggregate demand (£500m. at 1982 prices). Further, the extra imports of textiles could lead to some depreciation in sterling, making UK goods more competitive. Also, the *developing* countries would now have earned more foreign currency from their increased exports of textiles, and be able to purchase more UK exports. Professor Silberston calculates the *net* effect of abolishing the MFA on the *whole economy* of the UK to be an *extra* 37,000 jobs, over a five-year period.

Apart from quotas imposed as a result of its membership of the EC, the UK applies a variety of nationally imposed quotas. One survey revealed that the UK applied such quotas on 65 products, less than France and Italy which each had over 120 national quotas, but more than West Germany with 31.

Voluntary Export Restraints (VERs).   These are arrangements by which an individual exporter or group of exporters agrees with an importing country to limit the quantity of a specific product to be targeted at a particular market over a given period of time. In effect, VERs are quotas and the consequent welfare implications of their application are much as is demonstrated in Fig. 24.3. VERs have become a highly popular means of protection in recent years. In 1989, there were in excess of 250 of these arrangements in force. Most of them have been put into place by the US and EC with a view to restraining imports from Japan and the rest of the Far East. One estimate has put the proportion of US manufactured imports subject to VERs or restrictions under the MFA in the late 1980s at around 25%. Aside from textiles and clothing, which as we mentioned earlier, are covered under the later arrangement, VERs are most commonly found in areas such as motor vehicles, electronics and steel. Japanese car importers, for example, limit their share of the UK auto market to around 11%. Similar VER's are effective with other EC members. But one area of growing controversy concerns cars that are produced by Japanese manufacturers within the boundaries of the EC. The establishment of a number of plants, particularly in the UK, in recent years led to calls by some other members of the Community for these products to be included in the VER arrangement.

Subsidies.   The first three forms of protection we have described have all been designed to restrict the volume of imports directly. An alternative policy is to provide a subsidy to domestic producers so as to improve their competitiveness in both the home and world markets. The effect of this is demonstrated in Fig. 24.4.

Once again we assume that the world supply curve is perfectly elastic at P_w. Under conditions of free trade, the domestic price is set by the world price at P_w. Domestic production is initially OQ_1 with imports satisfying the excess level of demand which amounts to Q_2-Q_1. The effect of a general subsidy to an industry would be to shift the supply curve of domestic producers to the right. The domestic price will remain unchanged but domestic production will rise to OQ_3 with imports reduced to Q_2Q_3. If, however, the subsidy is provided solely for *exporters*, the impact on the domestic market could be quite different. The incentive to export may encourage more domestic production to be switched from the home market to the overseas markets which in turn could result in an increased volume of imports to satisfy the unchanged level of domestic demand.

Fig. 24.4 The effect of a general subsidy

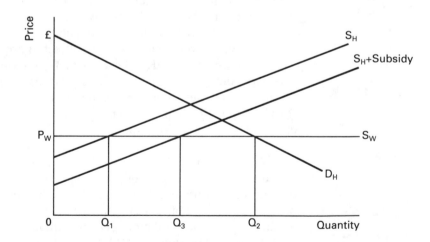

Subsidies have been quite widely employed over the last decade with agriculture a particularly significant beneficiary. The effective level of subsidy in the OECD agricultural sector has risen from 30% to 50% of the value of domestic production during the 1980s. The 1990 EC annual review of unfair US trade practices, for example, specifically focuses on the use of agricultural export subsidies. Meanwhile, the US has itself had cause to complain about the protection afforded to farmers in the EC through the Common Agricultural Policy. Producer subsidies in agriculture stand at 40% in the EC, while the corresponding figure for the USA is 28%. What actually constitutes a subsidy is itself, however, the subject of a certain amount of controversy. In the mid 1980s, a dispute erupted between the British Steel Corporation and the US authorities over aid being granted to the company by the British government. The only aid received had been general regional aid, available to all industries. The British view was that this should not be included in the definition of a subsidy. The Americans chose to differ, arguing that all aid, whether generally available or specifically targeted at a certain industry, constituted a subsidy and promptly imposed a duty of 19.3% on UK exports of steel plate to the US.

Exchange controls.   A system of exchange controls was in force in the UK from the outbreak of the Second World War until 1979 when, in order to allow the free flow of capital, they were abolished. They enabled the Government to limit the availability of foreign currencies and so curtail excessive imports; for instance, holding a foreign-currency bank account had required Bank of England permission. Exchange controls could also be employed to discourage speculation and investment abroad.

'Health' and 'safety' standards.   These are often imposed in the knowledge that certain imported goods will be unable to meet the requirements. The British Government used such standards to prevent French imports of turkeys and ultra-heat-treated (UHT) milk. Ostensibly the ban on French turkeys was to prevent 'Newcastle disease', a form of fowl pest found in Europe, reaching the UK. The European Court ruled, however, that the ban was merely an excuse to prevent the free flow of imports. It came to a similar conclusion in 1983 as regards the requirement that UHT milk should be 'filled and closed on registered premises'. Since only a British local authority could register such premises, it effectively outlawed the sale of foreign milk in Britain. A more recent case concerns the importation of American and Canadian meat into the EC. The Community alleged that the animals had been treated with certain hormones and so constituted a health risk. The US authorities regarded the EC claim as unjustified and an example of pure protectionism. It led to virtually no meat exports from the US to the EC market in 1989.

Time-consuming formalities.   In October 1982 France announced that all imported video recorders would have to go to the small customs post at Poitiers for clearance. With a staff of just eight, imports were inevitably delayed for weeks, giving a significant advantage to domestic producers. In 1990, the EC alleged that 'excessive invoicing requirements' required by US importing authorities has hampered exports from member countries to the US.

Import deposit schemes.   These require importers to deposit a sum of money with the central bank. In tying up cash, an import deposit effectively raises the cost of importing. Such a scheme was in force on one-third of UK imports from late 1969 until the end of 1970. It required a deposit of 50% of the value of the imported goods to be placed with the central bank *before* the customs would release the goods, repayable after 180 days. The scheme was fairly successful in reducing imports initially, but became less so as alternative methods of finance were found.

Public sector contracts.   Governments often give preference to domestic firms in the issuing of public contracts, despite EEC directives requiring member governments to advertise such contracts. Public contracts are actually placed outside the country of origin in only 1% of cases.

The case for protection

Protectionist measures may be applied on a selective or more widespread basis, with most of the measures currently in force falling into the first category.

Selective protection   A number of arguments have been used to justify tariff and non-tariff barriers applied on a selective basis:

1.   To prevent dumping.
2.   To protect infant industries.
3.   To protect strategically important industries.
4.   To maintain employment by preventing the rapid contraction of labour-intensive industries.

Dumping occurs where a good is sold in an overseas market at a price below the real cost of production. Under Article 6, GATT allows retaliatory sanctions to be applied if it can be shown that the dumping materially affected the domestic industry. As well as using GATT, countries within the EC can refer cases of alleged dumping for investigation by the European Commission. The Commission is then able to recommend the appropriate course of action, which may range from 'no action' where dumping is found not to have taken place, to either obtaining an 'undertaking' of no further dumping, or imposing a tariff. During the 1980s, the Commission initiated around 400 investigations into alleged dumping of products. As a result, there are currently 56 goods including CD players, photocopiers and dot-matrix printers, which are subject to EC dumping duties. Japanese exporters have suffered disproportionately from these restrictions. For example, video recorders from Japan were subject to a 29% duty. In an effort to circumvent the duties, there has been a growing trend towards establishing what are termed 'screw-driver' plants in Europe for the final assembly of the products. For example, when in 1984 a 28% duty was imposed on Japanese electronic typewriters, imports into the EC area amounted to 700,000. By 1988, a similar quantity were being *assembled* in various EC countries while only 35,000 were directly imported. Since the vast bulk of the production process was still taking place in the Far East, the EC reacted by bringing in limits on the extent of non-European content allowable in products if the dumping duty was to be waived. In the case of the typewriters, there was an agreement to raise the *local content* of the output to 40%. However, the effectiveness of this form of protection has been thrown into doubt by a 1990 GATT ruling which declared these conditions illegal, arguing that they constitute a discriminatory charge on Japanese companies operating in Europe.

The use of protection in order to *establish new industries* is widely accepted, particularly in the case of developing countries. Article 18 of GATT explicitly allows such protection. An infant industry is likely to have a relatively high cost structure in the short run, and in the absence of protective measures may find it difficult to compete with the established overseas industries already benefiting from scale economies. The EC has used this argument to justify protection of its developing high-technology industries.

The protection of industries for *strategic reasons* is widely practised both in the UK and the EC, and is not necessarily contrary to GATT rules (Article 2). The protection of the UK steel industry has been justified on this basis, and the EC has used a similar argument to protect agricultural production throughout the Community under the guise of the CAP.

General protection   The case for a more general form of protection as part of a long term strategy has been strongly advocated by a number of groups in the UK, such as the Cambridge Economic Policy Group (CEPG)[3] in the early 1980s. Their analysis might be studied in more depth as being typical of the reaction against freer trade. In the UK, general protection as a policy option went out of fashion in the mid-1980s as healthy inflows of oil revenues enabled the economy to recover strongly without the feared deterioration in the balance of payments. But this was not to prove sustainable. By the end of the decade, the current account had not only moved back into deficit but had also registered its largest ever shortfall of some £21bn. Protectionist sentiment still remains subdued despite this but advocates of a CEPG-style strategy could re-emerge if deficits once again start to form a constraint on economic activity. Contrary to GATT philosophy, the CEPG argued that import tariffs, correctly applied, would actually *increase* world trade. They noted with some irony that 'controls' already existed (i.e. in the early 1980s), but in the form of the large number of unemployed, whose reduced spending power had cut the demand for imports!

In proposing expansion (*not* contraction) as the only solution to economic crisis, the CEPG recognized, however, that the balance of payments could become a binding constraint, with a substantial part of any increase in income being spent on imports.

To support their argument, the CEPG pointed to the decline in the surplus gained through trade on manufactures (see Fig. 23.1), traditionally used to pay for the import of goods, and raw materials. This erosion of UK trade in manufactures becomes still more serious in view of the progressive increase in import penetration. In Table 23.5 we noted that 35% of total UK demand is now spent on manufactured imports, compared to only 17% in 1968.

To reflect these trends, the CEPG strategy was based on combining a fiscal stimulus to the economy with widespread import controls. Imports were not to be reduced but initially *restricted to their present level* and subsequently permitted to grow only when exports increased. In this way, whilst it could not be argued that imports were actually being cut, any acceleration in economic activity would no longer be choked off by a further deterioration in the current account position. This would then allow for stronger economic growth in the UK than would otherwise have been the case, and would result in a lower level of unemployment.

A rather different example of a general protectionist strategy is provided by Japan where the imposition of a whole array of tariff barriers, subsidies and regulations has created a hostile trading environment for many overseas companies. Although there are many factors which have contributed to the outstanding performance of the Japanese economy in recent years, the restrictions of imports have clearly played some part, providing the framework under which a large current account surplus has been amassed. This has in turn led to a strong Yen and a low level of core inflation.

Criticisms of protectionism

Retaliation   A major drawback to protectionist measures is the prospect of retaliation, which may arise in unexpected ways. For example, in July 1980 the UK imposed unilateral controls on the import of Indonesian clothes when that country exceeded its quota under the MFA. This involved imports worth around £10m. The Indonesian Government immediately retaliated by cancelling an order with British Aerospace valued at £40m., and began to reconsider other export contracts from the UK worth in excess of £350m. The risks of retaliation are perhaps even greater for measures of general protection. This was admitted by the CEPG, though they suggested that foreign producers would 'soon' recognize that import volumes into the UK would be even higher with import controls and an expanding UK economy than with no import controls and UK recession.

The consequences of retaliation could be especially serious for the UK, given the importance of trade within its economy. In 1988 UK exports totalled 19.8% of GDP (at market prices), which is higher than most of its major competitors (e.g. France 16.8%, Japan 9.7%, USA 5.7%).

The widespread protection surrounding the Japanese economy has become increasingly widely criticized in recent years. The near doubling in the size of the bilateral trade surplus with the US between 1984 and 1986 set in motion a chain of events which eventually led to the introduction of the *Omnibus Trade Act* two years later. Section 301 provides for the US to take retaliatory action against any countries deemed to be pursuing unfair trade practices.

The US also initiated the *Structural Impediments Initiative* in 1989 in an effort to seek market opening reforms from Japan. By mid-1990 Japan had agreed to strengthen its anti-monopoly law to control the activity of Japan's large industrial groups, and to reform its Retail Store Law so as to allow more large stores which, it is hoped, would import more foreign goods.

Misallocation of resources   We saw in Figs 24.1–24.3 that protectionism can erode some of the welfare benefits of free trade. For instance, Fig. 24.2 showed that a tariff (and Fig. 24.3 a quota) raises domestic supply at the expense of imports. If the domestic producers cannot make such products as cheaply as overseas producers, then one could argue that encouraging high-cost domestic production is a misallocation of international resources.

A related criticism also suggests that protectionism leads to resource misallocation on an international scale, but this time concerns the multinational. We saw in Chapter 7 that multinationals are the fastest-growing type of business unit in Western economies, and that they are increasingly adopting strategies which locate particular stages of the production process in (to them) appropriate parts of the world. Protectionism may disrupt the flow of goods from one stage of the production process to another, and in this sense inhibit global specialization.

On the domestic level, Turner (1980) found that profits were higher than normal in industries which were dominated by a few large firms, reflecting their use of market power. However, excess profits were smaller in the industries which experienced most foreign competition. Protectionist measures, by removing such competition, may therefore allow large firms to exert their latent market power, causing prices and profits to be raised at the expense of consumers.

Institutional problems The application of general protection is seen as being incompatible with continued membership of both the EC and GATT. Expulsion or withdrawal from the EC would mean, amongst other things, the loss of preferential access to European markets – the major destination for UK exports (see Table 23.2). However, Greece imposed import duties on industrial products in violation of EC rules in 1982, yet its continued membership of the EC has not been at issue.

More appropriate alternatives Those who advocate protectionism have been criticized for neglecting more appropriate alternatives. For instance, the National Institute[4] believed the CEPG to be unduly pessimistic about a strategy of reflation and devaluation. The National Institute suggested that if the devaluation was introduced in a gradual-step sequence, and a permanent incomes policy is imposed, then rises in costs, prices and wages may not erode the competitive benefit of devaluation. There will then be no need for the progressive series of devaluations, with inflationary effects, foreseen by the CEPG.

Many of these criticisms of protectionism are encapsulated in an OECD report (1985), *Costs and Benefits of Protection*. Amongst its conclusions were that:

1. The last decade has seen a marked growth in *non-tariff* barriers, despite a significant reduction in *tariff* barriers.

2. Trade restrictions have merely diverted imports from *more restricted* to *less restricted* areas.

3. Quota restrictions have caused *prices* to rise in the protected markets.

4. Protection has only raised employment *in the protected sectors* by 2–3%, and then only in the short run. In the *long run* the effect is much less, with a tendency for capital to be substituted for labour.

5. Protection by the *developed* countries restricts the ability of the *developing* countries to earn foreign currency, worsens the world debt situation, and distorts the investment plans of developing countries.

Conclusion

While the debate over protectionism may have died down in the UK in recent years, at an international level there has been growing concern as to the future of the free trade system. The latest GATT round has made very little progress on a range of controversial issues and a big divide still exists between the positions of the developed and the developing nations. Meanwhile, the latter part of the 1980s has witnessed a dramatic increase in the number of bilateral barriers to trade which have been imposed outside the GATT framework. For the time being, the volume of world trade is continuing to grow. But the threat of a downturn is increasing, which would carry serious implications for global prosperity. Perhaps the most encouraging aspect of recent developments has been the lessening of tension between the US and Japan. Talk of a trade war has receded somewhat as American companies began to obtain greater opportunity to enter the Japanese market. However, unless there is a renewed recognition of the *world-wide costs* of protectionism, the protectionist lobbies in various countries may still succeed in curbing the growth of international specialization and trade.

Notes

1. It could, however, be argued that the welfare loss is overestimated by this analysis. Area 3, though no longer received by the Government as tax revenue, may still be received by importers. Although only paying P_W to the foreign suppliers, the importers now receive P_W when selling $Q_5 - Q_4$ on the domestic market.
2. See chapter 2 of IMF (1988).
3. See, for example, Godley and May (1977) and Cripps and Godley (1978).
4. For a review of various possible strategies, see Allsopp and Joshi (1980).

References and further reading

Allsopp, C. and **Joshi, V.** (1980) Alternative strategies for the UK, *National Institute Economic Review*, 91, Feb.
Balassa, B. and **Michalopoulos** (1985) 'Liberalizing World Trade', *World Bank Discussion Paper*.
Cripps, F. and **Godley, W.** (1978) Control of imports as a means to full employment and the expansion of world trade: the UK case, *Cambridge Journal of Economics*, **2**.
Godley, W. and **May, R. M.** (1977) The macroeconomic implications of devaluation and import restriction, *Economic Policy Review*, 3, March.
Hamilton, C. B. (1990) *Textiles Trade and the Developing Countries*, The World Bank.
Hindley, B. (1988) Dumping and the Far East Trade of the EC, *World Economy*, **11**, 4 Dec.
IMF (1988) *Issues and Developments in International Trade Policy*. Washington.
OECD (1985) *Report on the Costs and Benefits of Protection*. Paris. See *Economic Progress Report*, 117, HMSO.

Silberston Report (1985), in *Economic Progress Report*, 117, HMSO.
The Economist (1982) Is free trade dead?, 25 Dec. p. 91.
Turner, P. P. (1980) Import competition and the profitability of United Kingdom manufacturing industry, *The Journal of Industrial Economics*, **29**, Dec.

Managing the economy

In this chapter the objectives of macroeconomic policy are discussed, along with the instruments for achieving them. After a short review of the interventionist theory of macroeconomic policy, we consider the conduct of policy in the UK. Adjusting the instruments of policy to 'best' meet a set of target values for various objectives seems to fit the actual conduct of policy in the UK until 1974. Since then, the emphasis has shifted away from such 'fine-tuning' and towards the adoption of medium- and long-term rules. This change of emphasis is well illustrated by considering the policies advocated by the Cambridge Economic Policy Group (CEPG) and by the monetarists. The chapter concludes by tracing the fortunes of the Medium Term Financial Strategy and assessing the contribution made by supply-side economics to macroeconomic policy.

The objectives of policy

The desire of most individuals is to live and work within an economic framework which gives them the prospect of steady employment, relatively stable prices and a rising standard of living. It is usually recognized that to achieve such a situation the economy must trade and 'pay its way' with other economies. Politicians realize that to attract votes and gain political power they must promise that these aspirations will be met, if only in the long run. Economic objectives at the macroeconomic level are therefore set in terms of full employment, price stability and rapid economic growth, together with long-term equilibrium in the balance of payments. All these objectives have attracted attention in the post-war period in the UK. Since they are unlikely to be achieved in their totality, they have usually been expressed in terms of target values. Whilst these target values have not always been explicitly stated, they seem to be influenced by achieved values within the recent past.

Full employment

For instance, it is recognized that full employment can never mean zero registered unemployment if only because of dynamic change within society. Following the Beveridge Report of 1944, a 3% rate of unemployment (about half a million) was used in the 1950s and 1960s as the 'acceptable' upper limit. Sadly, in the 1980s merely reducing unemployment below the 10% level might seem the effective target.

Stable prices

A similar point can be made regarding inflation. Stable prices have always been regarded as unrealistic, but the attainment of an annual inflation rate of around 2.5% seems to have been the approximate target in the first two post-war decades. More recently the reduction of the annual inflation rate to single figures or to a rate equivalent to that of our industrial rivals, would appear to have been the target set.

Economic growth

Economic growth has received relatively little specific emphasis in the UK, although most governments have expressed some enthusiasm for it! We have, generally speaking, enjoyed rising living standards and have compared ourselves (favourably) with our parents and grandparents rather than with our contemporaries in Europe, the USA or Japan. A well-known statement concerning economic growth as an objective was made by the late R. A. Butler in 1954, when he suggested a doubling of living standards every twenty-five years as an explicit target. This was greeted as being over-ambitious, yet it entailed an annual growth rate of GDP of less than 3%. The Economic Plan of 1965 sought a growth rate of 3.8% per annum, but this was quickly seen to be unattainable and this attempt at long-term planning was soon abandoned.

The balance of payments

The balance of payments is often described as an objective of economic policy, the target being either equilibrium or a surplus over a period of time in order that accumulated international debts might be repaid. This can hardly be related to the aspirations of individuals and is thought by many to be more properly described as a constraint upon the achievement of other objectives. Nevertheless, target figures have been set in the past, e.g. the 1953 Economic Survey called for a surplus of £450m. per annum as the target surplus on current account in the 1950s to finance the long-term capital outflow. It was not achieved, and since then the use of target figures has become less important. However a 'healthy' external account is still an important consideration of policy.

This list of objectives could be extended to include others, such as the redistribution of income and wealth, but target values for employment, inflation and underlying economic growth have received most attention. The recent record of achievement is displayed in Table 25.1.

Table 25.1 shows that the efforts of successive governments simultaneously to achieve the four major objectives have failed. However, this by no means indicates that it is 'worthless' for governments to intervene in the economy, as the situation could have been still worse without such intervention.

The instruments of policy

Governments would have no macroeconomic problems if market forces in the economy automatically lead to 'full employment' equilibrium, with stable prices, and a rapid economic growth. The bulk of the evidence seems to indicate that market forces alone have failed to achieve these objectives, either in full or even at 'satisfactory' values. Such 'market failure' essentially constitutes the case for intervention by governments. If governments *are* to

Year	Unemployment as a percentage of working population (excluding school-leavers)	Annual change in RPI (%)	Annual change in GDP (at factor cost) (%)	Balance of payments (current account) (£m.)
1972	3.1	7.1	2.7	+191
1973	2.1	9.2	7.1	−1,018
1974	2.1	16.1	−1.7	−3,317
1975	3.3	24.9	−1.1	−1,582
1976	3.5	15.1	2.6	−913
1977	4.7	12.1	2.6	−128
1978	4.6	8.4	3.2	+972
1979	4.1	17.2	1.8	−548
1980	5.4	15.1	−2.4	+2,797
1981	8.5	12.0	−0.8	+6,641
1982	9.8	5.4	1.6	+4,608
1983	10.4	5.3	3.2	+3,796
1984	10.7	4.6	2.4	+1,956
1985	10.9	5.7	3.6	+3,165
1986	11.2	3.7	3.3	−45
1987	10.3	3.7	4.3	−4,352
1988	8.3	6.5	4.7	−14,960
1989	6.4	7.7	2.0	−19,067

Source: CSO (1990).

intervene in the economy, there still remains the problem of selecting the appropriate instruments for achieving the targets they set themselves.

In general terms the policy instruments available to the UK Government are fiscal policy, monetary policy, prices and incomes policy, and policy instruments aimed at the balance of payments, such as the exchange rate or import controls. These policy instruments are sometimes called 'instrumental variables', i.e. variables over which the Government has some control, and the values of which affect the behaviour of the economy itself in some reasonably systematic way.

Fiscal policy

Fiscal policy[1] involves using both government spending and taxation to influence the composition and level of aggregate demand in the economy. Elementary circular flow analysis suggests that by raising the level of government expenditure and/or by reducing taxation, the level of aggregate demand can be raised (by a multiplied amount) with favourable consequences for economic activity and employment. Such an expansionary course of action might result in a larger budget deficit, or a reduced budget surplus, in this way affecting the Public Sector Borrowing Requirement (PSBR). This somewhat simplistic approach is the basis for fiscal interventionism as advocated by 'Keynesians',[2] and carried out with some success for over twenty-five years in the UK. The Budget is viewed not as an accounting procedure, with expenditure and revenue to be balanced as a matter of good housekeeping, but as an instrument of policy to be manipulated as a means to an end. Deficits are financed by borrowing, short or long term, from home and abroad, with the increased National Debt seen as a means of spreading the costs of current policy over future generations.

Practical problems abound. Although tax rates can be set, the revenues they will yield are difficult to predict as income levels can vary. Also government expenditure and tax receipts are subject to time-lags, which can have destabilizing effects. For instance, the Government may aim to raise spending to stimulate the economy during recession, but the effects may not be felt for several time periods, when the economy may be in a different situation. In other words, fiscal policy may move the economy away from desired values rather than towards them. There is even a problem in identifying the Government's fiscal stance. A contradictory fiscal policy will, if successful, reduce incomes and tax yield, and might also have the effect of raising some government expenditures such as unemployment benefit. If we look, therefore, at the Budget *out-turn* for evidence of the Government's fiscal stance, we may come to the wrong conclusion – the reduced tax yield and increased government expenditure may be the result of a contradictory fiscal policy, not evidence of an expansionary one! Problems such as these account in part for the relegation of fiscal policy in favour of monetary policy by Conservative governments during the 1980s.

Monetary policy

Monetary policy aims to influence monetary variables such as the rate of interest and the money supply, to achieve the targets set for the four major objectives. Although the rate of interest and the money supply are interrelated (see Ch. 16), for convenience we examine these separately.

The rate of interest – in practice there are many – is thought to be important because it is a cost of borrowing, influencing not only long-term investment decisions by firms but also their short term borrowing to overcome cash-flow problems. Interest rates may influence consumer spending on durable goods by affecting the cost of hire-purchase finance. Interest rates also influence household decisions as to the composition of the assets they hold. For example, low interest rates offer little reward for those acquiring financial assets, thus encouraging consumer expenditure on goods and services. The balance of payments is also affected by interest rate policy, as capital inflow and outflow depend on UK interest rates relative to those in other countries.

The money supply, as we saw in Chapter 16, 'matters' to both monetarists and Keynesians. To monetarists, money supply mainly affects prices, at least in the long run, whereas to Keynesians, the major impact is on output and employment. The measurement and control of money supply have therefore been widely regarded as an important policy instrument, and we return to this below.

Prices and incomes policy

Prices and incomes policy is used in an attempt to control inflation by directly influencing the rate at which prices, wages and salaries rise. Depending on political and economic belief, such a policy can be viewed as an irrelevance by the monetarists, or as a necessary means of influencing the institutional determinants of inflation by the Keynesians, particularly when expansionary fiscal measures are being used to overcome unemployment.

Since 1960 there have been few occasions in which this instrument of policy was not in use, either on a voluntary basis or in the form of statutory control. Prices have been directly controlled as well as wages, and wages themselves have been subject to various forms of restraint, such as 'freezes', or 'norms' for wage increases. The impact of the policy has, predictably, fallen most heavily on the public sector. Although during the operation of incomes policy the rate of wage inflation has usually been reduced below the previously prevailing figure, it has often been higher than the 'norm' set, and has always been followed, when controls have been relaxed, by a rapid and sharp increase in the rate of wage inflation.[3] It is difficult to test the overall effects of the use of this instrument of policy, but it is generally regarded as having been less useful in the long term. Prices and incomes policy was last used formally in 1979, but an incomes policy has been used informally since then, with the introduction of cash limits for the public sector acting as a constraint on wage increases.

The exchange rate

The exchange rate is one of the instruments which can be used to influence the balance of payments. With the exception of the devaluations of 1949 (30%), and 1967 (14%), the sterling exchange rate was essentially fixed under the International Monetary Fund (IMF) system. In 1971 the convertibility of the dollar into gold at a fixed price was abandoned and the IMF fixed exchange rate system broke down. Since mid-1972 the UK exchange rate has fluctuated, in theory according to market forces (a 'clean' float), but in practice often 'managed' by the authorities (a 'dirty' float). Although the pound fell to record low levels against the dollar in early 1983, it would have fallen even lower had the Bank of England not intervened on the foreign exchange market to buy the pound with its foreign currency reserves.

A change in the exchange rate will affect the relative prices of domestic- and foreign-produced goods and services. For example, a lower exchange rate makes UK goods cheaper in the foreign markets, and foreign goods more expensive in the UK market (see Ch. 22). Given appropriate elasticities for exports and imports,[4] a lower exchange rate will improve the balance of payments.

One major difficulty in a lower exchange rate policy is that this will have an adverse effect on domestic costs, both directly and indirectly. The rise in price of imported foodstuffs and finished manufactures will have an immediate and direct effect on the price level, because these items are included in the Retail Price Index (RPI). The rise in price of imported raw materials and semi-finished manufactures will also have an indirect effect on the price level, by raising domestic costs of production. Higher prices could also stimulate higher wage demands to protect real incomes, further fuelling inflation. In these ways the competitive advantage of devaluation may well be eroded, and the objective of price stability (or reduced inflation) adversely affected. Between 1985 and 1988, the government sought to target the exchange rate at particular levels against various currencies. This was in order to prevent sterling depreciating too rapidly, thereby endangering the control of inflation. The entry of sterling into the ERM at a relatively high rate of 2.95 DM to the pound was also to help contain inflationary pressure in the UK.

Import controls

Import controls are another policy instrument for affecting the balance of payments, but have been little used in the UK since the Second World War, other than to reduce import tariffs in line with other members of the General Agreement on Tariffs and Trade (GATT). Two examples may serve to illustrate their use. Between 1964 and 1966 there was an import surcharge scheme whereby most imported manufactured goods carried a levy of 15% in an attempt to reduce imports by over £550m. per annum. It was a partial success, reducing them by perhaps half the intended sum. In 1968–70 there was an import deposit scheme whereby half the value of imported manufactured goods had to be deposited with the Government for six months, with no interest paid. Little effect upon the balance of payments was discerned.

Renewed interest in import tariffs emerged in the early 1980s, stimulated by the CEPG who, initially at least, saw a direct and close relationship between the size of the Budget deficit and the size of the balance of payments deficit. If expansionary domestic fiscal policy is to overcome unemployment and stimulate investment, they advocate imposing tariffs to prevent the extra domestic spending from being satisfied by overseas suppliers. Their aim was not to reduce imports below the initial pre-expansion figure, but to prevent them from rising above that level.

Problems in managing the economy

Before we consider the theory of economic policy, some general points can be made concerning the objectives of policy and the instruments available to the Government.

Trade-off between objectives

With regard to objectives, the most obvious difficulty is that the objectives 'trade off' against each other. At the present time the policy instruments the Government has used to achieve the objective of lower inflation have imposed a cost of higher unemployment. Curbing the money supply has reduced the value of spending,[5] and raised interest rates, resulting in the closure of many firms, with the loss of jobs. Curbing government spending as part of monetary policy has also reduced employment in the public sector. A higher exchange rate up to 1981/82 and again from 1985 to 1988 made UK exports expensive, and imports cheaper, again reducing domestic output and employment. Lower inflation has therefore been achieved, but at the cost of higher unemployment. High interest rates and low economic activity have discouraged investment, adversely affecting another important policy objective, that of economic growth. This raises the question of 'weighting' the objectives against each other, e.g. how much extra unemployment and lower growth will be tolerated in order to reduce the inflation rate by a further x percentage points?

Interdependence of instruments

Policy instruments are not independent of each other. For example, fiscal policy has implications for the money supply and for the rate of interest. In turn, the domestic rate of interest will, by its effect upon short-term capital flows, influence the sterling exchange rate, and will also affect the money supply.

Instruments as objectives

It has to be recognized that policy instruments sometimes become objectives in their own right. This was the case with the exchange rate instrument which was used only twice in the post-war period up to the early 1970s. This was because preserving the value of the pound had itself become an objective of policy, so that it could no longer be used as a flexible instrument of policy. Again in February 1987 the UK agreed to the Louvre Accord in Paris which stated that a period of exchange rate stability was desirable. This made it more difficult to use the exchange rate as a policy instrument and in some respects it then becomes an *objective* of policy instead!

Political constraints

The set of policy objectives chosen, and the instruments used, may be constrained by the fact that it is politicians who are the ultimate decision-takers. Each course of action must therefore be evaluated in its political context. The use of some policy instruments may then be inhibited, as with the Conservative Government's reluctance formally to use a prices and incomes policy given its views on the efficacy of a free market system.

The theory of economic policy

Here we look at the basic theory of economic policy, concentrating on the 'fixed targets', the 'variable targets' and the 'satisficing' approaches to policy formation.

The fixed targets approach

Perhaps the best-known approach is that of Tinbergen (1952), the so-called fixed targets approach, which establishes the condition for the simultaneous achievement of fixed target values for a number of objectives. *Tinbergen's rule* states that if these target values are to be achieved simultaneously, then there must be at least the same number of instruments as there are objectives. The values of these instruments are determined by the desired-target values of the objectives, and they can then be assessed to see whether they are both feasible and acceptable to the decision-makers.

This rule can be illustrated in Fig. 25.1 where, for simplicity, the two-instrument/two-objective case is illustrated.[6] Instruments I_1 (monetary policy), and I_2 (fiscal policy), are plotted on the axes of the graph. Movements along each axis and away from the origin will be used to indicate 'expansionary' policy. On the horizontal axis, for example, close to the origin we have 'tight' fiscal policy, with high taxation and low government expenditure. Movement along the horizontal axis and away from the origin indicates that fiscal policy becomes 'easier', with taxation falling and government expenditure rising. The Budget moves from surplus into deficit, with the deficit becoming greater as the movement to the right continues. On the vertical axis, points close to the origin indicate restrictive monetary policy, with high interest rates and static, or slowly growing, money supply.

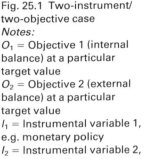

Fig. 25.1 Two-instrument/
two-objective case
Notes:
O_1 = Objective 1 (internal
balance) at a particular
target value
O_2 = Objective 2 (external
balance) at a particular
target value
I_1 = Instrumental variable 1,
e.g. monetary policy
I_2 = Instrumental variable 2,
e.g. fiscal policy

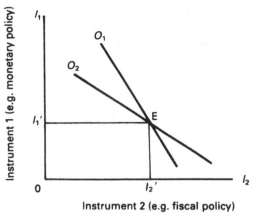

Movement along the vertical axis and away from the origin indicates an expansionary monetary policy, the money supply rising rapidly and interest rates falling.

The line O_1 shows the combinations of monetary and fiscal policy required to achieve the objective of *internal balance*, i.e. full employment (or something very close to it) with price stability (or a low and acceptable rate of inflation). O_1 will be negatively sloped, on the assumption that expansionary fiscal policy must be accompanied by contractionary monetary policy, if full employment is to be achieved without price inflation. If contractionary monetary policy did not accompany the expansionary fiscal policy then too high a level of aggregate demand would be generated, and with it price inflation.[7]

The line O_2 shows the combinations of monetary and fiscal policy required to achieve *external balance*, i.e. balance of payments equilibrium. It, too, is negatively sloped, reflecting the fact that expansionary fiscal policy raises domestic incomes, so increasing imports (and perhaps reducing exports). If balance of payments equilibrium is to be maintained, then these unfavourable effects on the current account must be offset by an improvement elsewhere in the accounts. This could be achieved by a contractionary monetary policy, which raises interest rates, attracting inflows of capital from overseas. Again, if fiscal policy is expansionary, a contractionary monetary policy will be necessary to preserve the external balance.[8]

Figure 25.1 shows that with two objectives (internal and external balance) and two instruments or instrumental variables (monetary and fiscal policy) then, by setting monetary and fiscal instruments at values I'_1 and I'_2 respectively, objectives O_1 and O_2 can be achieved simultaneously.[9] Tinbergen's rule is thereby illustrated.

Suppose now a third objective is added, perhaps a target rate of economic growth (Fig. 25.2). The line O_3 shows the combinations of monetary and fiscal policy required to achieve this target rate of economic growth. O_3 is positively sloped, on the assumption that an expansionary fiscal policy, involving extra government spending, will 'crowd out' private sector investment. Total investment can then only be kept at the level required to achieve growth rate O_3 by encouraging private sector investment through low

Fig. 25.2 Two-instrument/
three-objective case

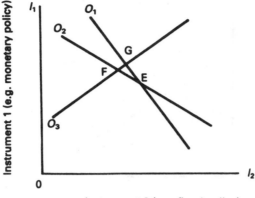

Instrument 2 (e.g. fiscal policy)

interest rates, i.e. by expansionary monetary policy. Expansionary fiscal *and* monetary policy are in this case required to achieve the target rate of economic growth O_3.

We can now see that it would be a fortunate and unlikely coincidence if O_3 happened to pass through point E, i.e. if all three objectives could be achieved with just two policy instruments. If, as in the figure, it does not, then we can only achieve two of the three objectives with our two policy instruments. For instance, we could be at G (O_1 and O_3 achieved, but not O_2) or at F (O_2 and O_3 achieved, but not O_1) or at E (O_1 and O_2 achieved, but not O_3). To achieve the third objective now requires a third policy instrument, perhaps exchange rate policy![10] If we cannot find extra policy instruments, Tinbergen's rule will be violated, i.e. there will be fewer instruments (here two) than objectives (here three). Except in the fortuitous case that all three objectives intersect, at G, F or E, then an *explicit choice* will have to be made between the conflicting objectives. In our example we must choose between G, F or E.

Tinbergen's approach has the great merit of being fairly simple to understand. It has encouraged governments to be explicit about their macroeconomic objectives and has stimulated the search for new policy instruments, such as flexible exchange rates or prices and incomes policy. Its emphasis on 'fine-tuning' the economy by introducing additional policy instruments, and changing their values, reflects the spirit of 'Keynesian' interventionism.

The flexible targets approach

In Tinbergen's approach, when we were unable to achieve all three objectives simultaneously because we lacked sufficient policy instruments, the target then became the achievement of any two, i.e. at G, F or E in Fig. 25.2. A choice had to be made between these alternatives. In contrast Theil (1956) suggested that the target could be more flexible, and that any position could be chosen within the triangle GFE. In this case no single objective is achieved, instead a compromise between the three is reached, all three being 'missed', but by a narrow margin in each case. This might be preferred to achieving two objectives by missing the third by a considerable margin.

Theil's flexible targets approach therefore presupposes that since all the objectives cannot be met there must be some 'welfare loss' whatever choice of objectives is made. This approach also assumes that a social welfare function can be defined for society as a whole, the aim then being to minimize the welfare loss for any choice made. The welfare function will take into account the *deviation* between the actual value achieved for any objective and its target value, with any such deviation indicating a loss of welfare. The problem then becomes one of minimizing a welfare loss function bearing in mind that the objectives are presumably 'weighted' with respect to each other.[11] For example, in the early 1980s a deviation between the actual and target inflation rate would appear to be weighted more heavily than a deviation between the actual and target unemployment rate. Weights W_1, W_2 and W_3 are introduced into the welfare loss function to be minimized below. The deviations between actual and target levels are conventionally squared in order to eliminate the problem of sign.

It follows that if the three objectives have *actual* values O_1, O_2 and O_3, and *target* values O_1^*, O_2^* and O_3^*, then the policy-makers would seek to minimize the social welfare loss function defined in terms of those three objectives, i.e.

$$\text{Minimize } U(O_1, O_2, O_3) = W_1(O_1 - O_1^*)^2 + W_2(O_2 - O_2^*)^2 + W_3(O_3 - O_3^*)^2$$

If there had been sufficient instruments to permit the simultaneous achievement of all three objectives, then $O_1 = O_1^*$; $O_2 = O_2^*$, and $O_3 = O_3^*$; in other words, the welfare loss function would equal zero. In terms of Fig. 25.2 all three objective functions (O_1, O_2 and O_3) have coincided at a single point. More sophisticated forms of such functions recognize that it is not only the extent to which the target objectives are fulfilled that matters, but also the values of the instrumental variables themselves. For example, high tax rates or higher interest rates may themselves reduce social welfare and might therefore be included in the loss function.

No one would suggest that political decision-makers study loss minimization functions of the form indicated above, but the approach is helpful in suggesting that attempts should be made to think seriously about the relative weights given to objectives,[12] and that if fixed target values are unattainable then flexibility might have to be accepted.

The satisficing approach

Both the Tinbergen and the Theil approaches suggest that the economy is 'fine-tuned' by the policy-makers,[13] i.e. instruments are continuously manipulated in order to achieve target welfare maximizing (or loss-minimizing) values. Mosley (1976) pointed out that in practice policy instruments are periodically manipulated, usually all at once, in response to a crisis. He has proposed a 'satisficing' theory of economic policy, which views the policy-maker as a 'satisficing' agent, i.e. one whose motive is not to achieve the best possible states at all times, but to achieve 'satisfactory' levels of performance. These 'satisfactory' levels are influenced, in the case of macroeconomic objectives, by recently achieved performance and are determined by compromise bargaining between such institutions as the Bank of England, the Treasury and the Cabinet. He suggests that a package of instruments will be used in order to respond to a 'crisis', which might be an unsatisfactory level of performance with respect even to one objective, with the strength of the response depending upon the amount by which the actual value differs from the 'satisfactory' level.

Testing the satisficing approach for the period 1946–71, Mosley found that *any* balance of payments deficit triggered a response – in other words only a zero or positive balance was regarded as 'satisfactory'. However, the unemployment figure considered 'satisfactory' varied over the years, following a rising trend. In 1953 it was below 1.6%, in 1965 below 2.5%, and by 1971 below 3.6%. Is below 10% considered 'satisfactory' in the early 1990s?

The fixed and flexible targets approaches to macroeconomic policy predict that policy-makers will seek to find new and effective instruments of policy in order simultaneously to achieve a growing number of economic objectives. If that search is not successful, then compromises between the target values of the objectives will be sought; more pragmatically, the policy-makers will accept quite broad ranges of values for the objectives and will intervene only when one (or more) of the target values becomes 'unsatisfactory'. In this last, 'satisficing', case the economy is 'managed by exception'.

Until the mid-1970s this reflected the interventionist 'Keynesian' approach which prevailed in the UK after the Second World War. Target values and achieved values for the objectives rarely diverged significantly, and it was generally accepted that policy-makers, armed with the predictions of increasingly sophisticated forecasting models of the economy, and using an increasing range of instrumental variables, could and should manage the economy by 'fine-tuning' it on to a desired path. However, as the 1970s progressed, the fine tuning and satisficing approaches to policy making were being replaced by theories which began stressing the inherently stable nature of the economy. These advocated the need to set 'rules' which policymakers should follow in the medium-term, instead of concentrating on short-term interventionism. The views of the Cambridge Economic Policy Group and the Monetarists will be developed in the next section, together with an assessment of monetarism and its changing impact on the policy making of successive Conservative governments during the late 1980s.

Post-war macroeconomic policy in practice

The first period – pre-1974

The major preoccupation as the Second World War ended was to put an end to the high levels of unemployment which had prevailed throughout the inter-war period when unemployment had averaged around 14%, even reaching 22% in 1932. The primacy of this objective was expressed in a famous sentence in the 1944 Government White Paper on Employment Policy: 'The Government accepts as one of their primary aims and responsibilities the maintenance of a high and stable level of employment after the War.' In the 1950s and 1960s unemployment figures of half a million led to reflationary measures, and the figure of 1 million unemployed (about 4% of the workforce) was first reached as late as 1972, when very strong measures were taken to expand demand and raise the employment level. Such expansionary measures usually took the form of fiscal activity (increased government spending and/or lower taxation), accompanied by relaxed hire-purchase controls and some stimulus to bank lending. This was the 'Keynesian' response to unemployment.

These measures had an effect upon the level of employment but also led to periodic balance of payments crises as the stimulus to aggregate demand raised not only incomes and employment but also imports. The resulting balance of payments crises could only be tackled, given our reluctance to use tariffs, by a deflation of aggregate demand resulting in greater unemployment. This 'stop–go' cycle had adverse effects upon the rate of long-term economic growth, which was a general objective of all post-war governments.

The average inflation rate was generally low (4.8% in 1946–50, 4.6% in 1951–55, 2.1% in 1956–60, 3.5% in 1961–65, 4,6% in 1966–70 and 8.5% in 1971–73), and was dealt with partly by adjusting aggregate demand but also by the use of a prices and incomes policy, itself a reflection of the Keynesian view that trade unions and other institutional features of the labour market are major factors in determining inflation.

Up to the early 1970s we can broadly say that macroeconomic policy was based upon 'Keynesian' principles, emphasizing the management of aggregate demand, mainly through fiscal policy, backed up by some form of prices and incomes policy. This kind of interventionist policy has been described as an attempt to 'fine-tune' the economy, adjusting the various policy instruments in order to achieve a set of policy objectives, and reflects the three approaches dealt with above. After 1974 the emphasis began to move away from 'fine-tuning', with its continuous exercise of government 'discretion' in varying instruments to achieve target values, and towards a more ordered path of set 'rules'.

The second period – post-1974

The subsequent period saw dramatic changes. Inflation and unemployment increased appreciably (see Table 25.1 above), and the Keynesian approach was increasingly criticized as a basis for macroeconomic policy-making.[14] New research programmes achieved prominence with their own theoretical bases, leading to new approaches to macroeconomic policy.

Money was increasingly recognized as an important factor, that is to say 'money mattered', and less emphasis was placed on the demand side of the economy and more on supply. Even to those for whom the demand side retained its Keynesian pre-eminence, there was an interest in the influence of net financial assets on consumer expenditure in addition to the influence of income. During the period two 'new' approaches seemed to reflect these trends – that of the CEPG and that of the monetarists. These two 'schools' of economic thought might at first sight seem to have little in common, for they advocated very different policy measures and disagreed about the way the economy worked. What makes them interesting from our point of view is that they agreed that the economy was inherently stable and that the Keynesian fine-tuning interventionist approach was inappropriate. They advocate the use of 'rules' to be followed, a tax rule on the one hand and a money growth rule on the other. Short-run intervention was seen as likely to be at best irrelevant, and at worst counter-productive.

The ideas of the CEPG became increasingly prominent in the period 1974–84. Although they emphasized the importance of aggregate demand in determining output and employment in the economy, they were critical of the orthodox Keynesian approach in a number of respects. First, they believed that fiscal intervention was actually destabilizing, for a variety of reasons: the underestimation of the multiplier; the existence of variable time-lags between implementing policy and its eventual impact on the economy; and the inadequacy of short-term forecasting models. Second, they alleged that the net result of fine-tuning the economy was to make things 'worse' rather than 'better'. Third, they also rejected the use of a prices and incomes policy to overcome inflation, believing it to be unnecessary to curb wage demands and the pressure of demand increases. In such periods the actual growth of real incomes will be high relative to workers' expectations, so that workers are *less* likely to press for the high wages which would feed a wage–price spiral.[15] In fact, the imposition of an incomes policy might actually make things worse, frustrating workers' expectations, and so leading to increased demand for wage rises. Fourth, they rejected the use of devaluation as a means of raising the competitiveness of domestic goods (and services) in home and overseas markets, and thereby improving the balance of payments. The CEPG claimed a very strong feedback from devaluation to domestic inflation rates, through its effect upon the prices of imported goods and raw materials. Higher prices will reduce workers' real incomes, so leading to increased wage claims, further price rises, and an erosion of the temporary advantage gained by devaluation. Indeed, they even proposed interference with the free trade policy advocated by the Keynesians, who believed that free trade was to the benefit of all countries.

The CEPG also differed from traditional Keynesians in seeing fiscal policy as possibly *contributing to* the balance of payments problem rather than correcting it. They identified a strong link between the balance of payments on current account and the size of the public sector surplus/deficit.

In the conventional manner let

I = investment expenditure,
G = government expenditure,
X = exports,
S = savings,
T = taxation receipts,
M = imports. Then, for equilibrium:

$$I + G + X = S + T + M$$

rearranging

$$X - M = S - I + T - G$$

i.e. the surplus on the balance of payments current account is, by definition, equal to the private sector surplus $(S - I)$ plus the public sector surplus $(T - G)$.

The private sector surplus is the sum of household and company *net* savings and this, it is claimed, is so small that it can be ignored. Household saving in the UK is normally balanced by investment in housing (channelled by building society deposits), and company saving is the major source of company investment. That being so then:

$$S - I \simeq O$$

and

$$X - M \simeq T - G$$

i.e. the balance of payments current account surplus/deficit is approximately equal to the public sector surplus/deficit, and changes in the latter will lead to approximately equal changes in the former. The explanation is that the effect of expansionary fiscal policy will be to raise incomes and imports faster than exports.

The policy implication of the approach typified by the CEPG was that an expansion of domestic demand to alleviate unemployment must be accompanied by the use of import controls. If the expansion is not accompanied by import controls, then the balance of payments will rapidly move into a considerable deficit, with devaluation or depreciation of the exchange rate unable to correct the deficit.[16] The favourable effects for employment of the expansionary fiscal policy will then be dissipated overseas as increased demand in the UK is met by increased purchases of foreign goods rather than domestically produced goods. Their reply to the argument that the imposition of import controls on the part of the UK would be met with retaliation from other countries, is that the aim would not be to *reduce* the level of imports into the UK but to keep the level from rising. If no other country is harmed there will be no need for retaliation! In fact, any rise in UK exports might subsequently create scope for imports to rise.

We have already seen that economists supporting the CEPG analysis believe that 'fine-tuning' the economy by pursuing an interventionist policy is actually counter-productive and destabilizing. They believe that the economy is relatively stable in the medium term and that the most appropriate policy is to apply a 'fiscal rule' within the context of a medium-term strategy. This rule takes the form of a composite tax rate – the par tax rate – set at such a level that desired targets for National Income (employment) and the balance of payments can be achieved in the medium term. This rule should be adhered to, and the par tax rate altered, *only* if the target values are themselves altered, or if there are major disturbances in the world economy, or in the trade-off between the employment and balance of payments objectives.

The monetarists

Monetarists similarly eschew the use of an armoury of policy instruments (instrumental variables) to achieve macroeconomic objectives. The monetarist economists believe that if the money stock is increased, real output is not affected in the long run, though prices are, i.e. control of the money supply is the key to the control of inflation.[17] They accept that in the short run changes in money supply will affect output as well as prices. However, there will be time-lags between the change in money supply and changes in output, making it inadvisable to use the manipulation of aggregate demand as a policy instrument for achieving target levels of output and employment. Output and employment will instead be determined at their 'natural' levels by microeconomic factors affecting aggregate supply. These are more easily influenced by measures designed to improve market efficiency or to increase the supply of factors of production.

Policy-makers are therefore encouraged to follow simple 'rules' which will influence the economy in the long run, and will not generally be subject to changes which might cause instability in the short run. The most obvious rule is to control the rate of monetary expansion, and to effect changes in it relatively gradually in order that disruption is not too great. To the monetarist the target rate for monetary expansion (given flexible exchange rates) becomes the proxy for the target rate of inflation, so that the 'target' is now set in terms of the value of the instrumental variable (money supply) rather than in terms of the objective (inflation). Short-run manipulation of the instrument to achieve the target objective was regarded as neither necessary nor even possible. Instead, the authorities are to control inflation through the long-run rate of monetary expansion. A rule for policy is therefore established.

This was the fundamental monetarist 'rule', but there was also general consensus amongst monetarists regarding other 'rules'. Most believe that the budget should be balanced and that government expenditure should be reduced to as low a level as possible. A balanced budget leaves policy-makers with a considerable degree of freedom as regards the all-important rate of money supply growth. Further, if government expenditure is low, then tax revenue can be low, so that market prices are less distorted by the imposition of taxes and the market mechanism works more efficiently. Public enterprise, such as the nationalized industries, should where possible be 'privatized' so that government expenditure and taxes can be reduced still further, and market prices prevail. Most monetarists also advocated a freely fluctuating exchange rate which will adjust differences between domestic and world inflation rates, so restoring competitiveness when necessary and protecting the balance of payments (see Ch. 22).

In the UK monetary targets were first formally set in 1976 when the IMF made limits on Domestic Credit Expansion (DCE) a precondition of a $3.9bn loan. The Letter of Intent which was sent to the IMF by the Labour Government confirmed a shift away from the Keynesian short-term management approach, via credit restrictions and interest rate, towards long-term control of monetary aggregates and the elevation of monetary policy to a central role. A package deal of measures was used in an attempt to control the money supply. Minimum lending rate was raised, supplementary special deposits (SSDs) were introduced to form 'the corset', banks were given priorities for lending purposes and the fiscal stance was tightened. The target aggregate chosen was $£M_3$, changes in which were accomplished by the measures mentioned in Chapter 16.

Medium-term economic strategy

An important turning point in economic policy took place in 1979 with the election of the Conservative government under the leadership of Margaret Thatcher. The main thrust of macroeconomic policy moved towards the evolution of a non-inflationary economic environment within which a market economy could rapidly flourish. As in many aspects of Economics, a major shift in policy making often originates from a modification of economic thinking. In this case, the theoretical basis for the anti-inflationary policy was the breakdown of the Phillips curve relationship (which seemed to have underpinned Keynesian macroeconomic policy ideas in the 1960s) and the emergence of Friedman's 'expectations augmented' version of the Phillips curve. This latter version of the Phillips relationship combined the Friedmanite inflationary expectations theory with the concept of the 'natural rate of unemployment' (see Chapter 17). As far as policy making is concerned, the intention was to achieve the goal of lower inflation by influencing aggregate demand (through the money supply) and by improving aggregate supply responsiveness, thereby creating a fall in the 'natural rate of unemployment'. The Thatcher government therefore introduced an economic strategy directed towards the medium-term, which had two main components.

The first main component was **macroeconomic** in nature and was in line with monetary thinking. It involved a *Medium Term Financial Strategy* (MTFS) whose aim was to use constraints on the money supply (see below) to decrease the growth of money GDP over time, and thereby cut the rate of inflation. This obviously reflected the predominant use of monetary policy as the government's main economic policy instrument and the subordination of fiscal policy. As far as the latter was concerned, the government aimed to decrease the Public Sector Borrowing Requirement (PSBR), mainly by reducing public expenditure, since it felt that that there was a close relationship between the size of the PSBR and the money supply. It was also argued that any increase in PSBR, and therefore in government borrowing, would mean that interest rates would have to rise in order to persuade the private sector to hold public debt.These high interest rates would, in turn, lead to a movement of funds from the private to the public sector, i.e. the private sector would be 'crowded out'. Therefore, the government saw the central aim of the MTFS as the control of inflation, which was to be achieved by reducing the growth of money supply and by keeping the PSBR under control. The second main component of the medium-term economic strategy was **microeconomic** in nature, making use of the so-called *supply-side policies* in order to improve the *output responsiveness* of the economy. In terms of the economic analysis used above, these supply-side policies sought to improve the workings of markets in order to decrease the 'natural rate of unemployment'. In the next section we will first follow the course of the MTFS before looking in more detail at the government's supply-side policies.

MTFS 1979–81

The MTFS was first published in March 1980. There have been annual policy statements since 1980 which set out *targets* for monetary growth and for the PSBR over a medium-term time horizon. As noted above, the prime aim of the MTFS was to eradicate inflation, in the belief that inflation actually caused unemployment by creating inflationary wage and price expectations. Creating a stable, non-inflationary framework was therefore seen as essential, and this became the cornerstone of policy. Table 25.2 summarises the main targets and outturns of the various versions of the MTFS between

1980 and 1990; by comparing targets and outcomes, the relative 'success' of the MTFS strategy can be gauged.

MTFS Targets	1980	1981	1982	1983	1984	1985	1986	1987	1988	1989	1990	Outturns
£M$_3$ (% p.a.)												
1980/81	7–11											20.0
1981/82	6–10	6–10										14.5
1982/83	5–9	5–9	8–12									10.0
1983/84	4–8	4–8	7–11	7–11								9.8
1984/85			6–10	6–10	6–10							9.5
1985/86			5–9	5–9	5–9	5–9						14.8
1986/87					4–8	4–8	11–15					18.0
1987/88					3–7	3–7		****				22.1
1988/89					2–6	2–6						22.4
M$_1$ (% p.a.)												
1982/83			8–12									11.0
1983/84			7–11	7–11								11.0
1984/85			6–10	6–10	****							
1985/86				5–9								
PSL$_2$ (% p.a.)												
1982/83			8–12									9.0
1983/84			7–11	7–11								12.3
1984/85			6–10	6–10	****							
1985/86				5–9								
M$_0$ (% p.a.)												
1984/85					4–8							5.5
1985/86					3–7	3–7						3.5
1986/87					2–6	2–6	2–6					4.0
1987/88					1–5	1–5	2–6	2–6				5.0
1988/89					0–4	0–4	1–5	1–5	1–5			7.5
1989/90							1–5	1–5	1–5	1–5		5.75
1990/91									0–4	0–4	1–5*	
1991/92									0–4	0–4	0–4†	
1992/93										0–4	0–4†	
1993/94											−1–3†	
PSBR (% of GDP)												
1980/81	3.75											6.00
1981/82	3.00	4.25										4.50
1982/83	2.25	3.25	3.50									2.75
1983/84	1.50	2.00	2.75	2.75								3.25
1984/85			2.00	2.50	2.25							3.25
1985/86				2.00	2.00							2.00
1986/87					2.00	2.00	1.75					1.00
1987/88					1.75	1.75	1.75	1.00				−0.75
1988/89					1.75	1.75	1.50	1.00	−0.75			−3.00
1989/90							1.50	1.00	0.00	−2.75		−1.25
1990/91								1.00	0.00	−1.75	−1.25	
1991/92									0.00	−1.00	−0.50	
1992/93										−0.50	0.00	
1993/94											0.00	

* Target range.
† Illustrative ranges.

Source: Healey (1990), Financial Times (1990).

Table 25.2 The MTFS 1980–90, targets and outturns

In the early period, £M$_3$ was chosen by the government as the most reliable indicator of spending, and targets for the growth of £M$_3$ were set in each annual MTFS statement. Unfortunately, in order to control £M$_3$, interest rates had to be raised to record levels of 17% in 1979; even then this did not seem to bring £M$_3$ within the desired bands. Interest rates remained high throughout 1980 and this pushed up the exchange rate, making UK exports uncompetitive in international markets. The continued attempts to get £M$_3$ and the PSBR under control led the government to tighten its fiscal policy in 1981 and although interest rates fell during the early part of the year, they were back to 16% by later that year. The early monetarist experiment, plus the world recession, led to a fall in manufacturing output by 19.6% between June 1979 and June 1981 and a loss of 23% of manufacturing employment (see also Ch. 1).

Two interesting developments grew out of this early monetarist experiment. First, a difficulty arose in finding a valid measure of money which faithfully reflected movements in UK spending. Unfortunately, £M$_3$ was becoming unreliable as a measure of UK spending. For example, as the interest rate rose, depositors were induced to shift from non-interest to interest bearing accounts. Such a shift would not change the total money supply £M$_3$, but merely redistribute it from accounts where it was more likely to be spent (non-interest bearing) to accounts where it was less likely to be spent (interest bearing). As a result, although figures for £M$_3$ were not recorded as having fallen much in this period, the *actual spending* of the population decreased more significantly. Second, it was becoming clear that economic policy, whether short- or medium-term in aim, was still unable to reconcile conflicting objectives. For example, controlling money supply and the PSBR involved a policy of high interest rates; but these increased industrial investment and also led to a fall in UK exports (as the exchange rate rose with interest rates). The early monetarist experiment was not immune to the traditional problems involved when trying to balance policy targets with policy instruments.

MTFS 1982–84

In 1982 the government overhauled the MTFS and began to abandon the policy of targetting a single monetary variable, i.e. £M$_3$. For example, it had become clear as early as 1981 that *narrower* definitions of money such as M$_0$ and M$_1$ were growing much more slowly than £M$_3$ and were reflecting more accurately what was happening to the real economy. As a result, other measures of money such as M$_0$, M$_1$, and PSL$_2$ began to be included as target aggregates, and £M$_3$ targets were adjusted to take into consideration some of the problems noted above. The doubling of unemployment between 1979 and 1982 also weakened the government's will to continue with its severe anti-inflationary policy. By Autumn 1982 interest rates had fallen to around 9% and remained reasonably steady until the middle of 1984, while at the same time the Lawson tax-cutting budgets from 1983 onwards provided some stimulus to aggregate demand. Much of the recovery of the 1982–85 period was due to a rise in consumer expenditure as earnings rose faster than inflation. This was further fuelled by a credit boom, brought about by easier access to credit and a fall in the savings ratio.

During this period the targets for the PSBR were gently eased, as money supply targets other than £M$_3$ were tried, with varying degrees of success. The government became more aware of the problems involved in using only monetary targets as the cornerstone of policy. Indeed 'squeezing' inflation out of the system by this method would not only be difficult, but may even be impossible. In a pragmatic sense, it seemed that by late 1984, both the government and the Bank of England had accepted that a 5% inflation rate might be a more realistic objective in the future. As money supply targets became less reliable, monetary policy began to shift towards targetting the exchange rate. This was to continue into the next period.

MTFS 1985–88

The government's MTFS took another turn at the begining of 1985 when economic circumstances created an exchange rate crisis. The government had shown increasing unease at the apparent rise in the underlying trend of UK inflation in 1984, together with the continued problem of unemployment. At the same time the dollar was at its peak. Thus ensuing loss of confidence in the UK led to a fall in the value of the pound to \$1.04; this caused the UK to experience inflationary pressure as the low exchange rate increased import costs. As a result of this volatility in the exchange rate, a more 'active' policy was adopted in order to stabilize the exchange rate at a 'desirable' level which would not increase inflation. It was felt that sterling would best be pegged to a stable currency such as the deutschmark, and for a while the unofficial government target for sterling was set at around 3.0DM to 3.2DM to the pound. It should be understood that the move towards stable and targetted exchange rates was not only a UK phenomenon. The major trading nations had agreed in the 'Plaza Accord' of October 1985 and in the 'Louvre Accord' of February 1987 to move towards co-ordinating their economic policies and to peg their currencies within agreed target zones.

What had clearly happened in 1985 was a shift in the role of monetary policy; instead of using the interest rate mechanism to control the *money supply*, it was now used to control the *exchange rate*. Inflation was now seen as being transmitted to the UK economy mainly through the exchange rate route. By November 1985, $£M_3$ was downgraded from a 'target variable' to one which was now only to be 'monitored'; since 1987, M_0 has been the only targetted monetary variable in government use. The 1985–88 period saw a gradual fall in interest rates and a more relaxed approach to monetary policy in general; the interest rate weapon being used increasingly to achieve the desired exchange rather than any specific money supply targets. At the same time the UK experienced boom conditions, stimulated by easier credit conditions and higher post-tax incomes. Consumer expenditure on both durable and non-durable goods (such as housing) led the growth of aggregate demand. The unemployment rate fell, but many saw the rise in inflation by the end of 1988 as the inevitable 'cost' of such a policy.

This period shows that following simple monetary *rules* cannot always bring simple solutions to the economy. It also shows the conflicting nature of targets and instruments. Some members of the government (including the Prime Minister) believed that interest rates should have been higher during this period, in order to control the money supply and therefore aggregate spending and inflation. Others, such as the Chancellor, Nigel Lawson, felt that the best course was to keep interest rates rather lower in order to prevent the sterling exchange rate rising above a certain target level against currencies such as the deutschmark and dollar. In this way we could still control inflation, but without squeezing the domestic money supply and credit too much. In the end, a rise in M_0 above its target values and clear signs of a resurgence in inflation meant that in March 1988, interest rates rose once more.

MTFS 1988–

Between 1988 and 1990 inflation again rose, from 6.5% to over 10%. Interest rates remained at a high level during this period; even so the growth of consumer demand proved difficult to control, with so many changes in the financial markets having made credit even easier to obtain. The result of the consumer boom was also felt on the current account, which had moved into a massive deficit of around £20,000m by 1989. At the same time, the PSBR policy was designed to 'complement and support the monetary stance'; since 1989, policy towards PSBR (or PSDR) has been 'tightened', with tax yields designed to rise to £1bn by 1991. The government continued to believe that it was important to keep fiscal policy within a 'stable' framework, and not to use it as a short term instrument of demand management. By the beginning of the 1990s, the MTFS no longer provided the clear guidelines for policy which had prevailed in the early 1980s.

Supply-side strategy

As was explained previously, the Conservative Government's medium-term economic strategy also revolved around improving the *output responsiveness* of the economy. Monetarists generally have sympathy with the view that output and employment are supply-determined, rather than with the Keynesian view that they are demand-determined.

Fig. 25.3 (a) The Keynesian approach; (b) the supply-side approach

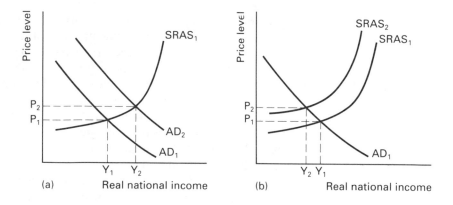

Figure 25.3(a) represents the familiar Keynesian view, with prices and output (Real National Income) being determined largely by changes in aggregate demand. Our main interest here is to contrast this familiar diagram with Fig. 25.3(b), which uses the same axes to reflect the monetarist or supply-side view of economics. Figure 25.3(b) implies that it is changes in supply conditions which largely initiate changes in prices and output. Mainstream monetarists would use the supply-side approach to determine the equilibrium levels of output and employment in the long run. We briefly consider some aspects of this approach which have attracted attention.

First, there is the suggestion that unemployment and social security benefits encourage people to spend more time searching for the type of employment they consider appropriate. As a result they remain on the unemployment register longer, the unemployment figures are swollen, and aggregate output is restricted from the supply side. An ancillary argument is that the difference between some low-paid jobs and the rate of unemployment benefit is so marginal that such jobs are not taken up. This problem is aggravated by the UK tax system, which may result in some workers, previously unemployed, paying marginal tax rates in excess of 100% when moving into low-paid jobs – the 'unemployment trap' (see Ch. 14). Unemployment and social security benefits may in these ways cause the short run aggregate supply curve to shift to the left, from $SRAS_1$ to $SRAS_2$ in Fig. 25.3(b), reducing the level of output and employment, and raising the price level higher than it would otherwise be.

The second suggestion is that, quite apart from the 'unemployment trap', taxation can affect the supply of labour (and so the level of output) through its disincentive effects. The corollary of this is that a cut in taxes might so stimulate work effort, and therefore output, that total tax revenue rises. In terms of Fig. 25.3(b) tax cuts would shift the supply curve to the right, i.e. from $SRAS_2$ to $SRAS_1$, so that output and employment would rise, and prices fall.

The third suggestion is that labour has priced itself out of the market, thereby reducing employment and output, because the trade unions have forced up the real wages of their members. It has been estimated by Minford and Peel (1981) that unions have 'marked up' members' wages by between 12 and 25%, so raising permanent unemployment figures by between 400,000 and 800,000,[18] although more recent research has put the average mark-up at 10% or less (Blanchflower 1986). Another important study (Layard and Nickell 1985) showed that the unemployment rate in the UK had risen by 11.83 percentage points between 1956 and 1983 and that union 'push' on wages accounted for 2.27 of those percentage points.[19] The policy implication is that trade union bargaining power should be curbed. In terms of *labour market* analysis the market wage is pushed above the equilibrium wage so that unemployment rises. In terms of the *goods market* in Fig. 25.3(b), the rise in labour costs shifts the aggregate supply curve upwards and to the left from $SRAS_1$ to $SRAS_2$. Output and employment are reduced and prices are higher than they would otherwise be.

Finally, there is the suggestion that the very high unemployment and low output figures prevailing in the UK exaggerate the true situation because there is a considerable 'hidden' or 'black' economy, encouraged by a desire to evade taxation. Some of the 'black' economy would be conducted in monetary terms (e.g. payment in cash to a local handyman), some in non-monetary terms by means of barter. The 'black' economy has always been with us, and estimates as to its size vary from 2.5% of GDP (the gap between expenditure and declared income) to 7.5% (Inland Revenue estimates of tax evasion) and even to 15%.

As explained above, successive Conservative governments have implemented a wide range of measures consistent with the approach of supply-side economics (shown in Fig. 25.3 as a shift in the aggregate supply curve downwards to the right). We will briefly summarise some of the practical changes which have to be implemented in an attempt to increase the efficiency of markets.

Taxation

Successive Conservative governments have believed that the taxation structure has become distorted over the years and should be changed in order to create more incentives and to induce more output (supply) responsiveness. For example, the decrease in tax allowances on mortgages in the late 1980s from £30,000 per *person* to £30,000 per *dwelling* was partly designed to curb the amount of investment in housing and to stimulate investment in company shares, i.e. to channel investment into more productive forms which would help stimulate output. Similarly, tax relief on life insurance premiums had been abolished in 1984, in an attempt to encourage people to invest in company equities. Again the rate of Capital Gains Tax had long been *less than* the basic rate of income tax, giving, for example, a better return to a person who bought and sold oil paintings than to a person buying company shares. In 1988 the CGT and the basic rate of income tax were equalised to prevent this bias. As well as bringing down personal taxation in order to stimulate incentives, successive governments have also decreased corporation tax for large companies, from 52% in 1983/4 to 25% by 1990; for small firms the rate was reduced from 35% to 25% in the same period. Those cuts in corporation tax were an attempt to stimulate reinvestment in capital stock.

Labour supply, efficiency and training

Successive governments have also believed in the need to improve the workings of the UK labour market, in order to make it more 'efficient' (i.e. labour should be mobile, well trained and free from institutional – e.g. union – bias). As far as *mobility* is concerned, the government felt that the UK labour market needed to be 'flexible', with workers induced to take up jobs rapidly. It was thought that this process was being inhibited by narrow differentials between the income of those out of work, thereby preventing active job search. Continuous adjustments have therefore been made in national insurance benefits and income related benefits over the past years, with the aim of widening the gap in income levels between those in work and those out of work.

To improve the *institutional problems* surrounding the labour market, successive Conservative governments have introduced a series of laws to regulate employment and the Trade Unions. The Employment Acts of 1980, 82, 88 and 89, together with the Trade Union Act of 1984, have weakened the control of unions (see Ch. 20). In the area of *training*, the government has attempted to introduce new schemes for the unemployed, such as the Restart Programme and Employment Training. In December 1988, White Papers entitled 'Training for Employment' provided the context for the subsequent launch of Training and Enterprise Councils (TECs) to improve the quality of training in local areas and to help the transition from education to work. Similarly, the Technical and Vocational Educational Initiative (TVEI) aims to influence the whole curriculum of schools and colleges to prepare pupils of 14–18 for the demands of working lives. These changes, together with others relating to the basic school curriculum, have been aimed at increasing the quality of the UK's stock of 'human capital'.

Industrial policies

Very briefly, it should be realized that the whole process of privatization fits well into the supply-side ideology. Successive Conservative governments have felt that companies in the private sector are better at using resources than those in government hands. It is therefore no surprise that the government has sought to place the main utilities into private hands over the last decade. The more 'lenient' attitude towards Mergers and Acquisitions during the 1980s has been another by-product of this general view that the private sector can better utilise resources.

Conclusion

We have seen how Keynesian interventionism placed a premium on finding a variety of policy instruments to achieve a number of target objectives. Until the 1970s the Keynes/Tinbergen/Theil approach was the theoretical basis for short-term macroeconomic policy. However, evidence began to accumulate that this activity could be counter-productive, even destabilizing. The search for alternative approaches was also encouraged by the oil crisis of 1974 which destroyed old-established trade-offs and relationships between objectives. In addition, the oil-price increases deflated the non-oil-producing economies of the West and stimulated inflation. 'Stagflation' and later 'slumpflation' became new problems which the traditional 'fine-tuning', interventionist theories could not easily handle. Emphasis switched to medium- and long-term strategies which now prevail over short-term fine-tuning. In the 1980s the setting of medium-term 'rules' for the conduct of policy became central to the ideas of groups of economists as diverse as the CEPG and the monetarists. However, attempts during the 1980s to adhere to various forms of the Medium Term Financial Strategy failed to provide a solution to the UK's macroeconomic problems. Much attention has been given in recent times to the supply-side of the economy, i.e. to the efficient operation of a market economy in which the state plays a more limited economic role. Nevertheless, as noted elsewhere in this book (e.g. Chs. 5–8), examples of 'market failure' still abound, and ironically more government intervention may be needed to remedy information defects and strategic alliances within the UK economy. Managing an economy is a difficult task and governments and their economic advisors will continue to grapple with the best ways of matching economic objects with policy instruments for some time to come.

Notes

1. For a survey of the conduct of fiscal policy from 1974 to 1981 see Savage (1982).
2. Keynesian economists are those who interpret Keynes's work in a certain way; whether they truly reflect Keynes's economics is a matter for debate.
3. For instance, in the 1978/79 period when the 'norm' was 5% per annum for wage changes, 12% was the figure achieved during the operation of the policy, and 20% was the rate experienced in the following six months.
4. That is, provided the Marshall–Lerner condition is satisfied, with the

sum of price elasticity of demand for UK exports and price elasticity of demand for imports into the UK greater than unity.

5. For instance, in Chapter 16 we noted that the money supply, M, times the velocity of circulation of money, V, would give the monetary value of spending.

6. This diagrammatic approach is that of Mundell (1962).

7. If points on O_1 indicate internal balance, then points off it indicate imbalance. Check that above and to the right of the line there will be inflation, whereas below and to the left there will be unemployment.

8. Similarly, if points on O_2 indicate external balance, then points off it indicate imbalance. Check that a balance of payments surplus will occur below and to the left of the O_2 line, and a deficit above and to the right.

9. Provided that O_2 and O_1 cross! Economic objective O_2 is shown as having a shallower slope than O_1. Can you see why? Start at E, and move up the O_1 line; expansionary monetary policy reduces interest rates, so that the short-term capital inflow will diminish, and the balance of payments will deteriorate. To keep it in balance, a lower National Income would be necessary in order to reduce the import flow. This could be achieved by contractionary fiscal policy, i.e. above E, O_2 must lie to the left of O_1.

10. If the exchange rate is lowered then O_2 might shift to the right and so pass through point G (which had previously been a balance of payments deficit position). All three objectives are now achieved.

11. Although the relative weights change as unemployment rises and inflation falls.

12. And to reflect the fact that 'overachievement' of target values may be deemed as harmful to social welfare as 'underachievement'. A balance of payments surplus would be viewed here as creating as much 'loss' as a balance of payments deficit.

13. For example work by Fisher, Pissarides and Caves. Fisher's work related to the UK between 1953 and 1968 and found the authorities willing to trade off $1bn of reserves for a 0.4% reduction in unemployment. Pissarides found the authorities indifferent between a 1% reduction in unemployment and a £789m. loss in reserves or a 26% increase in inflation!

14. Doubts grew as to the effectiveness of interventionist policy. Poor forecasting and the time-lags involved in putting policy measures into action resulted, it was claimed, in destabilization, i.e. the process of intervention made things worse.

15. There will be a reversed Phillips curve. (For Phillips curve see Ch. 17.)

16. The income effect of the fiscal policy on imports is assumed to be larger than the price effect of devaluation or depreciation on exports.

17. If $M . V \equiv P . T$, the equation of exchange where M = money supply, V = average velocity of circulation of money, P = average price level, and T = volume of transactions. Then, if both V and T are fixed (or change at a known rate), money supply M directly affects price level P. So $\Delta M = \Delta P$, and the inflation rate is determined by the growth of the money supply.

18. Minford and Peel (1981) argue that if such benefit were cut in real terms

by 15%, then, in combination with a similar reduction in the trade union mark-up, the number of permanently unemployed could be cut within three years by 1.25 million.

19. Interestingly this study found *demand* factors to be *at least as important* as union militancy in causing unemployment in the 1967–79 period, and *more important* in the 1979–83 period.

References

Allsopp, C. and **Graham, A.** (1987) The Assessment: Policy Options for the UK, *Oxford Review of Economic Policy*, **3**, no. 3.

Blanchflower, D. (1986) What effects do unions have on relative wages in Great Britain? *British Journal of Industrial Relations*, July.

British Business (1988) 8 April.

Budd, A. (1990) The Medium Term Financial Strategy Now, *Barclays Economic Review*, May.

CSO (1990), *Economic Trends*, Annual Supplement 1990; July 1990 and earlier editions.

Financial Times (1990) The Budget details, 21 March.

Griffiths, A. (1990) Shareownership and the Economy, *British Economic Survey*, **19**, no. 3, Autumn.

Healey, N. (1990) Mrs Thatcher's 'Fight Against Inflation: Ten Years Without Cheer', *Economics*, **26**, Pt. 1, Spring.

Layard, R. L. and **Nickell, S.** (1985) The causes of British unemployment, *National Institute Economic Review*, 111, Feb.

Minford, P. and **Peel, D.** (1981) Is the Government's economic strategy on course?, *Lloyds Bank Review*, **40**, April.

Mosley, P. (1976) Towards a satisficing theory of economic policy, *Economic Journal*, **86**, March.

Mundell, R. A. (1962) The appropriate use of monetary and fiscal policy for internal and external stability, *IMF Staff Papers*, **9**.

OECD, *Economic Surveys*, UK, July (1987).

Savage, D. (1982) Fiscal policy, 1974/5–1980/81: description and measurement, *National Institute Economic Review*, 99, Feb.

Theil, H. (1956) On the theory of economic policy, *American Economic Review*, **46**, May.

Tinbergen, J. (1952) *On the Theory of Economic Policy*. North-Holland Publishing Co., Amsterdam.

The UK has now been a member of the EC for over eighteen years and the EC itself has been in existence for over thirty years. During this period the matter of UK membership of the Community has never ceased to be a cause of great controversy. It would be true to say, however, that all major political parties now accept the *fact* of UK membership even if they differ quite widely in their overall approach and attitude to the Community and how it should develop. This chapter seeks to review the development and operation of EC policies and institutions, and in particular their impact upon the UK. Six major areas are considered, the Single European Act, the Community budget, the Common Agricultural Policy (CAP), commercial policy, trade and payments, and the European Monetary System (EMS).

Historical background

The historical background to the EC has been covered in some depth elsewhere.[1] In the thirty years since its foundation the EC has absorbed the two 'communities' which preceded it, i.e. the European Coal and Steel Community (ECSC) and the European Atomic Energy Community (Euratom). The ECSC had been established in 1952 to control the pooled coal and iron and steel resources of the six member countries – France, West Germany, Italy, Belgium, the Netherlands and Luxembourg. By promoting free trade in coal and steel between members and by protecting against non-members, the ECSC revitalized the two war-stricken industries, and it was this success which prompted the establishment of the much more ambitious European Economic Community (EEC), now officially known simply as the European Community (EC). The European Atomic Energy Community had been set up by treaty in 1957 with the same six countries, to promote growth in nuclear industries and the peaceful use of atomic energy.

The EC was formed on 1 January 1958 after the signing of the Treaty of Rome. This sought to establish a 'common market', by eliminating all restrictions on the free movement of goods, capital and persons between member countries. By dismantling tariff barriers on industrial trade between members and by imposing a common tariff against non-members, the EC was to become a protected free-trade area or 'customs union'. The formation of a customs union was to be the first step in the creation of an 'economic union' with national economic policies harmonized across the member countries. The original 'Six' became 'Nine' in 1973 with the accession of the UK, Eire and Denmark, and 'Ten' in 1981 with the entry of Greece. The accession of Spain and Portugal on 1 January 1986 increased the number of member countries to twelve.

Table 26.1 presents some of the important characteristics of the twelve

Table 26.1 The Twelve:
some comparisons

Country	Population (million) (1989)	Economically active population		
		Agric. (%) (1989)	Ind. (%) (1989)	Services (%) (1989)
Belgium	9.9	3.7	26.3	70.1
Denmark	5.1	6.4	26.2	67.4
France	55.7	8.4	28.5	63.1
W. Germany	61.3*	5.5	39.1	55.4
Greece	10.0	30.8	21.1	48.1
Eire	3.5	17.2	25.7	57.1
Italy	57.4	11.6	28.5	59.9
Luxembourg	0.4	4.3	28.6	67.1
Netherlands	14.7	5.2	26.2	68.6
Portugal	10.3	24.4	31.4	44.2
Spain	38.9	17.4	28.2	54.4
UK	57.0	2.3	27.6	70.1

* Note that the unified Germany has added to it the population of East Germany –
some 16.7m – making the population of Germany 78m; and the population of the
EC – 341m, compared to the present 324m.

	Share of EC GDP (%) 1989	EC Pop'n. (%) 1989	GDP per capita (PPP's) 1987	Unemployment (%) 1989	Inflation (%) 1989
Belgium	3.2	3.0	101	10.2	3.1
Denmark	2.4	1.6	114	9.2	4.8
France	20.5	17.2	109	10.8	3.7
W. Germany	26.0	18.9	114	7.3	2.8
Greece	1.1	3.1	54	3.0	13.8
Eire	0.7	1.1	64	17.8	4.1
Italy	17.7	17.7	104	16.7	6.3
Luxembourg	0.1	0.1	125	1.4	3.3
Netherlands	5.0	4.5	104	7.4	1.1
Portugal	0.8	3.2	54	6.8	12.6
Spain	6.7	11.9	74	17.8	6.8
UK	15.8	17.6	105	6.4	7.8

Note: GDP per capita is calculated on the basis of Purchasing Power Parities (PPP)
and is expressed as an index (EC = 100).

member countries. It shows how diverse they are in terms of population,
industrial structure, standard of living, unemployment level and inflation
rate.

A number of economic arguments have been advanced in support of the
EC:

1. By abolishing industrial tariff and non-tariff barriers at national frontiers,
   the EC has created a single 'domestic' market of around 340 million
   people, with opportunities for substantial economies of scale in
   production. By surrounding this market with a tariff wall, the Common
   External Tariff (CET), member countries are the beneficiaries of these

scale economies. The implementation of the 'Single European Act' will, by 1992, open the EC's internal frontiers completely.

2.   By regulating agricultural production through the CAP, the EC has become self-sufficient in many agricultural products.

3.   By amending the co-ordinating labour and capital regulations in the member countries, the EC seeks to create a free market in both, leading to a more 'efficient' use of these factors. A further factor, 'enterprise', is to be 'freed' through increased standardization of national laws on patents and licences.

4.   By controlling monopoly and merger activities, competition has been encouraged both within and across frontiers.

5.   By creating a substantial 'domestic' market and by co-ordinating trade policies, the EC hopes to exert a greater collective influence on world economic affairs than could possibly be achieved by any single nation.

These various policies have been supported by a number of other arrangements, including a common form of taxation, a common currency, and policies directed towards transport, energy, education, social improvement and regional aid. There are, today, few areas of economic life untouched by a specific EC policy or institution. Although our main concern in this chapter will be economic, we should not overlook the political objectives which lay behind the formation of the EC. As early as 1946, Winston Churchill had called for a 'United States of Europe' as a diplomatic and military counter to the Soviet Union. However, it was two Frenchmen – Robert Schuman and Jean Monnet – who were the founding fathers of the EC, with their vision of using economic involvement to tie Europe's warring countries together. Having attempted, on three occasions, to join the EC during the 1960s, the UK was finally accepted for membership in 1970, signed the Treaty of Accession in 1972, and became a full member with effect from 1 January 1973.

The UK's objectives in signing the Treaty of Accession in 1972 were a combination of the short- to medium-term economic, with the medium- to long-term political. There was an undeniable desire to share in the prosperity which the EC appeared to have stimulated for its six members since 1958. The fact that the average growth rate of the Six had been 4.8% per annum between 1961 and 1971, compared to the UK's 2.7% per annum, seemed to show that entry into the EC might offer a solution to some of the UK's growth problems. In this chapter we examine the effect of UK membership of the EC under six broad headings:

1.   The Single European Act;
2.   The EC budget;
3.   The Common Agricultural Policy, CAP;
4.   Commercial policy;
5.   Trade and the balance of payments;
6.   The European Monetary System, EMS.

For each of these headings we discuss both EC policy in general and how it has affected the UK in particular.

The Single European Act

The Single European Act, as it is widely known, came into force in July 1987. It constituted a major development of the Community and was based on a White Paper, 'Completing the Common Market' which had been presented by the Commission to the Milan meeting of the European Council in June 1985. It represented the first time, since 1957, that the original Treaty of Rome had been amended.

The Act looks towards creating a single European economy by 1992. The objective is not simply to create an internal market by removing frontier controls but to remove all barriers to the movement of goods, people and capital. Achieving a single European market will mean, amongst other things, work on standards, procurement, qualifications, banking, capital movements and exchange regulations, tax 'approximation', communications standards and transport. An early example of the type of development involved was the introduction, in January 1988, of the new customs form – the Single Administrative Document (SAD) – replacing over 150 pieces of national customs documentation with just one form. But this form will, itself, become obsolete when the final customs controls at EC internal frontiers are abolished in 1992.

The Single Act has also had political ramifications in that it has formalized the use of qualified majorities for taking decisions in the Council of Ministers and has given the elected European Parliament greater legislating powers.

The EC budget

Since 1970 the EC budget – the centralized source of funds used to finance EC institutions and policies – has been self-financing. Instead of asking each member country for a specified annual contribution, revenue is raised automatically in a number of ways:

1. Customs duties (CET);
2. Agricultural and sugar levies;
3. Value added tax (VAT); and, since 1988;
4. An amount up to 1.2% of national GNP.

All revenues raised through the Common External Tariff (CET) on industrial imports are paid directly to the EC Commission in Brussels, providing around 23% of total revenue. The same procedure is followed as regards agricultural and sugar levies on imports (see the operation of CAP, pp. 553–57), which provide around 6% of total revenue. The EC Commission in Brussels then returns 10% of the revenue received from industrial and agricultural levies to the member governments to cover administrative costs. In addition, the EC budget received from each country the revenue of a *maximum* 1.4% rate of VAT.[2] The actual rate of VAT levied has varied over the years from 0.78% in 1979, to a projected 1.24% in 1986[3], and an actual amount of over 1.4% in both 1986 and 1987. This source provides around 62% of total revenue.

From 1988 onwards revenue has been supplemented by an additional source in the form of up to 1.2% of each member's GNP paid directly from the national government budgets. In 1989 this raised 9.2% of total revenue.

Spending from the EC budget has increased from 3.8bn ECU in 1970 to around 46bn ECU (1 ECU = 73p; 1990) in 1989 (see Table 26.2). This represents a central EC expenditure of around £104 per head compared to UK government expenditure of approximately £2,700 per head. This expenditure is applied to numerous EC programmes, though support for agriculture takes up about two-thirds. Table 26.3 presents expenditure by policy area and shows the beginning of a tighter rein on agricultural support, and an expansion of regional and social programmes during economic recession.

Table 26.2 The EC Budget

1. Total Spend

Year	Amount (bn ECU)
1979	14.4
1985	25.4
1988	43.4
1989	46.1

2. Sources of Revenue

Source	% of total EC Budget
VAT	61.6
Customs Duties	23.4
GNP Related Element	9.2
Agricultural Levies	3.0
Sugar Levies	2.8

Source: derived from *Eurostat* 1990.

Table 26.3 European Community budget spending areas (1980–89) (%)

	1980	1982	1984	1986	1988	1989
Agriculture (CAP)	72.0	66.0	67.7	68.8	71.3	62.0
Common Fisheries Policy	N/A	N/A	0.4	0.6	0.5	} 9.6
Regional Fund	2.5	10.6	5.7	7.7	7.3	
Social Fund	2.4	3.6	6.5	6.8	6.4	7.3
Research, energy, industry, transport	0.5	1.6	6.9	2.4	2.4	3.5
Aid to developing countries	3.8	5.2	3.5	3.7	1.8	1.2
Balance†	18.8	13.0	9.3	10.0	10.1	16.4

† Spending on personnel and administration plus reimbursements to member governments for the cost of collecting tariffs and levies (approximately 4% of budget).
Source: see Table 26.4.

It must also be pointed out that the macroeconomic effects of such a relatively small budget are extremely limited in the conventional national sense. The revenue-raising powers of the Community are restricted to customs duties, VAT and, from 1988 onwards, a GNP-related element. None of these has more than a marginal effect on the national economies. In 1989, total EC spending was only 1.12% of members' total GNP.

In terms of expenditure policy, the Community budget has a very decided macroeconomic effect in spite of the small size of the EC budget in relation to the overall levels of government spending in the twelve member countries. In 1989, the Community's budget for agriculture was over £20bn and the effects of such spending on a European scale, and within a strict legislative framework, have been significant. The distortions created by the CAP are dealt with below and, in greater detail, by other sources (see, in particular, Barnes 1988).

The focus of concern, from the UK point of view, over the EC budget has centred upon the two issues of:

1. The unbalanced nature of the Community's expenditure policy; and
2. The net cost to the UK of the EC's revenue and expenditure policies.

The UK and the EC budget

It must be stressed that the terms 'net contributor' and 'net beneficiary' relate only to the EC budget and its relatively tiny amounts of expenditure, and *not* to the members' total experience within the Community. Merely to say that West Germany and the UK have usually been large net contributors to the budget has no bearing upon whether they have or have not benefited overall from membership of the EC. It is also important to understand that being a 'net contributor' does not imply a transfer of West German or UK funds to the EC. The budget is 'self-financing' to the extent that contributions to it are, by treaty, never the property of the member state. It is intended (although the results in practice are very different) to be a reallocation of resources from rich to poor in much the same way as national income tax. However, it is not so much its position as a net contributor to the budget that has worried successive UK governments, as the size of that contribution.

The calculation of the UK's net contribution involves the following procedure:

1. Industrial tariffs paid directly to EC; plus
2. Agricultural levies paid directly to EC; minus
3. Administrative costs of collecting the above; returned to UK Government; plus
4. VAT contribution (according to the rate set by Council); plus
5. Direct UK Government contribution (the GNP element)

equals gross contribution, minus

6. Amount due to UK for agricultural support (from Intervention Board); minus
7. Structural Fund payments.

equals net contribution (or benefit for some members).

As a major importer of both manufactured goods and food (see Ch. 23), the UK collects large amounts under items (1) and (2). The VAT rate, as a tax on the value added is, of course, fairly closely related to economic activity and therefore the VAT contribution is reasonably proportional across member countries. Summing items (1)–(5) gives the UK's *gross* contribution to the EC budget. However, the UK must set against this the revenue it received for agricultural support programmes, item (6), and for regional and social projects, item (7). Subtracting items (6) and (7) from gross contribution gives the UK's *net* contribution (or benefit).

Whereas the UK's gross contribution is relatively high compared with other members', her receipts from the EC budget, items (6) and (7), are relatively low. The UK receives little in terms of agricultural support because the operation of the CAP largely benefits less efficient producers, and not efficient ones like the UK. The modest increase in EC support for regional and social projects in the UK has been insufficient to correct this imbalance. As a result the UK has consistently found itself a net contributor.

Attempts to follow the history of British net payments to the EC budget are dogged by the changing nature of the agreements surrounding the budget and by the frequency of additional, 'emergency' payments made by member countries in order to keep the EC solvent whilst the larger budget issues were being settled.

The British Government publishes an account, each year, of its dealings with the EC in *The Government's Expenditure Plans*, and these have formed the basis of Table 26.4. There is little relationship between one year's figures and the next, however, and the table should be taken as an indication of the size of the problem only.

Table 26.4 The EC budget – UK payments and receipts by financial year

	1985/86	1987/88	1989/90
Gross payments	3,745	4,881	5,774
Public sector receipts	−1,936	−1,975	−2,334
VAT abatement	−823	−1,302	−1,271
Net payments	986	1,604	2,169

Source: The Government's Expenditure Plans: 1987–88 to 1989–90, vols I and II.

The 1984 budget reforms

Under the original structure of the Community budget from 1972 to 1982 the UK, one of the poorest members (being only sixth-ranked in terms of income per head) found itself the second-highest net contributor. In contrast, France had a higher income per head than the UK, but made the second-lowest net contribution.

The UK's net contribution was considerably reduced over the period 1980–84 by the Conservative Government's specially negotiated rebates, but there was still need for a permanent solution to the imbalance created by the methods adopted by the EC in both raising revenue and allocating expenditure. The regressive nature of the budget was widely acknowledged both within the Commission and in member governments but the problems of amending a system which benefited large and powerful voting groups in several countries were acknowledged as immense. Only the UK and West Germany were net contributors to the budget, the other eight countries (at that time) relying upon large and relatively inefficient farming communities to ensure sufficient flows of funds. The most important part of budget revenue – the then 1% maximum rate of VAT – was, in practice, exhausted in late 1983[3]. Neither the UK nor West Germany wished to see any additional revenue funded by merely increasing the maximum rate of VAT without guarantees of limits on agricultural spending. To this end, the EC Commission in 1983 looked at alternative methods of increasing budget revenue including an energy import tax that would increase budget revenue in such a way as to achieve two objectives at once. First, it would fall very lightly on the oil-rich UK, and relatively heavily on the main beneficiaries of the CAP; and second, it might help reduce Europe's energy dependency (energy constitutes some 34% of the EC's imports) by encouraging conservation and substitution. Another method suggested by the Commission was to use differential application of the rate of VAT. This would lead to high-income per capita countries, like France, Denmark and the Benelux countries, which are also substantial beneficiaries from agricultural support, paying higher VAT rates than the others.[4]

The settlement of the problem, at the Fontainebleau meeting of June 1984, was closer to the second of these propositions but did not go very far towards meeting British and West German fears about the CAP. The VAT ceiling was increased to 1.4% on condition that CAP expenditure was limited (which did not, in fact, happen). In 1986 the planned budget was a total of 35bn ECU representing an overall VAT rate of 1.244%. The new arrangements for the UK abatement, whereby the UK received rebates on its VAT payments, meant that there were in fact three separate VAT rates levied:

UK	0.727%
West Germany	1.213%
All others	1.260%

In practice, therefore, the 1984 arrangements represented a differential application of the rate of VAT, with other members paying a higher rate than the UK.

The 1988 budget settlement

The increase in the rate of VAT did not meet the need for increased expenditure for very long. The 1.4% rate was, in fact, exhausted before the end of the 1986 financial year and, in 1987, the member governments were forced into a series of 'emergency' funding decisions in order to cover agricultural spending and to meet the obligation of rebates to the UK. One such 'supplementary budget' had to be agreed in late 1987 in a form which simply put off around 4bn ECUs (£2.8bn) of agricultural spending until 1988.

During a meeting which lasted well into the early morning hours of Saturday, 13 February 1988, the Community Heads of Government agreed further radical reforms to both sides of the EC budget. On the expenditure side limits were agreed on agricultural spending and increases on the Regional and Social Funds. Spending on the CAP was limited to a fixed amount of about £19bn per year and its growth was limited to 75% of the increase in the rate of growth of the Community's GNP. At the same time the decision was taken to double expenditure on the Regional and Social Funds by 1993.

The Community's revenue was to be radically amended by the addition of a further source outside the VAT element.

From 1988 onwards each member state has also paid to the EC budget a sum equivalent to up to 1.2% of GNP. From that date, therefore, the sources of finance for the Community have been:

1. The CET;
2. Agricultural levies;
3. A rate equivalent to up to 1.4% of VAT;
4. Up to 1.2% of each member's GNP.

The Common Agricultural Policy

When the Treaty of Rome was signed in 1957 over 20% of the working population of the 'Six' were engaged in agriculture. In the enlarged EC of today that figure is 11.5%, ranging from the UK with 2.3% to Greece with over 30% (see Table 26.1). Since one in five of the EC's workers were involved in agricultural production in 1957, it came as no surprise that the depressed agricultural sector became the focus of the first 'common' policy, the CAP, established in 1962. The objectives of this policy were to create a single market for agricultural produce and to protect it from imports, the justification being to ensure dependable supplies of food for the EC and stability of income for those engaged in agriculture.

Both the demand for, and the supply of, agricultural products are, for the most part, inelastic, so that a small shift in either schedule will induce a more than proportionate change in price. Fluctuations in agricultural prices will in turn create fluctuations in agricultural incomes and therefore investment and ultimately output. The CAP seeks to stabilize agricultural prices, and therefore incomes and output in the industry, to the alleged 'benefit' of both producers and consumers.

There are, of course, a number of ways of achieving such objectives. Prior to joining the EC, the UK placed great emphasis on supplies of cheap food from the Commonwealth. The UK therefore adopted a system of 'deficiency payments' which operated by letting actual prices be set at world levels, but at the same time guaranteeing to farmers minimum 'prices' for each product. If the world price fell below the guaranteed minimum, then the 'deficiency' would be made up by government subsidy. Under this system the consumer could benefit from the low world prices whilst at the same time farm incomes were maintained. Although the UK system involved some additional features, such as marketing agencies, direct production grants, research agencies etc., it was by no means as complex as that which has operated in the UK since 1972 under the CAP.

Method of operation

The formal title for the executive body of the CAP is the European Agricultural Guarantee and Guidance Fund (EAGGF), often known by its French translation 'Fonds Européen d'Orientation et de Garantie Agricole' (FEOGA). As its name implies, it has two essential roles: that of guaranteeing farm incomes; and of guiding farm production. We shall consider each aspect in turn.

Guarantee system Different agricultural products are dealt with in slightly different ways, but the basis of the system is the establishment of a 'target price' for each product (Fig. 26.1). The target price is *not* set with reference

Fig. 26.1 EC agricultural pricing

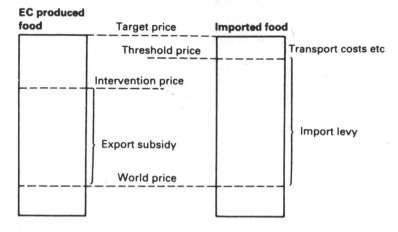

to world prices, but is based upon the price which producers would need to cover costs, including a profit mark-up, in the highest-cost area of production in the EC. The EC then sets an 'Intervention' or 'guaranteed' price for the product in that area, about 7–10% below the target price. Should the price be in danger of falling below this level, the Commission intervenes to buy up production to keep price at or above the 'guaranteed' level. The Commission then sets separate target and Intervention prices for that product in *each area* of the Community, related broadly to production costs in that area. As long as the market price in a given area (there are eleven such areas in the UK) is above the Intervention price, the producer will sell his produce at prevailing market prices. In effect the Intervention price sets a 'floor' below which market price will not be permitted to fall and is therefore the guaranteed minimum price to producers.

In Fig. 26.2, an increase in supply of agricultural products to S_1 would, if no action were taken, lower the market price from P_1 to P_2, below the 'Intervention' or 'guaranteed' price, P^*. At P^* demand is Q' but supply is Q^*. To keep the price at P^* the EAGGF will buy up the excess $Q^* - Q'$. In terms of Fig. 26.2 the demand curve is artificially increased to D_1 by the EAGGF purchase.

If this system of guaranteed minimum prices is to work, then EC farmers must be protected from low-priced imports from overseas. To this end levies or tariffs are imposed on imports of agricultural products. If in Fig. 26.1 the price of imported food were higher than the EC target price then, of course, there would be no need for an import tariff. If, however, the import price is below this, say at the 'world price' in Fig. 26.1, then an appropriate tariff must be calculated. This need not quite cover the difference between 'target' and 'world' price, since the importer still has to pay transport costs within the EC to get the food to market. The tariff must therefore be large enough to raise the import price at the EC frontier to the target price minus transport costs, i.e. 'threshold price'. This calculation takes place in the highest-cost area of production in the EC, so that the import tariff set will more than protect EC producers in areas with lower target prices (i.e. lower-cost areas).

Fig. 26.2 EC and the
guarantee system

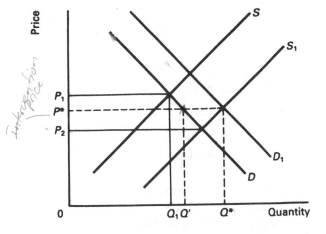

Should an EC producer wish to export an agricultural product then an export subsidy will be paid to bring his receipts up to the Intervention price (see Fig. 26.1), i.e. the minimum price he would receive in the home market.

Cereal products provide a useful case-study of the practice of import and export policy under the CAP. For example, import levies on common wheat in 1981/82 were at one time as high as 90% of the world price, which reflects the difference between domestic costs of production and world costs. For wheat, rye and barley together the EAGGF had to take over 2.4 million tonnes into stock in that year in order to maintain the Intervention, or guaranteed, price. Intense pressure on storage facilities forced 3 million tonnes to be exported (under subsidy) from stock in 1981/82, which still left 2.6 million tonnes in store. Unfortunately for the CAP, abundant harvests in cereal products throughout the world meant that these exports incurred large subsidy payments.

Recent reforms have had a significant effect on key sectors such as dairy products. In 1981 the EC was producing over 101 million tonnes of milk and consuming only 88 million tonnes. A series of national quotas since 1986 have reduced production to 92.3 million tonnes, in 1988. This remains some 5 million tonnes above consumption and still cost the EC 6.35bn ECU (about £4.3bn) in 1988.

The system outlined above does not apply to all agricultural products in the EC. About a quarter of these products are covered by different direct subsidy systems, e.g. olive oil and tobacco, and some products, such as potatoes, agricultural alcohol, and honey are not covered by EC regulation at all.

Guidance system The CAP was, as originally established, a simple price-support system. It soon became obvious that agriculture in the 'Six' required considerable structural change because too much output was being produced by small, high-cost, farming units. In 1968 the Commission published a report called *Agriculture 1980*, more usually known as the 'Mansholt Plan' after its originator, Commissioner for Agriculture, Sicco Mansholt. The plan envisaged taking large amounts of marginal land out of production, reducing the agricultural labour force, and creating larger economic farming units. The plan eventually led to the establishment of a Common Structural Policy in

Commodity (000's tonnes)		1986	1987	1988	1989 (est)
Cereals	UK	4,353 (96)	2,199 (40)	1,737 (27)	706 (15)
	EC	12,782 (36)	12,960 (37)	10,756 (31)	7,808 (23)
Beef	UK	72 (24)	61 (23)	32 (17)	8 (3)
	EC	553 (35)	625 (38)	623 (39)	122 (6)
Butter	UK	253 (325)	192 (275)	49 (76)	9 (15)
	EC	1,344 (260)	1,026 (231)	206 (47)	30 (7)

Source: The Government's Expenditure Plans 1990–91 to 1992–93.

1972, which for political reasons was to be voluntary and administered by the individual member states. The import levies of the EAGGF were to provide funds to encourage small farmers to leave the land and to promote large-scale farming units. However, whereas over 30% of CAP expenditure went on the guidance section in the early 1970s, in more recent years much less has been devoted to this use – as little as 3% of CAP expenditure in 1984–85.

Green currencies

These strange, hybrid currencies, were first created in 1969 in order to avoid the effects of the devaluation of the French Franc and the revaluation of the Deutschmark on farm incomes and consumer prices. As part of the move towards the CAP it was felt that the Community should have a common agricultural price system for its main products. The common administered price level is expressed in terms of ECUs (see below). Prices expressed in ECUs have to be converted into national currencies, with the rate at which 1 ECU exchanges against the national currency called the 'green' or representative rate. For example, if the common price for wheat was fixed at 30 ECU per kilogram, and the green rate for the pound was £1 = 2 ECU, then the UK farmer would receive £15 per kilogram for wheat. If the green pound was devalued to £1 = 1.5 ECU, then the UK price for wheat would rise to £20 per kilogram, and with it farm incomes. Whereas if the green pound was revalued to £1 = 3 ECU then the UK price for wheat would fall to £10 per kilogram, and farm incomes would also fall.

The Fontainebleau meeting agreed in 1984 that, in the light of the success of the EMS in holding exchange rates relatively constant, the system of 'green' rates and their associated MCAs would be gradually dismantled. In fact the UK has had a zero MCA rate for several years.

Changes in the value of the green pound are, therefore, significant for prices and farm incomes, making the 'green' rate politically sensitive. A lower green pound keeps the UK price of agricultural products and farm incomes high; conversely a high rate for the green pound benefits UK consumers. A further complication is the fact that the 'green' rate and the actual exchange rate may differ in the course of the year. Rather than change the 'green' rate, and thereby disrupt farm prices and incomes, the Community uses Monetary Compensation Amounts (MCAs). These are assigned in such a way as to bring the prices of agricultural goods in actual currency into conformity with those intended when the 'green' rates were last set.

The May 1990 agricultural prices settlement allowed a devaluation in the 'green rate' of sterling which more than offset cuts in agricultural prices which had been decided upon by the EC Council. This gave British farmers an increase of between 9% and 11% in their incomes (some of the weirder practical aspects of the CAP were well described in a Financial Times article; Dickson (1990).

The effects of the CAP

The failure of the guidance policy has meant the continued existence of many small high-cost producers in many areas of the EC, with correspondingly high 'target' prices. High target prices have in turn encouraged excess supply in a number of products, requiring substantial purchases by the EAGGF to keep prices at the guaranteed level, which led to the familiar butter mountains, wine lakes, etc. The net effect of the CAP has therefore been, via high prices, to transfer resources from the EC consumer to the EC producer. At the same time the CAP has led to a less efficient allocation of resources within the EC in that high prices have made the use of marginal land and labour-intensive processes economically viable. Arguably, resource allocation has been impaired both within the EC *and* on a world scale, in that the system of agricultural levies distorts comparative advantages by encouraging high-cost production within the EC to the detriment of low-cost production outside the EC. Finally, through its import levies and export subsidies the CAP introduces an element of discrimination against Third World producers of agricultural products, for whom such exports are a major source of foreign earnings.

These are, of course, by no means the only effects of the CAP. In many areas it has enabled small-scale farming communities to be maintained in circumstances where the alternative would be unemployment. It has also produced dependable food supplies for a continent whose agriculture has, historically, been neither efficient nor reliable.

Reform of the CAP

The growth of agricultural spending in the early 1980s placed increasing pressure on the EC's 'own resources'. By 1983 the 1% VAT ceiling had been breached and even the steady growth in imports (providing CET revenue) was not sufficient to meet the demands on the budget. The member governments were forced to agree to special additional payments to meet deficits which arose in 1983, 1984, 1985 and 1987. These 'intergovernmental advances' were significant (totalling some 1,981m. ECU in 1985) and resulted in the attempt by West Germany and the UK to achieve reductions in CAP expenditure in return for agreement to increase the VAT ceiling. In theory, the increase in the ceiling to 1.4% from 1986 onwards was supposed to be matched by reductions in CAP spending. These were to be obtained through measures, beginning in 1984, to cut dairy production (using quotas and a 'superlevy') and to control cereals surpluses.

A Commission report, *Perspectives* (EC 1985), revealed, however, that EC agricultural production continued to grow at between 1.5 and 2.0% per annum, whilst internal demand for agricultural production increased at only 0.5% per annum. The Commission wanted to see cuts in agricultural prices, a lowering of quantities eligible for export subsidies and more farmland being taken out of production, the problem of small farmers being resolved on a more openly 'social' basis through direct income support.

With no agreement on reform during 1986 or 1987, the CAP began to expand rapidly and the Council was forced to agree a series of 'supplementary' budgets and, in late 1987, to postpone some 4bn ECU of agricultural spending until 1988. The British Government continued to hold out for formal, legislative controls on CAP expenditure and for increases in spending in the Regional and Social Funds.

The breakthrough occurred at the Brussels Heads of Government meeting in February 1988 during which a further, new source of finance was sanctioned (up to 1.2% of GNP) in return for legislative limits on the CAP. In 1988 the CAP was limited to a fixed sum of 27.5bn ECU and it could only expand, in future years, by three-quarters of the average rate of growth in EC GNP.

Other significant limits were placed on the CAP in the form of a ceiling on cereal production (160 million tonnes), a cut in producer prices of about 3%, and a new 'co-responsibility' levy of 3% on larger farmers.[5] Funds were also allocated for a 'set-aside' policy under which around 20% of EC agricultural land was to be taken out of production for five years.

UK agriculture and the CAP

Although the EC is now the UK's major trading partner in food and food products, the British public remain uncertain as to how they have fared under the 'new' system. The common view seems to be that our trade in food products has deteriorated, that our food prices are higher than would have been the case, and that our farmers have fared well under the CAP. We shall examine each aspect in turn.

Whilst the UK continues to experience a deficit on trade in food products, that deficit is declining in real terms due to greater self-sufficiency. For instance, in 1970 the UK's trade deficit with the EC in food, beverages and tobacco was £1,341m. whereas in constant (1970) prices that deficit was only £638m. in 1980 and as little as £484m. in 1984. The UK now produces over 60% of its total food needs and over 90% of its cereal requirements.

Reaching a conclusion as to the effect of the CAP on UK food prices, is complicated by the need to assess what would have happened if the UK had not joined the EC. The evidence is complex and the figures confusing. As far back as 1969 the Labour Government had estimated a rise in food prices of between 18 and 25% on entry into the EC. More recently, it was estimated that UK food prices were 12% higher than would have been the case had we not joined (Johnson 1983). In contrast the EC's own statistical body estimates that UK food prices actually *fell* by between 6 and 9% over the period 1973–81.

The view that farmers have been greatly enriched by the CAP is also one with little foundation in fact. Real farm incomes throughout the EC were about 10% lower on average in 1981 than they were in 1973, with West Germany, France and the UK faring worst. UK farm incomes fell, in real terms, over the period 1973–83 by between 28 and 56%, depending on how one treats depreciation. In 1983 alone farm incomes fell by a further 6.6%.

All these estimates of trade flow, prices and farm income have assumed that the UK would have continued with its system of deficiency payments. In other words, that UK prices would have been kept close to world prices, that imports would be largely free of levies, and that farm incomes would be maintained by direct subsidy payments. This may not, in fact, be a valid assumption. The deficiency payments system encouraged high levels of food imports, to the benefit of consumers in terms of low prices, but to the detriment of the balance of payments, and of the Exchequer. As regards this last point there is evidence that the cost of the deficiency payments system would have been as high, if not higher, than that of the CAP. For instance, the Labour Party estimated the budgetary cost of a *return* to the deficiency payments system at about £1,800m. for 1981. Yet a study by Newcastle University for the same year estimated the current budgetary cost of UK membership of the CAP to be only £1,000m. (*Economist* 1982), a saving of £800m.

Although consumer prices may well have been higher under the CAP than they would have been under the deficiency payments system (the Institute of Fiscal Studies estimated, in 1987, that the CAP adds about £6 per week to the food bill of the average British family of four), the balance of payments and budgetary costs of the CAP have almost certainly been lower.

Commercial policy

Unlike agriculture, there is no common policy for the commercial life of the Community, and no single policy which could be given this name. Instead, there are a whole series of policies which include the Common External Tariff (CET), the Structural Funds, research and development initiatives, the moves towards 'European Company Law', and Competition policy. The CET is imposed on all industrial imports from non-EC countries, though with a few exceptions.[6] Since tariffs on industrial products traded between member countries have been dismantled, the application of the CET has created a protected free trade area or 'customs union' of some 320 million consumers.

The effect of creating a customs union is, however, double-edged. 'Trade creation' is the term used to refer to the extra trade between members of the customs union as a result of removing tariff barriers. Production of certain goods is then transferred from high-cost to low-cost producers within the customs union. It can therefore be argued that trade creation causes resources *within* the customs union to be used more efficiently. However, 'trade diversion' also occurs as a result of the CET imposed against non-members of the customs union. This may cause some production to be transferred from low-cost producers *outside* the union to high-cost producers inside. We shall see below that the two effects are extremely difficult to quantify. However, in general terms, the higher the original tariff between member countries, and the higher the original tariff against non-members, the more likely it will be that the efficiency gains from trade creation will outweigh the efficiency losses from trade diversion.

Apart from the CET, commercial policy merely consists of a number of *ad hoc* measures based on principles embodied in the Treaty of Rome, and which relate loosely to industry. We now briefly review a number of these measures.

The EC has a long history in regulating the production of steel, beginning with the ECSC itself, and more lately with the Davignon Plan for EC steel production. These have played an important role in adjusting EC steel output to world demand, particularly in times of world recession and intense competition from American and Far Eastern sources. The Community has also developed several 'policies' for assisting industrial development, for easing structural change and for funding new research. These now come under the heading of the 'Structural Funds' which include the older, separate 'Regional' and 'Social' Funds. The combination of these funds, together with the Guidance element of the CAP and other rural initiatives, is intended to result in fully integrated plans for the less developed regions of the Community.

The UK regularly receives about 15% of the Structural Funds. In 1990 this will result in our receiving – via Integrated Development Operations, local authorities and other statutory bodies – some £350m (increasing to around £450m by 1994) to support such diverse activities as road and telecommunication development in the North-east, support for manufacturers in Wales and Northern Ireland, training, retraining and job creation.

The EC Commission also attempts to oversee both the price of energy and its availability within the Community. It was instrumental in arranging the 'oil sharing' scheme under which the UK would guarantee certain quantities of oil to her partners in the event of shortage. It also supervises various energy research programmes financed by the EC at university level, including the Joint European Torus (JET) fusion research project. The EC has recently established a programme for co-ordinating research in information technology, aimed at helping European electronic and communication industries compete against US and Japanese producers. The European Strategic Programme for Research and Development in Information Technology (ESPRIT) is a ten-year programme, which began in 1984, covering 50% of the R & D costs of agreed projects.

In recent years the scope and the numbers of Community programmes for industrial research, development and collaboration have increased. Table 26.6 will give an idea of the variety of such programmes. In terms of overall expenditure the amounts involved are relatively small but the economic effects of the cross-national co-operation which are generated by such schemes are difficult to quantify. There is some evidence from the increase in

Table 26.6 Examples of EC research and collaboration programmes

BAP	Academic–industrial links in bio-engineering; established 1982 as BEP; 1986 as BAP
ESPRIT	Industrial links in high technology; established 1983
RACE	EEC-wide communications progamme; established 1985
BRITE	Advanced technology development; established 1985
SPRINT	An information technology programme; established 1988
COMETT	Academic–industrial links; established 1986

international takeovers and research collaboration that the programmes may be optimizing the use of research funding and promoting the development of technologies which might have a significant economic impact in the future.

The EC's competition policy, which seeks to control commercial practices which restrain trade (such as price-fixing, market segmentation and other 'cartel-like' activities) has been one of its lesser known but extremely active industrial interventions. (See Ch. 5 for mergers policy.)

The objective of competition policy is to eradicate distortions and imperfections in the operation of all kinds of market. The Commission has attacked price-fixing, dumping, transport cartels, technical standards, and public procurement policies. The targets have been as varied as the West German beer-standard (the *Reinheitsgebot* of 1516) and British car manufacturers.

UK industry and the EC

It is extremely difficult to evaluate the industrial effects of UK entry into the EC. Certainly the hope on entry was that the UK would secure 'dynamic gains' in this sector to offset the expected 'static costs' of the net budget contribution and higher food prices. The 'dynamic gains' were expected to include a boost to output and productivity from a large, protected market, with its potential for scale economies and greater export opportunities. However, for whatever reason, there seems little evidence in Table 26.7 of any 'dynamic gains' for UK manufacturing output after entry into the EC in 1973. In fact, the real output of UK manufacturing has fallen still further behind that of the other EC countries.

Table 26.7 Comparisons of manufacturing output (1970 = 100)

	1970	1975	1980	1985	1989
EEC (excluding UK)	100	108	133	133	152
West Germany	100	104	122	122	137
France	100	108	133	133	152
Italy	100	107	139	132	157
UK	100	102	110	113	126

Source: OECD (1987c, 1990).

The picture is no more encouraging when we turn from manufacturing output to manufacturing productivity. We noted in Chapter 1 that UK output per person employed in manufacturing is still well below that in other member countries. For instance, in manufacturing in the early 1980s, each person employed in UK manufacturing produced only $6,800 of output per annum, whereas the figure was $12,800 in France, $13,800 in West Germany and $16,000 in the Netherlands. In terms of hourly productivity, the UK rate was only 60% of that achieved in France, and around 50% of that in West Germany and the Netherlands. In fact Lord Kaldor suggested, prior to entry, that the alleged 'dynamic gains' might turn out to be 'dynamic costs', as the UK market in industrial products became more exposed to its European competitors with the dismantling of tariffs. It may be that the UK joined the wrong type of 'customs union'! If trade in agriculture and in service activities were freed between member countries, rather than trade in industrial products, then some of the alleged 'dynamic gains' might indeed have materialized. In Chapter 1 we noted that the trend towards service activities, though a feature of all advanced economies, has been most marked in the UK. It is arguable that it is in this sector that UK comparative advantages lie. The present industrial policy of the EC, which frees trade in industrial products whilst permitting (along with GATT) the protection of services, would seem to be to the particular disadvantage of the UK.

Trade and the balance of payments

The EC runs a deficit on its visible trade with the rest of the world, largely due to its need for substantial imports of fuel and raw materials. As regards invisible trade the EC is roughly in balance with the rest of the world. Of course, within these totals there are substantial net deficits and net surpluses within individual countries. In the early 1980s the EC visible trade balance with the OPEC countries had an annual deficit of around $25bn, whereas the net deficits with the USA and Japan were $17bn and $13bn respectively. Partly to offset these deficits there was a $10bn net surplus with countries in the European Free Trade Association (EFTA) and a $46bn net surplus with Africa.

The UK's trade with the EC

The UK's trade with the EC has shown important changes since the late 1960s. First, the area composition of UK visible exports and imports indicates a strong movement towards the Community. In 1969, for example, 29% of total UK visible exports were destined for the EC, whilst 26% of UK visible imports came from the EC. By 1987 the shares had increased significantly, to 45 and 53% respectively. Second, as can be seen from Tables 26.8 and 26.9, the UK's trade with the rest of the EC has shown little improvement in either visible or invisible terms. It is clear that the slight improvement in visible trade during the late 1970s and early 1980s was due, to no small degree, to Britain's exports of North Sea oil. The reduction in the value of these exports following that period has had a marked effect on the overall visible balance.

Table 26.8 United Kingdom balances with the EC 1974–88 (£m.)

	1974	1976	1978	1980	1982	1984	1986	1988
Balance on visible trade	−2,134	−2,186	−2,467	753	−1,167	−3,084	−8,382	−13,453
Balance on invisibles of which:	208	−264	654	−702	634	850	−783	−2,866
Private sector, public corporations and IPD*	611	555	984	977	2,346	2,771	1,367	689
Balance on current account	−1,926	−2,450	−3,121	51	−533	−2,234	−9,165	−16,339
Balance on current account (constant 1984 prices)	−6,599	−6,995	−5,639	71	−588	−2,234	−8,267	−13,741

* Interest, profits and dividends.
Source: CSO (1989b).

The nature of the EC, as a bloc which allows free trade in manufactured goods, has worked to the disadvantage of the relatively less efficient British manufacturers. Similarly, the fact that the EC remains a closed market with respect to both agricultural goods and invisibles (particularly the two areas of

Category	SITC*	1965	1970	1975	1980	1985	1987	1989
Food, drink and tobacco	(0,1)	0.20	0.24	0.27	0.54	0.47	0.50	0.50
Materials	(2,4)	0.64	1.03	1.00	1.33	0.86	0.82	0.78
Fuels	(3)	0.69	0.56	0.59	2.88	4.83	3.92	2.41
Semi-manufactured goods	(5,6)	1.33	1.39	0.93	0.92	0.76	0.78	0.76
Finished manufactured goods	(7,8)	1.41	1.25	0.92	0.88	0.66	0.69	0.70
Other	(9)	2.11	2.02	0.70	1.36	1.31	1.73	1.98

* SITC Standard Industrial Trade Classification.

Note: The export/import ratio (R/M) is the total value of exports (f.o.b.) divided by the total value of imports (c.i.f.).

Source: Compiled from CSO (1989a).

Table 26.9 Balance of Trade Ratios (UK/EC) 1965–89

British strength – insurance and banking) has restricted the UK from taking advantage of the areas in which she has had a small comparative advantage.

Table 26.9 presents the UK/EC balance of trade ratios for different commodity groups. If the ratio is below unity then the UK is a net importer, and if above unity a net exporter. The UK's performance has improved in food, drink, tobacco, materials and fuel, but has deteriorated in semi-finished and finished manufactures (see also Fig. 26.3). For instance, in food, drink and tobacco, the UK only exported to the EC in 1970 around one-quarter of its imports from the EC. However, by 1989 this ratio had increased to one-half. The improvement is even more dramatic in fuel, with the ratio increasing from just over one-half in 1970 to almost 4 in 1987, largely due to North Sea oil, though falling back to 2.41 by 1989 as oil reserves begin to deplete. On the other hand, the UK's performance on manufactures, both semi-finished and finished, shows a significant deterioration. For example in finished manufactures, whereas in 1970 we exported in value to the EC 1.25 times as much as we imported from the EC, by 1989 this ratio has fallen to 0.70; in other words, the UK moved from surplus to deficit in trade in finished manufactures.

Fig. 26.3 UK–EC trade 1987, % total UK–EC trade

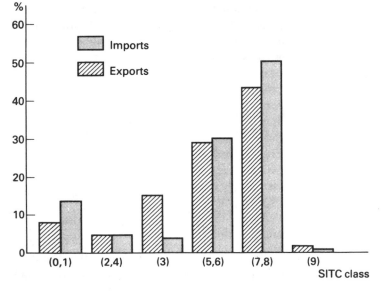

Although in general there has been an overall improvement in UK trade with the EC since 1970, it is narrowly based upon North Sea oil and is, perhaps, threatened by the progressive deterioration in UK/EC trade in manufactures. This deterioration of trade in manufactures is particularly worrying since exports and imports of manufactures together constitute some 66% of total trade with the EC whilst food, drink, tobacco and oil, together account for only 25%. A study by Winters (1982) has emphasized the problem, indicating that UK sales of manufactures in her home market would have been 17% higher without entry into the EC. In fact, UK accession into the Community may have led to trade creation for its partners, with European goods displacing UK goods in UK markets.[7]

The Balance of Trade Ratios demonstrate deterioration or improvement in specific types of product, but they should never be examined without bearing in mind the *overall size* of each product in the UK's export and import portfolio. Although minor improvements have been made in some SITC categories, the major trade items in manufactured goods have shown consistent deterioration.

In previous years there has been a tendency for some British economists to point to the country's relative strength in 'service' sectors and to claim that, once the EC creates a single financial market, the UK will begin to dominate the other member states on the basis of its powerful financial and insurance institutions. This claim may yet turn out to be justified but, as financial markets became freer during the late 1980s, the UK did not appear to benefit. By 1990 the UK was seeing the first deficits on invisible trade for many years.

The European Monetary System

A single currency within the boundaries of the twelve members, permitting trade at 'known prices', has been a long-standing goal of the EC. Such a currency would overcome the uncertainties created by currency fluctuations, which discourage medium- and long-term contracts and therefore international trade. A common currency and common exchange reserves, together with a European Central Bank, are the major features of European monetary union (EMU). The 'Snake', and later the EMS, were seen by many as steps towards European monetary union.

The 'snake' 1973–79

Consultations between the 'Six' and the three applicant countries between 1970 and 1972, led in 1973 to the establishment of a currency co-operation system called variously the 'Snake', or the 'Snake in the Tunnel'. It required each central bank to maintain its currency within a band of ±2.25% against the US dollar, limiting the fluctuations that could occur between member country currencies. This had the advantage of reducing uncertainty but it did restrict the use of the exchange rate as a policy instrument for adjusting trade deficits and surpluses between members.

The oil crisis of 1973 and ensuing world recession created balance of payments problems for many member countries. Fluctuations in the balance of payments in turn led to more volatile exchange rates, making it more difficult to maintain par values within the narrow bands of the 'Snake'. As a result the UK remained a member for only a few months, with France also leaving the system in January 1974. Although the 'Snake' itself continued, it did so in a truncated form, with three members outside (UK, Eire and France) and four non-members inside (Norway, Sweden, Austria and Switzerland). In effect the 'Snake' now contained only currencies with a historically close link to the Deutschmark and it was replaced in the late 1970s by the EMS.

European Monetary System (EMS) since 1979

The EMS was created in order to increase co-operation on monetary affairs within the Community, and like the 'Snake', was founded on the ultimate goal of European Monetary Union (EMU). The impetus came from the Commission under its then president, Roy Jenkins, supported by both Helmut Schmidt of West Germany and Valéry Giscard d'Estaing of France. The EMS was established in March 1979 with three main components, a European currency unit (ECU), an exchange rate mechanism, and the European Monetary Co-operation Fund (EMCF). In 1989 a fourth element was added – the Very Short Term Financing facility (VSTF). This is a means of funding deficits between member states to an unlimited amount, but for very short periods of time. Although the exchange rate mechanism was similar to the old 'Snake', the EMS as a whole was a much more sophisticated system.

The ECU is, potentially, the most radical of the EMS innovations. Whilst superficially similar to the old unit of account in which EC dealings used to be denominated, the ECU is far more than a *numéraire*. It is valued according to a weighted basket of all the EC currencies. Being a weighted average it is more stable than the exchange rate of any single currency (see Table 26.10). In addition to its role as a unit of account, it functions as an international reserve currency. Each member of the EMS 'buys' ECUs with 20% of their gold and dollar reserves, which are then held by a new EC institution called the European Monetary Co-operation Fund (FECOM according to its French initials). The central banks use their holdings of ECUs to buy each other's currencies and to settle debts.

The second element of the EMS is the exchange rate mechanism which is, essentially, a development of the 'Snake'. Like its predecessor, the new scheme sets a 2.25% divergence limit, but this time not against the more volatile individual currencies but against the ECU. The new scheme also differs from the old in that it encompasses a formally recognized method of 'warning' governments that they have to take action. Each currency has a 'divergence limit'[8] computed against each of the other currencies in the scheme which, because it does not include the 'home' currency whose divergence against itself is zero, is always slightly less than the official 2.25% limit. If a currency diverges by more than 75% of this limit it has reached its 'divergence threshold' and the Government will be expected to intervene, either to buy its own currency for ECUs (if the exchange rate has declined) or to sell it for ECUs (if the exchange rate has risen).

The European Monetary Cooperation Fund, the third element in the

Table 26.10 The European
currency unit (ECU)

Weighting of national currencies in the ECU (%)	
Deutschmark	30.10
French franc	19.00
Sterling	13.00
Italian lira	10.15
Dutch guilder	9.40
Belgian franc	7.90
Spanish peseta	5.30
Danish krone	2.45
Irish punt	1.10
Greek drachma	0.80
Portuguese escudo	0.80

Notes: The Luxembourg franc is linked with the
Belgian franc.

EMS, consists of all the heads of the central banks of the member states and
is intended to supervise the use of the 'official ECU'. This is the currency unit
as it was originally established, acting as a means of settling deficits between
the members, and supported by an IMF-type system of deposits of gold and
foreign currency. It holds the members' 20% deposits of gold and dollars, is
empowered to lend up to 25bn ECUs to countries in difficulties, and is
intended ultimately to become a central bank for Europe – the 'European
Monetary Fund' – acting to support the ECU against the dollar, yen, etc.

The final part of the Delors Plan aims to establish full Economic and
Monetary Union and will involve the setting up of a European Central Bank.
This may or may not be based on the EMCF itself, but such a bank will
certainly need to have powers similar to those wielded by the West German
'Bundesbank' or by the US Federal Reserve. Consequently, the institution
has already been dubbed 'Eurofed'.

The EMS is now regarded as one of the more successful of the EC's
policies and the ECU has exceeded even its supporters' hopes.

Until mid-1987 the development of the ECU as a private currency was
hampered by the refusal of the West Germans to recognize it. The ECU has
been developing as a major international bond currency and, indeed, as a
private European currency but the objections of the West Germans meant
that it could not be truly 'European'. In June 1987, however, the West
German Government removed their veto on the private holding of ECUs by
their citizens and thereby opened the way for further liberalization of capital
movements within the Community.

The ECU is now used throughout the EC as a basis for travellers' cheques[9]
and the Belgian Government even issued 50 ECU gold and 5 ECU silver
coins in 1987 to celebrate the thirtieth anniversary of the founding of the EC.

In 1989 Austria and Norway formally applied to be 'associated' with the
EMS.

The UK and the EMS

The UK is a member of the EMS but, until late 1990, was not a member of its
exchange rate system, which is now known not as the 'Snake' but as the
'parity grid'. The UK Government felt in 1978 that sterling would be too

volatile to cope with the confines of the parity grid system. Although the EMS contains provisions for currencies to be devalued and revalued, the UK anticipated a continual need to defend a weak pound within the grid, thereby putting pressure on its gold and foreign exchange reserves after its holdings of ECUs had been exhausted. The UK also held that the restricted variation in exchange rate against other member currencies would impede the use of the exchange rate as a policy instrument, in dealing with bilateral trade deficits with other member countries. Finally, by setting limits for sterling, the exchange rate could less readily be used for economic management in the UK, e.g. a high pound helping to curb inflation.

Currency	Sep. 1979	Nov. 1979	Mar. 1981	Oct. 1981	Feb. 1982	Jun. 1982	Mar. 1983	Jul. 1985	Apr. 1986	Aug. 1986	Jan. 1987
Bfr	0	+5.0	0	0	−8.5	0	+1.5	+2.0	+1.0	0	+2.0
Dkr	−2.9	0	0	0	−3.0	0	+2.5	+2.0	0	0	0
DM	+2.0	+5.0	0	+5.5	0	+4.25	+5.5	+2.0	+3.0	0	+3.0
Ffr	0	+5.0	0	−3.0	0	−5.75	−2.5	+2.0	−3.0	0	0
Ire	0	+5.0	0	0	0	0	−3.5	+2.0	0	−8.0	0
Lr	0	+5.0	−6.0	−3.0	0	−2.75	−2.5	−6.0	0	0	0
Dgdr	0	+5.0	0	+5.5	0	+4.25	+3.5	+2.0	+3.0	0	+3.0

Note: + = *revaluation;* − = *devaluation.*

Key: Bfr = Belgian franc and Luxembourg franc; Dkr = Danish krone; DM = Deutschmark; Ffr = French franc; Ire = Irish pound (punt); Lr = Italian lira; Dgdr = Dutch guilder.
Sources: Lomax (1983); European Commission (1985, 1987); *Guardian* (1986).

Table 26.11 Changes in EMS central rates 1979–88

Table 26.11 shows the readjustments which have taken place in the EMS parity grid up to mid 1988. The West Germans feel that these readjustments have been too frequent, allowing several countries to avoid the macroeconomic discipline originally intended by adopting the system. Ironically, having remained out of the parity grid due to fears of sterling's weakness, the UK Government experienced for a period the exact opposite. At least until the end of 1982 the problem would have been that of having to keep sterling down within the grid rather than of establishing a 'floor' for sterling.

As indicated in Chapter 23, UK trade has become less sensitive to price factors and therefore less easily influenced by exchange rate adjustment. Further, a third of UK trade is still invoiced in the dollar or in other EMS currencies,[10] reducing the importance of EMS currency fluctuations to the UK. For these reasons it has been suggested that the restrictions imposed on the *sterling exchange rate* by the EMS parity grid are, from the point of view of trade, less important to the UK than to other EC member countries. It would therefore seem that the restrictions imposed upon *UK demand management*, via the parity grid, have proved the greater deterrent to full UK participation within the EMS. However, the arguments in favour of the UK joining the EMS parity grid became stronger as the EC became more important in UK trade, and as dollar-invoiced oil took a smaller share in UK exports. The problem, now the UK has joined, will be the ability of the system to cope with three major currencies, in view of the difficulties it has experienced in coping with two, namely, the Deutschmark and French franc.[11]

It must be said, however, that the chronic 'British disease' of persistently high inflation will not be miraculously cured by entry into the Exchange Rate Mechanism. The UK's economic problems are extremely deep-seated and complex. They are associated not only with the way in which British governments are able to manage the economy (for example, in the lack of independence of the Bank of England) but also in the wage bargaining process and in expectations. Many would argue, further, that even deeper social and educational problems need to be solved. Even the strongest of supporters of Britain's participation in the ERM see it primarily as a further discipline on British governments, not as the solution to all the UK's economic ills.

European Economic and Monetary Union (EMU)

As long ago as 1969 the Commission funded the 'Werner Report' (Werner 1970) which acknowledged what it called the 'political wish to establish economic and monetary union' and set a target of completion by 1980. Unfortunately the severe economic traumas of the 1970s intervened and it was 1979 before even the first stage – the setting up of the European Monetary System (EMS) – was accomplished.

In 1988 the Council decided to look into the matter again and set up a Committee under the EC President, Jacques Delors. That Committee reported in June 1989 and the Council agreed to enter into Stage 1 on 1 July 1990. The 'Delors Report' saw the stages towards EMU being as follows:

Stage 1: the establishment of a Single European Market; stronger competition policies through the reduction of subsidies; improved coordination of economic and monetary policy; the joining of the ERM by all EC members; the reform of the Structural Funds (the old Regional and Social Funds); and the deregulation of financial markets.

Stage 2: a transitional phase during which the existing institutions of the EC would be strengthened and a European system of central banks would be set up.

Stage 3: full EMU would be anticipated by further expanding the regional and social policies (which would be necessary to underpin the enhanced competition between countries and regions which would ensue in the unified currency area); the Delors Plan also calls, at this stage, for 'irrevocably locked exchange rates' and for 'binding constraints on national budgets'.

The result of these phases – for which no precise time schedule has been set – was to be the establishment of a single European currency and full EMU.

The Delors Plan has encountered significant opposition from certain economists, ranging from those who believe that the system would be unworkable due to the strains placed on the poorer countries and regions, to those who believe that the objective is valid but that elements such as 'binding constraints on national budgets' are unnecessary. Among the more telling arguments is one which holds that a community in which there is complete freedom in the financial markets will not need to have a single currency established by decree. If corporations and people are allowed to hold and do business in whatever currency they wish, there will be an inevitable, free-market, move towards the strongest currency.

The first stage of the Delors Plan – the establishment of a true Single European Market (SEM) – had, of course, already been put in train by the Single European Act of 1987. As the fundamental base of the EMU structure, the Commission felt that it was necessary to set out clearly what the economic benefits would be. They therefore commissioned a group of senior economists, financiers and business people to investigate the issues. The Committee under the Chairmanship of Paulo Ceccini reported in 1988 (Ceccini 1989).

The Ceccini Report

Although published as a single report, the 'Ceccini Report' is simply the summary and conclusions of no less than 13 separate economic reports on aspects of the single market. It identifies two types of cost associated with what it calls, in shorthand, 'non-Europe'; i.e. a Europe of markets separated by physical, technical and fiscal barriers:[12]

- first are those barriers which have an immediate benefit when they are removed;
- second are those which will have benefits spread over a period of time.

It should be noted that both types include elements of both static and dynamic benefits.

The parts which make up the 'Ceccini Report' examined the single market from the point of view of micro-economic benefits (the removal of non-tariff barriers, economies of scale, X-efficiencies, etc.) and of macro-economic benefits (the supply-side shock and its effects on GDP, inflation rates, employment, production, etc.).

Using a variety of methods, the Report came up with significant benefits which might accrue to EC members as a result of the single market. These included the following:

- total gains of around ECU 216bn at 1988 prices (between 4.3% and 6.4% of EC GDP)
- price deflation of an average 6.1%
- an improvement to the EC's external trade of about 1%
- an improvement to budget balances of about 2.2%
- around 1.8m new jobs (a reduction in unemployment of about 1.5%).

The Reports are extremely detailed and are well worth examination in their own right as an example of the use of up-to-date theoretical models in economic analysis. In one area alone, that of administrative costs, the Report identified:

- 7,500 MECU (*million ECU*) in standard administrative costs of the current system for companies trying to trade across EC internal borders,
- between 415 and 830 MECU in delays to trade at border posts,
- between 4,500 and 15,000 MECU in business foregone by companies not wishing to become involved in the bureaucracy,

- between 500 and 1,000 MECU in government spending on border controls,
- a total cost – in administration alone – of between 12,915 and 24,330 MECU (£9.4bn–£17.7bn).

Conclusion

The purely economic effects of UK membership of the EC are extremely difficult to isolate; not least because it is necessary to establish some sort of credible model of what would have happened had we not joined. In simple terms there has been a continuing budget deficit, a clear welfare loss to UK consumers from the CAP, an observable displacement of UK manufactures in our domestic market and a continuing deficit on non-oil visible trade with the rest of the Community. Critics argue that we joined the wrong type of community! If, instead, of regulated agriculture, free trade in industry and protection of services, we had joined a community espousing free trade in agriculture and services, and regulation of industry, then the UK would indeed have been well served by entry.[13]

Against this, one has to take into account the recent attempts to solve the UK budget contributions, the increased UK self-sufficiency in food, the already parlous state of the UK manufacturing sector in 1973/74 and evidence, albeit flimsy, of increased industrial competitiveness since 1980. Membership has also made the UK a part of a powerful trading bloc, with all that this implies for bargaining strength, as perhaps evidenced in the terms secured for protection of industries such as textiles, footwear and steel. The 'bottom line' must take into account that the EC is much more than the sum of its economic parts. It is an attempt to achieve political as well as economic unity, across a continent that has been divided for millennia. It is against this backcloth that current EC leaders are tentatively seeking joint foreign policy initiatives and joint trade approaches to the USA and Japan.

Notes

1. See, for instance, Borchardt, Klaus-Dieter, *European Unification – The Origins and Growth of the European Community*, European Commission (1989) 3rd edn, Brussels.
2. This is now 1.4% of the total value of retail sales in member states of a common basket of goods and services.
3. This was the budgeted amount. In fact, the 1983 VAT percentage reached its upper limit of 1% due to two supplementary budgets, largely required to cover agricultural spending. In 1984, the upper limit was raised to 1.4%.
4. Under one proposal, once EC farm spending exceeds 33% of the total EC budget (currently it is 65%), then a differential rate of VAT is applied. A proposal on these lines was actually implemented in 1984.
5. The 'co-responsibility' levy is a method by which farmers are penalized for over-production of agricultural products. Up to a certain level of production the farmer is entitled to sell his goods either on the open market, or to the EC's Intervention stocks. Above that, agreed, level of

production the price allowed to the farmer will be reduced by a specific percentage called the 'co-responsibility' levy.

6. For instance, the Lomé convention gave preferential access to EC markets to some Third World industrial products.

7. Featherstone, Moore and Rhodes (1979) also concluded that UK trade in manufactures has been adversely affected by entry into the EC. There have, however, been dissenting opinions. Morgan (1980) calculated a net benefit of £0.3bn by the late 1970s in UK–EC trade in manufactures as a result of entry.

8. The divergence limit for any currency is calculated by the formula $\pm 2.25\ (1-w)$ where w is the percentage weight of the currency in the ECU. For West Germany this results in a limit of $2.25\ (1-0.301) = 1.57\%$.

9. ECU travellers' cheques were launched by Thomas Cook and the Société du Cheque de Voyage in 1985. They are now cleared by a consortium of thirty-five European clearing banks under the ECU Banking Association and are accepted by some hotels and restaurants

10. For a further analysis of the EMS and the UK's position, see Lomax (1983).

11. Much to most people's surprise the success story of the EMS has been the new currency unit, the ECU. The unit is now being used not only for settlements between EEC central banks and for denominating FECOM reserves but also for bond issues and for private bank deposits. By 1985 the ECU was the most widely used international currency for bond issues, with bank liabilities in ECU estimated to have reached $30bn by the end of that year (Bevan 1985).

12. *Physical barriers* include the border controls which remain in place for goods transport and the large amounts of paperwork still required for trade between member states. *Technical barriers* include the different regulations, laws, standards and public procurement systems operated by the member states. *Fiscal barriers* include the different VAT rates which exist in the member states and their very different excise duties.

13. An attempt to calculate the overall costs and benefits of EEC membership was published by the Institute of Fiscal Studies (1983). The study calculated the net overall cost of UK membership at some £3,580m. (6,284m. ECU) in 1983. More surprisingly, it found that West Germany, Italy, Belgium and France were also net losers, and that the result of EEC policies was a *total* net welfare loss to the ten members of about 13bn ECU.

References and further reading

Barnes, Ian (with Jill Preston) (1988) *The European Community: key issues in economics and business.* Longman.

Bevan, Sir Timothy (1985) The ECU – Europe's new currency, *Barclays Bank Review*, Nov.

Butler, Sir Michael (1988) *Europe: more than a continent.* Heinemann.

Ceccini (1989) *The European Challenge 1992 – The Benefits of a Single Market*, Wildwood House edition written by John Robinson.

CSO (1989a) *Overseas Trade Statistics of the UK*, Dec., and previous issues (1970; 1976; 1981; 1985; 1987).

CSO (1989b) *United Kingdom Balance of Payments*.

Dickson, T. (1990) *The European Market 1992*, Financial Times, 23 March.

The Economist (1982) 6 March.

European Commission (1985) *Perspectives*, Internal Commission Report.

European Commission (1987).

European Commission Report (1982) Com 82, 794 Final, Dec.

European Parliament (1984) *Programme for European Economic Recovery*, April.

Eurostat (1990) *Eurostatistics: Data for short term economic analysis* (March); (1989) *Basic statistics of the Community*, 26th edn.

Featherstone, M., Moore, B. and Rhodes, J. (1979) EEC membership and UK trade in manufactures, *Cambridge Journal of Economics*, Dec.

Federal Trust (1987) *Paving the Way: next steps for monetary cooperation in Europe and the world.* Federal Trust Study Group chaired by the Rt Hon. David Howell, MP.

Guardian (1986) 7 April.

Institute of Fiscal Studies (1983) *Report on the Costs of EEC Policies and UK Membership*, Dec.

Johnson, O. (1983) How golden is the harvest?, *Lloyds Bank Economic Bulletin*, May.

Lomax, D. F. (1983) Prospects for the European Monetary System, *National Westminster Bank Quarterly Review*, May.

Morgan, A. D. (1980) The balance of payments and British membership of the European Community, in: Wallace, W. (ed.), *Britain in Europe*.

OECD (1987a) *Economic Outlook*, June.

OECD (1987b) *Economic Surveys*, Dec.

OECD (1987c) *Main Economic Indicators*, Dec.

Pearce, Joan and Sutton, John (1986) *Protection and Industrial Policy in Europe.* Routledge & Kegan Paul.

Pelkmans, Jacques and Winters, Alan (1988) *Europe's Domestic Market.* Chatham House Paper No. 36, Routledge & Kegan Paul.

Roarty, Michael, J. (1987) The impact of the CAP on agricultural trade and development, *National Westminster Bank Quarterly Review*, Feb.

Werner (1970) *Report to the Council and the Commission on the Realisation, by stages, of Economic and Monetary Union in the Community*; EC Commission, Supplement to Bulletin 11.

Winters, L. Alan (1982) *British Imports of Manufactures and the Common Market.* Bristol University discussion paper, 82/127.

International money

In this chapter we review the rapid and significant changes that have continued to take place in the international monetary system. The early gold standard was, after a period of uncertainty, replaced by a system centred on the International Monetary Fund (IMF). The IMF sought to provide some stability in exchange rates by establishing 'par values' for currencies and by providing financial resources for countries experiencing balance of payments deficits. Since 1972 the IMF has continued to play a role in providing world liquidity, but has lost its stabilizing influence on exchange rates. Today, there are renewed worries about the level of world liquidity and indebtedness, and the current system of floating exchange rates has itself become a target for criticism. While nations and global institutions seek to meet the challenge of expanding trade and existing debt, the pace of change continues to accelerate. Events in Europe have dominated the process of change since early 1990 in the form of the issues of Economic and Monetary Union in the EC, the effects of the German reunion (GEMU), and the re-entry of the economies of Eastern Europe and the Soviet Union into the world economic and monetary system. We examine the present international monetary system in detail and consider the advantages and disadvantages of various alternatives. These include greater use of special drawing rights (SDRs), a return to gold, an enhancement of the role of the IMF, the long term effect of the European Monetary System (EMS), and even world monetary union.

International money refers to all those sources of finance which can be used to cover debts incurred by nations in their trade with each other. In the earliest times trade took place on a relatively simple basis; with goods exchanged either for other goods (barter) or for a few valuable commodities, the most important of which was gold. The growth of world trade in the nineteenth century made the settlement of debts with bartered goods or with gold and silver, increasingly difficult.

  Barter entails a number of obvious problems, not the least of which is the requirement of a 'double coincidence of wants' between buyer and seller,[1] yet it still remains an important element in world trade. Although total figures for world barter trade are difficult to formulate, many large trade deals are concluded on this basis. For example, Russian natural gas is exported in return for high-technology pipelines and pumping turbines. Similarly, in another 'deal' British Aerospace sold aircraft to Finland in return for imports of a wide variety of goods, from furniture to clothes, with British Aerospace acting as agent for these products in the UK.

  As the nineteenth century progressed it soon became apparent that, despite barter transactions, there was insufficient gold and silver to cover the increased totals of trade debt. Natural as well as political restrictions on the volume of gold mined meant that the value of gold output could not keep pace with the value of world trade. Between 1800 and 1913 gold output per head rose by an average of 7.3% per decade, whereas the value of world trade per head rose by some 33% per decade (Kenwood and Lougheed 1971). In fact, by 1913 approximately 85% of the world's money supply was in paper and bank deposits. The inadequacy of gold as a foundation for the world's system of payments was therefore becoming increasingly clear.

We might note that gold's contribution to the international monetary order was perhaps greater than its role as a means of payment. It was for some time the centrepiece of an entire system for correcting balance of payments disequilibria, a system which became known as the 'gold standard'.

The gold standard system

As the nineteenth century progressed, and as world trade expanded, the use of gold as a means of international payment broadened to take in almost all the major trading countries. Although a few, such as the USA, persisted for some time with silver, by about 1873 (with the passing of the Gold Standard Act in the USA) a gold standard payments system could be said to be in effect. The 'price' of each major currency was fixed in terms of a *specific weight of gold*, which meant that the price of each currency was fixed in terms of every other currency, at a rate that could not be altered. The gold standard was therefore a system of *fixed exchange rates*. Any difficulties for the balance of payments had to be resolved by expanding or contracting the domestic economy. A rather stylized account of the adjustment mechanism will highlight the main features of the gold standard system.

Suppose a country moved into balance of payments surplus. Payment would be received in gold which, because domestic money supply was directly related to the gold stock, would raise money supply. This would expand the economy, raising domestic incomes, spending and prices. Higher incomes and prices would encourage imports and discourage exports, thereby helping to eliminate the initial payments surplus. In addition, the extra money supply would lead to a fall in its price (the rate of interest), encouraging capital outflows to other countries which had higher rates of interest – a minus sign in the accounts. A payments surplus would, in these ways, tend to be eliminated. For countries with payments deficits, gold outflow would reduce the gold stock and with it the domestic money supply. This would cause the domestic economy to contract, reducing incomes, spending and prices. Lower incomes and prices would discourage imports and encourage exports. The reduction in money supply would also raise the price of money (interest rate) – encouraging capital inflows – a plus sign in the accounts. Payment deficits would, therefore, also tend to be eliminated. This whole system came to be regarded as extremely sophisticated and self-regulating. Individual countries need only ensure (a) that gold could flow freely between countries, (b) that gold backed the domestic money supply, and (c) that the market was free to set interest rates. Of course, this meant that countries with payment surpluses would experience expanding domestic economies, and those with deficits contracting economies.

There seemed to be a general acceptance amongst the major trading nations that currency and payments stability took precedence over domestic production and employment. What was perhaps not realized was that the apparent 'success' of the system in the forty years between 1873 and 1913 was largely due to the additional liquidity provided by sterling balances. The growing value of UK imports had led to an increase in the holding of sterling by overseas residents, who then used sterling to settle international debts.

If the supply of gold and other precious commodities could not keep pace with the expansion of world trade, the obvious alternative was to make use of 'paper'. In practice, of course, exporters would only accept paper and a 'paper' system could only be used on a worldwide basis when it fulfilled a number of useful criteria:

1. it had to be freely exchangeable on a global basis;

2. it had to be available in sufficient quantities;

3. it needed to be of a fixed value which did not depreciate rapidly;

4. its value, ideally, needed to be guaranteed in terms of some other precious commodity such as gold.

The paper currency, in other words, had to be 'as good as gold'.

For a brief period in the late Victorian and early Edwardian eras sterling fulfilled the bulk of this role. Sterling continued to play a part in the funding of international debt in what was called the 'Sterling Area' well into the 1960s.

Although several attempts were made to revive the gold standard after the First World War, these largely failed. The dominance of the UK in world trade began to fade during this period, restricting the supply of sterling as a world currency. The Great Depression of the late 1920s and early 1930s also encouraged many countries to adopt protectionist measures. In such an atmosphere countries became less willing to abide by the 'rules' of the gold standard. Gold flows were restricted, and money supply and interest rates were adjusted independently of gold flow to help domestic employment rather than international payments. Wages and prices became much more rigid as labour and product markets became less 'perfect', which further impeded the adjustment mechanism. For instance, any deflation that did still occur in deficit countries, led *less often* to the reductions in factor and product price needed to restore price competitiveness. Countries began therefore to resort more and more to changes in the exchange rate to regain lost competitiveness.

This breakdown of the gold standard system during the inter-war period found no ready replacement. The result was a rather chaotic period of unstable exchange rates, inadequate world liquidity and protectionism. It was to seek a more ordered system of world trade and payments that the Allies met in Bretton Woods, in the USA, even before the Second World War had ended. What emerged from that meeting was an entirely new system, under the auspices of the IMF.[2]

International money

The IMF system

Imbalances in world trading patterns, and imperfections in world money markets have at least three implications:

1. That deficits and surpluses rarely self-correct, so that foreign exchange reserves are required to fund persistent payments deficits.

2. That although surpluses and deficits are supposed to balance as an accounting identity[3] for the world as a whole, in practice surpluses are rarely recycled to debtor countries. The oil price increases of 1973 resulted in increased oil payments during 1974 equivalent to about 15% of world trade, and these proved extremely difficult to recycle. Table 27.2 gives an indication of the extent of the recycling problem during the 1970s and early 1980s.

3. That even though in theory the world must be in overall balance, in practice there is a substantial imbalance. As far as these missing balances are concerned, the OECD reported in 1983 a missing $60bn. A number of factors may be involved; time-lags in reporting transactions, the non-recording of arrangements conducted through tax havens, and the problem of using an appropriate 'price' to evaluate trade deals when exchange rates fluctuate several times between initiation and completion.

In order to settle deficits, theory tells us that deficit countries should be able to run down their foreign exchange reserves, or to borrow from surplus countries. Both methods have, in reality, proved next to impossible. The countries most likely to suffer deficits are those with low per capita incomes and few foreign exchange reserves. They are also in consequence those with low credit ratings on the international banking circuit, making borrowing from surplus countries difficult. It was in order to solve just these sorts of liquidity problems for deficit countries that the IMF was established. As well as providing foreign currencies in times of need, its other major objective was to promote stability in exchange rates, following the uncertainties of the inter-war period.

Before we consider how the IMF sought to fulfil these objectives, we briefly review its operation. It began in 1946 with just 39 members, but is now a giant international organization with 152 members, including China and the Eastern bloc countries of Hungary, Romania, Poland, Vietnam and Yugoslavia. It has an unwieldy board of governors, with one governor from each member country. However, day-to-day decisions are taken by an executive board of twenty-two members, seven of whom are appointed by the USA, West Germany, the UK, France, Japan, Saudi Arabia and China, with the remaining fifteen elected from geographical constituencies.[4]

Provision of foreign currencies

The IMF aimed to provide a pool of foreign currencies, which could be used by members to 'finance' temporary balance of payments deficits. This would give deficit countries time to 'adjust' their deficits, i.e. adopt policies which would eventually eliminate them. They could then avoid immediate and massive deflations aimed at cutting spending on imports, sudden moves towards protectionist measures, or reductions in the exchange rate to regain

price competitivene...
the IMF was therefore...
income and trade, whilst...
objective of encouraging sta...

To establish this pool of cur...
'quota', with the obligation to sub...
quota in gold or US dollars, and the...
Quotas were allocated in proportion to...
The size of each quota determined both t...
the country could 'borrow'.

Whenever a country wished to 'borrow' fore...
with an equivalent amount of its own currency. Th...
hold more than 200% of any country's quota in that...
it already held 75% of the quota in the domestic curren...
question could 'borrow', as a maximum, 125% of its own q...
currencies. The IMF would normally only allow a country to...
its quota in any one year. The first 25% of 'borrowing' was deen...
automatic right for each member, and was termed the 'reserve tra...
remaining 100% might entail conditions of use, and this part of the...
borrowing right was termed the 'credit tranche'. Under these Articles, t...
IMF was clearly set up as a rather conservative institution, with members
having to purchase ('borrow') foreign currency with that of their own.

Quotas were initially established at a total of $8.8bn in 1946, and
represented not only the initial 'borrowing rights' of member countries but
also their voting rights. Quotas have been increased on several occasions
since 1946, though the USA and a few advanced industrialized countries are
still almost as dominant now as they were at the outset. In 1989 quotas
totalled SDR 90bn (SDR = Special Drawing Right), with 1 SDR = $1.28
approximately. The USA, UK, France, West Germany, Japan, Saudi Arabia
and Canada alone accounted for 49% of both total quotas and total voting
rights. Within the overall SDR 90bn twenty-three industrial countries
contributed 56.8bn. Some examples of constituent quotas are as follows:

(SDR m., 1990 prior to quota increases of 50%)

USA	17,918	Japan	4,223
UK	6,194	Saudi Arabia	3,202
West Germany	5,403	Canada	2,941
France	4,482	and, Bhutan	2.5

In May 1990 the members of the IMF agreed to increase the overall quota
by 50% to SDR 135bn and to adjust the rankings of the 'top five' so that,
after the USA, West Germany and Japan will share joint second place and
Britain and France will share joint fourth place.

The last quota increase, some 47.5%, had been in February 1983.

Apart from the reserve and credit tranches, the IMF's ability to assist
countries in distress has been founded upon (a) 'facilities', each of which
draws upon the IMF's quota, (b) other instruments based on trusts or other
external finance, (c) two important practices through which the IMF acts as
intermediary; and (d) a world currency at the disposal of the IMF. These are
listed below, but considered in detail later when we examine world liquidity.

cing*
ncing*

Trust fund*
Bufferstock
Enlarged access

nt*
l Adjustment
Contingency

ts to borrow

ich is now either dormant or completed.

s and practices, and especially the
ed the nature of the IMF. It is no
of its Articles, simply reallocating a
vhich can intervene actively to find
ate new world money.

s.[5] By helping deficit countries to finance their deficits,
seeking to promote the smooth growth of world
at the same time helping to fulfil its second major
ble exchange rates.
encies, each new member was assigned a
scribe to the IMF 25% of the value of that
rest (75%) in its own domestic currency.
the member's share of world trade.
e amount paid in, and the amount
gn currency, it had to *buy it*
e IMF rules were never to
ountry's currency. Since
y, the country in
uota in foreign
borrow' 25% of
ed an
che'. The

**Exchange rate
stability**

Under the IMF system, each country could, on joining, assign to itself an
exchange rate. It did this by indicating the number of units of its currency it
would trade for an ounce of gold, valued at $35. The dollar was therefore the
common unit of all exchange rates. A country had a 'right' to change its
initial exchange rate (par value) by up to 10%. For changes in par value
which, when cumulated, came to more than 10%, the permission of the IMF
was required. The IMF would only give such permission if the member could
demonstrate that its payments were in 'fundamental disequilibrium'. Since
this term was never clearly defined in the Articles of the IMF, any substantial
payments imbalance would usually qualify. A rise in par became known as a
revaluation; a fall in par, devaluation. As well as changing par value, a
member could permit its exchange rate to move in any one year $\pm$ 1% of par,
but no more. Because the IMF system sought stable, but not totally fixed,
exchange rates, it became known as the 'adjustable peg' exchange rate
system.

The IMF also introduced – in 1961 – the idea of 'currency swaps' by which
a country in need of specific foreign exchange could avoid the obvious
disadvantages of having to purchase it with its own currency by simply
agreeing to 'swap' a certain amount through the Bank of International
Settlements. The swap contract would state a rate of exchange which would
also apply to the 'repayment' at the end of the contract.

Changes in exchange rate were a means by which deficits or surpluses
could be adjusted. For instance, a devaluation would lower the foreign price
of exports, and raise the domestic price of imports. The IMF system has,
however, been criticized in its actual operation for permitting too little
flexibility in exchange rates. Between 1947 and 1971 only six adjustments
took place: devaluations of the French franc (1958 and 1969), sterling (1949

and 1967), and revaluations of the Deutschmark (1961 and 1969). It is true, of course, that adjustments of exchange rates are subject to an extremely fine balance: too many adjustments and the system loses stability and confidence; too few and the system generates internal tensions of unemployment and/or lower real incomes which may eventually destroy it.

By 1971, continuing US deficits (the expense of the Vietnam War was a major contributory factor), paid in part with US dollars, had led to an overabundance of dollars in the world system. Under the IMF rules all dollars could be converted into gold at $35 per ounce, and as confidence in the dollar declined, US gold stocks came under increasing strain. Although the USA, even in 1971, still accounted for 30% of world gold reserves and 15% of total world reserves (gold, foreign currencies and SDRs), the enormous payments deficits of 1970 and 1971 ($11bn and $30bn respectively) imposed tremendous pressure on its gold and foreign currency reserves. President Nixon announced in August 1971 that the US dollar would no longer be convertible into gold.

The scrapping of dollar convertibility into gold at a *fixed price*, caused a crisis in the IMF exchange rate system, which had been founded on that very principle.[6] This was followed by two increases in the 'official price' of gold – in 1971 to $38 per ounce, and in 1973 to $42.22 per ounce – together with revaluations of other currencies against the dollar, and increases in the width of the permitted band within which currencies were allowed to drift from ± 1% to ± 2.25%. None of these had any lasting effect, however, as first sterling (in 1972), and then the dollar (in 1973) began to float freely against other currencies. By 1976 almost all IMF members had adopted some type of floating exchange rate system. The IMF meeting of that year in Jamaica officially recognized this new situation.

The floating exchange rate system

According to basic economic theory, a system of freely floating exchange rates should be self-regulating (see Ch. 22). If the cause of a UK deficit were, say, extra imports from America, then the pound should fall (depreciate) against the dollar. This would result from UK importers *selling* extra pounds sterling on the foreign exchange markets to buy US dollars to pay for those imports. In simple demand/supply analysis, the extra supply of pounds sterling will lower its 'price', i.e. the sterling exchange rate. As we saw in Chapter 22, provided the Marshall–Lerner elasticity conditions are fulfilled (price elasticity of demand for UK exports and imports together greater than 1), then the lower-priced exports and higher-priced imports will contribute to an improvement in the balance of payments, perhaps after a short time-lag (Thirlwall 1988).

As it has developed since 1973, however, the system has not been one of 'freely floating' rates. Instead, governments have tended to intervene from time to time to support the values of their currencies. For instance, the UK has intervened in recent times to prevent the pound falling when cheap imports were part of its anti-inflationary strategy. The setting, for internal reasons, of particular 'targets' for the exchange rate has therefore resulted in a system of 'managed' exchange rates, picturesquely described as a 'dirty floating system'. The major advantages and disadvantages of fixed vs floating exchange rates are shown in Table 27.1.

Table 27.1 Fixed vs floating exchange rates: the pros and the cons

Fixed	Floating
Advantages	
1. Exchange rate stability provides a basis for expectations	1. Automatic eradication of imbalances
2. Stability encourages increased trade	2. Reduced need for reserves – in theory, no need at all
3. Reduced danger from international currency speculation	3. Relative freedom for internal economic policy
4. Imposes increased discipline on internal economic policy	4. Exchange rates change in relatively smooth steps
5. Domestic price stability not endangered through import prices.	5. May reduce speculation (rates move freely up *or* down)
Disadvantages	
1. Requires large reserves	1. Increased uncertainty for traders
2. Internal economic policy largely dictated by external factors	2. Domestic price stability may be endangered through import prices
3. No automatic adjustment – danger of large changes in rates	3. May increase speculation through co-ordinated buying or selling

World liquidity

It is clearly unrealistic to expect a 'pure floating system' under present international conditions, so that there will be no automatic adjustment of deficits and surpluses by movements in exchange rates. This leaves the IMF with a continuing problem of financing sometimes persistent trade deficits with some form of international money, in a world in which exchange rates are neither fixed nor floating freely. The size of the problem may be gauged from the figures presented in Table 27.2.

Table 27.2 World balance of payments on current account ($bn)

	1973	1974	1975	1979	1980	1981	1983	1984	1985	1986	1987	1988	1989	1990
OECD	+10	−25	+2	−38	−75	−35	+47	−65	−72	−14	−48	−22	−50	−51
OPEC	+8	+60	+25	+70	+110	+60	−30	−10	−4	−34	−11	−26	−18	−11
Non-oil developing	−6	−24	−30	−35	−61	−72	−94	−24	−29	−15	−18	−26	−3	−12

Sources: OECD (1990).

Normal trading deficits and surpluses on current account were magnified by the upward movement of oil prices in the early and late 1970s. However, economic recession and falls in real oil prices in the 1980s meant that the advanced industrialized countries of the OECD moved back into (temporary) surplus, and that the overall surplus of the oil-exporting countries (OPEC) has returned to deficit. The world economic recession in the early 1980s contributed to a fall in world commodity prices, and since these are the major exports of the non-oil developing countries, their trading position further deteriorated, despite cheaper oil.

With such serious accumulations of international debt, in the non-oil developing countries *and* elsewhere (e.g. Poland, Yugoslavia, Brazil, Mexico), the level of world liquidity became a serious issue in the 1980s. The availability of credit through the IMF was found to be so limited that many countries turned to private banks for lines of credit at competitive rates. Before examining the current situation in more detail, it is useful to note the size and sources of world liquidity.

Size and structure of world reserves

As Table 27.3 demonstrates, *world official reserves* in 1989 totalled SDR 1,214.8bn ($1,554.9bn). This, of course, excludes various important

Table 27.3 Composition of official reserves (SDR bn)

	Gold*	Foreign exchange	IMF credits†	SDRs
1950	34.7	13.3	1.7	—
1960	41.1	18.6	3.6	—
1970	43.9	45.3	7.6	3.1
1975	141.1	138.8	12.6	8.7
1980	531.3	292.9	16.8	11.8
1985	361.3	348.3	38.7	18.2
1987	538.2	454.9	31.5	20.2
1989	623.9	544.1	26.5	20.3

* Market prices.
† Fund reserves.
Source: IMF (1989).

practices, such as the General Arrangements to Borrow (GAB) and Eurocurrency swaps, etc. (see p. 586), which themselves constitute *world liquidity*. Around 52% of world official reserves are in gold, and 45% in foreign currency, with over half of the latter made up of US dollars.[7] In fact, no less than 90% of the foreign currency reserves of France, West Germany, Switzerland, Japan and the UK are in US dollars. International Monetary Fund reserve positions (credits) provided around 2% of world official reserves in 1989; SDRs contributed a mere 2% of world official reserves in 1989 (see also Table 27.4). We consider both these sources in more detail below.

Size and sources of world liquidity

As we have noted, *world liquidity* is more than the total of world official reserves. The following is an inventory of its various components – gold, foreign currency, Eurocurrencies, IMF borrowing facilities, SDRs and a range of practices.

Gold Mined today in the greatest quantities by the Soviet Union and South Africa, gold represents a difficult commodity with which to underpin a major share of world trade. Its supply cannot be raised significantly to meet any

Reserve	Gold at market prices (%)	Gold at SDR 35/oz (%)
Gold	51.4	11.4
Foreign currencies	44.8	81.5
IMF fund reserves	2.1	4.0
SDRs	1.7	3.1
	100.0	100.0
Total reserves		
SDR (bn)	1,214.8	667.3
US$ (bn)	1,554.9	854.1

Source: IMF (1989).

needs for greater world liquidity, limited as it is by technical factors, such as the rate of extraction and new discoveries. For instance, during the 1970s world trade was increasing by 5% per annum in real terms, but world stocks of gold only increased by 2% per annum. Gold also faces strong political pressures, given the identity of its major producers.

Foreign currency   Around 50% of this is made up of dollar holdings (if we include Eurodollars – see below). Although clearly still important, the overwhelming dominance of the dollar in foreign currency holdings has begun to recede. In 1976 the holdings of US dollars and Eurodollars peaked at around 85% of world official foreign exchange reserves.

A new form of currency holding has appeared since 1979 in the form of the European currency unit (ECU). This is a new currency unit, based on a basket of all EC currencies, which has become part of the international reserves of the European central banks. It is 'created' by the European Monetary Cooperation Fund (FECOM), as part of the operation of the European Monetary System (EMS). European currency units therefore represent a new form of world liquidity, and are considered in more detail in Chapter 26.

Eurocurrencies   These are, strictly speaking, part of foreign currency reserves (around 35% of the total in 1989), though their impact on world liquidity is far more than their share of those reserves. One of the main types of Eurocurrency is the 'Eurodollar' which is not, in fact, European at all. The term refers to any US dollar which has been deposited in a non-US bank and which is, therefore, not subject to domestic US exchange and reserve regulations. It is because these 'Eurodollars' are not subject to the same reserve requirements as US 'native' dollars that they may profitably be loaned at lower rates of interest. Businesses, and increasingly governments, may therefore borrow Eurodollars as a cheaper way of obtaining the US dollars they require to finance their US purchases.

The market for Eurodollars is now extremely large, with some estimates putting it at over 1 trillion dollars ($1,000bn). Similar markets now exist in currencies other than the dollar, with these other currencies also held by 'non-native' national banks, and therefore outside any usual reserve requirements for their use. Governments are making more use of such

Eurocurrency markets to fund public sector enterprises and to build up their own foreign reserves. It is widely believed that official statistics only measure a part of the true value of Eurocurrency holdings. Because of this, and because they are cheaper and easier to use than the same currencies when subjected to national reserve requirements, Eurocurrencies can be regarded as making a contribution to world liquidity in excess of their contribution to world official reserves. Total Eurocurrency deposits were estimated at $2,800bn in 1987.

International Monetary Fund borrowing   Although part of world official reserves (see Table 27.3 above), borrowing from the IMF through its 'normal facilities' (reserve and credit tranches) does not *add* to *world reserves*. This is because such borrowing is usually 'purchased' with the borrower's domestic currency. However, it may still be regarded as adding to world *liquidity* when a less negotiable domestic currency is exchanged for a more negotiable international currency.

Reserve tranche.   This amounts to 25% of a member's quota, and may be 'borrowed' automatically, i.e. without IMF conditions.

Credit tranche.   Should further borrowing be needed the IMF will make available four 'credit tranches', each representing 25% of a country's quota and each carrying progressively tougher terms and conditions.
    The combination of a 'reserve' tranche and four 'credit' tranches, allows a country to borrow up to 125% of quota from the IMF.

Borrowing facilities.   There are, however, further facilities for borrowing, with varying degrees of strictness as to conditions attached. The credit tranche, together with the compensatory and contingency financing facility (CCFF) and supplementary financing facility (SFF) (see below), are usually regarded as the 'hard condition' facilities. Prior to 1979, only about 20% of IMF loans were of the 'hard' variety, but since 1979 this has risen to almost 75%. Conditions imposed often relate to fiscal or monetary aggregates; for instance, in 1983 Brazil was required to cut its public sector deficit from 6 to 2.5% of GDP in order to secure finance. Conditions may also include the level of the exchange rate, and may sometimes relate even to specific domestic policies. Kucinski (1982) reported that the IMF suggested the repeal of a Brazilian law, index-linking the wages of low-paid workers, in return for its $4.5bn dollar loan. Conditions are usually set after a 'review' by a group of IMF economists, who return from time to time to monitor progress.

Compensatory financing facility.   The CFF was introduced in 1963 to assist primary producing countries in difficulty due to a temporary fall in export earnings (e.g. crop failure or natural disaster). In May 1981 it was extended to assist with cereal import costs. It has an overall ceiling of 105% of quota.

Compensatory and contingency financing facility   – this superseded the CFF in August 1988. It has added the possibility of contingency financing to support agreed structural adjustment programmes.

Extended fund facility.   The EFF began in 1974 and was introduced to provide countries with more time to adjust their financial affairs. Most IMF loans had to be repaid in three to five years, but the EFF initially gave up to eight years for repayment, and now even longer. The 1983 Brazilian loan is repayable under this facility within ten years.

Oil facilities.   These were temporary facilities established in 1974 to assist countries whose balance of payments had been severely hit by rising oil prices. In theory the oil facility had an upper limit of 450% of quota (to enable less developed countries (LDCs) with very low quotas to receive significant assistance), but some countries received loans up to 800% of quota. The oil facilities were ended in 1976.

Bufferstock facility.   This was established in June 1969 to finance the building-up of bufferstocks by commodity producers at times of falling world prices. Up to 45% of quota is permitted.

In addition to its 'normal' resources the IMF has a variety of other instruments and facilities at its disposal:

1.   Supplementary Financing Facility
This is actually a separate Trust, established with the IMF as a trustee, in February 1979. It originally borrowed SDR 7.5bn from the oil producers to assist countries which had exceeded their Credit Tranche borrowing.[8]

2.   Enlarged Access Facilities
Set up in May 1981 after SFF money became fully committed, it allows members to borrow up to 150% of quota in a single year,[9] or up to 450% of quota over a three-year period. The intention is to assist countries with large deficits relative to quota. Saudi Arabia, Switzerland and the Bank for International Settlements have provided most of the funds for this facility.

3.   Structural Adjustment Facility.
In 1986 a new 'structural adjustment facility' was implemented in order to recycle the loan repayments to some of the Fund's poorer members the Low Income Developing Countries. This facility was originally established with resources of around SDR 3bn but this has proved inadequate for the task of assisting members in significant debt. The overall limit was 70% of quota. At the Venice Summit of June 1987 the Group of Seven[10] agreed to expand this facility to over SDR 9bn in 1990.

4.   Enhanced Structural Adjustment Facility.
At the Venice Summit it was agreed to expand the SAF on identical terms but with additional funds. Loans are now determined on need and there is no overall ceiling. However, the IMF operates a policy of 250% of quota as the maximum access unless there are 'exceptional circumstances'. Normal repayments are in 10 half yearly payments beginning $5\frac{1}{2}$ years and ending 10 years after the date of the loan.

5.   Trust fund facility.

Between 1976 and 1980 the IMF sold 25m. ozs gold at market prices. It used $4.6bn of the revenue to establish a trust fund to assist the LDCs. This facility ceased in 1981 when the fund had been exhausted. Over 104 developing countries having received $1.2bn directly as 'gifts' and around $3bn as loans.

Intermediation   The role of the IMF does not end with these various facilities. It has been an intermediary in arranging *standby credits* at times when currencies have come under severe strain. These credits have not usually been used, but have helped restore market confidence in a country's ability to withstand speculative pressure, which itself has often eased that pressure. It has also from time to time arranged finance from the Group of Ten countries,[10] as well as providing an entirely new world currency unit, the SDR.

Special drawing rights   These were introduced by the IMF in 1969, both to raise the total of world official reserves and to serve as a potential replacement for gold and foreign currency in the international monetary system. Special drawing rights were essentially a 'free gift' from the IMF to its members, which could be used to settle debt between countries. The SDR had no separate existence of its own, being simply a book entry with the IMF. It served as international money since it could be transferred to other countries in settlement of debt. The total of SDRs to be created was at the discretion of the IMF, but the allocation of that total was to be strictly in proportion to quotas. To make this new world currency acceptable, it was initially valued in gold, with interest rates paid on credit balances. Special Drawing Rights were later valued in terms of a basket of sixteen different currencies, the idea being to move away from depending on gold, yet to retain confidence in the value of the SDR by avoiding dependency on any single currency. In 1981 this rather unwieldy basket was replaced by a smaller basket of five major currencies, with the weightings as follows (1987):

	(%)
US dollar	51.0
Deutschmark	16.7
Yen	14.0
Sterling	9.6
French franc	8.7

By 1990 only SDR 21.5bn had been approved and SDR 20.3bn had been issued by the IMF, each SDR being worth approximately US $1.28 in 1990 terms. The fact that this total has been given to members in amounts proportional to the size of their quotas has not been without criticism, as it is the major trading countries which (as we have seen) have the largest quotas. There have been six issues of SDRs to date with the most recent (4.1bn SDR) being in January 1981.

Although the total issue of SDRs still represents only 2% of world liquidity, the SDR has recently acquired greater importance. First, the restriction of the 'basket' to five major currencies has given it greater credibility. Second, since 1981 the IMF has permitted full market rates of interest on holdings of SDRs, instead of only 60% of that rate as previously.

Third, SDRs can now be used for currency swaps and forward transactions, and can even be held by non-member countries.

General arrangements to borrow   In 1962 the ten largest IMF members plus Switzerland (which is not an IMF member) constructed the GAB. Each of the signatories contributed an amount of its own currency towards a fund which stood at $7bn in 1982. In January 1983 the fund was increased substantially to $19bn in order to help alleviate the world banking crisis. Until January 1983 the GAB had been an arrangement available only to signatories, but since then its resources have been available to any country in need.

'Swap' arrangements   In the 1960s the USA instituted a system of currency 'swaps' with other countries, whereby each central bank agrees to lend its own currency, or to acquire currency balances of the other, for a specified time period. Although these are relatively short-term arrangements, there is currently an additional $30bn which could be added to total reserves under such schemes.

The current international system – an evaluation

Although the functioning of the world exchange rate system is an issue in its own right, it has important implications for another issue, namely world liquidity. If exchange rates are prevented from, or are incapable of, adjusting balance of payments disequilibria, then prolonged periods of imbalance are inevitable. The adequacy of world liquidity to finance deficit countries then becomes an issue of great importance, both in terms of its size and its composition.

Adequacy of world liquidity

Where the question of the adequacy of world liquid assets is concerned the IMF uses a measurement known as the reserve/imports ratio (R/M ratio), a decline in which would spotlight greater difficulty in financing trade. The R/M ratio measured in weeks has declined steadily, on a global basis, from 52 weeks in 1938, to 11 weeks in 1982. Not only is this ratio of dubious value, but there is no agreement as to what its level should be. Critics suggest that the R/M ratio obscures the fact that the need for liquidity is to finance payment *deficits* rather than the value of trade. The size and duration of world *deficits* may depend more on the flexibility of exchange rates to payments imbalance, and the degree of international co-ordination of domestic demand management policies, than on the value of world trade. Any fall in the R/M ratio might then be more than offset by greater flexibility of exchange rates, or by more international co-ordination of policies. In any case, if a decline in the R/M ratio is to be construed as a problem, as it was during the 1960s, this implies a value judgement that the initial level of that ratio was 'just right'.

The adjustment of imbalances between deficit and surplus countries has also been a continuing problem over the past two decades. The large OPEC surpluses of the late 1970s (Table 27.2) were recycled by the world's major banks to the developing countries. The eagerness of those banks and the competition between them, drove interest rates down and repayment terms up. In spite of this, however, the developing countries, both those with and those without oil, ran into repayment problems and the 'debt crisis' of the late 1980s.

By 1990 the problem had ceased to be OPEC surpluses and had turned to the large and continuing surpluses being generated by West Germany and Japan. These have proved slightly easier to cope with given the almost bottomless demand for funds created by the equal and opposite deficits in the USA, UK and certain other of the developed countries.

There has been rather more consensus that the *composition* of world liquidity gives cause for concern. The introduction of SDRs by the IMF in 1969 reopened a controversy which has been raging since the 1920s between those economists, like Keynes himself, who wish to replace gold with some kind of international standard paper money (Keynes called his 'Bancor') and those, like some of ex-President Reagan's advisers, who wished to see the discipline and rigidity of a gold standard reintroduced.

International debt

The problem of international debt – especially that of the developing world – has always been with us. It would be fair to say, however, that never before has it taken on such a serious aspect as during the late 1970s and throughout the 1980s.

The increase in oil prices during the mid-1970s created a surplus for the oil-exporting countries which the banks of the USA and Europe were only too happy to recycle. Loans were advanced to Third World countries for many purposes and competition between the banks ensured not only that the rates of interest were extremely low but that the true extent of the problem was obscured for some time.

Table 27.5 Debt owed to major creditors ($bn; end 1985)

	Multilateral	IMF	Banks	Export credits	Official aid	Other	Total
MID*	32	17	308	52	10	30	449
Sub-Sah†	16	6	13	19	8	11	73
	48	23	321	71	18	41	522
% of total	9.2	4.4	61.5	13.6	3.5	7.8	100.0

	Debt per head ($)	GDP per head ($)	Debt as % of GDP ($)
MID*	840	1450	57.9
Sub-Sah†	220	280	78.6

* MID = middle-income debtors.
† Sub-Sah = Sub-Saharan debtors.
Source: OECD (1987b).

An indication of the extent of Third World debt can be gained from Table 27.5, which shows the position at the end of 1985 with respect to two major debtor regions – the fifteen so-called 'middle-income debtors' and the 'Sub-Saharan debtors'.[11] Table 27.5 shows, quite clearly, not only the large part played by the commercial banks but also the relatively small part played by the IMF.

A combination of economic pressure and world assistance through the IMF and the World Bank has resulted in the needs of major debtor countries being reduced. However, the total of debt outstanding to the accounts of the non-oil exporting LDCs is increasing inexorably. The IMF felt that debt would, nevertheless, continue to represent approximately the same proportion of Third World exports (see Table 27.6). This, of course, is

Table 27.6 Total debt – non-oil LDCs ($bn)

Year	Total debt	Debt/exports (%)
1986	1,100	187
1987	1,197	177
1988	1,234	166

Source: IMF (1987a).

Table 27.7 UK commercial overseas debt provisions. The provision of UK banks 1989–90

20 LDC debtors: breakdown of debt by main creditor group* (1989)

	Bank debt $bn	% of Total	Other private $bn	% of Total	Official debt $bn	% of Total	Total debt $bn
Venezuela	25.4	79.4	2.1	6.4	4.6	14.2	32.0
Mexico	69.8	69.7	1.9	1.9	28.5	28.5	100.3
Brazil	77.2	68.7	6.3	5.6	28.8	25.7	112.3
Bulgaria	6.6	66.3	1.0	10.4	2.3	23.2	10.0
Argentina	36.8	64.6	3.4	5.9	16.8	29.5	56.9
Ecuador	6.1	54.5	0.4	3.7	4.7	41.8	11.2
Chile	9.9	52.3	2.6	13.8	6.4	34.0	19.0
Costa Rica	2.1	45.4	0.4	8.8	2.2	45.8	4.7
Colombia	7.6	43.6	1.5	8.5	8.3	47.8	17.3
Philippines	11.8	39.9	2.1	7.0	15.8	53.2	29.6
Peru	8.0	39.2	2.2	10.8	10.2	50.0	20.4
Yugoslavia	6.6	37.3	0.8	4.7	10.2	58.0	17.6
Uruguay	2.4	32.2	3.9	52.9	1.1	14.8	7.3
Poland	8.8	21.7	1.5	3.8	30.1	74.4	40.4
Nigeria	6.8	21.2	4.2	13.1	21.1	65.7	32.1
Cote d'Ivoire	3.2	20.8	4.1	27.3	7.9	51.8	15.2
Morocco	3.6	17.5	0.1	0.3	17.0	82.1	20.7
Egypt	4.1	11.1	2.1	5.5	30.9	83.4	37.1
Jamaica	0.4	10.6	0.3	6.4	3.4	83.0	4.2
Bolivia	0.4	10.3	0.0	1.1	3.6	88.5	4.1

* Listed in descending order, according to percentage of debt accounted for by banks.

Source: Institute of International Finance.

dependent upon the expansion of developed economies and the continued steady growth of the world economy as a whole.

Resolving the debt problem   It is true to say that the years since the first oil boom of the early 1970s have seen the world grappling not only with the problem of recycling surpluses but also with the ever present threat of increasing amounts of debt.

This drama has been played out on a world stage on which the same actors have appeared time and again: Argentina, Brazil, Mexico, Peru, Nigeria, Venezuela, Kenya and Philippines, and many others.

A number of methods of resolving the 'debt problem' have been proposed. Almost all rely upon the intervention of the IMF. International debt is unique in that the debtor is under no real compulsion to repay. Within the boundaries of a nation-state the laws usually provide for both the means of recovering debt and the punishment of those in habitual debt. In international law, however, there are no such provisions or sanctions. It is possible for even the largest of debtors to renege on their obligations and – short of war – there is little or nothing that can be done about it.

Resolving the debt problem

The 1970s

As the 1970s came to a close the main worry of the developed nations was that a large debtor would renege on debts and would, thereby, throw one or more of the world's largest economies into massive recession. The mechanism would have worked through the balance sheets of the major banks (some of which were extremely heavily committed) to their share prices and, thence, to the overall confidence of the public in the financial sector. Significant efforts were made to avoid this and the IMF played a major role during the late 1970s and early 1980s in negotiating 'rescheduling' agreements in order to lessen the burden on the debtor nations. At the same time it attempted to encourage 'correct' economic policies which, it was hoped, would avoid the need for future loans.

The IMF's medicine was administered to countries such as Argentina, Brazil, Peru and Uruguay but, even where it was accepted by the governments, it ran into considerable resistance from the public of those countries who objected to the economic stringency required.

The 1980s

By the early 1980s, and under the pressure of another world recession, many debtor countries were on the verge of reneging on their debts. In 1985 the 'Baker Plan' looked towards solving the problem by ensuring that the IMF amended its programmes. The 'Programme for Sustained Growth' was agreed in Seoul in October 1985 and aimed to reduce the burden of the IMF's austerity policies and the pressure on social stability brought on by both the austerity policies and those attempting to cut imports.

Within the confines of its restricted financial resources the IMF became a net recipient of money by 1987. Whereas in 1983 the Fund had been lending over $10bn per year to help offset the problems of debt repayment and economic adjustment, by 1987 it was actually a net recipient. In 1987, therefore, the Fund took a decision to reduce the amount of 'high-conditionality' lending it was doing and to increase lending under the structural adjustment facility (from SDR 3bn in 1987 to over SDR 9bn in 1990).

Since 1982 the world economy has been growing more strongly (OECD growth has averaged around 3% per annum since then) and imports have grown particularly strongly (by around 7% per year). US and UK banks have managed to reduce their exposure to the risk of Third World debt. For example, in 1982 US banks' exposure to problem debtors amounted to 6.8% of their total assets (UK banks 9.8%) but by 1987 the equivalent figures were 5.4% and 6.9% respectively. Even so, for the major debtor countries the proportion of debt to exports grew from around 165% in 1980 to over 330% in 1987. The result was that a series of the most heavily indebted countries began to consider their options. Peru and Zambia placed limits on their debt-service repayments in 1987 and Brazil stopped paying interest due on their debts in February of that year. The annualized rate of inflation in Brazil in February 1987 was 377%.

World economic developments since the early 1980s have been mixed for the developing world. LIBOR (the London Inter-Bank Clearing Rate) fell by 5% between 1984 and 1988 and this had the effect of saving the debtor countries some $18bn per year in interest payments. On the same side of the balance sheet, oil importers such as Brazil have benefited from the reduction in oil prices.

However, because most of the major debt countries are net oil exporters, the reduction in prices has worsened their balance of payments situation and the reduced lending by commercial banks has restricted the sources of further assistance for them.

The 1990s

The late 1980s saw significant moves towards a more comprehensive and flexible approach to the ever-increasing 'debt problem'. This was due, in no small measure, to the reluctance of debtor countries like Mexico, Brazil, and Nigeria to put their economies under unsustainable pressure by continuing to meet their interest and capital repayment obligations.

Given total world debt in the MIDs and sub-Saharan states of over $1,300bn (of which over $450bn was due from Latin America) the resources of the IMF (an absolute maximum of around $115bn) were never going to be of significant help. Furthermore, the experience of the commercial banks during the late 1970s and early 1980s meant that they were not going to be interested in expanding their lending to those same countries.

In the event, 1989 and 1990 saw a number of moves towards a 'package' of measures which, together, have begun to relieve some of the 'crisis' atmosphere. On the one hand the IMF has continued to develop its facilities while, on the other, the commercial banks have begun to find ways around the roadblock of existing debt.

The IMF Way

The sheer scale of existing debt and the implications of failing to meet the problem head on are daunting. In 1990 several countries still bore immense debt burdens:

	$bn
Brazil	115
Mexico	100
Poland	40
Venezuela	35
Nigeria	32

In many cases a large proportion of the total debt was held by commercial banks. For example, banks held some $27bn out of Venezuela's total debt of $35bn. This situation has encouraged the development of 'joint' solutions (see below). The IMF, for its part,has continued to assist, where possible, through its existing facilities but the problems are almost intractable and have only begun to be addressed by combined action on the part of global institutions, national governments and the commercial banks.

World Debt – Some Examples

Poland
Total debt outstanding in 1990 stood at over $40bn of which around two-thirds was owed to commercial banks. The IMF recommended a package of policies in 1990 and these appeared to be having the desired effect of reducing inflation, raising domestic prices, increasing competition, and expanding output.

Nigeria
One of the most difficult cases of the 1990s Nigeria was viewed in the early '80s as the fastest developing nation in sub-Saharan Africa. Oil wealth had pushed GNP per head up to respectable levels and growth was accelerating.

Large scale international borrowing and the real fall in oil prices between 1986 and 1990, however, threw the process into reverse. The country's oil revenue, which was over $26bn in 1980, had fallen to just $9bn in 1990. GNP had fallen, over the same period, from over $1,000 to only $300 per head. By 1990 Nigeria's foreign debt stood at $32bn and it required $4.5bn per year – 60% of Nigeria's foreign exchange earnings – just to service it.

With population growth of around 3.3% per year it was estimated by the Nigerian government in 1990 that it could take the country 50 years to regain its 1980 standard of living.

Brazil
Perhaps the best known, because the largest, world debtor, Brazil had estimated total debts in 1990 of over $115bn, 60% of which was owed to banks. In that year interest and repayments of principal amounted to over $15bn.

It is not surprising, therefore, that Brazil took one of the strongest lines against the IMF and the banks. Like many others it began, unilaterally, to set guidelines for the amounts of interest repayments it would make in any one year. These were to be closely related to the amounts of export earnings Brazil was able to generate.

The Brady Way

Total debt outstanding to commercial banks forms a very significant proportion of total world debt. In 1989 alone, UK banks made provisions in their accounts exceeding £5bn ($9.3bn) against bad debts in the developing countries (see Table 27.6).

During the 1980s there was considerable concern that the extent of banks' exposure to this debt could topple the banks themselves and send developed economies into recession. That this did not happen was due to a combination of emergency action by the IMF, regular rescheduling agreements, cuts in interest rates, and debt write-offs on a steady and continuous basis. There is no way of knowing exactly how much money – in loss of interest and write-offs – was lost by the commercial banks throughout the developed world during this period.

Individual banks and countries took whatever action they could. However, such action was, by necessity, piecemeal and uncoordinated, until, in March 1989, the US Secretary of the Treasury, Mr James Brady, came up with a range of action for commercial banks combined with US government, World Bank or IMF support which, together, offered significant advantages for both debtors and creditors.

By the middle of 1990 four countries had entered into 'Brady Agreements' – Mexico, Costa Rica, the Philippines and Venezuela. Each agreement was actually a package of agreements between the country concerned and its banking creditors, the IMF and the World Bank.

The agreement with Venezuela, signed in March 1990, restructured almost $35bn of total debt (over $26bn of which was with the commercial banks). The package was supported indirectly by an IMF 'Extended Fund Facility' of $4.6bn over three years plus $755m in World Bank loans at low interest rates.

An unforseen advantage of the 'Brady' initiative has been the effect it has had on the value of world debt being traded across the financial markets. In March 1989 Mexican debt was trading at 33 cents on the dollar (US). By May 1990 it had risen to 44 cents and this new surge of confidence has enabled many third world countries to begin to 'securitize' their debt (i.e. to turn loans into bonds).

Debt Arrangements – Old and New, Traditional and Ingenious
Most countries borrowed funds in the 1970s and the early 1980s on the traditional basis of 'fixed term, fixed interest'. These are called 'General Obligation' loans.

When it became clear, in the early 1980s that a large proportion of this lending could not be repaid, the IMF, banks and governments began to devise ways of assisting the debtors and of trying to avoid the dread of any country 'reneging' on its debts.

Some of the techniques they used are as follows:

Contingent Debt
This means that the debt repayments are related closely to the debtor's 'ability to pay'. This is usually accomplished by linking the repayments directly to a fixed proportion of export earnings

generally or of exports of a specific product or commodity. In the case of 'Commodity Contingent Debt' the funding is – effectively – a form of pre-export finance (Currie & Vines, 1989).

Asset Backed Debt

This is one of the more ingenious ways of securing debt. In this sense, asset-backed debt is something we are all familiar with in the form of mortgages. The banks began, in the case of foreign loans, by securing the loans against traditional and logical assets such as ships, and aircraft but they have recently invented new forms of assets in the form of such things as telephone charges and credit card interest. In February 1990 the US investment bank, Saloman Bros, announced the first global issue of asset backed securities. Totalling $1bn, the issue was backed by credit card receivables from Citicorp.

Debt-for-Debt

Rather than have debtors refusing to pay interest or principal on the old debt, the banks offer them a new deal. The old debts are swapped, usually at a discount of up to 30%, for new long term bonds at very low interest rates. From the banks' point of view it is better to have something paid back eventually than to have the debtor renege on the whole debt. Such deals were signed with Argentina in 1987 and with Mexico and Brazil in 1989.

Cash Buy-Backs

Should a debtor come into some money the banks may agree to 'sell' the debt to them at a large discount in return for immediate cash. In 1988 Chile came into windfall earnings from rising copper prices and bought back large chunks of debt at a 40% discount.

Debt-for-Equity

In this scenario the debts are discounted for local currency with which the banks then buy equity in local companies. Chile, again, was one of the first states to use this technique but it is relatively rare. In spite of its obvious attractions, in money terms, to a debtor nation, it tends to be unpopular due to the increase in foreign ownership of local companies which it entails.

Table 27.7 UK commercial overseas debt provisions. The provisions of UK banks 1989–90

Bank	£m
Barclays Bank	983
Lloyds Bank	1,768
Midland Bank	846
National Westminster Bank	990
Standard Chartered Bank	427
	5,009

This total is believed to represent about 70% of the banks' total exposure.

Source: Financial Times 21st March 1990..

Reform of world liquidity

More use of SDRs   Recent attempts to alter the composition of international reserves in favour of SDRs have been largely frustrated by those who fear an erosion of international monetary discipline. The idea of a 'substitution account' has been proposed, which would allow countries to exchange their foreign currencies for SDRs (Johnston 1980). The idea was to reduce the exposure of world reserves to currencies in which confidence can ebb and flow with alarming speed. The SDR, by being based on a basket of currencies, is likely to be much more stable, and since there was only to be a substitution *between* reserve assets, the change in composition would not be inflationary in a world sense. The proposal for a substitution account was, however, shelved in 1983.

The reasons for this are complex but appear to be based upon several criticisms of the SDR system. First, SDRs are usually one of the least valuable assets in any government's portfolio of reserves. Because an SDR is an average of five different currencies it will, though stable, always be less valuable than the strongest, and it therefore tends to be amongst the first items disposed of in reserve asset portfolios. Second, the way in which SDRs have been allocated has favoured the richer countries. Each allocation of SDRs has merely been given out to countries on the basis of their quota with the IMF. Quotas are allocated in proportion to the value of trade, so that the richest countries have received the largest allocations of additional liquidity.

Some attempts have been made to make SDRs more acceptable. As we noted above, the SDR now yields a full market rate of interest on any holding, and is more negotiable than before. However, there is more resistance to the Third World suggestion that SDR allocations be used to expand the international liquidity of developing countries. Some, like Paul Bareau (1981), believe that aid should *not* be a function of the central monetary organization: 'in a domestic context giving SDRs as a form of aid to encourage trade would be tantamount to requiring the Bank of England to underwrite any deficiency in the UK social security system'.

More use of gold   Another suggestion has been to use gold to solve the twin problems of composition of world liquidity *and* exchange rate adjustment at one move. Bareau represents this view in his proposal for a new system in which several reserve currencies would be backed by gold, on an official basis and with an official price.

There are undoubted attractions in re-establishing gold in the world money system, not the least of which is the increased stability which such a system would bring to exchange rates. However, there are also serious reasons why such a return would be difficult to make. First, since the world began to experiment with the system of floating rates in the early 1970s, countries have discovered a potent tool in their economic armouries, namely being able to 'manage' their exchange rates in accordance with domestic economic policies. Second, it would anyway be difficult in practice to fix parities bearing in mind the extreme differences in rates of inflation and balance of payments performances. Third, a return to gold would tie increases in world liquidity to the production of gold – even if greater flexibility were allowed in the official price. We have already noted how the physical limitations of production restricted the real growth of the gold stock to a mere 2% per annum during the 1970s, well below the growth in the value of trade.

Despite such problems it is not inconceivable that gold may become more important in international payments. The US Congress set up a Gold Commission in 1981 to explore the possibility of again linking the dollar to gold. The EMS has also used gold as 25% of its base (see Ch. 26).

More use of the IMF   Rather less controversially, there have been recent attempts to restore the role of the IMF in order to help stabilize exchange rates and to provide greater access to world liquidity. The impetus for this has certainly been the world banking crisis of the 1980s, in which commercial banks have found themselves locked into loans with countries which can no longer even guarantee to pay debt interest. Mexico, Poland, Brazil, Romania and Yugoslavia have been the most visible cases in recent years. Yet the world debt problem is even more serious than these isolated cases suggest. In 1986, total borrowing by non-oil LDCs alone was estimated by the IMF to have reached a staggering $650bn. In contrast the IMF had theoretical finances totalling a mere SDR 90bn (i.e. $115.2bn). Even then its reserve requirements and current commitments meant that only one-third of this was actually available.

This environment has led to renewed efforts to harmonize exchange rate policies, and to provide greater liquidity, both of these under the auspices of the IMF. As regards the first objective, the five 'SDR' countries (the USA, West Germany, the UK, France and Japan – the 'G5' countries), have moved some way towards accepting responsibility for more stable exchange rates. At the Versailles economic summit in June 1982 they undertook to 'strengthen our cooperation with the IMF in its work of surveillance'. They also recognized their responsibility to maintain both the internal *and* external values of their currencies – a tacit recognition that the harmonization of internal policies is a prerequisite for external stability. The U-turn by the French Socialist Government in 1982 towards the more common counter-inflationary policies of the other four countries has strengthened such prospects. More recently the 'G5' countries took a historic decision with regard to the US dollar. At a meeting in the summer of 1985 they agreed to co-operate in an effort to reduce the value of the US dollar against all the other currencies. This represents a significant move away from the regime of 'floating exchange rates' which has existed since the early 1970s. The agreement is an explicit acceptance of the argument that volatile exchange rates have hindered the growth of world trade since 1972 and that a more stable system is required.

As regards the second objective, the provision of greater liquidity, the increase in IMF quotas by 47.5% in February 1983 and by 50% in June 1990, to a total of SDR 135bn, is a first step in this direction. We have already noted the January 1983 agreement to raise the GAB threshold to SDR 19bn, with these funds available for the first time to countries outside the Group of Ten members of the IMF.

World monetary union   In theory the best possible situation would be that of a completely integrated monetary system – monetary union on a world scale.

Part of this would involve a single world currency, which would bring freedom from exchange rate problems, and a greater certainty in the real price of trade. There would also be no need for foreign exchange reserves to support payment deficits. However, the dream may be more attractive than the reality.

A single world currency would in fact entail serious disadvantages. Countries would no longer be able to make use of exchange rate adjustment (e.g. devaluation) to raise their competitiveness. Instead, changes in the level of wages and/or unemployment would become the mechanism by which any trade imbalance between countries would be adjusted. The 'trade deficit' of the North-east region with the rest of the UK is a useful example. Since the North-east cannot devalue, and as wages are not significantly below those elsewhere in the UK, the outcome is higher unemployment in the North-east than elsewhere, despite the regional policies of successive governments.

The common European currency mooted in 1990 as the first step towards European monetary union would almost certainly result in similar problems. Regions of Europe with balance of payments difficulties are unlikely to be able to achieve an increase in their competitive edge by wage reductions, due to union resistance, so that they may be forced into situations of virtually permanent unemployment. It follows that European or world monetary union must involve more than a common currency. It must have some central control of demand management policy in the various world 'regions', with policies directed specifically towards helping the disadvantaged 'regions'. Even then some will experience particularly severe problems in trade, and will no longer have available one of the policy instruments for tackling these problems, namely exchange rate adjustment.

The reform of the world exchange rate regime

There are several significant implications of freely floating exchange rates even where they are constrained and 'partially managed' by national governments. Not the least of these is the effect that large capital movements can have on the domestic money supply. Inflows of capital need to be 'sterilized' – one method would be for the Government to borrow directly from the public – or the inflows will increase the money supply. If, for example, the banks were to hold the new inflows they would increase their reserves and, thereby, their lending capacity.

Williamson (1986) has proposed a system of 'target zones' for currencies which would, actually, be a midway system between pure floating and fixed rates. The zones would be agreed internationally and would be subject to automatic adjustment each month by reference to differences between bilateral rates of inflation. He recommends wide bands for the zones (+ or − 10%) and does not believe that there should be any obligation to act enforced upon the governments involved.

Like all such suggestions its success relies upon assumptions about the behaviour of governments and individuals which may not, in practice, be justified. It would, almost certainly, fall between the two stools of failing to meet the traders' need for virtually fixed rates and the governments' requirements for optimum freedom to use the exchange rate for domestic purposes.

Rybczynski (1987) argues, on the other hand, that currency flows in the late 1980s are such that only a system of freely floating exchange rates is able to cope. Some $150bn flow through the currency markets of London, New York and Tokyo *every day* and only about 10% of this money is related to trade.

Stabilizing exchange rates   There are a number of theoretical means of stabilizing exchange rates and providing the stability which the governments and the traders of the world appear to require:

1. A return to a fixed exchange rate regime either using gold or a mixed system such as the IMF's between 1945 and 1973;

2. A formal 'target zone' system which allows reasonable bands;

3. A system of international policy co-ordination which attempts to meet the problems on a wider base than merely that of the exchange rate itself.

There have been calls from a number of economists for a return to the discipline of the gold standard but few people believe that this, alone, would be practicable.

International discussions have, over the years since the breakdown of the formal IMF system in 1973, produced a clear trend towards the third of the options above. The relative success of the EMS since 1980 has given this process a further boost.

Two events, since then, have made the creation of, at the very least, an international understanding extremely important. The first has been the steady deterioration in the US trade and budget deficits; and the second was the stock market crash of late 1987 which was also partially due to the first. Increasing US deficits led, in 1985, to the so-called 'Plaza Accord' by which the major industrial countries agreed broad targets for their relative exchange rates. Further deterioration of the situation led, in February 1987, to the 'Louvre Accord' between six major countries (see Table 27.8 and Fig. 27.1).

Table 27.8 Deficits and surpluses: the big three and the rest ($bn)

Country	1986	1987	1988	1989	1990 (est)
USA	−141	−154	−132	−116	−108
W. Germany	38	43	45	51	52
Japan	86	82	79	77	72
Non-oil developing	−15	−18	8	−3	−12
OPEC	−34	−11	−21	−18	−11

Source: IMF (1989); UN (1990).

Under the *Louvre Accord* those six countries made the following agreements:

Surplus countries would attempt to:
(a) strengthen domestic demand;
(b) reduce their external surpluses;
(c) maintain internal price stability.

Deficit countries would attempt to:

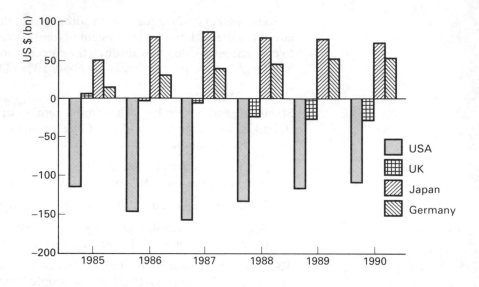

Fig. 27.1 Current account
comparisons (US$bn)

(a)   encourage 'steady growth with low rates of inflation';
(b)   reduce their domestic imbalances;
(c)   reduce their external deficits.

It was also agreed that all countries would try to 'foster the stability of
exchange rates around current levels'. When the 'Group of Seven' met in
June 1987 they affirmed the Louvre Accord in a new 'Venice Economic
Declaration' and also agreed to expand the IMF's structural adjustment
facility. The Accord was understood to have set 'upper limits' for most
currencies. Sterling's was believed to have been US$1.74 and DM3.00. By
early 1988, however, sterling had breached both of these limits (to US$1.85
and DM3.05 in March of 1988). The relative changes in exchange rates
throughout the period between the Plaza and the Louvre Accords may be
seen in Table 27.9 and Fig. 27.2.

Table 27.9 Index of bilateral
exchange rates 1985–88

Year	Yen/US$	DM/$	$/£	DM/£	Yen/£
1985	100	100	100	100	100
1986	71	74	114	85	80
1987	61	62	126	78	76
1988 (1st quarter)	53	57	133	76	71

Source: IMF (1988).

Following these agreements there was a significant expansion in the
economies of West Germany, Japan and the UK and a slight contraction in
those of the USA, Canada, Italy and France.

The Louvre Accord began to break down in late 1987 following the

Fig. 27.2 Exchange rates, bilateral rates 1985–88

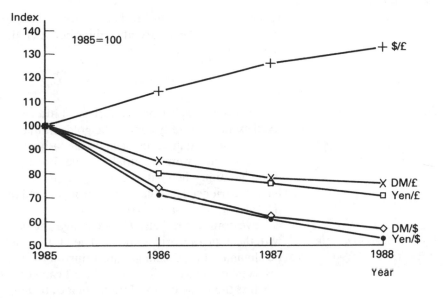

October stock market crash but these events also demonstrated the importance of international collaboration in avoiding the panic which might have turned the crash into a major world recession. Immediately following the events of 'Black Monday' when the UK stock market alone had US$135bn wiped off its books, the West German Government announced publicly that it had no intention of tightening its monetary policy. The USA, for their part, reaffirmed their commitment to the stability of the US dollar and the Federal Reserve Board expanded the US money supply and reduced domestic interest rates. Early in 1988 the West Germans and the Japanese also reduced their rates of interest.

By the middle of 1988 the worries of the world's major finance ministers were centred on an interesting series of policy targets and conundrums. The need to avoid world recession, and the effect this would have on the LDCs and the debt problem, meant that interest rates should be kept relatively low and that domestic demand should not be constrained in those countries with surpluses. Similarly, even in the major countries which were running deficits such as the USA, rates of interest needed to be maintained at a relatively low level in order to support currencies which were under pressure.

The main danger for the world economy lay in failing to co-ordinate economic policy between the surplus and deficit countries. Japanese domestic demand needed to be expanded if imports were to be encouraged and exports reduced. In the USA, on the other hand, the object was to restrain domestic demand so that exports could be built up and imports discouraged. The rate of interest had to be maintained at a level which would discourage domestic consumption whilst maintaining the dollar in a stable condition. The central banks of the world expended a great deal of their reserves during the spring of 1988 in defending the value of the US dollar and, therefore, in preventing a massive world recession.

Perhaps the most encouraging development in world money terms during the 1980s has been the willingness of the major seven economies not only to talk about target zones for their respective currencies but, more importantly, to think about the interrelationships between their economies and to act upon them.

Conclusion

The world has experienced a variety of international monetary systems. The fixed exchange rate system of the gold standard was, after the inter-war period of uncertainty, replaced by the 'adjustable peg' system of the IMF. Exchange rates were essentially stable, but could be adjusted by devaluation or revaluation when balance of payments crises developed. Since 1972 we have experienced a rather bewildering period of floating exchange rates, though with governments often seeking to 'manage' the exchange rate to achieve domestic targets. The exchange rate system is inextricably linked with the issue of world liquidity. The more rapidly payments disequilibria can be eliminated via exchange rate adjustment, the smaller the need for liquid reserves to finance deficits. It is the efficacy of exchange rate adjustment, as much as the value of world trade, that determines the world's true need for liquidity.

Whereas it was the problem of *liquidity* which most exercised governments and international institutions in the late 1970s and early 1980s, it is the problem of *exchange rate stability* which is considered of greater importance today. The ease of communication between major world markets, the reduction of exchange controls and the consequent growth of 'Eurocurrency' markets have brought about a situation in which it could be argued that the world is *too* liquid. Still more serious for world leaders, these new sources of liquidity are becoming increasingly difficult to control. An example is the growth of 'off-balance sheet' banking activities since 1980. Banks are no longer lending direct to customers but are either underwriting 'Euronotes' and other securities, or are arranging 'swaps' (exchanges of debt between companies or countries).

The exchange rates of the 1990s are therefore subject to pressures which are far removed from merely adjusting *current account* deficits. Changes in the *capital account*, linked to interest rate differentials, currency swaps, future rate options and the growth of Euronotes have all contributed to the volatility of exchange rates since 1980. While the US current account deficit *grew* from $9.2bn in 1982 to $102bn in 1984, the trade-weighted value of the US dollar *rose* over 23%. Clearly factors *outside* the current account must have led to the unexpected rise in the dollar. In fact the US Federal Reserve in 1985 has estimated *world capital movements* at between $20,000bn and $50,000bn, in support of trade flows of only $2,000bn in value. If these capital flows were mostly long term then the problem might not be too pressing, but there is evidence that a large majority is *short term* and *speculative*. This has led to much discussion about the merits of attempting to control capital flows using new techniques, such as a tax on currency conversions.

The solution to such problems must lie in meeting the *causes* of the destabilizing flows – e.g. differences in interest rates – and in attempting to establish a loose form of international co-operation in setting exchange rates. The implication of this is that a return to some form of *banded* exchange rate regime may be necessary, together with close co-ordination of economic policy. The 1985 'G5' agreement on the dollar and on economic policy co-ordination, and the 1987–88 agreements, can be seen as first steps in this direction.

Notes

1. That is, that the buyer should both desire what the seller has, and have what the seller desires.
2. The Allies met at Bretton Woods in New Hampshire in July 1944 to agree a world financial order which would, they hoped, avoid the disastrous problems which exacerbated the Depression of the late 1920s and early 1930s. They agreed to establish the IMF to stabilize exchange rates, and the International Bank for Reconstruction and Development (the World Bank) to aid in the reconstruction of the world economy through the issue of long-term loans. The British at Bretton Woods proposed a more radical and sophisticated plan based on the work of J. M. Keynes and centred on an 'International Clearing Union' (a central bank for central banks). There would have been an international currency called 'Bancor' and automatic overdraft facilities for the member countries. For a number of reasons, largely political, the Keynes Plan was rejected and the proposals of the US negotiator, Harry Dexter White, for the IMF were accepted instead.
3. An identity is something which is defined in such a way that it must hold. Double-entry bookkeeping in accounts means that + and − are, in total, equal.
4. The IMF is administered by a permanent staff located in Washington, DC, and headed by a managing director. The current MD is Mr Michel Camdessus who was appointed in 1987.
5. A lower exchange rate makes exports cheaper abroad, and imports dearer at home.
6. The dollar was the linchpin of the system of par values. It was fixed in price *re* gold (US$35 an ounce) and convertible into gold. All other currencies were then expressed in terms of this 'stable' dollar price.
7. Sixty per cent if we also include Eurodollar holdings.
8. Remember with four possible credit tranches, each at 25% of quota, the credit tranche as a whole gives a 'borrowing' right equal to the quota.
9. Normally a country could only 'borrow' 25% of quota in any one year.
10. The world's press have taken, over the past decade or so, to using shorthand for various world meetings. The use of the terms 'Group of Five', etc. have been a part of this trend. The Group of Five: the USA, Japan, the UK, West Germany and France. The Group of Seven: the 'Five', plus: Italy and Canada. The Group of Ten: the 'Seven' plus: Belgium, the Netherlands and Sweden.
11. The fifteen 'middle-income debtors' (MID) are: Argentina, Bolivia, Brazil, Chile, Colombia, Ecuador, Ivory Coast, Mexico, Morocco, Nigeria, Peru, Philippines, Uruguay, Venezuela, Yugoslavia. The 'Sub-Saharan debtors' are all those Sub-Saharan African states with the exceptions of Nigeria (in the MID countries) and South Africa.

References and further reading

Annual Report, Federal Reserve (1985).

Ainsley, E. M. (1979) *The IMF – Past, Present and Future*. University of Wales Press, Cardiff.

Bareau, P. (1981) *The Disorder in World Money: from Bretton Woods to SDRs*. Institute of Economic Affairs, Twelfth Wincott Memorial Lecture.

Currie, D. and **Vines, D.** (1989) *Macroeconomic Interactions between North and South*, Cambridge University Press.

Donnelly, Graham (1987) International economics, in: *Key Issues in Economics*. Longman.

HM Treasury (1987) International debt, *Economic Progress Report*, 190, July.

IMF (1987a) *International Financial Statistics*.

IMF (1987b) *World Economic Outlook*, Oct.

IMF (1988) *International Financial Statistics*, Feb.

IMF (1989) *International Financial Statistics*; vol. xlii, No. 11.

Johnston, G. A. (1980) World liquidity and the IMF Substitution Account, *Barclays Bank Review*, **55**, 3 Aug.

Kenwood, A. G. and **Lougheed, A. L.** (1971) *The Growth of the International Economy: (1820–1960)*. Allen and Unwin, pp. 90–1.

Kucinski, B. (1982) *Guardian*, 8 Dec.

National Institute Economic Review (1988) Feb.

OECD (1990) *Economic Outlook*.

OECD (1987b) *External Debt Statistics*. Paris.

Rybczynski, Tad (1987) The approaches towards the reform of the international monetary system, *National Westminster Bank Quarterly Review*, Feb.

Thirlwall, A. P. (1988) What is wrong with balance of payments adjustment theory? *The Royal Bank of Scotland Review*, 157, March.

UN (1990) *Monthly Bulletin of Statistics*, Vol. xliii, No. 12; March.

Veil, E. (1982) *The World Current Account Discrepancy*. OECD occasional paper, June.

Williams, R. *et al.* (1983) *International Capital Markets: developments and prospects*. IMF occasional paper, 23.

Williamson, John (1986) Managing exchange rates, *The Economic Review*, **4**, 1, Sept.

Transport is an important sector of the UK economy and has been the subject of increasing debate in recent years. This chapter will deal with certain aspects of that debate, notably the problems of road transport congestion and the move towards a more deregulated transport sector. The last 40 years have seen a dramatic change in the patterns of demand for transport. For example, in 1952 only 28% of passenger kilometres travelled were by car, taxi and motorcycle, while public transport (both road and rail) accounted for 62%. Today, however, the share has changed, with 85% of passenger kilometres now being by car, taxi and motorcycle. Such a substantial change has significant implications for road congestion and the environment. In this chapter we therefore concentrate mainly on the *road transport sector*, and on the car in particular.

Characteristics of transport

Firstly, transport is a service which is seldom demanded for its own sake and can be viewed as a 'derived demand'. In other words, the demand for the private car, public transport and freight haulage, is 'derived' from the need to transfer passengers and goods from one destination to another. Each journey undertaken can be seen as 'unique' in terms of both time and space, and cannot therefore be stored or transferred.

Secondly, the transport sector (both passenger and freight operators) is affected by the peak and off-peak nature of demand. There will be periods of maximum or peak demand, e.g. on a *daily* basis when commuters travel into a major conurbation to work, or on a *seasonal* basis when holidaymakers use road, rail or airline traffic during summer periods. Peak periods are present in the transport sector because of the derived nature of demand and because transport is consumed immediately and is therefore non-storable. Spare capacity at one time of the day or season *cannot* be used at another time of the day or season. Also the indivisibility of supply means that public transport may be running at full-capacity into the urban area in the peak period, but operating empty on the return journey. As a result there are often problems of over supply during off-peak periods.

Thirdly, the transport sector has, over the years, been subject to varying degrees of state intervention. When the Conservative Government was elected in 1979, the transport sector was characterized by public ownership and substantial government intervention, particularly in the provision of public transport. The 1980's saw a period of rapid change, with a substantial scaling down of state intervention in the sector. For example, the *1980 Transport Act* deregulated the long distance express coach market allowing increased competition. The National Freight Corporation was privatized in 1982 and subsequent years saw the deregulation of local bus provision as a result of the *1985 Transport Act*. Other transport companies were privatized, such as British Airways in 1987. Future years could see the privatization of BR and London Underground, as well as the private funding of new roads.

Fourthly, 'externality' effects are a characteristic of transport. These include effects such as pollution through emissions from car exhausts, noise from aircraft and motorways, and traffic congestion. At present 15% of the world's total emission of carbon dioxide comes from motor vehicles and the figure rises to 40% if we confine ourselves to the developed world (Glaister, Starkie and Thompson 1990). These costs are imposed on the community and are generally *not* taken into account by the transport provider (company or individual) who is usually only concerned with the *private costs* (such as fuel, wear and tear, etc.) of the journey undertaken. Intervention by the state has therefore been required to deal with these external effects, especially where companies or individuals have failed to take full account of the *social* implications of their actions. This has led, for example, to the compulsory wearing of seat belts and to safety tests on cars over a certain age in order to decrease accident and hospital costs.

Table 28.1 Passenger traffic

	Billion passenger kilometres/percentage														
	Road										Rail*		Air		All modes
	Buses and coaches		Cars and taxis		Motor cycles		Pedal cycles		All road						
		Per cent		Per cent		Per cent		Per cent		Per cent		Per cent		Per cent		Per cent
1978	50	11	373	79	7	1	5	1	435	92	35	7	2.7	1	473	100
1979	48	10	372	79	7	1	5	1	431	92	35	7	3.0	1	469	100
1980	45	9	395	80	8	2	5	1	453	92	35	7	3.0	1	491	100
1981	42	9	400	81	10	2	5	1	456	93	34	7	2.8	1	493	100
1982	41	8	411	82	10	2	6	1	468	93	31	6	2.9	1	500	100
1983	42	8	414	82	9	2	6	1	471	93	34	7	2.9	1	502	100
1984	42	8	434	82	9	2	6	1	491	93	35	7	3.4	1	529	100
1985	42	8	440	82	8	2	6	1	496	93	36	7	3.6	1	536	100
1986	41	7	462	83	8	1	5	1	516	93	37	7	3.7	1	557	100
1987	41	7	490	84	7	1	6	1	545	93	39	7	4.0	1	588	100
1988	41	7	519	84	7	1	5	1	572	93	41	7	4.6	1	618	100
1989	41	8	356	85	7	1	5	1	609	93	40	6	4.9	1	654	100

* British Rail plus London Transport Underground, the Strathclyde Passenger Transport Executive urban rail system and the Tyne and Wear Metro.

Statistics on personal travel by sea within Great Britain (or the United Kingdom) are not available.

Source: Department of Transport (1990), Transport statistics GB 1979–89.

Fifthly, other characteristics of transport may be gauged from the changing nature of travel over the last decade. Table 28.1 gives a summary of passenger travel in Great Britain over the period 1978–1988. It shows that there was an increase in passenger transport by 30% over the period, with travel by cars and taxis increasing 39%. *Cars* dominate passenger transport and have expanded their share of this sector from 79% to 84% over the period in question. Over the same period there has been a decline in *bus* and *coach* passenger kilometres, both in absolute and relative terms. In fact, bus and coach travel fell by 16% between 1978 and 1981, after which it has remained constant at between 7 and 8% of overall passenger kilometres travelled in Great Britain. Domestic air travel, although it has grown by 70% between 1978 and 1988, still only accounts for 1% of overall travel.

	Billion passenger kilometres							
	Private road vehicles		Buses and coaches		Rail excluding metro systems		All modes	
	1977	1987	1977	1987	1977	1987	1977	1987
Great Britain	358[3]	497[3]	51	41	34	38	408	576
FR of Germany	432	530[1]	69	61[1]	37	42[1]	538	633[1]
France	415	537	27	40	52	60	494	637
Italy[3]	326	400[1]	55	140[1]	42	42[1]	422	582[1]
Netherlands	102	141[1]	11	12[1]	8	9	122	162[1]
Spain	113	127[1]	29	34[1]	19	15[1]	160	176[1]
Japan	281	400[1]	87	100[1]	312	335[1]	681	835[1]
USA	3,600	4,500[1]	42[3]	38[2],[1]	17	19[1]	3,658	4,557[1]
USSR	–	–	345	470[1]	322	374[1]	–	–

[1] Estimated.
[2] Intercity transport only.
[3] National vehicles, cars and taxis.

Source: Adapted from Department of Transport (1989) Transport statistics GB 1979–89.

Table 28.2 Passenger traffic by mode: 1977 and 1987

Table 28.2 compares Great Britain with a number of other countries in terms of passenger kilometres travelled between 1977 and 1987. In all of these countries the major mode of transport is the private road vehicle (although there are no figures available for private road vehicles in the USSR). It is interesting to note that in Japan, 40% of all passenger kilometres travelled are by rail, although there has been a 42% increase in passenger kilometres travelled by private road vehicles between 1977 and 1987.

Finally, another characteristic of transport is the changing nature of the *freight* market. In terms of freight transport, Table 28.3 gives figures in billion tonne kilometres and percentage, by mode, over the period 1978–88. It shows that there has been a 25% increase in freight transported over the ten year period and, as with passenger transport, roads can be seen as the major form of transport, with 59% of the share in 1988.

One interesting point to note is the decline in rail tonne kilometres in 1984 which was attributable to the miners' strike when coal and coke were no longer transported by rail.

Also 95% of *passenger* users' expenditure was devoted to road transport in 1988. For *freight*, in terms of all road and rail haulage, some 97% of freight users' expenditure was on road in 1988. In 1987 households spent on average £28 per week on transport and travel, which accounted for 15% of household

All traffic	Billion tonne kilometres (Percentages)											
	1978		1980		1982		1984		1986		1988	
Road[1]	99.3	(56)	92.4	(53)	93.8	(53)	99.9	(55)	105.4	(56)	130.2	(59)
Rail	20.0	(11)	17.6	(10)	15.9	(9)	12.7	(7)	16.5	(9)	18.0	(8)
Water[2]	47.6	(27)	54.1	(31)	58.7	(33)	59.7	(33)	54.8	(29)	60.9	(28)
Pipeline[3]	9.8	(6)	10.1	(6)	9.3	(5)	10.4	(6)	10.4	(6)	10.8	(5)
All modes[4]	176.7	(100)	174.2	(100)	177.7	(100)	182.7	(100)	187.1	(100)	219.9	(100)

Notes:
[1] Figures include an estimate for the work done by vehicles under 3.5 tonnes gross vehicle weight.
[2] UK figures.
[3] Oil pipelines only (excluding offshore pipelines).
[4] Domestic air freight within the UK, while sometimes important in terms of speed of delivery for urgent items, is insignificant in volume.

Source: Adapted from Department of Transport (1989), Transport Statistics GB 1978–88.

Table 28.3 Freight transport by mode (in billion tonne kilometres and percentages)

expenditure. Of the £28, approximately £24 went on the purchase and running of motor vehicles (Transport Statistics GB 1989).

The demand for transport

The quantity of a good or service demanded is dependent upon a number of factors, such as its own price, the price of other goods or services (particularly close substitutes and complements), and income. For example, private car ownership is not only a function of the price of motor vehicles, but also of fuel prices, the price of alternative forms of transport, and income levels. Income is an important factor in determining both the demand for transport in general, and the *particular mode* of transport a passenger uses.

The Family Expenditure Survey (CSO 1990) gives 1988 figures for motoring expenditure, fares and other travel costs for households with different levels of income in the UK. It clearly shows that travel expenditure increases with income, with those households on a gross normal weekly income of under £45 having an average weekly expenditure on *motoring* (which includes the net purchase, maintenance and running of private motor vehicles) of £2.98, whilst those on a weekly income of £200–£250 have an expenditure of £21.41 and those on £650 and above per week have an expenditure of £52.25. For *all* households the average is £25.31. The figures for expenditure on *bus and coach* fares reveal that expenditure declines at higher income levels. Households on less than £45 spend 0.73 pence weekly; those on between £200 and £250 spend £1.21, however those on £650 and over spend only £1.13 on average per week, leading one to suggest that bus and coach travel is viewed in economic terms as an *inferior good*.

For *rail transport*, the Family Expenditure Survey reveals a different trend, with higher income groups spending more on that mode of travel. Those on a gross income of under £45 per week spend 0.25 pence of their income on rail travel; those on between £200 and £250 spend 0.96 pence, and those on £650 plus spend a total of £4.07 per week.

Predicting the demand for transport in the future is a difficult process since it depends on how the variables affecting demand change over time. For example, forecasts of car ownership predict an increase of over 60 per cent between 1988 and the year 2000. In 1988 there were approximately 18m private cars licensed in Great Britain, and for the UK as a whole there were 343 cars per 1,000 of the population. As Table 28.4 reveals, however, we have not as yet reached saturation level in terms of car ownership, for there are still 80 per cent of households in the lowest quarter of income who do *not* own a car.

Table 28.4 Number of household cars by household income quartile 1985/86

Household income Quarter	Percentage households		
	Number of household cars		
	None	One	Two or more
Lowest	80	19	1
Second	44	50	6
Third	20	62	18
Highest	7	46	47
All Households	38	44	18

Source: Department of Transport (1988) 'National Travel Survey 1985/86 Report'.

When the UK is compared to other industrial nations (Table 28.5) it can be seen clearly that we have a relatively low level of car ownership.

Table 28.5 Rates of car ownership and GDP per head 1988

Country	Cars per 1,000 people	GDP per head (in $US)‡
USA	565	19,600
West Germany	461	14,200
Sweden	398	14,700
France	394	13,700
Italy	392	13,000
United Kingdom	343	13,500
Denmark	310	13,700
Spain	250	9,500
Japan	240	14,400
Greece	144	7,000
Portugal	125	6,400

† Updated from Table 8, p. 28 in *National Road Traffic Forecasts* (GB) 1989.
‡ At current purchasing power parity exchange rates, 1988 provisional.

Sources: World Road Statistics, International Road Federation Monthly Bulletin of Statistics, United Nations Statistical Year Book.

With regards to forecasting car ownership, the Department of Transport used the *National Road Traffic Forecasts* 1988 (Goodwin 1990) to make the following observation:

'Many factors are likely to influence the growth of car ownership and use. They include income, the cost of buying and running cars, journey requirements (work and non-work), quality of public transport services and the way people's expectations and preferences about car ownership change over time. . . . It seems likely that car ownership will eventually reach a limit –

or 'saturation level' – as a larger proportion of the population acquires cars. Since no country appears to have reached this limit yet, the level of saturation must be assumed. For these forecasts, saturation has been assumed to occur when 90% of the driving age group of 17–74 year olds owns a car; (100% car ownership is unlikely because some people will be prevented or deterred by disabilities or other factors). On this basis, saturation would correspond to 650 cars per thousand people. The forecasts of growth in national car ownership are essentially about the rate and path with which the saturation level is approached.'

Forecasts of future traffic, particularly the private car, are essential for a central government which has to decide on the allocation of funds for future road development. For, as stated by the Department of Transport in 1989:

Traffic forecasts are important in assessing whether the benefits from a road improvement, over its life-time, justify the initial cost and in determining the standard of provision. They enable a balance to be struck between providing extra capacity before it is needed and the cost of adding to capacity at a later stage. Traffic forecasts also play a part in predicting the environmental impacts of traffic, such as noise and air pollution.

Such forecasts are difficult to determine owing to the high degree of uncertainty about the future and for this reason the basis of the forecasts involves two differing assumptions, namely that of low economic growth and that of high economic growth. The forecasts therefore provide a range of values ('scenarios') to cover the uncertainties involved. It is possible, however, for the outcome to fall outside the forecast range, with the Department of Transport being unable to forecast traffic levels accurately. A good example of this was seen with the M25, for which forecasts were undertaken in the 1970s when oil prices were high and economic growth low. This led the Department of Transport to *underestimate* the likely demand for transport along the route. For example, between 1982 and 1987 they forecast an increase in road traffic of between 9% and 16%, but the *actual* increase was 22%. The main reason for this was that the forecast assumed a growth of GDP of between 8% and 15% over the 5-year period, but GDP actually grew by 18%. Also the price of fuel was forecast to rise in real terms, whereas it actually fell.

The latest official forecast of traffic growth between 1988 and 2000 lies between 27 and 47%, with the wide range reflecting the varying assumptions of GDP growing between 26% (low assumption) and 46% (high assumption) over the twelve year period.

The supply of road space

In 1988 Great Britain possessed 354,315 kilometres of public roads, of which trunk roads and motorways comprised less than 5 per cent but carried 31 per cent of all traffic. Trunk roads, including motorways, are the responsibility of the Department of Transport in England and although the *general* shape of the road programme is stated as part of government policy in documents such as 'Roads for Prosperity' (Cmnd 693, 1989), *specific* schemes are subject to careful assessment, including their 'fit' within the overall scheme.

The Government's Expenditure Plans 1990–91 to 1992–93 give a

breakdown of expenditure on national roads. For 1988–89, new construction
and the improvement of roads accounted for 71% of the national road
expenditure. This included projects such as the extension of the M40 between
Oxford and Birmingham, the A1–M1 link in the East Midlands and the M66
in Manchester. The rest of the expenditure (29%) was allocated to
maintenance work. In 1990–91 it is estimated that the spending on new
construction will be £1,282mn, an increase of over 50% on 1987–88 and by
the end of 1989 there were some 530 schemes in the trunk road programme,
including 170 bypasses and relief roads. The government, as part of the
overall road building programme, published in May 1989 'Roads for
Prosperity'; this included plans to double the spending on roads to £12bn
over a ten year period. It also involved schemes to increase the size of the
road programme by a total of 2700 miles of new and widened roads, with the
aim of relieving congestion on certain parts of the road network.

Project Evaluation

With public sector resources being scarce and the demand for road schemes
being so high, it is necessary to appraise the need for *particular* road schemes.
It is not always possible to undertake a full appraisal of every road scheme, so
a first selection is made based on, for example, traffic flows. Once this has
taken place the projects deemed worthy of further consideration are then
assessed in more detail. This will involve traffic surveys, forecasts of future
demand (with and without the investment) and, if necessary, public
enquiries. In some instances it can take as long as 14 years for the planning
and construction phases to be completed. One method used to evaluate
alternative projects, taking account of the likely benefits and disadvantages,
involves *investment appraisal*. While it is possible to use the concept of profit
or financial returns to establish, for example, whether a local bus company
should operate, this is not applicable to road investment, where the users do
not pay directly for using the facility. In a situation where no prices are
charged for using roads, and where costs and benefits such as time savings
and effects on the environment are difficult to measure, then a different
technique to simple profit and financial returns is required. *Cost Benefit
Analysis* (CBA) enables comparisons to be made between the costs of a road
scheme and the benefits to road users so that decisions can be made regarding
the viability of the project. CBA was first used in the 1960s to evaluate the
M1 motorway. It led to the development of a computer-based technique
called COBA used by the Department of Transport. This has been modified
over the years and is applied to the majority of inter-urban road schemes.
COBA acts as a benchmark, since it places monetary values on certain road
user benefits, but the values *exclude* non-user or environmental costs and
benefits, namely pollution, noise, vibration and community severence,
because of the difficulty in calculating them accurately. For example, it is
difficult to determine what aspects of noise cause disutility. Is it loud noise,
intermittent noise or persistent noise? Even if this could be determined, what
monetary value should be put on the disutility! As well as excluding the
environmental factors, no attempt is made to evaluate the direct costs and
benefits of particular road projects to the regional or national economy,
because these are also considered to be too difficult to estimate.

Benefits   Road user benefits *included* in COBA cover journey time savings, savings in vehicle operating costs, and accident cost savings. Forecasts have to be made as to the *type* of journey (e.g. for work or for leisure) and how many trips of each type are undertaken, so that an estimate of the *time savings* can be made. Such time savings are divided into working time savings and leisure time savings, and together they make up roughly 80% of the major benefit for most road schemes. *Working time saving* is valued as a benefit to the employer, because it is assumed that it can be used in the production of a good or service. However it is debatable whether small increments of time saved have real economic value when aggregated over a large number of vehicles. For example, it is quite obvious that one hour saved on a work journey can be of benefit in terms of the output which could have been produced in that time, but it is less clear how important a time saving of 10 minutes would be. Also it is unclear, for example, whether a saving of 10 minutes to six road users is equivalent to a time saving of one hour for one road user. Non-working time is more difficult to calculate because there is no economic market for leisure time. The way *leisure time savings* are calculated is by observing the trade-off at the margin between work and leisure time. The Department of Transport places a value on leisure time which is equivalent to 40% of the average gross hourly wage rate. *Accident savings* are also difficult to calculate, because any monetary measure needs to take account of lost output and medical costs, and must make an allowance for personal suffering. COBA includes a figure of 19% of overall benefits attributed to improved safety. *Vehicle operating-cost savings* are calculated on the basis of fuel, oil, tyres, vehicle maintenance and depreciation.

Costs   The **cost** side of any COBA assessed scheme will involve a valuation of items such as the purchase of land, construction costs, maintenance costs saved on existing roads, and the costs of maintaining new roads.

Discounting   When undertaking a road scheme the majority of the costs will be incurred first, followed by a number of years of benefit, and this time-profile must be taken into account when assessing a road investment scheme. However because costs and benefits occur in different years it is necessary to express their values in terms of a particular year, i.e. the *present value* year. The technique of *discounting*[1] is used to obtain the Net Present Value (NPV) of a stream of future costs and benefits from a particular scheme, covering a thirty year period from the time the road is opened. The equation for the NPV can be shown as:

$$\text{NPV} = (B-C)_0 + \frac{(B-C)_1}{(1+r)} + \frac{(B-C)_2}{(1+r)^2} + \frac{(B-C)_n}{(1+r)^n}$$

In the equation, B refers to the benefits and C the costs (including the capital costs) of the particular road scheme. The *subscripts* 0, 1, .. n, refer to the number of years over which the costs and benefits are said to occur (namely thirty years), and r is the discount rate (which is presently set by the Department of Transport at 8%). The benefits (B) are assessed on a 'do-minimum' and 'do-something' basis. The *do-minimum* scheme is the existing road network with only minor improvements, and the *do-something* scheme is the existing road network plus the new road being proposed. There will be user costs associated with each network, namely the time it takes to travel on the route, the number of accidents and the operating costs of the vehicles. The *difference* between the user costs on the do-minimum and the do-something network is discounted to form the user benefit (B) of the new road scheme being proposed.

The costs (C) as stated above comprise the purchase of land, construction and maintenance costs. In terms of the above equation, if the NPV is *positive* then it indicates that the scheme is economically justified. In order to compare projects which are of different sizes, it is necessary to divide the NPV by the capital cost, thus producing the NPV/C *ratio* which can be used as a means of ranking projects. It has been estimated by the Department of Transport that the benefits to costs ratio on roads due to be started over the next four years is 2.5 to 1, which is seen to be roughly equivalent to a 20% economic rate of return in real terms.

As stated previously, the major benefits of a new road scheme are the savings in terms of time and reduced accidents, and these are based on *estimates* of future traffic flows. It is important therefore once a road scheme is in operation that figures of the *actual* flows are obtained, so as to establish how successful the original Department of Transport's forecast had been. The latest 1990 figures from the Department show that when comparing the forecast figures for 58 road schemes with actual flows, 57% of the schemes had actual flows *within an acceptable range* predicted by the initial forecast.

With the growth in vehicle kilometres being 42% between 1978 and 1988, the increase in the length of all public roads of only 5.36% (25% for motorways) would appear to suggest that road construction has not kept pace with the growth in vehicle kilometres, especially since the increase in average daily traffic on *each* kilometre of all roads has been 34% over the same period (52% on motorways). Road space is therefore a valuable and scarce resource, and if road congestion is to be controlled then policies need to be pursued either to ration the existing road space (e.g. by introducing a road pricing policy) or to expand the road space available. The following section will investigate in more depth the problems of urban road congestion, although a number of the issues also apply to inter-urban road congestion. The various costs of congestion will be considered and possible demand and supply remedies will be investigated.

Road transport congestion

Congestion costs arise because the addition of more vehicles onto a road network reduces the speed of other vehicles and so increases the average time it takes to complete any particular journey.

It is possible to gain some understanding of congestion by studying the relationship between speed and flow along a particular route. Figure 28.1 shows a *speed-flow curve* for the movement of vehicles along a particular road. It shows how motorists interact and impose delays and costs on each other. In a free flow situation (around point A) there is little or no interaction between vehicles and therefore speeds (subject to the legal speed limit) are

Fig. 28.1 Speed-flow curve

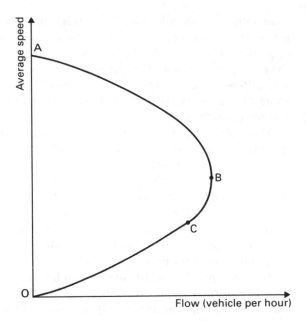

relatively high. However, as extra vehicles join the road, average speed is reduced; nevertheless an increased flow will still occur until point B is reached. The flow of vehicles depends upon the number of vehicles joining the road and the speed of the traffic. For the *individual user*, maximum efficiency is where the speed is at its highest, i.e. point A. In terms of the *system as a whole* however the maximum efficiency is at point B, before the speed-flow curve turns back on itself (i.e. where the maximum flow of vehicles is achieved). Once at point B, the road is said to have reached its capacity at the maximum flow level. Motorists may continue to enter the road after B because they may lack perfect information, thus slowing down the whole flow. Point C may therefore be used to represent the speed-flow situation during a peak period. At this point the traffic is in a stop-start situation, perhaps where the traffic flow is subject to a bottleneck. This gives rise to high *external* costs which the motorist is not taking into account. These costs will tend to increase the closer the road is to full capacity.

The costs of congestion

It is clear that a major strategy is needed to tackle the congestion problem, not only in urban areas but also on inter-urban routes. Congestion undermines competitiveness and hinders certain conurbations, particularly London, from attracting people and business. It also imposes a financial cost on the business community in terms of increased commuter times and delays in the delivery of goods. One estimate calculated that congestion costs are over £3bn per year in London and the six major English conurbations alone, and suggested that the total national congestion bill could be in the region of £10bn per year. (The British Road Federation 1988.)

The Confederation of British Industry estimates that delays on the M25 cost £1bn per year, and that London's inadequate transport system costs the nation around £15bn per annum, almost two thirds of which relates to

London and the south east. In the CBI report 'The Capital at Risk', published in 1989, the following figures were given for the averaged additional costs incurred in London and the South East. This information was compiled from data provided by those national companies which could compare their distribution costs in London and the South East with other areas. The results are shown in Table 28.6 and reveal that the £15bn per annum consists of, amongst other things, increased staff and vehicles requirements and additional fuel costs.

Table 28.6 Congestion costs in London and the South East

Average additional costs due to congestion incurred in London/South East	
Productivity lost due to lateness of staff	1%
Delivery time and cost penalties within M25	30%
Additional staff/drivers needed to beat congestion	20%
Additional vehicles needed	20%
Additional vehicle service/repair costs	20%
Additional fuel costs	10%
Estimated total additional transportation costs in the London area	20%

Statistics were compiled from information provided by national organizations that could compare distribution costs in London and the South East with other areas.

Source: Confederation of British Industry, 'The Capital at Risk', 1989.

Specific businesses such as British Telecom and the Royal Mail put the cost of congestion to themselves at £7.25m and £10.4m per annum, respectively. These costs were measured in terms of fleet inefficiency, lost driver's time, and extra vehicle costs. According to the CBI, every British household has to spend at least £5 per week *more than it needs to* on the transport of goods and services in order to meet the costs to business of road and rail congestion. This is equal to 2p on the basic rate of income tax. The CBI estimate that if traffic delays could be reduced, thereby raising average speeds by 1.5 mph, then London's economy would be better off by £1m per day. The problem is not of course limited to the UK; for example in the US, the Federal Highway Administration put the cost of congestion on urban freeways in 1984 at more than $9bn (*The Economist*, 18 Feb 1989).

In terms of traffic speeds, the situation has worsened over the last 20 years. In Central London, the morning and evening peak period travel speeds were 12.7 and 11.8 mph respectively in 1968–70, whereas by 1986–88 they had fallen (according to the Department of Transport) to 11.5 and 11.0 mph respectively. Figure 28.2 gives some indication of the causes of congestion. There has been a dramatic rise in the number of licensed vehicles over the period 1951 to 1988, made up almost entirely of 'private and light goods vehicles', in which category the private car predominates.

The theory of urban road transport congestion   An economic model can be used to simplify the various issues involved in transport congestion, as shown in Figure 28.3. The horizontal axis measures the flow of vehicles per hour along a particular route. The vertical axis measures the cost per trip, including time costs. Two demand curves are shown, both of which have a

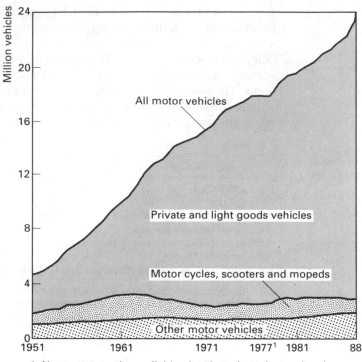

Fig. 28.2 Number of vehicles licenced: by type *Source:* CSO (1990).

1 No census results available, data have been interpolated.

negative slope because it is assumed that motorists will reduce their driving if the cost of driving increases. The demand curve D_1 refers to the *off-peak* demand for the route. It is the aggregate demand of all motorists who wish to use the route. If the cost per trip is C_0, and demand is D_1, then this will produce a flow of F_0 along the route. When making a journey, a motorist is not likely to take account of the congestion cost of that journey and may in fact only consider his or her own *marginal private cost* (MPC). MPC includes costs such as the price of petrol used and the opportunity cost of the time the motorist spends travelling. There can, however, be costs incurred on *other* road users which the individual motorist will not take into account. These are 'external costs' and include such things as the pollution and noise borne by society as a whole and the congestion borne by other road users. These are shown by the *marginal social cost* curve (MSC) in Figure 28.3. For simplicity Figure 28.3 assumes that congestion is the *only* externality; hence MPC is shown as equal to MSC for some range of traffic flow up to F_1 because there is no congestion until that flow is reached. (Of course if we allowed for the pollution which occurs from exhaust gases at low mileage, then MSC would be above MPC at all levels of traffic flow.) If motorists *did* take into account the social costs of a journey, then they might decide that the journey was not worth making, at least not at that time of day or by that particular route.

In the Figure it can be seen that the flow of traffic can increase up to F_1 without congestion, because it is possible for the additional cars to enter the road without slowing down any other driver. It can be seen, therefore, that there is no divergence between marginal private cost and marginal social cost. However at flows above F_1, congestion is apparent because additional

Fig. 28.3 Equilibrium traffic flow

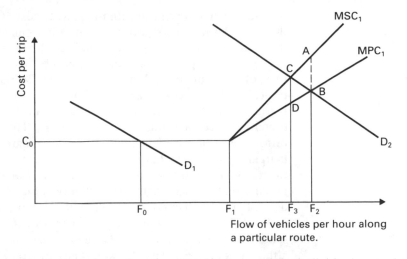

drivers slow down the overall traffic flow and the individual motorist's MPC per trip increases. Each motorist is now beginning to interfere with other road users, affecting their costs but ignoring those costs when deciding whether or not to make a particular trip. As the flow of traffic increases beyond F_1 there is also a *divergence* between the MPC and the MSC, as shown in the figure by lines MPC_1 and MSC_1 (MSC is equal to MPC plus the social cost of congestion). This is mainly brought about through increased travel times, as each additional driver entering the road imposes an extra delay (perhaps only small) on every other driver. If the demand for the route at the peak period is of the normal shape D_2, then the traffic flow will be F_2. Here F_2B will be the (private) cost per trip *to the motorist*, and the external costs which the motorist has *not* taken into account will be equal to AB. At a flow of F_2 there is therefore *allocative inefficiency*, as the 'real' or social cost of congestion has not been accounted for by the private motorist.

Policy options for urban road congestion – demand policies

There are various policies which have been designed to improve the use of existing road capacity. These include policies which can be introduced to influence the *demand* for road space; there are also policies designed to expand road capacity, which can be viewed as *supply* side policies. These various policies will be covered in this section. However at this stage it is also worth mentioning that there is a 'laissez faire' approach which is an alternative solution for permitting an equilibrium level of road transport congestion to emerge. For instance, if congestion gets 'too bad' in a particular region, then it may persuade companies and individuals to move to less prosperous regions which do not have the same level of congestion. The problem with this 'laissez faire' approach is that the transport network may be operating at, or near, full capacity at certain times, and therefore even small fluctuations in demand can cause long delays and create problems for safety. For example, in London, ambulances which reached accidents at an average speed of 25 mph in 1975, now reach accidents at an average of 11 mph (T. Bendixson 1989).

Road pricing   When undertaking a journey, each driver is comparing the private benefit of each trip with the private cost of each trip. Drivers will add their vehicles to the flow whenever their marginal private benefit exceeds their marginal private cost. New roads could be built to meet the demand during the peak period, or demand could be restrained, or a mixture of the two policies could be undertaken. In Figure 28.3 above the flow of F_3 could be achieved by placing a tax (a road price) of CD on the road user, so raising marginal private costs from MPC_1 to equal those of MSC_1; this would thereby reduce the traffic flow from F_2 to F_3. This road pricing option would bring about a 'more efficient allocation' of a scarce resource, because the marginal private benefit (as measured by the demand curve) is now equal to the marginal social cost curve. Road pricing is an option which is gaining in popularity. For road pricing to work most efficiently, the majority of road users should be charged, although public sector users where demand is inelastic should be exempt. Buses, which are efficient in the use of road space, would have a lower road price per passenger than the car, and although commercial vehicles would pay the road price they would benefit from reduced delays and more predictable travel times. D. Newbery, in a recent article, has commented that 'As road space is a valuable and scarce resource, it is natural that economists should argue that it should be rationed by price – road-users should pay the marginal social cost of using the road network if they are to make the right decisions about whether (and by which means) to take a particular journey, and, more generally, to ensure that they make the correct allocative decisions between transport and other activities'. (Newbery 1990.)

Urban road pricing which involves charging for road use, was suggested as a possible solution to the urban congestion problem as long ago as 1964, when the Ministry of Transport produced the Smeed Report. Road pricing could be introduced by using meters attached to cars in the form of an electronic numberplate. As a car entered a congested area or stretch of road, the meter would be activated by sensors in the road. A charge would then be registered and a bill for the congestion caused sent to the motorist periodically. As well as dissuading the marginal car user from using the road, it would also provide the authorities with revenue which could be used to construct more roads or to improve the public transport system. Research has been undertaken by the London Planning Advisory Committee (LPAC 1988) on road pricing schemes in Central London. It reported that, for a typical electronic road pricing scheme, the 'best' charge would be one of 0.70p per charging point, on the basis that the typical two-way trip would cross two or three charging points in each direction. It estimated that revenue, net of administration, would be £300m per annum and that vehicle kilometres in Central London would be reduced by approximately 15%, with a net economic gain of about £200m per annum (House of Commons Transport Committee, 1st Report, Roads for the Future, 1990).

One of the criticisms levelled at road pricing is its effect on increasing the inflation rate. However, if it succeeded in reducing the total costs of commercial activities, then this is a false worry. Road pricing should not be viewed as a revenue maximizing tax, but as an efficiency maximizing tax. It could then be the key to medium-term relief from congestion and could provide the funds for the long-term upgrading of roads and public transport.

At present, road users pay approximately £17bn per annum in road tax and petrol tax, which is substantially more than is spent on road construction and maintenance. The road users' payment of road tax is seen as a 'luxury goods tax' and therefore not as a specific transport tax. The tax on petrol is *not* related to the use of the road, particularly congested roads, and therefore does not promote the efficient use of scarce road space. Of course it could be argued that a tax on petrol is broadly related to road use, in that the more a car is used the more fuel tax is paid in total. The Chartered Institute of Transport stated in the conclusions of its report published in 1990 that a road pricing scheme for London should cover the area within the boundaries of the M25. The scheme would cost in the region of £80m per annum to administer, but could produce revenue in excess of £600m per annum. However, if a road pricing system were introduced, it would possibly prove unpopular with motorists because it would constitute an additional tax burden.

However, the theoretical case for road pricing is widely accepted by economists and a successful system has been demonstrated experimentally in Hong Kong (Hau 1990). Nevertheless there are a number of problems to be addressed when considering the implementation of a road pricing policy. First, there need to be accurate estimates of elasticities of demand and of marginal external costs (Glaister, Starkie and Thompson 1990). Second, the issue of equity and the problem of practically implementing the scheme, both need to be considered. For example, what charge should be made for congestion and how would it vary depending on the level of traffic and the time of day? Third, road pricing could be seen as an invasion of privacy, which was one of the reasons for it not being continued in Hong Kong after the initial experiment. However some writers view the lack of understanding of the new charges by car owners as a possible reason for its lack of success, for there was a failure to realize in Hong Kong that the charges of $2–$3 per day would replace the annual licensing fee (Newbery 1990).

Road pricing is certainly an option worthy of serious consideration.

Supplementary licences An alternative to road pricing in congested urban areas could be a system of *supplementary licences*. Such a system has, in fact, been in operation in Singapore since 1975. A vehicle owner would have to buy and display a licence if the vehicle travels into a designated area. In Singapore, motorists have to buy a licence to enter the business district between 7.30 am and 10.15 am. It has been found that traffic has fallen by as much as 76% during this period, which suggests that road users are sensitive to such a fiscal penalty. It is also interesting to note that the introduction of the supplementary licence did *not* lead to a large increase in the use of public transport in Singapore. This may have been due to the growth of car sharing, which could be viewed as a benefit of the scheme. The supplementary licensing scheme would also be beneficial in a congested area where the demand was not sensitive to the congestion tax. In terms of Figure 28.3 above, the aim would be to shift the demand curve D_2 to the left to reduce the traffic flow towards F_1. However, any licence system like this needs 'policing' and those found to be without a licence must be fined. In 1989 the London Planning Advisory Committee considered the supplementary licence scheme as performing less well than electronic road pricing, because it was less refined.

Finally, it is worth noting that road pricing (including supplementary licences) involves rationing the congested infrastructure at peak times, here by using the price mechanism, and is an example of 'the polluter pays' principle. Obviously important in such a scheme is the destination of the revenue collected. If it went into the general exchequer fund, then it may be presented as just another tax. However it could be directed towards the provision of new road capacity or towards improving the public transport network.

Subsidizing public transport   Another approach designed to shift the demand to the left in Figure 28.3 is *subsidizing public transport*. This method was used in the 1970's by a number of UK metropolitan councils. For example in Sheffield, bus fares were reduced by 55% in real terms over the period 1975–81. In addition to financial implications, the problem faced by this method is in persuading car users to *transfer* from private to public transport, since they often perceive themselves as being the *victims* of congestion rather than the *cause* of it. To be successful this policy requires a long-term improvement in public transport and a cross elasticity of demand between public and private transport substantially greater than zero. An added problem is that increased income levels lead to increased car ownership, thus lowering the demand for public transport. The Public Transport sector therefore becomes more reliant on certain groups of travellers, namely the young, the elderly and those on low incomes, i.e. on a market which is getting smaller (Goodwin 1990). The Department of Transport comments that 'The level of traffic on roads in London is a reflection largely of individual choice, not the non-availability of other modes of travel'. However, it could be the case that individuals are not paying the true cost of motoring, i.e. there are 'hidden subsidies' which have the effect of making single car occupancy an attractive proposition, particularly in the peak period. This results in an inefficient use of road capacity.

Parking restrictions   One policy which has been extensively used in urban areas since the 1960s is *parking restraints*. The aim has been, through parking meters and restrictions on on-street parking, to limit the supply of parking spaces, so reducing the demand for urban routes. This policy, too, has limitations in that removing parking facilities from a road essentially increases the size of the road and may therefore encourage extra traffic flows. At the same time, parking restraints encourage illegal parking which may add to congestion. This is one of the main reasons for the introduction of wheel clamps in Central London in 1986.

City Councils have sought to use pricing policies at their car parks to encourage shopping and other short stay motorists, while at the same time discouraging long stay commuters. However, the success of this policy has been hindered to some extent by their lack of control over privately operated car parks and by high volumes of through traffic in most congested areas. Parking charges are also unable to discriminate between length of journey or route taken. Pricing policies could be used to encourage motorists to park at peripheral, out of town, car parks, which could be part of a park-and-ride scheme. One such scheme is in operation in Oxford.

Limiting car ownership and use   There are two further ways of influencing the demand for road space. The first, is to *limit car ownership*. This could be achieved by imposing either import restrictions, a registration tax, or a system of rationing on cars. As yet, this is not something which has been advocated in the UK but it does occur in certain parts of the world, not only to deal with traffic congestion but also to save energy. In January 1990, the Singapore government increased the registration tax on cars by 500%, which meant that the average price of a new car had its registration tax increased by S$5,000, to S$6,000. This is viewed as an interim measure, with the government eventually introducing a quota system to limit the number of vehicles on the road. The second method is to introduce a system of *car sharing* which, if successful, would also shift demand to the left in Figure 28.3.

Policy options for urban road congestion – supply policies   As well as demand policies to deal with the urban road congestion problem, *supply side policies* (such as new road building) can be implemented. An urban road building strategy can be examined by the use of Figure 28.4.

Fig. 28.4 Equilibrium traffic flow: supply side policies

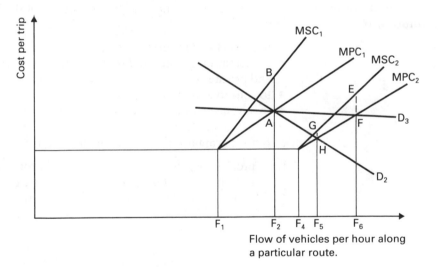

Flow of vehicles per hour along a particular route.

Increasing the number of lanes, or building new roads, will shift the marginal private cost and marginal social cost curves from MPC_1 and MSC_1 respectively, to MPC_2 and MSC_2. The diagram implies that before the road capacity was expanded, congestion occurred beyond a traffic flow of F_1, but now occurs at a point beyond F_4. The reason for this is that road construction increases road capacity, so that an increased flow is now possible before the costs of congestion appear. If demand is taken to be D_2, then a flow of F_5 will now use the road and although there will be some congestion (note that MSC_2 is greater than MPC_2 at F_5 by the distance GH) this will be somewhat less than the congestion *before* the new road expansion, which was AB in Fig. 28.4.

There is, however, a limitation with this strategy. If the road network is expanded and improved, then individuals who previously used public transport may now begin to use their own car. New traffic will therefore be *generated*, as those who did not make a particular trip previously are now encouraged to do so, and motorists who travelled via a different route may now be persuaded to use the route(s) in question. Also peak and off-peak travel can, to some extent, be viewed as substitutes, so that off-peak travel may fall. It could therefore be argued that increasing a road's capacity will result in more vehicles using the route, i.e. a case of supply generating its own demand. This means that the level of demand may well be underestimated. In fact demand could become almost perfectly elastic, as with demand curve D_3 in Figure 28.4. If this were to be the case, then the flow of traffic along the particular route would be F_6 and not F_5, and the social cost which had not been taken into account would be EF and not GH. The final situation may not, then, be significantly different from the initial external cost of AB in Figure 28.4. In other words, a similar congestion problem would still persist.

Government transport policy – regulation or competition?

Government Transport Policy has been influenced, over time, by a number of factors. The present aims and objectives of the Department of Transport are:

- to protect and improve safety;
- to increase efficiency and reduce unit costs of transport in both the public and private sectors;
- to conserve the environment; and
- to advance United Kingdom transport interests abroad.

In furthering these aims and objectives, public expenditure is incurred on:

(i)   promoting safety and environmental protection by regulation, licensing, testing, accident investigation, publicity, education and research;
(ii)   improving and maintaining a national road system;
(iii)   investing in local roads improvements, public transport, ports and airports;
(iv)   maintaining local roads, supporting local public transport operations and financing concessionary fares for the elderly and handicapped;
(v)   providing external financing required by nationalized transport industries.

Over the years, the state has attempted to influence transport in a number of ways:

Quality   This has mainly been concerned with safety. In 1930 the Road Traffic Act was introduced, which required both bus operators and freight hauliers to licence their vehicles with regional Traffic Commissioners. This policy was viewed, essentially, as one of protecting the public interest. This follows from the fact that, for both the road haulier and the bus operator, the capital costs of vehicle purchase are relatively low, so that there is a low barrier to entry into the industry. As a result profits can be driven down, which in turn could lead to operators trying to reduce their costs, with possibly adverse effects on safety standards. In recent years there have been a number of transport disasters and this has clearly made the whole area of transport safety a major political issue. An important question is whether increased competition will lead to reduced safety standards!

Quantity   The licensing system has also been used as a form of regulatory control. Successive governments have been of the opinion that quantitative controls on transport were necessary in order to make sure that existing capacity was fully utilized. Such controls have applied to the road haulage and bus industries. One of the implications of licensing has been the cross-subsidization of bus services. Until 1986, the provision of unprofitable services was closely linked to the granting of licences for route monopolies by the traffic commissioners. Although certain services, such as late evenings, weekends and certain rural routes, were unprofitable, they were viewed as being 'socially' worthwhile. The financial losses on such routes were supported from the profits which the operators earned on the more profitable routes, so that cross-subsidization clearly took place. However cross-subsidization was only possible as long as operators did have monopolies; with a deregulated bus sector this was less likely.

Ownership   Railways and parts of the road haulage and bus passenger transport sector are, or have been, under public ownership. The main reasons put forward for such ownership have been that if subsidization of such services was needed, then it would be easier for the government rather than private companies to control that particular operation. Government control would also allow for an improved co-ordination of services. The government's stance on state ownership has changed, however, in the last 10 years, as with the sale of the National Freight Corporation to its employees in 1982, and of the National Bus Company following the deregulation of the bus industry in 1986.

Resource allocation   A major area of direct government involvement in the transport sector concerns the large amounts of public expenditure invested in the road network. Expenditure on maintaining, renewing, improving and extending national roads is planned to be £1,814m for 1990–91, £1,893m for 1991–92 and £1,985m for 1992–93.

Government intervention in the transport sector, characterized by state monopolies, public ownership and investment based on state priorities, can be contrasted with a 'laissez-faire' approach. The latter involves leaving the sector to the workings of the free market, with quality, quantity and resource allocation being determined by consumer preferences. In a 'pure' laissez faire situation, transport services are provided by privately owned firms and the finance of those services is based on customer fares. In this free market there would be no statutory control on entry into the sector and no financial support for those operators facing difficulties. However the transport sector has *not* been left to the free market, for many of the reasons mentioned above, although there has been a move in recent years to allow certain parts of the transport sector to operate in a 'freer' market. This has been the case with the private financing and construction of the Channel Tunnel, the deregulation of the bus industry and the proposed private financing of road construction. In terms of more government involvement, there is a mounting case for government to seriously consider a road pricing policy to counteract the problems of road congestion which are hindering the efficient working of the market mechanism and resulting in a misallocation of resources. Certainly, with the revised traffic forecasts of May 1989, there is now a general consensus that road supply cannot realistically be expanded sufficiently to meet demand. The need for demand management policies has therefore become more widely accepted and these will become an increasingly important part of any government's transport policy in the foreseeable future.

Government's free market policy – case studies

Private road construction

In May 1989 the government published a green consultation paper entitled 'New Roads by New Means' which set out proposals for the private funding of roads. Private sector companies would now be invited to bid for contracts to design, construct and operate privately financed road schemes. As well as building new motorways, such schemes could include the introduction of fast lanes for cars constructed alongside existing roads.

To date there has only been a limited number of private sector projects, for example the Channel Tunnel, the Severn bridge and the Dartford river crossing. Despite this low number, the government does not perceive road building as purely a public sector monopoly.

The rationale for private sector roads is based on the premise that it allows (in theory at least) more roads to be built than would be the case if government funded road schemes were the only ones undertaken. Also, because private road builders would be using their own finance plus that of their shareholders, they would have to bear the risk of financial failure. This being so, greater care would be taken to ensure that projects were completed on time and within the financial constraints laid down. Essentially, it would mean that the risk would be transferred from the public sector to the private sector.

Roads would, of course, only be built if the construction company believed that demand was sufficient to generate an adequate return on the capital investment. The private road builders would charge for the use of such roads, which would ensure that the users paid directly for the resources they consumed. In return for being charged for the use of the road, the user would receive a higher quality road service. However there are a number of issues which need to be considered as regards private sector road projects. Tolls will need to be collected, and these can in themselves cause congestion. They may also create problems of road design, because the number of toll exits has to be limited. However the problem of toll collection could, to some extent, be dealt with by having vehicles fitted with an electronic identity plate. This would allow cars to pass through a toll point such that a pre-paid bank account is directly debited. Tolls would be based on what motorists were prepared to pay, although in monopoly situations (such as river crossings) the government would have to fix a maximum charge in line with the 'public interest'. It is likely, however, that private sector finance would only be attracted to those parts of the country which were experiencing relatively higher levels of economic growth, and that the public sector would have to provide for the less economically attractive regions.

Another question which needs to be addressed is whether any increased involvement by the private sector in road construction will lead to a net addition to the total road programme, or simply to a displacement of public sector expenditure on roads.

Again, it is not clear at what level the tolls would be set. A system of 'shadow tolls' has generally been ruled out by the government. A 'shadow toll' is one where the private construction company makes an agreement to build a road and is then reimbursed by the government, depending on the number of vehicles which use the road. One benefit of using such a 'shadow toll' would be that it would avoid the disruption of the traffic flow caused by the collection of actual tolls.

The private funding of road construction is in its early stages at present, but in the future the government does envisage a number of tolled roads. Private sector companies have been asked to present their proposals for schemes such as a northern relief road for Birmingham and a motorway between Birmingham and Manchester. For example, various joint ventures involving companies such as Tarmac and Balfour Beatty, and Trafalgar House and Sir Robert McAlpine, were considering the Birmingham relief road project.

Deregulation of the bus industry

Prior to 1930, the local urban and rural bus industry operated in a competitive market structure with no government regulation. There was fierce competition between rival bus companies (using surplus war vehicles) and this period was associated with a high number of accidents, unscheduled and irregular intervention by 'pirate' operators at peak times, and other types of wasteful duplication.

It was for these reasons that, in 1930, the *Road Traffic Act* was introduced, which was to form the basis of bus industry regulation for 50 years. Under the Act, Traffic Commissioners were responsible for the issue of road service licences (a licence being required for each route operated), the quality of vehicles and the level of fares.

The period 1930 to 1980 was therefore a restrictive one for the local bus service industry. A comprehensive public transport network was provided under a protectionist system, with a licence acting as a barrier to entry, since a licence gave the operator a monopoly on a particular route for the duration of the licence. In 1930 the industry was dominated by private bus operators but, as it developed, the state took a progressively larger role, as with the formation in 1968 of the National Bus Company (NBC) and the Scottish Bus Group (SBG). This meant that by 1986 the industry consisted of state owned operators, the local authority sector and independent companies which mainly operated in the contract hire sector (including school bus provision).

Changes were regarded as necessary by the mid 1980s. There had been a steady decline in patronage, with bus and coach passenger travel falling from 42% of total travel in 1953, to 8% in 1983. The growth in the use of the private car, fare increases in excess of the inflation rate, increased operating costs and the decline in the service provided, were seen as the chief reasons for the decline in bus/coach travel.

The Conservative government started on the changes with the *1980 Transport Act*, which abolished road service licences for long distance express coach travel, and with the decision to establish the 'trial areas' of Devon, Hereford and Worcester, and Norfolk, for local bus service deregulation. For long distance coach travel, the Act allowed companies which met certain safety standards to enter the market and to offer whatever service they chose. By 1989, passenger prices on the main trunk roads were 15% lower in real terms, and coach frequency 70% higher, as compared to the position prior to deregulation (Thompson and Whitfield 1990).

The 1984 White Paper on Buses stated:

'The total travel market is expanding. New measures are needed urgently to break out of the cycle of rising costs, rising fares, reducing services, so that public transport can win a bigger share of this market. We must get away from the idea that the only future for bus services is to contract painfully at large cost to taxpayers and ratepayers as well as travellers. Competition provides the opportunity for lower fares, new services, more passengers. For these great gains, half measures will not be enough. Within the essential framework of safety regulation and provision for social needs, the obstacles to enterprise, initiative and efficiency must be removed.'

The White Paper led to the *1985 Transport Act*, through which (by October 1986) road service licensing requirements were abolished outside London. Provision was also made in the Act for the privatization of the National Bus Company. The Passenger Transport Executives operating in metropolitan areas were to be converted into independent companies, still owned by the local authorities but which now had the option to privatize them. Local bus operators had to register their routes and times and to give sufficient notice of withdrawal of services. There was also the introduction of competitive tendering for the unprofitable bus routes.

So the main objective of the 1985 Act was to introduce competition into the bus sector, providing the opportunity for independent bus operators which did not offer licensed services before 1986, now to do so. There are a number of potential benefits from deregulation.

- Firstly, increased competition should allow greater choice for the consumer and provide a service which is more responsive to the preferences of the consumer.
- Secondly, there should now be a closer relationship between bus operating costs and the fares charged, the reason for this being the ending of cross-subsidization, whereby certain routes were overcharged in order to subsidize non-profitable routes. This was helped, of course, by the freedom of entry for new operators after 1986, which in principle should compete away any 'monopoly profits' from charging excessive fares on routes, unrelated to costs.

- Thirdly, there should be greater potential for innovation in bus travel under deregulation, which was less likely in the absence of competition. One such innovation following deregulation has been the introduction of mini-bus services.
- Fourthly, under deregulation, a reduction is likely in the subsidies obtained by bus operators to undertake unprofitable services. The revenue support from government had increased from £10m in 1972 to £520m in 1982. It could be argued that such subsidies created a protective wall behind which bus operators could operate inefficient services.

There are however reservations about deregulating the bus sector. Increased competition and the need to lower costs, possibly through reduced vehicle maintenance and training for drivers, could result in reduced safety standards. A view has also been expressed that free entry into the industry could add to the congestion problem, especially at peak times. This is particularly true with the increased use of mini-buses and with the additional number of stops introduced to put-down and pick-up passengers. However these possible problems may be overstated because some of the increased patronage is likely to be from car users transferring to buses, and in any case buses form only a small proportion of all road vehicles.

There are often low levels of demand for certain bus services, notably in the evenings and on Sundays. This could mean that such off-peak services, which are basically unprofitable, will be withdrawn or their frequency reduced. At the same time, services in high demand (mainly in conurbations at peak periods) will have a number of bus operators providing a duplicated service. This kind of competition could lead to a high turnover of bus operators and may stimulate collusion so as to avoid direct competition. Finally if a long established, regulated sector, is deregulated then the competitive free market which ensues may prevent a planned, integrated and co-ordinated transport sector from being offered, as is the case in many European cities.

The impact of deregulation   In terms of bus mileage, there was a 14% rise in 1987–88 as compared to 1985–86 (the year before deregulation). Unit operating costs (outside London) also fell by 20% in real terms during the period. However between 1985–86 and 1987–88, there was a fall of 5.5% in passenger trips. One reason put forward for this has been the confusion passengers have experienced due to the changes in service times, routes, and operators brought about through deregulation (Robinson 1989). A survey of a number of bus industry executives, undertaken by Harris Research on behalf of Peat, Marwick McLintock, viewed recent major trends as being one of small operators continuing to enter the market while at the same time rationalization was taking place, with small operators being taken over by larger operators keen to protect their local monopoly. There is therefore the likelihood that an oligopolistic market will develop in the bus sector, with smaller firms possessing 100 vehicles or less being vulnerable to competition. Some writers suggest that significant entry to the market has only occurred in a small number of areas, namely Manchester, Glasgow, Preston and Oxford, and that new entrants have in many cases failed to sustain their place in the market (Glaister, Starkie and Thompson 1990).

The Channel Tunnel

On the 20 January 1986, the governments of Britain and France gave their approval to the construction of a privately financed fixed-link route across the Channel. This was to be built by an Anglo-French private sector consortium called Eurotunnel. The tunnel is being financed totally by private sector money, since the Channel Tunnel Treaty prohibits government funds being used to finance the project. It is due to open on the 15 June 1993 and is likely to have a major economic impact on the UK economy and on the South-East in particular. There will be three separate tunnels, 50km long. Two of the tunnels will be used by trains which will transport cars, coaches and heavy goods vehicles between Britain and France on a drive-on/drive-off system; a third will act as a service tunnel. The tunnel was originally forecast to cost £4.87bn, but the cost is now estimated to be over £7bn. Technical advisors to the 200 international banks which have agreed loans and stand-by credits of £5bn to Eurotunnel, say that the cost could be as high as £8bn. It was also stated that this figure was a mid-point of their range of estimates. For example, the costs rose by 48% between November 1987 and October 1989 alone, and there are at least four reasons for this.

Firstly, there have been unexpected delays in tunnelling under the English coast because of the difficult ground conditions. Secondly, the building industry has been suffering from inflationary pressures. Eurotunnel forecasted that building costs would increase by 4.5% in 1988, whereas in fact construction costs in the South East of England increased by between 15% and 20%. Thirdly, the prices of the locomotives and rolling stock have increased from the original estimate of £245m in 1986 to a figure of £600m by July 1989. In 1986–87 forecasters were unsure as to the final cost but certainly part of the increased cost in rolling stock can be put down to changes in safety specifications (*The Economist*, Oct 7 1989). Fourthly, there have been increased costs in the tunnel railway itself. The cost of the rail terminals, signalling installation and the tunnel communications were initially estimated at £1.14bn. There have however been specification changes which meant that the cost, by early 1990, had reached £1.86bn.

The Channel Tunnel is likely to have an important impact on the economy in a number of areas. Firstly, there has been the creation of employment opportunities in the manufacture of £600m of rolling stock and the construction of the tunnel which, at its peak, employed just under 4000 workers. Once open it has been estimated by Eurotunnel that 3000 workers will be employed, mainly in the tunnels operation and maintenance. Secondly, the tunnel is likely to provide substantial competition for the cross-channel ferry companies, particularly on the Kent coast. It is forecast that the Channel Tunnel will take 42% of the cross channel passenger traffic by 2003, as seen in Table 28.7. In terms of freight, it is forecast that by 2003 the tunnel will account for 17% of the cross channel freight market.

Finally, with the creation of the Single European Market in 1992 the tunnel may lead to an even greater concentration of economic activity in the south east. Markets are increasingly being seen as European rather than

Table 28.7 Eurotunnel estimates of the total demand and the tunnel share of the cross-Channel passenger and freight traffic

Table 28.7 Eurotunnel estimates of the total demand and the tunnel share of the cross-Channel passenger and freight traffic

Passengers (million trips per annum)	1985	1993	2003
Total passenger market	48.1	67.1	93.6
Projected tunnel traffic	–	29.7	39.5
Freight (million tonnes per annum)			
Total freight market	60.4	84.4	122.6
Projected tunnel traffic	–	14.8	21.1

Source: Adapted from Channel Tunnel Joint Consultative Committee, (1988), HMSO.

British, and businesses deciding where to locate their factories may be drawn to the south east because of the tunnel and the links with the continent. All this may have implications for UK Regional Policy.

European Community Transport Policy

The EEC Treaty of Rome states that one of the objectives of the European Community is the adoption of a Common Transport Policy (CTP), which is seen as one means of achieving European integration and economic development. The CTP has aimed to support the free market mechanism and to foster competition but, unlike other common policies such as the Common Agricultural Policy, the CTP has had limited success. This has been mainly because the provision of transport services within member countries has been highly decentralized and fragmented. For instance, the transport policies of EC member countries have tended to differ widely with regards to state intervention, competition, regulation, and the finance and subsidization of public transport. The *Single European Act 1986* has been important in moving the EC towards a CTP in a number of areas, with the Commission of the European Community viewing the integration of the transport market as an important part of the programme for strengthening industry and trade in the community. However the continued use of restrictive practices in transport by member states has not helped the creation of a competitive free market in transport. As a result, the main thrust of transport policy has so far been on a piecemeal basis.

In *air transport* the main push has been towards deregulation, safety and establishing a common approach to countries which are not members of the EC. On most intra-European flights, passengers choose between aircraft belonging to countries at either end of the route, and pay the price approved by the governments of those two countries. However, after 1st January 1993 this will no longer be the case; from that time onwards all routes will be deregulated and it is expected that fares will fall and service frequencies will increase. However, a study by the London Business School shows that on routes which are dominated by business traffic, new entrants have experienced difficulty in competing against the established airlines once deregulation has taken place. This has been because of the strong brand identity created by existing operators and the fact that airlines contemplating entry have often had less favourable access to the computer reservation system. One of the main problems with deregulation is that the market could be dominated by a few large operators, i.e. be an oligopolistic market. This is borne out in the US where the deregulated market has eight major operators which together take 92% of the market.

With regards to *rail*, the EC has stressed the need for an EC railways network to strengthen economic co-operation and to help unify the market. All member states have adopted a similar, centralized organization for their railways, and as railways have been controlled by national governments it is not surprising that their operations have been restricted to the national territory. There is a need, however, for the creation of a community network, with the development of high speed lines and an improvement of existing services. This will be particularly important for taking advantage of the opportunities provided by the Channel Tunnel due to open in 1993. In this respect Britain is some way behind other European countries, with the development of a high speed rail link from the tunnel to London and beyond still problematic.

In the *road haulage* sector, movement has been restricted throughout the EC and competition is distorted by different national regulations which affect the use of capacity and regulate access to the industry. For example, a system of licences requires hauliers to apply for a limited number of permits in order to move goods between member countries of the EC. 'Cabotage', namely the collection and delivery of loads by a non-resident haulier in another member country, has in general been prohibited. However since the 1st July 1990, member states have been provided with 15,000 'cabotage' permits, valid for 2 months as part of an experimental scheme due to end in 1992. Even though the permits only represent 1% of the EC road transport market, they will enable hauliers to undertake business throughout the community, and the total number of permits will increase by 10% each year until 1992. This should mean a more efficient use of road transport capacity, thus reducing the number of empty vehicle movements.

Within certain member countries (although not in the UK) there is also restricted entry of firms into the road haulage industry; this policy is implemented through a quantitative control on permits. This has led to a black market in permits and the community is committed to their abolition by 1992. In the meantime, however, it is likely that monopoly profits will be earned by those possessing such permits. Tariff (price) controls also exist in some countries, although France plans to eliminate tariff regulation by 1991.

Conclusion

This chapter has attempted to identify, and analyse, a number of the current issues facing the transport sector, notably road congestion and the role of the state in transport provision. Transport, as a derived demand, is an important sector of the UK economy, accounting for some 15% of household expenditure and having a planned expenditure of £4,490m allocated to it in 1991–92 by the Department of Transport. The period 1978–88 has seen a 30% increase in the demand for passenger transport and this is expected to continue into the next century, with the car dominating. Income has been viewed as a major factor in determining that demand and its future growth. Forecasting the future patterns of demand is seen as essential for governments when deciding on the allocation of funds to possible new road developments. The increased reliance on the car has created a major problem of congestion, particularly in urban areas, and in recent years this has become more of a political issue. A number of possible solutions have been examined, originating from both the supply and demand sides. On the supply side, it is clear that it is not possible to provide sufficient road capacity to meet the likely growth in demand. Demand needs therefore to be 'managed', and demand side policies have been extensively used. However, road pricing has not, as yet, been implemented in the UK, although it is viewed by many to be the best method of dealing with the congestion problem.

The public sector plays an important role in the transport sector, both as regards its expenditure on such aspects as the national roads system and its ownership of parts of the sector, notably British Rail. The last ten years has, however, seen a move towards a transport sector operating in a 'freer' market. Certain parts of the sector have been privatized, the bus industry has been deregulated and there has been increased private sector involvement in the provision of the transport infrastructure. This chapter has sought to examine the possible reasons for this move towards a free market sector, together with the likely advantages and disadvantages.

Note

1. For an explanation of Discounting and Present Value see R. G. Lipsey (1989) An Introduction to Positive Economics, 7th edn, Weidenfeld and Nicolson.

References and further reading

Abbott, K. and **Thompson, D.** (1989) Deregulating European Aviation: the impact of bilateral liberalization. Centre for Business Strategy Working Paper, London Business School.

Bendixson, T. (1989) Better a Road Toll than a Death Toll. *The Observer* 29 January.

CSO (1990) *Social Trends*, 20.

Channel Tunnel Joint Consultative Committee (1988) Kent Impact Study, Overall Assessment, HMSO.

Chartered Institute of Transport (1990) Paying for Progress. A Report on Congestion and Road Use Charges.

Confederation of British Industry (1989) The Capital at Risk: Transport in London Task Force Report.

Department of Transport (1984) *Buses*, HMSO, (Cm 9300).

Department of Transport (1988) *National Travel Survey 1985–86 Report*, HMSO.

Department of Transport (1989) *National Road Traffic Forecasts (GB)*, HMSO.

Department of Transport (1989) Transport Statistics GB 1978–88, HMSO.

Department of Transport (1989) *Roads for Prosperity*, HMSO, (Cm 693).

Department of Transport (1989) *New Roads by New Means – Bringing in Private Finance*, HMSO, (Cm 698).

The Economist (1989) The city, the commuter and the car. 18 February, 1989.

The Economist (1989) Under water, over budget. 7 October, 1989.

Family Expenditure Survey (1988) Department of Employment, 1990.

Glaister, Starkie and Thompson, (1990) The assessment: Economic Policy for Transport, *Oxford Review of Economic Policy*. **6**. 2 Summer.

Goodwin, P. B. (1990) Demographic Impacts, Social Consequences, and the Transport Debate, *Oxford Review of Economic Policy*. **6**, 2, Summer.

Hau, T. (1990) Electronic Road Pricing: Developments in Hong Kong 1983–1989. *Journal of Transport Economics and Policy*.

House of Commons Transport Committee (1990) First Report Roads for the Future; **1** 198, HMSO.

London Planning Advisory Committee (1988) Strategic Planning Advice for London for the 1990's.

London Planning Advisory Committee (1989) Memorandum of Evidence to the Transport Committee, First Report Session 1989–90: Roads for the Future, 198, HMSO.

Newbery, D. M. (1990) Pricing and Congestion: Economic Principles Relevant to Pricing Roads. *Oxford Review of Economic Policy*, **6**, 2, Summer.

Robinson, D. (1989) Where will it all end? Bus Industry Special Report. Transport vol 10 No 5 September.

Thompson, D. J. and Whitfield, A. (1990) Express Coaching: Privatization, Incumbent Advantage and the Competitive Process, Centre for Business Strategy Working Paper, London Business School.

Treasury (1990) *The Government's Expenditure Plans, 1990–91 to 1992–93*. Chapter 7, Department of Transport.

A guide to sources

The following list, and associated discussion, is by no means intended to be exhaustive, but rather to highlight some of the more useful sources for statistical data and information on the UK economy. The sequence will be as follows:

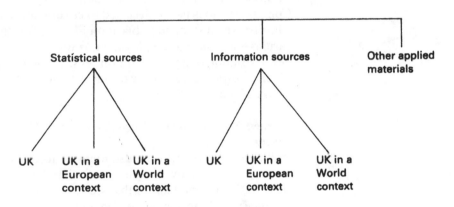

Statistical sources

The following contain important statistical series and, in some cases, articles commenting on those series or on related issues. The addresses given are those for enquiries about *orders* and *subscriptions*.

The UK economy

Guide to Official Statistics   HMSO Books, PO Box 276, London SW8 5DT.
     This is perhaps the most useful starting point in any search for statistical sources. First published in 1976, and now in its fifth edition, the guide covers virtually all official government statistics and some important non-official ones. Statistical sources are presented by subject area, with both regular and *ad hoc* publications outlined, as well as unpublished data available on request.

     The other UK statistical sources we consider are presented alphabetically.

Annual Abstract of Statistics (AAS)   HMSO, PO Box 276, London SW8 5DT.
     Annual Abstract of Statistics gives annual figures, wherever possible, for the previous ten years, in some 400 tables. It presents the major statistics of

the various government departments, grouped under eighteen section headings.

Bank of England Quarterly Bulletin (BEQB)　Economics Division, Bank of England, London EC2R 8AH.

The *Bulletin* is published quarterly, providing detailed statistics on assets and liabilities of the UK monetary sector institutions, though with less detail than in *Financial Statistics* (see below). Data are also provided for money stock components, government debt, official reserves, foreign exchange rates, comparative interest rates, and flow of funds analyses. Each issue contains a number of articles on recent economic and financial developments and on other topics in banking and finance.

Business Briefing　Border House, High St, Farndon, Chester CH3 6PK.

Business Briefing is published monthly by the British Chambers of Commerce and is partly designed to cover material included in *British Business* which stopped publication in 1989. It includes brief updates on various issues such as employment, training, taxation, etc. and reports on any new legislation or government surveys. It also has a Business Trends section which incorporates a variety of statistics on the UK economy previously covered by *British Business*.

Business Monitor (BM)　Business Statistics Office, Cardiff Road, Newport, Gwent, NPT 1XG.

Business Monitor presents summary information on the annual census of production, with a two- to three-year time-lag. The annual summary tables (PA. 1002) present data for the latest, and previous four years, for mining and quarrying, the manufacturing industries, construction, gas, electricity and water. Detailed data are presented, by Minimum List Heading, on output, employment and costs, for both establishments and enterprises in each industry group. Separate annual (PA) reports are also available for each Minimum List Heading, together with quarterly (PQ), and monthly (PM), reports.

Business Ratios Reports　The Business Ratio Manager, 23 City Road, London EC1Y 1AA.

Business Ratio Reports analyse 12,000 leading UK companies every year, in 150 individual sector analyses. A number of key accounting ratios are presented for the current and previous two years, including profitability, liquidity, stock turnover, capital usage, capital/labour, credit period and export ratios.

Economic Trends (ET)　HMSO, PO Box 276, London SW8 5DT.

Economic Trends is published monthly by the Central Statistical Office and contains tables and charts illustrating trends in the UK economy. Data are provided for the latest month, or quarter, as appropriate, and usually for at least the five previous years. As well as trends in the components of National Income, output and expenditure, trends in productivity, employment, trade, financial and corporate matters are outlined.

Employment Gazette (EG)   Department of Employment, Caxton House, Tothill Street, London SW1H 9NF.

Employment Gazette is a monthly publication of the Department of Employment. Each edition contains labour market data on employment, unemployment, vacancies, industrial disputes, earnings and retail prices. Special feature articles are also presented in each edition, examining specific issues affecting the labour market, such as women's pay, industrial relations, productivity, the New Training Initiative, etc.

Financial Statistics (FS)   HMSO, PO Box 276, London SW8 5DT.

Financial Statistics is a monthly publication of the CSO. Data are provided on a wide range of financial topics, for the latest month or quarter, and for at least the previous five years. Financial accounts are presented for various sectors of the economy, central and local government, the public corporations, the monetary sector, other financial institutions, industrial and commercial companies, the personal sector and the overseas sector.

Monthly Digest of Statistics (MDS)   HMSO, PO Box 276, London SW8 5DT.

Again this is a monthly publication of the CSO. It gives up-to-date statistics on the output of various industries, covering a wider range of industries than *Business Monitor*. Statistics are also presented on the components of National Income and Expenditure, on demographic topics, on the labour market and on a variety of social issues.

National Income and Expenditure   HMSO, PO Box 276, London SW8 5DT.

Published annually by the CSO the so-called *Blue Book* is the single most comprehensive source of data on National Income, output and expenditure, and their components. As well as data for the current calendar year, those of the previous ten years are also provided. For some tables, data are even presented for twenty calendar years on a consistent basis and, in an annual supplement, as far back as 1946.

Regional Trends (RT)   HMSO, PO Box 276, London SW8 5DT.

Regional Trends is an annual publication of the CSO, and presents detailed data on the Standard Planning Regions of the UK. *Regional Trends* includes a wide range of economic, social and demographic indices, highlighting regional disparities in the UK.

Social Trends (ST)   HMSO, PO Box 276, London SW8 5DT.

Much of the material in *Social Trends* is of interest to the social scientist in general rather than the economist in particular. Nevertheless, it gives a detailed breakdown of patterns of household wealth, income, and expenditure, together with demographic, housing and social trends.

UK Balance of Payments   HMSO, PO Box 276, London SW8 5DT.

The so-called *Pink Book* is the most comprehensive single source available for balance of payments statistics. Published annually, it breaks down visible trade, invisible trade, investment and other capital transactions, official financing, and external assets and liabilities, into their various components. Data for the previous ten years are presented for purposes of comparison.

The UK economy in a European context

Economic Survey of Europe   HMSO, PO Box 276, London SW8 5DT.
    Published by the UN annually. Data are presented by individual country, and by geographical groupings in Europe, including the Eastern bloc countries. Trends are identified for the various components of agriculture, industry, investment, consumer expenditure, National Income and foreign trade. The tables and charts are supplemented by written discussion.

European Economy   HMSO, PO Box 276, London SW8 5DT.
    European Economy appears three times a year, in March, July and November, and is published by the Commission of the European Community. The November issue contains an annual report on the economic situation within the Community. A statistical annex presents the main economic indicators on an annual basis, and is attached to each issue.

Eurostat   HMSO, PO Box 276, London SW8 5DT.
    Annual publications on the major indices of economic activity are provided by the Statistical Offices of the European Communities under the *Eurostat* heading.

The UK economy in a world context

International Monetary Fund publications   HMSO, PO Box 276, London SW8 5DT.
    World Economic Outlook. Published annually since 1980. This presents and analyses short- and medium-term projections for individual countries, together with a discussion of key policy issues. The industrial countries, the oil-exporting countries, and the non-oil developing countries, are considered as separate groups.

OECD publications   HMSO, PO Box 276, London SW8 5DT.
    OECD Economic Surveys. Individual country reports for the advanced industrialized economies, published annually.
    OECD Economic Outlook. Presents economic trends and prospects in OECD countries. Published twice a year in July and December.

United Nations publications   HMSO, PO Box 276, London SW8 5DT.
    UN Statistical Yearbook. Published annually covering a wide variety of indices of economic activity for developed and developing nations.
    World Economic Survey. Published every second year, examines fluctuations in the world economy, by individual countries and by groups of countries, for a variety of economic indicators. Problems and prospects are examined for the developed market economies, for centrally planned economies, and for the developing countries, together with the outlook for international trade.

Information sources

The following are helpful in locating new and past articles, in newspapers and periodicals. These often provide a fund of useful contemporary data on, and analysis of, applied issues. Also included are references to sources of documents and papers produced by various official and unofficial bodies.

The UK economy

British Humanities Index The Library Association, 7 Ridgmount Street, London WC1.

Published quarterly, this presents titles of articles, listed by subject and by author, for over 300 current periodicals.

Clover Newspaper Index Clover Publications, 32 Ickwell Road, Northill, Biggleswade, Beds SG18 9AB.

Published monthly, this index covers all the main daily papers such as the *Times*, *Financial Times*, *Daily Telegraph*, *Guardian* and *Independent*, as well as the Sunday papers. It provides a single comprehensive source of all the articles written in these newspapers and is valuable for tracing most subjects of economic interest to the reader.

Monthly Index to the Financial Times Financial Times Business Information Ltd, Bracken House, 10 Cannon Street, London EC4P 4BY.

Published monthly, this details all the articles, by subject, and by author, in the final edition of the *Financial Times* during that period.

Official publications These are particularly difficult to track down.

HMSO Government Publications, PO Box 276, London SW8 5DT.

Published monthly (and even daily as a flysheet) this provides an index to new reports by parliamentary (e.g. House of Commons select committees) and non-parliamentary (e.g. Cabinet Office) bodies.

Unfortunately a number of important reports from government departments and various official bodies are not included in the HMSO lists. A useful new publication seeks to document these.

Catalogue of British Official Publications. Chadwyck-Healey Ltd, 20, Newmarket Road, Cambridge CB5 8DT.

Published bi-monthly, this lists British official publications *not* published by HMSO. The majority of these publications are available on microfiche from the address above.

Also helpful are:

Government Statistics. A Brief Guide to Sources. CSO Press and Information Service, Great George Street, London SW1P 3AQ.

This is a free booklet from the Government Statistical Service listing the most important official statistical publications.

NEDO in Print. National Economic Development Office, Millbank Tower, Millbank, London SW1P 4QX.

This catalogue lists the reports currently available from NEDO. Reports by the various tripartite Economic Development Committees and Sector Working Parties are extremely valuable sources of data and comment for a wide range of economic sectors and applied issues.

Research Index   Business Surveys Ltd, PO Box 21, Dorking, Surrey RH5 4EE.

A monthly index, by subject heading, and by company name, to articles and news items of financial interest in over 100 periodicals, and in the national Press, during the previous period.

Reviews of UK Statistical Sources   Pergamon Press, Headington Hill Hall, Oxford OX3 0BW.

This is the successor to the previous series on *The Sources and Nature of the Statistics of the UK*, edited by M. Kendal. The reviews not only outline, but also evaluate statistical sources for a wide and expanding range of topics.

The Times Index   Research Publications Ltd, Reading RG1 8HF.

A monthly index, by subject heading and by author, to the pages of *The Times* newspapers (excluding the *Financial Times* – see above). Available on microfilm.

The UK economy in a European context

Publications of the European Community   Alan Armstrong Ltd, 2 Arkwright Road, Reading, Berks RG2 0SQ.

This annual catalogue contains all the publications, including periodicals, issued during the year by the Institutions of the European Community. There is a breakdown by subject heading.

The UK economy in a world context

HMSO International Organizations Publications   PO Box 276, London SW8 5DT.

This annual catalogue contains all items placed on sale by HMSO in that year for the international agencies and overseas organizations for which HMSO acts as agent. These include: the European Commission; the IMF; the OECD; and the UN, amongst many others.

Other applied materials

The following are a number of useful sources, readily available to the reader interested in applied economic issues.

Bank Reviews   Often available free, on application.
Barclays Economic Review, published quarterly, Economics Dept, Barclays House, 1 Wimborne Road, Poole, Dorset BH15 2BB.
National Westminster Bank Quarterly Review, published quarterly, The Editor, National Westminster Bank p.l.c., 41 Lothbury, London EC2P 2BP.
The Royal Bank of Scotland Review, published quarterly, 36 St Andrews Square, Edinburgh EH2 2YE.

British Economy Survey   Longman, Longman House, Burnt Mill, Harlow, Essex CM20 2JE.

A highly useful, twice-yearly, update on the current state of the British economy. Eight main sections: Industrial Structure; Public Sector; Monetary System; Public Finance; Industrial Relations and Employment; Balance of Payments; World Economy. Published in October and April.

Business Strategy Review   Oxford University Press, Pinkhill House, Southfield Road, Eynsham, Oxford OX8 1JJ.

This is produced three times a year by the London Business School's Centre for Business Strategy. It contains articles on practical issues which are relevant to decision making within modern business.

Economic Briefing   Central Office of Information, Hercules Road, London SE1 7DU.

This is published three times a year and replaces the long standing *Economic Progress Report*. It is directed more towards educational use than was the case with the EPR.

Economics   Economics Association, Maxwelton House, 41–43 Boltro Road, Haywards Heath, W Sussex RH16 1BJ.

This is the official journal of the Economics Association and is published quarterly. As well as containing articles on various aspects of Economics and related subjects, it also covers up-to-date teaching methods and reviews new literature.

Lloyds Bank Economic Bulletin   Group Economics Dept, Lloyds Bank, 71 Lombard St, London EC3P 3BS.

Monthly, on request. Each issue covers a topic of current interest, presenting economic principles in a manner understandable to non-economists. Also included is a section on changes in the main economic indicators.

Oxford Review of Economic Policy   Oxford University Press, Pinkhill House, Southfield Road, Eynsham, Oxford OX8 1JJ.

A quarterly publication which includes articles on various topics of current relevance. Some issues concentrate wholly on *one* contemporary topic, such as Exchange rates, Education and Training, Finance, Health Economics, etc.

The Economic Review   Philip Allan Publishers Ltd, Market Place, Deddington, Oxford OX5 4SE.

Five issues are published each academic year in September, November, January, March and May. *The Economic Review* is aimed at introductory students in economics, and relates economic theory to contemporary economic problems. Each issue contains main feature articles, and a teaching section which reviews the various ways of tackling typical examination questions.

The Economist   25 St James Street, London SW1A 1HG.

This is the internationally known weekly, published by the Economist Newspapers Ltd. It includes articles on subjects such as World Politics and

Current Affairs, together with Business, Finance and Science. It is an invaluable source of national and international business news and also has a useful update on basic economic statistics.

The Times 1000   Times Books, 16 Golden Square, London W1R 4BN.

This is a yearly update of the basic data on the world's top companies. It covers the top 1,000 UK companies and also the main companies of many other OECD countries. It also provides information on companies in the financial sector, such as Clearing banks, Acceptance houses and Discount houses, as well as an update on the year's main mergers and acquisitions.

Treasury Bulletin   HMSO, PO Box 276, London SW8 5DT.

This commenced publication in 1990 and is designed to contain more extended articles on economic events and economic policy than *Economic Briefing* (see above).

United Kingdom in Figures   Central Statistical Office, Press and Information Service, Great George Street, London SW1P 3AQ.

This pocket-sized abstract provides current facts and figures on population, employment, the environment, the standard of living and the National Accounts. Free from the above address.

Who Owns Who   Dun and Bradstreet, 26–32 Clifton St, London EC2P 2LY.

This is a yearly publication which includes a mass of essential information about companies and their subsidiaries. It enables readers to find the main subsidiaries of UK companies, whether in the UK or abroad. It can also be used to trace the parent firm if the name of the subsidiary is known. This publication is therefore invaluable for unravelling the pattern of ownership and control in UK industry.

Notes on Contributors

G. H. Black, F.C.A.   Formerly Senior Lecturer in Accountancy, Anglia Higher Education College (AHEC) and Chief Examiner in A-level Accounting for the University of London Schools Examination Board. Author of a number of books, including *Financial Accounting*, Woodhead-Faulkner, 1986. Responsible (with M. Smith) for Chapter 2.

G. Burton, B.A., M.Sc.   Senior Lecturer in Economics, AHEC, with special reference to macroeconomics. Involved in teaching at degree, BTEC and professional levels. Responsible for Chapters 11, 17, and 18.

J. Collier, B.Sc., M.A.(Cantab), Ph.D.   Senior Lecturer in Economics, AHEC, and Fellow and Director of Studies in Economics, Lucy Cavendish College, University of Cambridge. Author of a number of articles and books, including (with K. C. Pye) *The Organization in its Environment*, Hart-Davis 1985. Responsible for Chapters 7, 15, 16 and 22.

P. T. Fenwick, B.A., M.A.   Senior Lecturer in Economics at AHEC and formerly in Business Studies at the Cambridge College of Further Education. Previous management experience in the British car industry. Responsible (with R. Mills) for Chapter 20.

E. Fuller, M.Sc., A.C.M.A.   Senior Tutor and Deputy Director of Small Business Centre, Durham University Business School. Also consultant of long standing to the International Labour Organization and chairman of Headway Systems Limited, an advanced IT firm. He currently directs research in applications of advanced information technology for enterprise development and has produced and edited numerous publications in the field of enterprise including papers, articles, books, trainer manuals and expert systems. Responsible for Chapters 3 and 9.

M. A. Griffiths B.A., M.Sc.   Senior Lecturer in Economics, AHEC, previously Tutor in Economics at the University of Wales, Aberystwyth. Visiting Fellow of the Japan Foundation, Sophia University, Tokyo in 1978 and Industrial Research Officer at the Research Institute for the National Economy, Tokyo 1987/88. Author of articles on labour and trade, and responsible for Chapters 23 and 25, and Chapters 6, 21 and 29 (with S. D. Wall), Chapter 5 (with M. Smith) and Chapter 19 (with R. Prestwich).

S. Ison B.A., M.Sc.   (CV to come) Responsible for Chapter 28

D. Marshall, B.A., M.A.   Senior Lecturer in Economics, AHEC, with special reference to development economics. Involved with teaching at degree, BTEC and professional levels. Responsible for Chapters 1 and 8.

R. Mills, M.A.(Cantab)   Formerly Senior Lecturer in Economics and Industrial Relations, AHEC, and Tutor in Social Sciences in The Open University. Author of a number of articles on industrial relations in *Local Government Manpower*. Responsible for Chapter 4 and (with P. Fenwick) Chapter 20.

R. Prestwich, B.A., M.A., M.Phil., Ph.D.   Formerly Senior Lecturer in Economic Geography, AHEC. Education Coordinator, Minnesota Trade Office, St. Paul, MN, USA, and Adjunct Faculty, Dept. of Economics, Metro State University. Author (with P. Taylor) of *Introduction to Regional and Urban Policy in the United Kingdom*, Longman, 1990, and author of papers on regional economic development, industrial location and international trade. Responsible (with M. A. Griffiths) for Chapter 19.

K. C. Pye, B.A., M.Phil.   Formerly Principal Lecturer in Economics and Politics, AHEC and Director of Studies in Economics, University of Cambridge Board of Extra-Mural Studies, now Training Development Officer for the Clothing and Allied Products Industry Training Board. Previous experience in the British aircraft industry. Author (with J. Collier) of *The Organization in its Environment*, Hart-Davis, 1985. Responsible for Chapters 26 and 27.

S. Rubinsohn, B.A.   Portfolio Strategist with Capel-Cure Myers, and previously Lecturer in Economics at degree and professional levels, AHEC. Responsible for Chapters 12 and 24.

M. Smith, B.A., M.B.A., Ph.D.   Senior Lecturer in Accounting, Murdoch University, Perth, Western Australia. Formerly Head of Economics, King Edward VII School, Lytham, and Senior Lecturer in Business Studies, AHEC. Actively engaged in research on aspects of financial information, and regular contributor to 'Management Accounting' and *Accounting and Business Research*. Author of the spreadsheet text *Calculating with QL Abacus*, Longman, 1986. Responsible for Chapters 2 (with G. Black) and 5 (with M. A. Griffiths).

S. D. Wall, B.A., M.Sc.   Formerly Principal Lecturer in Economics, AHEC, with special reference to microeconomics. Consultant to the OECD on the impacts of information technology, and guest lecturer and examiner at the University of Cambridge. Author of a wide range of reports and articles on the economics of technical change, and (with P. Nicholson) of *Postal and Telecommunication Statistics*, Pergamon, 1986. Responsible for Chapter 10, and (with M. A. Griffiths) for Chapters 6, 21 and 29.

P. Wigley, M.A.(Cantab), M.A.(Lond)   Formerly Senior Lecturer in Economics, AHEC, with special reference to public finance, and Visiting Professor, Cuttington University, Liberia. Author of articles on labour markets, focusing particularly on the equal pay issue. Responsible for Chapters 13 and 14.

Index

Index entries are arranged in letter-by-letter alphabetical order, in which spaces between words are ignored. 'Banking system' therefore comes before 'Bank of England'. References to notes are indicated by 'n'. Headings starting with numbers are filed as though spelled out.